S0-AXY-905

ACCLAIM FOR THE WORD

A WIZARD'S BESTIARY is an ambitious and comprehensive compilation of imaginary-animal lore. The colorful text and abundance of both traditional and contemporary illustrations capture the rich variety of animal forms that the human imagination has reshaped over millennia. A valuable encyclopedic addition to the ever-growing shelf of books on fantastic creatures.

—Joseph Nigg
author of *The Book of Fabulous Beasts*

This gorgeous, sumptuously-illustrated book is truly a stunning contribution to the cryptozoological and zoomythological literature, one that is destined to remain a standard reference work on these subjects for many years to come. **—Karl P.N. Shuker, PhD**
author of *The Beasts That Hide From Man*

As we stand at the edge of the vast unknown, we all look in to see and for some, to investigate cryptic animate enigmas. Those of us who have been doing this for decades, as Zell-Ravenheart has, view the fantastic world of animal mysteries, ancient living wonders, and accommodating new species in different ways. Cultural insights, ethnic folklore, native traditions, and magical tales mix in and have their place in this phantasmagoria involved in the study of hidden animals. This book shares overlooked insights and incredible clues for the casual reader or the dedicated student of cryptozoology. A valuable resource. Highly recommended.

—Loren Coleman, co-author,
Creatures of the Outer Edge, Cryptozoology A to Z

Lively, entertaining and informative, this is the book I wish I had when I first began researching the lore of the world's magical creatures. No monster hunter can afford to be without it. **John Michael Greer**
author of *Monsters:
An Investigator's Guide to Magical Beings*

Oberon Zell! Who better to write such a book than this living legend from the magickal world. Here is the man who recreated living Unicorns, who traveled to the remote South Seas in search of genuine Mermaids. **—Amber K,** author of *True Magick*

Oberon Zell-Ravenheart's mighty tome is undoubtedly the one book that, more than any other, I was hoping someone, someday was finally going to write: namely, a definitive, encyclopedic study of the many and varied weird beasts, fabulous monsters, and diabolical creatures that are said to lurk in the darkened corners of our mysterious world.

Whether your interest focuses upon those elusive, hairy man-beasts such as Bigfoot and the Yeti;

the ghostly, black devil dogs of old England; the bloodsucking, vampire-like Chupacabras of Puerto Rico; or the many and mysterious long-necked serpents of the world's lakes, lochs and oceans, Zell-Ravenheart's title is one that I heartily recommend.

With entries on a dizzying array of beasts, such as the terrifying, cave-dwelling Aatxe of Spain; and the Boroka of the Philippines—which has the unfortunate habit of dining upon human flesh; as well as much welcome data on monsters of the movies; and a rich array of drawings, photographs, maps, and more, A WIZARD'S BESTIARY is a book that is destined to become a true monster-hunting classic.

—Nick Redfern
author of *Memoirs of a Monster Hunter*
and *Three Men Seeking Monsters*

Oberon Zell-Ravenheart's stunning new work lifts the curtain allowing the reader backstage to examine the elusive creatures of myths and legends. Bigfoot, Mermaids, Dragons and more, the Unicorn information alone is worth the price of admission. Not only a fascinating read but a comprehensive reference that you will find yourself going back to time and again. "Don't wait, don't hesitate, get a copy now!"

—Rick West, Dr. West's
Traveling Sideshows and Animal Menagerie

Acclaim for *Dragonlore* by Ash DeKirk:

I just received the book today, and I've had a hard time putting it down. I have never seen a more complete discussion of dragons, from around the world, and through the ages. If you have any interest in the legends and lore of dragons, this book is for you.

—Mark Mercier, Mobile, AL

Anyone with an interest in dragons will enjoy this book. I can think of at least two DMs who will be receiving this book as a Christmas/Yule gift from me. Please keep more of these books coming.

—FrogsDancing, Quakertown, PA

There are legends of dragons all around us—and they appear in fantasy novels and games as well as movies. Any fan of dragons will be thus delighted with DRAGONLORE, which examines the details of every species of dragon, gathers myths under one cover, and considers the impact and presence of dragons in popular culture. Black and white illustrations pepper an excellent overview that is a pick for any dragon fan, and any collection strong in fantasy.

—Midwest Book Review, Oregon, WI

Copyright © 2007 by Oberon Zell-Ravenheart and
Ash "LeopardDancer" Dekirk

All rights reserved under the Pan-American and International Copyright Conventions. This book may not be reproduced, in whole or in part, in any form or by any means electronic or mechanical, including photocopying, recording, or by any information storage and retrieval system now known or hereafter invented, without written permission from the publisher, The Career Press.

A Wizard's Bestiary
Edited by Kirsten Dalley
Typeset by Oberon Zell-Ravenheart
Cover design by Lucia Rossman/Digi Dog Design NYC
and Ian Daniels
Printed in the U.S.A. by Book-mart Press

To order this title, please call toll-free 1-800-CAREER-1 (NJ and Canada: 201-848-0310) to order using VISA or MasterCard, or for further information on books from Career Press.

The Career Press, Inc., 3 Tice Road, PO Box 687,
Franklin Lakes, NJ 07417
www.careerpress.com
www.newpagebooks.com

Library of Congress Cataloging-in-Publication Data
Zell-Ravenheart, Oberon, 1942-
      A wizard's bestiary / by Oberon Zell-Ravenheart and Ash "LeopardDancer"
      DeKirk
         p. cm.
      Includes bibliographical references and index.
      ISBN-13: 978-1-56414-956-5
      ISBN-10: 1-56414-956-0
         1. Animals, Mythical. I. DeKirk, Ash, 1978- II. Title.

GR820.Z45 2007
398.24'54--dc22

                  2007042608

A WIZARD'S BESTIARY

A MENAGERIE OF MYTH, MAGIC, AND MYSTERY

OBERON ZELL-RAVENHEART
AND ASH "LEOPARDDANCER" DEKIRK

New Page Books
A division of The Career Press, Inc.
Franklin Lakes, NJ

FOREWORD: CREATURES OF THE NIGHT

BY JACQUES VALLEE

Creatures of the Night—is it wise to force them out of the gloom where they linger, like the ancient Chimaera that was part goat, part lion, and part Dragon, and presided over the passage of the evening sun into the darkness? At dusk, like the Salamander, they emerge at the intersection of magical biology and human imagination. Gubernatis, in his erudite *Mythological Zoology*, believes the Salamander represents the moon which lights itself, lives by its own fire, has no ray of its own, and makes the rays (and hairs) of the sun fall off.

Before our friends Oberon and Ash, many scholars and sorcerers of every age, in their wisdom—or their temerity?—have attempted to catalogue and to elucidate the strange beings described by their contemporaries. The monsters did not always hide in the secret convenience of the dark. Some even dared to expose themselves in full daylight, the better to scare honest medieval folks out of their wits.

Thus we find in Schedel's *Chronicles of Nuremberg* (1493) the stupefying representation of a being with six arms, seen by astonished townspeople. A creature observed in Rome in 1530 had feet like a duck's, an enormous forked tail like a fish, the breasts of a woman, and a human face with straight ears, like those of a deer. Gesner published an engraving of it in Zurich in 1558.

Gessner's duckfooted mermaid 1558

Gessner's Sea Devil

Aldrovandi of Bologna relates the adventures of a horned hybrid in a book he published in 1642. As for Sebastian Munster, an illustration in his 1544 book titled *Cosmographie* clearly shows a woman kneeling (in adoration or begging for her life—or her virtue) before a tall biped with three heads: one belonging to a serpent, one to an eagle, and one to a lion. He grabs his genitalia while staring at her, in a manner suggesting that, monster or not monster, he is not immune to desire.

Gesner also shows us an engraving of a *Diable de Mer* (Sea Devil), which must have been actually captured by brave fishermen, because he states it was "painted from nature." The great Boaistuau himself regales us with true accounts of "a monster born alive on Earth, which was of human figure from the navel up, and the rest a dog" (Chapter xxxvii). In another part of his book (Chapter vii), he illustrates a report with an engraving of "a Monster of our own

time, about which the question is settled of whether demons can procreate and exercise the work of the flesh."

In the present volume, focused on creatures closely related to animals, rather than meta-humans like elves and Cyclops, we meet beings from myth and legend all over the globe. Under Oberon's gifted pen, they are brought to life again and become, in more ways than one, "familiar" to us.

We live in an age that claims rationality as its standard. It relegates any deviation from the academic norm to the realm of the impossible, alongside the Mermaid and the Unicorn—phantasms of a bygone era when folks were insecure and uneducated. So the reader should be prepared for a shock when opening this book: You will learn that there is a perfectly rational explanation for Mermaids, and that Unicorns *do* exist. Several of them appeared in this century and followed Oberon and his jolly friends in their adventures. I have touched a live Unicorn and can report how wonderful it felt to experience something that every academic knew as an absolute fact to be impossible.

We shouldn't sell scientists short, however. Contemporary biotech must have learned some of the lessons from old *grimoires*, because it is busy reinventing the Chimaera in the lab through genetic manipulations that hope to save lives and throw new light on the mysteries of biology, birth, disease, and the evolution of species.

They could also spell danger: As scary as the Gryphon may be, the chimaeras that contemporary labs are patenting with such entrepreneurial frenzy will be a thousand times more powerful. If cryptozoology gives any warning, it is that we only unleash such beasts at our peril. All the more reason to learn about them before it is too late. If Unicorns roam the land, what wonders will the Gargoyles belch out next, from the lofty spires of our ivy towers? If the Kraken is real, can Dragons be far behind?

Fortunately, as ancient tradition teaches, there are convenient medicines to cure the ravages of nightly monsters. Thus, against the poisonous venom of Salamanders, Pliny advises the seeds of the hairy and stinging nettle, mixed with the broth of a tortoise. We can only wish that all human nightmares could be healed with such simple remedies.

—Jacques Vallée
San Francisco, 21 May 2007

A WIZARD'S BESTIARY
TABLE OF CONTENTS

PREFACE 1 BY LEOPARDDANCER

Incipit liber de naturis bestiarum.
De leonibus et pardis et tigribus,
lupes et vulpibus, canibus et similiis.

Here begins the book of the nature of beasts.
Of lions and panthers and tigers,
wolves and foxes, dogs and apes.
—*Aberdeen Bestiary* (12th century)

 OR AS LONG AS I CAN REMEMBER, I've been interested in creatures regarded as mythical and legendary. My paternal grandparents instilled in me a sense of wonder regarding the world and all it contains. They also imparted a love of reading and learning that is still with me today. At an age when most children are still reading children's books, I was engrossed in tales of Coyote and Raven, of Herakles' trials and tasks, of Dragons, Gryphons, and Thunderbirds.

My grandmother had a great deal of Native American blood in her lineage. Even more, she embraced Native American spirituality, which she managed to blend quite well with her Christian beliefs. It was the Native American beliefs, however, that she passed on to me. These beliefs included a deep and abiding respect for the land and all of its creatures, be they hawk or Tlanuhwa, lizard or Dragon.

Growing up, I focused more and more on myths, legends, and the creatures within. Likewise, I became more and more addicted to reading in general. Through it all, I wondered: Was it possible that these creatures were real? What would they be like if they were real? Indeed, over the years I've seen many things that I could not explain. I could swear that I've seen the shadow of the Tlanuhwa. Certainly, it was the shadow of a bird far larger than any I've ever seen before (or since, for that matter). I could also tell you that, in a field along a route I used daily, I saw a great Earth Dragon basking in the sun. A second glance revealed only a moss-covered boulder that had never been there before, and is not there today. Then there are Master Oberon's Unicorns, and anyone who has seen them cannot deny their existence!

When I was still fairly young, I met those who would introduce me to the Dun'marran path, the path I still follow today. The Dun'marra are the People of the Dragon. Through this connection, I became very interested in the great beasts on which my path centers. I went on to study Dragonlore from around the world. Surprisingly enough, I found that Dragons exist wherever people live, from Africa and Asia to Europe and even the Americas. Within these pages, you will find Dragons and myriad other creatures of myth and lore—creatures such as the Gryphon, the Roc, the Unicorn, and the Yeti—that exist in many different cultures around the world.

Eventually I was led to the Grey School of Wizardry, where I am now privileged to teach alongside some of the best people I have known. I am honored to have worked with Master Oberon on this project.

I would like to dedicate this work in loving memory of Nina "Dancing Bear" Clark (1928–2006).

ACKNOWLEDGEMENTS BY OBERON

First, of course, I dedicate this book to Morning Glory, the love of my life and my cosmic soulmate, with whom I have been privileged to share these past 34 years of amazing adventures. This book has been our dream for three decades, and finally, here it is!

I would also like to acknowledge a few of the authors and pioneer researchers who inspired me to begin my own explorations into the mistry realms of fabulous and forgotten beastes: Roy Chapman Andrews, Bernard Heuvelmans, Ivan Sanderson, Peter Byrne, Doc Holiday, Roy Mackel, Richard Greenwell, and Grover Krantz.

I also thank some current researchers who have been kind enough to consult with me in various aspects of this book: Joseph Nigg, Loren Coleman, and Rick West.

I thank the curator of the Field Museum of Natsural History in Chicago, who took a young boy into the great museum's back rooms and vaults, and gave him the first fossils of a lifetime colletion. I no longer remember his name, but his influence remains.

I extend my appreciation to my old friend Tom Williams for his contributions to this book, drawn from our mutual interests in cryptozoology, and our shared adventures in pursuit of Unicorns and Mermaids.

Another dear friend who deserves mention here is Diane Darling—our partner in many adventures for over a decade, and keeper of the last Unicorn.

Thanks to the talented artists who contributed custom illustrations to this compendium: Joe Butt, Xander Carruthers, Ian Daniels, Ash DeKirk, Dana Keyes, Tam Songdog, and Tracy & Adam Swangler.

I thank my brother, Barry Zell, for his diligence and recommendations in proofing the chapters of this manuscript as they were being written.

And finally, I thank my dear friend Jacques Vallée for writing a perfect Foreword to this work.

PREFACE II BY OBERON

*...Now I will believe
That there are Unicorns; that in Arabia
There is one tree, the Phoenix' throne;
One Phoenix at this hour reigning there.*
—Shakespeare, *The Tempest* (3.3.21-24)

I HAVE ALWAYS HAD A DEEP FASCINA-tion and affection for animals of all kinds, both real and imaginary. Growing up in the suburbs of Chicago, I spent as much time as possible at the city's zoos and museums, visiting farms, and going on camping and fishing trips. I got all the *Golden Nature Guides* as they came out, and never missed Disney's "True Life Adventures" movies, *Wild Kingdom* on TV, and now, Animal Planet and the Discovery Channel. I have several sets of various animal encyclopedias, the *Time-Life Nature* and *Science* series, and entire shelves full of books on dinosaurs, nature, cryptozoology, and mythical monsters.

One of the most significant revelations of my youth occurred in elementary school, when, in the process of reading the *World Book Encyclopedia* volume by volume, I turned to the entry on dinosaurs, with a two-page spread of Charles Knight's iconic painting of a Triceratops facing off against a T-rex With a thrill that still sends shivers down my spine, I suddenly realized that *Dragons were real!* Just as the stories said, once upon a time the world really was ruled by huge and mighty reptiles. They lumbered over the land, they churned the seas, and, with wings as wide as those of an airplane, they commandeered the air. They were even more immense and diverse than the most imaginative tales had portrayed—*and they really existed!*

From that point on, I became absolutely obsessed with dinosaurs. I learned everything I could about those amazing creatures. Similar to a sports fanatic memorizing statistics of all the players, I memorized every dinosaur name I could find and all their identifying features: what their Greek names meant, when and where they lived, what they ate, and how big they were. My parents thought this was all rather amazing, as they couldn't even pronounce most of these names, and they'd ask me to come out at their parties and rattle off dinosaur stats for their guests.

This passion excited by dinosaurs naturally came to extend to other fantastic creatures of long ago, including those of myth and legend. I began visiting natural history museums, hunting for fossils, and collecting dinosaur models as soon as they started being made, which I would carefully paint in realistic colors and install in dioramas.

My library on these subjects grew, as did my collection of models, fossils, animal skulls, artwork, movies, and other memorabilia pertaining to the prehistoric and mythical menageries. Today I have perhaps one of the most extensive private collections of miniature dinosaur replicas in existence, going back nearly 60 years. Someday I need to open a museum.

Since childhood, I have brought home, raised, and kept all kinds of wild animals as pets and rescuees (I worked for many years with Wildlife Rescue), including frogs, salamanders, snakes, lizards, turtles, tarantulas, praying mantises, caterpillars and butterflies, ants, bats, owls, herons, opossums, deer, and wild pigs. I have maintained multiple terrariums and aquariums, both fresh and salt water (yes, I had my "Age of Aquariums"). And I have had my share of domesticated animals as well, from gerbils, guinea pigs, hamsters, rats, cats, and ferrets to goats and Unicorns—which brings us to the great Unicorn Adventure and the present book.

*Triceratops & T-Rex by Charles Knight,
Field Museum of Natural History*

One evening, in the summer of 1975, my wife and soulmate, Morning Glory, and I were sitting around the living room with friends discussing mythical beasties, and we decided to look up some of them in the *Encyclopedia Britannica*. Under "Basilisk" (see picture), I found a fascinating article relating the Cockatrice, Basilisk, Medusa, and a South American lizard to the Egyptian spitting cobra, and we conceived the idea of writing a book revealing the true origins and history of various "mythical" creatures and entities. Having just read Peter Beagle's charming *The Last Unicorn* (1968), we decided to title our proposed book *Creatures of Night, Brought to Light* (as the novel's Mommy Fortuna refers to her little mythic menagerie), and we began seriously and systematically collecting and filing legends, pictures, and accounts of sightings of everything from Nessie to Bigfoot.

Shortly thereafter, Morning Glory and I sold our house in St. Louis, bought and converted an old school bus, and set off across the country to find America and visit friends and correspondents. From museums, libraries, universities, and friends, we were introduced to dozens of books on the subject of esoteric zoology (or *cryptozoology*, as it is now called), including *On the Track of Unknown Animals* and *In the Wake of the Sea-Serpent,* both by Bernard Heuvalmans; *The Great Orm of Loch Ness* by F.W. Holiday; *The Lore of the Unicorn* by Odell Shepard; the books of Charles Fort, Willy Ley, Ivan Sanderson, Frank Edwards, Peter Costello, and countless others, which we devoured and then added to our collection. In Oregon, I met Bigfoot researcher Peter Byrne, and I became a regular contributor to *The Bigfoot News*.

After a few months of wandering, we came to roost in 1976 in Morning Glory's home town of Eugene, Oregon. We lived there for a year, teaching a course on Celtic shamanism and mythology at Lane Community College. We became actively involved with Oregonians Cooperating to Save the Whales, lobbying for a legislative boycott of whaling nations and urging the tuna fisheries to stop killing dolphins. Meanwhile, we continued our research in the library of the University of Oregon. We explored arcane mysteries and histories, and sought to unveil the truth behind the legends of Sea Serpents, Gryphons, the Phoenix, Bigfoot, Atlantis, Witches, Faeries, Elves, the Kraken, Dragons, Amazons, Mother Earth, Magick, ESP, and Unicorns.

In the course of our research, we discovered the lost secret of the Unicorns—how they were actually produced from ancient times to the Renaissance (see Chapter 4). In the summer of 1977, we abandoned our book project and moved to a 5,600-acre homesteading community in the mountains of Mendocino County, Northern California, to raise living Unicorns, which we did from 1980–85. During that time, we traveled all over North America exhibiting our Unicorns at Renaissance fairs, and appearing with them in countless TV shows, newspapers, magazines, and books. Finally, in 1984, our agents brokered an exhibition contract with the Ringling Bros. and Barnum & Bailey Circus, and for the next four years our Unicorns became the stars of the Greatest Show on Earth!

With the money from the Circus contract, we next mounted a diving expedition to New Guinea in search of real Mermaids—specifically, the unknown sea animals called *Ri* or *Ilkai* by the natives of New Ireland, where they were frequently seen. Find them we did, and, videotaping it all, we reported our findings to the 1985 annual meeting of the International Cryptozoological Society. We still have the videotapes, and someday we'd love to put together a documentary on that expedition (see Chapter 10).

These remarkable stories you will find in this book, along with many other marvels and wonders of the natural and unnatural world. Enjoy!

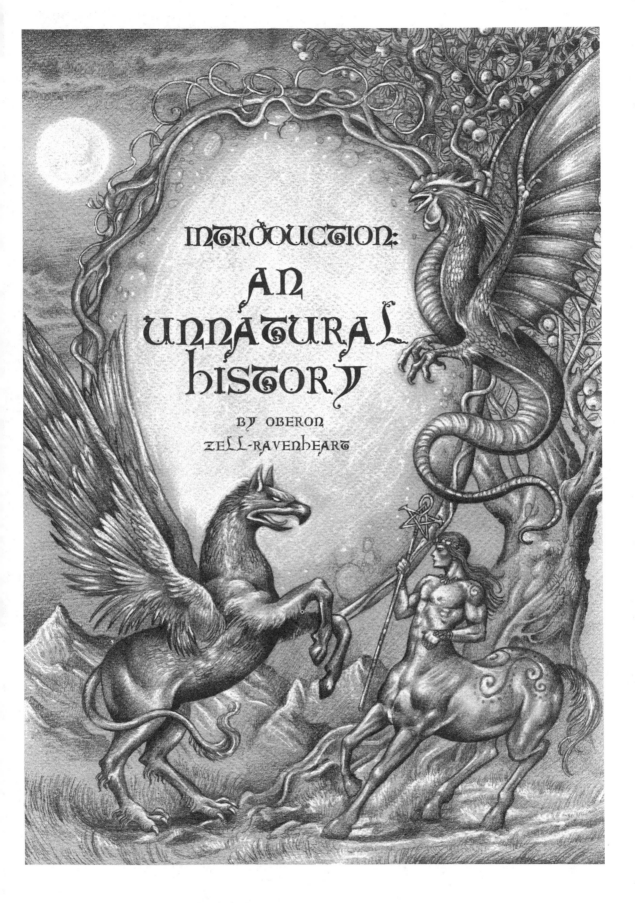

INTRODUCTION:
AN UNNATURAL HISTORY

BY OBERON
ZELL-RAVENHEART

But some day Unicorns will be remembered.
And Griffins will again be brave and strong.
A Phoenix will be seen on the horizon
And all forgotten creatures shall belong.
　　　　　　　　　　—Barbara Wersba
　　　　　The Land of Forgotten Beasts, 1964

 E HAVE ALWAYS BEEN FASCINATED with, intrigued by, and fearful of the "ghoulies and ghosties and long-leggedy beasties and things that go bump in the night," from which that old Scottish prayer begs us to be delivered. Humans have never been nocturnal, but, since before our ancestors came down out of the trees, our predators have been. Our very first magick—the pivotal creation that turned us from animals to humans—was fire. And through the long hours of darkness, we huddled around the tiny circle of firelight, beyond which lurked the Creatures of Night. Who knew what unseen and monstrous shapes lay hidden behind those red, green, and yellow eyes that glowed from the shadows behind our backs? What night terrors growled, roared, screamed, shrieked, hooted, and howled out there in the dark? We could only imagine.

And so we filled the Unknown with monsters, as noted in the blank spaces on of all those old maps. Many of them were quite real and quite dangerous, and many others were purely figments of our fevered imaginations. And we had no way of knowing which were which. We told stories. And, eventually, those stories got written down and compiled into books similar to this one.

This bestiary ("book of beasts") is but the latest in a long line of predecessors, and it only seems fair to introduce it with an homage to its proud lineage.

The Physiologus and the Bestiary

The bestiary as such is a peculiarly medieval European phenomenon. Although ancient writers such as Ctesias, Aristotle, and Pliny the Elder had described various animals, including many that were purely imaginary, the first to compile an intentional encyclopedia of all the world's known creatures was an anonymous writer known as the *Physiologus* ("naturalist"), who lived in Alexandria perhaps as early as the 2nd century CE. Although he was probably Egyptian, he wrote in Greek, and his book was so popular that, within a couple of centuries, it was translated into all the languages of Europe. Eventually, the name *Physiologus* became identified with the compilation itself.

The initial compilation included descriptions of perhaps 50 animals, trees, and minerals. Over the centuries, as travelers brought tales and reports from ever more distant lands, each copier and translator of the Physiologus bestiary added to it anonymously, filling in the blanks, and increasing the number of creatures included on the land, in the seas, and in the air. Though often distorted in descriptions and depictions, it has been estimated that 90 percent of the creatures listed are based on real animals. But the compilers had no way of making distinctions between actual or imaginary beasts—after all, the Unicorn certainly appeared no stranger than the hippopotamus, walrus, elephant, ostrich, kangaroo, pangolin, or giraffe—to say nothing of the platypus! And prehistoric creatures that were far more bizarre than the wildest imaginings of myth once walked the Earth. Imaginative reconstructions of their fossilized remains also contributed to the bestiaries.

The first bestiary in French verse was written by Philip de Thaon between 1121 and 1135, and was dedicated to Queen Adela, wife of Henry I. While the original *Physiologus* and all its predecessors consisted entirely of textual descriptions, later Bestiaries came to be lavishly and imaginatively illustrated—surely none more spectacularly than the magnificent, 12th-century *Aberdeen Bestiary*, listed in the inventory of the Old Royal Library at Westminster Palace in 1542 as *Liber de Bestiarum Natura*. This library was established by Henry VIII to house literary works rescued from the monasteries he dissolved. And, for centuries, monks had little to do but laboriously copy and re-copy old manuscripts, embellishing them as their only outlet for artistic creativity. The 13th century saw a veritable explosion of bestiaries, each attempting to outdo the others.

The Physiologus and his successors, however, were less interested in the natural history of these marvelous and mundane beasts, birds, and sea-monsters than they were in the allegorical symbolism that could be drawn from them to illustrate Christian values and morality. In presenting the animals we have chosen for this book, we are omitting all those allegorical references. (Interested readers may find them in T.H. White's charming *Book of Beasts* (1954), which is a translation of a late bestiary, with copious notes.) And we are not listing the bestiary's common and well-known animals. Rather, what you will find here are creatures of myth and legend.

"Gorgons, Hydras, and Chimeras Dire"

Fabulous monsters appear in the earliest myths and legends of all countries. In particular, the Greek heroic stories had the greatest influence on Western culture. For example, in Homer's *Odyssey,* Odysseus encounters the seductive *Sirens,* whose singing lures sailors to their doom upon the rocks. He also faces the paired terrors of the multi-headed *Scylla* and the maelstrom *Charybdis,* from which we derive the modern expression, "between a rock and a hard place." Among the 12 labors of Heracles, he had to kill the nine-headed *Lernean Hydra,* capture the golden-antlered *Arcadian Stag,* drive off the brass-feathered *Symphalian Birds,* tame the flesh-eating *Wild Mares of Diomedes,* and carry off the three-headed guard dog, *Cerberus*, from the gates of the Underworld!

Perseus beheaded the frightful *Gorgon Medusa,* whose gaze turned men to stone, and from her severed neck sprang the lovely winged horse, *Pegasus,* from whose back Bellerophon skewered the tripartite fire-breathing *Chimera*—with the head of a lion, the body of a goat, and the tail of a serpent. Perseus used Medusa's head to petrify the sea monster *Cetus,* thus rescuing the princess Andromeda to become his bride. Theseus slew the *Minotaur* in the heart of the Cretan Labyrinth. Jason and the Argonauts rescued the blind seer Phineas from the hideous *Harpies,* then went on to battle the *Dragon* guarding the fabled *Golden Fleece of Aries*, the constellation of the Ram.

The origin stories of all the gods and monsters of Greek myth were splendidly told by Hesiod (ca. 700 BCE) in his *Theogony.* He recounts how the Titans Keto and Phorcys engendered the Gorgons and the serpent-bodied *Echidna* ("Mother of Monsters"), who in turn bore the *Lernean Hydra,* the *Chimera,* the *Sphinx,* the *Harpies,* the two-headed *Orthus,* the three-headed *Cerberus,* and the vulture-eagle that gnawed Prometheus's liver. Even earlier, the ancient Sumerian *Enuma Elish* enumerated the monstrous brood of demons, scorpion-men, and horned serpents born to the primordial Dragon-Mother, *Tiamet,* who was slain by *Marduk* to create the lands and seas.

Historians and Geographers

The first writer to describe the exotic animals of various far-off lands was the Greek Herodotus (484–425 BCE). In *The Histories,* he told of the *Phoenix* that flew to Egypt to be resurrected every 500 years from Arabia; in that country also lived *Winged Serpents* and the *Cinnamon Bird* who built its nest of that precious spice. He reported dog-size *Giant Ants* (marmots) that dug up gold from the Indian desert, and repeated the story of the gold-guarding *Gryphons* of Scythia and the one-eyed *Arimaspians* who tried to steal their hoard.

Ctesias the Cnidian (ca. 400 BCE), a Greek serving as a doctor to the Persian royal court, wrote the book *Indica,* about a country he never visited. There were to be found a fierce, one-horned wild ass (the rhinoceros, often assumed to be the *Unicorn*), and the man-eating red *Martikhora* (tiger) with a human face and a scorpion's tail. He also mentioned the *Krokottas,* now understood to be the hyena.

In 44 CE, Pomponious Mela, the first Roman geographer, reported in his *De Chorographia* on the exotic creatures of Africa, including horse-eared birds called *Pegasies,* and horned ones called *Tragopomones.* Another denizen of the dark continent was the droopy-headed *Catobleblas* (gnu), with its petrifying, Gorgon-like gaze.

Pliny the Elder (23–79 CE), the world's first true naturalist, included all the creatures previously recorded, adding the *Yale*, with its swiveling horns, and the baleful *Basilisk* to the mythic menagerie of his *Natural History.* He also reported various sea monsters, including *Tritons, Nereids,* and the Sucking Fish (remora), which reportedly could hold a ship immobile.

Most writers following these [took them as the authority, prefacing their own entries with: "If Ctesias is to be believed…." *Dragons, Salamanders, Sea Serpents,* and many other creatures more and less bizarre and generally located in faraway lands found their way into the ever-expanding unnatural histories.

Travelers' Tales

In the Middle Ages, trade routes began opening up for Europeans, and enterprising merchants set out on the Silk Road to Arabia, India, and the Far East. Some explorers began to penetrate into sub-Saharan Africa as well. During this era, marvelous travelers' tales flourished, telling of exotic wonders, amazing discoveries, and romantic adventures far beyond the boundaries of the walled kingdoms of Europe. These stories were every bit as fascinating to medieval citizens as adventure tales and science fiction are to us today, with real as well as fictional explorers setting forth "to explore strange new worlds; to seek out new life and new civilizations; to boldly go where no one has gone before!"

With the advent of the Crusades (1095–1244), travel between West and East increased enormously, and soon, even remote hamlets in the British Isles had their returning crusaders, with their stories of the wonders of the Holy Land and Saracen civilization. The world had grown a whole lot bigger.

Many of the more imaginative travelers' tales were based on fantastical versions of the supposed adventures of Alexander the Great (356–323 BCE) as he conquered the known world all the way to India—and even to the heavens! Some of these fabrications were circulating as early as the 2nd century CE, but the legend reached its zenith during the 12th and 13th centuries, in the form of Alexander's alleged *Letter on India to Aristotle.*

The first and most famous European to travel across the entire continent of Asia and return to describe its nations, peoples, and animals was the Italian, Marco Polo (1254–1324). His account of 25 years of travel with his father and uncle changed the maps and vastly expanded the European worldview. However, although his descriptions of various legendary creatures are quite realistic, illustrators continued to rely on traditional interpretations.

Other travelers followed Polo, adding their accounts to the expanding bestiary. Genuine reports were overshadowed, however, by completely spurious fabrications, of which the most popular and influential were *The Letter of Prester John* (ca. 1175) and *The Travels of Sir John Mandeville* (ca. 1356). Prester John was the supposed Christian emperor of all the Indias, and the bogus letter described the marvels of his vast realm and invited the Byzantine emperor, Manuel, to visit. Over time, the location of Prester John's kingdom shifted to Africa, and generations of explorers sought to find it.

The fabricated Sir John Mandeville—the creation of an anonymous French or English author—presented a well-constructed amalgamation of material drawn from many classical and medieval sources. The narrative was taken seriously for generations as the first travel guide for pilgrims to the Holy Land, Persia, India, and far-off Cathay (China). Today it is considered the beginning of the travel-fiction genre.

All these accounts—both factual and fictional—served as preludes and inspirations for the great Age of Exploration (1420–1620), made possible by the adoption of the ingenious Chinese invention—the compass. Fleets of trading ships began traveling around the horn of Africa and into the Indian Ocean and the many islands of the East Indies. In 1492, notwithstanding the Viking excursions of half a millennium earlier, Europeans officially "discovered the New World." And finally, in 1606, Australia, the long-hypothesized southern Antipodes, completed the catalog of inhabited continents. (Frozen Antarctica wasn't discovered until 1820.) All these places had their local fauna, both factual and fictional.

Rational Disbelief

Throughout these centuries, creatures we now consider to be fabulous were generally accepted as part of the larger animal kingdom, and were never treated as a category in and of themselves. No zoological compilations distinguished between natural and unnatural history, and thus the bestiaries simply included the magickal beasts right along with the mundane ones.

By the 17th century, however, a new wave of rationalism was spreading across the Western world. Born in the twin fires of the Renaissance and the horrors of the Inquisition, the new philosophy sought to free humanity from the errors and shackles of superstition. The Scientific Revolution was officially christened with the founding of the Royal Society of London in 1660. Its Latin motto, *Nullius in Verba* ("on the words of no one"), signified a commitment to establishing truth through experiment rather than citation of authority. All things unprovable—including Dragons, Gryphons, Mermaids, Unicorns, and many other "Creatures of Night" which could not be brought to light—were dismissed with scornful derision by the new generation of scientists.

Sir Thomas Browne (2605–2682), in his *Pseudodoxia Epidemica* ("Vulgar Errors"), dealt the most crushing blow to traditional beliefs regarding many favorite beasts. Published in 1646, Browne's encyclopedic analysis challenges all the classical authorities—particularly Pliny—and devastatingly discredits such creatures as the Amphisbaena, Basilisk, Centaur, Gryphon, Phoenix, and Unicorn. However, while rejecting the accepted magical "vertues" of the Unicorn's horn (*alicorn*), Browne concedes that "there be many Unicornes."

For the next two centuries, fabulous animals were largely ignored by scholars, except as allegories in art and poetry, or in attempts to rationalize them as cases of mistaken identity and fallacious thinking. Their habitations were relegated to heraldry and fairy tales, such as those collected by the Brothers Grimm from 1812–1815.

Cryptozoology

But as new generations of explorers continued to penetrate hitherto unknown territory, they encountered persistent reports and rumors of unknown animals said to be lurking in impenetrable forests, jungles, deserts, marshes, murky lakes, and the fathomless depths of the sea. At first, these reported creatures were invariably considered mythical by scholars and scientists; but eventually, one at a time, specimens were obtained that confirmed their existence and expanded the index of known zoology. Spectacular examples included the chimpanzee and gorilla of Africa, the Komodo dragon of Indonesia, the elephant bird of Madagascar, and the giant squid—the legendary *Kraken* of Viking lore.

Many reported creatures, however, still remain elusive and unidentified, awaiting official discovery and scientific confirmation. These include such beasties as the Loch Ness Monster, Bigfoot, Sea Serpents, the Mongolian Death-Worm, and the dinosaurian Mokele-mbembe of the African Congo. To encompass these elusive monsters, Bernard Heuvelmans (1916–2001) coined the term *Cryptozoology*, the study of unknown animals. The line between modern *cryptids* (as they are called), and historical creatures of fable, myth, and legend, is ultimately nonexistent. All these beasties are lurking within these pages, and now you may set forth upon your own journey of discovery:

"Here be Monsters!"

I. THE MAGICKAL MENAGERIE

I. The Magickal Menagerie
A Glossary of Fabulous Beastes

"There be monsters of the deep, and beasts swim amid the slow and sluggishly crawling ships."
(—Avienus, lines 117–29 of *Ora Maritima*).

OST OF THE CREATURES CONSIDERED for inclusion in this glossary have been taken seriously and believed to have actually existed by those who have described and depicted them over the ages. Others are significant components of local and cultural myths, legends, and folklore. Yet another category we've included is fantastic animal representations, called *charges*, in European heraldry. These Fabulous Beasts still lurk deep in the hidden recesses of our collective cultural mythology. And sometimes, as with *cryptids* such as Bigfoot, the Kraken, and the Loch Ness Monster, actual sightings of which are reported by countless eyewitnesses, they even manifest in the flesh!

As this is a bestiary, we have restricted these entries to creatures considered to be animals of some sort—and even a few animate plants, or *plantimals*. While some of the entries may have human components (such as Centaurs, Fauns, Sirens, Harpies, and Mermaids), we have not included gods, demigods, demons, humanoid monsters and beings (Giants, Faeries, Ogres, etc.), or the "Monstrous Races" of medieval travelers' tales, said to reside in faraway lands. These will be covered in a future book.

We have also excluded mere literary and movie monsters, such as those created by Lewis Carroll, J.R.R. Tolkein, J.K. Rowling, and other authors, that appear solely in these works. A few exceptions will be made, however, for such creations as have transcended the bounds of their original literary or cinematic context to become part of our general cultural mythos—such as Tolkein's Ents, Lovecraft's Cthulhu, and the movie monsters Godzilla, King Kong, and the Creature from the Black Lagoon.

We have also chosen to omit "Nursery Bogies"—those terrifying spooks that parents in every culture have invented to frighten their children into submission and keep them from wandering off into dangerous places, such as fens and forests, marshes and millponds, wells and woodlands. Although these are multitudinous, they are not truly "Fabulous Beasts" in the same sense as our other entries, as no adults actually believe in their existence, or ever have.

The alphabet verses are by Elizabeth Barrette.

A is for Amphisien: two-headed,
Serpentine, and surely to be dreaded.
Touching nose to nose, it goes a-rolling
Past knights who thought they'd find it a-strolling.

Aatxer—A terrifying red bull in the Basque folklore of Spain. Dwelling among the canyons, caves, and gorges of the Pyrenees Mountains, he comes out on stormy nights to harass travelers. His younger self is called *Aatxegorri*. He is the nemesis of all *Unicorns* in Peter Beagle's fantasy novel and movie, *The Last Unicorn* (1968). His mate is *Beigorri*, a crimson cow.

Ababil—According to the Quran, these were huge birds that saved the city of Mecca in the year of Mohammed's birth (571 CE) by dropping bricks on an attacking army of elephants—possibly an explanation for a meteor shower. Ababil is now a local name for the common Barn Swallow (*Hirundo rustica*). See *Roc*.

Abada—A type of small *Unicorn* said to dwell in the African Congo. Said to be very shy, it is probably a Black Rhinoceros (*Diceros bicornis*). See *Abath*, *Cartazonus*, *Karkadan*, *Kere*, *Serou*.

Abaia—A gigantic eel of Melanesian mythology. It lurks at the bottom of freshwater lakes throughout the islands of Fiji, Solomon, and Vanuatu and protects the fish. If humans attempt to fish in its lake, the Abaia causes terrible rainstorms and floods to destroy them.

A Bao A Qu—A pathetic allegorical creature of Malaysian lore, it is said to lurk invisibly at the base of the winding stair of Chitor's Tower of Victory. When a pilgrim sets foot on the first step, the A Bao A Qu awakens. Silently it follows the climber, gaining substance, color, solidity, and perfection with each step. Its manifestation is complete only at the final terrace, and only if the pilgrim is an enlightened being. In all the centuries, this has only happened once. Otherwise, the A Bao A Qu tumbles back down as the climber descends, until it is once again no more than a vague, amorphous presence.

Abath—A female *Unicorn* said by 16th-century European writers to dwell in the forests of the Malay Peninsula of Southeast Asia. This was certainly the small and very rare Javan Rhinoceros (*Rhinoceros sondaicus*). See *Abada, Cartazonus, Karkadan, Kere, Serou*.

Abgal (or *Apkallu*)—These *Merfolk* of Sumerian myth were regarded as guardians of a sort, and teachers of the arts and sciences. They had the head of a man and the lower body of a fish. They are believed to have derived from the *Apsu*, of the entourage of Enki, god of wisdom. In Philistine-Assyrian myth, their king is Dagon, god of earth and agriculture.

Achiyalabopa—This celestial bird hails from Pueblo Indian myth. Its rainbow-colored feathers are said to be sharp as knives. It is reminiscent of the *Stymphalian Birds* that Heracles killed for his sixth Labor.

Achlis—A bizarre, elk-like beast of Northern European folklore, the Achlis has an enormous upper lip that forces the creature to eat by walking backwards. Having no joints in its hind legs, it is unable to rise from a lying position, and must rest by leaning against a tree at night. Clever hunters can capture it by partially cutting through its favorite tree. When the tree topples, so does the Achlis. It was described by Pliny the Elder (23 BCE–79 CE) in his *Natural History*. It is also known among the *Fearsome Critters* as the *Hugag*.

Acipenser—An unusual beastie of European myth whose anatomy hinders rather than helps it. These monstrous fishes have scales opening toward the front. This fish is actually the Sturgeon (*Acipenser*), which derives its scientific name from its mythological antecedent.

Adar Llwch Gwin—These bird-like creatures of Welsh Arthurian myth could understand human speech. They were commanded by Drudwas, and were used for magickal combat as well as for protection. They were so loyal to their master that they killed him after he ordered that they slay the first knight to appear on a field of battle. His opponents were delayed, making Drudwas the first to arrive. The Adar Llwch Gwin appear in the hit series *Final Fantasy*, in the guise of the *Chocobo*.

Adaro—These are *Merfolk* of the Solomon Islands. But nlike most Merfolk, the Adaro have actual legs and feet from which sprout their fishy fins. In addition to this oddity, shark-like dorsal fins adorn their heads. They live in the sun, travel to Earth on rainbows, and ride on waterspouts over land. They shoot people with flying fish, causing unconsciousness and sometimes death.

Aeternae—Ferocious beasts with sawedged horns reported as living in the northern plains of India in the 4th century BCE. They killed several of Alexander the Great's soldiers who challenged them. This may be the same creature as the *Antalops*, possibly the Asiatic Ibex (*Capra ibex sibirica*). See *Urus*.

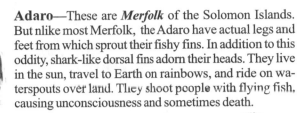

Afanc (or *Adang, Abhac, Abac, Addanc, Addane, Adanc, Avanc*)—An evil water beast of Welsh folklore, the Afanc resembles the *Hippocampus* or *Water-Horse* in appearance, sometimes with elements of a crocodile or beaver. Lurking for prey in river pools near Brynberian Bridge, the Afanc pulls in those who are unlucky enough to wander too close, and causes random flash floods to the surrounding areas. Other locations where it was seen include Llyn Llion, Llyn Barfog, and Llyn yr Afanc. The Afanc was eventually destroyed, some say by King Arthur himself. See *Aughisky, Kelpie*.

Agathodemon—A winged serpent in Gnostic lore said to bring good fortune. When equated with *Aion*, the god of time, it is shown with a lion's head on a man's body, and standing on a globe encircled by the signs of the Zodiac.

Agogwe (*Kakundakri* in Zimbabwe; *Sehit* on the Ivory Coast)—Small, furry hominids sighted in Tanzania, East Africa, and other locales in Sub-Saharan Africa. With grotesque features and aggressive behavior, they are 3–4 feet tall, bipedal, long-armed, and covered with a scraggly coat of thick, rust-colored hair over reddish-yellow skin. Some cryptozoologists suggest that they may be remnant *Australopithecines* (shown). See *Bigfoot*.

Ahani—A family of evil, predatory monsters in the mythology of the Navajo Indians of the American Southwest. The *Binaye Ahani* are limbless twins with deformed torsos. Filled with malice toward all creatures, the gaze of their eyes can kill. The *Thelgeth* are huge, headless monsters covered in shaggy hair, and the *Tsanahale* are giant, feathered bird-monsters resembling *Harpies*.

Ahool—Reportedly seen in Java and Vietnam, these are giant bats of an unidentified species. Named for their cry, they are said to be the size of a year-old child, dark grey, and with a head similar to that of a monkey. They resemble fruit bats, which are related to primates and thus really are a kind of flying monkey. The Malayan Flying Fox (*Pteropus vampyrus*) has a 6-foot wingspan. Despite its resemblance to the fruit bat, however, the Ahool is said to be a fish-eater. See **Alan**, **Guiafairo**, **Hsigo**, **Olitiau**, **Orang-Bati**, **Ropen**, **Sassabonsum**, **Vietnamese Night Flyers**.

Ahuizhotl ("Water Possum"; also called *Sun Dog*)—This vicious predator of Mexican and Central American myth resembles a medium-sized dog, with monkey paws and a human hand at the end of its prehensile tail. It snatches unwary fishermen and people walking too close to the shore, pulling them under the water to eat only their eyes, teeth, and nails. It is most likely based upon the Kinkajou (*Potos flavus*), also called the Honey Bear, which is the only member of the Carnivora with a prehensile tail. See **Glyryvilu**.

Aillen Trechenn—A three-headed Irish monster that hated all humans, especially heroes. Each Samhain (Hallowe'en) it emerged from a mound to wreak havoc until it was eventually slain by Amairgen.

Ai Tojon—A great, two-headed eagle of Siberian myth, the Ai Tojon lives at the very top of the World Tree, from which he shines forth light over all the world.

Aitvaras (identical to Latvian *Pûkis* and Estonian *Tulihänd*, *Pisuhänd*, *Puuk*; also known as *Kaukas*, *Damavykas*, *Spary•ius*, *Koklikas*, *Gausinëlis*, *•altvikšas*, *Spirukas*)—A Lithuanian household spirit that resembles a cock while indoors, but outdoors appears as a dragon about 2 feet long, with a serpentine body and four legs. In some districts it has wings and flies through the air trailing fire. It may hatch from an egg of a 9- to 12-year-old rooster, and if it dies it becomes a spark. An Aitvaras will lodge itself in a house, refusing to leave. Its presence brings riches into the household, but the wealth is usually stolen from the neighbors. An Aitvaras can be purchased from the Devil, but the price is the buyer's soul. Once bought, it is nearly impossible to get rid of. If injured, it can be healed just by touching the ground. See **Lidérc**.

Aja Akapad—A lightning-swift, one-legged goat in Hindu mythology. It represents the force of lightning as it strikes the Earth with a single kick.

Ajatar (also spelled *Aiatar* or *Ajattara;* related to the Lithuanian **Aitvaras** and the Estonian *Äi*, *Äijo*, or *Äijatar*)—An evil female serpent or **Dragon** from Finnish legend. Called "Devil of the Woods," or "Mother of the Devil," she suckles serpents that cause illness.

Akhekhu— An Egyptian desert serpent with four legs, thought by European travelers to resemble a **Gryphon** in some unspecified respects. However, the description is more reminiscent of a long-necked lizard, most likely the Nile Monitor (*Varanus niloticus*).

Akhlut—A spectral killer whale of Inuit myth, this creature is said to hunt the Alaskan ice in the form of a gigantic wolf. Avoid places where giant wolf tracks disappear near the edge of a floe, as this means that Akhlut is back in his killer whale form and lurking nearby. He may be hungry! See **Amarok**.

Akuma—Also called *Toori Akuma* or *Ma*, this demonic Japanese monster is terrifying and evil. With an enormous flaming head and eyes like coals, it flies through the air brandishing a sword. It brings bad luck to anyone who sees it.

Akupara—In the Hindu mythology of India, the Akupara is the gigantic cosmic turtle that supports the Earth upon the backs of four, eight, or 16 elephants standing on his shell. See **Father of All Turtles**, **Kurma**.

Al (or *Elk*)—This hairy, half-human, half-beast creature of Armenian, Libyan, and Persian folklore has fiery red eyes, tusks similar to those of a boar, iron teeth, brass claws, and copious, shaggy, snake-like hair. It lives in swamps, as well as damp, dark places such as stables and wet corners of houses, and attacks humans who wander into the wilderness. It becomes invisible when it dons a pointy hat covered with small bells. The Al actively hunts women—especially when they are incapacitated in childbirth, as newborn infants are its favorite delicacy. It carries scissors to cut the umbilical cord. It may also steal the woman's liver, and the victim and her child both die when the Al touches the liver to water, which it must do in order to eat the liver. The Afghan version of this creature is a ghoulish female beast, with long, floating hair and talon-like finger nails, that consumes human corpses.

Alan—Mischievous, half-human, half-bird creatures from the forests of the Philippines. With extended fingers on their backward-facing feet and stubby toes on their hands, they spend much of their time hanging upside down from trees. They are often very helpful toward humans, and supposedly served as foster parents to several legendary heroes whom they found lost in the forest as babies. This description, along with the locale, strongly suggests a giant fruit bat, such as the Malayan Flying Fox (*Pteropus vampyrus*), which has a 6-foot wingspan, although it only weighs up to 3.3 pounds. See *Ahool*, *Alan*, *Guiafairo*, *Hsigo*, *Olitiau*, *Orang-Bati*, *Ropen*, *Sassabonsum*.

Alicanto—A luminous bird of Chile that feeds on silver and gold ores in the mountains. The Alicantos that eat gold shine like the sun at night, and the ones that eat silver glow like the full moon. Prospectors follow these lights through the darkness, hoping to be led to rich veins of ore, but they generally just fall over a cliff. These myths certainly refer to Fireflys (*Lampyridae*). See *Cucuia*, *Ercinee*.

Alkonost—Similar to the *Harpy*, this horrible creature of Siberian myth has the upper body of a human female and the lower body of a gigantic bird of prey. She dwells in *Rai*, the Land of the Dead, where her grim task is to torment the souls of the damned. Her antithesis is the *Sirin*. But in Slavic myth, the Alkonost is the *Bird of Paradise*, with a voice so sweet that all who hear it lapse into forgetfulness. She lays her eggs on the seashore and puts them into the water. The sea is then calm for six or seven days, at which point the eggs hatch, bringing a storm. See *Halcyon, Geraher*.

Allocamelus—A beast of English heraldry, with the body and legs of a camel and the head of an ass.

Alloés—Described in the 16th century by Thevet in his *Cosmography*, this New World sea creature resembled a cross between a goose and a fish, with a long, bird-like neck, and flippers instead of wings and feet. It may have been the Great Auk (*Pinguinus impennis*), extinct since 1844.

Almas (or *Albasty, Abnuaaya, Abnuaaya, Almasti, Bekk-Bokk, Mongolian Wild Man*)—Said to dwell in the Altai Mountains near Tien Shan in the province of Sinkiang, Mongolia, these "wild people" live like animals and are covered with hair, except on their hands and faces. Although this description would seem to describe some sort of unknown ape, some cryptozoologists have suggested that the Almas may be remnant Neanderthals. See *Chuchunaa*, *Wudewasa*, *Yeti*.

Alphyn—A fantastic heraldic beast with a body similar to that of a wolf, and the front legs and belly of a dragon. It also has long, pointed ears, a long, thin tongue, and a knotted tail.

Altamaha-ha—An aquatic mystery creature sighted by many witnesses since 1969 in the Altamaha River, the surrounding waterways and marshes of the South Georgia coast, and also in Florida. It is about 20 feet long and as big around as a man's body, with front flippers and a horizontal fluked tail. It is described as very elongated, resembling something between an alligator, an eel, and a dolphin, with large, protruding eyes and an alligator-like snout armed with large, conical teeth. It has a serrated ridge down the back and a low dorsal fin. It has often been seen stranded on the banks of the river and cavorting on the surface like a dolphin. These descriptions suggest it is a freshwater dolphin .

Amarok—A spectral wolf of Canadian Inuit myth, the Amarok will overtake and devour any who are foolish enough to venture out alone at night. See *Akhlut*.

Amikiri — Small flying creatures of Japanese folklore, with crablike claws and long, serpentine tails. They cut up mosquito nets, fishing nets, and laundry hung out to dry.

Ambize—A creature from the Congo River delta area of West Africa, where it was also called the *Angulo* ("Hog Fish"). It was described by 16th-century European sailors as having the head of a pig on the body of a huge fish. Weighing more than 500 pounds, it also had human arms and hands and a round, flat tail similar to a beaver's. Its meat tasted like pork. This description is certainly reminiscent of an African Manatee (*Trichechidae senegalensis*). See *Hoga, Igpupiara*.

Amhuluk—Serpentine *Lake Monsters* in the folklore of the Oregon Indians. They metamorphose into many different forms, each more terrible than the last. Animals that fall into the enchanted waters of their lakes are also transformed into monsters.

A-Mi-Kuk—A huge and hideous sea-monster in the folklore of the Inuits of the Bering Straits. With a slimy skin and four long, human arms instead of legs, it preys on fishermen. It can "swim" through the earth, pursuing its quarry to lakes far inland.

Ammut (or *Ammet, Amemet, Amermait, Am-Mit, Amam;* meaning "Bone Eater")—A terrible female monster in the Egyptian Underworld, she has the head of a crocodile, a lion's mane, a leopard's forelimbs and spots, and the hindquarters of a hippopotamus. The Egyptians called her "the Devourer of the Dead." She personified divine retribution for all the wrongs one had committed in life. In Osiris' Hall of Justice, the hearts of the dead were weighed against Ma'at's feather of truth, and those who failed to pass the test were fed to Ammut.

Amphisbaena (Greek, "goes both ways"; also called *Amphista, Anksymen, Anphine, Fenmine,* or *Amphivena,* "Mother of Ants," which it feeds upon)—A snake-like reptile of Libya with glowing eyes and heads at both ends of its body. If cut in half, both halves will rejoin. It moves in either direction by placing one of its heads in the other's mouth and rolling along like a wheel. According to Pliny, wearing a live amphisbaena will protect pregnant women, and wearing a dead one will cure rheumatism. The Amphisbaena is also a real animal, a kind of legless, burrowing "worm lizard" (*Amphisbaenidae*) whose tail is shaped exactly the same as its eyeless, earless head. There are 158 different species. They grow up to 20 inches in length, and crawl equally well forward or backward (but they don't roll like a wheel!). See *Amphisien, Hoop Snake*.

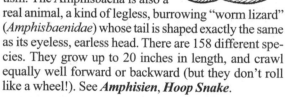

Amphisien (or *Amphisaena, Amphisbeme*)—A bizarre heraldic variant of the **Cockatrice**, depicted as a **Dragon**-serpent with two heads, one in the usual place and the other at the end of its tail. It has birds' legs and feet and Dragon wings. *Amphisaena* is also a bronchial ailment caused by the ingestion of amphorae.

Amphitere—Beautiful, feather-plumed or serpentine **Dragons** similar to the Aztec **Quetzalcoatl** or the Egyptian **Apep**. Amphiteres were reputed to possess great wisdom and knowledge, as well as some form of associated power, such as the ability to hypnotize. Many also guarded hordes of treasure, but, unlike typical treasure-hording Dragons, they took on the task out of obligation rather than out of a liking of shiny things. It was said that armed men would grow from the teeth of an Amphitere planted in fertile ground, and would be absolutely loyal to the sower.

Anaye—A group of malevolent sibling monsters of Navajo Indian mythology. There are four kinds: the limbless *Binaye Ahani*; the headless *Thelgeth*; the *Tsanahale* bird; and an unnamed creature whose f u r grows like roots into the desert rocks. Considered to be the fatherless children of wicked women, they are the source of all misery, fear, and evil in the world. They are vanquished by the sons of the Sun and Water, but their other siblings—Cold, Poverty, Famine, and Old Age—continue to plague us.

Angka—An enormous Arabian bird, large enough to carry off an elephant. Much like the **Phoenix**, it lives for 1,700 years, burns itself to ashes, and rises again. Because of its great size, it is also associated with the **Roc**. The Arabs believed that they were originally created as perfect birds, but over time, they devoured all the animals on Earth and started carrying off children. The people appealed to God, who prevented the Anka from multiplying; thus it eventually became extinct.

Angont—A gigantic, poisonous serpent in the folklore of Eastern Canada's Huron Indians. Indeed, the very flesh of this monster is deadly, much like that of poison arrow frogs. It lurks in forbidding and desolate places, from which it uncoils across the land to inflict pestilence and calamities upon humanity.

Aniwye—A giant skunk-monster in the folklore of Canada's Ojibwa Indians. Similar to its smaller brethren, the Aniwye uses a nasty spray as a defensive or offensive weapon. It has a taste for human flesh, and can understand human languages.

Anthalops (or *Alce, Alcida, Talopus, Calopus, Panthalops*)—A large antelope whose curved horns have saw-toothed edges with which it can cut down large trees. In Babylonian myth, this creature was called **Aptaleon.** Descriptions and drawings seem to indicate the Sable Antelope (*Hippotragus niger*) as the most likely inspiration for this creature, but a strong case has also been made for the Reindeer (*Rangifer tarandus*), as an important aspect of the myth shows that the Anthalops often gets its horns stuck in branches of the Herecine Shrub (*Hircus-cervus*), and

Fabricus wrote that reindeer did indeed have saw-shaped horns. However, because reindeer live only in the far north, this identification seems unlikely. See **Busse, Calopus, Parandrus**.

Antukai (or *Atunkai*)—According to native Oregon Indian legend,

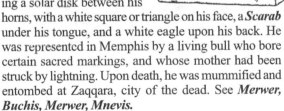

this was originally a grizzly bear that fell into the waters of the lake serpent **Amhuluk** and was turned into a huge beaver or otter-like monster that hunts people. During the Pleistocene era, there was a colossal beaver (*Castoroides ohioensis*) in North America. It was 8.2 feet long and weighed 485 lbs.

Anzu (or *Zû, Imndugud*)—A gigantic, benevolent storm-bird in ancient Mesopotamian mythology. Similar to a **Gryphon**, it has a lion's body and the head of an eagle with a saw-like beak; though it was sometimes said to have the body of an eagle and the head and torso of a bearded man. Later versions gave it two heads. It is the attendant of the great primordial serpent **Dragon**, **Tiamet**, and the thunderclap of its mighty wings brings welcome rains to the parched desert. See **Uma Na-Iru**.

Apalala—A frightening water-serpent of India that ruled the source of the Swat River in the state of Peshawar, now Pakistan. It was tamed and converted by the Buddha, a scene often illustrated in Buddhist art. See **Lake Monsters, Makara**.

Apis—(also *Hap*, or Greek, *Epaphus*) A gigantic black bull in ancient Egyptian mythology, sacred to the creator-god Ptah. He was represented as bearing a solar disk between his horns, with a white square or triangle on his face, a **Scarab** under his tongue, and a white eagle upon his back. He was represented in Memphis by a living bull who bore certain sacred markings, and whose mother had been struck by lightning. Upon death, he was mummified and entombed at Zaqqara, city of the dead. See **Merwer, Buchis, Merwer, Mnevis**.

Apocalyptic Beasts—In the New Testament's final *Book of Revelation*, three Beasts are prophesied to appear at the time of the *Apocalypse* ("Lifting of the Veil"), and will initiate *Armageddon*, the great battle between Good and Evil that will precede the Second Coming and the Day of Judgment. The first Beast will come

out of the sea, and will have the body of a leopard, the paws of a bear, and seven leonine heads bearing ten horns and ten crowns. The second Beast will arise from the Earth. It will have the same bodily form, but with only one head and short horns. The third Beast resembles the first except that it is red in color, and upon it will ride the "Scarlet Woman" or "Whore of Babylon," representing all corruption in religion and politics. See **Hydra**

Apotharni—A race of male and female **Centaurs** described by Conrad Lycosthenes in his *Prodigorum ac Ostentorum Chronicon* (1557). Dwelling in marshy areas, both sexes are bald-headed and have goatees on their chins. See **Onocentaur, Hippocentaur**.

Apres—A Heraldic bull with a short tail similar to that of a bear.

Aptaleon—This mythical Babylonian beast could saw down trees with his horns, but could get caught and held in a thicket or a bush called *erechire*. Probably based on antelopes, it appears in British heraldry and carvings in Churches. See **Calopus, Antelops**.

Areop-enap—On the South Pacific island of Nauru, Areop-enap, the Ancient Spider, created the world out of an immense clamshell. Finding two smaller, horn-shaped snail shells inside, he placed them at either side to form the sun and the moon. Then he enlisted a caterpillar named **Rigi** to pry open the lid of the clamshell, and Rigi's salty sweat became the sea. The bottom part of the shell formed the Earth and the upper lid, the heavens. After Rigi became a butterfly, he flew between them to keep them separate.

Arion—A magickal winged **Pegasus**, offspring of the grain-goddess Demeter and the sea-god Poseidon in their horse-god/-goddess guises. Arion has a rather unique feature in that both of his right feet are actually human hands. The name has been given to the common garden slug (*Arion hortensis*).

Argus Fish—One of a number of bizarre sea monsters depicted in Olaus Magnus' newsletter, *Monstrum in Oceano Germanica* ("Monsters of the North Sea," Rome, 1537). The 72-foot-long creature is shown with several additional eyes on its flanks, and is therefore named for *Argos*, the thousand-eyed Titan of Greek mythology whose eyes were placed in the tail of the peacock. This is clearly a representation of a Whale Shark (*Rhincodon typus*), whose dramatic "tic-tac-toe" markings of

white lines and dots do indeed give the impression of many eyes along its sides. It is the world's largest fish, officially recorded at 40 feet long, with reported lengths up to 70 feet.

Aries—A great winged ram from Geek mythology. Its name is *Chrysomallus*, "The Ram with the Golden Fleece," and it is that legendary fleece that

becomes the quest of the Argosy. The story goes that when young Prince Phryxus of Thessaly was accused by his wicked stepmother of causing a famine in the land, he fled to Colchis on the back of Chrysomallus. Arriving safely, he sacrificed the ram to Zeus and hung its fleece in the temple, from whence it was eventually stolen by Jason and the Argonauts. Zeus placed Chrysomallus himself in the heavens as the constellation of Aries the Ram. Recent archaeological research has revealed that the people of ancient Colchis used wooly sheepskins to filter gold particles from the rivers.

Asipatra—This *Stymphalian Bird* of Indian myth has razor sharp claws and wings. Asiparta lives in *Yamapura*, the Underworld, where it tortures condemned souls.

Asootee—In Hindu mythology, this is the enormous world-serpent with its tail in its mouth that encircles the entire universe— turtle, elephants, and Earth. See *Jormungand*.

Aspidochelone (Latin, "Shield Turtle"; also *Aspidodelone*, **Fastitocalon**, or "Devil Whale")—A sea monster similar to a giant whale or turtle, so immense that, when it is basking on the surface, sailors mistake its back for an island and land on it. When they build a fire, however,

the "island" plunges into the depths, dragging the ship and crew to a watery doom. European sailors often told tales of its existence and sightings. Arabian writers called it the **Zaratan**. See *Father of All Turtles*, *Imap Umassoursa*, *Jasconius*.

Aspis (Latin, "Asp")—A two-legged *Dragon* of medieval Europe, depicted both with and without wings. Its bite causes instant death, and it is so poisonous that even touching its dead body is fatal. But it can be easily overcome by music, upon hearing which it jams its tail into one ear and presses the other to the ground.

Ass-Bittern—A creature of British heraldry with the body of an ass and the head of a bittern bird (*Botaurus stellaris*).

Audumbla—This immense cow was the second being after the giant Ymir to appear from the melting ice of Niflheim in the Norse creation myth. Her milk nourished Ymir, and her licking of the ice revealed the first gods.

Aughisky (also *Each Uisge* or *Alastyn*)—A shape-shifting Irish water monster, virtually identical to the Scottish **Kelpie** and the Welsh **Afanc**. Appearing as a tame horse, it invites weary travelers to mount it, whereupon it plunges into the nearest water, drowns them, and devours everything but their livers. As long as the rider keeps the Aughisky away from water there is no danger, but any sight or scent of water means certain doom. Despite its horselike ears, it can sometimes appear human. See **Horse-Eel**, **Kelpie**, **Peiste**, **Water-Horse**.

Auvekoejak—A sea monster found in the waters around Greenland. Inuit descriptions of these creatures resemble **Merfolk**, except that they are covered in fur rather than scales. The same creature was called **Havstrambe** by the Norse of Iceland and Scandinavia. It has been equated with the Northern Fur Seal (*Callorhinus ursinus*) as well as the Stellar's Sea Cow (*Hydrodamalis gigas*), which Arctic explorers exterminated by 1768. See **Ikalu Nappa**, **Margygr**.

Avelerion (also *Allerion, Ilerion, Yllerion*)—Eagle-like birds of prey, there is only one pair living in the world, in Asia or India. The spurious 12th-century *Letter of Prester John* described them as having fiery, razor-edged feathers, similar to **Stymphalian Birds.** At the age of 60 years they produce two or three eggs, and when the eggs hatch after 40 days, the parents drown themselves in the sea, a scene witnessed by representatives of all other birds. In heraldry they are often represented without a beak or feet, similar to footless **Martlets**. They are seen on the coat-of-arms of the Lorraine family, and depicted on the *Mappa Mundi* ("Map of the World") disk of Hereford Cathedral in England (c. 1295).

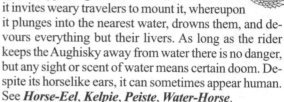

Axex—Similar to a **Gryphon**, this Egyptian creature sports a hawk's head and wings on the muscular torso of a large feline. Three curved appendages atop its head resemble the crest of a rooster. The Axex has sometimes been confused with the winged British scavenger known as the **Opincus**.

Az-i-wû-ghûm-ki-mukh-'ti
—A fearsome creature of Inuit folklore said to resemble a walrus, but with the fanged head and legs of a dog, the tail of a fish, and shiny black scales. It can kill a man with a single swipe of its tail. See *Equus Bipes*, *Marine Boar*, *Rosmarine*, *Sea Hog*

B is for Baku, the eater of dreams,
Gubbling nightmares, swallowing screams.
Head of an elephant, tail of an ox –
Still it will come through, no matter the locks.

Babai—A creature of the Egyptian Underworld, that assists *Ammut*, the Eater of the Dead, in disposing of any deceased who fail the test of Ma'at's Feather of Truth.

Badigui (or *Diba, Ngakoula-Ngou*)—A gigantic water snake said to dwell in the Ubangi-Shari of equatorial Africa. It browses on tree branches without leaving the water, and strangles hippos but does not eat them.

Baginis—Half animal and half woman, these beautiful creatures of Australian folklore have clawlike fingers and toes. They capture men, but let them go after raping them.

Bagwyn—A hybrid creature only rarely depicted in European heraldry. It has the body and tail of a horse and the head of a heraldic antelope, with long horns curved backward.

Bahamut—An enormous, dazzlingly bright fish with the head of a hippo or elephant. In Moslem myth, it floats in a fathomless sea, supporting on its back an immense bull named *Kujuta* with 4,000 eyes, ears, nostrils, mouths, and feet. The bull in turn carries a gigantic ruby mountain, upon which stands an angel who holds the six hells. Above these is the Earth, and above the Earth, the seven heavens. Some say that beneath the sea is the Realm of Fire, where writhes *Falak*, a vast serpent whose mouth contains the six Hells. See *Behemoth*, *Labbu*, *Makara*.

Bahri—A human-headed bird of Moslem myth, similar to the Greek *Siren*.

Baikal Lake Monster—Lake Baikal in Siberia is the world's largest body of fresh water. More than 4,900-ft deep, it contains more than 20% of the Earth's fresh water, and harbors more species of animals and plants than any other lake on the planet. One of these is reported to be a gigantic sturgeon, even larger than the record of 27 feet for a Russian Sturgeon (*Acipenser gueldenstaedtii*). Some think this monster is a mutant spawned by the massive pollution of the lake by the Baikalsk Pulp and Paper Mill, which has been dumping approximately 640,000 cubic feet of untreated waste into Lake Baikal every day since 1966. See *Flathead Lake Monster*, *Mother of the Fishes*, *Whitey*.

Bakbakwakanooksiwae—A monstrous, vicious, man-eating bird in the Kwakiutl Indian folklore of Canada's northwest coast. He is also called *Hokhoky*, "Cannibal-at-the-North-End-of-the-World." He and his mate, *Galokwudzuwis*, hunt down people, smash in their skulls, and gobble their brains.

Baku—A benevolent dream monster of Japanese folklore. It has the body of a tapir, the head of an elephant, the mane of a lion, the tail of an ox, and the legs and paws of a tiger. When invoked upon first awakening, by saying "O Baku, eat my dreams!" it gobbles up any lingering nightmares, so that the dreamer may have a peaceful day.

Balam—Supernatural Jaguar guardians of the Four Directions in the folklore of the Quiché Indians of Mexico. Their names are: *Iqi-Balam* ("Moon Jaguar"), *Balam-Agab* ("Night Jaguar"), *Balam-Quitzé* ("Smiling Jaguar"), and *Mahu-Catah* ("Famous Name"). In their roles as guardians of nature, they protect the villages, the people, and their cultivated land.

Balena—A female sea monster mentioned but not described in the 2nd-century Alexandrian *Physiologus*. The term eventually came to be applied to the great baleen whales (*Mysticeti*).

Bar Juchne (or *Bar Yacre*)—In Talmudic Jewish legend, this is an enormous bird, similar to the *Roc*, whose wingspan can eclipse even the sun. It preys on cattle and even humans. It was said that once upon a time an egg fell from a Bar Juchne nest, shattering 300 trees and flooding 60 villages. See *Anka*, *Ziz*.

Barliate (or *Annes de la mer, Barchad, Barnacha, Bernekke, Bernaca, Bernicle, Barnacle Goose, Tree Goose*)—A type of Goose that was believed to begin life as a kind of barnacle

growing from trees or attached to driftwood. It is based upon actual Goose-Neck Barnacles (*Lepas anatifera*).

Barmanu ("Big Hairy One")—A kind of hairy hominid reported from eastern Afghanistan, as well as the Shishi Kuh Valley in the Chitral region of Northern Pakistan. Similar to the American **Skunk Ape**, it is noted for its revolting stench. See **Bigfoot**, **Yeti**.

Barometz (Tartar, "Little Lamb"; or *Tartary Lamb*, *Barbary Lamb*, *Scythian Lamb*, *Vegetable Lamb*, *Lycopodium*)—In Hebrew legend, this is a woolly, sheeplike creature from the Middle East that is also half vegetable. Formally called *Planta Tartarica Barometz*, they are produced from little gourds and attached to shrubs by very short stems. Once they have eaten all the grass within reach, they die of starvation. Barometz was considered a delicacy as its meat supposedly tastes like crab, and its blood like honey. Its bones were used in rituals to give the power of prophecy. The "vegetable lamb" is generally assumed to be the Cotton Shrub (*Gossypium*), but it has also been explained as a Wooly Fern *(Cibotium barometz)* that grows in the Middle East and is used as a styptic. Yet another excellent candidate is *Polypodium barometz*, an Asian fern with thick roots growing along the surface of the ground, which are covered in a dense wool, and when cut, ooze a blood-red fluid.

Basket Monster—In African Zulu folklore, this creature appears to be an open baby basket. But if an unwary mother places her baby inside, the basket grows legs and scuttles away like a crab.

Basilisk (from Greek, *basileus*, "Little King"; or Latin, *Regulus*, "Prince"; in French, *Basilic* or *Basili-coc*)—Born from the blood of Medusa's eyes, the Basilisk is described as a monstrous serpent crowned with a dramatic frill, crest, or crown, for which it is called the "King of Serpents." It is so poisonous that it leaves a wide trail of deadly venom in its wake, and its gaze is likewise lethal. It poisons streams, withers forests, and causes birds to drop out of the sky. Its enemy is the weasel and mongoose. In actuality, the Basilisk derives from the Egyptian Spitting Cobra (*Naja nigricollis*), which grows to 7 feet long, and sprays lethal poison from its fangs with great accuracy into the eyes of its victims. There are also small South American lizards called Basilisks (*Basiliscus*), but they have none of the attributes of their legendary namesake. See also **Cockatrice**, **Muiriasc**, **Scoffin**.

Batsquatch—A bizarre, bat-winged nocturnal primate said to dwell in the dense forests surrounding Mount St. Helens in the state of Washington. It has purple skin, red eyes, and a simian head with bat-like features. Some cryptozoologists speculate that it may be an unknown species of giant fruit bat. See **Ahool**, **Alan**, **Big Bird**, **Guiafairo**, **Hsigo**, **Kongamato**, **Olitiau**, **Sassabonsum**.

Batutut—A small, red, apelike creature reported to dwell in the rainforest of the Malaysian state of Sabah, it is considered to be related to the little, frog-eating hairy hominid known as the **Teh-Ma**, and the Vietnamese **Nguoi-Rung**. See **Orang Pendek**.

Beast of Brassknocker Hill—In a 1979 sighting, this creature was seen stripping the bark and branches from trees in an area of England. Local small wildlife also began to decline. Finally, an eyewitness reported seeing a 4-foot-long, bear-like creature with two dramatic white rings circling its eyes. Although supposedly still unidentified, this could only be an Andean Spectacled Bear (*Tremarctos ornatus),* probably escaped from a menagerie. Gerald Durrell's Jersey Zoo has several of these.

Beasts of Elmendorf—These hairless, blue-skinned, canine-like creatures have been terrorizing the farms of East Texas since 2004.

Beast of Gévaudan—A vicious, wolf-like beast that ravaged the countryside of southeastern France from 1764–1767. It was said to have killed more than 100 people and many cattle, ripping out their entrails. It was described as looking something like a wolf, with a shaggy coat, long legs, and glaring eyes. Many believed it to be a werewolf. When local hunters failed to kill it, King Louis XV sent his own soldiers, to no avail. In 1767, it was finally killed by Jean Chastel, who shot it with two silver bullets. It turned out to be a Striped Hyaena (*Hyaena hyaena*), escaped from the private menagerie of Antoine Chastel, Jean's son. *Brotherhood of the Wolf* (2001) is an excellent film of these events. See **Crocotta**.

Behemoth (or *Enoch*)—An exaggerated Biblical version of the hippopotamus, appearing in the Book of Job (40:15-19). The word comes from the plural of the Hebrew *b'hemah*, meaning "kingly beast." Thus any large, heavy, and other-

wise unknown animal can be called a "Behemoth." In Jewish legend, the Behemoth is a monster of formidable strength, often portrayed in battle with the *Leviathan*. In Christian apocryphal tradition, the Behemoth is identified with Satan, as a monster that must be destroyed. Some cryptozoologists have proposed that the Behemoth may be a reference to the *Mokele-M'Bembe*. See ***Bahamut, Hadhayôsh***.

Beithir—A giant eel or water-snake said to inhabit secluded waters of the Scottish Highlands. Witnesses report its length at 9 to 10 feet, and it has been seen moving over land. This may be a Conger Eel (*Conger conger*), which is known to attain that size. Many eels can squirm through wet grass from one pond to another. Or, it could be a typical *Lake Monster*.

Benu—This heron-like bird is white with red legs and a crest of long feathers sweeping back from the crown of its head. The word *Benu* in Egyptian means both Purple Heron (*Ardea purpurea*) and palm tree. Much of the *Phoenix* mythology is based on Egyptian myths of the Benu, as it was said to rise from its burning tree with such melodious song that even the gods were enthralled. The Benu was a symbol of the sun-god Ra, reborn each morning in the fiery dawn. It was also identified with Osiris, as it resurrected itself from death.

Ben-Varrey and **Dinny-Marra** (or *Dooinney Marrey*, Manx, "Man of the Sea")—These *Merfolk* dwell around the Isle of Man. Dinny-Marra are the males, which tend to be friendly and easy to get along with. The females are called *Ben-Varrey*, and they delight in enchanting human sailors with their beautiful songs, then luring them to their deaths. See *Merrow*, *Havfrue, Havmand*.

Bergman's Bear—A giant, short-haired black bear from Russia's Kamchatka Peninsula. A pelt was examined in 1920 by Swedish zoologist Sten Bergman, who named it *Ursus arctos piscator*. It is believed extinct, but sightings are still reported. See *Short-Faced Bear*.

Bessie—A *Lake Monster* reported since the 19th century in Lake Erie in Canada, "South Bay Bessie" has been described as a serpentine creature, more than 40 feet long, with a diamond-shaped head and humps along its back. Its colors range from dark green to black. It is also said to have a pair of long "arms," similar to a giant squid. See *Devil's Lake Monster*.

Betikhân—A *Faun*-like creature of Indian myth, the

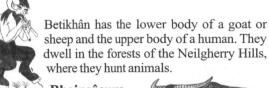

Betikhân has the lower body of a goat or sheep and the upper body of a human. They dwell in the forests of the Neilgherry Hills, where they hunt animals.

Bhainsâsura—A destructive monster in Hindu folklore, it looks like a gigantic water buffalo. It appears at the time of harvest, and unless appeased by an offering of a pig, it will trample the crops in the fields. The Bhainsâsura is based on a creature from the *Mahâbhârata* called *Mahisha*, which is vanquished by Durgâ. See ***Con Tram Nu'Ó'C***.

Bialozar—A gigantic, eagle-like bird of Polish folklore, much like the *Roc*. In Russia, the same bird is called the *Kreutzet*. The Bialozor is also a real bird found regularly year-round in Poland. Its English name is the Gyrfalcon (*Falco rusticolus*), a bird that resides only in northern forests.

Biasd Bheulach—A monstrous phantom beast that haunts the Ordail Pass, on the Isle of Skye off the coast of Scotland, where its nocturnal howling and shrieking terrifies travelers. In the tradition of the *Black Dogs*, it is also said to appear as a grotesque, one-legged man.

Bicha—A human-headed bull monster in Spanish folklore. See *Minotaur*.

Big Bird—In 1976, residents of the Rio Grande Valley in Texas were terrorized by a 5-foot-tall, gorilla-faced creature with blood-red eyes and bat-like wings. No sightings have been reported since. See *Batsquatch*.

Big Fish of Iliamna (or *Giant Fish of Iliamna*)—As described in the legends of the Tanaina Indians of subarctic Alaska, this ferocious fish attacks fishing boats amid the floating ice, biting chunks out of the bottom until they sink so it can eat the fishermen.

Bigfoot (or *Sasquatch*)—A giant *anthropoid* ("man-ape") reported for centuries in the ancient forests of the American Pacific Northwest. More than 3,000 sightings have been recorded. Eyewitnesses report that that they are 7 to 8 feet tall, weigh up to 400 pounds, and are covered in shaggy, dark brown hair. The many huge footprints found, and subsequently often cast in plaster, are the basis of its name. It is thought to be related to the *Yeti* of Nepal and the *Yowie* of Australia, as well as similar creatures around the world. See *Kapre, Skunk-Ape*.

Bird of Paradise (or *Manucaudiata, Manuqdewata*, "Bird of the Gods")—A glorious bird with spectacular, long flowing plumage of iridescent gold, red, and green, it was said to live in Paradise feeding only on dew. Having no feet, it rests by entwining two extra long tail feathers around a branch. It makes no nest; the female lays her eggs in a depression on her mate's back, and the eggs hatch while the bird is in flight. It seems the entire legend derives from the stuffed skins of two such birds that the Sultan of Batjan, in the Moluccas, presented to the captain of the *Victoria*, the first ship to circumnavigate the world, as a gift to the King of Spain. It was simply the custom of the natives who prepared the specimens to remove the skin without retaining the feet. Thus the scientific name given to the species is *Paradisea Apoda*: "footless of Paradise." See *Martlet*, *Phoenix*.

Bishop Fish—A sea creature depicted in 16th-century bestiaries as looking somewhat like a robed Bishop of the Catholic Church. They have a mitered head, a scaly body with two claw-like fins instead of arms, and a fin-like cloak. In the 13th century, one was captured in the Baltic Sea and taken to the King of Poland. Upon being shown to some Bishops of the Church, it gestured for release, which was granted. In 1531, another was caught off the coast of Germany, but it refused food and died after three days. These were certainly Angel Sharks (*Squatina*), an unusual group of sharks with flattened bodies and broad pectoral fins similar to those of rays. According to J.W. Buel, "it is frequently called Monk-Fish on account of its rounded head, which seems to be enveloped in a hood, and also because of a habit it has of rolling its eyes in a kind of reverential and supplicatory manner." It was a common taxidermy practice to creatively cut up and manipulate preserved rays into weird "creatures" called *Jenny Hanivers*. See *Flying Fish*, *Monkfish*.

Bitoso—An ordinary-sized, multi-headed demonic worm of Romanian folklore, which caused stomachaches leading to loss of appetite. Hence its nickname, "the faster" (the verb, not the adjective). This sounds like a mythologized version of internal parasites, such as the Trichina Worm (*Trichinella spiralis*) or Tapeworm (*Cestoda*)—of which the largest grow to a stunning 100 feet in length.

Bixie—A kind of Chinese *Chimera*, the Bixie is a winged lion with horns.

Black Bird of Chernobyl—In the days preceding the infamous April 26, 1986 meltdown of the Chernobyl nuclear power plant in the Ukraine,

employees reported seeing a large, dark, headless man with gigantic wings and fire-red eyes. After the explosion, as Soviet helicopters circled the smoldering reactor, dropping clay, sand, lead, and extinguishing chemicals on the flames, some of the workers described a "20-foot bird" gliding through the radioactive smoke. Parallels to the *Mothman* phenomenon are uncanny. See *Frieburg Shrieker*, *Man-Dragon*, *Owlman*.

Black Devil #1—A jet-black *Centaur* in the mythology of the Mayan Indians of the Yucatan.

Black Devil #2—A jet-black stallion of Shoshone Indian myth. The Black Devil has fiery red eyes and sharp teeth. It is said to stalk and eat humans.

Black Dogs (or *Hellhounds*)—Large and menacing black canines with glowing red eyes, that figure prominently in the folklore of the British Isles. These creatures can be as small as a calf or as large as a bear, and they usually move with utter silence, save for the clicking of their claws. They haunt lonely roads on dark nights, following or appearing alongside of wanderers, who suddenly feel a cold dread and despair that chills the heart and raises the hairs on the back of the neck. "Black Dog" is somewhat of a misnomer as they can be many different colors. Some have horns, others have saber teeth, and still others can shapeshift into a human, a headless person, a bear, or a white rabbit. Most of these beasties look like a mastiff, but others are said to be a more shaggy type of dog. Although Black Dogs are generally regarded as evil, some are benevolent and others, merely indifferent. In various times and places they are called by different names. See Chap. 27: "Demonic Dogs."

Bledmall (or *Bladmall*, *Bledmail*, "Sea Monster")—Irish sea monsters that frighten local sailors and fishermen. No descriptions have been given regarding their appearance.

Bo—A voracious, horse-like creature of Chinese legend, with the razor-sharp teeth and claws of a tiger and a single horn atop its head, similar to a *Unicorn*. It is impervious to all man-made weapons and can emit a thunderous roar like the sound of rolling drums. See *Ki-Lin*.

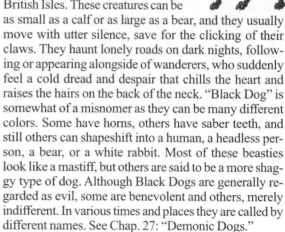

Boars, Wild—Many myths of peoples throughout the world tell of legendary giant wild boars. These include the *Calydonian Boar* (or *Aetolian Boar*) of ancient Greece, hunted by many heroes in an epic adventure. Norse myths feature *Gullinborsti* ("Golden-bristled"), a mighty wild boar crafted of metal in the forge of the Dwarves, and who draws the chariot of Freyr, god of fertility. There is also the porcine mount of Freya, wife of Odin, called variously *Hildesvin* ("Battle Swine") or *Slidringtanni* ("Terrible Tusk"). *Saehrimnir* ("The Blackened") feeds all the assembled Aesir and slain warriors of Valhalla, regenerating by the following dawn to repeat the daily cycle of being hunted, slain, roasted, and consumed. In the Welsh *Mabinogion*, *Ysgithyrwyn* (or *Twrch Trwyth*, *Torc Triath*, *Porcus Troit*, *Porcus Troyn*, *Troynt*) was the colossal king of the wild boars. Once a human king, he is transformed by the gods as a punishment. *Hwch Ddu Gota* ("Bob-tailed Black Sow") is a gigantic black pig of Welsh folklore that was said to gobble up the final celebrants at the Celtic festival of Samhain (later Hallowe'en). Hindu mythology tells of *Verethraghna*, a ferocious giant boar with enormous tusks and a terrible temper, that is sent by Mithra to plague humans who offended the god. *Kamapu'a* ("Pig Child") is a giant boar of Hawaiian mythology who roots up the islands from the sea with its huge snout.

Boas—A kind of serpent monster first described in Pliny's *Natural History* (77 CE). According to the *Physiologus*, "the Boas is a snake found in Italy; it is of a vast weight; it follows flocks of cattle and of gazelles, fastens on their udders when they are full of milk and sucking on these, kills the animals; from its ravaging of oxen, bos, it has got its name Boas." Later depictions gave it wings, large ears, and sometimes two legs. The name *Boidae* is now applied to large constricting snakes, mostly of the New World. Primitive Ophidians, such as Pythons, retain small ventral spurs which are remnants of hind legs, and are oviparous, hatching shell-less eggs within the body of the mother to give live birth.

Bocanach—A huge, frightening spectral goat that menaces night wanderers on lonely Irish roads. See **Black Dogs**.

Bolla (or *Bullar*)—A serpentine monster in the folklore of southern Albania. It has four legs, small wings, and faceted silver eyes. When it wakes from its yearlong hibernation on St.George's Day (April 23), it devours the first human it sees. After 12 years, it metamorphoses into a horrific, fire-breathing flying **Dragon** with nine tongues called **Kulshedra**. Sometimes described as an immense hairy woman with pendulous breasts, Kulshedra causes drought, requiring human sacrifice in propitiation.

Bonnacon (or *Bonasus*, *Bonachus*)—An Asian beast with the body and mane of a horse and the head of a bull. Depicted as red in color, its horns, according to the *Physiologus*, are "curled around upon themselves with

such a multiple convolution that if anybody bumps against them he does not get hurt." But its most famous attribute is its burning, napalm-like excrement and terribly foul fart, "which covers three acres; and any tree that it reaches catches fire." It is usually identified as the European Bison, or Wisent (*Bison bonasus*), or even the now-extinct Aurochs (*Bos primigenius*), but the description better fits the African Gnu, or Wildebeest (*Connochaetes gnou*). See **Catoblepas**.

Booa—A fierce nocturnal creature reported from Senegal, East Africa. It is described as resembling a giant, strangely-colored Hyena. Its name is derived from the cry it makes. See **Crocutta**.

Boobrie—An enormous, web-footed water bird said to haunt salt wells and lochs of Argyllshire in the Scottish Highlands, where it will catch and devour any beast or human venturing too close to the water's edge. It has a terrifying roar like that of a bull instead of a normal birdcall, and is said to be a metamorphosed form of the **Each Uisge**, or **Water-Horse**.

Boroka—An odd creature of the Philippines (particularly the Iloko), the Boroka has the head and breasts of a woman, the body and four legs of a horse, and the wings of an eagle. Boroka hunt and eat humans, being especially fond of young children.

Al Boraq—(or *Borak*, *Burak*, "Bright-shining")—In Moslem mythology, this is a fabulous flying steed. It has an equine body and neck with a luxurious mane, eagle's wings, a peacock's tail, a human head with long, donkey-like ears. It is pure white, but its wings, tail, and mane are studded with colorful, sparkling gems and pearls. Its breath is like sweet perfume, and it can understand all human languages. Originally the mount of the Archangel Gabriel, it travels farther in one pace than the eye can see. Mohammed rode it from Mecca to Jerusalem and back in but a moment, and ascended upon it to heaven.

Boreyne—A heraldic creature with a barbed tongue, curly horns, a dorsal fin like a fish, the forelegs of a lion, and the hind legs of an eagle.

Brag—Appearing as a misshapen black horse, this spectral steed might be seen on lonely moors and roads of England's Northern Counties, where it lures wanderers to their death. See **Kelpie, Phooka**.

Brosnie—A 16-foot-long, bioluminescent, aquatic reptile with a serpentine head, this creature inspires terror in the fishing communities of Russia's Lake Brosno and along the Volga River. See *Lake Monsters.*

Broxa—A bird from Eastern European Jewish folklore, believed to suck the milk from goats during the night. In the Middle Ages, however, it was claimed that these creatures had developed a taste for blood, similar to vampire bats.

Brucha—Irish monsters with fiery eyes and sharp iron spikes all over their bodies. They trample the trees and vines in orchards and vineyards, then roll on the fruit to impale it on their spines and take it back to their young ones. A similar story is told in the *Physiologus* about *Ercius*, or Urchin the Hedgehog (*Erinaceinae*), which is probably the basis of the Brucha.

Buata—A gigantic, supernatural wild boar monster with huge tusks in the folklore of New Britain, it hunts people and can speak and understand human language. But it is very stupid and can easily be tricked out of taking a victim.

Bucentaur—A creature with the torso of a man and the body of an ox, with cloven hooves. Ity is related to *Centaur* and *Onocentaur*. The Cretan *Minotaur* is sometimes thus portrayed. See *Hea-Bani.*

Buchis (Greek, "Bull"; also *Bukhe, Bukhe* See)—A great bull in Egyptian mythology, sacred to the god Menthu at his temple at Hermonthis. His hair grows backwards, and changes color every hour of the day. See *Apis*, *Merwer*, *Mnevis.*

Bulaing—Monstrous serpents of the Karadjeri Australian Aboriginal Dreamtime. See *Rainbow Serpent.*

Bulchin (or *Bicorne*, "Two-Horned")—A female monster of medieval European folklore, depicted as a fat panther with a horned human head, and wearing a broad grin. Often carved on 16th-century church misericords, she was said to feed on henpecked husbands. Her scrawny mate, which preys on obedient and submissive wives, is the *Chichelvache.*

Bull of Inde—A gigantic ox in Indian folklore with an impervious yellow hide and massive horns that pivot in any direction. If trapped, it gores itself to death rather than be captured alive. See *Catazonon*, which may describe the same animal.

Bunyip ("Evil Spirit"; also *Moolgewanke, Tuntabah, Tunatpan, Wee-Waa*)—A fierce, bellowing water-monster said to dwell at the bottom of still swamps, lakes, rivers, and *billabongs* (water holes) of the Australian outback. Described

as about the size of a calf, and resembling a dark, hairy seal or hippo. Sometimes said to possess long arms and enormous claws, it has also been depicted as having tusks, fins, scales, wings, a long tail, and even feathers. In Tasmania, it is called the *Universal Eye*, and is portrayed as serpentine. It is greatly feared as a man-eater. Some cryptozoologists postulate that it may have been *Diprotodon*, a large, Ice-Age marsupial hunted by the early Aborigines and depicted in rock art. See *Lake Monsters*.

Burach Bhadi (or *Wizard's Shackle*)—An enormous, leech-like water monster inhabiting shallow lochs and river fords in the Western Isles near Scotland, and also reported in Perthshire. It has nine squinty eyes atop its hideous head and back. If anyone attempts to ride through the water, it attaches itself to the horse's legs and pulls horse and rider under in order to suck their blood. See *Lake Monster*, *Mongolian Death Worm*, *Orm*.

Buru—A reptilian monster reported to dwell in the marshy lakes of a remote valley in the Himalayan Mountains, until it was hunted to extinction in the 1940s. According to the Apu Tani people, the Buru was about 12 to 15 feet long, with stumpy, clawed legs and armored plates along its back and tail. Three rows of short, blunt spines ran down its back. It was mottled blue-black in color, with a pale underbelly. Its triangular head had flattened teeth, except for four sharp fangs in its upper and lower jaws. It was a shy animal and kept far away from people, hiding in the swamp during the dry season, but appearing in the rainy season when the swamp became a lake. This description matches very closely various Cretaceous Ankylosaurs like Hylaeosaurus (shown). However, some cryptozoologists believe it may just be an undiscovered species of giant lungfish.

Busse—Reported to dwell in Scythia, the Busse was the size and shape of a bull, greybrown, with the head and antlers of a stag. It was said that it could change its color to camouflage itself from hunters. This is believed to be a description of a Reindeer (*Rangifer tarandus*), which molts seasonally, changing from dark grey-brown in summer to white against the winter snow. See *Tarandrus.*

Butatsch-Ah-Ilgs—A huge, hideous, shapeless, swollen stomach ringed with flaming eyes, it was said to dwell in the depths of the Luschersee, a lake in Switzerland believed to be the gateway to Hell. No one dared fish in those waters, nor graze their flocks on the surrounding hillsides. See *El Cuero*, *Freshwater Octopus*, *Glyryvillu*, *Hueke Hueku*, *Invunche*, *Manta*, *Migas*.

C is for Cockatrice, bringer of death,
Wilting whole forests with one noxious breath.
Dragon-tailed rooster with wings like a bat –
Crowing, it ruins its whole habitat.

Cacus (Greek, "Wicked")—This monster of Greco-Roman myth was the progeny of Hephaestos and the Gorgon Medusa. It had a huge, spherical body on long legs, similar to a gigantic misshapen spider. Three fire-breathing, venom-spewing, humanoid heads sprouted from its scrawny neck. It hid by day in a cave above the River Tiber in Etruria, Italy, emerging at night to ravage any living creatures it could find, dragging them back to its lair. Heracles encountered and killed it as he returned from his 10th Labor.

Cait Sith (or *Cat Sith, Cu Sith,* "Fairy Cat")—A huge and evil feline of Scottish myth, the Cait Sith is the size of a large dog. It is all black with a  white patch on the chest, shaggy, bristling fur, and an arched back. It is a popular blazon in Scottish heraldry, and is commonly seen at Hallowe'en. See *Wild Cats*.

Caladrius (or *Charadrius, Caladre*)—A miraculous white river-bird of medieval European folklore, with the ability to diagnose whether a patient will live or die. If the bird refuses to look at the patient, his or her death is sure to follow. It draws out illness—especially jaundice—from a sick person into itself, turning its feathers grey. Then it flies out into the sun, where the poison melts away, restoring the bird's pure white plumage. Discovered in Persia by Alexander the Great, its dung cures cataracts in the eyes. Scientists have assigned the name *Charadiidae* to the plovers, but T.H. White believed it to be a Wagtail (*Motacilla alba Linn*), which is still held in superstitious awe in Ireland for the skull-like markings on its head.

Calchona—A great dog-monster in Chilean folklore, it has a long, white, woolly fleece like that of an unshorn ram, and a thick, tangled beard. Haunting mountain passes, it terrorizes travelers, frightening their horses and stealing their food. See *Black Dogs*.

Calopus (or *Chatloup*)—A goat-like creature with serrated horns, said to live along the banks of the Euphrates River in Persia. It has a body like that of a wolf, a snout like a boar's, a beard like a goat's, tail and teeth like a lion's, and spines down its back. It has cloven hoofs in front, and back feet like a Dragon's. Mentioned since the time of ancient Babylon, its earliest known depiction was carved in a block of wood in Raveningham church, Norfolk, England, dating from around 1383. Most likely based on the Sable Antelope (*Hippotragus niger*), the Calopus can use its horns to cut through thickets or even fell trees. The name has also been assigned to a family of edible mushrooms, *Boletus calopus*. See *Aptaleon*, *Antalops*, *Urus*.

Calygreyhound—A hybrid heraldic creature with the body of an antelope, the head of a wildcat, the front claws of an eagle, and the hind legs and hooves of an ox. Often it was depicted with ram-like horns. Appearing on the crest of the De Vere family, it symbolizes swiftness.

Camahueto—A sea monster in the folklore of the Chiloé Islands near Chile. Described as resembling an aquatic horse or bull, it begins life in the high mountain streams, and migrates downstream to the sea as it grows, gouging out gullies in the river banks along the way with its terrible claws and fangs. In these lairs it lies in wait for shipwrecked sailors to devour them.

Cameleopard (or *Cameolpardel, Cameleopardalis*)—Supposedly the offspring of a camel and a leopard, it is about the size of a camel, but has the spotted skin of a leopard and two sharp, curving horns. Ancient Sumerians believed that it possessed both the speed and voracious appetite of the predatory leopard. Represented in heraldry and as a circumpolar constellation, it is clearly identified with the Giraffe (*Giraffa camelopardalis*).

Camoodi—An enormous serpent in the native folklore of Guiana, in South America. Sometimes mistaken for a huge, fallen tree-trunk, it is the protector of the Camoodi Forests. It may be derived from the giant Green Anaconda (*Eunectes murinus*, "good swimmer"), which reaches lengths of more than 30 feet—possibly far greater, according to some accounts. See *Mawadi*, *Sterpe*, *Sucuriju Gigante*.

Campacti (or *Cipatli*)—In Aztec folklore of Mexico, this is the vast primordial **Dragon** from whose slain body the Earth was formed. It was depicted as a fish-like crocodile. See also *Tiamet*.

Campe—A monster in the Greek legend of the *Tita-nomachia* ("Battle of the Titans") who guards *Tartarus*, the underworld pit where the *Centimanes* ("hundred-handed ones") and *Cyclopes* ("wheel-eyes") are imprisoned.

Camphurcii—A fish-eating composite sea creature dwelling in the coastal waters off the Island of Molucca, in Indonesia. It is described by Thevet in his 16th-century *Cosmography* as having the body and forelegs of a deer, the webbed hind feet of a goose, and a great, single horn extending more than 3 feet from the center of its forehead, like a *Unicorn*.

Canvey Island Creatures—Several strange marine monsters that washed up on the shores of Britain's Canvey Island in 1954. They had round, ruddy bodies, froglike mouths, bulbous eyes, prominent gills, and two stubby legs with webbed feet. They had no arms, so it was assumed they would have stood erect bipedally, in which case they would have been 3 to 4 feet tall. Eventually an ichthyologist identified the carcasses as Anglerfish (*Lophius piscatorius*), whose fleshy, jointed pectoral fins are easily mistaken for short legs with feet. A 68-pound specimen was caught off the shore of Canvey Island in 1967.

Capricornus (Greek, "Goat-horn")—First mentioned in Sumerian myth as an attendant of Ea, god of the waters, it was originally described as a fish with a human head, and was associated with the constellation of *Sukhur-Mashu*, the "Goat-Fish." In Greco-Roman mythology, the great *Dragon Typhon* is transformed into a goat-fish upon chasing the goat-god Pan into the Nile River. Zeus then places the creature in the heavens as the constellation *Capricorn*. See *Suhur-Mas*.

Carbuncle (or *Carbunkel, Carrabuncle*)—A small, squirrel-like creature of Paraguay, with a ruby (*carbuncle*) set in its forehead, the Carbuncle comes from tales of early South American exploration by Spanish conquistadors. The same name was also applied to a creature said to be the source of freshwater pearls found in Killarney Lake, Ireland.

Caretyne—A fire-breathing heraldic creature with the body and horns of a bull and a porcine snout. White with yellow spots, it appears on the badge of a Tudor-period courtier.

Caristae—"Birds which can fly through the flames without harm, burning neither their body nor their feathers" (Albertus Magnus, c.1200–1280).

Carrog (Welsh, "Torrent")—A monster said to dwell in the Conway Valley in County Gwynedd, Wales. When roused, it washes the valley clean from end to end.

Cat-Fish—A creature of European heraldry depicted as a cat in the front parts, with a fish's lower body and tail. In Chinese legend, it causes earthquakes.

Cath Pulag (Welsh, "Cat with Sharp Claws"; also *Capalus, Chapalu, Cath Paluc, Cath Balug,* or *Cath Balwg*)—This phantom feline of Welsh and Arthurian myth hunts both cats and people to satisfy its ravenous appetite. The Cath Pulag has a spotted pelt and massive claws. It is conjectured to have originally been a leopard imported into Anglesey by a Welsh king. See *Wild Cats*.

Catoblepas (Greek, "that which looks downward"; also called *Gorgon*)—A bull-like creature of Ethiopia and southern Egypt. It is covered in iron scales like those of a  *Dragon*, with tusks like a boar's, and no hair except on its porcine head, which always droops downward on its scrawny neck. It eats poisonous plants, and if frightened, it belches noxious fumes. Pliny claimed that "all who met its gaze expired immediately." Because of this, it is also called the "Gorgon," after the Gorgons of ancient Greece, of which Medusa, with her gaze that turned men to stone, was the most famous. Early accounts of the Catoplebas describe a herbivorous creature with hooves, but by the 1600s this description had changed to a scaly, winged beast with large teeth and claws. Cuvier suggested that it was based on the Gnu, or Wildebeest (*Connochaetes gnou*). See *Bonnacon*.

Ccoa—A catlike monster in the Quechua Indian folklore of Peru. It is grey with dark, horizontal stripes, and has a huge head with great, fiery eyes that spit hail. It causes destructive storms and crop failure, and must be placated with offerings throughout the growing season. Its name has been adopted as an acronym for the Cougar Club of America.

Ceasg—These Scottish *Mermaids* are very dangerous. Half-human and half-salmon, they can only be killed if their souls can be found and destroyed. The souls, however, are housed in special containers that are hidden away in the depths of the ocean. If a person is lucky enough to trap a Ceasg, then they will be granted three wishes. Ceasg have been known to marry humans, and the children of these unions become great sailors.

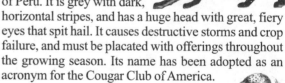

Celestial Horse—A Chinese creature resembling a white dog with a black head, it has fleshy wings with which it can fly. See *Pegasus*.

Celestial Stag—A deer of Chinese legend, capable of human speech. Dwelling in the Heavens and beneath the Earth, it guides lost miners to veins of precious ores and gems. But if it ever touches the surface of the Earth it dissolves into jelly

Celestial Tigers—Four guardians and rulers of the Cardinal Quarters in Vietnam's Annamite mythology. The *Blue Tiger* rules the East, governing spring and plants. The *Red Tiger* (reported from the Sunderbans area of eastern India) rules the South, controlling summer and fire. The *White Tiger* (now commonly seen in zoos) rules the West, autumn, and metals. And the melanistic *Black Tiger* is the ruler of the North, monarch of winter and water. All of these except the blue one represent actual recorded color variants of Tigers (*Panthera tigris*). But, in 1910, in China's Fujian Province, American missionary Harry R. Caldwell encountered "a tiger coloured deep shades of blue and Maltese."

Celphies—Ethiopian creatures with a bovine body, "whose hind feet from the ankle up to the top of the calf were like a man's leg, and likewise his forefeet resembled a man's hand" (Solinus, *Collection of Remarkable Facts*, 200 CE). This sounds very much like Olive Baboons (*Papiocynocephalus anubis*). See *Cynocephali*.

Centaur (also *Ixionidae*, in reference to their supposed human progenitor, Ixion)—Mythological half-man and half-horse, originally envisioned as a full man with the hindquarters and rear legs of a horse growing from his back. Later it came to be depicted with the man's torso grafted onto the horse's shoulders (properly, a *Hippocentaur*). They originally dwelt on Mount Pelion in Thessaly, northern Greece. Most were savage and lascivious, often carrying off human women. After a particularly noxious episode at the wedding of Hippodameia and Pirithous, king of the Lapiths, where they got drunk and attempted to abduct the bride, they were driven from Thessaly in a famous battle. But the Centaur Cheiron was a kind and wise teacher who tutored Aesclepius, Jason, and Achilles, and freed Prometheus by relinquishing his own immortality in trade. Zeus placed him in the heavens as the constellation Sagittarius. The myth of the Centaur is believed to be derived from garbled descriptions of early horsemen by people who had never before seen horses being ridden. See *Apotharni, Bucentaur, Hippocentaur, Ichthyocentaur, Onocentaur*.

Centauro-Triton—A scale-less variety of *Ichthyocenaur* in Greco-Roman mythology, with the dorsal fin and tail of a dolphin.

Centipede (Greek, "Hundred-Footed")—An immense, man-eating monster living in the mountains near Lake Biwa, Japan. The *Dragon King* of that lake asks the famous hero Hidesato to kill it for him. The hero slays it by shooting an arrow, dipped in its own saliva, into the brain of the monster. The Dragon King rewards Hidesato with a never-emptying bag of rice which feeds his family for generations. The name also refers to an arthropod, of which the largest—*Arthropleura* of the Carboniferous Era—was 11 feet long! The biggest living species is the Amazonian Giant Centipede (*Scolopendra gigantea*), which attains 14 inches in length. See *Con Rit*.

Centycore (or *Centicore*)—A bizarre hybrid creature said by Solinus (c. 258 CE) to inhabit the plains of India. It has a horse's hooves, lion's legs, elephantine ears, a bear's muzzle, a monstrous mouth, and a single ten-point antler protruding from its forehead. It has the voice of a man, and has no mercy. Although described very differently, it is equated in heraldry with the *Yale*.

Cerastes (or *Hornworm*)—A monstrous serpent in medieval European folklore, which buries itself in the desert sands, showing only the four ramlike horns atop its head. When curious creatures approach to investigate, it strikes out with its poisonous fangs and drags them beneath the sand to be devoured, much like the ant-lion insect. It is derived from the 2-foot-long North African Horned Asp (*Cerastes cerastes*), which is common in Egypt, and which does indeed bury itself in the sand.

Cerberus (or *Kerberos*, Greek, "Demon of the Pit")—Cerberus is the great, 3-headed black dog with the tail of a *Dragon*, who guards the gates of *Erebos*, the Greek Underworld ruled by Hades and Persephone. He lets anyone in, but allows none to leave. His heads denote the past, the present, and the future, and they devour all things. A child of the giant Typhon and *Echidna*, originally Cerberus is described as having 50–100 heads. He is dragged out of Hades' realm by Heracles as his final Labor. Wherever Cerberus's saliva falls, the poisonous aconites sprout (also called monkshood or wolf's bane). Later, the poet Orpheus charms the beast to sleep with the music of his lyre. In Roman mythology, the Trojan prince Aeneas and Psyche are able to pacify Cerberus with honey cakes (one for each head!). See also *Garm, Sharama, Xolotl*.

Cerynean Hind (or *Arkadian Hind*)—A mighty, magickal deer with golden antlers and hooves of brass, which Heracles was charged by King Eurystheus to capture alive as his fourth Labor. Ranging the slopes of Mount Cerynaea in Greece, the Hind was sacred to Artemis, goddess of the hunt. It induced a compulsion in hunters to pursue it until they died of sheer exhaustion. It was so swift of foot that it took Heracles a full year to get close enough to lame it with an arrow in the leg. He then bound the wound and carried the prize back to Eurystheus, at which point it was released. See **White Hart**, **Zlatorog**.

Cetus (or *Ketos*)—A ferocious sea monster of Greek myth whom Poseidon sent to ravage the coast of Philistia (modern Israel) in retaliation for the Queen's boast that her daughter Andromeda was as beautiful as the *Nereids*, or sea-nymphs. To appease the sea-god, Andromeda was chained to a rock at Jaffa as a sacrifice, but as Cetus approached, the hero Perseus flew by, having just slain Medusa. Perseus petrified the monster with the severed head of the Gorgon, saving the princess, whom he subsequently married. Cetus is described as having a dog-like head on a vast bloated body, with a huge tail divided into two flukes. It is commonly portrayed as a monstrous whale, from which derives the scientific name for whales and dolphins: *cetaceans*. Indeed, according to Pliny the Elder, "The skeleton of the monster to which Andromeda in the story was exposed was brought by Marcus Scaurus from the town of Jaffa in Judaea…it was 40 feet long, the height of the ribs exceeding the elephants of India, and the spine being 1-foot 6-inches thick." Clearly this was a whale! Immortalized in the heavens as the constellation *Cetus*, it often appears among other sea-creatures on medieval maps.

Chai Tung (or *Hai Chiai*)—A variety of Chinese **Unicorn**. See **Ki-Lin**.

Chamrosh (or *Cynogriffin*)—A fabulous creature of Persian myth, living beneath the Soma tree upon which the mighty **Senmurv** roosts. Similar to a **Gryphon**, with the head and wings of a bird upon the body of a dog, it gathers the ripe seeds that are shaken from the tree each time the great bird alights, and distributes them throughout the land. See **Ziz**.

Chan—An immense clam in Chinese folklore, whose exhalations form wondrous undersea palaces of coral. Very likely a description of the Giant Clam (*Tridacna gigas*) that inhabits coral reefs of the South Pacific and Indian oceans. These can weigh more than 400 pounds and measure as much as 5 feet across.

Chancha con Cadenas (Spanish, "Sow Harnessed with Chains"; also *Chancho de Lata*, "Tin Pig")—A creature of Argentine folklore, it haunts the slums and riverside towns around Córdoba and Buenos Aires, where it runs along the railroad tracks and telegraph wires, making a deafening din. But as soon as one looks for the source of the racket, the phantom pig vanishes.

Charybdis—Daughter of Gaia and Poseidon, this ambitious sea-nymph flooded land to enlarge her father's kingdom. As punishment, Zeus transformed her into a horrific sea monster in the form of a vast, disembodied mouth gaping at the surface, sucking in both air and water in a vast vortex and spewing them forth three times a day. Devouring all passing ships, this maelstrom is set on one side of a narrow strait, across from an equally dreadful monster, the **Scylla**, whose six long necks support ferocious, toothy heads. In the *Odyssey*, Odysseus loses his ship and many men to these twin terrors, barely managing to survive himself. Traditionally, Charybdis has been located in the Strait of Messina off the coast of Sicily, opposite a rock called Scylla. But the whirlpool there is seldom dangerous, and scholars have recently suggested that a more likely location would be near Cape Skilla in northwest Greece. There are also families of crabs and butterflies called *Charybdis*. See **Cìrein Cròin**.

Cheeroonear—These predatory creatures of Australian legend hunt and devour humans. They walk upright, trailing extremely long arms along the ground, and have canine heads.

Cherufe—A giant lava monster in the folklore of the Aracanian Indians of Chile and Argentina, it lives in the magma of volcanoes in the Andes Mountains and preys on young maidens. Two warrior daughters of the sun-god control the monster with magickal swords that can freeze it. But occasionally it breaks free, causing volcanic eruptions and earthquakes. To appease the Cherufe, virgin girls are sacrificed by tossing them into the mouth of the volcano.

Chiang Liang—A Chinese monster with the body of a **Panther**, the head of a tiger, and a human face. It has long hoofed legs, and is often shown with a snake in its mouth.

Chichevache (French, "Scrawny Cow"; also *Chichifache*, "Thin Face," or *Thingut*)—Mate to the over-fed

Bulchine (or *Bicorne*), it is frequently depicted on medieval church misericords as a scrawny, undernourished cow with a miserable-looking human face. It was said to feed only on submissive and obedient wives, for want of which nourishment it starved to death.

Chimera (or *Chimaera*, "Goat")—A fire-breathing composite monster of Greek myth with the body of a goat, the head of a lion, and the tail of a dragon. Oddly, it is often shown with multiple heads, which is quite different from the way it is described. The offspring of *Echidna* and Typhon, it terrorizes the country of Lycia, in Asia Minor. It is slain by the Corinthian hero Bellerophon from the back of *Pegasus*, the flying horse. The myth likely originated from an eponymous mountain in that country, where ignited emissions of natural gas were seen. According to Servius (4th century CE), "Flames issue from the summit of Mount Chimaera. There are lions in the region under the peak. The middle parts of the hills abound with goats, and the lower with serpents." Eventually, *Chimera* became a term for all improbable inter-species hybrids, and is commonly applied today to genetically modified organisms. Is it also the scientific name of a weird little fish, *Chimaera affinis* (shown), intermediate between sharks and bony fishes.

Chio-tuan—A variety of *Ki-Lin*, the Chinese *Unicorn*. It is said that in the 13th century, a scouting expedition of Genghis Khan encountered one in the desert north of India, which the Emperor was planning to invade. It looked like a deer, with green fur and a single horn, and it spoke to the soldiers, saying, "It is time for your master to return to his own land." When this was reported to the great Khan, he called off his plans for the invasion.

Chonchón—A dangerous creature said to dwell in Chile, it is in the shape of a human head with enormous ears, which serve as wings for its flight on moonless nights. Chonchónes are visible only to Wizards, and are said to possess the same magickal powers. See *Flying Heads*, *Leyak*.

Ch'ou-T'i—A composite creature of Chinese folklore, described as having a head at each end, similar to an *Amphisbaena* or Dr. Doolittle's *Pushmi-Pullyu*. It lives in the country west of the Red Water.

Chuchunaa (Tungus, "Outcasts"; also *Mulen*, "Bandit"; and *Siberian Snowman*)—These Siberian hairy hominids, or "Man-Apes," have been seen clothed in animal skins, leading some researchers to speculate that they may represent a relic population of Neanderthals.

They have been described by eyewitnesses as being tall and human-like, with broad shoulders, a protruding brow, long, matted hair and occasionally unusual fur coloration. See *Almas*, *Marked Hominid*, *Wudewasa*.

Chupacabra (Spanish, "Goatsucker")—A truly bizarre creature reported for decades throughout Central America, Mexico, and Puerto Rico. It is described variously by different witnesses, mostly farmers, who fear it as a predator of their livestock. Some claim it walks on four clawed feet, some on two. It has red or black eyes, often a long tail, and sometimes even batlike wings. It is 3 to 5 feet tall when standing upright, with smooth or scaly skin, and sometimes with hair or spines down its back. See *Itcuintlipotzotli*.

Chuti—A ferocious cryptid inhabiting the Choyand and Iswa Valleys of Nepal, and often depicted in traditional art. It has a striped, tiger-like body and a canine head. This is certainly the Striped Hyaena (*Hyaena hyaena*). See *Leucrocotta*.

Cigau—An aggressive mystery cat of Sumatra, with unmarked tan fur, a short tail, and a ruff encircling its neck. It is somewhat smaller but more heavily built than the Sumatran Tiger (*Panthera tigris sumatrae*). See *Seah Malang Poo*, *Yamamaya*.

Cigouave—A predatory monster of Haitian Voodoo folklore, it has the body of a lion or *Panther* and a humanoid head, and is derived from 16th-century missionary descriptions of the Indian *Manticore*.

Cîrein Cròin (Gaelic, "Grey Crest"; also *Curtag Mhòr a' Chuain*, "Great Whirlpool of the Ocean"; *Mial Mhòr a' Chuain*, "Great Beast of the Ocean"; and *Uile Bhéisd a' Chuain*, "Monster of the Ocean")—According to Scottish folklore, this is the most enormous Sea Serpent that has ever existed, able to swallow entire whales in a single gulp. This is very likely a reference to the Corryvreckan whirlpool, located between the islands of Scarba and Jura in Argyll and Bute. At its wildest, this maelstrom forms a vast, swirling cauldron 300 feet wide and 100 feet deep, and has been known to suck ships to their doom. See *Carybdis*, *Great Norway Serpent*.

Clifden Water-Horse—Similar to other *Water-Horses*, these are described as semi-aquatic, equine monsters, said to dwell in Lough Auna and Lough Shanakeever, two glacial valley lakes north of Clifden, Ireland. See *Horse-Heads*, *Lake Monsters*.

Cockatrice—Originating as the serpentine *Basilisk*, the North African Cockatrice is depicted as a rooster with a Dragon's tail and bat-like wings, and so poisonous that its very glance or breath kills. It can rot the fruit on a tree from a distance, and any water from which it drinks will be polluted for centuries. It is said to be born from a cock's egg, hatched by a toad. Similar to the Basilisk, its only foe is the weasel. Both Cockatrice and Basilisk derive from the Egyptian Spitting Cobra (*Naja nigricollis*), which sprays poison from its fangs with great accuracy into the eyes of its victims. A popular heraldic beast, its name was later applied to a venomous lizard of Armenia, and a huge brass cannon of Tudor times.

Cock-Fish—A heraldic monster with the head, wings, and clawed feet of a rooster, and the tail of a fish.

Cocodryllus (or *Corkendril*)—Though often bizarrely depicted, this is just a monstrous, 30-foot-long version of the crocodile, colored in vivid crocus or saffron hues. Nile Crocodiles (*Crocodylus niloticus*) of Egypt and Estuarine Crocodiles (*Crocodylus porosus*) of Indonesia and northern Australia can grow to this size, but they are basically grey in color, with yellowish underbellies.

Coje ya Menia (Portuguese, "Lion of the Water"; or *Dilali*, *Mourou-Ngou*)—A large, amphibious animal reported in the area of the Kuango River in east Angola, Africa. Slightly smaller than a hippopotamus, it normally lives in the river, but comes out on land during the rainy season, when its mighty roars may be heard at night. It is known to attack and kill hippos, which flee the area. Although some claim it has a horse's body and a lion's mane and claws, it is most probably a Nile Crocodile (*Crocodylus niloticus*). See *Kasai Rex*.

Colo-Colo—A baleful nightmare demon in the folklore of the Araucanian Indians of Chile, it hovers over sleepers and sucks their saliva until they succumb by dehydration to fever. Similar to the *Cockatrice*, it is hatched from the egg of a black cock.

Con Tram Nu'Ó' C—A huge, supernatural water buffalo in the folklore of the Annam of Thailand. It can cross great distances over any surface, including water, almost instantly. Anyone who can find a hair of this creature will be able to do the same. See *Bhainsâsura*.

Conopenii—Giant, fire-breathing horse of Persian mythology, with the head of an ass.

Con Rit—An enormous *Centipede*-like creature discovered washed up on the coast of Along Bay, Vietnam, in 1883. Called *Con Rit* ("centipede"), it was 60 feet long and 3 feet wide, dark brown on top and yellow underneath, with a segmented body of 3-foot by 2-foot chitinous hexagonal segments. 28-inch-long filaments protruded from both sides of each segment. Cryptozoologist Karl Shuker believes that the Con Rit is an invertebrate, perhaps a gigantic *isopod* or an undiscovered form of aquatic *chilopoda*. See *Many-Finned Sea Serpent*.

Coonigator—Ferocious mammal-reptile hybrid creatures seen raiding campground dumpsters around Mount Pelier, Vermont. Described as being raccoon-sized with thick, grey fur, its face exactly resembles that of an alligator. Sightings have increased in recent years.

Corc-Chluasask—Supernatural progeny of the Scottish and Irish *Tairbh-Uisge*, or Water-Bull, these appear as monstrous calves with velvety hides and split ears. To protect their herds, farmers on the Isle of Skye used to kill any calf born with malformed ears.

Cornu—In Irish legend, this is a demonic black bird that St. Patrick banished to Lough Derg, where it lives on the miserable penitential island called St. Patrick's Purgatory.

Cows of Näkki—Bovine water monsters in Estonian folklore, they are driven up from the depths by the monstrous *Näkki* (a giant *Water-Horse* similar to the Irish *Kelpie*). It is said that if one of these could be captured, it would give superior milk. See *Tairbh-Uisge*, *Water-Bull*.

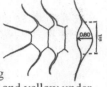

Creature from the Black Lagoon—A humanoid fish appearing in three Universal movies: *The Creature from the Black Lagoon* (1954); *Revenge of the Creature* (1955); and *The Creature Walks Among Us* (1956). In the first film, a paleontology expedition along the Amazon River discovers the Black Lagoon and its prehistoric inhabitant. The scientists capture the creature, but it escapes. It returns to kidnap the female research assistant, and the others have to rescue her. The Creature has entered our universal cultural mythology, and many similar creatures have been reported over the years. When Jenny Clack of the University of Cambridge discovered a fossil amphibian in what was once a fetid swamp, she gave it the Greek name *Eucritta melanolimnetes* ("Creature from the Black Lagoon"). See *Frogman*, *Gatorman*, *Gillman of Thetis Lake*, *Green-Clawed Beast*, *Intulo*, *Lizard Men*, *Loveland Frog*, *Mill Lake Monster*, *New Jersey Gator-Man*, *Pugwis*, *South Carolina Lizard Man*.

Crocho—An immense bird, said to dwell on Cape Daib (Cape Corrientes) at the tip of Africa. It was reputed to be 60 paces from wingtip to wingtip, and able to carry off elephants. According to Fra Mauro (1459), in 1420, an Indian junk putting in at the coast discovered an egg of this bird that was "as big as a butt" (a large cask holding a volume of 126 gallons). See **Roc**.

Crocotta (also *Corocotta*, *Cro-cotte*, *Crocuta*, *Curcrocute*, *Cynolycus*, *Leucrota*, *Rosom-acha*, *Akabo*, *Alazbo*, *Zabo*, *Lupus Vesperiti-nus*)—An ass-sized dog-wolf of India with a leo-nine body, deer-like legs with cloven hooves, and a human-like voice with which it lures its victims. Instead of teeth, it has bony jaws to crush its prey, which it then swallows whole. It must turn its entire head to focus its immobile eyes. This is a derivation from the much earlier **Leucrotta**. Ctesias referred to this creature as the *Cynolycus* ("Dog-Wolf"). Also called *Yena*, *Akabo*, *Alzabo*, *Zabo*, *Ana*, and many other names, it is a scavenger clearly identified with the Hyaena (*Crocuta crocuta*), but confused with elements of the antelope. See **Rompo**.

Crodh Sidhe (Gaelic, "Fairy Cows")—In Irish folklore, these "sea-cows" live in the ocean and graze on seaweed. They are white or speckled, with red ears. They may reflect a memory of marine mammals such as the Stellar's sea cow (*Hydrodamalis gigas*), which Arctic explorers had exterminated by 1768.

Cthulhu (or *Great Cthulhu*)—A hideous, primordial alien being created by horror fantasy writer H.P. Lovecraft (1890–1937), Cthulhu has become a cult icon whose popularity has spread far beyond its literary origin, figuring prominently in role-playing games, T-shirts, bumper stickers, parody songs and slogans, and even plush dolls. In his "Cthulhu Mythos," Lovecraft conceived a secret world beneath our own, inhabited by ancient races and dark "Elder Gods." Ruler of them all is Great Cthulhu, an octopus-headed monstrosity who plunged from the stars millions of years ago with his kin, ruling the world from the city of R'lyeh. When R'lyeh sank beneath the Pacific Ocean, all of its denizens fell into a sleeping death, awaiting a time when the city will rise again and they will be reawakened to ravish and slay across the world.

Cucuio (or *Cocuie*, *Fire-Bug*, *Fire-Beetle*)—A tiny West Indian bird that gives off its own light. This thumb-sized creature has four wings and bright shining eyes. It is said that poor people in Cuba and the Antilles capture them for lanterns, but must release them in the morning to recharge. These are clearly tropical Fireflies (*Lampyridae*), of which more than 2,000 species are known. Creole women are said to arrange the glowing larvae in their hair and garments, where they produce a dazzling effect superior to jewels. Ancient Chinese also sometimes captured fireflies in translucent containers and used them as short-term lanterns. See **Alicanto**, **Ercinee**.

El Cuelebre—A vast, winged flying serpent of Spanish folklore, it guards a great treasure hidden in a cavern or under a waterfall. But anyone who finds it will never return. See **Amphitere**.

El Cuero (Spanish, "Cowhide"; also *El Trelquehuecuve*; *El Bien Peinado*, "The Smooth-headed One")—Reported lurking in the glacial waters of Lago (Lake) Lacar, in the Southern Andes Province of Neuquen, is a large and dangerous water monster, described as resembling a flat skin similar to a cowhide, with clawed tentacles and multiple eyes. According to legend, it originated from a donkey's hide that fell into the water and came alive, engulfing every living thing it encountered by folding itself around them. It suns itself on the rocks and causes windstorms. It sounds very similar to a giant octopus, except that it lives in fresh water. A species that fits the description very well is the Japanese Pancake Devilfish (*Opisthoteuthis depressa*). See **Butatsch-Ah-Ilgs**, **Glyryvillu**, **Freshwater Octopus**, **Hueke Hueku**, **Invunche**, **Manta**, **Migas**, **Oklahoma Octopus**.

Cynamolgus—This Arabian "Cinnamon Bird" brings cinnamon from afar to build its fragrant nest at the top of a tall palm tree, where spice gatherers shoot it down with leaden arrows. Its legend is conflated with that of the **Phoenix**, which is said to build its nest of cinnamon and other Arabian spices.

Cynocephali (Greek, "Dog-Headed")—Said to be very common in Ethiopia, they are described as having a black, hairy, humanoid bodies with the head of a dog. These ferocious creatures have been identified with Olive Baboons (*Papio cynocephalus*). However, the 3-foot-tall Indris Lemur (*Indri indri*) of Madagascar also bears a striking resemblance to a short, dog-headed human, especially as it often stands or sits upright. See **Celphies**, **Manticora**, **Sphinx**, **Wulver**.

Cynoprosopi—*Dragons* of the Sahara Desert, akin to the **Ying-Lung** of China. They are covered with shaggy fur, have dog-like heads, muzzles with profuse beards, and bat-like wings. They prey upon goats and antelope.

D is for Dragon who flies from afar,
Each armored scale shining bright as a star.
Gold is its treasure and greed is its game,
Guarded by legend: the fierce dragon-flame.

Dadhikra (or *Dadhikravan*)—A beautiful cosmic white horse in Hindu mythology of India, exactly resembling the **Pegasus**. Flying across the sky on eagle's wings, it personifies the new moon.

Dard—An Austrian lizard-monster with the mane of a horse and the head of a cat. It lives in a lake and may sometimes be seen basking on the shore. See **Kelpie**.

Dea—A kind of **Salamander** lizard listed in an English bestiary from 1220, it lives in fires, upon which it feeds.

Deer-Centaur—A variation of the **Centaur**, with a deer's body instead of that of a horse. See **Centaur**.

De Loys' Ape—An ape-like creature—one of a pair—that was shot, killed, and photographed in 1920 by Swiss geologist Francois De Loys, during an expedition to the jungles of Venezuela. Other than this unique photo, apes are entirely unknown in the Western Hemisphere. In 1929, Dr. George Montadon named it *Ameranthropoides loysi* ("Loys' American anthropoid"). Skeptics have dismissed the image as nothing more than a Spider Monkey (*Simia paniscus*), which has an adult body length of only 20 inches. But recently, fossilized remains have been found of a giant, prehistoric howler-spider monkey, which, if still living, could account for this specimen. Interestingly, in *Sea and Land* (1887), J.W. Buel reports that: "Dr. Lund has furnished us with descriptions of the Brazilian orang outan, which he calls the Caypore, obtained principally from the legends of the natives." And in the early 19th century, German naturalist Alexander von Humboldt heard stories from the Orinoco about furry, human-like creatures called *Salvaje* ("Wild"). These were said to build huts, capture women, and eat human flesh. All ape-like creatures reported from South America are collectively dubbed *Mono Grande* ("Large Monkey"). See **Giant Monkeys, Memegwicio**.

Dendan—Gigantic black fish of Arabian legend. If they come into any contact whatsoever with humans—even the mere sound of a human voice—they die.

Devil Bird (or *Ulama, Maha Bakamuna*)—A large, elusive bird found only in the densest mountain jungles of Sri Lanka and India, its extremely loud cry sounds eerily similar to a human in pain, hence its name. Although westerners assert that it's a mere figment of superstition, a live specimen was rescued from attacking crows in 2001. The largest owl in Sri Lanka, it is now called the Forest Eagle Owl (*Bubo nipalensis*). See **Strix**.

Devil Fish (also *Sea Devil, Sea Bat*)—A huge and powerful sea monster described by J.W. Buel as having "eight long arms attached to a broad, flat body, in the center of which are its leering eyes and cavernous mouth, around which are several horny spines." The name and the eyewitness reports clearly identify it as the giant Manta Ray (*Manta birostris*), of which the largest known specimen had a 25-foot "wingspan" and weighed 6,600 pounds. However, these fish do not have tentacles, which makes the description a bit puzzling, as it seems to conflate the manta ray with a cephalopod—for example, the Pacific Giant Octopus (*Enteroctopus dofleini*), which may grow to more than 30 feet long and weigh more than 100 pounds. See **Cuero, Glyryvilu, Iémisch, Manta**.

Devil's Lake Monster—A **Lake Monster** said to inhabit the deep, cold, salty water of the mist-shrouded Devil's Lake in Sauk County, Wisconsin. The local Nakota Indians have stories of this creature going back many centuries; one of the earliest recounts a fatal attack on a canoe full of warriors by something with many tentacles, similar to a **Kraken**. See **Bessie, Cuero, Freshwater Octopus, Lusca**.

Devil Monkeys—Reported throughout the American Midwest and as far north as Alaska, these are described as baboon-like creatures with powerful, kangaroo-like hind legs. They are extremely aggressive, attacking people and even cars. See **Goatman**.

Dhumarna (Sanskrit, "Smoke-colored")—King of the **Sea-Serpents** in Hindu mythology. Like Attica's legendary King Cecrops (shown), he is a snake from the waist down but human above, similar to a **Naga**.

Didi (or *Dru-di-di, Didi-aguiri*)—A small (up to 5 feet tall) hooting ape or hominid with red or black fur reported for centuries to be inhabiting the montane forests of Brazil, Suriname, and Guana. Some of the descriptions overlap those of the much larger **Mapinguary**. Named for the range of shrieks and whistles they emit, it's very likely they are a type of Howler Monkey (*Alouatta*), of which nine species are currently recognized. With body lengths of up to 3 feet, these are among the largest of New World monkeys.

Dingonek—Said to dwell in the rivers and lakes of western Africa (primarily in the area of former Zaire), the Dingonek is approximately 12 feet long, with a squarish head, saber-like, canine teeth, a long horn, and a poisonous "stinger" on the end of its tail. Its skin is scaly and mottled, like that of a Pangolin (*Manidae manis*). This description is reminiscent of the 8-foot-long Pleistocene Giant Pangolin (*Manis palaeojavanicus*) (shown), fossils of which have been found on the Indonesian islands of Java and Borneo. See **Mokele-Mebembe**, **Veo**.

Dipsa—A deadly serpent so small that people can step on it without seeing it. Its lethal venom is so painless that victims are dead before they even realize they have been bitten. T.H. White suggests that this may be the Common Krait (*Bungarus caeruleus*) of India (shown). See **Seps**, **Syren**.

Diwe—Huge, horned monsters of Iranian folklore that hunt and devour lone travelers.

Djieien—A giant, six-foot-tall spider in Seneca Indian folklore of the northeastern United States. Its invincibility came from the fact that it hid its heart beneath the floor of its lair. But the hero Othcigwenhda, missing the monster with a thrust of a sharp stick, inadvertently stabbed the ground and pierced the hidden heart, thus killing Djieien immediately. See **Tsuchi-Gumo**.

Dobhar-Chú (Gaelic, "Water Hound"; also *Dorraghow*, "King of the Lakes," and *Dhuragoo, Dorraghowor, Dobarcu, Anchu*)—A voracious, man-eating, otter-like creature in Irish folklore, considered the Father of All Otters. Reported back at least to 1684, it is described as being "half-wolfdog and half-fish," 6 to 8 feet long, with short, white fur and a dark brown cross on its back. Some, however, say it is hairless, with slimy black skin. Because of its ferocity, locals call it the "Irish Crocodile."

Dodu—A very aggressive ape reported from the southern Cameroons of Africa. It is dark grey, stands 6 feet tall, and is mostly bipedal. It has only three fingers on each hand, and three clawed toes on each foot. It attacks gorillas and leaves little piles of sticks on the ground.

Dog-Centaur—A variation of **Centaur** with the body of a large dog. See **Centaur**.

Dolphin (or *Delphine*)—The swiftest creatures in the sea, it is said that they can jump over most ships. They are supposedly attracted to human voices, and gather together to sing when music is played. When Dolphins play and leap in waves they forecast storms. There is said to be a kind of Dolphin in the Nile River with a serrated back, which kills crocodiles by slicing open their soft underbellies.

Dover Demon—A strange, melon-headed humanoid creature reported to have been seen along the roadside at night by several teenagers in the Boston suburb of Dover, Massachusetts, in April of 1977. They said its thin body was about 4 feet tall, with peachy, smooth skin. It had long limbs and fingers and large, orange eyes. It has not been seen since. Was it a space alien? No one knows.

Draco (Latin, "Dragon"; from Greek, *draconta*)—Depicted in classical Greco-Roman art as a great, bat-winged serpent, it was later said to inhabit caves in India and Ethiopia, where it preyed upon elephants.

Draconcopedes—In medieval European folklore, these are serpents with a woman's head and breasts. The serpent in the Garden of Eden was often so depicted.

Dracs (from Latin, *draco*, "Dragon")—Predatory water monsters said to inhabit the depths of the Rhône River in France, where they terrorized the town of Beaucaire by dragging victims from boats. *Drac* is the word for **Dragon** in Catalan and other languages.

Dragon—A gigantic reptilian creature, frequently possessing bat-like wings and fiery breath. Some are capable of human speech. There are many varieties, living in all the Elements: Earth, Water, Fire, and Air. Wingless, legless dragons are called *Lindorms, Wyrms, or Wyrms*. Those with legs but no wings are called *Drakes*. A Dragon with two limbs and two wings is called a *Wyvern*. Dragons with feathery rather than leathery wings are called *Amphiteres*. Dragons exist in cultures the world over.

Eastern Dragons tend to be wise and benevolent creatures of clouds, rain, and bodies of water. *Western Dragons* tend to be crafty and evil, and many were slain by various heroes and knights. Some Dragons are based on known creatures, such as crocodiles, giant monitor lizards (such as the Komodo Dragon, *Varanus komodoensis*), the rib-winged flying lizards of Madagascar (*Draco volens*), and the remains of dinosaurs. And others—such as the **Mokele-Mbembe** of the Congo swamps, or the **Loch Ness Monster** and its kin—may still be lurking in unexplored regions and dwelling in deep lakes throughout the world.

Dragons of Ethiopia—

Great, serpentine **Dragons** up to 35 feet long, with one or two pairs of wings. They were said to prey on elephants. They may be derived from the Nile Crocodile (*Crocodylus niloticus*) or the Reticulated Python (*Python reticulatus*), both of which may reach that size (but neither have wings!). See **Draco**, **Pa Snakes**.

Dragon Horse—This creature of Chinese mythology resembles a horse, but has the head of a **Dragon** and scales instead of fur. Though some Dragon Horses can fly, none of them have wings; indeed, Dragon Horses are more often seen as water dwellers. Considered divine messengers, these creatures fly between the Heavens and the Earth, revealing the meaning of the Yin/Yang symbol.

Dragon Kings—The five immortal Dragon Kings dwell under the sea in elaborate crystal palaces. One is chief over all, and the others represent one of the four Cardinal Directions: North, South, East, and West. Their names are *Ao Ch'in*, *Ao Jun*, *Ao Kuang*, and *Ao Shun*. They all answer to the Jade Emperor, who tells them where to distribute the rains. The Dragon Kings are said to be 3 to 5 miles long, with shaggy legs and tails and whiskered muzzles. Their slinky, serpentine bodies are covered in golden scales. It is said that when the Dragon Kings rise to the surface, waterspouts and typhoons are created, and when they take to the air, massive hurricanes result. Only the exceptional are allowed to meet with these great ocean sovereigns.

Dragon-Mermaid—This female creature of Celtic myth enables childless couples to conceive, but requires a sacrifice in return. If she is refused, she lays a curse upon the family.

Dragon-Tygre—A heraldic beast with the body of a **Dragon** and the head of a tiger. The European take on the Asiatic Dragons.

Dragon-Wolf—A heraldic beast with the body of a **Dragon** and the head of a wolf. Another creature reminiscent of the Asian Dragons.

Drake—A wingless **Dragon** or **Lindorm** in Swedish folklore, this term may also apply to Elemental Dragons, such as Fire-Drakes, Sea-Drakes, Ice-Drakes, etc. It is also used for male Dragons. See **Orm**, **Python**.

Drekavac (Slavic, "One that cries while yelling")—A terrifying night creature in Slavic mythology, sometimes described as an animal, sometimes as a bird. Some believe it is a soul of an unbaptized child; all agree that its yell is horrifying. There are regional variations, but its height when walking on all fours is about 3 feet. It lurks in deep caves and tunnels, sometimes in packs.

Duah—Gigantic flying predators reported in Papua New Guinea. They have a 24-foot, leathery wingspan, a toothless beak, and a long, large head crest, precisely matching the presumed extinct pterosaur *Pteranodon*. Likewise, they are oceanic fish-eaters, though there are reports of vicious and fatal attacks on humans. This is likely to be a Bismark Flying Fox (*Pteropus neohibernicus*). Recognized by science as the world's largest living species of bat, it has a wingspan of 5.5 to 6 feet and is native to New Guinea and the Bismark Archipelago. However, these fruit bats do not eat fish or attack people, so perhaps this is an unknown cryptid. See **Kongamoto**, **Pterodactyls**, **Ropen**, **Snallygaster**.

Dunnie—A kind of shape-shifting **Phookah** haunting the area of Northumbria, England. It materializes as a plowhorse, donkey, or pony. If anyone attempts to harness it, however, the Dunnie disappears, laughing, leaving the person holding an empty harness.

Dzu-The (Sherpa, "Big Thing")—The largest of the three types of **Yeti** (distinguished by size), according to the Sherpas of Tibet. The others are the middle-sized **Meh-Teh** and the smaller **Yeh-Teh**, with *teh* meaning a flesh-and-blood animal. The Dzu-Teh normally walks on all fours, rising to its hind feet only when it runs. Some researchers think this is the Himalayan Black Bear (*Ursus thibetanus*), which often preys upon yaks.

E is for Enfield,
    from Ireland's
    fame,
Fox-headed wolf of
    the hero's acclaim.
After a battle, it watches
    and waits,
Guarding slain chieftains
    and minding their fates.

Each Tened (Gaelic, "Fire-Horse")—In Irish folklore, this flaming phantom horse carries off evil-doers, who are compelled to ride it, burning, for all eternity.

Easg Saint (Gaelic, "Holy Fish")—According to legend, a pair of these sacred fish lived in a well

near a church in Ireland, eating hazelnuts that fell from the tree above the well. These imparted magickal qualities to the fish, including the ability to speak. Killing the fish brought divine retribution.

Ebu Gogu—The native name for small, hairy, inarticulate cave dwellers first reported by Portuguese sailors visiting the Indonesian island of Flores in the 16th century. Sightings continued well into the 19th century. Then, in 2003, the sub-fossil remains of seven diminutive hominids were discovered on the tiny island. Officially designated *Homo floresiensis* ("man of Flores"), they were immediately dubbed "Hobbits" in the popular press. Ranging in height from 3 to 4 feet, they appear to have been a dwarf island race of *Homo erectus*.

Echencis (Greek, "ship-detaining"; also *Remora*, *Mora*)—A tiny "sea-serpent," only 6 inches long, that can stop a ship under full sail by attaching itself to the hull. Said to dwell in polar seas, it freezes the air and water to hold a ship fast in an icy grip; thus, it is considered the arch-enemy of the fire-dwelling **Salamander**. The suckerfish, or Remora (*Echeneis naucrates*) (shown) attaches itself to large sharks. See **Murex**, **Scolopendra**.

Echidna—The "Mother of Monsters" in Greek mythology. Daughter of Gaea and Tartarus, she was a beautiful woman from the waist up, but her lower body was that of a monstrous snake with speckled skin. By her Titan husband Typhon, she bore children that were equally horrible: **Cerberus**, **Orthus**, the **Hydra**, the **Harpies**, the **Chimaera**, and the vulture that ate Prometheus' liv-

er. She also bore the **Sphinx** by her son Orthus. She dwelt in a cave near Scythia, where she was eventually killed by the 100-eyed Argus Panoptes. The name *Echidna* has been given to the little egg-laying "spiny anteater" of Australia.

Eer-Moonan—Ferocious monsters of the Australian Aborigine Dreamtime, they have the bodies of dogs, the heads of echidnas (spiny anteaters), and the feet of human women. They hunt humans with deadly stealth.

Eikthymir (Teutonic, "The One With the Oak-like Antlers")—The great cosmic stag of Norse myth that stands on the roof of *Valhalla* and browses the vast World Tree, *Yggdrasil*.

Elephant-Tiger—A fabulous creature in Thai folklore, with the body of a mighty elephant and the proportionally large head of a ferocious tiger. According to legend, it was captured by the hunters of King Phan, and then mated with his best elephants, breeding the invincible war elephants that later routed the armies of Phan's enemy, King Kong. It is paraded in effigy in the annual celebration of that victory.

Emela-Ntouka (Lingala, "Killer of Elephants"; also *Chipekwe*, *Groot Slang*)—A large, amphibious creature said to dwell in the Likouala swamps of the Congo, in Lake Banweolo, Cameroons, and in other swamps of the West African coast. It is slightly smaller than the hippos it kills and feeds upon. It has a smooth, dark green, grey, or brown body without bristles, a crocodile-like tail, and a single ivory horn like a rhino's with which it disembowels elephants. Its elephantine footprints show three-toed claw marks. One was killed in 1934, but no scientific study was done. Some cryptozoologists have noted the similarity of this description to the Cretaceous ceratopsian, *Monoclonius*; however, those animals were herbivores. See **Coje ya Menia**, **Kasai Rex**, **Mokêle-M'Bêmbe**, **Ngoubou**.

Empusa (or *Empousa*, pl. *Empusae*)—A shapeshifting female monster in Greek folklore, she is human from the waist up, with one leg of an ass and the other of brass. The goddess Hecate sends Empusa to harass lone travelers on dark country roads. Appearing as a **Black Dog**, a mule, an ox, or even a beautiful woman, she scares to death or eats anyone she encounters. *Empusa* is also a genus of the *Empusidae* family of mantis insects, which includes the praying mantis.

Encantado (Portuguese, "Enchanted One")—Creatures of Brazilian folklore that dwell in an underwater paradise called the *Encante*. The term may apply to spirit beings or shapeshifting serpents, but most often it refers to freshwater dolphins that have the ability to transform into humans. The dolphin referred to is called the *Boto*, or Pink River Dolphin (*Inia geoffrensis*), which lives in the Amazon River. See *Selkie*.

Enfield—A hybrid beast of Irish heraldry with the body of a lion, the chest of a greyhound, the hindquarters and tail of a wolf, the front legs and talons of an eagle, and the head of a fox. It was said to protect the bodies of fallen chieftains for proper burial.

Enfield Horror—A mystery monster spotted in Enfield, Illinois. Witnesses described it as grey, with three legs, two arms jutting out of its chest, and two pink eyes the size of flashlights. Police investigators found doglike prints with six pads.

Ents (Anglo-Saxon, "Giant"; Elvish, *Onod*, pl. *Onodrim*)—Historically referring to any number of large, roughly humanoid creatures, Ents are best known today as the ambulatory, humanoid trees from J.R.R. Tolkien's fantasy world of Middle-Earth. A wise and ancient race, they appear to have been inspired by the talking trees found in folklore throughout the world. Their appearance and size varies according to the species of trees they shepherd. The long-lost females are called *Entwives*.

Epirotes—In Greco-Roman mythology, this gigantic serpent guards the sun-god Apollo's walled garden of *Dragons*, divinatory descendants of the Delphic *Python*.

Ercinee (or *Hercynian Birds*)—Luminous birds of Germany's Hercynian Forest (*der Hertzwald*), whose feathers shine with bright phosphorescence to light their way through the darkest night. While there are no known phosphorescent birds, there are a number of such insects, of which the brightest by far is said to be the great Lantern Fly (*Lanternaria phosphorea*) of South America. It was believed, on the authority of Maria Sibylla Merian, that the huge, hollow structure on the front of its head, the so-called lantern, was luminous at night. Linnaeus adopted the statement without question and assigned several specific names, such as *lanternaria, phosphorea,* and *candelaria* in recognition of this, thus enshrining a myth which subsequent observations have failed to confirm. See *Alicanto, Cucuio*.

Euroa Beast—In early 1890, residents of Euroa, Australia, claimed that their village was being terrorized by a 30-foot long, unidentifiable reptilian monster. A representative of the Melbourne Zoological Gardens, equipped

with a big net, organized a search party of 40 trackers. They discovered a set of huge footprints, but these unfortunately terminated before the creature could be found. Was this a gigantic Estuarine Crocodile (*Crocodylus porosus*), or could it have been the supposedly extinct giant monitor lizard, *Megalania* (*Varanus prisca*) (shown)? See *Kurrea, Whowhie*.

F is for Firebird, silver and gold,
Lighting the room when its fair wings unfold.
Hearing its song heals the body and soul,
Even of grief that no balm could console.

Falcon-Fish—A creature of European heraldry with the body of a fish and the head and talons of a falcon. Oddly, it also has doglike ears.

Fandrefiala—A snake of Madagascar, which, according to local legends, will plunge tail first from a tree like a spear to stab animals passing beneath. This could be a reference to the Paradise Tree Snake (*Chrysopelea paradisi*) or other Asian snakes that can actually glide through the air by flattening their bodies. See *Jaculus*.

Farasi Bahari (or *Sabgarifya*)—Fabulous emerald-green horses that live in the Indian Ocean. On certain nights of the year, the stallions graze on an island off the coast of Africa, where horse breeders leave their mares in hopes that a mating will produce mighty green foals with incredible endurance owing to a lack of lungs. See *Hippocampus*.

Father of All Turtles—An enormous sea-turtle of Sumatran legend, and one of several varieties of *Sea Serpents* distinguished by Bernard Heuvalmans (1916–2001), the father of cryptozoology. There have been four recorded sightings of such a creature in different oceans. Some think it may be the 14-foot-long Cretaceous sea-turtle *Archelon* (shown). See *Akupara, Aspidochelone, Kurma*.

Fauns—In Greco-Roman mythology, Fauns are mischievous creatures with the legs, ears, short horns, and tails of deer or goats, and the faces and upper bodies of young men. They are children of the god Faunus, "the kindly one," and can cause nightmares. At times, they can also be quite cheerful. The charming Faun Tumnus is an important character in C.S. Lewis' *Narnia* books. See *Satyrs*, *Selin*, *Silvan*, and *Betikhân*.

Fastitocalon ("Floater on Ocean Streams")—A stony-skinned sea monster the size of a whale, resembling a small rocky island fringed with sand and seaweed. It is very dangerous, luring ships' crews to disembark for shore leave, then plunging with them into the depths to devour them. Absent any human victims, it emits a sweet perfume from its mouth that lures shoals of fishes within, swallowing them by the thousands. See *Aspidochelone*, *Imap Umassoursa*, *Jasconius*, *Zaratan*.

Fating'ho—A shaggy, black-haired, bipedal, apelike creature sighted by an entomologist in Guinea, West Africa, in November of 1992. According to native tradition, it is neither a chimpanzee nor a gorilla. It has not been identified by science.

Fearsome Critters—A term coined by 19th-century American and Canadian lumberjacks to encompass an endless and entertaining assortment of imaginary animals with colorful names which were claimed to inhabit the vast timber woods of North America. Invented as preposterous explanations for the unknown dangers and difficulties that sometimes claimed the lives of loggers, these wacky beasts were created to impress gullible tourists and newcomers to the logging camps. Fearsome Critters ranged from downright silly to bizarre and terrifying hybrids.

Fei Lian (or *Feng Bo*, "Wind Lord")—A celestial monster in Chinese mythology, with the body and legs of a stag, the spots of a leopard, and the tail of a serpent. Its sparrow-like head has bull horns. It controls the fierce storm winds, releasing them from a bag at whim.

Fêng Huang (or *Fum Hwang*)—The Chinese *Phoenix*, the *Fêng* is male and the *Huang* is female; together the pair symbolizes everlasting love. These beautiful birds stand about 9 feet tall. They have the breast and sinuous neck of a swan, the head and comb of a pheasant, the face of a swallow, the back of a tortoise, and the 12-feathered tail of a peacock. This descriptions fits remarkably well the Ocellated Pheasant, or Rheinart's Crested Argus (*Rheinarta ocellata*), found in central Vietnam and the Malayan peninsula. The form of the Fêng Huang represents the six celestial bodies, and its shimmering, striped plumage displays the five fundamental colors (yellow, green, red, black, and white). It will not eat any living thing, including plants. One of the *Ssu Ling*, the four spiritual creatures of China—the others being the *Lung Wang* (Dragon), the *Gui Xian* (Tortoise), and the *Ki-Lin* (Unicorn)—the Fêng Huang stands at the South, and represents the season of summer. It is a symbol of high virtue, representing Yin and Yang, and the primordial force of the Heavens. Its appearance is an omen of good fortune, bringing peace and prosperity. Its chicks are called *Yoh Shoh*.

Fenrir, the Fenris Wolf (*Fenriswulf* or *Fenrisúlfr*; also called *Hrodvitner*)—A huge and terrible monster in the form of a wolf, he is the eldest of three horrific children of the malicious Norse God Loki and the Giantess Angboda. Knowing that Fenris, Loki, and the Giants will one day destroy the worlds of Gods and men, the Gods had the Dwarves fashion a magickal fetter to constrain the beast. This apparently delicate ribbon was woven of six impossible things: the footsteps of a cat, the roots of a mountain, the beard of a woman, the nerves of a bear, the breath of a fish, and the spittle of a bird. Fenrir was then chained to a rock a mile below the Earth, with a sword between his jaws. But, at Ragnarok, Fenrir will break his chains and join the Giants in their final battle against the Gods.

Ferla Mohr (Gaelic, "Big Grey Man")—An aggressive grey ape that stands 20 feet tall and lives in mountainous areas of Scotland. There are legends of such giant apes throughout the British Isles, where they were greatly feared.

Figonas—Winged cosmic serpents who were the creators of all life in the mythology of the Melanesian people on the Solomon Island of San Cristoval. The greatest of these is *Aguna*. He created the first man, who was so helpless that Agunua also had to create a woman to make fire, cook, and weed the garden. *Hatuibwari* is considered the primal ancestress of the human race. Her vast serpentine body has a human torso, with four pendulous breasts to nourish all creatures. She also has four eyes and two enormous wings.

Fillyloo (also *Gowrow, Golligog, Gollygog, Moogie*)—A giant lizard-monster or *Dragon* in the Native American legends of the Ozark mountains, which it was reported to frequent in the 19th century. As described by V. Randolf in 1951, it was said to be at least 20 feet long, with boar-like tusks.

Fin People—Half fish and half human, these *Merfolk* bask on the shore during the summer near Eynhallow village

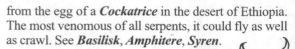

in Scotland's Orkney Islands. According to legend, once the humans of Eynhallow were in communion with the Fin People of *Finfolkaheen*, a mirror village beneath the waves. If any of the Fin People could succeed in seducing a human, they would lose their fish tail and could live on land.

Firebird (Russian, *Zshar-Ptitsa*)— A miraculous celestial bird of Russian fable, with shining feathers of gold and silver and sparkling crystal eyes. Pearls fall from its beak when it sings, and its song can heal the sick and cure blindness. A single fiery tail feather can light up an entire room. It grazes in the garden of its owner, Tzar Dalmet, but at night it sometimes sneaks into the nearby orchard of Tzar Vyslav Andronovich to steal his golden apples of youth, beauty, and immortality. It is considered to be the Russian *Phoenix*, and its origin may likewise have been in *Bird of Paradise* skins.

Fire-Drakes—Great, fire-breathing, bat-winged *Dragons* inhabiting marshes in the British Isles and mountain caverns of northern Europe, where they guard hordes of treasure.

Fish Pig—One of many fanciful sea-creatures often depicted in the oceans of medieval maps. This one has strange tentacles surrounding its head, and may actually be intended as a representation of a Giant Squid (*Architeuthis*). See *Kraken.*

Flying Fish—A strange sea-creature caught off the northwest coast of Italy in the 16th century. About 5 feet long, it had a huge head, wide wings, and a long tail. It frightened members of the royal court where it was exhibited. From the depiction it appears to have been a cow-nosed ray (*Rhinoptera bonasus*). See *Serra.*

Flying Heads (or *Big Heads*)— Weird aerial disembodied heads in the folklore of the Iroquois Indians of the eastern United States. They have flashing fiery eyes, huge, wing-like ears, and great, gaping, snarling mouths. Gnarly claws protrude from under their long scraggly hair, which holds them aloft as they are carried by the storm winds, hunting unwary humans. See *Chonchón*, *Leyak.*

Flying Serpent of Isa—A monstrous serpent of medieval Christian legends, reported by travelers as being hatched from the egg of a *Cockatrice* in the desert of Ethiopia. The most venomous of all serpents, it could fly as well as crawl. See *Basilisk*, *Amphitere*, *Syren*.

Focas—"A Sea-Bull, very strong and dangerous. He always fights with his wife until she dies, and when he has killed her he casts her out of his place and seeks another, and lives with her very well until he dies, or until his wife overcomes him and kills him. He always stays in one place, and he and his young live by any means they can" (*Physiologus*).

Fo Dogs (or *Dogs of Fo*; also *Foo Dogs*, *Kara-Shishi*, *Shiski Dogs*, *Lions of Buddha*)—Chinese temple guardians. They have a body like that of a winged lion, a bushy tail, and a broad, doglike head, sometimes with a horn on the forehead. They are always shown paired—the males with one forepaw rested on a ball, and the females with puppies at their feet.

Freiburg Shrieker—A terrifying, black, *Mothman*-like creature with huge wings that blocked the entrance to a coal mine in Freiburg, Germany, on September 10, 1978. As miners approached to go to work, it let out a series of unbearable piercing shrieks, driving them back. An hour later, an enormous explosion destroyed the mine. When the smoke cleared, the strange apparition had disappeared, and the lives of the men were saved. See *Black Bird of Chernobyl*, *Man-Dragon*, *Owlman*.

Freshwater Octopus—Although there are no known species of cephalopods able to live in fresh water, there have been numerous reports of octopus-like creatures hailing from lakes in Indiana, Kentucky, Oklahoma, and West Virginia, as well as in the monster-infested Ohio River. They are always described as being "ugly," grey in color, and about 3 feet long. They seem similar to *Octopus burryi* and *Octopus filosus/hummelinki*. With about 300 species of octopus catalogued to date, it is possible that a freshwater variant might turn up, though probably not as impressive as J.R.R. Tolkein's "Watcher in the Water!" See *Devil's Lake Monster*, *Oklahoma Octopus*.

Frogman—A 3-foot-tall creature reported by eyewitnesses in Juminda, on the coast of Estonia in the fall of 1938. It had brownish-green skin, no neck, human-like hands, and a hump in the front of its body. Its mouth was like a large slit. See *Loveland Frog.*

Fuath (Gaelic, "Hatred"; also *Arrachd* or *Fuath-Arrached*)—Shapeshifting water monsters in the folklore of the Scottish Highlands. Dwelling in rivers, lochs, and the open ocean, they have webbed feet, yellow hair, a tail, no nose, and dress in green. There are several subspecies: *Beithir* is a monstrous serpent that haunts the corries and mountains of Glen Coe. The *Brollachan* is a shapeless entity said to be responsible for many weird or inexplicable occurrences. The *Fachen* (or *Fachan, Fachin*) is a horrible, birdlike monster with a single eye in the middle of its forehead, a mangled arm jutting out from its chest, and a single leg growing at an awkward angle. It is covered in feathers, with a tuft of them like a cock's comb on its head. Roaming desolate back roads in search of human prey, whom it mutilates before killing, it ruffles up its feathers like a turkey before leaping upon its victim. The *Peallaidh* ("Shaggy One") inhabits the upland rivers and forests of Perthshire, Scotland. A lowland variety is called the *Shellycoat*. *Fuath* has become a generic term for any nature spirit, but particularly the evil kind. See **Urisk**, **Vough**.

Fur-Bearing Trout—A species of trout said to be living in lakes and rivers of the northern United States and Canada, where the water is
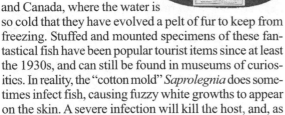
so cold that they have evolved a pelt of fur to keep from freezing. Stuffed and mounted specimens of these fantastical fish have been popular tourist items since at least the 1930s, and can still be found in museums of curiosities. In reality, the "cotton mold" *Saprolegnia* does sometimes infect fish, causing fuzzy white growths to appear on the skin. A severe infection will kill the host, and, as the fungus continues to grow afterward, dead fish covered in this "fur" can occasionally be found washed up.

G is for Gryphon, an eagle before
Leonine hindquarters even the score.
Vigilant guardian, strong in attack –
Many's the thief who's turned into a snack.

Gaasyendietha—A fire-spitting cosmic dragon in Seneca Indian folklore of the northeastern United States. It dwells in lakes and rivers, but flies through the night sky as a blazing meteor. See *Jurik*.

Gaffs—In the jargon of carnival and circus freak shows, gaffs are fabricated "creatures" created by skilled taxidermists and exhibited in presentations designed to lure gullible paying customers in to see them. Modern exam-

ples include *Mermaids, Jackalopes, Wolpertingers, Chupacabras, Furbearing Trout*, and *Bigfoots*. The foremost modern creator of sideshow gaffs is Doug Higley, whose exhibits of realistic oddities are usually aptly titled, "What is it?" See *Jenny Hanivers*.

Gagana—A miraculous bird of Russian folklore, with copper claws and an iron beak. Often invoked in spells and incantations, it is said to live on the wondrous otherworldly *Booyan Island*, which is located in the Eastern Ocean near Paradise.

Gainjin—The first animals in the mythology of the Papuans of Keraki, they descended to Earth from the heavens to help in the creation. Only two remained after it was finished: *Bugal* the snake, and *Warger* the crocodile.

Gamayun—Another miraculous prophetic bird of Russian folklore inhabiting the magical Booyan Island, along with other fabulous creatures and holy men with healing powers. This one has a human head.

Gandharvas (Pali, *Gandhabbas*)—A kind of shaggy, *Centaur*-like creature of India, they have the bodies of horses, but with human heads atop equine necks. They drive the Horses of the Sun. Entertainers of the gods and keepers of the heavenly beverage, *soma*, they are famed for their lovely music, and they also teach the medical arts to humanity. They dwell in fabulous, mirage-like palaces, and may be found in forests, mountains, or clouds. The word *Centaur* may derive from *Gandharva*.

Gansas—A swan-like bird with only one web-footed leg, which has one talon. They migrate annually to the moon.

Garafena—A magickal snake of Russian folklore, it lies upon a golden artifact on the fabled Booyan Island and is invoked in spells against snake bites.

Gargouille—A legendary great *Dragon* that lived in the marshes of the Seine River and ravaged the countryside around the town of Rouen in France. It was particularly noted for causing waterspouts, and upsetting boats to drown and devour boaters and fishermen. The monster was slain in the 7th century by St. Romain, then Bishop of Rouen. He tied two criminals to stakes to bait the Dragon, and when it appeared, he transfixed it with his crucifix, tied his bishop's stole around its neck, and led it docilely into Rouen, where it was killed by the townsfolk. From that time on, all monstrous building decorations, antefixes, and waterspouts have been called **Gargoyles**. See **Tarasque**.

Gargoyle—Grotesque carvings of humanoid and animal monsters often found on the eaves of Gothic buildings and churches throughout Europe. Originally designed as ornamental water spouts to direct rainwater clear of a wall, in medieval times they acquired religious significance as protectors of humans and averters of evil.

Garm (or *Garmr*)—The blood-spattered, four-eyed *Hellhound* that guards the gates to Niflheim—land of the dead and the dread domain of the goddess Hel in Norse mythology. From his post in the cave of Gripa, he allows no one to leave. Garm has been compared to the Greek *Cerberus,* as both are ferocious dogs that guard the entrance to the Underworld in their respective mythologies. See *Sharama, Xolotl.*

Garuda (or *Taraswin*, "Swift One")—A gigantic, man-like bird of Hindu mythology that is the celestial mount of the god Vishnu. It has the body, wings, talons, and head of an eagle-vulture (*lammergeier*), but with a human face and limbs. Its colors are gold, scarlet, and green. It is the sworn enemy of the snakelike Nagas. Emblemizing royalty throughout Southeast Asia, it is also the symbol of the Indonesian Garuda Airlines. In Thailand it is called *Galon* or *Khrut.*

Gatorman—Reports of these bizarre, human-reptile hybrid creatures lurking in the Florida Everglades and other large swamps in the American Southeast date back to the mid-1700s. They are said to be about 5 feet long, with a child-sized head and body, four stubby, gator-like legs with webbed feet, and a long, muscular tail. They are covered with greenish scales, and have a mouth full of razor-sharp teeth.

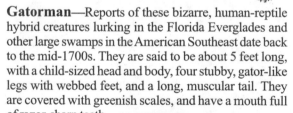

Alleged photos are obviously *Gaffs.* In the summer of 1973, a similar gator-humanoid hybrid was sighted by numerous witnesses in New Jersey's Newton-Lafayette area. And in 1977, New York State Conservation Naturalist Alfred Hulstruck reported that the state's southern region was inhabited by "a scaled, man-like creature [which] appears at dusk from the red, algae-ridden waters to forage among the fern and moss covered uplands." See *Intulo*, *Lizard Men*, *New Jersey Gatorman*, *Mill Lake Monster.*

Gengen Wer—In the Egyptian creation myth, she is the cosmic goose that lays the egg from which all living things are hatched.

Geraher—A seabird mentioned in medieval bestiaries, she lays enormous eggs, which causes her great agony, then hides them at the bottom of the sea to protect them from predators. When the eggs hatch, she leads her chicks to the shore to feed. See *Alkonost, Halcyon.*

Gçush Urvan (or *Gosh, Gôshûurûn, Gôshûurvan*)—A vast cosmic cow in Persian mythology, she contained the seeds of all plants and animals. For 3,000 years she grazed upon the barren Earth until she was killed by Mithra. From her body emerged a pair of cattle plus 282 pairs of other animals, and from her legs arose 65 species of vegetation. One version of the myth has her as a bull. See *Hadhayôsh.*

Ghul (pl. *Ghilan*)—Shapeshifting creatures of Arabic lore that haunt lonely places, where they lure travelers away from their companions to devour them. They can be killed with a single blow, but if a second blow is struck, they come back to life. No doubt this is the origin of *Ghoul*, the graveyard-haunting corpse eater of Western lore.

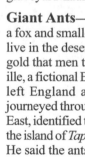

Giant Ants—Described as "larger than a fox and smaller than a dog," these animals live in the deserts of India, where they dig up gold that men tried to steal. Sir John Mandeville, a fictional English knight who left England around 1322 and journeyed throughout the Middle East, identified their homeland as the island of *Taprobana* (Ceylon).

He said the ants separate the gold from the dirt as they excavate their burrows. In the heat of summer, the aggressive ants stay in their holes during the day, and men come on camels or horses and take the gold. In other seasons, men send in horses carrying empty baskets. The ants, who cannot abide anything empty, fill the containers with gold, and then the horses are recalled. These creatures have been identified as Red Marmots (*Marmota caudata*), large rodents living in colonial burrows like those of prairie dogs. *Marmot* means "mountain ant," and to this day, people living above the Indus River collect gold dust from their burrows.

Giant Monkeys—Reports of these from around the globe probably involve several species. They range from 4 to 6 feet tall, with barrel chests, thick arms, powerful legs, and bushy tails. Smaller ones are said to resemble kangaroos. They have fierce-looking, baboon-like faces and pointy ears. Their fur may be short to shaggy, and varies from red to black. Their three-toed tracks are 12 to 15 inches long, with

the larger ones being thinner. American versions are often called "Devil Monkeys," or, more recently, *Napes* (an acronym for "North American apes"). Chimpanzee-like primates reported from the forests and swamplands of the southeastern and midwestern United States, these appear to be smaller than and distinct from the large bipedal hairy hominids, such as **Bigfoot**. A famous example is the 5-foot-tall, grayish *El Campo Ape Man*, encountered in 2004 by residents of El Campo in Matagorda County, Texas. A large, apelike creature sighted in the area around Clanton, Alabama, in the fall of 1960 was called *Booger*. It made cries "like a woman screaming," and left big footprints in the sand along a creek. The *Fouke Monster*, a large, hairy "man-ape" reportedly stalking the backwoods and creeks of Miller County in Arkansas, has been known to attack and kill animals. One three-toed footprint measured 13.5 inches long. See **DeLoys Ape**, **Memegwicio**.

Giant Salamander—Huge amphibians, 5 to 9 feet long, sighted in several lakes and rivers of California's Trinity Alps since the 1920s. The largest known salamander in North America is the Pacific Giant Salamander (*Dicamptodon tenebrosus*), but it never grows more than a foot long. However, the Japanese Giant Salamander (*Andrias japonicus*) (shown), the largest known in the world, reaches 6 feet in length and lives more than 80 years!

Giant Sloth of Patagonia—Huge, red-haired creatures roaming the forests of Patagonia in South America have been reported since the 1890s. Cryptozoologists believe they could be *Mylodons* (shown), giant ground sloths with thick, orange fur thought to be extinct for 10,000 years. They weighed 450 pounds and stood 10 feet tall, using their sturdy tails to balance themselves upright. Patagonian Indians tell of hunting the *Iemisc* or *Mapinguari*, a terrifying creature that lived in the mountains. This animal was the size of an ox, with short legs. It had reddish fur, a soul-wrenching scream, and a horrible stench. It was nocturnal and slept during the day in burrows. The Indians found it difficult to penetrate the animal's hide with their arrows. A small section of apparently fresh Mylodon hide was found by a rancher named Eberhardt in a Patagonian cave in 1895. Nearby human remains suggested that it had been hunted by people. The skin was studded with bony nodules and would have been impervious to the teeth of Pleistocene predators as well as Indian arrows. See **Mapinguari**.

Gigelorum (or *Giol-Daoram*)—Found in Scotland, this smallest of all creatures nests in a mite's ear and cannot be seen by the naked eye.

Gillman of Thetis Lake—A man-sized, gilled, amphibious humanoid said to inhabit Thetis Lake on Vancouver Island, British Columbia, Canada. It emerged from the lake on August 19, 1972, and attacked two boys. Nearly 5 feet tall and weighing about 120 pounds, it was covered in silvery-grey scales and had webbed hands and feet with sharp protrusions with which it slashed one of the boys. A few days later two other young men encountered the same creature, which they described as having a monstrous face with dark, bulbous eyes, a fish-like mouth, huge ears, and six sharp projections on its head connected by a thin membrane. It reminds one very much of the 1954 movie, **The Creature from the Black Lagoon**. See **Green-Clawed Beast**, **Lizard Men**, **Pugwis**.

Girtablili (or *Girtablulu*)—Scorpion men and women of Babylonian mythology who guard the pass into the Mashu Mountains where the sun rises. They were depicted with a human upper body, arms, and head, but with the lower body, legs, and tail of a scorpion. The males have a snake-headed penis. They are mentioned in the *Epic of Gilgamesh*, and images of them appear on Babylonian and Assyrian seals and talismans against psychic attack.

Glashtyn—A Manx version of the **Water-Horse**, or **Phooka**. Like them, it may appear as a handsome young man, but his horse ears are a dead giveaway. See **Aughisky**.

Globsters (or *Blobs*)—Mound-like, amorphous carcasses that have washed up on ocean beaches of Bermuda, New Zealand, and Tasmania. Roughly cylindrical in shape with a flattened underside,

they have varied in size from 8 to 30 feet long. Virtually unidentifiable masses of fibrous collagen, they have no internal skeleton—neither of bone nor cartilage—and their rubbery skin is as tough as a car tire and covered in thin hair. Some appear to have gill-like slits, small mouths, and long fleshy lobes or tentacles along the sides, but no eyes have been reported. Although considered by many to be storm-ravaged carcasses of the (as yet unconfirmed) *Octopus giganteus*, it has recently been determined that they are the boneless remains of Sperm Whales (*Physeter macrocephalus*), consisting of the huge "melon" and strips of blubber from between the ribs. See **Lusca**, **Tumu-Ra'i-Fuena**.

Glyryvilu (or *Guirivulu*; also *Vulpangue*, "Fox-Serpent")—A freshwater **Lake Monster** dwelling in Chile's Andean Mountains. In some districts it is described as a fox-headed snake or a puma with the head of a fox. Its long tail terminates in a vicious claw, with which it seizes its victims. As it swallows them whole, its mouth

and belly extend like those of a snake. Elsewhere, it is said to be a gigantic fish or *Dragon*. And yet another version says it is flat and disc-shaped, similar to a ray, but with tentacles like those of an octopus and eyes around its perimeter. A marine animal that fits the latter description very well is the Japanese Pancake Devilfish (*Opisthoteuthis depressa*) (shown). See *Ahuizhotl*, *Cuero*, *Devil-Fish*, *Freshwater Octopus*, *Iémisch*, *Manta*.

Goatman—A malevolent, goat-human hybrid creature reported around the United States. Some witnesses say it is a man with a goat's head, whereas others say it looks more like a *Satyr*, and yet other reports combine the two. Its reported height varies from 6 to 12 feet. It has attacked pets and even cars—sometimes with an ax. See *Devil Monkeys*.

Goayr Heddagh—In Manx folklore, a luminous spectral goat that haunts lonely roads and menaces nocturnal travelers in the same fashion as a typical British *Black Dog*. See *Shuck Dog*.

Godzilla (Japanese, *Gojira*, "Gorilla Whale")—Popularized in about 30 Japanese films since his first appearance in 1954, this colossal, dinosaur-like reptile has become part of our world cultural mythology. Towering 500 feet tall and spewing atomic fire, this radioactive monstrosity is said to have been created by nuclear bomb testing in the Pacific, either releasing some prehistoric beast from eons of entombment beneath the sea, or mutating an island lizard such as the Galapagos Marine Iguana (*Amblyrhynchus cristatus*). The films invariably feature Godzilla demolishing the city of Tokyo, though in a 1998 American version by TriStar Pictures, he attacks New York City. As a symbol of thermonuclear destruction, Godzilla has become a kind of anti-hero figure, even saving the Earth from alien invaders.

Gollinkambi (or *Vithafnir*)—A great golden rooster that perches on the highest branch of the Norse World Tree, *Yggdrasil*, and watches for signs of the coming *Ragnorak*, the Doom of the Gods.

Gorgoniy—A mythical beast of Russian folklore that protects Paradise against mortals who would invade it.

Grant—From the folklore of the British Isles, this spectral colt with glowing, red eyes always walks on its hind legs. First mentioned in 1212 by Gervase of Tilbury, its appearance at the edge of a town sets the dogs to barking, warning the townsfolk of an immanent fire. See *Brag, Phooka*.

Great Norway Serpent—An enormous *Sea Serpent* reported dwelling in the North Sea. Black and scaly, with a long mane of hair, it is said to be 200 feet long and 20 feet thick. It inhabits coastal caves, and on summer nights it emerges onto the land to feast on livestock. See *Cìrein Cròin, Havhest, Sjøorm.*

Green-Clawed Beast—While swimming in the Ohio River near Evansville, Indiana, on August 21, 1955, Mrs. Darwin Johnson was suddenly clutched around the knee by a large, claw-like hand. Kicking free of the unseen attacker, which kept trying to drag her under, she eventually made it to shore. She was treated for multiple contusions on her leg, which bore a green, hand-shaped stain that remained for several days. See *Creature from the Black Lagoon, Gillman of Thetis Lake, Lizard Men, Pugwis.*

Grendel—A monster from the 8th-century Anglo-Saxon epic, *Beowulf.* The name derives from an ancient word *grindill*, meaning "to bellow," and Middle English *grindel*, meaning "angry," and suggesting a loud, deep-throated growl. Grendel's physical appearance is never described, and most illustrators interpret him as an Ogre. Originally, however, a *Grendel* was a type of serpentine monster, or *Worm*. Depending on its habitation, it was referred to as a *Grendel-pond*, a *Grendel-pit*, or a *Grendel-wood*. Beowulf's Grendel was called a *Grendel-mere* because it lives in a large, brackish pond full of coarse ferns. In the epic, Denmark's King Hrothgar builds a mead-hall near Grendel's lair. Hating the sounds of raucous merry-making, Grendel creeps into the hall while all are sleeping and kills 30 men, dragging their bodies into the swamp

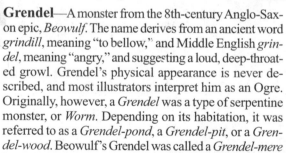

to be devoured. After several nights of this, the court abandons the hall. 12 years later, the 21-year-old Geat hero Beowulf sails to Denmark and offers to destroy the monster. He and his men stay in the mead-hall, and when Grendel appears, Beowulf cuts off one of its arms, mortally wounding the beast. Unfortunately, the next night, Grendel's mother, whose existence had been unsuspected, returns to avenge her son. Beowulf tracks her back to the swamp to slay her in a bloody underwater battle.

Gryphon (or *Griffin*, "to seize"; also *Gryph, Gryphus, Epimacus*; and *Gryps* or *Grypes*, meaning "curved, having a hooked beak")—A popular heraldic creature with the posterior and tail of a lion, and the head, wings, and claws of a mighty eagle. It also has prominent ears, like those of a horned owl. It is depicted in the paintings and sculptures of the ancient Babylonians, Assyrians, and Persians. Gryphons were said to take gold from the stream Arimaspias, which the one-eyed people of the region tried to steal. In actuality, the Gryphon is the Vulture-Eagle (*Gypaetus barbatus aureus*) or *lämmergeier*, meaning "lamb-stealer." The bird is sometimes called a "lion eagle" or a "bearded vulture" because of the "mane" of long ragged feathers around the its head. The largest and most powerful of all raptors, with a 10-foot wingspan, it is the eagle of Zeus. Despite its name, the Griffin Vulture (*Gryps fulvus*) is a different bird. A Japanese version of the Gryphon is called a *Kirni*. See **Heliodromos, Keythong**.

Grylio—An evil, **Salamander**-like reptile described in medieval bestiaries. It climbs into fruit trees and poisons the ripe fruit. Not only does the fruit become deadly, but also any water into which it falls. The name has been given to the Pig Frog (*Ranna grylio*). But it should be noted that many newts secrete potent toxins through their skin as a defense against predators. The Rough-Skinned Newt (*Taricha granulosa*) of the Pacific Northwest produces more than enough tetrodotoxin to kill an adult human foolish enough to swallow the animal or drink water in which it has lain. In order to take effect, the toxins must enter the body by being ingested or entering a break in the skin. See **Basilisk**.

Gryllus ("Grunting Pig")—A bizarre monster of Greco-Roman myth, originally depicted as having a porcine face in its belly and human-like legs. It came to refer to any creature with its head placed directly upon its legs. The name has been given to the family of insects popularly called crickets, as well as to cricket frogs.

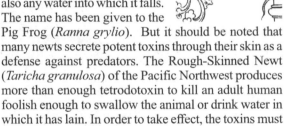

Guardian of the Fishes—A giant, fish-like Estonian water-monster that can also walk on land. Its most notable feature is a saw-toothed ridge running the length of its back, suggesting that it is most likely a Russian Sturgeon (*Acipenser*), which is known to reach at least 27 feet. See **Baikal Lake Monster, Mother of the Fishes, Whitey**.

Gugalana (or *Gudanna*)—Anu's monstrous Bull of Heaven from the Sumerian *Epic of Gilgamesh,* his poisonous breath can kill 200 warriors. Gugalana is the first husband of the Goddess of the Underworld, Ereshkigal. Gilgamesh and Enkidu fight and butcher him, but in retaliation, Anu causes Enkidu to sicken and die. This is a reference to the constellation Taurus, and the precession of the Equinoxes.

Guiafairo—A great, grey flying creature reported from West Africa, where it hides in caves and hollow trees during the day, emerging only at night. It has clawed feet and a human-like head. Cryptozoologists speculate that it may be an unknown species of giant bat, or the Hammerhead Fruit Bat (*Hypsignathus monstrosus*). Hammerheads are the largest African bats, and are dark gray with black wings spanning 3 feet. See **Ahool, Alan, Hsigo**, *Olitiau*, **Orang-Bati, Ropen, Sassabonsum**.

Guita ("Kicking Mule")—A Spanish **Dragon** slain long ago, whose great green effigy is now paraded in the festivals of Corpus Christi in Catalona as a talisman against evil. It has a black face with rolling eyes and huge fangs in an open red mouth, from which fireworks issue to simulate its fiery breath. See **Tarasque**.

Guivre—A vicious French monster with the body of a snake and the horned head of a **Dragon**. Said to inhabit forests, pools, and swamps, it is depicted in French heraldry. See **Kelpie**.

Gui Xian (or *Xuánwu*)—The great *Black Tortoise* of Chinese mythology, sometimes called the *Black Warrior of the North*. Representing the North and the season of winter, it is one of the four **Ssu Ling**, or "Spiritual Creatures," that stand at the four corners of the Earth. The others are the **Lung Wang** (**Dragon**) in the East; the **Fêng Huang** (**Phoenix**) in the South; and the **Ki-Lin** (**Unicorn**) in the West. The Black Tortoise is usually depicted as both a tortoise and a snake, with the snake coiling around the tortoise.

Gulon (or *Jerff*) This disgusting beast from Scandinavian legend was described by Aldrovanus and Gesner as a cross between a lion and a hyena, with sharp claws and the tail of a fox. It is often used as a symbol of gluttony, as it is said to squeeze itself between two trees in order to vomit or defecate what it has eaten to make room for more. In Germany this animal was known as the *Vielfras*, and was compared to both the weasel and the Wolverine (*Gulo gulo*), which bears its name. It entered American lumberjack lore as a ***Fearsome Critter*** called the *Gumberoo*.

Gurangatch—An immense lizard-fish from the Dreamtime lore of the Aborigines of New South Wales, Australia. This water-monster can tunnel through solid rock from pool to pool, causing rivers to overflow their banks.

Gwenhidwy (or *Gwenhudwy*)—A Welsh ***Mermaid***, said to be a shepherdess of the waves, of which every ninth one is a ram. The sight of her brings good fortune. See ***Havfine***.

*H is for Hippocampus, an ocean
Creature half-horse, half-fish, grace in motion
Pulling Poseidon's chariot, swimming
Swift under water, under stars dimming.*

Habéby (or *Fotsiaondré*, "white sheep")—A sheep-sized nocturnal beast said to inhabit the Isalo range of Madagascar. It has cloven hooves, a long muzzle, long furry ears, large staring eyes, and a white coat with buff or black spots.

Habergeiss—A three-legged Alpine bird of Austrian folklore whose nocturnal moaning and screaming presages an impending death. It is represented at the annual Perchtenlauf festival each January 5 as a goat-like hobby horse with snapping jaws.

Hadhayôsh (or *Hadhayâoshi, Sarsaok*)—In the Zoroastrian mythology of ancient Persia, a mighty ox that carried the first humans over the primordial ocean. At the time of the *Frashkart*—the ending of all things—its fat will be used to create an elixir of immortality, called *haoma*, for the resurrection of the righteous. It is equated with the ***Behemoth*** of Hebrew legend. See ***Gçush Urvan***.

Haetae—A leonine creature of stone. It feeds on fire and therefore guards against it and all other forms of disruptive or violent change. It can challenge time itself, bite the sun or moon, and create an eclipse. The Haetae also symbolizes water and justice. Statues of Haetae were installed at the gate outside the Kyongbok Palace in South Korea to protect the royal line and the nation.

Hafgygr ("Half-Woman")—A female water-monster of Norse myth, she dwells in stagnant pools and murky swamps. See ***Grendel's Mother***.

Hai Ho Shang (also *Sea Bonze* or *Sea Priest*)—A great, belligerent sea monster of Chinese folklore, with the body of a fish and the head of a Buddhist monk. It is fiercely territorial, very aggressive, and fully capable of capsizing a seagoing junk, drowning all aboard. Medieval European writers translated its name as "Sea Buddhist Priest," equating it with the ***Monk-fish***. This creature is evidently based upon the Angel Shark (*Squatina*), (shown), also called the monk-fish. See ***Merfolk***.

Haietlik (or *Heitlik*, "Lighting Serpent")—A giant water-monster in the legends of the Clayoqut and Nootka Indians of Canada's Pacific coast. It has a serpentine body like an elongated alligator, with a huge, horse-like head. It inhabits lakes and inland waterways and aids hunters and fishermen. Carrying a Haietlik skin was considered essential for whalers. The earliest recorded sighting was in 1791. See ***Haikur***, ***Horse Heads***, ***Lake Monsters***, ***Sea Serpents***, ***Water-Horse***.

Haiit—An arboreal beast recorded in 16th-century European writings, and said to dwell in central Africa. It has a large furry body, a very small tail, three-toed feet with long claws, and a face similar to that of a human. Most likely this was a Common Chimpanzee (*Pan troglodytes*).

Hai Riyo (or *Tobi Tatsu, Schachi Hoko*)—A fabulous Japanese flying creature with the feathered wings and lower body of a bird and the head of a ***Dragon***. They are related to the ***P'eng-Niao*** of China, and are similar to the ***Amphiteres*** of Europe and the plumed serpents of the Americas. See ***Quetzalcoatl***, ***Ying Lung***.

Hai-Uri—A one-legged, one-armed, one-sided monster in the folklore of the Khoikhoi natives of Africa. Nearly invisible, it relentlessly pursues human prey by hopping over all obstacles with remarkable speed and agility.

Hakenmann ("Hook Man")—A vicious, predatory sea monster in the coastal folklore of northern Germany. Similar to other ***Merfolk***, it has a humanoid torso and head with the lower body of a gigantic fish. See ***Halfway People***, ***Havfrue*** and ***Havmand***.

Hakulaq—A huge female sea-monster in the folklore of the coastal Tsimshian Indians of America's Pacific Northwest. She uses her child as bait, so that when humans try to rescue the baby from the water, she follows and swamps their boats with stormy waves. This is reminiscent of the Stellar's Sea Cow (*Hydrodamalis gigas*), exterminated by whalers in 1768.

Halata—"A sea beast that does unnatural deeds, for when she feels her young move, or stir in her body, than she pulls them out and looks at them. If she sees that they are still too young, she puts them in again and lets them grow until they are bigger" (*Physiologus*).

Halcyon (also *Alcyone* or *Altion*)—A Mediterranean seabird that is said to lay its eggs on the beach sand in midwinter, at the highest tide and amid the fiercest storms. Thereupon, the weather immediately calms for seven "brooding days" up to the chicks' hatching on Winter Solstice, followed by seven "feeding days." These 14 days of midwinter calm are therefore called by sailors "Halcyon days." The sacred day of the Halcyon is December 15, beginning the Halcyon Days festival, a time of tranquility. This bird is equated with the Belted Kingfisher (*Ceryle alcyon*) (shown). See *Alkonost, Geraher*.

Halfway People—Giant *Merfolk* in the folklore of the Micmac Indians of eastern Canada, their upper bodies are humanoid, whereas their lower parts are those of huge fish. They sing to warn people of approaching storms, but if shown disrespect, they invoke terrible tempests and turbulence. These may have been based on Walruses (*Odobenus rosmarus*) or the extinct Stellar's Sea Cow (*Hydrodamalis gigas*). See *Hakenman*, *Havfrue and Havmand*, *Margygr*.

Halulu—Man-eating birds of Hawaii whose feathers are composed of water from the sun. They can assume human form.

Hanuman—The popular monkey-god of India, the son of the monkey nymph Anjana and fathered by Vayu, the wind god. Yellow in color with an endless tail, he is a god of speed and strength and patron of athletes and warriors. In the Hindu epic, the *Ramayana*, Hanuman helps Rama (an avatar of Vishnu) rescue his wife, Sita, when she is abducted by the demon king Ravana. The Hanuman Langur (*Semnopithecus entellus*) is named for him, and considered his avatar. These sacred monkeys are allowed to roam freely in Hindu temples. See *Sampati, Sinhika*.

Harpies (Greek, *Harpyiai*, "snatchers" or "swift robbers"; also *Arepyiai*, "slicer" or "tearer")—Foul and hideous sisters with the gnarled faces and withered breasts of old hags, and the wings, bodies, and clawed feet of vultures. Their names are: *Aello* ("rain-squall"), *Celaeno* ("storm-dark"), *Okypete* ("swift-flying"), and *Podarge* ("swift-foot"). Originally personifications of the storm winds, hurricanes, and whirlwinds, they are also known as the "Hounds of Zeus." They can fly as fast as lightning, and their task is to carry souls of the dead to Hades. Everything they touch becomes contaminated with an awful stench. They fear only the sound of a brass instrument. Jason and the Argonauts vanquished them on the Quest of the Golden Fleece.

Havfine ("Sea-Woman")—Norwegian *Mermaids* with a fish's tail and a woman's torso. They are wave-herders; when the storm waves are driven like fleecy sheep upon the shore, any sailors still at sea are in danger of shipwreck. See *Gwenhidwy*, *Merfolk*, *Havfrue* and *Havmand*.

Havfrue and **Havmand** (or *Hav-strambe* in Greenland; also *Auvekoejak*)—*Merfolk* of Danish folklore, a female is called *Havfrue* or *Havfinë* ("sea-woman"), and a male is *Havmand* or *Havman* ("sea-man"). They have blue skin and green or black hair, and tend to be very unpredictable—one moment kind, the next vicious. It is considered very unlucky to see one. They can live in either salt or fresh water. The "Little Mermaid" of the Hans Christian Anderson story was a Havfrue. See *Margygr*, *Sea Trow*, *Dinny-marra* and *Ben-varrey*.

Havhest ("Sea-Horse")—A gigantic *Sea Serpent* of Scandinavian folklore, with a horse-like head. It has glittering yellow eyes, a long mane down its back, and front flippers like those of a seal. Its tail is two-lobed like that of a fish, and its double row of fangs may grow to 6 feet long. On top of all this, it breathes fire! It is a sinker of ships, but has only been seen a few times since the 19th century. See *Great Norway Serpent*.

Heavenly Cock (or *Bird of Dawn*)—A golden-plumed, three-legged Chinese rooster that crows three times a day—at dawn, noon, and sunset. From his perch in the vast *fu-sang* tree, the first crowing stirs the heavens and awakens all creatures. The eggs he lays produce red-combed chicks from which all the roosters of Earth are descended.

鶏

Hedammu—A vast, all-devouring *Sea Serpent* in the mythology of the Hurrians of ancient Mesopotamia. See *Musmahhu*.

Heliodromos—A fusion of *Gryphon* and vulture in medieval European lore and heraldry. It is known today as the Griffin Vulture (*Gryps fulvus*).

Hellhounds—A particularly demonic aspect of the traditional British *Black Dogs*, they are believed to hunt and drive lost or damned souls into Hell, Annwfn, or the Underworld. Their master is the Lord of Death. See *Cerberus*, *Cwn Annwfn*, *Coinn Iotair*, *Gabriel Hounds*, *Garm*, *Ki Du*.

Hercynian Stag—A mighty stag built like an ox, with a single, branching palmate horn growing from the center of its forehead—sort of a *Unicorn* moose. This may represent a remnant memory of the extinct Pleistocene Irish elk, *Megaloceras* ("great horn"), or an interpretation of its fossil remains. See *Sadhuzag*.

Herren-Surge—A seven-headed serpent of Basque legend. Although wingless, it can fly. It lives underground and devours unattended livestock. See *Apocalyptic Beast*, *Balaur*, *Chudo-Yudo*, *Hydra*, *Ihuaivulu*, *Illuyankas*, *Kaliya*, *Kraken*, *Leviathan*, *Ladon*, *Lotan*, *Musmahhu*, *Naga Pahoda*, *Orochi*, *Scylla*, *Thu'ban*.

Hibagon—A foul-smelling hairy hominid sighted in Hiwa, Japan, in 1972. Resembling a gorilla, it is about 5 feet tall, with a bristle-covered face, glaring eyes, and a snub nose. Hibagon footprints can be 10 inches long and 6 inches wide. See *Almas*, *Barmanu*, *Bigfoot*, *Skunk Ape*, *Yeti*, *Stinking Ones*.

Hînqûmemen ("Engulfer")—A unique kind of *Lake Monster*, this is an actual living body of water in the folklore of the Coer d'Alene Indians of British Columbia. If anyone takes water from the lake, the rest of the water will come after them as a flood and drown them.

Hippalectryon—The fabulous Cock Horse in Greek mythology, it had the foreparts of a horse and the wings and tail feathers of a rooster. Later, the Hippalectryon became a sort of comic symbol for ridiculous pomposity, especially of military leaders with plumes in their helmets.

Hippocampus (Greek, *hippos*, "horse," and *kampos*, "sea monster"; also *Hydrippus*, "Water Horse")—An aquatic monster or sea horse in classical Greco-Roman mythology, it has the head and forelegs of a horse with the body and tail of a fanciful fish. Its equine forefeet terminate in finlike flippers rather than hooves. It is the mount of Poseidon or Neptune, King of the Sea, and a team of them draw his chariot. The scientific name *Hippocampus* has been given to the peculiar little fish we call the seahorse, of which the largest species is only 14 inches long. See *Kelpie*, *Horse-Heads*, *Sea Horse*, *Water-Horse*.

Hippocentaur ("Horse-Centaur")—This is the full name of the *Centaur*, which has a horse body and four legs, with a human torso growing from the equine shoulders. Other "Centaurs" might have the body of a bull (*Bucentaur*), an ass (*Onocentaur*), or even a fish (*Ichthyocentaur*). The original version of the generic *Centaur* had a full human figure (including regular human legs) with the addition of a horse's hindquarters.

Hippocerf (Greek, *Hippocervus*, "Horse-Deer")—A creature of European heraldry that is deer-like in the front, and equine in the back. Because of its opposing elements, it symbolizes indecision. This animal may have been the Pleistocene Irish Elk (*Megaloceros*), presumed extinct for more than 10,000 years. See *Hercynian Stag*, *Sadhuzag*, *Sianach*.

Hippogriff (Greek, *Hippogryph*, "Horse-Gryphon")—Similar to a *Gryphon*, having the head, wings, breast, and claws of an eagle, but with the hind parts of a horse instead of a lion. Living far beyond the seas in the Rhiphaean Mountains, the Hippogriff is the result of the impossible breeding of a mare with a male Gryphon (whose favorite food was horseflesh). A large and powerful beast that can fly faster than lightning, it appears in Ludovicio Ariosto's *Orlando Furioso* (1516) as a mount for the Wizard Atlantes.

Hirguan—A large, shaggy manape in the folklore of La Gomera in the Canary Islands. See *Bigfoot*.

Hiyakudori—A two-headed bird in Japanese myth. Resembling the *Bird of Paradise*, it symbolizes the union of two famous lovers.

Hoga (or *Andura*)—A huge, fishlike *Lake Monster* reportedly dwelling in the Mexican lake of Themistitan. It

has a head and ears like a pig's, with very thick whiskers or long barbels around its mouth, and great fangs or tusks. It can change color to be red, yellow, or green. This is most likely the Caribbean Manatee (*Trichechus manatus*). In addition to the overhanging leaves of the *hoga* tree that it browses at the lakeshore, it is believed to also consume fish and any animals that get too close to the water. The South American version, called *Andura*, is probably the Amazon Manatee (*Trichechus inunguis*), but it may be the Amazon River Dolphin (*Inia geoffrensis*), or *bouto*. See **Ambize**, **Igpupiara**, **Sea Hog**.

Ho-Oo—This is the Japanese *Phoenix*, the *Ho* being the male and the *Oo* being the female. It comes to Earth to do good deeds for people, and its appearance heralds the dawn of a new era. The bird then ascends back to heaven to await the next cycle. Much like the Chinese Phoenix, the **Feng-Huang**, the Ho-Oo has been adopted as a symbol of the royal family, particularly the Empress. It represents the sun, justice, fidelity, and obedience.

Hoop Snake—A venomous snake of American folklore, said to grasp its tail in its jaws and roll along the ground, like a wheel, in pursuit of prey. At the last moment it straightens out, skewering the victim with its pointy tail. This reminds one of the **Ouroboros**, or the **Amphisbaena**. Some cryptozoologists believe this is a distorted description of the Sidewinder Rattlesnake (*Crotalus cerastes*) of the southwestern deserts. The Mud Snake (*Farancia abacura*) is popularly called the Hoop Snake or "stinging snake" for the sharply pointed tail with which it prods its prey.

Horned Alligator— A *Lake Monster* in the folklore of the Kiowa Indi-  ans of America's southern plains. Described as a great, gator-like beast, it has two horns on its head which are considered powerful medicine for healing as well as poisoning. See **Horned Serpents**.

Horned Serpents (or *Great Serpents*)—Enormous serpentine Dragons, usually aquatic, of Native American lore. They are extremely long with great, gaping mouths and horns atop their heads. The horns may be straight, curved, or branched. Some horned serpents have snake heads, whereas others have heads similar to a horse's. These beasties may be benevolent or malevolent toward humans. Most are scaled like snakes, but some, such as Misikinpik, have fur.

Oftentimes, eating the flesh of the horned serpent would grant one great wisdom or even turn one into a horned serpent. These creatures are prevalent throughout Native North America, often in the guise of deities or demigods. Specific names include: *Doonongas* (Seneca), *Kichiknebik* (Iroquous, Lenape and Algonquin), *Kolowisi* (Zuni), *Misikinpik* (Cree and Algonquin), *Onniont* (Huron), *Tatosok* (Abenaki), *Tcinto-Sakto* (Cree), *Tcipitck-aam* (Micmac and Maliseet), *To Kas* (Klamath), *Tzeltal* (Chiapas), *Kinepikwa, Kitychi-at'Husis, Mishipzhiw, Oyaleroweck* and *Sisiutl*. See **Lake Monsters**.

Horse-Eels (also *Water-Horses* or *Horse-Heads*)—A common description of **Lake Monsters** throughout the world, these are immense, undulating, serpentine creatures with a head and neck similar to that of a horse, complete with "ears." Some witnesses, however, describe these appendages as horns, so the animals may also be called **Water-Bulls** or **Horned Serpents**. Sometimes they are said to have glowing red or yellow eyes, great fangs, and the ability to breathe fire. See **Haietlik**, **Haikur**, **Havhest**, **Kelpie**.

Horses of the Sun—In many ancient cultures, the sun was seen as a chariot driven by a divine charioteer, and drawn across the sky by mighty celestial horses. In Greco-Roman mythology, four great winged **Pegasi** pull the chariot of Helios, the sun-god. In the Vedic mythology of India, the seven dawn-red horses that pull the chariot of Suraya, the Hindu sun-god, are called the *Gandarva*, after a Sumerian sky-dragon. In Norse myth, two giant horses pull the chariot of Sunna, the Norse sun-maiden. In another Norse legend, the sun chariot is pulled by a celestial horse named *Skinfaxi* ("Shining Mane"), and the moon chariot is pulled by *Hrimfaxi* ("Frost-Mane").

Hounds of the Wild Hunt —These spectral dogs serve the gods of death. When storms rage over the moors, folks say that the Wild Hunt is riding out, hungering for human blood or the souls of unbaptized babes. Anyone who catches sight of these terrible hounds will sicken and die within the year.

Hraesvelg ("Corpse-Eater" or *Windmaker*)—A vast,  eagle-like bird of Norse mythology that nests upon the icy peaks of the frozen north. Her eaglets are the frigid winds blasted forth by the flapping of her mighty wings. See **Bmola**, **Roc**.

Hsigo (or *Hsiao*)—These Chinese creatures are exactly like the flying monkeys from *The Wizard of Oz*. They have apelike bodies with a dog's tail, a birdlike head, a human face, and wings. They are probably based on the fruit bats, or "flying foxes," of India, Asia, Indonesia, and Australia. The wingspan of the largest species, the Malayan Flying Fox (*Pteropus vampyrus*), can measure 6 feet across, although it only weighs up to 3.3 pounds. These monkey-size bats are not related to the other insectivorous bats, but are genetically closer to primates. See *Ahool, Alan, Olitiau, Orang-Bati, Ropen, Vietnamese Night Flyers*.

Hua-Hu-Tiao—A monstrous, supernatural white elephant with immense wings in the mythology of Chinese Buddhism. From time to time it breaks free of its confinement to wreak havoc upon the world, killing and eating all creatures and people. It is eventually killed by the warrior hero Yang Ching, who, after being swallowed, hacks it to death from the inside. See *Kholomondumo*.

Huallepén (or *Guallipen*)—A Chilean *Water-Monster*, with the body of a sheep, the head of a calf, and twisted legs. It lurks in desolate pools and watercourses, and will mate with cows or ewes pastured nearby. The ill-begotten progeny may be recognized by their deformities of face and limb. It is very bad luck for a pregnant woman to encounter a Huallepén or its offspring, as her child will then be born similarly malformed.

Hueke Hueku ("The Leather")—A dreaded aquatic creature inhabiting lakes and rivers of South America. Natives say that when it floats on the surface of the water, it resembles a stretched animal skin. This sounds very like the creature known as *El Cuero*, "The Hide," which might be a type of *Freshwater Octopus*. A species that fits the description is the Japanese Pancake Devilfish (*Opisthoteuthis depressa*). See *Migas, Oklahoma Octopus*.

Hui—A giant, human-headed dog in Chinese folklore. It is fleet-footed, can leap all obstacles, and is unafraid of humans. Its appearance forebodes a typhoon.

Humbaba (also *Huwawa* or *Kumbaba*)—In the ancient Sumerian *Epic of Gilgamesh*, this is the monstrous guardian of the legendary Cedar Forest of Lebanon. His immense humanoid body is covered with scale plates; his leonine legs end in vulture talons; his head is adorned with bull horns; and his long tail has a head of a snake at the end. Gilgamesh the King, and his companion, Enkidu the Wild Man, defeat Humbaba in order to cut down the trees.

Huma—A *Bird of Paradise* in Persian and Hindu mythology that dwells in the heavens and never touches the Earth. The Huma joins both the male and female natures together in one body, each having a wing and a leg. Similar to the *Phoenix*, it consumes itself in fire every few hundred years, only to rise renewed from the ashes. A compassionate bird, it avoids killing for food, preferring to feed on carrion. Great blessings and good fortune come to any who see or touch it—especially if its shadow falls on them. See *Simmurgh.*

Huspalim—An Ethiopian creature described by traveler Ambroise Pare (1517–1590) as resembling a giant marmot with hairless, red-spotted skin and round paws. Its oversized head had a monkey-like face with tiny, round ears. On the Island of Zacotera, these were kept in cages to be eaten; but their tough meat had to be beaten thoroughly to tenderize it. See *Thanacth*.

Hvcko Capko (Seminole, "Long Ears")—A stinking creature in the folklore of the Seminole Indians of Florida. Its body is grey with a horselike tail, and its head is like a wolf's, but with huge ears. It lives in desolate places and presents no direct threat to people, but it is to be avoided as a carrier of disease. Fortunately, its ghastly stench makes that easy to do! See *Skunk Ape*.

Hydra (also *Exedra*, or *Lernean Hydra*)—A hideous, many-headed *Dragon* that dwelt in the marshes of Lerna in Argolis, Greece. A monstrous child of *Echidne* and *Typhon*, her enormous canid body sprouted nine or more heads on serpentine necks. One head was immortal, but if any of the others were cut off, two more grew back in its place. Heracles and his nephew Iolaus killed her as the second Labor, and Iolaus burned the stumps of each head that Heracles severed. The oldest images of this monster appear to depict a giant squid (*Architeuthis*). Hydra is also the largest of the star constellations, and was among the 48 listed by Ptolemy. The name has been applied to microscopic tentacled water creatures. See *Apocalyptic Beast, Balaur, Chudo-Yudo, Herren-Surge, Ihuaivulu, Illuyankas, Kaliya, Kraken, Leviathan, Ladon, Lotan, Musmahhu, Naga Pahoda, Orochi, Scylla, Thu'ban*.

Hydrus (or *Idrus*)—A bizarre, three-headed serpent described in the *Physiologus* as dwelling on the banks of the Nile River in Egypt. The mortal enemy of the *Coco-*

dryllus, or Crocodile (*Crocodylus niloticus*), it is said to slather itself with mud, slip down the Cocodryllus's throat, and rip open its stomach from inside. See ***Ichneuman***.

Hyman Topodes—According to Solinus's *Wonders of the World* (4th century), this is a pathetic, goat-like creature of Libya. Its legs are so bowed that it cannot walk, but can only drag itself along in a slow shuffle.

Hypnale—According to the *Physiologus*, this species of asp induces sleep in its prey with hypnosis and then kills. Based on the Egyptian Cobra (*Naja haje*), this is supposed to have been the kind of snake that Cleopatra used to end her life.

I is for Ichthyocentaur, a beast
Part man, part horse, part fish, all strangely pieced.
Finned tail threshing foam, it dives, it leaps free
Drawing its power from the fertile sea.

Iak Im (or *Yagim*)—An immense shark of Kwakiutl Indian myth, from the Pacific Northwest. It attacks fishermen, capsizing the boats and devouring the occupants. May be based on a prehistoric *Megalodon* ("great-tooth").

Icegedunk—From the area around Victoria, British Columbia, Canada, this is a strange species of terrestrial pinniped, with small ears and a muscular torso tapering into a slender midsection. Its body terminates in a bizarre, rear-wheel-like appendage, which provides them locomotion. Unfortunately, locals claim that these creatures are on the verge of extinction.

Ice Worms—Glacier-dwelling worms invented in 1898 by a young journalist for Alaska's *Klondike Nugget*. His article claimed that due to recent cold weather, huge numbers of these worms were squirming out of the ice to "bask in the unusual frigidity." The tall tale soon became a local phenomenon, inspiring the town of Cordovas to inaugurate an annual Ice-Worm Festival. Although everyone assumes that these creatures were purely imaginary, genuine Ice Worms (*Mesenchytraeus solifugus*) had been discovered in 1887 on Alaska's Muir Glacier. Feeding on snow algae, they are only an inch long and

can be black, blue, or white. *Solifugus* is Latin for "sun-avoiding," as Ice Worms emerge only at night, retreat-ing into the ice before dawn. At a temperature of 40 degrees F, its membranes melt and the worm is liquefied.

Ichneumon (or *Egyptian Rat*)—A ferocious Egyptian weasel mentioned by Pliny, Plutarch, and Strabo as the natural enemy of the asp, the ***Basilisk***, and the ***Cocodryllus*** (crocodile). Exactly like the ***Hydrus***, it is said to cover itself with protective mud, then slip down the Cocodryllus's throat and devour its insides. It is assumed to be the Mongoose (*Herpestidae*, "snake-killer"), but this author (OZ) believes it to be the Meercat (*Suricata suricatta*).

Ichthyocentaur (Greek, "Fish-Centaur")—As described in the *Physiologus*, this is an aquatic variation of the ***Centaur***, with the torso, arms, and head of a man, the forelegs of a horse (or sometimes a lion), and the lower body and tail of a dolphin or fish, similar to a ***Hippocampus***. It symbolizes fertility.

Iémisch (or *Vulpangue* "Fox-Serpent")—A Patagonian monster with the body and prehensile tail of a serpent and the foreparts of a fox. It kills its victims by constriction with its tail. See ***Glyryvilu***, ***Tatzelwurm***.

Igpupiara (or *Hipupiara*, "Dweller in the Water")—A kind of monstrous Brazilian ***Merbeing***, with a humanoid torso and a fishlike lower body and tail. Its head resembles that of a seal, and its five fingers are webbed. This would certainly seem to be the Amazon Manatee (*Trichechus inunguis*). Numerous sightings and attacks attributed to the Igpupiara were reported in the late 1500s through early 1600s. It was said to lure humans into the water, where it ate only their eyes, nose, breasts, genitals, fingers, and toes, leaving the mutilated corpse to wash up on the beach. Although this pattern of predation sounds more like Pirahnas (*Pygocentrus*), the attackers may actually have been Amazon River Dolphins (*Inia geoffrensis*). In Brazil, the Portuguese name for this species is *boutu vermelho*—"red dolphin"—for its bright pink coloration. See ***Ambize***, ***Hoga***.

Ikalu Nappa—***Merfolk*** dwelling in Arctic seas, according to Inuit legend. Possibly derived from the Stellar's Sea Cow (*Hydrodamalis gigas*), which European Arctic explorers exterminated by 1768. See ***Auvekoejak***.

Ilkai (also *Ri*; Pidgin, *Pish-meri*, "fish-woman")—A local name for an ocean-dwelling creature often seen around the island of New Ireland, north of New Guinea.

Normally living in the open sea, it swims into the sheltered coral coves at dawn and dusk to graze on eel grass growing on the shallow bottom. It is described as resembling a **Mermaid**, with a whale-like tail and breasts and genitals identical to those of humans. Females sit upright in the water to nurse their babies, which they cradle in their armlike flippers. The Ilkai is, in fact, the origin of the legends of **Merfolk**. Both legends are based on a real but rare animal, a *sirenian*, known to zoology as the Indo-Pacific Dugong (*Dugong dugon*).

Ilomba—A supernatural vampiric water snake in the folklore of Zambia and Zaire, in Africa. Created by sorcery, its head bears the visage of the sorcerer who created it. Its victims can be revived as zombie slaves to its master, but if it is killed, or if it dies from lack of prey, its creator also dies.

Imap Umassoursa—An island-monster of the Arctic sea, in the folklore of the Greenland Inuits. It rises up underneath boats and capsizes them into the frigid waters. See *Aspidochelone, Fastitocalon, Kraken, Zaratan*.

I-Mu Kuo Yan—Anthropomorphic bird creatures of Chinese legend, with feather-covered bodies similar to those of humans, but with bird wings in place of arms. These creatures are shy and avoid human contact. See *Tengu*.

Indrik the Beast—A miraculous two-horned beast of Russian folklore, known as the Lord of Animals. He lives on the Saint Mountain and rules the water along with snakes and crocodiles. The Earth trembles when he stirs, and legend tells that he once saved the people from a terrible drought. His name—a distorted version of *Unicorn*—was given to *Indricotherium* (shown), a gigantic hornless rhinoceros that lived in Asia 20-30 million years ago. The largest land mammal ever to have lived, it was 30 feet long, 18 feet tall at the shoulder, and weighed 20 tons.

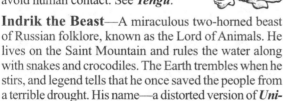

Ingheena—An African ape, or *quadrumana* (four-handed animal), reported by travelers Mr. and Mrs. Bowditch in the late 1800s, from the vicinity of the Gaboon River. They had not seen it themselves, but according to the natives, "these huge creatures walk constantly upon their hind feet, and never yet were taken alive; they watch the actions of men, and imitate them as nearly as possible....They build huts nearly in the shape of those of men, but live on the outside; and when one of their children dies, the mother carries it in her arms until it falls to pieces; one blow of their paw will kill a man, and nothing can exceed their ferocity." (Buel, 1887) These were, of course, Lowland Gorillas (*Gorilla gorilla*), considered mythical at that time, when it was believed that all great apes were orangutans.

Ink Monkey (or *Pen Monkey*)—A tiny monkey known in China since at least 2000 BCE, but now apparently extinct. Only 4 to 5 inches long, it was the traditional pet of scribes, and was said to help prepare their ink (or eat it!). It may have been the 4-inch-long Pygmy (*Tarsius pumilus*), identified in 1987, or another, as-yet-unidentified species of tarsier.

Intulo—In Zulu folklore from the South African province of KwaZulu Natal, this is a lizard-like creature with human characteristics. See *Gator-Men, Lizard-Men, Mill Lake Monster*.

Invunche ("Master of the Hide")—A truly hideous vampiric monster of Chilean folklore, resembling an enormous inflated animal skin or bladder. It occupies a cave that can be reached only through a narrow tunnel which passes under a lake. Although the Invunche cannot leave its lair, it has a minion, the *Trelquehuecuve*, that abducts young girls caught swimming or fetching water, and brings them to the Invunche, which drains their blood. See *Cuero*.

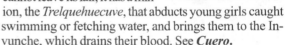

Island Beast—A sea monster of such immensity that sailors land on it, mistaking it for an island, whereupon it submerges and drowns them all. Various tales describe it as a titanic turtle, a prodigious whale, or a colossal cephalopod. See *Aspidochelone, Fastitocalon, Imap Umassoursa, Jasconius, Kraken, Zaratan*.

Itcuintlipotzotli—A bizarre Mexican creature the size of a terrier, with hairless skin, a wolfish head, no neck, a short tail, and a huge hump running the length of its back. It was illustrated in a 1780 book by a Jesuit priest, and one was reported killed in 1843 near Mexico City. Could this be the same creature as the **Chupacabra**?

Iwanëi—In the folklore of Equador's Jívaro Indians, these are serpent demons that manifest in various forms to kill their victims. One of these is *Panji*, a gigantic anaconda. Another is *Mancanèi*, a deadly water snake. See **Camoodi, Mawadi, Sterpe, Sucuriju Gigante.**

Iya—An immense, formless man-eating monster with horribly fetid breath, in the folklore of the Lakota Indians of North America.

J is for Jersey Devil, four feet tall,
Dog-headed and horse-hooved, and that's not all.
Bat-winged, rat-tailed, it runs up walls and trees.
Then it disappears – poof! – and no one sees.

Jackalope (also *Antelabbit, Horny Bunny, Aunt Benny, Stagbunny*)—A popular fantasy critter of the western United States, the Jackalope is a jackrabbit with small antlers like those of a deer or pronghorn antelope. The legend is atributed to writer Douglas Herrick (1920–2003) of Douglas, Wyoming, in 1932. Postcards showing jackalopes were sold in the U.S. in the 1930s, and stuffed examples may still be found in bars and taxidermy studios. Horned hares also abound in European legends—particularly in Germany and Austria—all of which were probably inspired by rabbits infected by the *Shope papilloma* virus, a common but temporary fibromatosis of the ears that causes hornlike bony tumors to sprout from the skull. Illustrations of horned hares in scholarly works by European naturalists in the 16th–18th centuries were probably similarly inspired. However, a horned gopher (*Ceratogaulus*; syn. *Epigaulus*) actually existed in North America during the Pliocene era. See **Jenny Hanniver, Miraj, Raurackl, Wolpertinger.**

Jaculus ("Javelin")—A 9-foot-long flying serpent with small wings (and sometimes forelegs) mentioned by the Roman poet Lucan (39–65 CE) in his *Pharsalia*. Pliny claimed it had two tongues, one with barbs. It guarded Arabian spice trees such as Frankincense, from which it would launch itself like a javelin to sink its fangs into its victim's throat. It also collected shiny objects, including gold and precious gems, leading some to speculate that it is based on a bird with such habits. The name has been given to a number of colorful, 3-foot-long flying snakes (*Chrysopelea paradisi*), or "paradise snakes" of Southeast Asia, India, and Ceylon. They launch themselves from branches, spreading their ribs and flattening their bodies in a concave airfoil to "swim" through the air, thus enabling them to glide considerable distances. See **Amphitere, Fandrefiala.**

Jagleop (or *Jagulep*)—A hybrid of a jaguar and a leopardess, bred at a Chicago zoo in the early 1900s. This spotted female became one of the parents of the controversial *Lijagleop*, which was mistaken for the legendary "Congolese Spotted Lion," or *Marozi*. See **Pardus**.

Jarapiri—A local spirit-monster, human above the waist and serpent below, associated with Wimbaraka, northwest of Alice Springs, Australia. See **Nagas**.

Jasconius (Latinized Irish, "fish")—A great sea-monster encountered by the Irish monk St. Brendan (484–578 CE) during his legendary seven-year voyage to the Promised Land of the saints.

The monks had disembarked onto a stony island to celebrate Easter mass, and were stoking a fire to boil a pot when the island began to move under them like a wave. As they all rushed back to their boat, the "island" swam away. Then Brendan told them that God had revealed to him in a dream that the supposed island was in reality a monstrous fish: "The foremost of all that swim in the ocean. He is always trying to bring his tail to meet his head, but he cannot because of his length. His name is Jasconius." See **Aspidochelone, Fastitocalon, Imap Umassoursa, Island Beast, Zaratan**.

Jengu (plural *Miengu*)—A water-spirit in the traditional beliefs of the Sawa ethnic groups of Cameroon, Africa. They are described as beautiful, **Mermaid**-like beings with long, wooly hair and gap-toothed smiles. They live in rivers and the sea and bring good fortune to those who worship them. They can also cure disease and act as intermediaries between worshippers and the world of spirits. Among the Bakweri, they are called *Liengu* (plural *Maengu*), and are important elements of a young girl's rite of passage into adulthood.

Jenny Hanivers—Properly speaking, these are skates or rays that have been altered to look like **Dragons** or sea monsters, and mummified expertly enough to appear quite real. The term is said to be derived from Anvers (modern Antwerp) in Belgium, which was supposedly a major center for their creation. Other manufactured composite creatures created by taxidermists include the **Baslisk, Cockatrice, Jackalope, Wolpertinger,** and **Fur-Bearing Trout**. The most popular manufactured creatures are "*Mermaids*" composed of monkey bodies with fish tails grafted onto them—for example, P.T. Barnum's famous "Fiji Mermaid." Most early mermaids were manufactured in the Orient as curiosities and souvenirs for travelers. Today these are treasured collector's items, and are still being made for the carnival sideshow trade, where they are known as *Gaffs*.

Jersey Devil—One of the most famous American "Mystery Monsters." Since its first appearances in the early 19th century, it has been seen by more than 2,000 people in and around the state of New Jersey. It is described as a 3- to 4-foot-tall birdlike creature, with 2-foot-long wings, a boxy head like a dog's or horse's, glowing eyes, and a piercing scream. It has diminutive forelimbs, cranelike hind limbs with horselike hooves, and a long, ratty tail. It is covered in brown or black fur, except for its bare-skinned black wings. Its strange hoof prints have gone up trees, leapt from roof to roof, and disappeared in the middle of roads and open fields. Speculations as to what it could be have included the rare Sandhill Crane (*Grus Canadensis)*, a prehistoric *Pterodactyl*, or a supernatural demon. See *Kongamato*, *Snallygaster*.

Jidra—A voracious plant-animal hybrid mentioned in *Zoology des Talmuds*, by L. Lewysohn (1858), as well as in medieval traveler's tales and the folklore of the Middle East. Growing on a long vine from roots implanted in the ground, the Jidra is a kind of human-shaped pumpkin, with magickal bones prized as an aphrodisiac when powdered and added to wine. It devours anything it can reach within the radius of its vine, but if the vine is severed, it dies screaming. See *Mandragora*.

Jinshin-Mushi ("Earthquake Beetle")—A bizarre, bug-like creature whose burrowings are said to cause earthquakes in Kyoto, southern Japan. Its immense, scaly body has 10 hairy spider's legs and a *Dragon*'s head. See *Jinshin-Uwo*, *Kami*.

Jinshin-Uwo ("Earthquake Fish")—This 700-mile-long eel carries all the Japanese islands on its back. Its head lies beneath the city of Kyoto, and a massive rivet driven into the ground in the temple gardens of Kashima secures the country to its back. The lashing of its mighty tail causes earthquakes. See *Jinshin-Mushi*, *Jörmundgand*, *Kami*, *Moshiriikkwechep*.

Jongari (also *Binjour Bear* or *Gayndah Bear*)—A 3- foot-tall, bipedal, bear-like creature reported in the area of Gayndah, Queensland, Australia. One was photo-

graphed in 2000. Aboriginal lore associates these creatures with legends of small, hairy people who once inhabited the land before the Europeans came. The myth may have

originated with the Giant Koala (*Phascolarctos stirtoni*) (shown), an arboreal Pleistocene marsupial which was about one-third larger than the modern Koala.

Jörmungandr ("Huge Earth-Monster;" or *Midgårdsormen*)— The *Midgard Serpent* of Norse myth, it surrounds Middle-Earth (*Midgard*), the world of humans, with its tail in its mouth. Jörmangund is the second of three children of Loki and the Giantess Angrboda. The first is the *Fenris Wolf*, and the third is Hel, Goddess of the Underworld. Seeing that the serpent is growing fast, and knowing that it will someday cause great evil, Odin throws it into the ocean that surrounds the Earth, where it eventually encircles the whole world. At the time of *Ragnorak*, Jörmungand and Thor will destroy each other. See *Asootee*.

Juma—A hybrid monster described by the 16th-century writer John Baptist Porta as a cross between an ass and a bull.

K is for Kraken, a gigantic squid:
Tentacles writhing, a sharp beak amid.
Vikings told tales of it swallowing ships,
Dragging down sailors in suckery grips.

Kadimakara—Gigantic prehistoric monsters in the Aboriginal folklore of Central Australia. According to the legends, they originally lived in the sky, but in ancient times they fell to Earth, where they lived for a long time until the blazing sun burned them all up, leaving only their bones—which we call dinosaurs.

Kafre (or *Cafre*)—An enormous, man-eating boar-monster in the folklore of the Philippine Islands. The Kafre is covered in thick black hair and has huge tusks. Its favorite food is humans, particularly lost hunters. Although it can walk upright like a man and understand human speech, it is very stupid and can easily be tricked out of a victim. In New Britain, the same creature is called *Buata*.

Kallicautzari (also *Callicantzari* or *Kalkes*)—Hairy, **Satyr**-like humanoids with equine ears and tails, described and depicted in the folklore and vase paintings of ancient Greece. Some are dwarfish, but others are as much as 20 feet tall. They are covered with rough shaggy hair, with caprine or canine heads and long, scraggy beards. They walk bipedally on cloven hooves, and live under Earth, gnawing at the roots of the World Tree. They emerge only in midwinter, when they create havoc, destroying crops and livestock, smashing houses, and raping women. See **Fauns**.

Kamaitachi ("Sickle Weasel")—Vicious, weasel-like creatures of Japanese folklore, they move too quickly to be seen. They always hunt in packs of three: the first one knocks the prey down, the second slashes its throat, and the third heals the wound so they can repeat the process until the victim is dead.

Kami—A gigantic catfish (*namazu*) thought to dwell beneath the Japanese islands, and held responsible for causing earthquakes. According to legend, the god of Deer Island thrust his mighty sword through the earth, transfixing the fish's head. From then on, whenever the ground shakes, the god quiets it by laying his hand on the granite hilt, which still protrudes near the shrine of Kashima. *Kami* is also the name given to Japanese Shinto Nature-Spirits. See **Jinshin-Mushi, Jinshin-Uwo**.

Kappa— River-dwelling Japanese creature of Shinto mythology, with the body of a tortoise, long, scaly limbs, the head of a monkey, and long hair. It lives on blood and cucumbers, and flies through the air on enchanted cucumbers with dragonfly wings. If treated with courtesy, the Kappa is friendly; if it is ill-treated, however, it will eat its tormentor. The Kappa has a hollow atop its head filled with fluid, which is the source of its power. If you bow to a Kappa, it will bow back— and spill the fluid, rendering it helpless. Pouring water into the hollow restores the Kappa's power. Similar to other reptiles, Kappas become sluggish in cold weather and hibernate during the winter. There are two distinct species: those that dwell in lowland waters; and others, called *Yamawaro*, that live in mountain streams. See *Ikaki*.

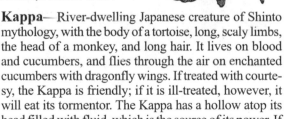

Kapre—Giant hairy hominids in the folklore of the Philipine Islands, they are said to be 7 to 9 feet tall and covered in long, shaggy brown hair. The Kapre lives in groves of bamboo, acacia, and mango, and may be encountered sitting under a tree smoking a pipe of tobacco. It is usually friendly and helpful to humans, especially women, but it also has a mischievous side, leading travelers astray in the forest. See **Bigfoot**.

Kar-Fish—Said to have the keenest eyesight of all creatures, this great fish encircles the Tree of Life in the Zoroastrian mythology of ancient Persia, guarding against the evil lizards of Ahriman.

Kargas—A Turkish variation of the **Gryphon**.

Karina (or *Kuntiak*)—A fearsome female owl-demon in the Islamic folklore of the Hausa, Nana, and Swahili tribes of Africa. It can also appear as a dog, a snake, or even a woman, and inflicts the evil eye upon people, crops, and livestock, causing them to sicken and become infertile. It is probably derived from the *Sheeree* of Berber lore—a nocturnal bird with human breasts living in the High Altlas Mountains that enters nurseries at night to suckle infants. This avian creature is also equated with *Lilith* of Sumerian mythology—an owl-goddess that was later transformed in Hebrew tradition into the first wife of Adam and mother of the demonic *incubi* and *subbubi*. In Indonesia, she is called *Kuntianak*. See **Harpy**.

Karkadann— (Sanscrit *Kartajan*, "Lord of the Wilderness." Also *Karkadan, Karkadanno, Karmadan, Cartazoon, Carcazonon*) A large and predatory **Unicorn** reported by Aelian (170-235 CE) as dwelling in the deserts and mountain wastes of India, where it contended with lions. Also called *monoceros* ("one-horn"), it is described as having thc head of a stag, teeth like a wolf, the body of a horse or bull, the feet of an elephant and the tail of a boar or lion. It is white or orange in color, with a long reddish mane and a sharp black spiraling horn. The Karkadann is quite beligerent, attacking even elephants. It was very swift, and could never be taken alive by hunters, as, like the **Bull of Inde,** it would kill itself first. Only the ringdove could charm the savage beast. This fearless little bird would perch upon the Karkadann's horn and sing, much to the delight of its host. In return, the Karkadann made its home near ringdove nests, protecting them from harm. This is clearly a description of the one-horned Indian Rhinoceros (*Rhinoceros unicornis*). See **Abada, Abath, Kere, Scythian Ass, Serou.**

Karora—One of the legendary *Creating Creatures* of the Australian Aborigines, it is said to be the ancestor of the little Bandicoot (*Peramelidae*).

Kasai Rex—Another of the supposed "living dinosaurs" reported from the jungles of Central Africa. In 1932, a Swedish plantation owner named Johnson and his native servant traveling through the Kasai valley witnessed one attack and devour a rhinoceros. He described it as a 40-foot-long lizard, with a long, thick tail and leonine legs, and long, sharp teeth in huge jaws. It was dark red, with vertical black stripes like a tiger's down its neck, back, and tail. See *Coje ya Menia*, *Emela-Ntouka*, *Megalania*.

Keelut—A hairless version of the British *Black Dog*, in Inuit folklore. It haunts lonely regions of polar Canada and Alaska, following and attacking nocturnal travelers.

Kelpie—A water-monster of Scottish legend that lurks in freshwater lochs, marshes, and rivers, preferring torrid rapids to placid pools. Normally it is an ugly black beast, part horse and part bull, with two sharp horns. But it can shapeshift into the form of a beautiful white horse. If anyone mounts this horse, it gallops into the water and drowns the rider, whom it then eats. Occasionally, however, it helps a miller by keeping the mill-wheel turning at night. See *Aughisky*, *Glashtyn*, *Horse-Eel*, *Lake Monsters*, *Tangie*, *Water-Horse*.

Kere—A ferocious variety of *Unicorn* in Tibetan legend. See *Karkadan*, *Scythian Ass*, *Tsopo*.

Kerkes—A Turkish version of the *Phoenix*. Tradition says it lives for 1,000 years and then consumes itself by fire, arising renewed to live another millennium. This cycle will repeat 7 times 7, or 49 times, until the Day of Judgment comes. The mystical tree *Ababel*—the "Father Tree" in the *Quran*—shoots out new branches and vegetation at every resurrection of the Kerkes.

Keto—A horrific sea-monster of ancient Greek myth, she is the wife of Phorcis, the sea-god. Their children are the Gorgons and their grotesque sisters, the Graeae.

Keythong—A male *Gryphon*, represented in heraldic symbolism with spikes or jets of flame springing from its shoulders in place of wings.

Khaiyr Beast—A *Lake Monster* dwelling in the actively volcanic Lake Khaiyr, in the remote Yanski area of Yakutsk in eastern Siberia. It was first reported by a Russian mineralogist, Mr. Glad-

kika, who was in the region to sample rare mineral deposits. As he sat on the lake shore, a jet-black, long-necked, small-headed animal resembling a *Plesiosaur* emerged from the water to graze on the long grass growing on the bank. A few days later, the expedition chief and two of his assistants observed the creature in the center of the lake. Their description matched Gladkika's, but added a prominent dorsal fin—a feature only found in fish and cetaceans. All witnesses agreed that the monster's skin was so black as to appear almost blue.

Khara—A gigantic, three-legged *Unicorn* ass in Zoroastrian mythology of ancient Persia. It has a single horn and nine mouths, and with its six eyes—two in front, two in back, and two on the top of its head—it is an all-seeing guardian warding humanity from evil.

Kheglen—A cosmic elk in Siberian mythology that steals the sun and is pursued across the sky by Main-Mangi, the great bear-mother. Main-Mangi eventually kills Kheglen and releases the sun, ending the winter. Kheglen is the constellation of Ursa Minor, Main-Mangi is Bootes, and the ski tracks of the pursuit are the Milky Way. This seasonal saga is reenacted annually in ceremonies of spring's return.

Khepra (or *Khepri*)—The cosmic scarab beetle of ancient Egyptian mythology that forms the sun and pushes it across the sky, just as the tiny dung beetle (*Scarabaeus sacer*) rolls a ball of dung. Images of Khepra are icons of Egypt itself.

Khyung—The high-flying cosmic eagle of outer space in Tibetan folklore. Mount of the gods and patron of mediums and lamas, he is hatched from the egg already full-grown, signifying the latent potential for true enlightenment. See *Garuda*.

Ki-Lin (also *Kilin, Qilin, Ky-Lin, Chai Tung, Lu,* or *Hai Chiai*)—A Chinese variant of the *Unicorn*, with the head of a *Dragon*, a lion's mane, the body of a stag, the tail of an ox, and, of course, a single horn. Its body radiates the five sacred colors—blue, red, yellow, black, and white—and its voice rings like a temple bell. First reported in the year 2697 BCE in the palace of the Chinese emperor Huang-ti, the *Ki* is the male aspect, and the *Lin*, the female. The Ki-Lin is king of the 360 beasts of the Earth, and one of the four auspicious animals—the *Ssu Ling*, or Spiritual Creatures of China. The gentle creature will not tread upon insects, nor eat living grass. Symbolizing wisdom, justice, and righteousness, it appears only during the time of an upright ruler or before the

Ki

Lin

birth or death of a sage, such as Confucius. The Ki-Lin is one of the six varieties of Chinese Unicorn. The others are the *Hiai Chai*, the *Ki lin*, the *King*, the *Kioh Twan*, the *Poh*, and the *Too Jon Sheu*. Some researchers believe that that this single-horned, semi-aquatic stag may actually be a rare or extinct subspecies (or mutated individual) of Chinese Water Deer (*Hydropotes inermis*). See *Hai Chai*, *King*, *Kirin*, *Kioh Twan*, *Poh*, *Sin-U*, *Too Jon Sheu*.

Kimpurushas—*Centaur*-like

creatures of Hindu mythology, they are entirely equine except for their human heads. They serve as minions of Kubera, ruler of the treasure-guarding *Yakshas*, whose kingdom is in the northern Himalayas. See *Kinnaras*.

King Kong (*Meg-aprimatus kong*)—A

fictional gigantic gorilla from the classic 1933 film of that name, with remakes in 1976 and 2005, and numerous sequels and spin-offs. Similar to *Godzilla*, Kong has become an iconic figure of world mythology. He inhabits Skull Island, southwest of Sumatra, along with dinosaurs and other prehistoric monsters. An American filmmaker captures the giant ape and takes him to New York City to be exhibited as the Eighth Wonder of the World. Kong escapes and climbs the Empire State Building, where he is shot and killed by airplanes. But it is really a case of "beauty killed the beast," as he is only trying to protect the beautiful actress Ann Darrow, whom he comes to adore.

King Otter—Dwelling in the River Conon

in Scotland, the King Otter is larger than ordinary otters. Its pelt is impervious to all weapons. If you can catch one, it will grant you one wish in exchange for its freedom. See *Dobhar-Chú*.

Kingstie—A gigantic, blackish, serpentine or

eel-like *Lake Monster* reported by many witnesses for more than 200 years in the Kingston area or eastern portion of Lake Ontario, Canada. Estimates of its size have varied from 20 to 40 feet long. Some reports have added details such as a long mane, a large tail, small limbs, fiery eyes, and antler-like horns.

Kinich Ahau—A fiery sun-bird and solar deity in the mythology of the Mayan Indians of the Yucatan Peninsula. See *Quetzalcoatl*.

Kinnaras—Half-bird, half-human musicians of Hindu mythology who entertain at the Himalayan court of Kubera, king of the Yakshas. They are wise and cultured. The Sanskrit word *Kinnara* derives from the same root as the Greek *Centaur*. See *Kimpurushas*.

Kirata—Composite creatures in the folklore of ancient India, they are tigers from the waist up and human from the waist down. Males are striped like a tiger all over, but females are golden, and beautiful enough to seduce humans. They subsist primarily on fish, but will also eat human prey.

Kirin (or *Kirien*)—The multicolored Japanese *Unicorn*, equivalent to the Chinese *Ki-Lin*. The Kirin is so gentle that it will not step on a blade of grass or injure an insect. It only appears when a certain constellation is in the heavens and a truly great man is born. Japan also has the single-horned *Sin-U*, which has leonine features and an infallible sense of justice, sometimes appearing in courts of law to acquit the innocent and slay the guilty.

Kirtimukha (Sanskrit, "Face of Glory")—A monstrous disembodied lion's head in Hindu fables of India. A guardian of doorways, it has protruding eyes, thick, horn-like eyebrows, and a mane of flames.

Kitsune (Japanese, "Fox")—In Japanese folklore, foxes are imbued with great intelligence, long lives, and magical powers, including the ability to shapeshift into human form and appear as young girls, beautiful women, or old men. Japan has two native subspecies of foxes: the Hokkaido Fox (*Kita kitsune*) and the Japanese Red Fox (*Hondo kitsune*). See *Kumiho*.

Kludde (also *Oschaert*)—A shapeshifting spectral beast of Belgian folklore. It haunts desolate roads of the Flemish countryside, and the only warning of its presence is the rattling sound of the chains that cover it. It preys upon nocturnal travelers by jumping on their backs and weighing them down, growing heavier and heavier with each step. No one can ever hope to outrun or escape it, for the faster one walks, the faster it follows, often slipping through the trees like a giant snake. It usually appears as a monstrous *Black Dog* walking on its hind legs, but it can also appear as a horse, a giant, hairy black cat, a frog, a bat, or a horrible black bird. In any shape, however, it is identified by the blue flame flickering about its head.

Koguhpuks ("Earth Moles")—Gigantic subterranean beasts in the folklore of Siberia and the Inuits of Alaska's Bering Straits. Extremely photophobic, they die upon exposure to light. Therefore, they emerge only once a year on the longest, darkest night (Winter Solstice). Huge bones of *Mammoths* found in spring in the thawing permafrost are said to be the remains of Koguhpuks that were caught on the surface at dawn. See *Tien-Schu*.

Kongamato ("Overwhelmer of Boats")—Numerous reported sightings of these large, leathery-winged flying creatures from swampy regions of Zambia, Congo, Angola, and Kenya have led cryptozoologists to speculate that that there may be a relic population of *Pterodactyls* still living in Africa. They are black or red, and are named for their proclivity for capsizing canoes. A witness in 1923 described them as smooth-skinned, with toothy beaks and wingspans of 4 to 7 feet. Another said the wings made a loud thunderous noise. All witnesses immediately identify it with pictures of *pterosaurs*. However, some researchers think this may be just a Hammerhead Bat (*Hypsignathus monstrosus*), Africa's largest fruit bat, whose black wings span more than 3 feet. See *Ahool*, *Alan*, *Guiafairo*, *Olitiau*, *Sassabonsum*, *Snallygaster*, *Wyvern*.

Koresck—A Persian *Unicorn* depicted as part goat and part horse, and honored as a royal beast.

Koskolteras Rhombopterix—A *Plesiosaur*-like *Lake Monster* supposedly dwelling in Lake Koskol, in the former Russian province of Kazakhstan. The earliest accounts of this creature were broadcast on a Soviet radio program in 1977. It was dubbed *Koskolteras Rhombopterix* by an anonymous researcher in homage to Sir Peter Scott's scientific designation of the *Loch Ness Monster*. See *Baikal Lake Monster*, *Brosnie*, *Khaiyr Beast*, *Kokkol*.

Kraken (or *Krabben*, *Skykraken*)—An immense, many-tentacled sea monster, capable of dragging entire sailing ships down into a watery grave. Vikings reported encountering squirming tentacles of the *Kraken* that covered acres of sea. These are actually Giant Squids (*Architeuthis*, "ancient squid")—deep-sea cephalopods the size of whales (which are, along with sleeper sharks, their only predators). Only recently have the first giant squids been captured alive, but many dead ones have washed up on beaches over the centuries. In April 2003, a juvenile specimen of a gigantic new species was recovered in Antarctic waters. It was named *Mesonychoteuthis* ("colossal squid"). In February of 2007, one was caught alive! See *Hydra*, *Lotan*, *Scylla*.

Kting Voar ("Jungle Sheep"; or *Ling Dong*, "Mountain Goat")—A caprid or arien cryptid from Cambodia (*Kting Voar*) and Vietnam (*Ling Dong*), it has 20-inch-long twisting horns, a purported set of which was purchased by biologist Wolfgang Peter in a market in Ho Chi Min City. No other evidence of its actual existence has been found.

Kudan—A human-headed bull from Japanese folklore, with three eyes on each side of its body and horns down its back. It always speaks truth, and is sought out as an oracle of things to come. See *Takujui*.

Kujata—The vast and mighty bull in Moslem myth that stands astride the cosmic fish *Baharmut*. Kujata bears a gigantic glowing ruby on his back, upon which stands the angel who carries the Earth on his shoulders. Kujata is said to have 4,000 eyes, 4,000 ears, 4,000 mouths, 4,000 nostrils, and 4,000 legs.

Kul (or *Kulili*)—Freshwater *Merfolk* of Assyrian myth, with the typical configuration of the upper body of a human and the lower body of a fish. *Kulullu* are the males and *Kuliltu* the females. Generally hostile to humans, they dwell in lakes, pools, and wells, which they stir up and pollute to render the waters undrinkable. They can be mollified by music, and singing a paean to them will secure their lifetime friendship. See *Abgal*.

Kulshedra (or *Kucedre*)—The final stage of metamorphosis of the Albanian *Bolla*. Usually appearing as a nine-tongued, fire-breathing *Dragon*, it can also appear to be a hairy old woman with pendulous breasts. It causes droughts, the cessation of which requires propitiary sacrifices.

Kumiho—A cruel and vampiric nine-tailed supernatural fox in Korean folklore, it is what an ordinary fox becomes after living 1,000 years. Similar to the Japanese *Kitsune*, it can metamorphose into a beautiful woman—sometimes even a bride, in which form it seduces men and kills them. But unlike the Kitsune, the Kumiho is always malevolent and predatory toward humans.

Kunaplpl (or *Guanapipi*)—A *Water Monster* in Aboriginal lore of Arnham Land, northern Australia. It lurks in streams, where it swallows young boys fishing. It is eventually persuaded by an eagle owl to regurgitate them, an event that is reenacted in boys' puberty rites.

L is for Lamia, Lybia's queen
Turned to a monster to vent Hera's spleen.
Tail of a serpent, but woman above –
Always remembering Zeus, her lost love.

Kurma—The vast cosmic turtle of Hindu mythology. Its carapace forms the vault of the heavens, and its plastron is the foundation of the Earth—particularly the Indian subcontinent. When the Hindu gods churn the ocean of milk (the Milky Way) to create many things and beings, they ask Kurma to dive to the bottom to support the mountain they use for a dash, with the great serpent *Sesha-Naga* as a rope. See *Akupara, Father of All Turtles*.

Kurrea—In the Australian Aborigine Dreamtime, this is a monstrous, swamp-dwelling reptile with a voracious appetite. It threatens to eat everyone, so the hero Toola is sent to kill it. But when his spears merely bounce off its armored back, Kurrea turns to pursue him, burrowing through earth and rocks as easily as water. As it closes in on him, Toola leads it to his mother-in-law, Bumble Tree. Kurrea takes one look at her, screames in terror, and dives into the earth, leaving a great hole. It never returns to bother humans again. Could this story possibly reflect a memory of the enormous prehistoric monitor lizard, *Megalania* (*Varanus prisca*)? See *Euroa Beast, Whowhie*.

Kusa Kap—A gigantic hornbill bird inhabiting one of the many tiny islands in the Torres Strait, which separates New Guinea from the northern tip of Queensland, Australia. With a 22-foot wingspan, this avian prodigy is said to carry dugongs aloft in its mighty claws, much as the fabled *Roc* is said to carry off elephants. The sound of its wings in flight is said to resemble the roar of a steam engine—a characteristic feature of the Rhinoceros Hornbill (*Buceros rhinoceros*) (shown), 4 feet long with a wingspan of 5 feet.

Kw'ên—An immense fish, miles in length, that once dwelt in the North China Sea. Eventually it metamorphosed into a truly vast bird called the *P'êng*.

Kyeryong—A creature of South Korean folklore that resembles a cross between a chicken and a *Dragon* (much like a *Cockatrice*). In a mountain by this name, there is a pool in which the female Kyeryong dwells. Women shamans bathe in this pool to obtain magickal powers. *Alyeong*, the first queen of Shilla, was said to be the child of a Kyeryong.

Labuna—A vast fish in Islamic mythology that swims in the lower ocean and supports on its head the mighty bull that holds the Earth upon his horns. See *Bahamut, Kujuta*.

Labynkr Monster—A *Lake Monster* inhabiting Lake Labynkr, Russia. It was first reported in 1964 by hunters whose dog had chased a deer into the lake. Both animals disappeared abruptly beneath the surface. Suddenly, the placid water began to froth, and up came a large, black monster with a prominent dorsal fin. It emitted a horrible shriek before resubmerging. Later that year, a Soviet research team sighted three large objects some 900 feet from shore. These appeared to submerge and resurface simultaneously, suggesting they were all parts of the same animal. See *Brosnie, Khaiyr Beast, Kokko, Koskolteras Rhombopterix.*

Lake Monsters—A class of unidentified large aquatic monsters reported by many eyewitnesses to be dwelling in the depths of lakes, lochs, swamps, and other bodies of water throughout the world. Nearly all of these lakes are extraordinarily deep and icy cold, which casts doubt on the possibility of these creatures being reptilian. They are commonly described as having bulky, undulating, wormlike or serpentine bodies and long necks with small horselike heads, superficially resembling submerged sauropod dinosaurs or *Plesiosaurs*. However, the rarity of sightings suggests that these animals are not air-breathing. Despite countless eyewitness reports spanning many centuries, and even a number of photographs, no actual specimen or other substantive evidence of their existence has yet been produced. See *Horse-Eels*.

Lamassu (or *Lama*)—Winged lionesses with human heads that guard the gates of Assyrian and Babylonian temples and palaces. They were said attack all but the purest good or the purest evil. Their male counterparts are called *Shedu*. See *Sphinx*.

Lamia—Once the beautiful Queen of Lybia, Lamia was seduced by Zeus, king of the Greek gods. His jealous wife, Hera, killed Lamia's children and turned her into a hateful monster—a woman above the waist and a serpent below. In this form she bore more children, the vampiric *Lamiae* or *Lamya*, which prey particularly upon sleeping children. Their reptilian bodies have a woman's head and breasts, with cloven hind hooves, a horse's tail, and feline forelegs. *Lamia* is also the name of a friendly Mermaid in Basque folklore of southern France and northwestern Spain.

Lampalugua—A gigantic predatory lizard with enormous claws in the legends of the Araucanian Indians of Chile. It devours both cattle and people.

Laskowice (or *Leschia*)—*Satyr*-like creatures of Slavic folklore, with typical hairy bodies, goats' feet, and human torsos. They are guardians and protectors of the forests and the creatures that dwell therein, particularly wolves. See *Faun*.

Lavellan—A Scottish beast resembling a rat or mouse. Although it could supposedly sicken cattle just by being near them, the cattle could then be cured by dipping the Lavellan's skin in their drinking water. The Water Vole (*Arvicola terrestris*) (shown) was supposed to have similar powers, and is thus probably the same animal.

Lau—An immense, *Plesiosaur*-like creature with a long, tapering neck and a donkey-like body with flippers, said to lurk in the dense papyrus swamps around Lake No in southern-central Sudan, East Africa. Bristling tendrils protrude from the animal's muzzle, aiding it in snaring prey. It was brought to international attention in 1914 when a group of Shilluk natives killed a specimen in the swamps of Addar to use its bones in protective amulets. This beast is often compared with the *Lukwata* of Lake Victoria, which is connected to Lake No by the White Nile. The two animals share many characteristics, including a taste for human flesh. They have also both been said to emit a cry like the trumpeting of elephants. See *Lake Monsters*.

La Velue (French, "Shaggy Beast"; also *Peluda, Peallaidh*)—A gigantic snake-headed monster in the folklore of medieval France. It had huge tortoise feet and a long tail, and was covered in straggly, green tendrils resembling thick, tangled grass tipped with nasty stingers. It supposedly ravaged the countryside along the Huisine River, destroying crops, livestock, and people with its burning breath and voracious appetite. When hunters approached, it

retreated into the river, causing the banks to overflow and flood the land. Eventually it was slain by the avenging fiancé of a maiden it had devoured. He hacked off its vulnerable tail, and it died instantly.

Leelanau—A *Lake Monster* inhabiting Lake Leelanau in Leelanau County, Michigan. It is described as having a long, stump-like neck, an equally long tail, and two large eyes. It first appeared after a dam was built in the late 1800s; this raised the water level 10 to 12 feet higher, thus creating a marshy environment where the creature was said to thrive. It has been many years since the last reported sighting.

Lenapizka ("True Tiger")—An amphibious *Lake Monster* in the folklore of the Peoria Indians of Illinois.

Leongalli—A Mongolian *Dragon* with a serpentine body and a leonine head and forequarters, quite similar to the European *Tatzelwurm*.

Leontophontes—As described in the *Physiologus*, these are "certain creatures of moderate size" that people burn in order to get the resulting poisonous ashes, which they sprinkle onto meat to kill lions, "should the lions eat the least little bit of it." These may actually be plants rather than animals, as Arnica is also known as Leopard's Bane, and Dandelion belongs to the genus *Leontodon*.

Leopon—Hybrid progeny of a lioness and a male leopard. Bred in Japanese and Italian zoos, they have the size and strength of a lion and the climbing abilities of a leopard. The males have sparse manes. Perhaps such pairings in the wild could account for reports of the legendary spotted lion, or *Marozi*. See *Jagleop, Liger, Pardus, Tion*.

Leucrocota (Greek, "White Wolf-Dog"; also *Crocotta*)—An Ethiopian animal first described by Pliny the Elder in his *Historia Naturalis* (77 CE). It is the size of a donkey, "with cloven hooves, the haunches of a stag, the neck and tail of a lion, the head of a badger, and a mouth that extends to the ears; it imitates the sound of the human voice." In place of teeth, it has ridges of bone in its jaws. It is clearly based on the hyena (*Crocuta crocuta*). See *Chuti*.

Leviathan (or *Livjatan*, "Coiling")—A vast and terrible primordial monster of Hebrew mythology, that encircles the world in the abyssal depths of the cosmic ocean. Said to be more than 900 miles long, with seven

heads and 300 eyes, it is the Ugaritic god of evil. It is nearly always referenced with its enemy, the **Behemoth**, and the name has been applied to various gigantic sea monsters, including whales and **Sea Serpents**. The seven heads, of course, link it to the **Hydra**. Some crypto-zoologists suggest it could be a reference to the **Sirrush** of the Ishtar Gate of Babylon, itself perhaps a living dinosaur. But this author (OZ) believes it is most likely originally based on the Nile Crocodile (*Crocodylus niloticus*). See **Apocalyptic Beast**, **Balaur**, **Chudo-Yudo**, **Herren-Surge**, **Hydra**, **Ihuaivulu**, **Illuyankas**, **Kaliya**, **Kraken**, **Ladon**, **Lotan**, **Musmahhu**, **Naga Pahoda**, **Orochi**, **Scylla**, **Thu'ban**, **Tiamet**.

Leyak—A supernatural monster of Balinese folklore, usually depicted in the form of a flying head with entrails dangling from it. There are only three of them, one male and two females. They have large fangs and very long tongues, and images of them are often hung on walls as house decorations. They seek pregnant mothers about to give birth in order to eat their babies or suck their blood. See **Flying Heads**.

Lidérc (also *Lüdérc*, *Ludvérc*, *Lucfir*, *Iglic*, *Ihlic*, *Piritusz*, *Mit-mitke*, *Ördögszeretõ*, *Csodacsirke*, "Miracle Chicken"; also *Ördög*, "Devil")—A demonic creature of Hungarian folklore, said to be hatched from the first egg of a black hen incubated under a human armpit or in a heap of manure. It attaches itself to people and assumes a human form to become their vampiric lover, bringing nightmares, similar to an *incubus* or *succubus*. The Lidérc hoards gold, which makes its owner rich, but it also causes illness and death. Haunting cemeteries, it appears by night as a fiery light, a will-o'-the-wisp, or a bird of flame. To banish the Lidérc, it must be persuaded to perform an impossible task, such as hauling sand with rope or carrying water with a sieve. See **Aitvaras**.

Liger—The gigantic progeny of a female tiger and a male lion, this hybrid weighs 1,000 pounds and stands 12 feet tall, making it by far the largest cat on the planet. Its pelt is a tawny orange, bearing the stripes of its mother as well as the spots of its father. The male has a moderate leonine mane. See **Jagleop**, **Leopon**, **Murozi**, **Pard**, **Tigon**.

Lightning Monsters—Sky-dwelling monsters of Zambian mythology, Africa. They have the foreparts and heads of goats, with the hind parts of crocodiles. They bounce between the heavens and the Earth during storms on elastic threads like bungee cords, creating lightning thereby. See **Lightning Serpents**.

Lightning Serpents (or *Lightning Snakes*)—Great sky-dwelling serpents in Australian Aborigine mythology that descend to the Earth and rebound to the heavens during storms, thus creating lightning. This contact between Earth and sky releases the life-giving rains. See **Lightning Monsters**.

Lik—A vast and ancient water serpent in the folklore of Gran Chaco, South America. With palm trees growing along its mossy back, it is the guardian of the fish that dwell in lakes and rivers. See **King of the Fishes**, **Lake Monsters**.

Lindwurm (Swedish, "Dragon"; also *Lindworm* or *Lindorm*)—Gigantic serpentine invertebrate from Germanic and Scandinavian legend, sometimes depicted with small wings, but incapable of flight. Numerous witnesses over the centuries describe the creature as being 10 to 20 feet long, with an unwieldy, legless body as thick as a man's thigh and black or green-gold in color, and a yellow-flamed belly. It has a horselike head and mane, a mouth full of sharp white teeth, and large, glowing red eyes. Very aggressive and able to attain great speed, it can take down a man on a galloping horse. When killed it emits a foul odor in its final death throes. First reported by Marco Polo, who encountered these creatures crossing the steppes of Central Asia, they began appearing in Europe during the Middle Ages. Although the Asian variety thrived on dry land, the European subspecies preferred marshes and streams. They haunted churchyards and ancient burial mounds, guarding their treasures and living on decaying human remains. Symbolizing war and pestilence, they devoured cattle and people. See **Lake Monsters**, **Mongolian Death Worm**, **Orm**.

Lion-Griffon—A class of Mesopotamian **Gryphon** with the head and foreparts of a lion, and the wings, legs, and hindquarters of an eagle or Gryphon. It can be seen in European heraldry, as well as in the sculptures and bas-reliefs of ancient Assyria and Persia, where it was associated with the war-god, Ninurta.

Little Manitou—An enormous, arboreal, horned water-serpent that emits sparks of flame, from the folklore of the Otsitsot Indians of the United States.

Liver—A cormorant-like bird said to have frequented the pool near where the city of Liverpool, England was built. It is depicted on the arms of Liverpool.

Lizard Men (or *Homo subterreptus*)—Strange reptilian-humanoid creatures reported from around the world, resembling the *Creature from the Black Lagoon* from the movies. Perhaps the most famous is the *Lizard Man of Scape Ore Swamp*, near Bishopville in Lee County, South Carolina. First reported in 1988, it is a 7-foot-tall creature with glowing, red eyes and rough, green skin. See *Intulo*, *Gatorman*, *Lizard Man*, *Loveland Frogmen*, *Mill Lake Monster*.

Llamhigyn y Dwr (Welsh, "Water Leaper")—An enormous, malignant, toadlike water-monster of Welsh folklore, with a tail and batlike wings instead of legs. It lurks along mud shoals and riverbanks where fish and sheep are plentiful, startling fishermen and curious sheep into falling into the muddy water to be devoured.

Loathly Worm—Monstrous serpentine *Dragons* with two front feet and no wings. Often depicted in medieval bestiaries and psalters, they were held responsible for the blighting of large regions of Europe. Perhaps the most famous was the Lampton Worm (shown). See *Lindwurm*, *Orm*, *Worm*.

Loch Awe Monster—Gigantic eels said for centuries to dwell in Scotland's Loch Awe. One of the few written accounts of these creatures comes to us from Timothy Pont (c.1562–1614), who described them as "big as ane horse with incredible length," and said they had frightened most of the fishermen away from the loch. See *Beithir*, *Lake Monsters*.

Loch Ness Monster (or *Nessie*)—The most famous of all *Lake Monsters*, inhabiting the murky 755-foot depths of 23-mile-long Loch Ness in the Scottish Highlands. Its bulky, undulating body has reported lengths up to 30 feet long, and has sometimes shown several humps above the surface. Its head and neck are proportioned similarly to those of a horse or giraffe, and topped with small, hornlike

projections. From its earliest recorded appearances in 565 and 690 CE, sightings have continuing sporadically through the centuries; however, the number of sightings increased dramatically after the construction of a public motorway along the Loch in 1933. In 1975, the scientific name of *Nessiteras rhombopteryx* ("Ness wonder with diamond-shaped fins") was bestowed upon this creature by Sir Peter Scott. Although it is popularly presumed to be a living *Plesiosaur*, this author believes they are actually invertebrates—probably some sort of gigantic, aquatic slug. See *Champ*, *Lizzie*, *Morag*, *Ogopogo*, *Orm*.

Lokapala Elephants—  In Hindu mythology, these are eight immense elephants that stand upon the shell of the cosmic turtle *Akupara* and support the disk-shaped Earth. Each male-female pair of pachyderms is assigned a quadrant, or *Lokapala*, and a guardian deity is mounted on each. They are as follows: North, *Himapandara* (god Kubera); Northeast, *Supratika* (god Prthivi); East, *Airâvata* (god Indra); Southeast, *Vamana* (god Yama); Southwest, *Kumuda* (god Sûrya); West, *Anja* (Varuna); Northwest, *Pushpadanta* (god Vâyu).

Long Necked Sea Serpent (*Megalotaria longicollis*, "Giant Sea Lion with a Long Neck")—A 15- to 65-foot-long Plesiosaur-like sea creature with a long neck, several humps, and the ability to move in vertical undulations. The head has a distinctive horse-like appearance, sometimes with hair and whiskers. It is believed by most cryptozoologists to be a long-necked, short-tailed sea lion. However, this writer (OZ) believes they are marine versions of the gigantic aquatic invertebrate typified by the Loch Ness Monster. There have been 82 recorded sightings from all the world's seas. See *Caddy*, *Sea Serpents*, *Lake Monsters*.

Lorelei—Beautiful female *Merfolk* of Germany who are said to guard magickal treasure hidden along the Rhine River, as well as magickal and spiritual knowledge. They are most famous from the Teutonic saga, the *Nibelunglied*.

Lough Fadda Beast—A long-necked *Lake Monster* inhabiting Ireland's Lough (Lake) Fadda. The first report came in 1954, when several boaters encountered a "long-necked monstrosity" which suddenly thrust its head through the water and bore toward them. "The head was about 3 feet out of the water, in a long curve," and its mouth was wide open, revealing whiteness within. At the last moment, the creature dove beneath the boat, then reemerged on the other side, displaying two distinct humps on its back. See *Horse-Eel*, *Loch Ness Monster*, *Water-Horse*.

Lough Ree Monster— A *Lake Monster* dwelling in Lough Ree, in County Meath, Ireland. St. Cronan Mochua, who founded the Church and Abbey of Balla in 616 CE, first chronicled the beast of Lough Ree after a group of hunters refused to pursue a stag that fled into the lake, for fear of the vicious monster that dwelled therein. Three priests encountered it in 1960, when a large, black, eel-shaped animal reared its head not 300 feet from shore. See *Horse-Eel*.

Lou Carcolh—In French folklore, a gigantic, snail-like mollusk with hairy tentacles and an enormous shell, that leaves a slimy trail behind it. Its lair is a huge cave beneath the town of Hastingue in the Les Landes region of southwestern France. It drags victims into its cave with its tentacles and consumes them. See *Sarmatian Sea-Snail*, *Tuba*.

Loveland Frogs—Several bipedal, reptilian, froglike creatures seen by multiple witnesses (including police officers) along the roadsides near Loveland, Ohio, in 1955 and again in 1972. They were 3 to 4 feet tall, with leathery, green skin, froglike heads, and webbed hands and feet. One of the alien creatures held a wand-like object above its head from which sparks shot out. See *Frogman.*

Lubolf—A hippopotamus-like creature with fangs. See *Behemoth*.

Lukwata—A carnivorous cryptid reported from Africa's Lake Victoria, which borders Uganda, Kenya, and Tanzania. Although some witnesses report it as a typical long-necked *Lake Monster*, it is more commonly described as having a square head and a brownish body resembling that of a dolphin and a white underbelly. Many local natives maintain that the Lukwata is a colossal 12-foot-long catfish, possibly a Wels (*Silurus glanis*) (shown), which is known to reach 10 feet in length and weigh 330 pounds. Natives claim that the Lukwata often fights with crocodiles, their primary natural enemy. See *Lau*.

Lung—The Chinese word for *Dragons*, especially the five-toed Imperial Dragons, guardians of the Earth's waters. They inhabit the rain clouds and breathe smoke and flames from their nostrils. Each holds a pearl of wisdom in its open mouth, and each has a particular area of responsibility (denoted by the word that precedes *Lung*). For example, *Shen Lung*, the Spiritual Dragon,

is the beautiful, multicolored, five-toed Imperial Dragon of China and the master of the wind-borne rains. Only the Emperor of China was allowed to wear his image—others were forbidden, under penalty of death. *Lung Wang*, the Azure Dragon, is the Dragon King. Representing the East and the season of spring, he is one of the four *Ssu Ling*, or "Spiritual Creatures," that stand at the four corners of the Earth.

Lusca (or *Giant Scuttle, Him of the Hairy Hands*)—A gargantuan octopus reportedly dwelling in the crystal waters of the Bahamas, off the coast of Florida. They are said to inhabit large limestone marine caves called "blue holes," and possibly "banana holes" on land. One native guide maintained that the arms of the Giant Scuttle are about 75 feet long, but they are not dangerous to fishermen unless they can grip the ocean floor and the boat at the same time. This as-yet-unconfirmed cephalopod has been assigned the scientific name of *Octopus giganteus*. See *Globster*, *Manta*, *Tumu-Ra'i-Fuena*.

Lwan (also *Luan* or *Lwan Shui*)—A majestic, gigantic pheasant of Chinese legend. When the Lwan changes the color of its feathers, it gains a different name: a Lwan with black feathers is called *Yin Chu*; one with a red head crest and red wings is called *Fung*; a pure white Lwan is a *Hwa Yih*; one with sapphire blue feathers is a *Yu Siang*; and a Lwan with golden feathers is known as *To Fu*.

Lybbarde—Supposedly the progeny of a lioness and a panther, the Lybbarde resembles a leopard. In heraldry, it is the symbol of boldness.

Lympago (also *Mantygr, Man-Tiger, Montegre, Satyral*)—A man-lion or man-tiger from medieval heraldry. It has the body of a lion or tiger, and the head of an old man with horns. Sometimes the horns resemble those of an ox, and the feet are more like a dragon's. See *Manticora*.

Lynx—A catlike creature described in medieval bestiaries as having the body of a *Panther* with the head of a dog. Its bright, far-seeing eyes can penetrate the darkest gloom to fix upon its sleeping prey.

Lyon-Poisson—A heraldic sea lion with the foreparts and head of a lion and the body and tail of a fish. See *Hippocampus.*

M is for Mermaid, half woman, half fish:
Vision of beauty, a sailor's fond wish.
With magic mirror and comb in her hand;
Waves of the ocean obey her command.

Mada—A huge and terrifying predatory monster in the folklore of India. It has an enormous mouth with great, protruding fangs, and a voracious appetite for living creatures—including humans.

Madidi Monster—A creature resembling a sauropod dinosaur reported from South America: "In 1907 Lieutenant-Colonel Percy Fawcett of the British Army was sent to mark the boundaries between Brazil and Peru. He was an officer in the Royal Engineers and was well known as a meticulous recorder of facts. In the Beni Swamps of Madre de Dios Colonel P. H. Fawcett saw an animal he believed to be Diplodocus.... The Diplodocus story is confirmed by many of the tribes east of the Ucayali" (*The Rivers Ran East* by Leonard Clark, 1953).

Mahamba—A gigantic crocodile living in the Lake Likouala swamp region of central Africa's Republic of the Congo. It has been reported to reach an impressive 50 feet in length, and to devour entire rafts and canoes, along with their occupants. Natives insist that the animal is a unique species, quite distinct from the familiar Nile crocodile (*Crocodylus niloticus*). Could this possibly be a surviving example of the monstrous *Phobosuchus* ("Fearsome Crocodile") (shown)? That giant Cretaceous predator was about 50 feet long, with a 6-foot-long head and 4-inch-long teeth.

Mahisha (also *Mahishâsura*, ***Bhainsasura***)—A huge, destructive monster of Hindu mythology, similar to a ***Bucentaur*** with the head of a water buffalo. It was slain by the hero Skanda, or, in another version of the myth, by Kali-Durga. See ***Kimpurushas.***

Maka—A vast cosmic serpent of the void in Egyptian mythology, that continually attacks the sun-god Ra on his daily journey across the sky. See ***Apep***, ***Mehen***.

Makalala ("Noisy")—A giant carnivorous bird seen in the 1870s in a region of Africa inland from the coast of Zanzibar. Taller than an ostrich but capable of flight, it has long legs and the powerful beak of a bird of prey. It is named for the sound it produces by clapping together the horny plates at its wingtips. Considered to be an extra-large variety of the Secretary Bird (*Sagittarius serpentarius*) (shown), it has been given the name *Megasaittarius clamosus* ("noisy giant secretary bird").

Makara ("Sea Monster")—A monstrous elephant-fish of Hindu legend, said to dwell in the Indian Ocean. From its most common depiction as a guardian on Hindu temple gates, it may be the same creature as the **Loch Ness Monster**. The elephant-like "trunk" resembles Nessie's long neck and small head, and the "ears" resemble the fins or flippers. However, it is also variously depicted as a grotesque crab; part crocodile and part bird; or a deer with the tail of a fish. It is the steed of the gods Ganga, Varuna, and sometimes Vishnu, and it represents the Zodiacal sign of ***Capricorn*** on the Hindu calendar. See ***Lake Monsters***, ***Water-Elephant***, ***Yali***.

Mali—A monstrous, shapeshifting, invincible hippopotamus in Gavoland, Mali, that devoured all the rice in the fields until it was slain by the hero Fara Make.

Mamba Mutu—A fearsome aquatic cryptid dwelling in Lake Tangankiya and the Lukuga River in Burundi, Africa. It is described as half-human, half-fish, and is said to kill people, suck their blood, and eat their brains.

Mamlambo (or *Brain Sucker*)—A monstrous ***Water-Horse*** said to inhabit the Mzintiava River near Mt Ayliff in South Africa. Xhosa tribal legends of this horrifying creature date back centuries. It is described as 60 to 70 feet long—including the tail—with a crocodilian torso and legs, a long, serpentine neck, and a horselike head. Its eyes glow in the dark with an eerie green luminescence. See ***Lake Monsters***.

Mammoth (from Russian *mamantu*, "that-which-lives-beneath-the-ground")—Highly evolved prehistoric elephants that were widespread across the Northern Hemisphere during the Ice Age and hunted extensively by early humans. In Mongolia, Manchuria, and Siberia, more recent legends account for the frozen specimens by claiming that they lived underground, and died as soon as they came into the sunlight. The shaggy-haired Woolly Mammoth (*Mammuthus primigenius*) was a spectacularly successful and prolific species, ranging from Spain to North America. There have been occasional claims that some might still survive in the vast and sparsely inhabited forests of the Siberian Tiaga.

Man-Dragon of China—A large, dark, manlike creature with wings, first reported at the beginning of 1926, when it was seen hovering over one of the world's largest dams, the Xia-on Te Dam in the southeastern foothills of China. On January 19, 1926, the dam collapsed, spilling more than 40 billion gallons of water onto farms and villages below and killing more than 15,000 people. Survivors came to believe that the Man-Dragon's appearance had been intended as a warning. See ***Black Bird of Chernobyl, Frieburg Shrieker, Mothman, Owlman.***

Mandragora (or *Mandragore, Mandrake*)—A unique plant that grows in the East, near Paradise. Its root grows in the form of a man or woman, and it shrieks horribly when torn from the ground. It is of great use in medicine and magick, but anyone who hears its cry goes mad or dies. It is therefore advised to tie a hungry dog to the plant by a cord and place a piece of meat beyond its reach. To get at the meat the dog will drag up the shrieking plant, keeping its master safely out of hearing range. The Mandrake (*Mandragora officinarum*) is a member of the psychotropic Nightshade family (*Solanaceae*).

Man-Eating Tree of Madagascar (or *Crinoida*)— A fantastic carnivorous plant allegedly discovered in 1878 on the island of Madagascar, where virgins were said to be sacrificed to it. The trunk was similar to an 8-foot-tall pineapple, topped with eight long, broad leaves, 11 to 12 feet long, that drooped to the ground. In the center of these was a liquid-filled hollow, surrounded by many 5- to 8-foot-long tentacles. The sacrificial victim was forced to climb the tree and drink from the hollow, whereupon the tentacles and leaves enveloped and crushed her. This legend may have been inspired by Africa's weird but harmless *Welwitschia mirabilis* (shown), discovered in 1860. See ***Ya-te-veo.***

Manetuwi-Rusi-Pissi ("Water Tiger")—A *Lake Monster* in the traditions of the Shawnee Indians of the southern United States, it is a guardian of lakes and fishes. See ***Guardian of the Fishes.***

Mangarsahoc (or *Mangarisaoka,* "whose ears hide its chin")—A large beast of Madagascar, with round, horselike feet and very long ears that fall over its eyes when it walks downhill. It makes a loud cry like that of a wild ass. Natives believe that the mere sight of it will bring bad luck.

Manipogo—A *Lake Monster* reported by many witnesses in Canada's Lake Manitoba, as well as nearby Lake Winnipeg, Lake Winnipegosis, Lake Dauphin, Lake Cedar, Dirty Lake, and Lake Memphrémagog, where it is called *Memphre*. Known by local Indians since they first settled the area, the creature is described as being 12 to 24 feet long, dark green or muddy-brown in color, and resembling a giant eel or snake with a single hump in the middle of its elongated body. It head resembles that of a snake, a sheep, or a deformed horse. On August 10, 1960, three were seen swimming together, and two years later one was photographed. See ***Ogopogo.***

Manta—A gigantic Sea-Monster in the folklore of Chiloc, Chile. The oceanic equivalent of the freshwater *Cuero* ("hide"), it is described as resembling a flayed cowhide with clawed tentacles and tail, and eyes all around the edges with four more on top. Although the name seems to allude to the giant Manta Ray (*Manta birostris*), which is certainly flat and can span up to 25 feet in length and weigh up to 6,600 pounds, the tentacles imply a cephalopod, such as the Pacific Giant Octopus (*Enteroctopus dofleini*), which may grow to more than 30 feet long and weigh more than 100 pounds. Mantas were said to sometimes climb out on land to sun themselves, and cause violent gales upon their return to the sea. This suggests carcasses washed ashore after a storm, which would account for the appearance of a stretched cowhide. See ***Cuero, Devil-Fish, Lusca, Migas, Tumu-Ra'i-Fuena.***

Manticora (from Persian *Mard-khor,* "Man-Eater"; also *Martikhora, Martiora, Manticore, Mantichora, Manticory, Manticoras, Mantiquera, Mantiserra, Mancomorion, Memecoleous, Satyral*)—A red lion-like creature of India with the face of a man, mane of a lion, tail and stinger of a scorpion, three rows of iron teeth, and a beautiful, musical voice similar to a trumpet or flute. It is certainly based on the Royal Bengal Tiger (*Panthera tigris tigris*), but it also seems to include elements of the Porcupine (*Hystrix leucura*) and the Hamadryas Baboon (*Papio hamadryas*). See ***Lympago, Cigouave.***

Many-Finned Sea Serpent (or *Cetioscolpenda aelani,* "Aelian's Cetacean Centipede")—An elongated creature up to 70 feet long, with segments and many lateral projections resembling dorsal fins, but turned backwards.

Found in the Western Atlantic, Indian, and Pacific Oceans, this creature is also known as the *Great Sea Centipede*, or **Con Rit**. It may be an invertebrate. There have been 26 recorded sightings, plus possible remains found on a beach in Vietı

Many-Humped Sea Serp

Plurigibbosus novae-angliae, "Many-Humped Thing from New England")—A 15- to 65-foot, medium-length-necked, long-bodied **Sea-Serpent** believed by many cryptozoologists to be an *archeocetacean* (ancient whale) such as *Zueglodon* (*Basilosaurus*). Found only in the North Atlantic, it has a series of humps or a crest along the spine like that of a sperm or grey whale. There have been 82 recorded sightings, a famous example of which is *Cassie*, the *Casco Bay Sea Serpent* of Maine, reported from 1777 into the 1950s.

Mapinguari (or *Isnashi*, *Alux*)—A mysterious creature said to live in the dense Amazon jungle of Brazil, with hair so thick it is invulnerable to weapons. According to the local Indians, it is about 6 to 15 feet tall, with reddish hair, large teeth and claws, and a horrible odor. Its call is said to be very humanlike, consisting of a long, loud, single vocalization that gradually lowers in pitch. Some cryptozoologists believe this might be a giant ground sloth, such as *Mylodon* or *Megatherium*, thought extinct for 10,000 years. They had bony nodules in their skins that served as protective armor. See **Giant Sloth of Patagonia**.

Marakihan—A large **Sea-Monster** with the body of a fish and the head of a man, supposedly found around the islands of New Zealand. It has a long tubular tongue with which it draws canoes and small boats into its mouth and devours them.

Margygr—A type of **Merbeing** of Greenland folklore, described as hideously ugly, with a flat face and piercing eyes. It may be based on the Walrus (*Odobenus rosmarus*) or the Stellar's Sea-Cow (*Hydrodamalis gigas*), hunted to extinction by 1768. See **Auvekoejak**, **Hakenmann**, **Halfway People**, **Havfrue**.

Marine Lion—A scaly leonine sea creature with an almost human voice. One was supposedly captured alive in the Tyrrhenian Sea in 1540 and presented to Marcel, Bishop of Castre, but it died shortly thereafter.

Marine Saurian—A 50- to 60-foot-long crocodile, or crocodile-like animal such as a *Mosasaur* or *Pliosaur*, found in the Northern Atlantic and Mediterranean. This could be an Estuarine Crocodile (*Crocodylus porosus*), but it would be a long way from its Indonesian and Northern Australian habitat. There have been nine recorded sightings. See **Sea-Serpents**.

Marked Hominids—Hairy hominids resembling **Bigfoot** but smaller and more human-looking in build. They are smelly social creatures that live in the forests and mountains of the frozen north. They come in several colors: some have light-colored manes, such as *Old Yellow Top*; others have patches of light-colored fur surrounded by darker fur; and some appear to be nearly albino. Sturdy, muscular creatures with large eyes and big bellies, they are nocturnal and omnivorous. See **Chuchunaa**, **Momo**, **Old Yellow Top**.

Marmaele—Small **Merfolk**, human in the upper part and fish-like below the waist. Bishop Erik Pontopiddan, in his *Natural History of Norway* (1752), states that they vary in size, from "the bignesse of an infant of half a year old" to a child of 3, and were thought to be the progeny of Mermaids and Mermen. Local fishermen sometimes caught them: "They tell us that these creatures then roll their eyes about strangely, as if out of curiosity, or surprise, to see what they had not seen before." Some were brought home and fed on milk, in the hope that they would foretell the future; but they were always returned to the sea within a day. The detail of the rolling eyes strongly suggests the Angel Shark (*Squatina*), also called **Bishop Fish**.

Martlet—A little footless bird of European heraldry, thought to have been inspired by the swallow or hummingbird, which are rarely seen to perch. It is depicted with ruffles of feathers in place of legs, and was thought to be unable to land, even sleeping and mating on the wing. See **Bird of Paradise**.

Mastertown Monster—A large unknown animal that appeared near the town of Masterton, New Zealand, in May of 1883. It had a broad muzzle, short legs, and curly hair. When the fearful townsfolk loosed their dogs upon the beast, one of the canines was flayed. This was enough to discourage the other dogs, which swiftly ran away. Tantalizingly, the account ends there. See **Bunyip**, **Bobhar-Chu**, **Euroa Beast**.

Mashernomak—A predatory **Lake-Monster** in the folklore of the Menominee Indians of North America.

Mawadi—Gigantic ana-condas of Brazil that capsize canoes, cause floods, and kidnap women. Their Queen is Huito, Mistress of the Waters. These are certainly  based on the Green Anaconda (*Eunectes murinus*, "good swimmer"), which reaches lengths of more than 30 feet, perhaps longer. See *Camoodi*, *Sterpe*, *Sucuriju Gigante*.

May's Point Mystery Fish—A piscine cryptid said to be lurking in a murky tributary of Cayuga Lake, one of Upstate New York's Finger Lakes. Dozens of nocturnal anglers claim to have seen this creature. Approximately 4 feet long, with a large hump, a round tail fin, and intricate, tribal-like patterns on its sides, this ichthyological anomaly has been likened to a *Coelacanth* by at least one eyewitness.

Mbielu-Mbielu-Mbielu ("One with planks growing out of its back")—A dinosaur-like creature of the African Congo. Pygmy fishermen report seeing it half-submerged in water with algae growing on its back, which is said to have several flat "planks" protruding from the skin. Although no one has ever seen the full body, legs, and tail of the creature, it is claimed that it is peaceful and herbivorous. The "planks" suggest the back plates of a *Stegosaurus*, but these Jurassic dinosaurs were not believed to be aquatic. See *Muhuru.*

Megalania (*Varanus prisca*)—A much larger pre-historic version of the Komodo Dragon, 15 to 20 feet long and weighing 1,000 to 1,300 pounds. Although it is believed to have been extinct for 40,000 years, sightings of living specimens are occasionally reported from Australia and New Guinea. See *Euroa Beast*, *Kasai Rex*, *Kurrea*, *Tanihwa*, *Whowhie*.

Melusina—A legendary figure in several European noble lineages, each of which gives a slightly different version of the story. The general theme is that a nobleman falls in love with a beautiful woman named Melusina whom he meets at a fountain in the woods. She agrees to marry him, on the promise that he will respect her need for total privacy on one day a week (or one day a month). Years go by happily and they have several children, but inevitably, the husband's curiosity gets the better of him, and he spies on his wife during her retreat. He sees her lying in her bath, with the lower half of her body ending in the tail of a serpent or fish—the result of an ancient curse. Her secret discovered, Melusina flees in shame, but she continues to watch over her children down through the generations. She is depicted in heraldry as a two-tailed *Mermaid* emblazoned on the crests of several royal houses claiming descent from her.

Merbeing—A generic term for amphibious humanoid cryptids. The marine varieties all have fishlike lower bodies, but the freshwater types have legs and often venture onto land. 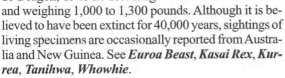 They are also carnivorous, and more aggressive than their marine counterparts. Both types have large oval eyes. Some have smooth skin, whereas others appear to have short fur or even patchy scales. Some of the fresh-water Merbeings display a row of spikes down their backs. Most resemble the *Creature from the Black Lagoon*. See *Honey Island Swamp Monster*, *Lizard Man*.

Merfolk/Mermaid/Merman ("Sea-Woman"/"Sea-Man")—From the waist up, this sea-creature resembles a man or woman, but its lower body resembles that of a fish. The stories often say they long for a soul. They are well-known from ancient mythology and sailors' tales throughout the world. Often confused with *Sirens*—even giving that name to a class of marine mammals (*Sirenia*)—females are often shown sitting on rocks combing their long hair to entice sailors to their doom. These legends can all be attributed to known sea mammals, such as the Dugong (*Dugong dugon*), a sirenian of Indonesia that has a long, sleek body, a large, whale-like tail, and breasts (on the females) identical to those of women. In heraldry, Merfolk symbolize eloquence in speech. The heraldic Mermaid is commonly shown with a comb and a mirror, and described as a "mermaid in her vanity."

Merhorse (or *Halshippus olai-magni*, "Sea-Horse of Olaus Magnus")—A 30- to 60-foot-long, large-eyed *Sea Serpent* with an equine head and neck. Often described as having whiskers and long, horselike manes, they have been seen in both salt and fresh waters throughout the world, with 71 recorded sightings. It is believed to be some sort of pinniped, such as a seal or sea lion, seen in the typical "periscope" position. See *Sea Serpents*, *Lake Monsters*.

Mermicoleon (or *Formicoleon*)—The "Ant-Lion," a creature generated by a translator's error. A word meaning "lion among ants" was mistranslated as a ferocious composite of lion and ant. The  name is now applied to insects that prey on ants by digging a conical sand pit and lying in wait underground for ants to slip in.

Merrow (From Gaelic *muir*, "sea," and *oigh*, "maiden"; also *Murchuacha, Moruadh, Moruach, Muir-Gheilt, Samhghubna, Suire*)— **Merfolk** of Ireland. The ugly males have short, flipper-like arms, green skin, teeth, and hair, and tiny, narrow eyes. The beautiful females, on the other hand, have flowing hair, translucent skin, and dark eyes. All have webbed fingers. Though they are happy, carefree creatures, it is considered bad luck to see one, as it usually heralds the coming of a terrible storm. They can intermarry with humans, producing web-fingered children with scaly skins. See **Havfrue** and **Havmand**.

Michi-Pichoux (also *Michi-Pichi, Michipechik, Mitchipichi, Matchi-Manitou*)—A terrifying **Underwater Panther** in the folklore of the Cree Indians of eastern Canada, where it dwelled among the islands of the St Lawrence River. It was described by French priest Father Louis Nicholas in his *Histoire Naturelle* (1675) as a hairy, tiger-like beast more than 18 feet long, with huge, clawed feet and a paddle tail like a beaver's. Its enormous head had fangs more than 2 feet long, and it preyed upon humans, especially children.

Migas—An aquatic monster dwelling in the upper reaches of the Congo River in central West Africa. It is described much like the **Cuero** of South America: a huge flat creature with long tentacles. It would seem to be a giant octopus, but no species of freshwater cephalopod is currently known to science. See **Freshwater Octopus, Hueke Hueku, Lau, Migas, Oklahoma Octopus.**

Mil— An Irish sea monster that sucks up the waters of the ocean and spews them forth again, causing the tides. See **Parata**.

Milcham—A Talmudic Jewish version of the **Phoenix**. It was the only animal not to eat from the Tree of Knowledge in the Garden of Eden, and was rewarded with the gift of immortality from the Tree of Life. It lives in a walled city for 1,000 years, at the end of which time it is consumed by fire, leaving an egg to begin a new cycle.

Mill Lake Monster—A strange creature reported from the Charles Mill Lake in Mansfield, Ohio. It was first seen emerging from the lake in March of 1959. Witnesses described it as an armless humanoid, standing more than 7 feet tall, with luminous green eyes. A second re-

port came in 1963, and others have trickled in over the years. Some have even claimed to have found footprints of gigantic webbed feet on the shore See **Gatorman, Lizard Men, New Jersey Gatorman, Orange Eyes**.

Mimick Dog—A fabulous creature believed by medieval Europeans to have inhabited ancient Egypt. It resembled an ape, with a snout like that of a hedgehog. An ability to mimic human behavior made them suitable as servants for the lower classes. This is probably an only slightly distorted reference to the Olive Baboon (*Papio cynocephalus*), which was, in fact, trained by ancient Egyptians for various tasks— including picking olives. See **Cynocephali**.

Minhocão (or *Miñocão*, from Portuguese, *Minhocar*, "earthworm")—An immense black earthworm said to dwell in the Andean highlands of South America. Some think it is 150 feet long and 15 feet wide, with a horny, armored hide that crushes trees as if they were blades of grass. Other witnesses say it is about 75 feet long, with two horns or tentacles protruding from its head. As a burrowing animal, the Minhocão is commonly blamed for houses and roads collapsing into the earth, as well as mysterious trenches so big they divert rivers and destroy orchards. Very similar to the *Sandworms* of Frank Herbert's *Dune* novels, the last sighting was in 1870. The largest known earthworm is the Australian *Megascolides,* which has been measured at over 10 feet long, with the diameter of a garden hose. See **Sterpe**.

Mi-Ni-Wa-Tu—A gigantic river monster in the folklore of the Teton Indians of Missouri. It is covered in red fur, and has a huge head with a single horn above a Cyclopean eye. Its long tail is flattened vertically like that of an alligator, with saw tooth projections along the upper edge. As it moves swiftly through the water, it creates a high bow wave in front, and an iridescent sheen on the water behind. In the early spring, it cracks the ice on the frozen Missouri River. Seeing it brings convulsions and even death.

Minocane—A heraldic beast that is half child and half spaniel.

Minotaur (Greek, "Bull of Minos")— A ferocious monster with the body of a powerful man and the head of a carnivorous bull. There was only one, named *Asterion*—the hideous cannibalistic offspring of Crete's Queen Pasiphae and a beautiful white bull. King Minos kept him in an underground maze called the *Labyrinth*, which Daedalus buildt specifically to imprison the beast. Minos fed him on

tributary sacrifices of Greek youths until the hero Theseus entered the Labyrinth and slew the monster.

Miqqiayuuq— A malicious water monster in the folklore of the Inuits of eastern Hudson Bay, Canada. A hairy, faceless creature, it lives under the ice of frozen lakes and upends buckets that are lowered to collect drinking water.

Mi'raj—A large, carnivorous, rabbit-like creature of Islamic folklore, with yellow fur and a single spiraling black horn. Supposedly found on an unnamed island in the Indian Ocean, it was feared by sailors, for it was swift enough to overtake deer and antelopes, and powerful enough to overcome pigs and cattle. See *Jackalope, Unicorn*.

Mishipizhiw ("Master of Fishes"; also *Mishipissy* or *Miskena*)—A giant **Lake-Monster** in the traditions of the Ojibwa and Algonquin Indians of the Great Lakes area of the United States. It was described as catlike, with a saw-toothed ridge down its spine and a long, sinuous tail which it used to whip up storms and whirlpools. The distinctive saw-toothed back almost certainly identifies it as a Lake Sturgeon (*Acipenser fulvescens*), which in Russia is known to reach lengths of 27 feet. See *Baikal Lake Monster, Guardian of the Fishes, Pal-Rai-Yuk, Underwater Panther, Whitey*.

Misiganebic—A 30-foot-long serpentine **Lake-Monster** in the traditions of the Algonquin Indians of the Great Lakes region of the United States. It has a horselike head, and its dark green body shines with multihued iridescence. These creatures are said to inhabit Lake Deschênes, Lake Désert, Lake Bitobi, Lake Pocknock, the Blue Sea Lakes, the Cedar Lakes, and Lake Trente-et-un Milles, where their task is to clean the waters. See *Horse-Eel*.

Mngwa ("the strange one"; also *Nunda*)—A ferocious gray cat, said to be the size of a donkey, that stalks the East African country of Tanzania. English contact with this animal began in the 1900's. Patrick Bowen, a hunter who once tracked the Mngwa, noted that the beast's prints were like those of a leopard but much larger. It also had brindled fur quite different from a leopard's. Bernard Heuvelmans speculated that it might be an abnormally colored variant of a known species, or perhaps a larger subspecies of the golden cat (*Profelis aurata*) (shown).

Moa—An enormous wingless bird of New Zealand believed extinct since around 1800, when the Maoris claim to have killed and eaten the last one. However, sporadic sightings suggest that some may have survived even into the 20th century. Of 21-38 known species, the largest were *Diornis robustus* and *Apteryx maxima,* both of which stood 12 feet tall.

Moehau (or *Moeroero, Maero*)—In the folklore of the Maori natives on the South Island of New Zealand, this is hairy hominid smaller than a man, with bony fingers and long claws. Said to live in trees and eat birds, they are solitary creatures, but would kidnap people if given the chance. Those living in the mountains are called *Moeroero*, whereas those in the interior are called *Maero*. Sightings have been reported since the 1840s.

Mokêle-M'Bêmbe (Lingala, "one who stops the flow of rivers"; also *Iriz Ima, N'yamala*)—A mysterious amphibious creature depicted in ancient rock paintings, reportedly inhabiting the Likouala swamp region of the Republic of Congo. It is said to be the size of an elephant, with short legs, three-clawed feet, leathery grey or reddish-brown skin, a reptilian head atop a long, flexible neck, and a long, muscular tail similar to that of an alligator. Some witnesses mention a single tooth or horn. This description is compellingly similar to a small sauropod dinosaur. It is herbivorous but also aggressive, and ferociously attacks and kills hippos and humans. Sightings of this creature have been reported since 1776, with numerous sightings by local villagers and explorers since 1913. One was even killed around 1959, but all those who ate its flesh died. See *Emela-Ntouka, Muhuru*.

Momo (short for "Missouri Monster")—A large, stinky hairy hominid reported from the backwoods of Missouri. It has so much fur that you cannot see its face. See *Bigfoot, Skunk Ape*.

Mongolian Deathworm (Mongolian, *Allghoi Khorkhoi,* "intestine worm")—Living deep within the sand dunes of the southern Gobi Desert, this creature's bulky, dark red, wormlike body is reported to be around 2 to 4 feet long. Supposedly, anything it touches turns yellow. It kills its victims instantly, either by spraying acid-like venom or by emitting a powerful electric charge from a range of several feet. For most of the year it hibernates under the desert sands, emerging to hunt only at night. It is particularly active in June and July. *Driloleirus americanus* is a 3-foot-long pink earthworm that smells like lilies and spits. Long thought extinct, a living specimen was discovered in 2005 in the Palouse soils of the Idaho/Washington border. See *Orm*.

Monkfish (or *Angel-Fish*)—A sea creature widely reported by medieval seafarers, and sighted often from 1200–1600 in the North Sea. Ambroise Paré (1517–1590), in his *On Monsters and Marvels*, described it as a kind of fish with a humanoid head and a monk's tonsure, cowl, and cape. During this same period, a similar creature called the *Hai Ho Shang* was reported in China. They are commonly depicted simply as large squids, artistically arranged and preserved as *Jenny Hanivers*. However, the actual animal referenced is the rare and unusual Angel Shark (*Squatina*). According to J.W. Buel, "it is frequently called Monk-Fish on account of its rounded head, which seems to be enveloped in a hood, and also because of a habit it has of rolling its eyes in a kind of reverential and supplicatory manner." See *Bishop Fish*.

Monoceros ("One Horn"; also *Karkadann*, *Carcazonon*)—A type of *Unicorn* described by Pliny the Elder in his *Historia Naturalis* (77 CE). It has the body of a horse, the feet of an elephant, the tail of a boar, and the head of a deer, with a 4-foot-long black horn projecting straight out from its forehead. This is clearly the single-horned Indian Rhinoceros (*Rhinoceros unicornis*). From the 17th century onward, however, the name was applied to the Narwhal (*Monodon monoceros*), also called *Monoceros Marinus*, or "Sea Unicorn." This creature was described as a huge, serpentine fish with an enormous, straight spiral horn projecting from its head, with which it attacked and sank ships.

Monster of Brompton—A typical *Lake-Monster* sighted during the 1970s in Lake Brompton, Lycoming County, Pennsylvania. It was grey-green, with a three-humped back extending about 8 feet above the surface. It had a horselike head with bristles around the mouth. Its rapid passage left a 250-foot-long wake in the murky waters, frightening the fishermen trying to avoid it. See *Horse-Eels, Merhorse*.

Monster of Lake Fagua—A *Lake-Monster* said to dwell in Lake Fagua, Chile, and described in a broadsheet published in 1784. It had a long, serpentine body, wings, and two "tails"—one which was pointed and used like a spear, and another which had circular suckers to hold its victims. It also had a humanlike face, great, donkey-like ears, huge horns, and a long mane like that of a horse. The first part of this description sounds like a large squid, but what are we to make of the rest?

Mo-O (or *Mo-Ko*)—A great Polynesian sea-*Dragon* that once moved an entire oyster bed from one island to another.

Morhon—A type of heraldic whale that has two blowholes and a mane like a lion's.

Moshiriikkwechep (or *Mohiriikkwchep*, "World Backbone Trout")—In Japanese mythology, a vast fish that lies in the mud beneath the ocean and supports the world on its back. Its periodic wriggling causes earthquakes and tsunamis. See *Jinshin Uwo, Jormundgund, Kami*.

Mother of the Fishes—An immense fish said to dwell in the River Elster, in Voightland, a district of Germany. It is the guardian of the fishes, but causes catastrophe if seen by any human. This could be a reference to the giant Lake Sturgeon (*Acipenser*), which can approach 30 feet in length. See *Baikal Lake Monster, Guardian of the Fishes, Mishipizhiw, Pal-Rai-Yuk, Whitey*.

Mothman—A mysterious flying creature that was first sighted in 1966 by a number of witnesses in and around Point Pleasant, West Virginia, following a number of UFO sightings. Named for a character in the *Batman* TV series, it was described as 5 to 7 feet tall, grey or brown in color, with huge wings, no head, and glowing red eyes on its upper body. It flew across the night sky at speeds estimated at 100 miles per hour, emitting a high-pitched shriek. It has been held responsible for the deaths of small animals and pets. A book by John Keel called *The Mothman Prophecies* (1976) was made into a movie in 2002. See *Black Bird of Chernobyl, Frieburg Shrieker, Man-Dragon, Owlman*.

Mourou N'gou—Leopard-like creatures with blue and white spots, said to inhabit lakes and rivers of the Central African Republic. They have hairy tails and, unlike other cats, leave clawed prints. They hunt in pairs and are not afraid to attack humans.

Muhuru—Another possible living dinosaur reported to be dwelling in the jungles of Kenya, West Africa. It is described by eyewitnesses as a heavily armored reptilian beast, with large, bony plates jutting out of its spine and an intimidating club-like tail. This sounds uncannily similar to the Jurassic ornithiscian dinosaur, *Stegosaurus* ("roofed-lizard"). See *Emela-Ntouka, Mbielu-Mbielu-Mbielu, Mokêle-M'Bêmbe*.

Muirdris (or *Smirdris, Sinach*)—A fearsome *Lake-Monster* of Irish legend, with spikes all over its body and numerous teats on its belly. It could swell up like a puffer fish. According to the legend, it dwelt in

Loch Rudraige, in County Devon, where it was slain by the hero Fergus Mac Léti.

Muiriasc (or *Murrisk, Rosualt*)—An Irish sea-monster that inhabited the plain near Croagh Patrick. Its effluvia caused misery wherever they were directed. If it spewed into the water, all the fishes died; if it belched fumes, all the birds dropped dead; and if it breathed vapor over the land, it killed all living things like a plague. See *Basilisk*.

Muirselche (Gaelic, "Sea Snail")—An Irish sea-monster that could suck anyone or anything into its gigantic maw. It was defeated by the Dagda, legendary chief of the Tuatha de Danaan, whose chanted spell caused it to ebb away. This would seem to be a reference to the tides, and especially to a *tsunami*. See *Sughmaire*.

Mulilo—A 6-foot-long, black, sluglike creature reported in the Congo region of Africa, along the border between Zaire and Zambia. It is highly dangerous, with deadly poisonous breath. See *Mongolian Death Worm, Orm*.

Muljewang—Water-monsters of Australian Aboriginal legend, believed to inhabit Lake Alexandrina and the Murray River. They are described as half man, half fish, and are often said to be hiding beneath large clumps of seaweed.

Murcat (or *Murchata*)—A sea-cat the size of a horse encountered by the Irish monk St. Brendan on his legendary voyage to the Island of Promise: "Bigger than a brazen cauldron was each of his eyes; a boar's tusks had he; furry hair was upon him; and he had the maw of a leopard with the strength of a lion, and the voracity of a hound." This was surely a walrus.

Murena (or *Muriena*)—Described in the *Physiologus* as an eel that rolls itself into a circle, the females are said to be so highly sexed that they will mate with serpents. Thus fishermen lure them by hissing like a snake. They can be killed with difficulty by a cudgel blow, but easily with a whip. However, the tail has a life of its own, and must be dispatched along with the head. Although the scientific name *Murena* has been given to the Moray Eels, these are actually Lampreys (*Petromyzontidae*), which, during the Middle Ages, were a popular food among the European upper classes, especially during fasting periods, because they taste much meatier than most true fish. King Henry I of England died from eating "a surfeit of lampreys."

Murex—A monstrous purple fish described by Pliny the Elder in his *Historia Naturalis* (77 CE) as having such strong jaws that it could latch onto a ship and hold it fast. While Pliny equated this creature with the **Echeneis**, or remora, the name has become applied to a genus of marine gastropods, including *Murex brandaris* and *Murex trunculus*, from which Tyrian purple dye was made.

Murghi-I-Adami—Two fabulous birds of medieval Islamic folklore, resembling peacocks with human faces and speech. It was said that anyone who could overhear them talking together would learn much of interest. See *Zägh*.

Murphysboro Mud Monster—A shrieking, 7-foot-tall, white-haired apelike monster reported on May 25, 1972, by more than 200 witnesses around Murphysboro in central Illinois. See *Bigfoot*.

Murray—A dinosaur-like reptile first reported in 1999 in 100-mile-long Lake Murray in Papua New Guinea. Described by eyewitnesses as being "as long as a dump truck," it is a bipedal, amphibious animal, approximately 6 feet in width, with two short forelimbs, legs "as wide as palm tree trunks," a long neck, and a slender tail. Its head resembles that of a bull, with large eyes and teeth as long as a man's fingers. Its back is said to have "largish triangular scoops," and its skin resembles that of a crocodile. This description sounds very much like a *Theropod* dinosaur. The bull-like head is suggestive of *Carnotaurus* (shown). See *Emela-Ntouka, Mokêle-M'Bêmbe, Muhuru*.

Muscaliet—A small fruit-eating creature of Persia with a body like that of a rabbit, and legs and tail like those of a squirrel, enabling it to leap from branch to branch. Its ears are similar to those of a weasel, and its muzzle resembles that of a mole. It has bristles like those on a pig and the tusks of a boar. When it climbs a tree it destroys the leaves and fruit. It nests in a hollow beneath the tree, and it is so hot that the tree to dries up and dies. (from the *Bestiaire of Pierre de Beauvais*)

Musimon (or *Tityrus*)—A heraldic animal similar to a goat, but with the head and additional horns of a ram.

Mustela (or *Sea Weasel*)—"She gives birth to her young like other beasts, and if she perceives that they will be discovered, she swallows them again into her body, and then seeks a place where they may be without danger, and then she spews them out again" (*Physiologus*).

Myakka Ape—A hairy hominid reportedly dwelling in the swamps around Sarasota, Florida. It is described as resembling a chimp or orangutan. See *Bigfoot*, *Giant Monkeys*, *Skunk Ape*.

Mystery of the Waters—A generic and euphemistic term for dangerous *Lake-Monsters* in the traditions of the Coeur d'Alene Indians of British Columbia, Canada.

*N is for Naga, the bringer
    of rain,
Also empowered to make
    rivers drain:
Half-man and half-serpent,
    wholly divine,
Guardian set before
    temple and shrine.*

Näcken (also *Bäckahäst*, *Näkki*, *Nikke*, *Nicker*, *Nickur*, *Nicor*, *Nickel*, *Ninnir*, *Nikyr*, *Nykur*, *Nykkjen*, *Nøkk*, *Nøkke*, *Nøkken*, *Haikur*)—A water-monster of Scandinavian and Icelandic folklore. It is usually described as a great white *Water-Horse*, similar to the Scottish *Kelpie* but with its hooves turned backward. Should anyone attempt to ride it, the Näcken plunges into the water, drowning its victim. When it emerges onto land at dawn or dusk, it may appear as either a *Centaur*-like creature, a golden-haired boy wearing a red cap, or an old man with a dripping green beard. In Estonia it is associated with whirlpools, which suck down boats and their crews to be devoured. See *Cîrein Cròin*, *Each Uisge*.

Nagas/Naginis ("Cobra")—Serpent-people of India. Nagas are male, and Naginis, female. They resemble humans from the waist up, and snakes from the waist down. Sometimes they have multiple heads and varying colors. The four classes of Naga—Heavenly, Divine, Earthly, and Hidden—are grouped according to their function: guarding the heavenly palace, giving rainfall, draining rivers, or guarding treasures, respectively. It is said that they will eventually destroy the world with fire. In Burma, Nagas are part serpent, part *Dragon*, and part crocodile. They give rubies to those they favor and protect many royal people. In Indonesia, Thailand, and Malaysia, however, Nagas are giant black water snakes or multiheaded sea-Dragons that terrorize fishermen. Their images are often used as temple guardians. The name has been applied to the Indian Cobra, *Naja naja*.

Nahuelito (or *Patagonian Plesiosaur*)—A *Lake-Monster* reported to be inhabiting Argentina's Lago (lake) Nahuel Huapi. For centuries local Indians have told of a gigantic creature with no head, legs, or tail dwelling in the lake. George Garrett, who saw it in 1910, said it "appeared to be 15 or 20 feet in diameter, and perhaps 6 feet above the water." In 1922, American gold prospector Martin Sheffield reported seeing an aquatic animal that moved like a crocodile, but bore an extended, swanlike neck.

Nakk (or *Nakki*)—*Merfolk* of Estonian and Finnish folklore, said to have been transformed from unrecovered victims of drowning. The males are malevolent, enticing people with their beautiful singing only to devour them. The pretty, fish-tailed Nakk maidens comb their long green hair with golden combs. The Finnish Nakki females have gleaming white bodies and breasts so long they can throw them over their shoulders.

Nandi Bear (or *Chimisit*, *Kerit*, *Kikambangwe*, *Koddoelo*, *Ikimizi*, *Sabrookoo*, *Shivuverre*)—An unknown large predator said to dwell in Kenya, Africa. With a sloping back and other ursine features, it was named after the Nandi tribe, who fear it as a vicious creature. They call it the "Brain Eater," and say it waits on a low-lying tree branch above a path for someone to pass beneath. Then it swipes off the top of their skull and eats their brains, leaving the rest of the body. This was probably the Atlas Bear (*Ursus arctos crowtheri*), the last known specimen of which was killed by hunters in northern Morocco in the 1870s. However, Bernard Heuvelmans makes a strong case for the Honey Bear or Ratel (*Mellivora ratel*), a bear-like African badger that reaches 3.5 feet in length.

Nasnas (or *Nesnás*)—A bizarre creature mentioned in Gustave Flaubert's *Temptation of St Anthony* (1874). Resembling half of a human, with one eye, one cheek, one hand, one leg, half a torso, and half a heart, it dwells in the wilderness of Hadhramaut and Yemen, and is capable of human speech. A bat-winged variety is said to live on the island of Ráïj—possibly Borneo. This would certainly be a large fruit bat.

Ndzoodzoo—A fierce variety of *Unicorn* in the native folklore of South Africa, it attacked humans on sight. Said to be common during the 19th century in the area of Makooa, north of Mozambique, it was the size of a horse and had a horn 2 and one-half feet long. This horn was flexible when relaxed, and could be curled like an elephant's trunk while the animal slept. But the horn became stiff and hard when the beast was enraged. The females were hornless. Hmmn...

Nee-Gued—A local name for the *Yeti* in the folklore of Sikkim, India It lives in the Kanchenjunga Mountains.

Nependis—A hybrid creature of European heraldry, depicted as part boar and part ape. It embodies the worst qualities of both animals.

Neugle (also *Nogle, Noggle, Nuggle, Nuggie, Nygel*)—A typical *Water-Horse* in the folklore of Scalloway in the Shetland Islands north of Scotland. It resembles a horse with a green mane and has a peculiar tail like a wheel curling over its back. It appears saddled and bridled, prancing invitingly on the shore, but should anyone mount it, the Neugle plunges into the water, drowning—or at least drenching—its victim, whereupon the beast disappears in a dancing blue flame. See *Aughisky, Glashtyn, Horse-Eel, Kelpie, Lake Monsters, Tangie, Water-Horse*.

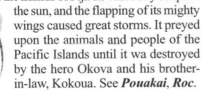

Ngani-vatu (or *Ngutu-lei*)—A gigantic predatory bird in the folklore of the islands of Fiji. Its vast body eclipsed the sun, and the flapping of its mighty wings caused great storms. It preyed upon the animals and people of the Pacific Islands until it wa destroyed by the hero Okova and his brother-in-law, Kokoua. See *Pouakai, Roc*.

Ngoima—An enormous eagle said by local natives to inhabit the forests of the African Congo. With a wingspan of 9-13 feet, it preys upon monkeys and goats. Its plumage is dark brown above and paler beneath. Its legs and talons are as large as a man's forearms and hands. This is certainly an exaggerated description of the rarely seen monkey-eating Crowned Eagle (*Stephanoaetus coronatus*), the most powerful raptor in Africa.

Ngoubou—A mysterious African animal described as having a large head-shield and tusks, much like a ceratopsian dinosaur. They are said to live in herds and vie with elephants over territory. See *Emele-Ntouka*.

Nguma-Monene—A giant African snake with a forked tongue and alligator-like ridges running down the length of its back. Said to reach 130 feet in length, this constrictor preys upon humans as well as animals. While on patrol over the African Congo in 1959, Belgian helicopter pilot Col. Remy Van Lierde took this photo of a gigantic snake, 40 to 50 feet in length. It was dark brownish-green with a white belly, and had a triangular head measuring about 3' by 2'. As the helicopter flew in lower, the snake reared up 10 feet into the air and looked as if it would strike at the copter if it flew any closer. See *Pa Snake, Python, Sucuriju Gigante*.

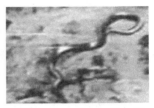

Nguoi-Rung ("Forest People"; also *Khi Trau*, "Buffalo Monkey")—A hairy hominid reported from the jungles of Vietnam. Descriptions are inconsistent—the creature varies from small to large, and is covered in hair ranging from grey to brown to black. They are said to come to campfires and sit among the men, but they do not speak. See *Nittaewo, Orang Pendek, Yeti*.

Nidhogg (also *Niðhöggr*, "Corpse Tearer" or "Malice Striker")—In Norse mythology, a monstrous serpent that gnaws constantly at the roots of the world tree, *Yggdrasil*, which supports the nine worlds. Nidhogg also tears at the bodies of the dead in the underworld domain of the dread goddess Hel.

Ningyo—These Japanese *Merfolk* are rather unique. They have the entire body of a fish, but with a human head. They are benevolent toward humans, warning against storms and other misfortunes. They are probably based on Dugongs (Dugong dugon). See *Abgal, Ilkai*.

Nittaewo (or *Nittawo*)—Tiny hairy hominids from the jungles of Ceylon and Sri Lanka. Said to be between 3 and 4 feet tall, they may have been Siamangs (*Symphalangus syndactylus*). In the late 18th century, the now-extinct Veddahs of Leanama rounded up the last Nittaewo and drove them into a cave. Brushwood was heaped before the entrance and burned for three days, suffocating the victims. See *Nguoi-Rung, Orang Pendek, Yeti*.

Nixie (or *Nix, Nixe*)—Freshwater *Merfolk* in Germanic and Scandinavian folklore. The name is derived from Old High German *nihhus*, meaning "crocodile," and refers to a great water-monster. Depending on the country, they are described variously as green *Mermaids*, grey *Water-Horses*, bird-woman *Sirens*, or aquatic *Centaurs*. All are predatory beings that entice mortals to a watery doom.

No-Kos-Ma—A gigantic, black, bear-like creature with an enormous snout, from the folklore of the Cree Indians of Canada.

Norman Lake Reptile—In 1964, North Carolina's Catawba River was dammed, transforming it into Lake Norman. With a length of 34 miles and a surface area of 32,510 acres, this is one of the largest manmade lakes in the American Southeast. It is also said to be inhabited by a monster that witnesses describe as fishlike in appearance, at least 14 feet long, with a slender body, thick, whisker-like appendages, flippers, and a "scabby looking" dorsal fin. The whiskers suggest a colossal catfish or, most likely, a Sturgeon (*Acipenser*) (shown).

Nuckalavee—An Irish parody of the *Centaur*, it has a rotten stench, and its breath can wilt crops and sicken livestock. It is an ugly amphibious sea-monster with a large, hideous head, a great, gaping mouth, and a single, burning red eye. It has froglike webbed feet rather than hooves. Its hairless skin is thin, moist, and transparent, giving it a flayed appearance. Black blood courses through yellow veins, and the pale sinews and powerful muscles are visible as a pulsating mass. These vicious creatures despoil their surroundings and kill for pleasure. But a human who is pursued by a Nuckalavee can escape by crossing fresh water, which the beast cannot abide.

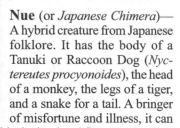

Nue (or *Japanese Chimera*)—A hybrid creature from Japanese folklore. It has the body of a Tanuki or Raccoon Dog (*Nyctereutes procyonoides*), the head of a monkey, the legs of a tiger, and a snake for a tail. A bringer of misfortune and illness, it can also transform into a black cloud and fly around.

Nupperabo—The flabby, dough-like guardian of *Jingoku,* the underground hell of Japanese folklore.

Nyaminyami—A mated pair of *Lake-Monsters* living in the depths of Lake Kariba, located in the Mashonaland West Province of Zimbabwe, Africa, near the southwestern border of Zambia. They also occasionally venture into the Zambenzi River. For centuries these creatures have been worshiped as gods by the Tonga, who call them the *Nyaminyami.* They are described by natives as scaly, serpentine creatures with fishlike heads, whereas others have reported sightings of gigantic, almost whale-like, humpbacked animals. Some claim that at least one of the Nyaminyami has reached a length of 120 feet.

Nyan (also *Avagráh, Gara, Gráha, Tanti-gáha*)—A monstrous, wormlike creature that inhabits rivers and marshes of Bengal and Burma in India. It preys upon large animals, including elephants, coiling about them like a *Python* and dragging th under the water to be consum This is probably the same cre as the *Bu-rin*, a giant Burmese water snake, 40 to 50 feet long. Said to be incredibly dangerous, it has attacked swimmers and even small boats. See *Dragons of Ethiopia, Mongolian Death Worm, Orm, Pa Snakes*.

Nzefu-Loi ("Water-Elephant")—An amphibious elephant-monster reported to be dwelling in the Congolese jungles of Africa. It has a body almost as big as a hippo's, but with a very long neck, a horselike tail, and ivory tusks. The appearance of a swimming elephant, with its trunk upraised, bears an uncanny resemblance to many descriptions and depictions of *Lake Monsters*. See *Makara, Mokele-M'bembe, Trunko*.

O is for Ouroboros who swallows
Its own tail, and the body soon follows –
Ever eating, eternally growing,
Standing for cycles, and never slowing.

O Goncho—An immense, winged white *Dragon* of Japanese legend, that dwells in the waters of Yamahiro. Every 50 years it metamorphoses into a golden bird with a haunting cry like the howl of a wolf. This periodic transformation and howling presages disasters, such as famine.

Odontotyrannus (Greek, "Toothy King")—An enormous amphibious monster that lived along the River Ganges in India, according to ancient Greek writers. It was covered in black scales and sported three huge horns on its head. Its vast mouth could consume an elephant. Certainly based on the crocodile, it was said to have attacked Alexander the Great (356–323 BCE) and his Macedonian army, killing and eating many soldiers and animals.

Oggie—A *Lake-Monster* said to be dwelling in New York's Onondaga Lake, considered by the Environmental Protection Agency to be one of the most polluted lakes in the United States, probably due to the discharge from Oswego's

Nine Mile Island nuclear power plant. In the summer of 1977, local cub scouts witnessed what they described as a dragon swimming offshore. The beast was soon named *Oggie,* thus begetting another Lake-Monster legend. But according to the oral history traditions of the Onondagas and Iroquois, there has always been a monster in the lake.

Ogopogo (or *N'haaitk, Naitakas, N'ha-a-tik,* Salish, "Snake-in-the-Lake")—A **Lake-Monster** inhabiting Lake Okanagan in British Columbia, Canada. The Shushwap Indians called it *Naitaka* ("Long Fish"). Said to dwell in a cave under an island in the middle of the lake, it was depicted in rock paintings and given effigy offerings of propitiation. Witnesses have described a creature resembling an enormous log, 15–20 feet long and 1–2 feet in diameter, with a horse- or goat-like head and an undulating serpentine form with several humps. It is also described as having either saw-toothed ridges on its back like a sturgeon, or a smooth back with several fins. See **Champ, Loch Ness Monster, Water-Horse.**

Olitiau—A gigantic, black, bat-like creature of the African Cameroons encountered by zoologist Ivan T. Sanderson (1911–1973) and naturalist Gerald Russell in 1932. It had "pointed white teeth set about their own width apart from each other" and "Dracula-like wings." Sanderson later speculated that the beast was "an exceptionally large specimen of the Hammerhead Bat (*Hypsignathus monstrosus*)." Hammerheads (shown) are the largest African bat species; they are dark gray with black wings spanning 3 feet, and have elongated, doglike snouts. See **Ahool, Alan, Guiafairo, Hsigo, Kongamato, Orang-Bati, Ropen, Sassabonsum.**

Oilliphéist (or *Oillepheist*; Gaelic, "Great Fabulous Beast")—An enormous **Dragon** or **Lake-Monster** said to have gouged the channel of the Shannon River in Ireland. Generally benign, it became enraged upon learning that St Patrick was coming to exorcise it, and swallowed a drunken piper, who continued to play inside the monster's belly until the beast disgorged him in disgust.

Oklahoma Octopus—A tentacled creature lurking in the depths of Lakes Thunderbird, Oolagah, and Tenkiller in Oklahoma. Long feared by the local Indians (who likened it to a leech), this animal has been described as roughly the size of a horse, with a leathery, reddish-brown skin, small beady eyes, and multiple tentacles. It is said to be a voracious predator and violently territorial. See **Cuero, Freshwater Octopus, Hueke Hueku, Migas.**

Onachus—A beast of Galatia in Asia Minor (Turkey) that burned everything it touched. The *Tarasque* was said to be the offspring of the Onachus and the **Leviathan.**

Onocentaur (or *Onoscentaurus, Monocentaur*)—A kind of **Centaur** with the torso and arms of a man, and the lower body of an onager or wild ass. Said to never sleep, it was described in the 3rd-century *Physiologus* and later bestiaries, and by Isidore of Seville (c. 560–636). In Christian symbolism, it represents hypocrisy and sensuality, and is sometimes considered to be related to **Satyrs.** The Onocentaur was closely associated with the **Siren,** and the two were often said to dwell near one another.

Onza (from Latin *Uncia,* "Cheetah;" or Aztec, *Cuitlamiztli*)—A large mystery cat said to inhabit the Sierra Madre Occidental mountains in northwestern Mexico. A specimen killed in 1986 proved to be a Mountain Lion (*Puma concolor*).

Onyx Monoceros—A Persian version of the **Unicorn,** described by Ctesias as having a white body like that of a mule, a purple head with blue eyes, and a massive horn that is red at the base, black on the shaft, and red at the tip. It is clearly based on the magnificent white Arabian Oryx (*Oryx leucoryx*), which can appear to have but one horn in profile, or if one is broken off.

Opinicus (or *Epimachus*)—A heraldic term for the Gryphon, probably derived from the Greek *Ophinicus,* the constellation of the Serpent. In European heraldry, the Opinicus is shown with the body of a lion, the wings and head of an eagle or dragon, and, oddly, the tail of a camel. It may have the front claws of an eagle, or all four legs may be leonine. Opinici are born without wings, which develop as they grow. In the Middle Ages, Arab traders would often sell coconuts and antelope horns to crusaders, claiming that they were the eggs and horns of the Opinicus. Shy nocturnal herbivores, Opinici are said to stalk the streets of modern London after dark, eating leftover fruits and vegetables found in the alleys behind markets.

OpkYen—A huge, spherical water-monster in the folklore of the Cheremis/Mari people of Russia. It inhabits large lakes, wide rivers, and inland seas, where it swallows entire boats with its immense, toothy mouth. See **Pamba.**

Orang-Bati ("men with wings")—Predatory nocturnal flying primates from the obscure Indonesian island of Ceram—the second largest island in the Moluccas group. The natives of Ceram describe these soaring simians as approximately 5 feet tall, with black, leathery wings, blood-red skin, and a long, thin tail. Emitting a "mournful wail," they are said to abduct infants and small children. During the day they retreat into a network of caves in an extinct volcano, Mount Kairatu. This description, as well as the locale, strongly suggests a giant fruit bat, such as the Malayan Flying Fox (*Pteropus vampyrus*), which has a 6-foot wingspan. These are not related to the other insectivorous bats, but are genetically closer to primates. See **Ahool, Alan, Hsigo, Ropen, Vietnamese Night Flyers**.

Orang Dalam—Hairy hominids of Malaysia, said to be 6–9 feet tall with red eyes. Males have much hair about their head, chest, arms, and legs. They give off a powerful odor likened to monkey urine. At first contact they appear friendly, making overtures and approaching slowly. Then they invariably become frightened and flee into the jungle. This is certainly the Bornean Orangutan (*Pongo pygmaeus*), called *Mias-Pappan* in Borneo. See **Orang Pendek**.

Orang Pendek—("little man"; or *Orang Letjo*, "gibbering man"; also *Sedapa, Batutut*)—A hairy hominid reported to be dwelling in the millions of acres of rain forests on the island of Sumatra in Indonesia. Standing 2.5–5 feet tall, its brownish skin is covered with short black or brown hair, and it has a long, black mane. It has no tail, and its arms are shorter than an ape's. It walks mostly on the ground, and its footprints are very similar to a human's. The creature eats mostly fruits and small animals, and is seen fairly often by locals, who say it has a language of sorts, although the Sumatrans cannot understand it. This may be the Sumatran Orangutan (*Pongo abelii*), the smaller and rarer of the two species of orangutans. However, some researchers have proposed that the recently discovered "hobbits" of nearby Flores island are also likely candidates. See **Batutut, Nguoi-Rung, Orang Dalam, Nittaewo, Yeti**.

Orc (or *Orcus, Orco, Orke, Orque*)—As described by Pliny the Elder in his *Historia Naturalis* (77 CE), this is a vast sea-monster with great toothy jaws that preys upon whales. Ludovicio Ariosto (1474–1573) identified it with the beast that threatens Andromeda and which Perseus slays. The name has been applied to the Orca (*Orcinus orca*), or Killer Whale—a highly intelligent, black-and-white whale notorious for eating marine mammals, including baleen whales. And J.R.R. Tolkien adopted the term for the Goblins of Middle Earth in his epic *Lord of the Rings* (1964). See **Cetus, Tsemaus**.

Orm (Norse *Ormr*, "Dragon"; or *Worm, Vurm, Wyrm*)—This is a general term for serpentine **Dragons**, especially those that are wingless and legless. Since F.W. Holiday's book, *The Great Orm of Loch Ness* (1968), it has also come to be applied to **Lake-Monsters**, especially those thought to be invertebrates.

Orobon—According to Arabs of Mount Mazovan, this is a ferocious, fishlike predator inhabiting the region of the Red Sea. It was described in medieval bestiaries as being about 10 feet long, with a head like a catfish's, webbed clawed feet, and a hide like that of a crocodile—which is most likely what the creature was based upon. However, considering the description of the head, it may have been a Wels Catfish (*Silurus glanis*), which is known to reach 10 feet in length and weigh 330 pounds. Perhaps this arises from a confusion of two separate animals.

Orthus (or *Orthos, Orthros, Orthrus*)—In Greek myth, a monstrous two-headed dog that guarded the cattle of Geryon. Orthus was the brother of three-headed **Cerberus** and the offspring of **Echidna** and Typhon. Orthus was clubbed to death by Heracles during his tenth Labor.

Ouroboros (or *Oroborus, Uroboros*; Greek, "tail devourer")—In Egyptian mythology, this is the vast Serpent of Eternity that, in an endless cycle of destruction and renewal, continually consumes its own tail as it grows longer at the front end. It frequently appears in alchemical illustrations to symbolize cyclicality and primordial unity. It is thought to have been inspired by the Milky Way, as some ancient texts refer to a serpent of light residing in the heavens.

Ova—A hairy hominid with backward-pointing feet, said to inhabit the Volga region of Russia. It menaces travelers by tickling them to death, but its vulnerable spot is a hole under its left armpit; touching it here renders it helpless.

Owlman—This giant, owl-like creature has been sighted in the coastal town of Mawnan in Cornwall, England, since 1976. It is described as man-like, with silver-grey feathered wings, pointed ears, huge, glowing eyes, and a black beak. Its long bird legs terminate in large black talons. Similar creatures have been reported in the United States in the Allegheny Mountains, the Ozarks, and the Pacific Northwest, by Indians and

early settlers, who called them *Great Owls* or *Big-Hoot*. In *Thunderbirds! America's Living Legends of Giant Birds* (2004), Mark A. Hall postulates that the **Moth-man**, reported in 1966, may also be such a creature.

P is for Pegasus, king of the steeds,
Who is a mount such as each hero needs.
Form of a horse with the wings of a bird,
He is a legend of whom all have heard.

Paiyuk—Evil water-elk creatures that prey upon humans in the folklore of the Ute Indians of Utah.

Pal-Rai-Yuk—A *Water-Monster* in the folklore of the Alaskan Inuits, who paint its picture on their canoes as a ward against the fearsome beast's attacks. It inhabits creeks and river estuaries, and is very long, with two heads, six legs, three stomachs, two tails, and a saw-toothed ridge down its back. These features suggest that it is based on mating sturgeons (*Acipenser*). See *Baikal Lake Monster*, *Guardian of the Fishes*, *Mishipizhiw*.

Palulukon—Vast water-serpents in the legends of the Hopi Indians of the American Southwest. The Palulukon represent the element of water; thus they are weather workers in charge of bringing the rains. It said that the world is carried through the cosmic ocean on the backs of two of these colossal beasts. Their turning causes earthquakes. If mistreated, the Palulukon can dry up wells, rivers, and water holes and cause droughts. See *Jinshin-Uwo*, *Jormungandr*.

Pamba—An immense *Lake-Monster* believed in native legend to inhabit  Lake Tanganyika, Tanzania. Its mouth is so huge that it can swallow a canoe and its occupants. It also turns the water red, so when fishermen see this they know to stay away. See *OpkYen*.

Panther (or *Panthera, Pantera, Pantere, Painter, Love Cervere*)—According to the *Physiologus*, the Panther is a large cat with "a truly variegated colour, and it is most beautiful and excessively kind." It was most famed for its aromatic belches (said to smell like allspice), emitted after it has slept for three days following feasting, and which attract its prey. These were bottled and sold as expensive perfumes,

leading to a confusion with the musk-producing African Civet Cat (*Civettictis civetta*). The favored mount of the Greek god Dionysus, the Panther's only natural enemy is the **Dragon**, which is immune to its fragrant breath. *Panther* does not denote a single species; it can refer to any large cat—especially one in a black phase, when it is called a "Black Panther." These may be mountain lions, leopards, or jaguars. Thus the African lion is *Panthera leo*, and the leopard is *Panthera pardus*. The heraldic Panther is always shown "incensed," with flames issuing from its ears and mouth. Sometimes it is depicted as an ordinary feline, but in German heraldry it has four horns, cow's ears, and a long, fiery red tongue.

Papstesel (or *Pope-Ass*)—A bizarre hybrid creature said to have been found during a flood in 15th-century Italy. It had a scaly woman's body like a Lamia's, with the head of an ass. One foot was clawed and the other hoofed, and one arm resembled an elephant's trunk. A cock-headed tail and the face of a bearded man decorated its backside. It was used as a symbolic depiction of Papal corruption during the 16th century.

Pard (or *Pardal, Pardus, Pantheon*)—This feline is described in the *Physiologus* as "a parti-colored species, very swift and strongly inclined to bloodshed. It leaps to the kill with a bound." It mates "adulterously" with the lion to produce the leopard. From the zoological names of the Lion (*Panthera leo*) and the Leopard (*Panthera pardus*), it is clear that what medieval bestiaries called the Pard is, in fact, the leopard. Likewise, the leopard in these texts is what we now call the Cheetah (*Acinonyx jubatis*), as the cheetah has spots like a leopard's and a scruffy mane like a lion's. Also, cheetahs run in small family groups, a level of organization somewhere between the lion's pride and the leopard's solitude. Thus, the leopard was thought to be a cross between *Leo* (lion) and *Pard* (leopard), hence *Leo-Pard*. Eventually "Pard" was dropped, "leopard" was adopted for the animal formerly called the Pard, and the leopard acquired its rightful name, "cheetah."

Pa Snakes—Gigantic serpents of Africa that prey upon elephants. When they eat an elephant, it takes them three years to spit out the bones. This is clearly an exaggeration of the Reticulated Python (*Python reticulatus*), the record measured size of which was 33 feet long. See *Dragons of Ethiopia*, *Nyan*.

P'êng (or *Pyong*)—A vast bird of Chinese legend that is the metamorphosed form of the huge fish called *Kw'ên*. Its outspread wings cover the sky from horizon to horizon. It lives in the north, but each year it rises thousands of feet into the air and flies toward the south, bringing the typhoon season. In Japan, the same bird is called the *Pheng*. It is said to be so big that it can carry off a camel. See *Kreutzet, Pheng, Roc, Simmurgh, Ziz*.

P'êng-Niao—Bird-Dragons of Chinese myth. They either have the head of a *Dragon* and the wings and lower body of a bird, or a completely serpentine body with feathered scales and birdlike wings, legs, and feet. See *Amphitere, Hai Riyo*.

Pegasies—Ethiopian birds with horselike ears. As recorded by Pliny the Elder in his *Historia Naturalis* (77 CE), the *Pegais* was a great bird with the head of a horse that lived in Scythia. Possibly a reference to the Shoebill Stork (*Balaeniceps rex*).

Pegasus (from Luwian, *pihassas,* "lightning")—Sired by Poseidon, god of the sea, this magnificent winged white horse sprang from the neck of the Gorgon Medusa when Perseus beheaded her. The only one who ever tamed and rode him was Bellerophon, who slew the *Chimera* from his back. Described as blood-red in the original myth, Pegasus later came to be depicted as pure white. Symbolizing fame, eloquence, and contemplation, the graceful Pegasus was the heraldic emblem of the Knights Templar.

Pegasus Dragon (or *Flying Horse*)—According to J.W. Buel (1887), this is a bizarre little fish, only 4 inches long, with a movable snout like that of a sturgeon or sucker fish. Its flattened body is encased in armor plates, and its tail resembles that of a crocodile. Related to the little Sea Horse (*Hippocampus*), it is supposedly able to fly using its enormous pectoral fins. Today these are known as Seamoths, of the family *Pegasidae*. However, they cannot fly. The one illustrated here (from Buel) is the Short Dragonfish (*Eurypegasus draconis*).

Peiste (or *Piast*)—An Irish term for *Lake-Monsters*, generally described as amphibious Worms or Dragons. See *Orm*.

Peridexion Tree—(Latin: *Peridixion,* also *Circa dexteram, Environ destre, Paradixion, Pendens, Perindens*) A tree growing in India that attracts doves, who gather in its branches because they like its sweet fruit. There they

are safe from the *Dragon*, who would eat the doves if he could. But he fears the shadow of the tree, and stays on the sunny side of it. Doves that remain in the shadow are safe, but any who leave it are caught and eaten by the Dragon.

Peryton—A fusion of deer and bird, the fierce green or light-blue Peryton has the antlered head and forelegs of a stag, and the wings and hindquarters of a bird. It casts the shadow of a man until it kills one. Then, after drenching its body in the victim's blood, its shadow assumes its proper shape, and it can never again kill another human. Supposedly originating in Atlantis, Perytons were prophesied by a Sibyl to bring about the fall of Rome. A 16th-century rabbi in Fez wrote that at the time of Hannibal's attack on Rome (211 BCE), Perytons attacked the fleet of Roman general Publius Cornelius Scipio near the Strait of Gibraltar, but were driven off when Scipio ordered his soldiers to use their shields as mirrors, blinding the beasts with reflected sunlight.

Phoenix (often spelled *Fenix* in medieval bestiaries)—She resembles a flame-colored cross between a peacock and a pheasant (the name means "reddish-purple one"). The Phoenix comes from Ethiopia, where every 540 years she lays a single egg in a nest of cinnamon and frankincense, which she fans with her wings until it bursts into flame and consumes her. When the egg, warmed by the embers, hatches, she is reborn from the ashes. For this reason, the Phoenix was adopted by Christians as a symbol of resurrection and immortality, and was a badge of Queen Elizabeth I. An important component of the legend may be found in the trade of *Bird of Paradise* skins from New Guinea, dating from 1000 BCE, when the island was first discovered by Phoenician seafarers. The most common species exported was Count Raggi's Bird of Paradise (*Paradisea raggiana*), the male of which sports profuse sprays of scarlet feathers under its wings. When these are activated in its courtship dance, it looks as though the bird is dancing amid flames. See *Benu, Fêng Huang, Firebird*.

Phooka (or *Pooka, Puka*; Welsh *Pwca*; Cornish *Bucca*; Manx *Buggane*)—A mischievous, shapeshifting *Water-Horse* in Irish folklore. It may even serve as a House-Elf, or Brownie. Interestingly, Irish children call snails "pookas," and exhort them to extend their horns in a nursery rhyme. See *Kelpie, Tuba*.

Phorcids—In Greek mythology, these are the monstrous children of Ceto, daughter of Gaea by Phorcys, the Old Man of the Sea. They include **Echidna**, mother of monsters; the seven-headed Dragon of Ladon; and the triple sisterhoods of the Graeae and the Gorgons.

Physeter (Greek, "Blower"; also *Whirlpoole*)—The sperm whale (*Physeter macrocephalus*). It was said to create whirlpools by spouting them from its blowhole.

Piasa—A creature of local legend dating back to 1673 when Father Jacques Marquette, in recording his famous journey down the Mississippi River with Louis Joliet, described the Piasa as a grotesque monster painted high on the bluffs along the Mississippi River, where the city of Alton, Illinois, now stands. According to Marquette's diary, the Piasa "was as large as a calf with horns like a deer, red eyes, a beard like a tiger's, a face like a man, the body covered with green, red and black scales and a tail so long it passed around the body, over the head and between the legs."

Pi-Hsi—This Chinese deity of rivers is part **Dragon**, part horse. See **Horse-Eel**, **Lake Monsters**, **Water-Horse**.

Pihuechenyi—Giant winged vampiric serpents in the folklore of the Araucanian Indians of Chile. See **Amphitere**, **Lamia**.

Pinatubo Monsters—**Lake-Monsters** reported from the Zambales region of the Philippine island of Luzon, where as many as five huge, black serpentine creatures have been seen swimming in the Tikis River. Local Aetas insist that these animals are unlike any eels, fish, or snakes they have seen. The first reported sighting was on November 5, 2002, when an Aleta boy mistook one for a floating log until it moved. Two months later, several witnesses observed a 7-foot-long, 3-foot-wide black creature undulating silently down the river.

Piranu—An Argentinian water-monster in the form of a great black fish with the head of a horse and large eyes. It lives in deep rivers and overturns boats that intrude upon its territory. See **Lake Monsters**.

Pish-Meri (Pisin, "Fish-Woman")—The word for **Mermaid** in the *pisin* lingua franca of Papua New Guinea. The most popular representation is the Mermaid depicted on the labels of Chicken-of-the-Sea tuna cans, from which natives concluded that the cans contained Mermaid meat. However, the term is also applied to a living sea-creature—the Indo-Pacific Dugong (*Dugong dugon*), which is the basis of nearly all legends of **Merfolk**. See **Ilkai**.

Pisuhand (or *Pukis*, *Pukys*, *Puuk*)—In the folklore of the Baltic states, these are small serpentine **Dragons**, only 2 feet long, that fiercely guard each house and its treasures. They take the form of cats when on the ground, but Dragons when they fly through the air. See **Tulihand.**

Pithon—A heraldic bat-winged serpent or snake. (If the wings resemble those of a bird, the creature is usually referred to as a winged serpent, or **Amphitere**.)

Plesiosaurs (Greek, "Near Lizard")—Long-necked aquatic reptiles contemporary with the dinosaurs. They had squat, flattened bodies, short tails, and four flippers. Supposedly exterminated 65 million years ago along with the dinosaurs, creatures resembling them continue to be reported worldwide as **Sea-Serpents** and **Lake-Monsters**. In most cases, these reports are based only on the sight of a longish neck, but in 1955, naturalist Alexander Laime saw three such creatures sunning themselves fully on rocks at the summit of the Auyan-tepui in Venezuela. Two French explorers to the same area said they saw a similar animal in 1990.

Ponik—A **Lake-Monster** inhabiting Lake Pohenegamook in Quebec, Canada. According to eyewitnesses, it resembles an overturned canoe about 36–40 feet long, with a ridge down its back, a head like an earless horse's or cow's, and long, catfish-like whiskers. Some witnesses have reported three humps and two large flippers.

Porci Marini (Latin, "Sea-Pigs")—The name for *Dugongs* in the *Physiologus*. See **Ambize**.

Poua-Kai (or *Pouki*)—A monstrous predatory bird of Maori legend. It hunted livestock and people until the last one was trapped in a great net and stabbed to death by the hero Hau-o-Tawera. This legend was based on a real creature, the giant Haast's or Harpagornis Eagle (*Harpagornis moorei*) that once lived on the South Island of New Zealand. Exterminated only 600 years ago, it was the largest eagle to have ever lived. A female weighed 35 pounds and stood 4 feet tall, with a wingspan of 10 feet. See **Ngani-vatu**.

Pterodactyls (Greek, "Wing-Fingered"; or *Pterosaur*, "Winged Lizard")—With their wings of webbed skin, these prehistoric flying reptiles are the very image of a **Wyvern**. Although supposed to have been extinct for 65 million years, sightings of

apparent living Pterosaurs are still reported from time to time. In April 1890, two cowboys in Arizona allegedly killed an enormous bird-like creature with smooth skin and featherless wings like a bat's. Its face resembled an alligator. They dragged the carcass back to town, where it was pinned, wings outstretched, on the side of a barn. A photo was purportedly published in the local newspaper, the *Tombstone Epitaph*. In February, 1976, southwest of San Antonio, Texas, three schoolteachers were driving to work when something looking like a *pteranodon* with a 20-foot wingspan swooped low over their car. See **Duah**, **Kongamato**, **Mothman**, **Ropen**, **Snallygaster**, **Thunderbird**.

Pugwis—A carnivorous amphibious humanoid said to have tormented the Kwakiutl Indians of the British Columbia's Puget Sound region for centuries. Its description greatly resembles the **Creature from the Black Lagoon** (1954 movie). See **Gillman of Thetis Lake**, **Lizard Men**.

Python—In Greek mythology, a monstrous female serpent born from the mud and slime that remains after the great flood of Deucalian. She dwelt in a chasm beside the Castellian Spring on the slopes of Mt Parnassus, guarding an oracular cave until the sun-god Apollo killed her with his arrows and established his temple on the site. This battle was ceremonially reenacted annually in celebration of the founding of the Delphic Oracle, whose priestesses were called *Pythonesses*. From this legend, the name *python* was designated for the giant snakes of the Old World, some of which reach lengths of more than 30 feet. See **Dragons of Ethiopia**, **Giant Congo Snake**, **Nyan**, **Pa Snakes**.

*Q is for Quetzalcoatl, a snake
Feathered and winged, who can make the sky shake.
Thunder and lightning are symbols of his,
Cosmic Creator who made all that is.*

Quanekelak—The cosmic whale in the mythology of the Bela Bela Indians of northwestern Canada. It has the body of a man and the head of an **Orca,** or killer whale.

Queensland Tiger—A medium-sized marsupial cat sighted in the forests of Queensland, Australia, in  the 1940s and 50s. It has stripes across its back, and sharp claws with which it disembowels prey as large as kangaroos. This is a different animal than the Tasmanian Tiger (*Thylacinus cynocephalus*), which is more wolf-like, but it may be related to the catlike Spotted Tiger Quoll (*Dasyurus maculates*) of eastern Australia. Heuvelmans, however, equates the Queensland Tiger with the supposedly extinct marsupial lion, *Thylacoleo.*

Questing Beast (or *Glatisant*)—A hybrid creature of British Arthurian legend, said to have the torso of a leopard, the hindquarters of a lion, the head of a snake, and the feet of a stag. Other descriptions have included iron-like scales and prodigious amounts of slime. The rumblings of its stomach sound like the baying of 40 hunting hounds. The Beast perpetually seeks fresh water to quench its unbearable thirst, but whenever it drinks, the water is fouled by its poisonous saliva. Said to have been begotten by the Devil with a princess who accused her brother of rape after he rejected her advances, it is a symbol of incest and anarchy. It appears several times in Mallory's *Le Mort D'Arthur*, where it is obsessively pursued by Sir Pellinore, and after his death, by Sir Palomedes. See **Grylio**, **Peiste**.

Quetzalcoatl (Nahuatl, "Feathered Serpent;" also Mayan, *Kukulk'an;* Quiché-Maya, *Guk'umatz*) —The great cosmic feathered serpent and culture hero of Mesoamerican legend. He is credited with creating and fertilizing the Earth, and introducing agriculture and civilization to the people. His symbols are lightning, thunder, and thunderbolts (meteorites). When a comet appeared, it was considered to be him. The myths often describe him as the divine ruler of the mythical Toltecs, who, after his expulsion from Tollan, travel south or east to set up new cities and kingdoms. Many different Mesoamerican cultures—such as the Maya, K'iche, Pipil, and Zapotec—claim to be the only true descendants of Quetzalcoatl, and thus of the Toltecs.

*R is for Roc, a gargantuan bird
Carrying elephants off from their herd,
Feeding its hatchlings on entire goats.
Angered, it drops giant boulders on boats.*

Racumon—A monstrous, hurricane-creating serpent-god in the folklore of the Carib Indians on the island of Dominica, in the West Indies.

Rahab (or *Rager*) A titanic and powerful *Sea-Serpent* of primordial chaos, mentioned in Biblical scripture: Isaiah 30:7, 11; Psalms 89:9-10; and Job 9:13 and 26:12-13. See *Leviathan*.

Raichô ("Thunder Bird")—A fabulous giant rook or crow-like bird in Japanese folklore. It lives in a tall pine tree, and its raucous calls summon the storms. This is also the name of a real bird, *Lagopus mutus*, a kind of ptarmigan or grouse.

Raiju ("Thunder Animal")—The pet of Raijin, the Shinto god of lightning in Japanese mythology. This demonic little creature has the body of a cat or weasel, the agility of a monkey, and the sharp claws of a *Tanuki* (*Nyctereutes procyonoides*). Composed of fire, he is the embodiment of the phenomenon of ball lightning. He becomes frenzied during storms, leaping about in trees, fields, and even buildings in frantic terror and making a cry like thunder. A tree marked by lightning is said to have been scratched by Raiju. He tries to hide by digging into human navels, so it is best to sleep on your stomach during a thunderstorm! See *Ratatosk*.

Rainbow Serpent —The sky-spanning rainbow envisioned as a vast, multihued, cosmic serpent —often seen as a creator being. Such creatures appear in the mythologies of many cultures, but particularly among the native peoples of Australia, Central and West Africa, Melanesia, Polynesia, and the Caribbean. They are associated with fresh water and floods, and may be benevolent or malevolent toward humans. In Australia, he is a creature of the *Alcheringa*, or Dreamtime, with different local names in various regions. The Warramunga refer to him as *Wollunqua*—a creature so immense that he can travel many miles without his tail ever leaving his waterhole. The Wik Mungkan of central Cape York Peninsula, Queensland, call him *Taipan*. This name has been assigned to a genus of large (up to 10 feet long), fast, highly venomous Australian snakes, one of which, the Fierce Snake (*Oxyuranus microlepidotus*), has the most toxic venom of any land snake in the world. In 2000, Queensland University zoologist Dr. Michael Lee and colleagues proposed that the legend of the Rainbow Serpent may have been inspired by an extinct 20-foot-long python, *Wonambi naracoortensis*. In

Africa, *Aido Hwedo* (or *Oshumare*) is a vast cosmic snake that supports the earth upon her back. Another is the *Damballah* of Voodoo myth, a snake which is the center of the Da Cult of Dahomey, West Africa. He is the consort of Aido Hwedo.

Ratatosk—The squirrel that runs up and down the Norse World Tree, Yggdrasil, carrying messages and insults between the eagle or cock *Gollinkambi*, who roosts at the top of the tree, and the serpent *Nidhogg*, who gnaws at its roots. When lightning is seen flashing between heaven and earth, it is Ratatosk running his errands. Unfortunately, being a squirrel, he often garbles the messages, sowing discord between the highest and lowest beings. See *Raiju.*

Ravenna Monster—A bizarre prodigy first described in *De Conceptu et Generatione Hominis* by Jacob Rueff (1554). Born in Ravenna, Italy, in 1511 or 1512, "it had a horn on the top of its head, two wings, was without arms, and only one leg like that of a bird of prey. It had an eye in its knee, and was of both sexes. It had the face and body of a man, except in the lower part, which was covered with feathers."

Re'em (or *Reem*)—A gigantic wild ox mentioned in Biblical scriptures. There was said to be only one pair at a time, living at opposite ends of the Earth. After 70 years apart, they came together for one day, and, after mating, the female killed the male. After 12 years of gestation, the female bore twins—a male and a female—herself dying in childbirth. And the cycle repeated. The Re'em is mentioned nine times in the Old Testament: in Job 39:9-10; Deuteronomy 33:17; Numbers 23:22, 24:8; Psalms 22:21, 29:6, 92:10; and Isaiah 34:7. Although this word has been commonly translated as "Unicorn," the animal is believed to have been the giant Aurochs, or *Urus* (*Bos primigenius*). The last one, a female, died in 1627 in the Jaktorów Forest, Poland.

Rift Valley Monster—A large, sail-backed lizard reported from Kenya. This description sounds like the gigantic carnosaur *Spinosaurus* (shown), which inhabited Africa in the Cretaceous era, 95-93 million years ago. Other prehistoric sail-backed reptiles included *Dimetrodon, Edaphosaurus*, and *Ouranosaurus.*

Rigi—In the creation myth of the 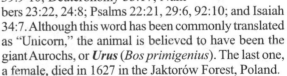 Nauru people of the South Pacific, this is the caterpillar that helps the Ancient Spider, *Areop-Enap*, create the heavens and the Earth by prying open a giant clamshell. His sweat from that effort becomes the salty sea, and after his metamorphosis into a butterfly, he constantly flies between the shells to keep them apart.

River Griffin—These lovely creatures are commonly spotted along the Eel River in Mendocino County, California. They feed mostly on fish and sometimes other river creatures smaller than themselves. They don't swim, but drop out of the sky and dive to catch fish. Like all Mendocino river-dwellers, River Griffins also love red wine and dark chocolate.

Rizos—A massive *Black Dog* with huge claws in the folklore of modern Greece. It haunts lonely roads at night, terrifying wanderers. It may attack if it is touched, but usually it just vanishes.

Roc (Persian, *Rukh*; also *Rucke*)—A gigantic bird of Madagascar, famed from the journals of Marco Polo and the *Arabian Nights* stories of Sinbad, and said to be large enough to carry off elephants. It is described as resembling an immense eagle or vulture, but in reality, this was the enormous, flightless "Elephant Bird," or *Vouron Patra (Aepyornis maximus)* (shown), which reached 11 feet in height and weighed 1,100 pounds. Its eggs were 3 feet in circumference, and had a liquid capacity of 2.35 gallons. These were the largest to have ever existed on Earth. This awesome avian was exterminated by humans in the 16th century. Because Vourons had insignificant wings and down-like pilli rather than true feathers, they were thought to be only the chicks of truly colossal flying adults. In two of the four *Arabian Nights* stories featuring the Roc, it retaliates for the killing of its chick by dropping boulders on ships. Gigantic "feathers" said to be from the Roc were actually dried fronds of the Raffia Palm (*Raphia*), which reach an impressive 80 feet in length. And Peter Costello suggests that the huge Wandering Albatross (*Diomeda exultans*), with wingspans up to 17.5 feet, could have also contributed to the legend of the Roc. See *Angka*, *Bar Yacre*, *Crocho*, *Kreutzet*, *Pheng*, *Simurgh*, *Thunderbird*, *Zägh*, *Ziz*.

Rods (or *Skyfish*)—Aerial anomalies that sometimes appear in photographs, usually in the

form of a long bar with small bulges along the sides. The first official report occurred after inspection of video footage taken on March 5, 1994, which appeared to yield

images of unknown flying animals. Since the advent of home video technology, photos of these creatures have increased exponentially worldwide. Some people believe that Rods are a type of new or alien life form. A more prosaic explanation is that they are actually the products of fast-flying insects being exposed in photographs. The elongated bars are the bodies of insects in motion, and the multiple bulges along the sides are their wing beats.

Rompo—A nocturnal scavenger beast from India and Africa that feeds on human corpses. It has a long body and tail, the head of a hare, the ears of a man, a mane of hair, the forefeet of a badger, and the hind feet of a bear. This description resembles a Hyaena (*Crocuta*). See *Crocotta*, *Leucrotta*.

Ropen ("Demon Flyer")—A *Pterodactyl*-like creature reported from the jungles of New Guinea since the 1950s. It lives in caves along the islands of New Britain and Umboi, and only flies at night. It has leathery wings spanning 3–4 feet, a narrow, tooth-filled beak, a head crest, webbed feet, and a long tail culminating in a diamond-shaped flange. It is said to feast on decaying flesh, often harassing funerals to attack the corpse. The description is uncannily similar to a *Rhamphorynchus*, believed to have been extinct for 65 million years. But it is far more likely to be a Bismark Flying Fox (*Pteropus neohibernicus*). Recognized by science as the world's largest living species of bat, it has a wingspan of 5.5–6 feet and is native to New Guinea and the Bismark Archipelago. See *Duah*, *Kongamato*, *Snallygaster*.

Rosmarine (or *Rosmarus*, *Rosmer*; all meaning "Horse of the Sea")—A fantastical depiction of the walrus, shown with tusks pointing up rather than down as they are in actuality. In Norwegian waters the same giant sea-monster was called *Roshwalr* ("Horse-Whale"), *Ruszor*, or *Cetus Dentatus* ("Toothed Whale"), and was described as having a bulky, smooth body of a whale and the head of a horse. A severed head of one was sent to Pope Leo X in 1520, and was drawn at the time, and later described by naturalist Ambroise Paré (1517–1590). It has been clearly identified as a Walrus, which has been given the scientific name of *Odobenus rosmarus*. See *Sea Hog*, *Sea Horse*.

Rumbus—"The Rumbus is a large fish, strong and bold, but he is a very slow swimmer; therefore he cannot get

very much food by swimming. Therefore he lays down in the ground or mud and hides there, and all the fish that he is able to overcome, as they come near him he takes them and eats them" (*Physiologus*).

S is for Sphinx, an enigma
at best;
Woe betide pilgrims who
trouble her rest.
Head of a woman, but lion
beneath –
Fail at the riddle, and fall to
her teeth!

Saber-Toothed Cats—Thought to be extinct since the end of the Ice Age, Saber-Toothed Cats continue to be reported from remote parts of the world. The *Tigre de Montagne* ("Mountain Tiger") is described by the Zagaoua natives of Chad, West Africa, as being the size of a lion, with red fur and white stripes, no tail, and a pair of huge fangs. When a Zagaoua hunter was shown pictures of animals both extant and extinct, he identified the Tigre de Montagne as *Machairodus*, the African saber-toothed tiger, believed to have died out a million years ago. Saber-tooths have also been reported from the mountains of Ecuador, Columbia, and Paraguay, South America, where a "mutant jaguar" with 12-inch-long saber-teeth was killed in 1975. Zoologist Juan Acavar, who examined the body, believed that the animal was in fact a *Smilodon populator*, supposedly extinct for 10,000 years.

Sadhuzag—A hybrid animal of medieval bestiaries, the size of a large bull, with the body of a deer and the bearded head of a goat. It has 74 flutelike hollow horns over its head and body, through which it emits either a melodious call to make all listen to and admire it, or a fearsome bellow to terrify the bravest hunter. It is often compared to the *Leucrotta* or *Yale*, but the description of its size and multiple horns sounds more like a Reindeer (*Rangifer tarandus*) (shown), or even the magnificent extinct Irish Elk (*Megaloceros giganteus*), whose many-tined antlers spanned 12 feet across. See *Hercynian Stag, Hippocerf, Sianach*.

Safat—A winged serpent with the head of a *Dragon*, from medieval bestiaries. She dwells high above the clouds and is rarely seen on Earth, as she spends all her time flying and never comes to rest. As she soars on high, she lays her eggs, which hatch while they are falling. Only the shells reach the ground, and if part of a shell is eaten by an animal, the poor creature will go mad. See *Amphitere*.

Sahab—A North Sea monster reported by Olaus Magnus (16th century) as having washed up on a Norwegian beach. It had a huge body, with several feet cloven like those of a cow, and one long, extended foot with which it supposedly caught its prey. See *Globsters, Kraken*.

St. Attracta's Monster—An amphibious *Lake-Monster* of Irish folklore. It roared like a lion, and had boar's tusks, fiery eyes, and ram's ears. It also had a horse's mane, fiery breath, a whale's tail, and one eye in its forehead. It struck fire from the rocks with its iron nails. Its lair was the island of Inis Cathaig (now Scattery Island) in the Shannon River estuary. It was vanquished by St. Senan, a 6th-century bishop who founded a monastery on the island. But it was named for St. Attracta, a nun who established a local safehouse for travelers. See *Auvekoejak, Havstrambe, Ikalu Nappa, Margygr*.

Saio-Neita ("Sea Maiden")—A *Mermaid* in Lapp folklore of Finland and northern Norway.

Salamandra (or *Salamander, Stellio, Dea*)—Brilliant-colored lizards or small *Dragons* that can live in flames and molten lava, and so cold that they are able to extinguish fires. Fireproof asbestos fibers were said to be "salamander wool." Paracelsus (1493–1541) gave their name to Fire Elementals. These myths are based on the European Fire Salamander (*Salamandra salamandra*), which hibernates in dead wood, often ending up in the fireplace as it crawls out of the logs, awakened by heat. When frightened, it exudes a harmless milky fluid that can actually extinguish weak flames. The Salamandra sometimes appears as a symbol for fire insurance. It is also said to be poisonous, and it is true that many newts secrete potent tetrodotoxins through their skin as a defense against predators. See *Grylio*.

Samebito ("Shark-Man")—A Japanese sea-monster that is half human and half shark, with a black body, big, glowing green eyes, and a pointy little beard. The Samebito inhabits a vast underwater kingdom, and has little contact with humans. When one does find itself on land, it is usually in some sort of trouble. But they are honest creatures, and will repay any kindness offered them. A Samebito is featured in the tale of the noble hero Totaro, who invites the exiled monster to live in a lake near Totaro's castle and feeds him. When Totaro falls in love with Tamana, whose greedy father demands 10,000 jewels for her dowry, Samebito's tears of sympathy become precious gems, thus enabling the couple to wed.

Samvarta—One of seven gigantic sea mares in Hindu legend of India. With churning fires in their bellies, they inhabit each of the seven seas. At Doomsday, they will arise from the waters and their fires will spread over all the lands, consuming everything.

Sarajevo Jumping Snake (or *Pos-tok,* "The Jumper")—A poisonous snake of Yugoslavia said to be able to jump several times the length of its body. Its average length is around 3 feet, but it may grow much larger. Color varies from slate grey to dark reddish brown. Herpetologists have identified it as the Nose-Horned Viper (*Vipera ammodytes*) (shown). However, these cannot really jump, but only lunge when striking as any viper does.

Sarmatian Sea Snail—A monstrous marine mollusk described by Ambrose Paré (12517–1590) in his *On Monsters and Marvels* as inhabiting the Sarmatian (Baltic) Sea, where it grazes the shoreline at low tide. It has four hook-like legs, glowing eyes, and a long, multicolored tail. Its branching horns have glistening globular tips. The biggest of all known snails is *Syrinx aruanus*, an Australian marine species that can grow up to 30 inches in length, and weigh up to 40 pounds. See *Lou Carcolh*, *Tuba*.

Sasquatch (Salish *se'sxac*, "Wild Man")—A term coined in the 1920s by Canadian journalist J.W. Burns to consolidate more than 150 local names for a giant hairy hominid that was seen by Indians for centuries in forests from Alaska down through British Columbia, Canada. Long portrayed in native masks and costumes such as the one shown here, it was first seen by white men in 1811, and since then hundreds of sightings and encounters have been reported. It is said to be 6–9 feet tall—sometimes as much as 12 feet—weighing 600–900 pounds, and covered with shaggy black or reddish-brown hair. It has long arms, and an apelike face with a flat nose. Walking upright like a man, it leaves humanlike footprints up to 20 inches long. It also has a distinct and very foul odor, like a combination of skunk and wet dog. See *Bigfoot*, *Skunk Ape*.

Sassabonsum—A huge evil bat-monster in the folklore of Ghana, West Africa. With red hair, hooked wings, and backward-pointing feet, it swoops upon people and carries them off at the bidding of the Mmoatia, or pygmy sorcerers. This is probably the Hammerhead Fruit Bat (*Hypsignathus monstrosus*), the largest bat in Africa, with a 3 foot wingspan. See *Ahool*, *Alan*, *Guiafairo*, *Olitiau*, *Orang-Bati*, *Ropen*.

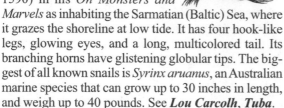

Satyr (or *Silvani*, "Forest People")—A bipedal, manlike creature, sometimes shown with horse ears and tail, but more commonly with the shaggy legs, cloven hooves, ears, and small horns of a goat. Notoriously lascivious, they are usually depicted with erections, chasing or frolicking with Nymphs, and playing pipes. Companions of Dionysos, they are considered to be the children of the Greek god Pan, and have been particularly identified with anthropoid apes, such as orangutans (named by Linnaeus *Simia satyrus*, "satyr monkey") and chimpanzees (*Pan troglodytes*). In Greek drama, actors costumed as Satyrs often performed parodies, called *satires*. Medieval Christian artists used their image to represent devils and demons. Clinically obsessive hypersexuality in men is called *satyriasis*. See *Faun*, *Silen*, *Silvan*, *Sphinx*.

Satyre Fish—A compound heraldic monster with a *Satyr*'s head, a fish's body, and wings. See *Sea Satyr*.

Sa-Yin ("Master of the Fishes")—A *Centaur*-like *Lake-Monster* from the folklore of the Toba Pilaga Indians of the Gran Chaco region of Paraguay, South America.

Scitalis (or *Scytale*; from *scitulus*, "elegant")—A serpentine winged *Dragon* with only two front legs, and multicolored scales so beautiful that animals and humans stop to admire it—whereupon the sluggish reptile strikes them down and devours them. Its poison is so fiery that anyone it bites is consumed in flames. It glows with such inner heat that even in a severe frost it will come out of its den to shed its skin. T.H. White suggests that it may be the "superbly marked" Rhinoceros Viper (*Bitis nasicornis*), found in the forests of West and Central Africa.

Scolopendra—According to Aristotle, this was a 2-foot-long centipede. But by the 16th century it had become a huge, spouting, whale-like *Sea-Monster* with numerous appendages hanging from its underside. These were thought to be legs by which it propelled itself over the water. It was said that, if hooked by a fisherman, the Scolopendra would vomit out its stomach, release the hook, and then swallow its stomach back again. This was probably the carcass of a large shark—a Great White (*Carcharodon carcharias*), a Whale-Shark (*Rhincodon typus*), or a Basking Shark (*Cetorhinus maximus*)—with many Remoras (*Echeneis naucrates*) attached to it. It is not unusual to find such carcasses with their innards spewed out. See *Echeneis*.

Scylla (from *skulle*, "Bitch")—A horrific *Sea-Monster* that lurks in a cave in the Strait of Messina, between Italy and Sicily, attacking ships and devouring their crews—including that of Odysseus. Originally, in Homer's *Odyssey*, she is a lovely sea-nymph who is punished for her transgressions (what these are varies in different versions) by being transformed into a hideous, tentacled monstrosity: a beautiful woman above the waist, but with the heads of six ferocious dogs (each with three sets of teeth) on long, serpentine necks sprouting from her mid-

section, and supported below by 12 dogs' legs. Scylla's necks are each 5 feet long, and when they are fully extended, she is 15 feet tall. She was pictured in classical art as a fish-tailed *Mermaid* with four to six dog heads ringing her waist. However, medieval artists unaccountably depicted her as having torso and head of a woman, the body of a wolf, and the tail of a dolphin. She is always referenced along with another Sea-Monster, *Charybdis*, the great whirlpool that sucks in ships and their crews. Scylla is eventually turned into a rock of that name, and she and Charybdis thus become the origin of the phrase "between a rock and a hard place." Scylla is another example of the beast elsewhere known as the *Hydra* or *Kraken*, which is actually the Giant Squid (*Architeuthis*).

Scythian Ass—A very early version of the *Unicorn*, reported by Herodotus (484–425 BCE). It was described as a large grey animal living in Scythia, with a single horn projecting from its forehead. The horn was valued for medicinal properties and as an antidote to poison, as it was said to be able to contain waters of the Underworld River Styx. This is clearly a Northern White Rhinoceros (*Ceratotherium simum cottoni*). See *Abada*, *Abath*, *Cartazonus*, *Karkadan*, *Kere*, *Serou*.

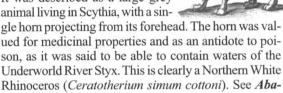

Sea-Bear (or *Ursine Seal*)—A sea-creature of cold northern regions, found in great numbers on the coast of Kamchatka and the Kurile Islands. It is still hunted extensively for its thick, soft wool, the "sealskin" of commerce. This is the animal we now call the Northern Fur Seal (*Callorhinus ursinus*).

Sea-Dog—A hybrid creature of English heraldry, in the shape of a dog but with webbed feet, a paddle-like tail, a long dorsal fin, and fish scales instead of hair. Possibly an artist's very loose interpretation of a beaver, the Sea-Dog is often included among other marine *Chimeras*, such as the *Mermaid*, *Sea Lion*, *Sea Horse*, and *Capricorn*. It is a popular symbol of seaports and sailors, who are popularly called "sea-dogs." And there are also the Dogfish Sharks (*Squalidae*). Philoponus (Padre Buel), who sailed with Columbus, claimed to have witnessed an attack by Sea-Dogs, "which, with snorts and growls terrible to hear, overturned the boats and devoured the luckless Spaniards as though they had been fresh beefsteaks the size of a man's hand."

Sea-Dragon—A heraldic beast with the foreparts of a dragon and a fish's tail. The name has been given to the Leafy Sea Dragon (*Phycodurus eques*) and the Weedy Sea Dragon (*Phyllopteryx taeniolatus*), both of them charming little fishes related to the Seahorse (*Hippocampus*), which are decorated with leafy projections to camouflage them among seaweed.

Sea-Elephant (or *Elephant Seal*)—A huge carnivorous *Sea-Monster* said by J.W. Buel to measure as much as 30 feet in length and 180 feet in circumference, "a prodigy much larger than the mightiest Jumbo, or the Mastodon of Petersburg." Named for its great size as well as its elephantine proboscis, the Elephant Seal (*Mirounga*) is indeed the largest member of the order Carnivora. The biggest known bull measured 22 feet in length and weighed 3.75 tons.

Sea-Gryphon—According to Philoponus (Padre Buel), who sailed with Columbus, five West Indians came to visit Columbus "seated on the back of a Sea-Gryphon, an immense animal having a scaly back, fringed collar, a lashing tail and a hog's head. It was also furnished with four huge paws, each paw having three fingers; it also had tremendous wings and fins—a very savage looking monster to behold." See *Sea-Hog*.

Sea-Hare—A ferocious predatory *Sea-Monster* of medieval European lore, it has the body of a fish, and the head, ears, and legs of a hare. The name has been applied to a type of sea slug, a large herbivorous mollusc of the suborder *Anaspidea* ("without a shield") (shown). The long, earlike projections on their heads inspired the common name. Their skin contains a toxin which protects them from predators.

Seah Malang Poo—A heavily built, tiger-like mystery cat living in the karst limestone mountains of Thailand's Sok National Park. It has brown and black stripes. One was supposedly shot in the 1930s, and the skin sent to Thailand's national museum. See *Cigau*, *Yamamaya*.

Sea-Hog (or *Marine Boar/Marine Sow*)—A huge, scaly fish of medieval sailors' tales. According to naturalist Ambroise Paré (1517–1590), one was seen in the North Sea in 1537. It had the body and head of a huge boar, with a fishlike tail and reptilian forelegs. It also had prominent tusks, which clearly identifies it as a Walrus (*Odobenus rosmarus*). A heraldic version of this tusked beast, with a quarter moon behind its horned head, *Dragon*'s feet, eyes on its sides and belly, and a fish's tail, was called the *Wonderful Pig of the Ocean*. See *Rosmarine*, *Sea Horse*.

Sea-Horse (or *Morse*)—A giant fish of British and Scandinavian folklore, with the head, mane, and foreparts of a horse, and cloven hooves. The same animal was also reported by early explorers of northern Canada, who called it *Equus Bipes* (Latin, "Two-Footed Horse"). Equally at home on land or sea, it was often seen basking on ice floes. According to Ambroise Paré (1517–1590), one was presented to the Pope in Rome. It appears in heraldry as the **Hippocampus**, with webbed feet instead of hooves, and a long dorsal fin down the back. Both names (Sea-Horse and *Hippocampus*) have been given to little fishes that are remarkably similar to the mythic beast. But the original animal of the legend was undoubtedly a Walrus (*Odobenus rosmarus*)—probably a tuskless female. See **Rosmarine**, **Sea Hog**.

Sea-Lion—Another hybrid creature of European heraldry, with the head and foreparts of a lion and the body and the tail of a fish. The name was adopted for the Pacific pinnipeds (marine mammals) of the family *Otariidae*, which have external ears, long front flippers, and the ability to walk on all four flippers on land. In the case of the California Sea Lion (*Zalophus californianus*), the much larger males also have bushy manes.

Sea-Satyr—A strange, fish-tailed sea-creature in the general form of a **Merman**, but with the head of a horned beast, arms ending in pinchers, and short, webbed hind feet. See **Satyre Fish**.

Sea-Serpents—Any one of a wide variety of huge, serpentine sea-monsters which have been reported over the centuries by seafarers. Some appear to be gigantic snakes, enormous eels, immense seaslugs, or even prehistoric creatures, such as long-necked **Plesiosaurs**. Bernard Heuvalmans (1916–2001), the father of cryptozoology, distinguished seven varieties based on consistent descriptions. These are: **Long-Necked**, **Merhorse**, **Many-Humped**, **Many-Finned**, **Super-Otter**, **Super-Eel**, and **Marine Saurian**. Some sightings may have been the tentacles of Giant Squids (*Architeuthis*). Others have turned out to be nothing but long masses of seaweed. Although there have been many well-documented sightings, no confirmed specimens of truly unknown animals have ever been retrieved. However, the Oarfish (*Regalecus glesne*), also called the Ribbonfish, certainly looks the part, and is the longest living bony fish. In 1808, a 56-foot-long specimen washed ashore in Scotland.

Sea-Stag—A heraldic beast with the foreparts of a stag and a fish's tail.

Sea-Trow—This Shetland Island *Mermaid* resembles other Merfolk, but is able to transform its fish tail into human legs and walk the land. Hans Christian Anderson's story *The Little Mermaid* is based on such a creature, as is the 1984 movie *Splash!* See **Havfrue** and **Havmand**.

Sea-Wolf—A heraldic beast with the foreparts of a wolf and a fish's tail.

Selchies (or *Silkie*, *Selkie*; Orcadian, "seal"; also **Roane** [pl.])—These shy  seal-people from the Orkney and Shetland islands of Scotland, Ireland, and Britain do not follow the pattern of most **Merfolk**. Rather than sporting fishtails and human bodies, the Selkies and Roane appear as seals while in the water. However, they can remove their sealskins and walk upon land as humans do. The species of seal said to have this magickal ability is not the Common Seal (*Phoca vitulina*), but only the Grey Seal (*Halichoerus grypus*). An angered Selkie can raise fierce storms to sink the boats of seal hunters or any others who offends him. The Scottish Roane are more gentle-natured, but both can be captured by taking their skins. If a Selkie or Roan thus captured is forced into a marriage, they will be a faithful and loyal spouse, albeit somewhat sad. But if ever they should recover their sealskin they will return to the ocean and not look back. People born with webbed hands or feet are said to be "Selkie-born." See **Fin People**.

Seljordsorm (or *Selma*)—A monster dwelling in 12-mile-long Lake Seljordsvatnet, near Telemark, Norway. First sighted in 1750, it has been seen more than 100 times since. It is usually described as serpentine, about 30 feet long, with a snakelike head and several humps on its back. In 1880, a 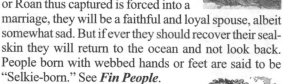 woman managed to cut one in half. The lower portion slithered back into the lake, but the front part of the beast remained on shore, where it rotted away without any tissue samples being taken.

Senmurv (or *Senmurw, Simyr, Sinam*)—A fabulous flying creature from Mesopotamian and Persian mythology that combines features of a mammal, fish, and bird. It is sometimes depicted with the body of a dog and the head and wings of a bird; or, with the body of a bird, the head and paws of a dog, and the tail of a fish. Sometimes it is even shown with the body of a musk ox, the head of a dog, and the wings of an eagle, often roosting upside down like a bat. It is said to be the union of earth, sea, and sky. It roosts in the oldest Soma Tree, which bears the seeds of every plant in the world. When the Senmurv alights or rises, the ripened seeds fall, and they are gathered and distributed by the **Chamrosh**, a similar creature resembling a **Gryphon**-dog. Eventually its legend became merged with that of the **Simurg**, which in turn gave rise to the Slavic **Simargle** and the Ukranian **Simorg**. See **Ziz**.

Seps—A small serpent whose venom dissolves the bones and the body from the inside out. Isidore of Seville (7th century) writes: "The deadly seps devours a man quickly so that he liquifies in its mouth." T.H. White suggests that this may be the Common Krait (*Bungarus caeruleus*) of India. See **Dipsa**.

Serou—A Tibetan form of the **Unicorn**, said to be very aggressive. Certainly this is a reference to the one-horned Indian Rhinoceros (*Rhinoceros unicornis*), which inhabits the foothills of the Himalayas. See **Abada**, **Abath**, **Cartazonus**, **Karkadan**, **Kere**, **Scythian Ass**.

Serpopard—A mythical feline from ancient Egypt, with the body of a leopard and the long neck and head of a serpent, featured extensively on decorated cosmetic palettes from the pre-dynastic period. Examples include the Narmer Palette and the Small Palette of Hierakonopolis, in which the creature's long neck is used as a framing feature, forming the cosmetic area in the former, or surrounding it in the latter.

Serpent King—The ruler and guardian of all snakes in Swedish folklore.

Serpent of Eden—A sentient serpent in the Garden of Eden, as described in the Bible in Genesis 3:1–5: "The Serpent was the most subtle of all the wild beasts that Yahweh God had made…." It has been vilified for tempting Eve to eat the fruit of the Tree of Knowledge, when it asked her if Yahweh had said she could eat from any of the trees. When she said no, that they were not to eat of the tree growing in the middle of the garden, under pain of death, the serpent replied: "You shall not surely die. God knows that on the day you eat of it, your eyes shall be opened, and you shall be as gods, knowing good and evil." And this, of course, is exactly what happened. The Serpent is usually shown in medieval religious art as a snakelike creature coiling about the Tree, but details vary over time. Early images show it with the horselike head more typical of a **Lake-Monster**, whereas later depictions give it a human head. Sometimes it has a crown, forelegs, or the wings and tail of a peacock. Eventually it came to represent all evil in the world, and became equated with the Devil. See **Draconcopedes**.

Serra (or *Serre*, *Sarre*, *Sarce*, *Scie*, *Flying Fish*, *Sawfish*)—A huge flying fish, with enormous fins like bat wings and the head of a lion. It would pursue a sailing ship for miles, but would eventually fold its wings drop back into the sea from exhaustion. Because the *Physiologus* described it as having a serrated cock's comb, with which it sawed open ships by swimming under them, some ancient authorities equated it with the Sawfish (*Pristis*). But it seems more likely to be a fusion of the Flying Fish (*Exocoetidae*) and the Manta Ray (*Manta birostris*), both famed for their soaring leaps out of the water.

Sevienda—A version of the **Phoenix** dwelling in India. Nicolo de Conti (ca.1395–1469), a Venetian merchant who traveled for either 25 or 36 years through India, Asia, and Africa, said it had a beak full of holes. Similar to the Phoenix, it was consumed by fire and regenerated from the ashes as a little worm or caterpillar.

Shachihoko—A Chinese **Water-Monster** with the body of a carp and the head of a tiger. Covered all over with poisonous spines when it is in the sea, it can transform into a tiger on land. It became a popular form of **Gargoyle** on medieval Japanese buildings.

Shadhahvar (or *Shadavar*)—A predatory Persian antelope with a single hollow, branching horn. The wind blows the horn like a flute, and animals are drawn toward the pleasant music. Then, the Shadhahvar kills them. See **Unicorn**.

Shag Foal (or *Tatter Foal*)—A shaggy horse or donkey that haunts lonely roads in Lincolnshire, England, frightening nocturnal travelers. See **Black Dogs**, **Buckland Shag**.

Shamir—A tiny insect or worm of Jewish legend that can carve wood and stone and even shatter glass. The size of a grain of barley, it was said to have inscribed the 10 Commandments into the stone tablets that Moses brought down from Mt. Sinai. Another legend tells how it was captured and used to cut the stones for King Solomon's Temple. The myth was probably inspired by the larvae of wood-boring beetles.

Shang Yung (or *Shang Yang, Rainbird*)—A fabulous one-legged bird that can change its height. It heralds the return of the rainy season and warns of floods. It draws water into its beak from rivers and seas, and blows it out in the form of rain onto the thirsty land; therefore, it is often petitioned in time of drought. Chinese children hop about hunched over on one foot, chanting, "It will thunder, it will rain, 'cause the Shang Yang's here again!"

Sharama—In Hindu mythology of India, this is the mighty dog that herds the cows of Surya, the sun-god, each morning to begin the day. Its offspring are the *Sharameyas*,  great, fearsome, four-eyed hounds that guard the entrance to the Afterworld, ruled by Yama, god of death. Their names are *Syama the Black* and *Sabala the Spotted*. Yama sends them out to find the dead and lead them to his bright kingdom. Therefore the dead are given raw meat to pacify the hounds. See *Cerberus*, *Garm*, *Xolotl*.

Shedu—Similar to the *Lamassu*, this winged beast from Assyrian-Babylonian mythology has a human head and the body of a bull. It guards temples and palaces.

Shielagh (or *Seilag*, *Seileag*)—A *Lake-Monster* dwelling in Scotland's 17-mile-long Loch Shiel, just south of Loch Morar (home of *Morag*). It is described as a 70-foot-long beast with three large humps along its back. The earliest recorded sightings go back to 1874, and continue through the turn of the 20th century. Then the animal was not seen again until 1997–'98, when a new spate of sightings were reported, including one in which four creatures were seen simultaneously.

Shoopiltie—A fearsome *Sea-Monster* in the folklore of the British Shetland Isles. It appears as a prancing pony on the shore, but can also take the form of a handsome youth with horse's ears. It lures unwary humans onto its back, then dashes into the water to drown and devour them. See *Cabyl-Ushtey*, *Eaèh Uisge*, *Kelpy*, *Nix*.

Short-Faced Bear—On Russia's remote Kamchatka Peninsula, local reindeer hunters insist that a 1-ton giant bear, with a small head, narrow body, and long legs, still exists. This description fits the prehistoric Short-Faced Bear (*Arctodos simus*), the biggest bear that ever lived. Standing 9 feet tall on its hind legs, this ferocious carnivore is believed to have been extinct for 10,000 years. See *Bergman's Bear*.

Shunka Warak'in—A  great, wolflike beast said to inhabit the great plains of North America. The name means "carries off dogs" in the language of the Ioway Indians. Some cryptozoologists speculate that the Shunka Warak'in may be a Dire Wolf (*Canis dirus*), or some other surviving Pleistocene predator. A purported specimen was shot in Montana around the turn of the 20th century. It was mounted and displayed at a general store and museum in Henry Lake, Idaho, where the owner called it "Ringdocus." Its current location is unknown, but to this author (OZ), it appears to be a Brown Hyaena (*Parahyaena brunnea*).

Sianach ("Monster")—A monstrous, ugly, aggressive, predatory deer in Scottish folklore. It was not to be hunted, but avoided. This may be a reference to the mighty Irish Elk (*Megaloceros*) of the Ice Age (shown), whose antlers spanned 12 feet. See *Hercynian Stag*, *Hippocerf*, *Sadhuzag*.

Silen (pl. *Sileni*)—A race of humanoids in Greek mythology, they are human from the waist up, but with a horse's legs, tail, and ears. Their father and leader is Silenus. Later, Romans equated them with the *Satyrs*. Human children are occasionally born with tails; this author (OZ) once met such a child—with a lovely horsetail, just like those in the old pictures. See *Kallicantzari*.

Silvan (pl. *Silvani*)—Romano-Etruscan versions of the Greek *Satyrs*, with similar goat-man characteristics. They are said to be followers of Silvanus, god of gardens and woodlands. See *Fauns*, *Silen*.

Simargl (or *Semargl*, *Semargl-Pereplut*)—A large, *Gryphon*-like dog with wings from Slavic mythology. In the *Book of Veles*, he is the father of Skif, the founder of Skifia (Scythia). See *Chamrosh*, *Senmurv*, *Simurgh*.

Simurgh (or *Sîna-Mrû*, *Simarghu*, *Simurg*, *Sumargh*: "30 Birds")—The magnificent King of the Birds in Arabian legend, representing divine unity. Its beautiful feathers are prized for their healing properties. Like the *Roc*, it is so huge that it can carry off an elephant or a camel, but it is also known to take human children into its nest to foster them. Derived from the *Senmurv*, it dwells in the mountains of Alberz in northern Persia. Like the *Phoenix*, this wise and peaceful bird lives for either 1,700 or 2,000 years. Some accounts claim it is immortal, nesting in the Tree of Knowledge. It is said to be so old that it has seen the destruction of the world three times over. A bird of the same name attended the Queen of Sheba. It had metallic orange feathers, a silver head, a human face, four wings, a vulture's talons, and a peacock's tail. See *Angka, Anzu, Chamrosh, Imdugud, Ziz*.

Singa ("Lion")—A creature of variable appearance in the folklore of the Batak people who live in the mountains of Sumatra. Its portrayals range from leonine to buffalo-like to anthropomorphic. It usually has a long face and large, round eyes, with prominent eyebrows almost like antlers. As a protective image, it is the dominant theme of Batak decoration, and can be found on houses, utensils, coffins, jewelry, and so on.

Sin-You (or *Sin-U*)— A variety of the Japanese **Unicorn**, or Kirin, which has leonine features and an infallible sense of justice. Legends tell of its being brought into courts of law to judge murder cases. If an accused is guilty, the Sin-You stands still, looks him squarely in the eye, and then impales him through the heart with its horn.

Sirens (or *Sirene, Sireen, Syrene*; pl. *Sirenes, Seirénes, Sirenae*)—These are depicted as part woman, part bird, or with woman's body, a fish's tail, and a bird's feet. Daughters of Phorcys, their individual names are: *Aglaope* ("Beautiful Face"), *Aglaophonos* ("Beautiful Voice"), *Leucosia* ("White One"), *Ligeia* ("Shrill one"), *Molpe* ("Music"), *Parthenope* ("Maiden-Face"), *Pisinöe* ("Mind-Persuader"), *Raidne* ("Improvement"), *Teles* ("Perfect"), *Thelxepeia* ("Soothing Words"), and *Thelxiope* ("Persuasive Face"). Various traditions placed them on an island called Sirenum Scopuli, near Sicily; on Cape Pelorum; on the island of Anthemusa; in the Sirenusian islands near Paestum; or in Capreae, which was surrounded by cliffs and rocks. Wherever they dwell, their haunting voices lure sailors to their doom. Odysseus survives by plugging his crew's ears with wax and tying himself to the ship's mast. Eventually Sirens became equated with **Mermaids**, and the name *Sirenidae* was given to an order of marine mammals, including dugongs, manatees, and sea cows. It is believed, however, that the seductive song of the Sirens was actually that of the Nightingale (*Luscinia megarhynchos*) heard from offshore.

Sirin—A brightly-plumaged Russian version of the **Siren**, with the head and breasts of a woman on the body of a bird (usually an owl). They live in "Indian lands" near Eden or around the Euphrates River, singing sweet arias of future joys to dying saints, who thus forget their worldly woes and die in peace. But ordinary men who hear them forget everything and follow them unto death. The antithesis of the Sirin is the *Alkonost*.

Sirrush (or *Mushrush, Mušh-uššu*)—Depicted on the Ishtar gate of ancient Babylon, this draconic reptile has a snakelike head and neck, with the forefeet of a cat and bird claws for hind feet. Apparently intended to represent a living animal, this bas-relief suggests the existence of a surviving dinosaur—possibly the African *Mokêle-M'Bêmbe*. In Babylonian mythology, Sirrush is one of the **Dragons** attendant upon the great *Tiamet*. At the time the Ishtar gate was carved, Nebuchadnezzar was King of Babylonia. In the Bible, Daniel 14:23-29 states that his priests kept a "living dragon" in the temple, which they worshipped, and which Daniel killed. See *Sta, Mafedet*.

Sisemite (or *Chichimite, Ulak, Uluk, Yoho, Yuho*)—A **Bigfoot**-like hominid with long hair that reaches the ground and notably long walking strides. It is said to inhabit the Guarunta Mountains of Central America. The Chorti Indians of Guatamala consider them to be the guardians of all wild animals.

Sisiutl—A monstrous **Sea-Serpent** in the traditions of the Bella Coola, Haida, and Kwakiutl Indians of Canada's Pacific coast. It is variously described as a salmon-serpent, a horned serpent, or even as a two-headed serpent. Sometimes it is depicted as finned and four-legged with huge fangs—often with two serpentine bodies emerging from either side of an enormous head. Anyone who meets its gaze will be turned to stone. Sisiutl is an assistant to Winalagilis, the war god, and its powers are sought by warriors. See *Basilisk*.

Sjøorm ("Sea-Worm")—Gigantic **Sea-Serpents** of Norwegian legend. They hatch on land as little snakes, but grew bigger and bigger as they eat ever-larger prey. When the land can no longer support their vast bulk, they retreat to the sea, where they continue to grow. See *Great Norway Serpent, Orm*.

Skahnowa—A monstrous turtle in the folklore of the Seneca Indians of the northeastern United States. It aids the horned serpent **Doonongaes** in hunting human and animal prey.

Skoffin (or *Scoffin*)—A terrible bird-**Dragon** of Icelandic legend. Sometimes described as a crowned and winged serpent, its stare is lethal to all, including its own species. When two Skoffins meet, they both die. They can only be killed by silver bullets into which a cross has been cut. See **Basilisk**, **Cockatrice**.

Skoll—In Norse myth, one of the two gigantic wolves that pursue the chariot of Sunna, the sun-maiden. When he catches and swallows it, the world is darkened in an eclipse. His brother is *Hati*, who chases the moon and eats it away each month.

Skrimsl (or *Skirimsl*)—A gigantic **Sea-Serpent** in Icelandic folklore. It inhabited the sea around Lagarfljot, where it was seen throughout the Middle Ages and into the 18th century. It was considered harmless, as its power had been bound by St. Gudmund until Doomsday. In recent years, however, a bizarre, worm-like **Lake-Monster** has been reported in Iceland's Lake Lögurinn (20.5 miles long and 367 feet deep), which some believe to be a reincarnation of the legendary Skrimsl. See **Orm**.

Skunk Ape (or *Southern Big-foot*)—A large hairy hominid reported in Florida, with more than 100 sightings during the 1970s–80s. The earliest published report was in 1942, in Suwannee County, by a man who claimed that the creature rode on his running board for half a mile. Their presence is announced by a revolting stench similar to rotting cabbage. Eyewitnesses usually describe them as having reddish-brown fur, but their color can range from black to white. Albino specimens commonly have bald heads and nostrils the size of half dollars. They have long, dangling apelike arms with clawed fingers, and they tend to snort. Tracks suggest that there are two species: the larger has three toes and an aggressive disposition, whereas the smaller five-toed variety is shy and harmless. The mention of red fur has led some researchers to speculate that an escaped Orangutan (*Pongo*) may be the basis of the sightings. See **Barmanu**, **Bigfoot**, **Hibagon**, **Honey Island Swamp Monster**, **Hvcko Cappo**, **Momo**, **Myakka Ape**, **Stinking Ones**.

Sleipnir ("smooth," "gliding")—The eight-legged grey horse of Allfather Odin in Norse mythology, and the greatest of all horses. He runs faster than the wind, traveling in the air, over land, and down into the regions of Hel—a nine-day journey. His mother was the wicked god Loki, who took the form of a mare when the stallion *Svadilfari* bore his giant master to Asgard, realm of the gods. See *Al Borak*, *Balios*, *Naras*, *Sivushko*.

Snake-Griffin—A heraldic hybrid with the foreparts of a lion, the wings and hind legs of an eagle, and the head of a snake. Heinz Mode feels that this is just a variant of the **Dragon**, and should not be separately designated. See **Gryphon**.

Snallygaster (or *Snollygoster*)—A **Pterodactyl**-like beast said to inhabit the Blue Ridge Mountains near Braddock Heights, Maryland. The first German settlers in the 1730s were terrorized by a monster they called *Schnellgeiste* ("quick spirit"). It was described as half reptile, half bird, with a metallic beak and razor-sharp teeth. It swooped silently from the sky to carry off its victims and suck their blood. Seven-pointed stars made to keep the Snallygaster at bay can still be seen painted on local barns. In February and March of 1909, local residents reported a creature with "enormous wings, a long pointed bill, claws like steel hooks, and an eye in the center of its forehead." It screeched "like a locomotive whistle." The Smithsonian Institute offered a reward for the hide, and President Theodore Roosevelt considered postponing an African safari to personally hunt the beast. A wingless derivative is known in Florida folklore as the *Snoligaster*. See **Duah**, **Kongamoto**, **Ropen**, **Wyvern**.

Solaris—"The Solaris is a fish so named because it is glad to be on land in the sun. It has a large head, a wide mouth, and a black skin, and is slippery as an eel. It grows large and is very good to eat" (*Physiologus*).

Song-Sseu—A Chinese bird with the body of a hen pheasant and the head of a woman. As the first mating call of the pheasant was a signal for young people to come out and dance, its image was embroidered on the ceremonial dance gowns of marriageable princesses.

Sphinx (from Greek *sphingo*, "to strangle"; or possibly from Egyptian *shesep ankh*, "living image")—A composite creature with a lion's body and paws and the head of a human or other animal. In ancient Assyria, it appears as a temple guardian called the **Lamassu**. Three types of Sphinx appear as guardians in Egyptian statuary, all with the wingless body of a crouching lion: The *Criosphinx* has the head of a ram; the *Hierocosphinx* is falcon-headed; and the *Androsphinx*, such as the Great Sphinx of Giza, has the head of a man. The Greek *Gynosphinx* has the head and breasts of a woman, with eagle wings. The offspring of **Orthus** and **Echidna**, the Gynosphinx is a demon of death, destruction, and bad luck. She is famous for posing the following riddle to trav-

elers: "What goes on four legs, on two and then three; but the more legs it goes on the weaker it be?" If they replied correctly, they were allowed to pass; but if they failed, she devoured them. Oedipus gave the correct answer, whereupon the mortified Sphinx killed herself. Pliny the Elder believed that Sphinxes were apes. Indeed, the Guinea Baboon (*Papio papio*) is still called a Sphinx. See *Celphies*, *Cynocephali*.

Ssu Ling—The four sacred "auspicious animals," or Spiritual Creatures, that stand at the four corners of the Earth in Chinese mythology. They also represent the seasons of the year and constellations of the Chinese Zodiac. The *Lung Wang* (Azure Dragon) represents the East (spring); its element is wood, and it brings the regenerating rains, embodies the positive *yang* principle, and represents the Emperor. The *Fêng Huang* (*Vermilion Phoenix*, or *Red Bird*) rules the South (summer); its element is fire, and it brings drought, embodies the negative *yin* principle, and represents the Empress. The *Ki-Lin* (Unicorn; alternatively *Baihu*, the *White Tiger*) governs the West (autumn); its element is metal, the key to sovereignty. And the *Gui Xian* (Black Tortoise, also called *Dark Warrior*) rules the North (Winter) along with a snake (shown); their element is water.

Sta (or *Mafedet*)—A hybrid creature in ancient Mesopotamian and Egyptian and mythology. It has the quadrupedal body of a lion with the head and neck of a serpent. Similar to the *Sirrush* of Babylon.

Stellione (or *Stellio*)—A lizard or newt with a weasel's head, covered with shiny spots like stars. It is so deadly to scorpions that the mere sight of it paralyzes them with fear. It sometimes appears in heraldry. Albertus Magnus (1200–1280), in *De Animalibus*, declares it to be the same as the *Salamander*.

Sterpe—Gigantic worms or serpents reported from Nicaragua. See *Mawadi*, *Minhocão*, *Sucuriju Gigante*.

Stinking Ones— Malodorous, white-skinned hairy hominids occasionally seen and smelled in the jungles of Malaysia. See *Barmanu*, *Hibagon*, *Hvcko Cappo*, *Yeti*.

Stoorworm ("Great Serpent")—An immense *Sea-Serpent* dwelling in the North Sea, so vast that its body could cover all of northern Europe. It threatened to flood all the British Isles unless appeased by human sacrifices. When the King's daughter was slated to be next, her father offered half his kingdom to whomever would slay the *Dragon*. Young Assipattle shoveled slow-burn-

ing peat into the worm's mouth, burning it up from inside.

Storsjöodjuret ("Great Lake Monster"; or *Storsie*)—A horned or long-eared *Lake Monster* said to inhabit Lake Storsjön in the province of Jämtland, Sweden. Reported since 1635, descriptions have varied over the years, leading some to speculate that there is more than one mysterious creature inhabiting the lake. Most witnesses have described it as serpentine, with multiple humps, a feline- or canine-like head, and greyish skin. It is 20–30 feet in length, with large eyes and a gaping mouth.

Strix (Greek, "Owl"; or *Striga*; pl. *Striges*)—A vampiric night bird of Roman legend that feeds on human flesh and blood. Various myths tell of people being transformed into these dreaded creatures. Pliny, in his *Natural History* (77 CE), writes that its name was once used as a curse, but beyond that he can only aver that the tales of them nursing their young must be false, as no bird except the bat suckles its young. Although they may have been bats originally, they have since been completely identified with owls, such that the genus *Strix* is assigned to these nocturnal birds. In the Middle Ages, the term was applied to Witches, such as the Romanian *Strigoaic*, the Albanian *Shtriga*, and the Italian *Strega*. See *Devil Bird*.

Stvwvnaya—A *Lake-Monster* in the folklore of the Seminole Indians who inhabit the Florida Everglades. It has a single long horn, reputed, like that of the *Unicorn*, to have aphrodisiacal qualities. It may be summoned from the watery depths by singing, allowing some of its horn to be pared off.

Stymphalids (or *Stymphalian Birds*)—Similar to cranes in size and general shape, these are man-eating birds with brass beaks, claws, and feathers which they can shoot from their wings like arrows. Named for the marshes of Stymphalia (Lake Stymphalos) in Arcadia, Greece, where they live, they terrorize the neighboring countryside until they are driven off and many killed by Heracles in his 6th Labor. The surviving birds settle on the island of Ares in the Euxine (Black) Sea, where Jason and the Argonauts later encounter them on their Quest of the Golden Fleece. Swiss ornithologist Michael Desfayes has proposed that these were actually the rare Hermit Ibis, or Waldrapp (*Geronticus eremite*) (shown), which has bronze-colored wings, a crest, and a long, blood-red beak. It survives today in Turkey. See *Achiyalabopa*, *Asipatra*, *Avelerion*.

Su—A ferocious and untamable beast said to live in chilly Patagonia, where it is hunted for its warm coat. According to Topsell: "When the hunters that desire her skinne,

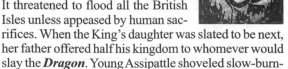

set upon her, she flyeth very swift, carrying her yong ones upon her back, and covering them with her broad taile.... This cruell, untamable, impatient, violent, ravening, and bloody beast, perceiving that her natural strength cannot deliver her from the wit and policy of men, her hunters...first of all to save her young ones from taking and taming, she destroyeth them all with her own teeth; for there was never any of them taken alive...." The description of the mother carrying her young on her back, covered by her bushy tail, suggests the Patagonian Opossum (*Lestodelphys halli*), which lives in a colder climate than any other opossum.

Sucuriju Gigante

("Giant Snake"; or *Sucuri, Sucuruiú, Boiúna, Liboya, Jibóia*; Spanish *Matora*, "Bull Eater")— Truly gigantic anacondas reported throughout the 20th century from the Amazon jungle in South America. Although the largest species, the Green Anaconda (Greek *Eunectes murinus*, "good swimmer"), is known to reach 37.5 feet, some explorers claim to have encountered and even killed monsters far larger, from 60 to 80 ft.

Sughmaire ("Sea Sucker")—A tidal monster of Irish legend, brought to Ireland from India by Fionn MacCumhail to drain a lake. There are said to be nine of these vast creatures throughout the world, sucking and in spewing out the tides in all the seas and harbors. See *Muirselche*.

Suhur-Mas ("Ram-Fish")—The original ancient Sumerian version of the *Capricornis*, associated with the same constellation of the Zodiac. It has the head and foreparts of a goat and the tail of a fish. See *Sea-Goat*.

Suileach—A great, many-eyed *Lake-Monster* that dwelt in the Lough of Swilly in County Donegal, Ireland. It terrorized the surrounding countryside until it was vanquished by St Colum Ceille (521–595), never to be seen again.

Super Eels—A group of large and possibly unrelated eels. Partially based on the *Leptocephalus giganteus* larvae (shown), later proven to be normal in size. Heuvelmans theorized eel, *synbranchid*, and *elasmobranch* identities as possibilities. Seen throughout the world, there have been 23 recorded sightings. See *Sea Serpents*.

Super Otter (also *Hyperhydra egedei*, "Egedi's Super Otter")—A 60–100 feet, medium-necked, long-bodied Sea Serpent resembling an otter. Believed by many

cryptozoologists to be an *archeocetacean* (ancient whale), it moves in numerous vertical undulations (6–7). Once reported near Norway and Greenland, if it ever really existed, it is now presumed to be extinct. There have been 28 recorded sightings. See *Sea Serpents*, *Lake Monsters*.

Surma—In Finnish mythology, this is a monstrous guardian of the gates to the Underworld, ruled by the goddess Kalma. It is a huge open mouth with gigantic fangs, leading to a bottomless gullet. Departed souls pass by Surma unmolested to enter the land of the dead, but any who attempt to leave, or any foolish mortals who venture near, are torn to pieces and swallowed into eternal oblivion. This is very similar to an actual cave entrance, with stalactites and stalagmites as the "fangs." See **Tlatecuhtli**.

Swamfisk—A predatory fish of Norwegian legend that wraps itself in a cocoon of putrid slime in order to appear dead and rotting. Small scavengers attracted to this apparent carcass are then gobbled up. This is surely the Hagfish (*Myxine glutinosa*) (shown), which exudes a copious envelope of gelatinous slime as a defense mechanism when it is alarmed. Interestingly, some of the 90 species of tropical Parrotfishes (*Scaridae*) also secrete a thick cocoon of mucus each night as a sort of sleeping bag.

Syren (or *Sirena*)—A monstrous, winged white serpent indigenous to Arabia mentioned in medieval bestiaries. It can cover the ground faster than a galloping horse and fly even faster. Its poison is so toxic that its victims are dead before they even feel the bite. T.H. White suggests that this may be based upon the Common Krait (*Bungarus caeruleus*) of India. See *Amphitere*, *Dipsa*, *Flying Serpent of Isa*, *Seps*.

Syrenka ("little mermaid")—A Polish freshwater *Mermaid*, also known as *Melusina*. With sword and shield, she is emblazoned on the coat of arms of the city of Warsaw (shown). The image evolved gradually over the centuries, from an original *Dragon* with a man's head to the present Mermaid, made official in 1622. Only the sword and shield remained the same. According to legend, in 1294, Melusina from the River Vistula led Duke Boleslaus of Mazovia to a fishing village, and ordered him to found there the city that became Warsaw.

Sz ("sword ox")—A Malaysian *Unicorn* that resembles an emaciated ox or water buffalo, with a single sharp-edged antelope-like horn.

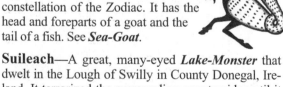

T is for Tarasque, a river-
dweller,
Sheathed in scaly armor
that's quite stellar.
Body of a serpent, lion-
headed,
It leaves many river-sailors
shredded.

Takujui—A Japanese monster, similar to the **Kudan**, with a human
head on the body of a beast, eyes
on its flanks, and spines down its
back. It is an auspicious creature, ap-
pearing only in times of wise government. See **Ki-Lin**.

Tangie— (Danish, "seaweed") A
malevolent **Seahorse** inhabiting Britain's Shetland and
Orkney Islands. It looks like
a scruffy pony with a long shaggy mane of sea wrack; or
it may appear as a Merman. It terrorizes lone travelers
along the lochs at night—especially young women, whom
it abducts and devours.

Tanihwa—Gigantic guardian reptiles
in the traditions of the Maori natives of
New Zealand. They live in deep pools
in rivers, in dark caves, or in the ocean,
especially where there are dangerous
currents or breakers. Some can tunnel
through the earth, causing landslides and
uprooting trees in the process. Others
are said to have created harbors by carving out channels to the sea. In the ocean,
they usually appear as a large shark or
whale, but in inland waters, they resem-

ble a giant Tuatara (*Sphenodon*) with a row of spines
down their back. They are protectors of their respective
tribespeople, attacking any outsiders upon sight. *Horomatangi*, the gigantic aquatic lizard and creator of the
great Karapiti blowhole, does not prey on people, and
sometimes even helps them. But it often attacks canoes,
and especially modern powerboats. *Hotu-Puku*, on the
other hand, hunted and devoured people, and was so
strong and fast that none could escape it. Eventually it
was killed by a party of hunters who lay a net across the
entrance to its cave and taunted it to come running out
into the snare, where it was speared until dead. *Huru-
Kareao* dwells in a lake near Tongariro, where it protects the villagers by wreaking vengeance upon their enemies. If an *Ihu-Mataotao* is killed and its belly cut open,
its victims will emerge undigested. And *Parata* sucks in
and spews out the waters of the oceans with its cavernous mouth, thereby accounting for the tides. Scientists
have named a fossil Mosasaur *Taniwhasaurus oweni* in
honor of the Taniwha.

Tanuki (or *Mujina*)—Mischievous
shapeshifters of Japanese folklore. They
are akin to **Kitsune**, though they are often gullible and absentminded. This is a
real animal, the "Raccoon-Dog" (*Nyctereutes procyonoides*). Tanuki are of-
ten depicted as being chubby with huge testes. They wear
leaf hats and often carry sake jugs. Tanuki statues are
often placed outside of bars to beckon customers inside.

T'ao T'ieh ("glutton")—
One of the oldest known
Chinese monsters, with one
head and set of forelimbs
but two huge, fat-bellied bodies, each with its own hind
limbs and tail. These can be based on anything from tigers to humans. Its head is disproportionately large, with
a cavernous mouth lined with rows of pointy teeth. This
six-legged beast represents gluttony, and it is painted on dishes as a subtle admonition against overindulgence at the dinner table. T'ao T'ieh is one of the
creatures featured in the PS2 game *Culdcept*.

Tarandrus (or *Tharandus,
Parandrus, Parandus,
Parander*)—A shaggy
grey animal resembling an
ox, with branching horns
like a stag's. Said to dwell

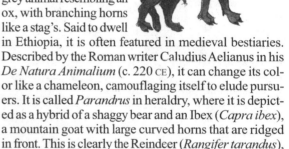

in Ethiopia, it is often featured in medieval bestiaries.
Described by the Roman writer Caludius Aelianus in his
De Natura Animalium (c. 220 CE), it can change its col-
or like a chameleon, camouflaging itself to elude pursuers. It is called *Parandrus* in heraldry, where it is depicted as a hybrid of a shaggy bear and an Ibex (*Capra ibex*),
a mountain goat with large curved horns that are ridged
in front. This is clearly the Reindeer (*Rangifer tarandus*),
which molts seasonally, changing from dark grey-brown
in summer to white against the winter snow. See **Busse**.

Tarasque—A ferocious, amphibious river-**Dragon** of the Rhone
Valley in southern France. Larger
than an ox, it has six legs, the head of a
lion, the paws of a bear, and a scaly
body with a long, serpentine tail ending in a sharp barb.
The hard, leathery shell on its back is covered with spikes.
It is subdued by St. Martha, who ties her belt around its
neck and leads it docilely back into the town of Nerlue,
where the villagers kill it. Afterward, the town's name is
changed to Tarascon, and annual processions continue
to commemorate this event. In depictions, the Tarasque
closely resembles an *ankylosaur* or a *glyptodont*.

Tarbh Uisge (or *Tairbe Uisge, Tairbh-Uisge, Taroo-Ushtey,
Cabyll-Ushtey, Theroo Ushta*;
Gaelic, "Water Bull")—A slimy
or velvety black **Water-Monster** with

bovine horns, no ears, and flaming nostrils. Its nocturnal cries have been compared to the crowing of a rooster. Docile and shy, it is found only in tiny isolated pools, deep in the Highlands of Scotland and Ireland, from whence it emerges at night to mate with local cows. Calves born of these unions are called **Corc-Chluasask** ("Split-Ears"), as they only have half ears. On the Isle of Skye, any calves born with malformed ears are killed immediately to protect the herds from ill fortune. The Manx version, *Taroo-Ushtey*, lives in freshwater swamps and pools and is not considered as dangerous. See *Lake Monsters, Taroo-Ushtey, Water-Horse*.

Tatzelwurm ("Clawed Worm"; also *Springworm*, "Jumping Worm"; *Stollenworm*, "Hole-Dwelling Worm"; *Tunnel Worm*; *Mountain Stump*)—A mysterious European reptile, generally described as a cigar-shaped lizard with a catlike head. It has been seen often over the centuries in the Swiss, Bavarian, Italian, and Austrian Alps, where it is said to be a hole-dwelling creature about 2-5 ft long, so poisonous that even its breath can kill a human. In France, where it is called *Arassas*, it is said to inhabit caves high in the French Alps. Descriptions of its appearance vary greatly as to the number of legs (two, four, or none), and skin (smooth, lumpy, scaly, or hairy). Some say it has a dorsal ridge running down its spine and tail, with scales on its warty body interspersed with red veins and bristles. It is highly aggressive and attacks without warning, rearing up and jumping up to 2–3 yards in one bound. It has been seen even as far south as Sicily, where, in 1954, several farmers reported a long serpent with a cat's head and forelegs attacking their pigs. Many depictions resemble Skinks (*Scincidae*), the largest of the lizard families with about 1,200 known species. Most lack a neck and have relatively small legs. Several genera (for example, *Typhlosaurus*) have no limbs at all, while others, such as *Neoseps*, have only vestigial limbs. Other depictions of the Tatzelworm resemble the *Ajolote*, or Two-Legged Worm Lizard (*Bipedidae bipes*) of Mexico, suggesting that this may be a larger European species.

Telchines—Spiteful *Sea-Monsters* resembling *Merfolk* in Greco-Roman mythology. They have thick bodies with flipper limbs and heads like dogs. Their gaze paralyzes anyone who angers them. Skilled in metallurgy, they forged the sickle with which Kronos castrated Ouranos, as well as the trident of Poseidon/Neptune. Originating in the Cycladic islands

of Crete, Cyprus, and Rhodes, they were scattered throughout the seven seas after attempting to abduct Aphrodite. These seem very likely to be seals. See *Selchie*.

Tengu (or *Ten-Gu*)—Winged creatures of Japanese myth, they are part human and part bird, with glowing eyes and large, beak-like noses. There are several varieties, some benevolent and others malevolent. Most commonly they are portrayed as humanoids with avian features, with the low-ranking *Karasu Tengu* and *Ko-Tengu* (or *Konoha Tengu*) being the most birdlike. These have faces that may be red, green, or black, and they often have human ears and hair. Their beaks are sometimes lined with sharp teeth, and they have clawed, birdlike hands and feet. Their wings and tails are feathered, and sometimes also their bodies. Coloration varies, but they are generally depicted with red clothing, hair, or skin. Residing in a fortress on Mount Kurama, north of Kyoto, they sometimes carry ring-topped staffs called *shakujo* to fight with or to ward off evil magic. The Karasu Tengu preys upon humans, which it is big enough to carry off.

Thanacth—A tailless black animal about the size and shape of a tiger, with a manlike head and frizzled hair. As described by Ambroise Pare (1517–1590) in his *On Monsters and Marvels*, and also by Thevet in his *Cosmography* (16th century), it was imported to the Middle East from India as a food animal. The description, however, sounds eerily human. See *Huspalim*.

Theow—A heraldic creature resembling a wolf with cloven cow hooves instead of paws.

Three-Legged Ass—A rather odd *Unicorn* of Persian mythology, with an immense white body as big as a mountain, three hoofed legs, six eyes, nine mouths, and a hollow golden horn with 1,000 branchlets. According to the Pharsian *Bundahish*, "its food is spiritual, and its whole being is righteous." Amber is its dung. It stands in the middle of the ocean, and uses its magickal horn to purify the seas of all uncleanliness.

Thunderbirds—Huge flying birds common to the mythology of many North American Indian tribes. They are usually described as gigantic eagles whose eyes flash lightning, and whose wing beats create thunder; they are said to carry off buffalos or even whales. Thunderbirds have been sighted throughout the United States, but mostly in the West and Midwest. They are commonly identified with the California Condor (*Gymnogyps californianus*), or even the Andean Condor (*Vultur gryphus*), whose wingspan is known to reach more than 15 feet. Some cryptozoologists have proposed that they may be the Pleistocene vulture *Aiolornis Incredibilis*, which had a wingspan of 17 feet. Recently, fossils have been found of an Argentine Teratorn, which stood 5 feet tall and had an astonishing wingspan of 24 feet. As Thunderbirds are often portrayed with long crests at the backs of their heads, they have also been equated with large *Pterodactyls*—specifically, *Pteranodon*. See *Angka*, *Crocho*, *Keneun*, *Kreutzet*, *Oshädagea*, *Pheng*, *Roc*, *Ropen*, *Simurgh*, *Tinmiukpuk*, *Ziz*.

Thunder Horse—A huge and terrifying horse-monster in the traditions of the Oglala Sioux Indians of Nebraska, Wyoming, and South Dakota. It plunges to the Earth during storms, and its hoofbeats create thunder. In 1875, paleontologist Othniel Marsh was shown enormous bones which the Sioux claimed were from a Thunder Horse. He identified them as huge, rhino-like relatives of horses that lived about 35 million years ago. In honor of the legend, he named it *Brontotherium*, "Thunder Beast" (shown).

Tiamet—The great Cosmic World-Serpent or *Dragon* of ancient Mesopotamian mythology, equated with salt water and the Milky Way. She has a vast, invincible body, with two forelegs, two great horns on her head, and an enormous tail. In the Babylonian epic, the *Enuma Elish*, she and her consort Apsu/Abzu (personifying fresh water) create the heavens and the Earth and engender the gods, who rebel against them. Tiamet is slain by Marduk, and her body dismembered to provide lands and stars. Her flowing blood becomes rivers. See *Jormungand*, *Leviathan*, *Typhon*.

Ti-Chiang—A celestial bird of Chinese mythology. It has three pairs of feet and splendid scarlet feathers, but no eyes or beak.

Tien-Schu (or *Tyn-Schu*, *Yn-Schu*, "The Mouse That Hides Itself")—A creature mentioned in a 5th century BCE Chinese book called *Ly-ki*: "It constantly confines itself to subterraneous caverns; it resembles a mouse, but is of the size of a buffalo or ox. It has no tail; its color is dark; it is very strong and excavates caverns in places full of roots and covered with forests." A 16th-century Chinese naturalist writes: "It dies as soon as it is exposed to the rays of the sun or moon; its feet are short in proportion to its size…. Its eyes are small; its neck short. It is very stupid and sluggish." These descriptions may refer to the Pleistocene Wooley Rhinoceros (*Coelodonta antiquitatis*)

(shown), whose frozen bodies have been discovered in thawing tundra. They give the impression of huge burrowers that had recently emerged from underground, only to die at the surface. See *Koguhpuks*.

Tieholtsodi (or *Teehooltsoodi, Tieholtsali, King of the Ocean*)—A great *Water-Monster* in the Navajo Indian creation myth of the American Southwest. It is described as a giant otter with smooth fur and enormous, buffalo-like horns on its head. In one tale, it causes the great deluge. When it abducts two women, Coyote steals two of its children. The angry monster floods the world, forcing the first people to flee up to the next level, our present Earth. The rain-god Tonenili and the fire-god Hastegini rescues the people and returns Tieholtsodi's children, but continues to cause minor flooding from time to time as a reminder. This and similar deluge legends seem to reflect the sudden rise in sea level that occurred at the end of the last Ice Age, 10,500 years ago. The waters rose 400–600 feet, flooding vast areas of inhabited land.

Tigon (or *Tion*, *Tiglon*)—An exceedingly rare hybrid of a male tiger and a lioness. As it is almost impossible to get these fierce antagonists to mate, there are only a few of these animals in existence, all owned by private collectors. Smaller in size but similar in appearance to the more common *Liger*, Tigons have orange coats with alternating stripes and spots. Males have a modest mane. Their roar sounds like a synthesis of those of both parents. Like most hybrids, they have fairly short life spans.

Tikbalang—A dangerous monster of Philippine folklore. Dwelling in secluded swamps, it is sort of an inverted *Centaur*, having the lower body of a man and the head and foreparts of a black or brown horse. Its knees rise above its head, hiding its equine face, but it can also appear human—even as one known to its victim. Like the *Black Dogs* of Western Europe, it pursues lone nocturnal travelers and leads them astray, never to be seen again. However, just as in the case of being "Pixie-led," victims may find their way back by turning their shirts inside out. It is said that if it rains with the sun out, a Tikbalang is getting married.

Tikoloshe—A hairy amphibious creature in the folklore of the Xhosa natives of South Africa. It is about the size and shape of a baboon, but walks upright, with its long arms trailing on the ground. It can appear human, and even turn invisible. Once confined to the rivers of the Transvaal, it has lately been seen in the Natal and even in urban Johannesburg. It is notorious for raping and strangling women, and for robbing and murdering rich men.

Tirisuk—A massive reptilian quadruped, or **Dragon**, of Inuit legend. It has two leathery "feelers" and a colossal set of jaws, which it uses to ensnare its victims.

Tityron—A heraldic animal that resembles a cross between a sheep and a goat.

Tlatecuhtli—An immense frog in Mexican Aztec mythology. It is associated with Coatlique, the rattlesnake-headed mother goddess of life, death, and rebirth. Its vast, fanged mouth is the entrance to the Underworld, land of the dead. This description is reminiscent of an actual cave, with the "fangs" as the stalactites and stalagmites. See **Surma**.

Tokandia—A large jumping quadruped of Madagascar. It climbs up into trees and utters humanlike cries, but it does not have a human face. This description fits the 200-pound Giant Lemur (*Megaladapis*) (shown), the largest lemur to have ever existed, believed to have been extinct for 1,000 years. Although it was the size of a small bear, it was nonetheless arboreal, similar to a colossal koala. See **Tratratratra**.

Tompondrano—A gigantic **Sea-Monster** of Madagascar, covered with armored plates like a crocodile's. In 1926, some fishermen reported that its phosphorescent head could be seen under water. This is certainly an Estuarine Crocodile (*Crocodylus porosus*), the largest of all living reptiles. Normally confined to Indonesia, they are known to reach 30 feet in length. The reported phosphorescence is created by the disturbance of bioluminescent plankton.

Too Jou Shen—A Chinese animal with a leonine body and head, cloven hooves, and a short, blunt horn projecting from the center of its forehead. Two pairs of these form a portion of the avenue of stone figures leading up to the Ming tombs, aboput 80 miles north of Peking.

Torngarsoak—A gigantic white spirit-bear in the legends of the Inuits of the Hudson Strait, Labrador, Canada. His lair is a deep cave on Ungava Bay, where he rules the seals and whales. He is the

mightiest of the great Polar Bears (*Ursus maritimus*), of which the largest recorded specimen weighed 1,960 pounds and stood 12 feet tall.

Tragopan (pl. *Tragopomones*)—According to Pliny, a horned bird endemic to Ethiopia. Medieval bestiaries describe it as a huge brown bird with two enormous ram's horns on its purple head. *Tragopan* is now the scientific name for a genus of Asian pheasant, *Tragopan satyra*—commonly called "horned pheasants" because of the two brightly-colored, fleshy horns on their heads that they can erect during courtship displays. The name is a composite of *tragus* ("billy goat") and the raunchy, half-goat deity, *Pan*, and also alludes to Pan's **Satyr** companions.

Tratratratra (or *Trétrétrétré*)—A furry arboreal primate reported to be dwelling on the island of Madagascar in 1658. It was the size of a child, with a humanlike face and ears, ape feet, and a short tail. This description, particularly the humanlike face, perfectly matches the chimpanzee-sized lemur, *Palaeopropithecus ingens* (shown), thought to have been exterminated in the 16th century by the first Europeans to settle the island. See **Tokandia**.

Tritons—**Mermen** of Greek lore, they are not nearly as attractive as some of their kin in other parts of the world. They have forked fish tails, a mouthful of sharp teeth, green hair, gills, and pointy ears. They are commonly shown bearing a trident and blowing a "Triton's Trumpet" seashell (*Charonia tritonis*). Male Tritons delight in playing malicious tricks on hapless sailors, earning them a reputation for lasciviousness and deceit. Ambroise Paré (1517–1590), in his *On Monsters and Marvels*, reports that a male and female Triton were sighted in the Nile River of Egypt. However, a famous preserved "Triton" exhibited in the 2nd century at the Temple of Dionysos in Tanagra, Boiotia, Greece, where it was said to have been captured in the local river, was certainly an Angel Shark (*Squatina*).

Troll Fisk ("Giant Monster Fish")—A general Scandinavian term for all **Sea-Monsters**, according to Erik Pontoppidan (1698–1764), Bishop of Bergen, Denmark.

Trunko—A bizarre, 45-foot-long carcass that washed ashore on November 1, 1922, on Margate Beach in KwaZulu-Natal, South Africa, after several people witnessed an epic battle between three gigantic **Sea-Monsters**. Two of these beasts were readily identified as whales, but the third was utterly unclassifiable. The carcass that washed ashore that evening bore a 5-foot-long headless neck, or "trunk" (hence the name), as well as a 10-foot-long, prawn-like tail, all of it covered with a coat of 8-inch-long, snow-white hair. After rotting for 10 days with no scientific investigation, the carcass was washed back out to sea, never to be seen again. This was probably a Basking Shark (*Cetorhinus maximus*) carcass, which witnesses had observed being torn apart by Orcas. See *Makara*.

Tsemaus (or *Ts'um'a'ks*)—A great *Sea-Monster* in the folklore of the Indians of British Columbia, Canada. Inhabiting the Skeena River estuary, it is described as a gigantic fish with a huge dorsal fin so sharp that it can cut a man in half. This is surely the *Orca*, or Killer Whale (*Orcinus orca*), the largest species of dolphin. See *Orc*.

Tsenahale—A vast eagle from the mythology of the Navajo Indians of the American Southwest. It was slain by Nayanezgami with an arrow of lightning. As it fell from the sky, its feathers turned into smaller birds, which became the mountain eagles. See *Thunderbird*.

Tsopo—An aggressive variety of *Unicorn* in Tibetan legend. This is actually the one-horned Indian Rhinoceros (*Rhinoceros unicornis*), which inhabits the foothills of the Himalayas. See *Karkadan*, *Kere*, *Scythian Ass*.

Tsuchi-Gumo—A monstrous invincible spider of Japanese legend. It preyed upon the populace until it was finally trapped in its cave with a steel net, and then roasted to death in a fire. Similar giant spiders are often featured in Japanese folktales, and also appear in the fantasies of J.R.R. Tolkein and J.K. Rowling. In these narratives, travelers and heroes exploring ancient castles, dank caverns, or dark forests come upon passages strung with great webs; they get caught, and must free themselves by killing the spider. See *Djieien*.

Tsuckinoko (or *Bachi-Hebi*)—In Japanese folklore, a large snake with a fondness for alcohol, said to be able to jump 3 feet. It has a very fat body, like a flattened triangle in cross section, with a distinct, arrow-shaped, catlike head, a narrow neck, and a skinny little tail—very similar to the African Gaboon Viper (*Bitis gabonica*). Some cryptozoologists have speculated that it may be a mutant variant of the Pit Viper, *Agkistrodom halys*. There have been many sightings, but no captured specimen.

Tuba (pl. *Tubae*; also *Tööm Ahr*)—A yardlong, snail-like cryptid with a coiled shell and a horned head resembling a mountain goat's. It is purported to inhabit caves in the Khangay and Altai Mountains to the west of Mongolia. Though it crawls on the ground like any snail, it can also climb walls and ceilings of caves by using its sticky mu-

cus secretions, which also protect it from predators. Its diet consists entirely of mold, though in rare cases Tubae are said to kill and eat small invertebrates. In Mongolian mythology, good fortune attends to anyone who finds one, provided the person does not harm it. A terrestrial gastropod of such size is not inconceivable, and the antennae of snails have often been compared to horns and ears. The largest known land snail is the Giant African Snail or Ghana Tiger Snail (*Achatina achatina*), which can measure up to a foot long. See *Lake Monsters*, *Lou Carcolh*, *Mongolian Death-Worm*, *Orm*, *Phooka*, *Sarmatian Sea Snail*.

Tumu-Ra'i-Fuena—An immense spotted octopus of Tahitian folklore, whose prodigious tentacles, like the Force of *Star Wars*, permeate and hold together every part of the Earth and the heavens. See *Lusca*, *Manta*.

Tursus—A marine monster of Finnish legend, described as having the body and head of a walrus with a human torso and arms. Derived in name from the *Thursir* (Frost Giants) of Norse myth, it is considered to be the basis of the *Rosmer*, or *Rosmarine*, which is the Walrus (*Odobenus rosmarus*).

Turtle Lake Monster—A *Lake-Monster* reported to inhabit Turtle Lake, 74 miles northwest of North Battlefield, in Saskatchewan, Canada. Eyewitness descriptions vary with respect to length (10–30 feet), skin texture (smooth or scaly), and shape of the head (resembling that of a horse, dog, or pig). The monster has been a subject of local legend for centuries; Indian folklore has it that anyone foolish enough to intrude on its territory will never return.

Turul (Turkish: *togrul* or *turgul*, "peregrine falcon")—A mythological great falcon in the origin myth of the Magyars of Hungary. In the legend, Emese, mother of Álmos, the founder of Hungary, dreams that a Turul has impregnated her, telling her that her child will become the father of a great nation. Later, the leader of the Hungarian tribes dreams that eagles have attacked their horses and a Turul has saved them, indicating that they must move. The Turul then guides them to the land of Hungary. Monuments to the bird may be seen throughout the country.

Tyger—A heraldic creature with the body of a wolf, a lion's mane and tail, no stripes, and a curiously pointed snout with tusks in the lower jaw. It is called a Tyger to distinguish it from the more typical tigers depicted in heraldry. Although the female is a fierce and protective mother, she is easily hypnotized by her own reflection, which allows her cubs to be stolen by a man holding a mirror. It is based upon the Persian Tiger (*Panthera tigris virgata*), which, unlike the Bengal Tiger (*Panthera tigris tigris*), is not striped. Although thought to be extinct since 1970, there have been several alleged sightings since then in the mountains of Iran.

Typhon—A giant, fire-breathing *Dragon* of Greek myth, taller than a mountain, with serpentine arms and legs, bird wings, and 9, 50, or 100 snakelike heads whose eyes blaze fire. He was eventually overcome by Zeus in the Battle of the Titans and imprisoned in Tartarus, deep beneath Mt. Aetna, where his convulsions are said to cause typhoons. On *Echinda*, he fathered such monsters as *Cerberus*, the *Chimera*, the *Hydra*, the *Sphinx*, the *Nemean Lion*, and the vulture/eagle that ate Prometheus' liver. See *Leviathan*, *Tiamet*.

U is for Unicorn, cloven of hoof,
Fearsome if cornered, but shy and aloof.
Hunters have long sought its magical horn,
Slaying more Unicorns than there were born.

Ugjuknarpak—A monstrous predatory mouse in the legends of the Inuits of Alaska. It hides under an overturned kayak, from which it snatches human victims with its extremely long, prehensile tail. It has superior hearing and great speed, and its hide is impervious to all weapons. No one dares approach its island lair.

Uktena—A giant, winged water-serpent of Tennessee and the Carolinas. It bears a precious gem upon its horned head, but no one can take it, for the monster's very breath is deadly to all creatures. See *Basilisk*, *Piasa*, *Unktehi*.

Uma Na-Iru ("Roaring Weather Beast")—A kind of inverted *Gryphon* of Mesopotamian myth, having the foreparts of a lion and the wings, back legs, and tail of an eagle. Rain issues from its mouth, and it serves as the mount of the storm-god, Adad. Rain clouds were called "Adad's bull-calves."

Underwater Panther (or *Michi-Pichoux*, "Great Lynx"; *Gichi-anami'e-bizhiw*, "Fabulous Night Panther"; *Ukena, Great Underwater Wildcat, Copper Cat*)—Powerful creatures in the mythology of certain American Indian tribes, particularly those in the Great Lakes region. They combine features of several animals, including the body and tail of a mountain lion, the horns of a deer or bison, the scales of a snake, the feathers of a bird, and many others. Said to inhabit the deepest parts of lakes and rivers, some were believed to be helpful, protective creatures, but usually they were feared as malevolent monsters that brought death and misfortune.

Unicorn (or *Licorn, Hippoceros*)—A cloven-hoofed animal with a single straight or spiral horn growing perpendicularly from the center of its forehead. Its horn is called *alicorn*. There were several different "species" at different times and periods in history, derived either from bulls, rams, goats, antelope, or deer. The best-known is the lovely caprine ("goatlike") Unicorn depicted in a number of famous Renaissance tapestries. In actuality, these were real animals whose horn buds were fused into one by a secret process which Dr. Franklin Dove rediscovered in 1933, and which this author (OZ) applied in 1980 to produce the first authentic living Unicorns in modern times.

Unnati—A beautiful celestial bird with a woman's head in the Hindu mythology of Nepal. She is the consort of Garuda.

Unktehi (or *Untekhi*)—Gigantic horned water-serpents in the folklore of the Lakota Indians of the American Midwest. Inhabiting waterfalls and other deep-flowing waters, they are the guardians of the Missouri River, and are constantly at war with the *Thunderbirds*.

Upas Tree ("Tree of Death"; also *Mancenillier, Manchineel, Manzanilla*)—A poisonous tree of Java, said to be so deadly that any creature approaching would be killed by its noxious emissions, resulting in miles of desolation and death in the surrounding region. In actuality, this is the Arrow Poison Tree (*Antiaris toxicara*), whose sap is used in making poison arrows. However, the deadly emanations attributed it are actually carbon dioxide emissions from volcanic fissures on this island. A similar poisonous tree (*Hippomane mancenilla*) grows in the West Indies, where its sap is also used for poison arrows.

Uraeus (Greek, *ouraios*, "cobra")—In Egyptian mythology, a huge venom-spitting cobra that coils around the solar disc of the sun-god, Ra. It was identified with the cobra goddess, Uajit or Wadjet. The symbol of sovereignty of the Pharaoh, the Uraeus was also called the Eye of Ra, which could spit fire against his enemies. This is the Egyptian Cobra (*Naja haje*), commonly called Uraeus Serpent.

Uridimmus ("Man Lion")—A hybrid creature of Mesopotamian mythology, portrayed as human above the waist and a lion below. Walking upright and carrying a staff, he represents the god of truth, justice, and righteousness.

Urisk (or *Ùruisg*, Gaelic, "Water Man")—A Scottish version of the Greek *Faun* or *Satyr*, with the upper body of a man and the lower parts of a goat. They are said to live in waterfalls in the Highlands, where they chase women, kill sheep, and frighten nocturnal travelers walking on lonely roads by suddenly appearing alongside them. But they are not entirely malevolent, as they also help farmers with the herding of their sheep. They are said to meet occasionally in great assemblies. This is one of the monsters generally referred to as *Fuath*.

Urus (or *Re'em*)—An ox-like animal the size of a large bull in European bestiaries, with huge, sawtooth horns with which it cuts down trees. When it drinks seawater it becomes disoriented, stabbing the ground or entangling its horns in trees, and can easily be captured. This animal was actually the Aurochs (*Bos primigenius*), progenitor of domestic cattle, of which the last known specimen, a female, died in 1627 in the Jaktorów Forest, Poland.

Uwabami—A monstrous flying serpent of Japanese legend, sometimes portrayed with wings, sometimes without. It flew down and scooped up human victims in its enormous jaws, until it was slain by the hero Yegara-no-Heida.

V is for Vouivre who sees through a gem Useful to mages and wanted by them. Draconic body and feminine face Doom foolish heroes who threaten her space.

Van Lake Monster (or *Vanna, Canavar*)—A *Lake-Monster* dwelling in frigid Lake Van in eastern Turkey, 5,160 feet above sea level. Hundreds of eyewitnesses have described a creature 50 feet long, with dark,

mottled skin, two small eyes atop its head, and sharp, triangular humps on its back. The earliest sightings date back only to 1995, but these include photos and videos.

Veo—A nocturnal cryptid reported to be living on the Micronesian island of Rintja. It is said to be the size of a horse, with huge claws and a long head. It has large, overlapping scales covering everything except its head, lower legs, belly, and the end of its tail. It feeds on ants and termites. This description matches that of the 8-foot-long Pleistocene Giant Pangolin (*Manis palaeojavanicus*) (shown), fossils of which have been found on the neighboring islands of Java and Borneo. See *Dingonek*.

Vietnamese Night-Flyers—Flying humanoids with batlike wings, sighted by three U.S. Marines in 1969, near Da Nang, South Vietnam. According to the soldiers' report, three naked, hirsute, feminine figures, all approximately 5 feet tall, flew over their post in the dead of night. The Marines claimed they could hear the flapping of their leathery black wings. These were certainly Malayan Flying Foxes (*Pteropus vampyrus*), the largest known fruit bats. The females have two breasts as humans do, and can have wingspans of 6 feet. See *Ahool, Alan, Hsigo, Orang-Bati, Ropen*.

Viper (or *Guivre, Wivre, Woutre*)—Poisonous snakes believed to reproduce by the female taking the male's head in her mouth, whereupon he spits his semen down her throat. During this oral copulation, the female, "driven mad by lust," bites off the male's head. She retains the fertilized eggs inside her until they hatch, and then gives birth to one a day. Eventually the others become impatient and burst out of her sides, killing her. This account was attested by Pliny the Elder (*Natural History*, Book 10, 82), and Isadore of Seville (*Etymologies*, Book 12, 4:10-11). Various *ophidophagic* ("snake-eating") snakes support this myth, as they may be discovered in the act of swallowing another snake as large as they are.

Vodianoi (or *Vodyanoi, Vodyany, Vodnik*)—A Russian *Water-Monster* variously described as resembling a gigantic ugly fish; a floating mossy log with wings; an old man with a blue face, green hair, and white beard; or a scaly or furry beast with huge paws, glowing eyes, sharp horns, and a long tail. They lurk in rivers, pools, swamps, and mill ponds, where they lure unwary humans to a watery death—unless cockerels are periodically sacrificed to them in propitiation.

Vorota Beast—A *Lake-Monster* reported from isolated Lake Vorota in the Sordongnokh tablelands of Siberia. Renowned geologist V.A Tverdokhlebov sighted it in July of 1953. He described a creature approximately 30 feet long and 6 feet wide, with a head that bore a pair of strange, light-colored markings. It also had a prominent dorsal fin that appeared to be set backwards compared with those of dolphins or sharks. It swam with vertical, porpoise-like undulations, and leapt from the water—making a tremendous splash—before submerging. This sounds like an Orca (*Orcinus orca*), or killer whale, but how could one get into this lake?

Vough—Female **Water-Monsters** of Scottish legend. Usually garbed in green, they have manes of yellow hair running down their backs to their tails, webbed hands and feet, and no noses. They fear light but have been known to marry humans and produce progeny. This is another of the evil monsters generally referred to as **Fuath**.

Vouivre (or *Wouivre, Wyvre, Wivre*) —A peculiarly French variation of the **Wyvern**, depicted as a **Dragon** with the head and breasts of a beautiful woman. She sees by means of a ruby, garnet, or diamond set between her blind eyes. This magickal gem is coveted by sorcerers, who attempt to steal it while she is sleeping or bathing. The Vouivre inhabits mountainous regions, lurking in ruined castles or monasteries, where she guards hoards of treasure. She will only attack a clothed person, so the best defense is to strip naked, whereupon she will flee.

Vritra (or *Vrtra, Vitra*, "Encloser")—A vast monster of Hindu mythology, usually depicted as a three-headed serpent encircling the world and causing drought by withholding the rains. Sometimes, however, Vritra is portrayed as a gigantic spider. As one of the evil *Asuras,* Vrita is the enemy of the god Indra, who eventually slays the monster and releases the rain clouds that Vritra had held captive in the mountains.

W is for Wyvern, serpent-shaped,
Bat-winged, eagle-clawed,
from which few escaped.
Red and green, the Wyvern in heraldry
Stands for war and envy and plague, all three.

Waheela—A wolfish creature said to inhabit Alaska and Canada's Northwest Territories. It is larger and more heavily built than ordinary wolves, with a wide head, big feet, and long white fur. Witnesses describe it as being about 4 feet high at the shoulder. Its hind legs are shorter than its front legs, and its tracks indicate widely spaced toes. Solitary creatures, they are never seen in packs. According to native legends, the Waheela is an evil sprit that tears the heads off its victims. Its description matches that of the Pleistocene Bear Dog (*Amphicyonid*), presumed extinct for 10,000 years.

Waitoreke (Maori, "Water-Dweller"; or *Kaureke*) —A small, otter-like cryptid reportedly inhabiting the South Island of New Zealand. Because no placental mammals are indigenous to New Zealand, it may be an aquatic monotreme, such as the duck-billed platypus.

Wakandagi (or *Wakandagi Pezi*) —A serpentine **Water-Monster** in the legends of the Mohawk and Omaha Indians of the central United States. Said to inhabit the Missouri River, it hurls exploding spheres of water at intruders upon its territory. Usually seen only through a mist, its head bears antlers like a stag's, and its hoofed front legs are also deer-like. See **Lake-Monsters, Tcinto-Sakto, Unktehi, Weewilmekq.**

Wallowa Lake Monster—A *Lake-Monster* reported to be dwelling in a deep glacial lake in Oregon. This horned amphibious beast has terrified local Nez Perce Indians for generations. It has been described by some eyewitnesses as being 75 feet long, with seven humps along its back. Other witnesses, however, insist that there are two distinctly different species living in the lake: the first measures 12 feet in length, with a serpentine, **Dragon**-like body, and a head resembling a hog's fused with a shark's; and the second is only about 8 feet long, with a head like a buffalo's and eyes 14 inches apart. Other witnesses claim the creature bears a large, rhinoceros-like horn.

Water-Horse—An amphibious beast with a horselike head, believed to lurk in the depths of many rivers, lakes, swamps, and pools of the British Isles. It is often described as grey or black horse whose hooves point backward. It can change its shape at will. If one mates with an ordinary horse, its progeny will always lie down in the water when crossing fords. Its temperament ranges from relatively docile to voraciously carnivorous. A Water-Horse may entice a man to ride it over a river, but if he should mention the name of Christ, the beast will drop him into the water. See *Kelpie*, *Lake-Monsters*, *Nykur*.

Wccwilmekq (or *Wiwilemekq*)—A serpentine *Water-Monster* in the traditions of the Algonquin and Maliseet-Passamaquoddy Indians of the eastern United States. It is variously described as a giant worm, a stag-antlered water-serpent, a great spiny sturgeon, or a crocodilian sea-monster with huge horns. It lurks in rushing waters, such as waterfalls, rapids, and whirlpools. Its horns contain all its power, conferring great courage and magick upon anyone who can manage to take scrapings of them. See *Orm*, *Unktehi*, *Wakandagi*.

Wendigo (or *Windigo*, *Windago*, *Wiendigo*, *Witigo*, *Witiko*, *Wee-Tee-Go*)—A Canadian hairy hominid similar to Bigfoot, but considered by the local Ind'ans to be quite different—and far more dangerous, as it preys on humans. The most feared creature in Inuit and Algonkian folklore, it is described as a lanky, 15-foot-tall "man-beast" covered in matted fur, with glowing eyes, long, yellow canine teeth, and a hyperextended tongue. But some eyewitnesses insist that the creature is hairless, with a sallow, jaundiced skin. Popularized by Algernon Blackwood's short story, *The Wendigo* (1907), legends of this beast date back centuries. This name has also been applied to an alligator-like monster said to inhabit Berens Lake, Ontario, where it tears up fishing nets.

White Chest—A serpentine *Lake-Monster* in the folklore of the Araucanian Indians of Chile. Said to inhabit Lake Aluminé, it has enormous strength. It attacks livestock that come to the water's edge to drink, dragging them into the depths to be devoured. See *Glyryvilu*.

White Hart—In Welsh folklore, a magickal white stag that leads pursuing heroes into legendary adventures, deep into the forbidden forest and to the very borders of Faerie or the Otherworld. It is featured in the *Mabinogion* tale of "Pwyll, Prince of Dyfed," as well as Mallory's *The Death of Arthur*. See *Cerynean Hind*.

White Panther—A luminous, white feline creature said to have emerged centuries ago from the waters of the River Huron, by Lake Erie. Its appearance was hailed by spectacular meteorological displays. A group of Wyandot Indian hunters wounded the beast, gathering its blood into medicine bundles, which they used as hunting charms on both animal

and human prey. This evolved into a powerful and brutal brotherhood. In the 18th century, the cult was condemned by Europeans as demonic sorcery, and its members were executed.

Whitey—An unhealthy looking *Water-Monster* reported to be dwelling in the White River, near Newport, Arkansas. The first sightings came in 1915, when witnesses reported seeing a single white hump "as big as a boxcar" in the river, and 14-inch-long, three-toed tracks along the banks. On July 1, 1937, Bramblett Bateman and County Deputy Z.B. Reid saw "something appear on the surface of the water" that was 12 feet long and 4–5 feet wide. Bateman said: "I did not see the head nor tail, but it slowly rose to the surface and stayed in this position for some five minutes." In 1971, the creature was seen again: "It looked like it was peeling all over," said one witness. Others reported a bony lump on the head and a spiny ridge along the back. It made a bellowing sound. Whitey is said to be 30–40 ft long, with a scaly, grey-white skin that is peeling in different areas. Cryptozoologist Roy Mackal proposed that it was a male Northern Elephant Seal (*Mirounga angustirostris*) that came up the Mississippi into the White River. The elephant seal is a huge creature; the biggest known bull measured 22 feet long and weighed 3.75 tons! The molting skin, tracks, voice, and particularly the bony projection on the forehead, all fit this identification. See *Baikal Lake Monster*, *Mishipizhiw*, *Pal-Rai-Yuk*.

Whowhie—A monstrous lizard in the legends of the Aboriginal people of Australia's Murray River area. It terrorized the region, devouring many people, especially children. After a particularly devastating raid on a village, the people tracked the monster to his lair in a cave, where he was sleeping off his meal. They burned brushwood at the entrance, fanning smoke into the cave for seven days until Whowhie finally emerged, coughing and blinded—whereupon the people rushed at him with clubs and spears until he was dead. This tale suggests an actual encounter with the gigantic Pleistocene Monitor Lizard, *Megalania* (*Varanus prisca*), which reached 20 feet in length and weighed up to 1,300 pounds—a true Dragon if ever there was one! See *Eurora Beast*, *Kurrea*.

Wihwin—A horselike *Sea-Monster* with huge fangs, in the folklore of the Mosquitos tribe of the Caraibes Indians of Honduras, Central America. During the hot dry months, the Wihwin leaves the ocean and prowls the land seeking human prey. It returns to the sea when the rains come. See *Kelpie*, *Sea Serpent*.

Wikatcha—A feline *Water-Monster* in the folklore of the Creek Indians of Oklahoma. According to the legend, this water-cat mated with a woman from the town of Coosa. When her family determined to drown the child of this union, the mother appealed to Wikatcha, and the enraged father raised a flood that washed away the entire town. The survivors founded the city of Tulsa, but neither the woman, her baby, nor Wikatcha were ever seen again. See *White Panther*, *Yenrish*.

Winged Serpents of Arabia

—According to Herodotus (484–425 BCE), these creatures resembled water snakes with batlike wings. In the spring they flew in a great horde from Arabia toward Egypt, where they were met in a narrow gorge by Sacred Ibises (*Threskiornis aethiopicus*), which destroyed them all. This is why the Egyptians so revered the ibis. The Winged Serpents have been identified as Desert Locusts (*Schistocerca gregaria*).

Wishpooshi

—A colossal beaver with huge claws dwelling in a vast lake in Washington State. According to Nez Perce Indian legend, this monster wished to be the only one to fish in the lake, and so he drove away or killed anyone who approached. The people appealed to Coyote, the trickster, who engaged Wishpooshi in a titanic battle, churning the water, creating great channels and gorges, and draining the lake. Finally, Wishpooshi swallowed Coyote, who then killed the beast by stabbing his heart from inside his body. From the immense carcass, Coyote created the tribes of the Chinook, the Yakima, and the Klickitat. During the Pleistocene era, a gigantic beaver called *Castoroides ohioensis* roamed North America, possibly inspiring this legend. It was more than 8 feet long, weighed 485 pounds, and had 6-inch-long teeth.

Wolpertinger

(or *Wolperdinger*)—A composite creature said to dwell in the Alpine forests of Bavaria in Germany. Most commonly a stag-antlered rabbit or squirrel, it may also have wings and fangs. Similar creatures include the Swedish *Skvader*, the *Rasselbock* from the Thuringian Forest, the American *Jackalope*, and the antlered chicken, *Elwedritsche*, of the Palatinate region. Stuffed Wolpertingers, created by taxidermists using parts of real animals, are often displayed or sold as souvenirs in their "native regions." Similar to the Jackalope, the Wolpertinger was probably inspired by sightings of wild rabbits infected with the *Shope papillomavirus*, which produces antler-like tumors on the animal's head and body. See *Gaffs*.

Wudewasa

(Anglo-Saxon, "Wood-Men;" or *Wodewoses*, *Woodhouses*, *Ooser*)—Hairy hominids popularly referred to as "European Wild Men." They appear in many medieval paintings, church carvings, and illuminated manuscripts. They are often shown holding large, rude clubs, sometimes wearing simple kilts of green leaves. Clearly distinguished from apes and monkeys, they were frequently represented by costumed actors in plays, masques, and dramas. Some researchers feel that they might have been relict *Neanderthals*. See *Bigfoot*, *Chuchunaa*, *Faun*, *Satyr*.

Wuhnan Toads

—Huge, white-skinned, amphibious toads infesting deep, water-filled gorges in the desolate and mountainous region of central China's remote Hubei province (known as Wuhnan). For generations they have plagued local fishermen, who have even resorted to dynamite in their attempts to destroy these voracious beasts. In 1987, an expedition of nine scientists from Peking University journeyed to the area to study its aquatic fauna. As they were setting up their cameras and cables along the shore of a lake, three large animals surfaced and began swimming towards them. The creatures resembled toads and were more than 6 feet long, with pale skin and large, gaping maws. Suddenly, one of the beasts shot forth a gigantic tongue, snagging one of the camera tripods and dragging it back into the water. Then the remaining toads emitted a horrific shriek and disappeared into the depths of the lake.

Wulver

—In Shetland Islands folklore, a hybrid creature with the body of a man and the head of a wolf. Covered in short, brown hair, it lives in a cave halfway up a hill and fishes in deep water. Harmless if unmolested, it will sometimes leave fishes on the windowsills of poor folk. It sounds like a baboon, but what would one be doing in the Hebrides? See *Cynocephali*.

Wyrm

(or *Worm*, *Wormkind*, *Vurm*, *Orm*; from Norse, *ormr*, "dragon")—A common term for evil serpentine *Dragons* in regions of the British Isles that were settled by Vikings a millennium ago. Worms inhabit foul, dank places, such as boggy marshes, fetid swamps, ancient ruins, and sometimes even rivers, lakes, and wells. They prefer hidden lairs near swampy lakes that connect with the sea at high tide, thus allowing these monsters to pass from one environment to the other. Their heads are like those of Dragons or horses, with huge, bulging eyes, great fangs, and often horns. See *Grendel*, *Lindwurm*, *Loathly Worm*, *Orm*, *Loch Ness Monster*, *Peiste*.

Wyvern (or *Wivern*)—A kind of flying serpentine **Dragon** with bat wings, two avian hind legs with eagle talons, and a long, barbed tail. Basically, it resembles a **Pterosaur**, such as *ramphorhynchus*. One variant is the *Sea-Wyvern*, which has the tail of a fish. Wyverns have been described as the largest form of Dragon, able to prey on such huge creatures as elephants and rhinos. In heraldry, the Wyvern symbolizes war, pestilence, envy, and viciousness. The default coloration of a heraldic Wyvern is green with a red chest, belly, and underwings. See **Cockatrice**, **Jaculus**, **Lindworm**.

X is for Xan, a remarkable bug
Living in jungles in lairs damp and snug.
Mentioned by Mayans and Kichers as well,
Many have met it – but few live to tell.

Xan—A fabulous insect-monster mentioned in the sacred texts of the Mayan *Popul Vuh* in Guatamala. It is actually the *Anopheles* mosquito, which still figures in the folklore of the Kicher Indians. As the carrier of deadly malaria and the killer of untold numbers of victims, the Xan is one of the most dangerous creatures in this bestiary!

Xexeu—Gigantic birds in the mythology of the Cashmawa Indians of South America. Similar to the North American **Thunderbirds**, they are responsible for bringing the clouds together to create huge storms. Most likely these creatures derive from the magnificent Andean Condor (*Vultur gryphus*), with its 10-foot wingspan.

Xian Yao—A disgusting and hideous monster in Chinese folklore, with a serpentine body and nine human heads. The companion of **Gong-Gong**, the Black **Dragon**, the two of them go about fouling lakes and rivers with their excrement and turning them into fetid swamps.

Xolotl—A huge and monstrous Underworld dog in the mythology of the Aztec Indians of Mexico, similar in many ways to the North American *Coyote*. His legs and feet are turned backward, and he can point his ears in all directions. Every evening he catches the golden ball of the sun, dragging it down into the Underworld until the next morning. He is said to have created the first humans and to have given them fire, but he also caused various disasters. Attempting to avoid death, he underwent many transformations, finally becoming the little, perpetually larval amphibian, the Axolotl (*Ambystoma mexicanum*). See **Cerberus**, **Garm**, **Sharama**.

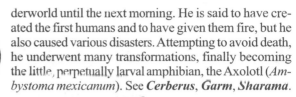

Y *is for Yale, a spotted black cow*
Whose horns can swivel around on its brow.
Tailed like a lion and tusked like a boar,
Not front nor behind is safe from its gore.

Yale (also *Yala*, *Jall*, *Eale*)—First mentioned by Pliny the Elder, the Yale is a spotted black bovine the size of a horse, with the tail of an elephant or lion and the tusked jowls of a boar. Dwelling in the Middle East and India, it bears 2-foot-long horns which it can rotate at will, one pointing forward and the other backward. The Nandi Tribes in Kenya used to train the horns of their cattle in this way, and these were known as "Kamari cows." The Yale is more likely based on the Indian Water Buffalo (*Bubalus bubalis*), which has horns that can measure up to 14 feet across. Some have claimed—erroneously—that it can swivel its horns forward when threatened. *Yael* is the Hebrew word for mountain goat, which is also said to be as big as a horse. When the Yale is used in heraldry to symbolize preparedness, the horns are always shown parted rather than parallel. See **Centicore**.

Yali (or *Yalaka*)—A hybrid monster of Hindu legend, combining the predatory aspects of a lion with the musculature, tusks, and trunk of an elephant. Often depicted in Indian temple sculpture to symbolize man's struggle over the elemental  forces of nature, these voracious beasts are said to be *vyala* ("wicked" or "vicious"). See **Makara**.

Yamamaya—A mystery cat resembling a tiger reported to be dwelling on the Ryukyu island of Iriomote, south of Japan. The size of a large dog, it may be an unknown species of tiger or leopard. See **Cigau**, **Seah Malang Poo**.

Yannig (or *Yannig An Od*)—A nocturnal **Sea-Monster** in the Breton folklore of Brittany in northern France. After dark, it comes out of the sea seeking human prey. It makes calls like the hooting of an owl, and if anyone answers, the monster instantly swoops down upon them.

Yata Garasu—A three-legged crow of immense proportions. In Japanese mythology, the Yata Garasu serves as a divine messenger.

Ya-te-veo ("I can see you")—A fabulous carnivorous tree of Central America, described by J.W. Buel, in his 1887 *Land and Sea*. It uses the multiple squid-like tentacles atop its trunk to capture prey in the same manner

as the little Cape Sundew (*Drosera capensis*). Elsewhere in the Americas, similarly described predatory plants are referred to as the *Brazilian Devil Tree, Brazilian Monkey-Trap Tree, Mexican Snake Tree,* and *Nicaraguan Dog-Devouring Tree*. See *Man-Eating Tree of Magagascar*.

Yeck—A small, shapeshifting spirit in the folklore of India. A Yeck usually appears as small furry creature wearing a white cap. It is strong enough to lift mountains and it enjoys leading humans astray. But anyone who can steal its cap gains the power of invisibility.

Yenrish—A *Lake-Monster* of Huron Indian legend, the Yenrish is a water-cat or panther said to inhabit the depths of Lake Eerie. See *White Panther*, *Wikatcha*.

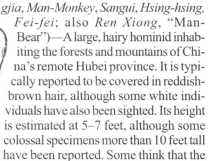

Yirén (Chinese, "Wild Person"; or *Yiren, Yeh Ren, Chinese Wildman, Wildman of Shennongjia, Man-Monkey, Sangui, Hsing-hsing, Fei-fei*; also *Ren Xiong*, "Man-Bear")—A large, hairy hominid inhabiting the forests and mountains of China's remote Hubei province. It is typically reported to be covered in reddish-brown hair, although some white individuals have also been sighted. Its height is estimated at 5–7 feet, although some colossal specimens more than 10 feet tall have been reported. Some think that the Yeren may be a surviving *Gigantopithecus*, while others suggest it may be a relict population of mainland Orangutans (*Pongo pygmaeus*), supposedly extinct in China since the Pleistocene. Recently, tests done on Yeren hair samples have shown that they belong to an unidentified creature completely unknown to China. See *Almas*, *Yeti*.

Yeti (or *Gin-sung, Metoh-kangmi, Nyalmo, Rakshi Bompo, Rimi, Thloh-Mung, Wildman of the Himalayas, Abominable Snowman*)—A snow-dwelling man-ape living high up in the cold, desolate Himalayan mountains of Tibet and Nepal. Eyewitnesses describe it as 7–10 feet tall, and covered in long, coarse hair—silver-white in the snowy mountains and orange-brown in the

forests. Similar to its American cousin, *Bigfoot*, the only evidence for its existence consists of hair samples, footprints, and vague sightings. According to the Sherpas, there are actually four types of *Yeti*, all distinguished by size, with the *teh* in the name of each implying a flesh-and-blood animal. The largest (13–16 feet tall) is the *Nyalmo* or *Dzu-Teh* ("Big Thing"), the medium-sized one (7–9 feet tall) is the *Rimi* or *Meh-Teh* ("Manlike Thing"), and the smaller (man-sized) and best-known is the *Rakshi Bompo* or *Yeh-Teh* ("That Thing There"). Many believe that the Yeh-Teh is simply the Nepal Gray Langur monkey (*Semnopithecus schistaceus*—fairly common in the higher plains of the Himalayas), and that the Dzu-Teh is really a Himalayan Black Bear (*Ursus thibetanus*). Then there is the *Teh-Lma* ("That There Little Thing"), the least known, said to be only 3-4 feet tall, covered in reddish-grey hair, with hunched shoulders and a pointy head. It eats frogs and other small animals. See *Yirén*.

Ying-Lung (or *Proper Conduct Dragon*)—Rather unique Chinese *Dragons* with fur instead of scales, and usually with feathered wings as well. They are guardians of the waters of the Earth and the clouds of heaven.

Yowie—An Australian hairy hominid, similar to the *Yeti* or *Bigfoot*. It is described as 6–14 feet tall, more human than ape, with broad shoulders and no neck. It is covered in longish hair that ranges from black or dark brown through shades of red and tan to almost white. Dark brown or reddish are the most common colors. It leaves footprints up to 16 inches long and 8 inches wide. The first report from European settlers dates to 1881, but the Aborigines had always known of them, calling them *Youree*. Like most hairy hominids worldwide, they are said to have an overpowering stench. Smaller individuals are quite shy and are probably juveniles, whereas the taller ones are bolder and often aggressive. Some even think they may represent a relict population of *Homo erectus*, known to have inhabited Pleistocene *Sunderland* (now the islands of Indonesia).

Ypotamis—An ungainly beast found in medieval travel lore, it was described as a monstrous aquatic horse that delighted in attacking and devouring fishermen. This creature is undoubtedly what we know today as the

Hippopotamus (*Hippopotamus amphibious*—"Amphibious River Horse"), an ill-tempered creature that needs little provocation to attack boats. See **Behemoth, Lubolf.**

Ypotryll—A heraldic beast with the head of a boar, the body of a camel, the feet of a goat, and the tail of a snake. It has huge tusks and teeth, glowing red eyes, and a gigantic penis.

Ythgewinnes (Old English, "Wave-Thrasher")—A species of sea **Dragon** that swims along the surface. Vikings carved these onto the prows of their ships to try to ward off real Dragons.

Yu Lung ("Fish Dragon," or *Dragon-Carp*)—In Chinese mythology, a **Dragon** with the fins and tail of a fish. Originally a celestial carp, it is transformed after leaping the Dragon's Gate waterfall and flying to heaven. It represents high aspirations and success in examinations.

Z is for Zaratan, built like a whale
Big as an island and fierce as a gale.
Sleeping, it's covered with boulders and trees –
Woken, its ride sends strong men to their knees!

Zägh—A gigantic bird of Islamic legend, it has a human head and the ability to understand and speak all human languages. See *Angka*, *Crocho*, *Kreutzet*, *Murghi-I-Adami*, *Pheng*, *Roc*, *Simurgh*, *Thunderbird*, *Ziz*.

Zaratan—An Arabic version of the immense island-whale or titanic turtle known in the West as the **Aspidochelone** or **Fastitocalon**. Its vast back is festooned with rocks and crevices overgrown with trees and greenery. Sinbad the Sailor encountered this monster in the first of his legendary voyages. See *Father of All Turtles*, *Imap Umassoursa*, *Jasconius*.

Zebroid—The generic term for all zebra hybrids. Zebras (*Equus Hippotigris*—"horse-tiger") are able to interbreed with all other equine species, including the Donkey (*Equus asinus*), resulting in a *Zebrass* or *Zonkey*.

Ziz (or *Renanim*, the *Sekwi*, "The Seer"; "Celestial Singer"; "Son of the Nest")—

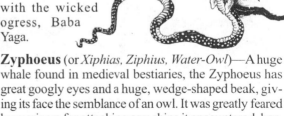

An enormous bird of Hebrew legend, much like the **Roc**. It is so huge that when it stands in the middle of the ocean, the water only comes up to its knees. It can block out the sun with its vast wings and has incredible strength. As the legend goes, once upon a time one of its addled eggs broke, washing away 300 cedar trees and drowning 60 villages. Equated with the Persian **Chamrosh**, the Ziz was said to have been created to protect all the small birds that would otherwise have died out long ago. According to rabbinical tradition, the meat of this bird will be served, along with that of the **Behemoth** and the **Leviathan**, at a great victory feast at the end of the world. Corresponding to the giant archetypal creatures of Persian mythology, the trio of the Behemoth, Leviathan, and Ziz was traditionally a favorite decorative motif for rabbis living in Germany. See *Bar Juchne*, *Thunderbird*, *Wuchowsen*.

Zlatorog—A pure white goat similar to a Chamois (*Rupicapra rupicapra*) with horns of gold. It browses on the highest crags of Mount Triglav, in Slovenia. If you can catch one, it will grant your wishes. But the Zlatorog is highly intelligent and will lead hunters on grand chases, often to their deaths.

It is also the symbol of Slovenia's most popular beer, Lasko Zlatorog. See *Cerynean Hind*, *White Hart*.

Zmei Gorynych—Similar to the *Nagas* of India, this creature of Russian and Slovenian folklore has the body of a snake with the head and/or upper torso of a man. Notorious for abducting lone women, he is associated with the wicked ogress, Baba Yaga.

Zyphoeus (or *Xiphias, Ziphius, Water-Owl*)—A huge whale found in medieval bestiaries, the Zyphoeus has great googly eyes and a huge, wedge-shaped beak, giving its face the semblance of an owl. It was greatly feared by mariners for attacking any ships it encountered, boring holes in them and sinking them. This was originally based on the Swordfish (*Xiphias gladius*), but the name has been given as well as to Cuvier's Beaked Whale (*Ziphius cavirostris*) and the Giant Beaked Whale (*Ziphiidae Berardius*).

CREEPERS
1. THE BALEFUL BASILISK
AND OTHER VENOMOUS VERMIN
By Oberon Zell-Ravenheart

Upon thy eyeballs murderous tyranny
Is in grim majesty to fright the world.
Look not upon me, for thine eyes are wounding.
Yet do not go away. Come, Basilisk,
And kill the innocent gazer with thy sight;
For in the shade of death I shall find joy—
In life but double death, now Gloucester's dead.
—Shakespeare, 2 Henry VI (3.2.49-55)

Ian
Daniels

 HIS ENTIRE BOOK HAD ITS GENESIS IN the legend of the Basilisk. One evening, in the spring of 1976, my wife and soulmate, Morning Glory, and I were sitting around the living room with friends discussing mythical beasties, and we decided to look some up in the *Encyclopedia Britannica.* Under "Basilisk" I found a fascinating entry linking the Cockatrice, Basilisk, Medusa, a South American lizard, and a deadly Egyptian snake, and we conceived the idea of writing a book revealing the true origins and history of various legendary and mythical creatures. We began seriously and systematically collecting and filing legends, illustrations, and accounts of sightings of everything from Abadas to Zaratans. This research led to many amazing adventures over the next 30 years, including raising Unicorns and diving with Mermaids. But here is where it all began.

THE BALEFUL BASILISK

"The Basilisk is so exceedingly cruel that when it cannot kill animals with the venom of its gaze it turns then to the herbs and plants, and looking fixedly upon them makes them wither up."
—Leonardo da Vinci (1452-1519), *The Notebooks*

King Alexander and the Basilisk

Alexander the Great was lord of the whole world. He once collected a large army and besieged a certain city, around which many knights and others were killed without any visible wound. Much surprised at this, he called together his philosophers and said, "My masters, how is this? My soldiers die, and there is no apparent wound!"

"No wonder," replied they; "on the walls of the city is a Basilisk, whose look infects your soldiers, and they die of the pestilence it creates."

"And what remedy is there for this?" said the king.

"Place a mirror in an elevated situation between the army and the wall where the Basilisk is; and no sooner shall he behold it, than his own look, reflected in the mirror, will return upon himself, and kill him." And so it was done.
—*Gesta Romanorum* ("Deeds of the Romans") 13th century

The baleful ***Basilisk*** (in French, *Basilic* or *Basili-coc*) is a special kind of Dragon with a very complicated history and etymology. Originally said to have been born from the blood of Medusa's eyes after Perseus beheaded her, the Basilisk is described as a monstrous serpent crowned with a dramatic frill, crest, or crown, for which reason it is called the "King of Serpents." Its name derives from the Greek *basileus,* meaning "little king," and its Latin name, *Regulus,* means "prince." It is so poisonous that it leaves a wide trail of deadly venom in its wake, and its gaze is likewise lethal. Indeed, it is said that, just as Medusa can, the eyes of the Basilisk can turn a victim to stone. It poisons streams, withers forests, and drops birds out of the sky. Its only natural enemy is said to be the weasel or mongoose, which is evidently immune to its deadly arsenal. But Aelian (175–235 CE) says that the Basilisk also fears roosters: "At the sight of one it shudders, and at the sound of its crowing it is seized with convulsions and dies." During the first century CE, travelers crossing the deserts of North Africa would take along cockerels as protection against Basilisks.

Fig. 1.
Basilisk
as serpent

Albertus Magnus (1200–1280), in his *De Animalibus*, r e l a y s the opinion of "natural scientists" that the Basilisk does not actually emit lethal rays from its eyes, but "rather, the cause of the corrupting influence is the visual energy which is diffused over very long distances because of the subtlety of its substantial nature; herein lies its ability to destroy and kill everything." He also says that the ancients strewed Basilisk ashes in their temples to keep out spiders and other venomous creatures, and that "silver melted in the ashes of a Basilisk takes on the splendor, weight and density of gold."[1] Bulfinch says that, in classical times, Basilisk skins were hung in temples to Apollo and Diana to ward off swallows, snakes, and spiders.[5] Ah, but first you have to find and kill a Basilisk!

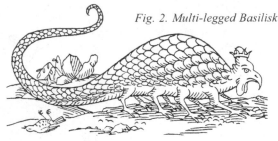

Fig. 2. Multi-legged Basilisk

Let's go back to the beginning. The legend of the Basilisk starts with a snake. In his *Natural History,* Pliny the Elder (23–79 CE), says it is "not more than 12 inches long, and adorned with a bright white marking on the head like a sort of diadem. It routs all snakes with a hiss, and does not move its body forward in manifold coils like the other snakes but advances with its middle raised high. It kills bushes not only by its touch but also by its breath, scorches up grass and bursts rocks." In this statement by history's first real naturalist lie several important clues to the true identity of the Basilisk.[1]

For one thing, it is a small creature—according to Pliny, only a foot long. No doubt this is why its Greek name is a diminutive: "*little* king." The distinctive feature of raising its body high is most significant, as this behavior is uniquely characteristic of only one family of snakes—the cobras—all of which are able to raise the first thirds of their bodies vertically. Moreover, most cobras have species-specific markings on their heads, often in the form of a diadem.

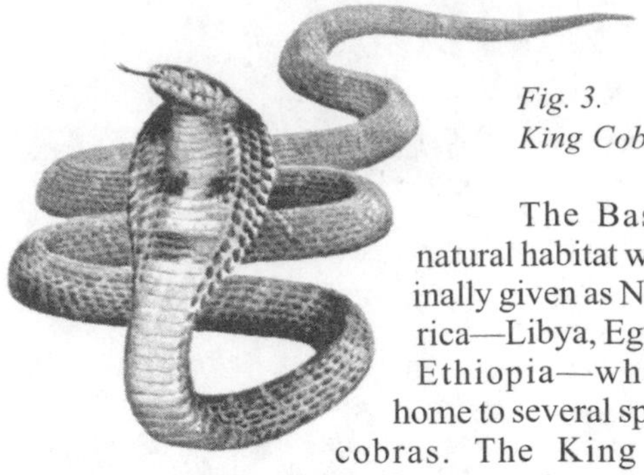

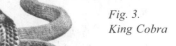

Fig. 3.
King Cobra

The Basilisk's natural habitat was originally given as North Africa—Libya, Egypt, and Ethiopia—which is home to several species of cobras. The King Cobra (*Ophio-phagus hannah*) has been advanced as the original Basilisk, but, at 18.5 feet long, this is the largest of all the world's venomous serpents, and can hardly be described as "little"! A full-grown king cobra can rear up to look a tall man directly in the eye—a most unnerving experience, I'm sure, and easily giving credence to a fabulous monster. In India, it is widely worshiped as *Nagaraja* ("King of Snakes").[2]

In actuality, the Basilisk derives from the Egyptian Spitting Cobra (*Naja nigricollis*), which grows to seven feet long, and sprays lethal poison from its fangs with uncanny accuracy into the eyes of its victims, blinding them instantly and rendering them helpless against its bite. This is the basis of the poisonous breath of the monster, which, as it turns out, is not mythical at all.

Fig. 4. Egyptian Spitting Cobra (Naja Nigricollis)

But it is legendary. From its serpentine origins in a real snake with deadly "breath," the legend of the Basilisk was carried through the centuries across lands where the actual animal did not exist. One of Europe's earliest printed books was the *Dialogus Creaturarum* ("Dialogues of Creatures"), printed in the Netherlands in 1480 by Pieter van Leu. This anonymous work seems to have been the first to identify the Basilisk as "a kind of lizard." When a colorful little lizard with elaborate crests on its head and back was discovered in Central America, it was immediately given the name of basilisk (*Basiliscus*). It is also popularly called the "Jesus Christ lizard" for its ability to run across the surface of water, but it has none of the deadly attributes of its fabulous namesake.

Fig. 5. Central American Basilisk

The archenemy of the Basilisk became mythologized as the **Ichneumon**, or Egyptian rat. This was a ferocious Egyptian weasel described by Pliny, Plutarch, and Strabo as the natural enemy of the Asp, the Basilisk, and the *Cocodryllus* (crocodile). It was said to cover itself with protective mud, then slip down a crocodile's throat and devour its insides. It is commonly assumed to be the Mongoose (*Herpestidae*, or "snake-killer"), an Indian weasel which is, in fact, the deadly enemy of cobras—as in the famous Rudyard Kipling story, "Rikki-Tikki-Tavi." But given the Basilisk's African habitat, its traditional nemesis is far more likely to be the Meercat (*Suricata suricatta*), popularized in Disney's *The Lion King* (1994) and the Discovery Channel's *Meercat Manor*. These charming and social little weasels have been documented on film performing elaborate rituals centered on deadly cobras.

Fig. 6.
Ichneuman (Meercat)
Nicholas Waldt, 1580

ᴛhE COCᴋAᴛRICE

Around 1180, English naturalist Alexander Neckham stated that a Basilisk had to be hatched from an egg laid by an aged rooster, which he called a "Basil-Cock." Soon, however, the term *Cockatrice* or *Cockatrix*—originally referring to any hybrid chimerical creature—started being used interchangeably for Basilisk. Here we see the parallel evolution of a new monster called the **Cockatrice**, which was said to be born from an egg laid in a dung hill by a 7-year-old cock that had mated with a serpent during the "dog days" when the star Sirius was in the sky. The egg was spherical rather than ovoid, and had no shell but only a tough membrane. It was then incubated and hatched by a toad. Thus the hatchling combined the features and habits of its parents and incubator.[3]

Fig. 7. *Cockatrice hatching*

A denizen of North Africa, the Cockatrice came to be depicted as a rooster with a dragon's tail and bat-like wings, so poisonous that its very glance or breath would kill. It could rot the fruit on a tree from a distance, and any water from which it drank would be polluted for centuries. To medieval Christians, it represented sin and sudden death. As with the Basilisk, its only foe was the weasel. A popular Heraldic beast, its name was later applied to a venomous lizard of Armenia, as well as to a huge brass cannon of Tudor times.

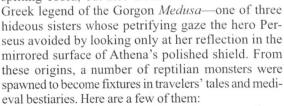

Fig. 8.
Cockatrice

Interestingly, it is a fact of biology that old roosters do indeed often develop egg-like masses in their bodies. As Aristotle (384–322 BCE) observed: "Substances resembling an egg… have been found in the cock when cut open, underneath the midriff where the hen has her eggs, and these are entirely yellow in appearance and of the same size as ordinary eggs."[4] And of course, the Cockatrice itself had to have its own progeny, such as the **Flying Serpent of Isa**. This was a monstrous snake of medieval Christian legends, reported by travelers as being hatched from the egg of a Cockatrice in the desert wastelands of Ethiopia. The most venomous of all the serpents, it could fly as well as crawl.

DEAᴅLᴉ GAᴢERS AɴD LEᴛhAL BREAᴛhERS

Fig. 9. *Medusa*
by Caravaggio

The Basilisk's ability to poison victims with its breath and turn them to stone with its gaze derives not only from the spitting cobra, but also from the Greek legend of the Gorgon *Medusa*—one of three hideous sisters whose petrifying gaze the hero Perseus avoided by looking only at her reflection in the mirrored surface of Athena's polished shield. From these origins, a number of reptilian monsters were spawned to become fixtures in travelers' tales and medieval bestiaries. Here are a few of them:

The **Skoffin** was a terrible bird-Dragon of Icelandic legend, clearly derived from the Cockatrice. Sometimes described as a crowned and winged serpent, its stare was lethal to all, including its own species. When two Skoffins met, they both died. This

creature could only be killed
by silver bullets into which
a cross was cut.

Fig. 10. Skoffin

The **Muiriasc** (or *Rosualt*) was an Irish monster
said to inhabit the plain near Croagh Patrick. Its effluvia caused misery wherever they were directed. If
it spewed into the water, all the fish died; if it belched
fumes, all the birds dropped dead; and if it breathed
vapor over the land, it killed all living things as a plague
would. How very like a Basilisk!

The **Svara** was a great yellow Dragon of Armenian
legend, with a single long horn, enormous ears, and
prodigious fangs. Its venom poisoned the entire surrounding region until it was slain by the hero, Keresapa.

The **Aspis** (Latin, *Asp*) was a two-legged Dragon
of medieval Europe, depicted both with and without
wings. Its bite caused instant death, and it was so
poisonous that even touching its dead body would be
fatal. But it could be easily overcome by music, upon
hearing which it would jam its tail into one ear and
press the other to the ground. This is an ironic myth
because, unlike all other reptiles, snakes have no ears
and are stone deaf.

*Fig. 11.
Aspis*

The **Questing Beast**, or *Glatisant*, was a hybrid creature of British Arthurian legend, said to have
the torso of a leopard, the hindquarters of a lion, the
head of a snake, and the feet of a stag. Other descriptions have included iron-like scales and prodigious
amounts of slime. The rumblings of its stomach sound-
ed similar to the baying of 40 hunting hounds. The
Beast was perpetually seeking fresh water to quench

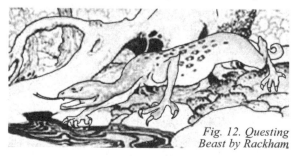

*Fig. 12. Questing
Beast by Rackham*

its unbearable thirst, but whenever it drank, the water
was fouled by its poisonous saliva. Said to have been
begotten by the Devil with a princess who accused her brother of rape after he rejected her
advances, it is a symbol of incest and anarchy. It
appears several times in Mallory's *Le Mort D'Arthur*,
where it is obsessively pursued by Sir Pellinore and,
after Pellinore's death, by Sir Palomedes.

Fig. 13. Catoblepas by Topsell (1658)

And then there is the **Catoblepas** (Greek, "that
which looks downward"; also called *Gorgon*). This
bull-like creature of Ethiopia and southern Egypt was
said to be covered in iron scales similar to those on a
Dragon. It had tusks like a boar's, and no hair except
on its porcine head, which always drooped downward
on its scrawny neck. It ate poisonous plants, and would
belch noxious fumes if frightened. Pliny claims that
"all who met its gaze expired immediately." Because
of this, it is also called the Gorgon, after the Gorgons
of ancient Greece, of which Medusa, with her gaze of
stone, was the most famous. Early accounts of the
Catoplebas described an herbivorous creature with
hoofed feet, but by the 1600s this description had
changed to a scaly, winged beast with large teeth and
claws. Cuvier suggested that it was originally based
on the Gnu, or Wildebeest (*Connochaetes gnou*).

Here are a few more venomous serpents of myth
and legend that may be identified with real-life snakes:

The **Uraeus** (from Greek, *ouraios*, "cobra")—A
huge, venom-spitting cobra in Egyptian mythology
that coils around the solar disc
of the sun god, Ra. It was identified with the cobra goddess Uajit,
or Wadjet.
The symbol
of sovereign-
ty of the Pha-
raoh, the Uraeus
was also called
the Eye of Ra,
because Ra could

*Fig. 14.
Uraeus*

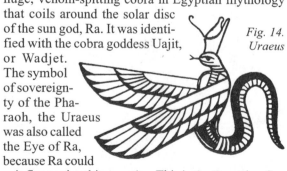

spit fire against his enemies. This is the Egyptian Cobra (*Naja haje*), commonly called the uraeus serpent.

The **Seps**—A small serpent whose venom dis-

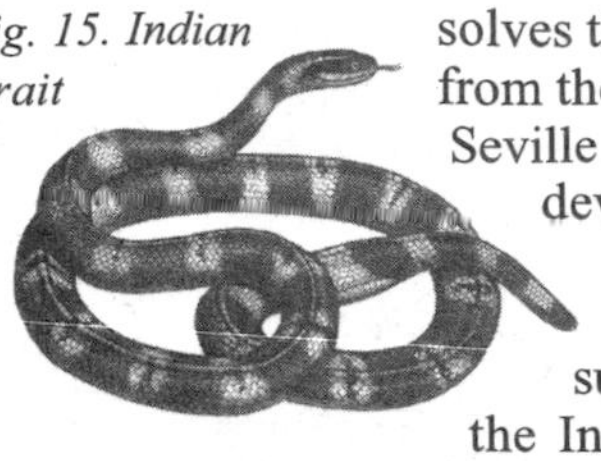

Fig. 15. Indian Krait

solves the bones and the body from the inside out. Isidore of Seville says: "The deadly seps devours a man so quickly that he liquifies in its mouth." T.H. White suggests that this may be the Indian Krait (*Bungarus caeruleus*). Its venom is four times as potent as that of the Indian cobra![5]

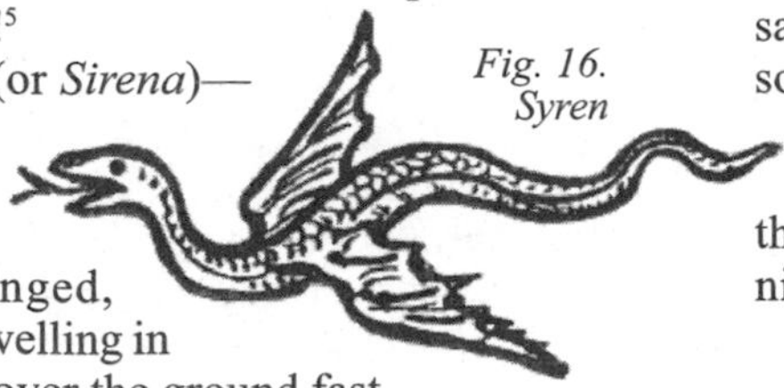

The **Syren** (or *Sirena*)—According to medieval bestiaries, this is a monstrous, winged, white serpent dwelling in Arabia. It can cover the ground faster than a galloping horse, and fly even faster. Its poison is so toxic that its victims are dead before they even feel the bite. White suggests that this creature may also be based upon the Indian krait.[5]

Fig. 16. Syren

SALAMANDRA & KIN

Fig. 17. Salamandra

Salamandra (or *Salamander, Dea*) are brilliantly colored lizards or small Dragons that can live in flames and molten lava, and are so cold that they are able to extinguish fires. Paracelsus (1493–1541) gave their name to Fire Elementals, listing them with the other three Elementals: Gnomes (Earth), Sylphs (Air), and Undines (Water). Appropriately enough, the Salamandra sometimes appears today as a symbol for fire insurance.

Salamanders were also considered to be highly poisonous. According to Pliney, "The Salamander casteth up at the mouth a certain venomous matter like milk, let it but once touch any bare part of a man or woman's body, all their hair will fall off, and the part so touched will change the color of the skin to a white morphew." He adds that the vile venom of a Salamander can infect trees, fruit, water, and even entire nations. If one so much as touched stove wood, anything cooked over it would be poisoned.[22]

These myths are based upon the European Fire Salamander (*Salamandra salamandra*), a colorful little black and yellow amphibian which hibernates in dead wood, often

Fig. 18. Fire Salamander

ending up in the fireplace as it crawls out of the burning logs, awakened by the heat. They do, in fact, exude a harmless milky fluid when frightened, which can actually extinguish weak flames. Moreover, it is true that many newts secrete potent tetrodotoxins through their skin as a defense against predators.

Until the middle of the 17th century, fireproof asbestos fibers were believed to be "Salamander wool." Although they were sometimes drawn as hairy, real salamanders are, of course, entirely smooth skinned, so it came to be said that the wool was from cocoons they wove, as silkworms do. Garments woven from these fibers could be cleaned by throwing them into a fire. Pope Alexander III had a prized tunic of Salamander's wool, as did the Emperor of In-

Fig. 19. Hairy Salamander

dia. This information provides a possible explanation for Pliny's description of the effect of their fluids upon human skin, for this is similar to what happens with asbestos poisoning, which causes skin cancer.[4]

In medieval Christian symbolism, the Salamander represents those who pass through the fires of passion and of this world without stain. Therefore, it stands for chastity, loyalty, impartiality, virginity, courage, Jesus, Mary, and the faithful. Interestingly, the Salamander is also used to symbolize the flames through which it passes, and so is also a symbol of fire, temptation, and burning desire. It was considered the "King of Fire," and as such it represented Christ, who baptized with the flames of the Holy Spirit.[6]

Fig. 20. Crowned Salamander of Francis I

The **Stellione** (or *Stellio*) is a lizard or newt with a weasel's head, covered with shiny spots like stars. It is so deadly to scorpions that the mere sight of it paralyzes them with fear. It sometimes appears in heraldry. Albertus Magnus (1200–1280), in *De Animalibus*, declares it to be the same creature as the Salamander.

*Fig. 21. Stellione
by Matthaus
Merian*

The **Scitalis** (or *Scytale*; from *scitulus*, "elegant") is a serpentine, winged Dragon with only two front legs and multicolored scales so beautiful that animals and humans are compelled to stop and admire it—whereupon the sluggish reptile strikes them down and devours them. Its poison is so fiery that anyone it bites is consumed in flames. Similar to the Salamander, it glows with such inner heat that even in a severe frost it will come out of its den to shed its skin. T.H. White suggests that it may be derived from the "superbly marked" rhinoceros viper (*Bitis nasicornis*), found in the forests of West and Central Africa.[5]

Fig. 22. Scitalis

The **Grylio** is an evil, Salamander-like reptile described in medieval bestiaries. It was said to climb into fruit trees and poison the ripe fruit. Not only would the fruit become deadly, but also any water into which it fell. The name has also been given to the pig frog (*Ranna grylio*).

It should be noted that many newts produce potent toxins in their skin secretions as a defense against predators. The rough-skinned newt (*Taricha granulosa*) of the Pacific Northwest produces more than enough tetrodotoxin to kill an adult human foolish enough to swallow the animal or drink water into which it has fallen. In order for the toxins to take effect, they must be ingested or enter via a break in the skin, but this can easily occur on a camping trip if one drinks water from a pool with newts in it.

TATZELWURMS & DEATHWORMS

The **Tatzelwurm** is a mysterious, hole-dwelling, European reptile, generally described as a cigar-shaped lizard, about 2 to 5 feet long, with a cat-like head. It is said to be so poisonous that its mere breath can kill a human. Known variously as the Clawed Worm, the *Springworm* or Jumping Worm, the *Stollenworm* or Hole-Dwelling Worm, the Tunnel Worm, or the Mountain Stump, many sightings of this creature have been reported over the centuries in the Swiss, Bavarian, Italian, and Austrian Alps. In France, where it is called *Arassas*, it is said to inhabit caves high in the French Alps. The many descriptions of its appearance vary greatly as to the number of legs (two, four, or none) and texture of the skin (smooth, lumpy, scaly, or hairy). Some say it has a ridge running down its spine and tail, with scales on its warty body interspersed with red veins and bristles. It is highly aggressive and attacks without warning, rearing up and jumping 2-3 yards in one bound. It has been seen as far south as Sicily, where, in 1954, several farmers reported a long serpent with a cat's head and forelegs attacking their pigs.

*Fig. 23.
Tatzelwurm 1*

Many depictions of the Tatzelwurm resemble skinks (*Scincidae*), the largest of the lizard families with about 1,200 known species. Most lack a neck and have relatively small legs. Several genera (for example, *Typhlosaurus*) have no limbs at all, whereas others, such as *Neoseps*, have only vestigial limbs. Other depictions of the Tatzelwurm resemble the *Ajolote*, or Two-Legged Worm Lizard (*Bipedidae bipes*) of Mexico, suggesting that this may be a larger European species. A number of these cryptic creatures have been reported killed or found dead, but regrettably, no specimens have been preserved for study. If one is obtained, it may turn out to be related to the New World Gila Monster (*Heloderma suspectum*) and the Mexican Beaded Lizard (*H. horridum*), presently the world's only known venomous lizards. But there have been no sightings in recent decades, and the legendary Tatzelwurm may already be extinct.[7]

Fig. 24. Tatzelwurm 2

Dwelling deep within the dunes of the southern Gobi Desert is a horrible creature known as the **Mongolian Deathworm.** Locals call it *Allghoi Khorkhoi* (Mongolian, "intestine worm"). In Kazakhstan, it is known as the *Büjenshylan*. Its bulky, dark red, worm-like body is reported to be around 2–4 feet long. Supposedly, anything it touches turns yellow. It kills its victims instantly, either by spraying acid-like venom, or by emitting a powerful electrical charge from a range of several feet. Burrowing under the desert sands and emerging to hunt only at night, it hibernates most

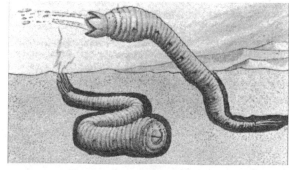

Fig. 25. Mongolian Deathworm by Phillipa Foster

of the year, becoming active in June and July.[7]

Driloleirus americanus is a three-foot-long pink earthworm that spits and, strangely, smells similar to lilies. Long thought extinct, a living specimen was discovered in 2005 in the Palouse soils of the Idaho/Washington border.

A six-foot-long, black, slug-like creature called *Mulilo* has been reported in the Congo region of Africa, along the border between Zaire and Zambia. It is reputed to be highly dangerous, with deadly poisonous breath.

AMERICAN ASPS

Fig. 26. Copperhead

North America has only four types of venomous snakes, three of which are pit vipers. They all share common features: triangular heads, thin necks, thick bodies, and diamond-shaped markings all down their backs. These are water moccasins and copperheads (both *Agkistrodon*),

Water Mocassin

Rattlesnake

and rattlesnakes (*Crotalus*). There is only one species of Copperhead (*A. contortrix*) and one of Water Moccasin (*A. piscivorus*), but there are eight different species of rattlesnakes in the United States.

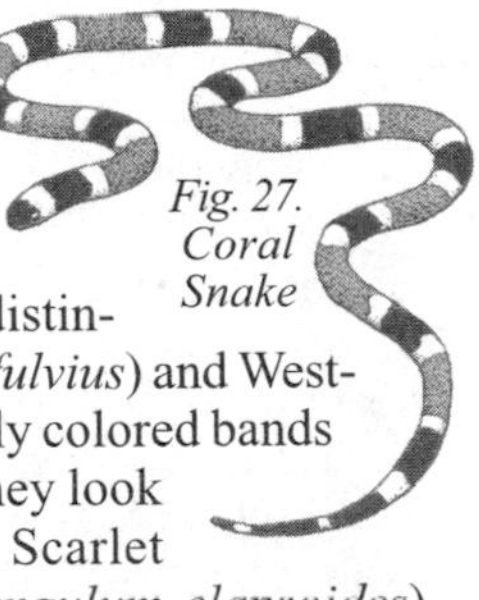

The fourth kind of venomous snake is an *elapid*, related to cobras (and thus, remotely, to the Basilisk). This is the Coral Snake (*Micrurus*), of which there are two virtually indistinguishable species—Eastern (*M. fulvius*) and Western (*M. tener*). They have brightly colored bands of red, yellow, and black, and they look almost identical to the pretty Scarlet King Snake (*Lampropeltis triangulum elapsoides*). There is a simple rule to tell them apart, based on the order of the colors of their bands: "Red and yellow, kill a fellow; red and black, venom lack."

Fig. 27. Coral Snake

Fig. 28. Scarlet King Snake

North America also has its share of mythical venomous snakes, such as the **Hoop Snake**, which, in pursuit of prey, is said to grasp its tail in its jaws and roll, like a wheel, along the ground. At the last moment it straightens out, skewering its victim with its pointy tail. This is reminiscent of the *Ouroboros* and the *Amphisbaena*. Some crypto-

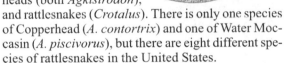

Fig. 29. Hoop Snake

zoologists believe this is a distorted description of the Sidewinder Rattlesnake (*Crotalus cerastes*) of the Southwestern deserts. But it is the Mud Snake (*Farancia abacura*) that is popularly called the hoop snake or stinging snake, for the sharply pointed tail with which it prods its prey.

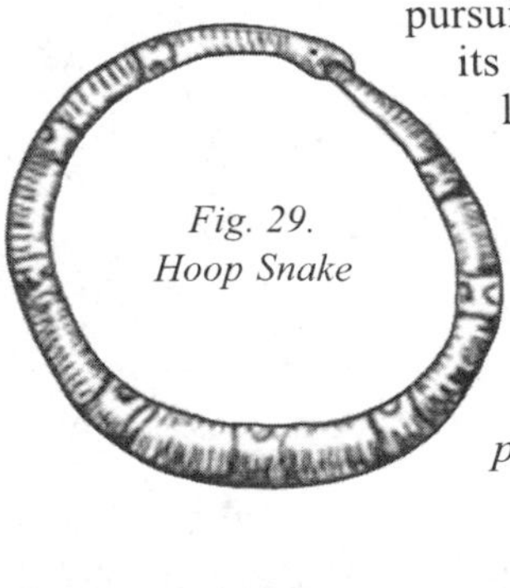

The **Uktena** is a giant, often winged water serpent of Tennessee and the Carolinas. It is said to have a precious gem upon its horned head, but no one can take it, for, similar to the Basilisk, the monster's very breath is deadly to all creatures.

Fig. 30. Uktena

The **Angont** is a gigantic, poisonous serpent in the folklore of the Huron Indians of Eastern Canada. The very flesh of this monster is deadly, similar to that of the Poison Arrow Frog (*Dendrobatidae*). It lurks in forbidding and desolate places, from which it reaches out with its long coils to inflict pestilence and calamities upon humanity.

And finally, there is the **Sisiutl**, a monstrous Sea Serpent in the traditions of the Bella Coola, Haida, and Kwakiutl Indians of Canada's Pacific Coast. It is variously described as a salmon-serpent, a horned serpent, or even a two-headed serpent. Sometimes it is depicted with fins, four legs, and huge fangs, often with two serpentine bodies emerging from either side of an enormous head. According to the mythic narratives, anyone who meets its gaze will be turned to stone. Sisiutl is an assistant to Winalagilis, the war god, and its powers are therefore sought by warriors.

Fig. 31. Sisiutl

MONSTER MOVIES: THE BALEFUL BASILISK

I know of only two movies that have featured Basilisks: *Harry Potter and the Chamber of Secrets* (2002), and a made-for-TV movie on the Sci-Fi Channel titled *Basilisk, the Serpent King* (2006). I am unaware of any Cockatrice or Salamandra in films. However, Medusa appeared in both *The 7 Faces of Dr. Lao* (1964) and Ray Harryhausen's *Clash of the Titans* (1981).

2. COSMIC SERPENTS

By Oberon Zell-Ravenheart

Forth from the dark recesses of the cave
The serpent came; the Hoamen at the sight
Shouted; and they who held the priest, appall'd,
Relaxed their hold. On came the mighty snake,
And twined in many a wreath around Neolin,
Darting aright, aleft, his sinuous nexk,
With searching eye and lifted jaw, and tongue
Quivering; and hiss as of a heavy shower
Upon the summer woods. The Britons stood
Astounded at the powerful reptile's bulk,
And that styrange sight. His girth was as of man,
But easily could he have overtopp'd
Goliath's helmed head; or that huge king
Of Basan, hugest of the Anakin.
What then was human strength if once involv'd
Within those dreadful coils! The multitude
Fell prone and worshipp'd.
— Robert Southey, *Madoc, The Curse of Kehama*

Oberon Zell

ERPENTS ARE UNCANNY AND MYSTErious creatures. Highly evolved, legless reptiles, they slither swiftly through the undergrowth, drop from trees, swim in both fresh and salt water, burrow into the earth, and even glide through the air. Periodically shedding their skins entire, they heal all of their scars to appear renewed and rejuvenated. And all serpents are predators, killing in manners unique to their kind—either by constriction or by the injection of deadly venom.

A deep fear of and even revulsion for serpents seems to be deeply imprinted on the psyches of all primates—including most humans. But while Western culture regards them as the very essence of evil itself, in certain mythologies they are considered to be wise and immortal benefactors and teachers of the Mysteries—especially those of sex.

Snakes evolved from earless, eyeless, legless lizards called *caecilians*, which are still in existence. Although our eyes and those of all other vertebrates derive directly from those of ancient fish, the eyes of serpents are unique in the animal kingdom for having been reinvented from sacratch. They have no eyelids, and so are unable to close their eyes in sleep or blink. Although snakes never re-evolved their lost ears, they developed unique organs for sensing infrared radiation, enabling them to hunt warm-blooded prey in the dark.

Although no modern reptiles bear live young, some serpents, such as garter snakes and boa constrictors, do. They accomplish this by hatching shell-less eggs inside the mother—a process called *oviviparity*. Many protect their eggs and young, and some—such as the king cobra of Kipling's *Riki-Tiki-Tavi*—even mate for life.

And finally, some snakes are known to be the longest of all reptiles, with recorded lengths of more than 30 feet, in the case of anacondas and pythons. But, as we shall see, reports from jungle explorers suggest that some may reach lengths of more than twice that.

CELESTIAL SERPENTS

Many myths and legends describe the sky-spanning vista of the Milky Way as the body of a vast, celestial serpent encircling the entire universe. The oldest example in Western mythology is *Tiamet*—the great Cosmic World-Serpent of ancient Mesopotamia, equated with salt water and the Milky Way. She has a vast, invincible body, with two forelegs, two great horns on her head, and an enormous tail. In the Babylonian epic, *Enuma Elish*, she and her consort Apsu/Abzu (personifying fresh water) create the heavens and Earth and engender the gods, who rebel against them. Tiamet is slain by Marduk, and her body dismembered and dispersed to provide lands and stars. Her flowing blood becomes rivers.

Fig. 1. Marduk slaying Tiamet

In the Akkadian mythology of later Mesopotamia, *Labbu* is the celestial serpent of the Milky Way.

He is slain by the god Tišpak.

Ancient Egyptian mythology gives us **Ka-en-Ankh Nereru**, who arcs across the night sky from horizon to horizon in the form of the Milky Way. In a rather backward journey, the solar barge of Ra enters its caudal vent each sunset, and emerges at the other end from its mouth at the following dawn, renewed for another day.

Apep is the mighty Moon Serpent of Egyptian mythology that emerges from the primal abyss when the world is formed, much like the Babylonian *Tiamet*. Apep represents storms, night, and death, and is associated with Set, the evil god of chaos. Apep is always trying to devour the sun-god, Ra. When he succeeds, the result is a solar eclipse, but he is always forced to regurgitate the blazing sun. Eventually Apep is bound by Horus, and chopped to pieces by Osiris.

Fig. 2. Mehen coiling over the boat of Ra

Another vast cosmic serpent in Egyptian myth is **Mehen**, who coils over the boat of Ra and protects him from the evil *Apep* as the sun-god sails through the darkness of the Underworld on his nightly return journey from the west to the east. The entrance to the Egyptian Underworld is guarded by the enormous serpent **Namtar**, who also protects the sun-god, Ra, on his voyages through the darkness from dusk to dawn. And **Maka** is yet another cosmic serpent of the void in Egyptian myth, who continually attacks Ra on his daily journey across the sky.

In the mythology of ancient Greece, this vast serpent of eternity is named **Ouroboros**, meaning "Tail Devourer," for, in an endless cycle of destruction and renewal, it continually consumes its own tail as it grows longer at the front end. It frequently appears in alchemical illustrations and to symbolize cyclicality and primordial unity. Numerous ancient texts refer to a serpent of light residing in the heavens.

Fig. 3. Ouroboros by Theodoros Pelecanos (1478)

Degei is the immense, sky-spanning cosmic serpent in the folklore of the Fiji Islands. He feeds and mentors the first man and woman, teaching them knowledge of speech, agriculture, fire, cooking, and sex.

In Hindu mythology, **Asootee** is the enormous world-serpent with its tail in its mouth, that encircles the entire universe —turtle, elephants, and Earth.

Fig. 4. Asootee encircling the universe.

WORLD SERPENTS

On a more terrestrial level, various cultural myths tell of a gigantic serpent that encircles the Earth, or from whose body living creatures are produced. The most famous of these is **Jörmundgandr** ("Huge Earth-Monster"), the *Midgard Serpent* of Norse mythology that surrounds Middle-Earth *(Midgard*, the world of humans) with its tail in its mouth. Jörmungand is the second of three children of Loki and the giantess, Angraboda. The first is the Fenris Wolf, and the third is Hel, Goddess of the Underworld. Seeing that the serpent was growing quickly, and knowing that it would someday cause great evil, Odin threw it into the ocean that surrounds the Earth, where it eventually encircled the whole world. At the time of *Ragnorak*, Jörmungand and Thor will destroy each other.

Fig. 5. Jörmundgandr, the Midgard Serpent

Ahi is a monstrous world-serpent in the Vedic myths of India. Embodying the snows of winter that hold the water in the mountains, Ahi drinks up all the waters of the Earth and then coils itself about the mountains. It is slain by the god Indra with his thunderbolts, thereby releasing the rains of spring.

Kholomodumo is a vast, all-consuming serpent-monster in the mythology of the Sotho tribes of southeast Africa. It devours all creatures and humans except for one woman; she bears twin sons who then slay the monster and release all of its victims from its belly to repopulate the Earth.

Umai-Hulhya-Wit is a vast, primordial, cosmic water-serpent in the creation myth of the Diegueno Indians of California. It is tricked by the first people into a brushwood dwelling, which is then set alight. The monster explodes, sending out into the world all the cultural artifacts (arts, languages, rituals, music, legends, and so on) that sustain humanity.

The **Figonas** are winged cosmic serpents who are the creators of all life in the mythology of the Melanesian people on the Solomon Island of San Cristoval. The greatest of these is *Aguna*. He creates the first man, who is so helpless that Aguna must also create a woman to make fire, cook, and weed the garden. *Hatuibwari* was considered the primal ancestress of the human race. Her vast, serpentine body has a human torso with four pendulous breasts to nourish all creatures. She also has four eyes and two enormous wings.

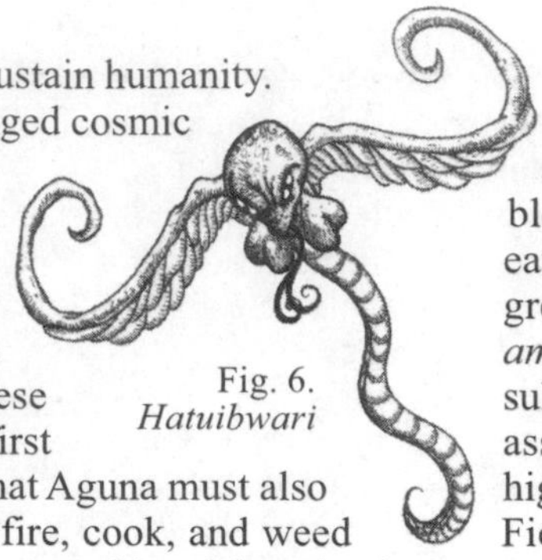

Fig. 6. Hatuibwari

In Islamic mythology, **Falak** is the cosmic serpent who lurks in the Realm of Fire beneath the world-supporting monster *Bahamut*, and whose mouth contains the six Hells. *Dabbat* is the vast serpent that will arise out of the Earth on Judgment Day to destroy the world of unbelievers.

Lik is a vast and ancient water-serpent in the folklore of Gran Chaco, South America. With palm trees growing along its mossy back, it is said to be the guardian of the fish that dwell in lakes and rivers.

And in the American Southwest, Hopi Indian legend tells of vast water-serpents called the **Palulukon**. Two of them, floating in the great cosmic ocean, support the Earth upon their backs. Their turning causes earthquakes.

RAINBOW SERPENTS

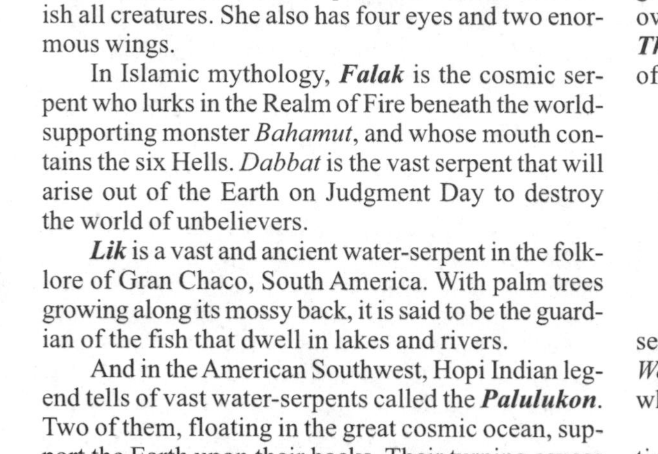

Fig. 7. Rainbow Serpent by Oberon

The sky-spanning rainbow is often envisioned as a vast, multihued cosmic serpent. Such creatures appear in the mythologies of many cultures, but particularly among the native peoples of Australia, Central and West Africa, Melanesia, Polynesia, and the Caribbean. The **Rainbow Serpent** is associated with fresh water and floods, and may be benevolent or malevolent toward humans. In Australia, he is a creature of the *Alcheringa*, or Dreamtime, with different local names in various regions. The Warramunga refer to him as **Wollunqua**, and they say he is so immense that he can travel many miles without his tail ever leaving his waterhole. The Kabi of coastal Queensland call him **Dhakhan**, and say he has the tail of a fish. Normally dwelling in deep mountain lakes, he travels between them in a rainbow.

In Arnham Land, the rainbow serpent is a cosmic python called **Julunggul** or *Yurlunggur*. Angered at the pollution of a waterhole from the menstrual blood of one of the primordial Wawilak Sisters, he eats both women and inundates the entire Earth in a great flood. In the Western Desert he is called *Wanambi*. The Wik Mungkan of central Cape York Peninsula, Queensland, call him **Taipan**. This name has been assigned to a genus of large (up to 10 feet long), fast, highly venomous Australian snakes, one of which, the Fierce Snake (*Oxyuranus microlepidotus*), has the most toxic venom of any land snake in the world.

Bobi-Bobi is a vast heavenly serpent that creates game animals for people to eat, and sacrifices one its own ribs to make the first boomerang for hunting. **Thugine** is a great black sea-serpent dwelling offshore of the Northern Territories.

Fig. 8. Sea Serpent by Matthaus Merian (1718)

Other regional names for the Australian rainbow serpent include *Langal*, *Mindi*, *Ngalbjod*, *Wullungu*, *Woinunggur*, *Worombi*, *Yero*, *Ungud*, and *Ungur*—which is also a term for the Dreamtime itself.

Other monstrous serpents of the Karadjeri Dreamtime are called the **Bulaing**. There are also the *Lightning Snakes*—great, sky-dwelling serpents that descend to the Earth and rebound to the heavens during storms, thus creating lightning. This contact between earth and sky releases the life-giving rains. And *Aranda* is a huge water-serpent of the Emianga region. It lurks in the deepest rivers and billabongs where it lies in wait for unwary humans, whom it swallows whole in one gulp.

Queensland University zoologist Dr. Michael Lee and colleagues have proposed that the legend of the Australian rainbow serpent and other such creatures may have been inspired by an extinct 20-foot-long python, *Wonambi naracoortensis*.

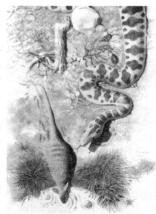

Fig. 9. Wonambi naracoortensisis

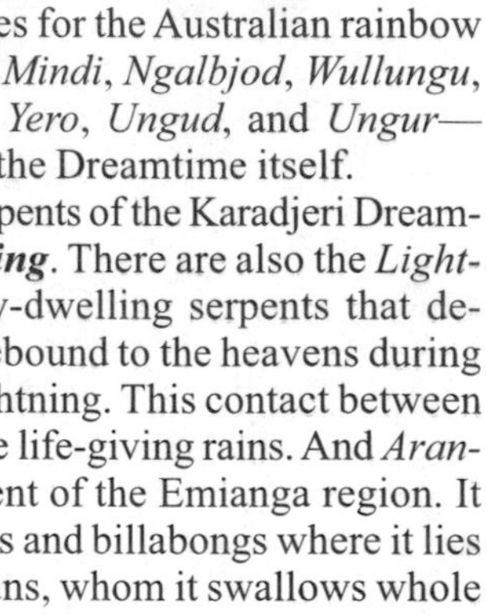

Damballah (or *Damballa Hwedo*) is the great cosmic rainbow serpent in the Voodoo mythology of Haiti, which has its origins in the cult of *Da* among the Fon people of Dahomey, West Africa. The colors of the rainbow encompass everything from his red masculine head to his blue feminine tail. Within his seven coils he holds the primordial ocean, the air, and the heavens above. His excrement becomes the mountains of the Earth. His consort is **Aido Hwedo**, the great rainbow serpent of Dahomey folklore that carries the god Mawu in the creation of the world. She eats vast amounts of iron, but when she cannot find enough she eats her own tail, as Ouroboros does. Her excrement also becomes the mountains of the Earth, eventually adding so much weight that Mawu places Aido Hwedo under the Earth to support it, where her writhing causes earthquakes.

In the traditions of the Yoruba natives of Nigeria, West Africa, the great rainbow serpent is called **Oshumare**.

borneo serpents

Throughout the world, **Lake-Monsters** and **Sea-Serpents** are commonly described as immense, undulating, serpentine creatures with horselike heads, necks, and ears. Some witnesses, however, say that the ears look more like horns, so the same animals may also be called *Water-Bulls* or *Horned Serpents*. Sometimes they are said to have glowing red or yellow eyes, great fangs, and even the ability to breathe fire. In the British Isles and other countries of the Old World, the equine heads and necks of such creatures are often noted, giving rise to legends of *Kelpies*, *Water-Horses*, *Horse-Eels*, *Seahorses*, and *Horse-Heads*. But in North America, where horses were unknown until the Spanish conquistadors brought them in the 16th century, the distinctive horns provided a common identity for these enormous aquatic "serpents" that are prevalent in the mythologies of many tribes.

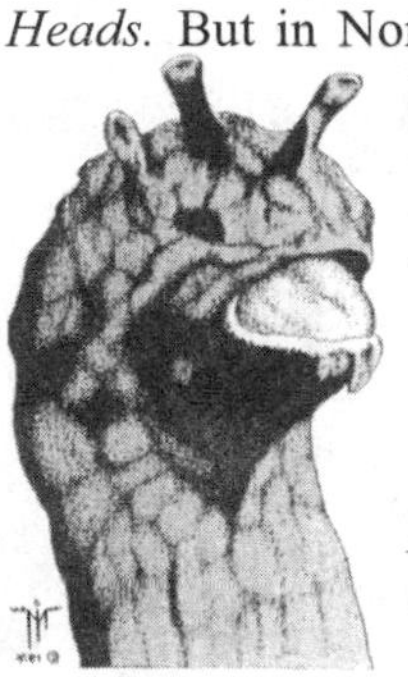

Fig. 10. Head of Loch Ness Monster from underwater photo taken 8/9/72 by Academy of Applied Science

I believe that Horned Serpents, Long-Necked Sea-Serpents, and classic Lake-Monsters are not reptiles at all, but gigantic aquatic slugs with heads and fleshy feelers like those of a snail. Today it is the oft-sighted Lake-Monsters, such as *Champ*, *Ogopogo*, and *Colossal Claude*, that are most known to the public. But such creatures have figured in Native American myths and legends for centuries—if not millennia.

American Horned Serpents (or "Great Serpents") are described as extremely long, with great, gaping mouths and two horns atop their heads. Like the Water-Horses of northern Europe, they may be benevolent or malevolent toward humans. Anyone who eats their flesh will become a Water-Serpent.

Fig. 11. Avan Yu, horned serpent of the underworld. Pueblo Indians, San Ildefonso, New Mexico.

In Canada, **Tcinto-Sakto** ("Long-Horned Serpent") is a giant serpent in the folklore of the Cree Indians, with branching horns like those of a stag. Different varieties can be blue, yellow, or white. **Tcipitckaam** (also called *Unicorn Serpent* or *Lake Utopia Sea-Monster*) is a serpentine Lake-Monster in the folklore of the Micmac and Maliseet of Nova Scotia, where it is believed to inhabit Lakes Ainslie and Utopia. According to legend, long ago two Maliseets were canoing on Lake Utopia, when suddenly the monster appeared and chased them from one end of the lake to the other. Since the arrival of Europeans in the late 1700s, new sightings have been reported every few years. It is described as having the body of an alligator and the head of a horse, with a long red or yellow spiral horn projecting from the center of its forehead.

Fig. 12. On Niont by Tracy Swangler

In the northeastern United States, **Doonongaes** is an enormous Horned Serpent in Seneca mythology. Normally dwelling in deep river pools, he occasionally emerges to sun himself on the banks. He and his companion, **Skahnowa**, the monster turtle, prey upon humans and large animals. The Hurons tell of a giant Horned Serpent called **On Niont**. It carved deep clefts in rocks and mountains with its single huge horn, which was prized for its magickal properties, much like the horn (*alicorn*) of a Unicorn.

In the traditions of the Algonquin Indians of the eastern United States, **Weewilmekq** is a serpentine Water-Monster described as a giant worm, a stag-antlered Water-Serpent, or a great spiny sturgeon. It lurks in rushing waters such as waterfalls, rapids, and whirlpools.

Fig. 13. Weewilmekq by Ash DeKirk

Moving across the country, **Kichiknebik** ("Great Horned Serpent"; also called *Kitsinac-Knebik*) is an immense horned rattlesnake in the folklore of the Iroquois, Lenape, and Al-gonquin Indians of the Great Lakes region. It protects people crossing the water in stormy weather. Able to travel swiftly through water or over land, it is large enough to swallow an entire buffalo.

Fig. 14. Untekhi

In the American Midwest, the **Unktehi** (or *Untekhi*) are gigantic, horned Water-Serpents in the folklore of the Lakota Sioux. Inhabiting waterfalls and deep-flowing waters, they are the guardians of the Missouri River, and are constantly at war with the Thunderbirds. **Wakandagi Pezi** is a serpentine Water-Monster in the legends of the Mohawk and Omaha tribes. A type of *Unktehi*, it is said to inhabit the Missouri River, where it hurls exploding spheres of water at intruders in its territory. Usually seen only through a mist, its head bears antlers like a stag's, and its hoofed front legs are also deer-like.

Hiintcabiit is a monstrous Water-Serpent in the legends and folklore of the Arapaho Indians of the western United States. It inhabits mountain lakes and rivers, and, like many of its kin throughout the world, it has two horns atop its head.

In the deserts of the American Southwest, Navajo folklore describes **Teehooltsoodi** as a Lake-Monster similar to a giant otter, with smooth fur and enormous buffalo horns on its head. In one tale, it causes the great deluge.

Fig. 15. Kolowisi

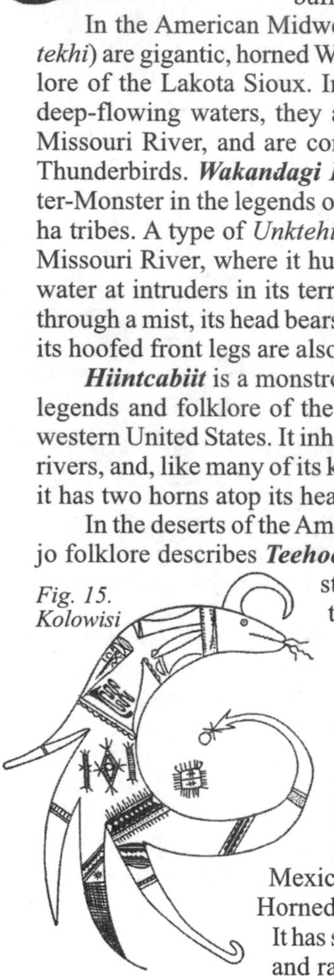

Tzeltal is a gigantic Horned Serpent in the mythology of the Chiapas Indians of southern Mexico. And **Kolowisi** is a great Horned Serpent in Zuni legend. It has sharp fins all over its body and razor-sharp teeth.

SACRED SERPENTS

Python was a monstrous female serpent born from the mud and slime that remained after the great flood of Deucalian. She dwelt in a chasm beside the Castellian Spring on the slopes of Mt. Parnassus, guarding an oracular cave of Gaea, until the sun-god Apollo killed her with his arrows and established his temple on the site. This battle was ceremonially reenacted annually in celebration of the founding of the Delphic Oracle, whose priestesses were called *Pythonesses*. And in Greek myth, a gigantic serpent named *Epirotes* guards Apollo's walled garden of **Dragons**, divinatory descendants of the Python of Delphi. From this legend, the name *python* was designated for the giant snakes of the Old World, some of which reach lengths of more than 30 feet. In fact, when classical authors wrote of Dragons or *Dracones,* they actually meant giant snakes—specifically pythons.

Fig. 16. Apollo slaying the Delphic Python

A sentient serpent in the Garden of Eden is described in the Bible in Genesis 3:1–5: "The Serpent was the most subtle of all the wild beasts that Yahweh God had made…." It has been vilified for tempting Eve to eat the fruit of the Tree of Knowledge, when it asked her if Yahweh had said she could eat from any of the trees. When she said no, that they were not to eat of the tree growing in the middle of the garden, under pain of death, the serpent replied: "You shall not surely die. God knows that on the day you eat of it, your eyes shall be opened, and you shall be as gods, knowing good and evil."[1] And this, of course, is exactly what happened. A fresco dating from 1291, in the chapel of the Abbave de Plaincourault, in France, depicts vividly the hallucinogenic *Amanita muscaria* mushroom as the infamous apple of Eden. The Serpent is usually shown in medieval religious art as a snakelike creature coiling about the Tree, but details vary over time. Early images portray it with the horse-like head of a typical Lake-Monster. Later depictions give it a human head, and sometimes even female breasts (a *Draconopede*). It may be shown with a crown, forelegs, or the wings and tail of a peacock. Eventually it came to represent all evil in the world, and was equated with the Devil.

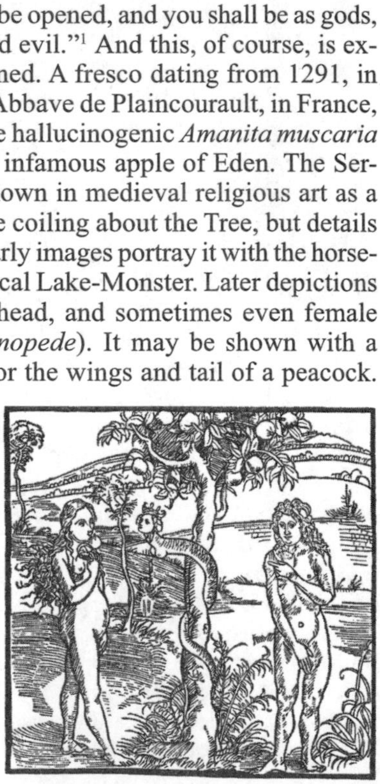

Fig. 17. The Serpent in the Garden of Eden by Albrecht Durer (1493)

Fig. 18. Ananta Sesha serving as Lord Vishnu's couch.

Ananta Sesha ("Infinite") is the thousand-headed cobra of Hindu myth. His movements churn the waters of the primal sea of milk, producing the sacred elixir of immorality. His mouths spit fire and his bite is poisonous. He will destroy the world at the end of the age, but for now his coils serve as a couch for the preserver-god, Vishnu, shading him with the spread hoods of Ananta's multitudinous heads. The son of Ananta Sesha, is **Vasuki**, the World-Serpent. When the gods churned the great Ocean of Milk to create the world, Vasuki was used as the rope.

Kaliya is the multiheaded King of the Serpents in Hindu mythology. This poisonous black monster dwells in the depths of the river Yamuna, emerging each night with a host of serpentine minions to ravage the countryside. After losing a battle with the god Krishna, Kaliya and his hordes are driven into the depths of the ocean.

Fig. 19.Kaliya defeated by Krishna

Nagas and **Naginis** are serpent-people of India. Nagas are male, and Naginis, female. They resemble humans from the waist up and snakes from the waist down. Sometimes they have multiple heads and varying colors. There are four classes of Naga—Heavenly, Divine, Earthly, and Hidden—all categorized according to their various functions (guarding the heavenly palace, giving rainfall, draining rivers, or guarding treasures, respectively). It is said that they will eventually destroy the world with fire. In Burma, Nagas are part serpent, part dragon, and part crocodile. They give rubies to those they favor and protect many royal people. In Indonesia, Thailand, and Malaysia, however, Nagas are giant black Water-Snakes or multiheaded Sea-Dragons that terrorize fishermen. Their images are often used as temple guardians. The name has been applied to the Indian cobra, *Naja naja*.

In Buddhist tradition, the King of the Nagas is **Muchalinda** (or *Vasuki*), a giant cobra that winds itself seven times around the Bo tree under which the Buddha meditates, spreading his hood to shelter the Buddha from a storm.

In Indonesian mythology, the gigantic King of the Serpents is **Naga Pahoda**, which dwells in the depths of the sea. When the god Batara Guru scattered dust to form land, Naga Pahoda rose up and squeezed it into many scattered islands.

Dewi Sesir is a Balinese sea goddess shown in carvings as a winged serpent with a woman's face and breasts.

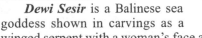

Fig. 21. Nagini

Shah-Mar is the great King of the Snakes in Armenian folklore. He dwells in a cavern high in the mountains, attended by many servant serpents.

In the folklore of Papua, New Guinea, an enormous serpent called **Make Make** represents the sun-god, Wunekau.

SUPER SERPENTS

In the annals of cryptozoology, there have been numerous compelling reports, mostly from South America, of truly gigantic snakes. Because fossils have been found of immense prehistoric serpents—such as Garstin's Giant Snake (*Gigantophis garstini*), which is believed to have attained lengths of 35 feet or more—there is no a priori reason why such monsters could not exist. Indeed, because large constrictors such as boas, pythons, and anacondas continue to grow throughout their lives, the only theoretical limits to their size may be their life spans and the ability of their skeletal frames to support the sheer weight of such mass. The latter does not apply to aquatic serpents, such as anacondas, as the water supports their great bulk. Indeed, an enormous anaconda allegedly measured in the 1940s by a Columbian petroleum geologist was 37.5 feet long. *Gigantophis* first appeared approximately 40 million years ago in the southern Sahara, where Egypt and Algeria are now situated, and may have died out only as recently as 30,000 BCE. Known only from a small number of fossils, it may have preyed on the pig-sized ancestors of modern elephants.[2]

Fig. 22. Gigantophis

It is likely that many of the legends of cosmic serpents may, in fact, be based on human encounters with these very real creatures, such as the following.

*Fig. 23. **Sucuriju Gigante***

From the Amazon jungle of South America come reports of the **Sucuriju Gigante** ("Giant Snake"), also known as *Sucuri, Sucuruiú, Boiúna, Liboya, Jibóia*; or the Spanish *Matora,* meaning "Bull Eater." These truly gigantic anacondas have been sighted throughout the 20th century; some were claimed to reach lengths of 120 feet. And several explorers claim to have encountered and even killed monsters 60–80 feet long. On a 1907 mapping expedition of the Amazon, Colonel Percy Fawcett claimed to have shot and measured a 62-foot-long specimen, as illustrated here by Bernard Heuvelmans, the father of cryptozoology:[3]

Fig. 24. Col. Fawcett's encounter with a 62-ft anaconda (from a drawing by his son, Brian)

In 1922, Father Victor Heinz saw an immense serpent on the Amazon River, near the town of Obidos. He said it was at least 80 feet long, with a body as thick as an oil drum, and it raised a huge wake as it swam down the river. And painter Serge Bonacase told Huevelmans of killing a Sucuriju in 1947, in the swamps between the Rio Manso and the Rio Cristalino.[4] Its body measured more than 65 feet long, and its triangular head was 24" by 20". Similar sightings have been reported as recently as 1995, along with enormous tracks and shed skins. Several have supposedly been killed by natives, but bodies are always quickly disposed of.

Native folklore of Guiana tells of an enormous serpent called **Camoodi**. Sometimes mistaken for a huge fallen tree trunk, it is said to be the protector of the Camoodi Forests. Monstrous worms or serpents called **Sterpe** have been reported from Nicaragua. And in Brazil, gigantic anacondas that capsize canoes, cause floods, and kidnap women are known as **Mawadi**. Their

Queen is *Huito*, Mistress of the Waters.

But truly giant snakes are not confined to South America. Africa is said to be the habitat of **Pa Snakes**—gigantic serpents that prey upon elephants. When they eat an elephant, they do not spit out the bones for three years. This is clearly an exaggeration of the Reticulated Python (*Python reticulatus*), the record measured size of which is more than 33 feet long.

Fig. 25. Pa Snake attacking an elephant

The **Nguma-Monene** is a giant African snake with alligator-like ridges running down the length of its back. It has a forked tongue like a snake's, and is said to reach 130 feet in length. It is a constrictor that preys upon humans as well as animals. While on patrol over the African Congo in 1959, Belgian helicopter pilot, Col. Remy Van Lierde took this photo of a gigantic snake, 40–50 feet in length. It was dark brownish-green, with a white belly and a triangular head measuring about 3" by 2". As the helicopter approached, the snake reared up 10 feet in the air and looked as if it would strike at the helicopter if it flew any lower.[5]

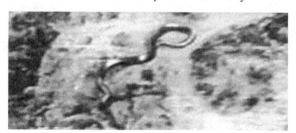

Fig. 26. Giant Congo snake photographed by Col. Remy Van Lierde, 1959.

The **Nyan**—also known as *Avagráh, Gara, Gráha,* or *Tanti-gáha*—is a monstrous, wormlike creature inhabiting the rivers and marshes of Bengal and Burma in India. It preys upon large animals, including elephants, coiling about them as a python does and dragging them under the water to be consumed. This is probably the same creature as the *Bu-rin*, a giant Burmese water-snake, 40–50 feet long. Said to be incredibly dangerous, it has attacked swimmers and even small boats.

In Japan, the monstrous *Serpent of Omi* plagued the region of Omi in Japan until it was slain by Prince Yamato Take, son of King Keiko.

And in North America, the Lakota Sioux have a legend of *Zuzeca* ("The Snake"), a massive, python-like serpent that is the source and patron of hidden things, concealed knowledge, lies, treachery, and deceit.

Fig. 27.
*Zuzeca by
Rosebud Elementary School*

the world's largest snake

Since the early 1900s, the Wildlife Conservation Society and the Bronx Zoo in New York City have offered a substantial reward for the delivery in good health of a live snake more than 30 feet long. The prize money—initially $1,000, and now up to $50,000—remains unclaimed.

According to *The Guinness Book of World Records*, the longest snake ever measured was a 39.4-foot reticulated python that was killed in 1912 on the Indonesian island of Sulawesi. A close second was a 38.3-foot African Rock Python (*Python sebae*) shot on Africa's Ivory Coast in 1932.

But in his 1931 book, *Snakes of the World,* the renowned herpetologist and former curator of the Bronx Zoo, Raymond Ditmars, writes, "In all of these years, in an endeavor to obtain record measurements [of reticulated pythons] from authoritative sources, the figures stand at 33 feet and another a few inches over 30 feet." Of the African rock python, Ditmars states, "It appears doubtful if this snake attains a length

of much over 20 feet and the average run of adult examples is 16 to 17 feet." And in a recent survey of more than 1,000 wild anacondas measured in Brazil, the largest was around 17 feet long and weighed 100 pounds.

The biggest snake ever held in captivity was the aptly named Colossus, a reticulated python at Pittsburgh's now-defunct Havilland Zoo. Upon his death in 1966, Colossus had reached a length of 28.5 feet and a weight of more than 300 pounds. He was succeeded by Samantha, a 26-foot reticulated python at the Bronx Zoo who died of old age in 2002. The current living record holder is Marci, a 25-foot reticulated python on display at the San Antonio Zoo.[6]

Oberon Zell

monster movies: cosmic serpents

The brilliant film adaptation, *The 7 Faces of Dr. Lao* (1964), based on the 1935 novel by Charles Finney, *The Circus of Dr. Lao*, includes the primordial Giant Serpent. Although many people thought that King Kong battled a huge prehistoric snake in the original 1933 movie, it is actually a *Tanystropheus*, a 20-ft-long Triassic lizard with a 10-foot-long neck. But in the 1976 remake, Kong does wrestle with a mighty serpent. *Conan the Barbarian* (1982) features a gigantic serpent guarding a temple treasure. *Thunder of the Gigantic Serpent* a.k.a. *Terror Serpent* (1988), tells of a pet snake that grows and grows. *Anaconda* (1997) and its 2004 sequel, *Anacondas: The Hunt for the Blood Orchid*, are based on the legend of the *Sucuriju Gigante*. A series of forgettable movies involving gigantic boas and pythons include: *Python* (2000), *Python II* (TV—2002), *Boa* a.k.a. *New Alcatraz* (2002), and, finally, the inevitable *Boa vs. Python* (TV—2004).

3. DRAGONS

By Ash "LeopardDancer" DeKirk

Th'old Dragon under ground
In straiter limits bound,
Not half so far casts his usurped sway,
And wrath to see his Kingdom fail,
Swindges the scaly Horrour of his foulded tail.
—John Milton,
On the Morning of Christ's Nativity

Ian Daniels

HAT IS A DRAGON? IN MODERN times the concept of the Dragon has become extremely stereotyped. What is the first thing that pops into your mind when you hear the word *Dragon*? Most likely it will be the winged, fire-breathing terror of European myth. But that is not all a Dragon can be, as we shall see. In many cases, snakes and Dragons are intertwined in the mythos of a culture. Dragons such as *Wurms* or *Wyrms* can be reminiscent of giant snakes. These are also known as Serpent-Dragons. The *Lindorm* or *Lindwurm* is a Wurm with a pair of wings. In other cases Dragons and lizards are intertwined. *Drakes* are Dragons that lack wings and look just like giant lizards. The *Wyvern* is a winged Dragon lacking forelimbs. And of course there is the typical, four-legged, winged variety. Winged serpents are just that—snakes with wings. Their wings may be feathered or webbed with skin, and they may have up to four sets of wings, though one is the norm. Hydra are Dragons with multiple heads. Most Dragons are considered scaly and reptilian, but there are Dragons that sport feathers and fur. Wherever man has dwelt, so there have been Dragons.

WESTERN DRAGONS

Dragons are a very common theme in European myth and legend. Vikings painted Dragons on their shields and carved Dragon heads on the prows of their longships. Dragons are especially prominent in heraldry. The heraldic Dragon is most often associated with King Arthur and was likely created by him. The Arthurian Dragon has four legs; the ribbed wings of a bat; the belly of a crocodile; eagle talons; and a serpentine tail. The heraldic Wyvern looks much like the Arthurian Dragon, except that it lacks front legs. Other heraldic Dragons have a wolflike head, the body of a serpent, eagle talons, bat-like wings, and a barbed tongue and tail.

In earlier times most European Dragons were actually symbolic of good things, much as their Asian cousins were and are. However, in medieval times the Dragon became symbolic of all things evil. It repre-

sented the devil, hell, sin, darkness, destruction, war, greed, and so on. Following is a small sampling of European Dragons.

Aitvaras—A Lithuanian Dragon that can shape-shift into a black cat. It was seen by some as a source of good luck and by others as a demonic being. The Aitvaras would attach itself to a family or person and bring good luck and fortune to the household. Unfortunately, many people viewed association with the Aitvaras as a form of sorcery or witchcraft.

Alklha (or *Alicha, Arakho*)—In the Buriat mythology of Siberia, this Dragon is so huge that its black wings, when spread across the sky, allow no light to reach the Earth. Periodically it attempts to devour the sun or the moon, causing an eclipse until the heat forces it to disgorge them. The craters on the moon are the marks of its teeth.

Fig. 1. Alklha by Tracy Swangler

Amphitere—A legless winged serpent with a dragon-like head, usually found in Wales and England. They have eyes like a peacock's tail, and wings that sparkle or glitter. The wings may be feathered, or membranous like a bat's. Amphiteres are 6–9 feet long and covered in heavy scales. They were reputed to possess great wisdom and knowledge, as well as some associated power, such as the ability to hypnotize. Many also guarded hordes of treasure, but, unlike typical treasure-hording dragons, they took this task out of obligation rather than out of a liking of shiny things. It was said that armed men would grow from the teeth of an Amphitere planted in fertile ground, and would be absolutely loyal to the sower.

Fig. 2. Amphitere by Ian Daniels

Balaur—A large Dragon of Romanian folklore and fairy tales, it has fins, feet, and multiple serpent heads (usually three, sometimes seven or even 12). It represents evil and must be defeated by Făt-Frumos in order to release the Princess. The term is now applied to a harmless Romanian snake, *Coluber jugularis balaur*.

Bolla (or *Bullar*)—A serpentine monster in the folklore of southern Albania. It has four legs, small wings, and faceted silver eyes. When it wakes on St George's Day (April 23) from its year-long hibernation, it devours the first human it sees. After 12 years, it metamorphoses into a horrific, fire-breathing flying Dragon with nine tongues called **Kulshedra.** Sometimes described as an immense hairy woman with pendulous breasts, Kulshedra causes drought, requiring human sacrifice in propitiation.

Carthiginian Serpent—The Roman army confronted this giant Serpent-Dragon along the Bagrada River. It was about 120 feet long and dwelled in the river. The serpent was slain by the army, and the skin of the giant beast kept in the temple on Capitol Hill until about 133 BCE, after which it disappeared.

Chudo-Yudo—A monstrous, multiheaded, fire-breathing Dragon of Russian folklore. Considered the controller of the waters, it was propitiated at times of drought. Its mother is the wicked Witch, Baba-Yaga, and its brother is Koshchei the Deathless.

Fig. 3. Chudo-Yudo

Cirein Croin—These great Sea-Serpents of Scottish myth are so large that they can swallow whales whole. They have greyish scales and a great crest upon their heads. Indeed, *Cirein Croin* means "Grey Crest."

Dahak—In the Zoroastrian mythology of Persia, this is an evil three-headed Dragon determined to destroy all that is worthy in the world. Its body is composed of lizards and scorpions. Chained beneath a mountain by the hero Thraotona (in some versions, Atar), it will break free at the end of time and wreak havoc upon the Earth. In Islamic mythology, this creature is called **Dabbat** or *Dabbatu 'L-Ard*.

Fig. 4. Dahak

Derketo—A whale-monster of Babylonian myth with the foreparts of a Dragon. It was created by the goddess Ishtar, and its birth caused the great flood.

Y Ddraig Goch—The Red Dragon of Wales, national emblem of the country. Its antagonist is *Gwiber* ("Viper"), a winged white Dragon.

Fig. 5. The Red Dragon of Wales

Dragon of Ladon—A scaly monstrosity with 100 heads, it was placed by the goddess Hera in the Garden of the Hesperides to guard the sacred golden apples of immortality. Heracles killed it during his 11th Labor, and Hera subsequently placed it in the heavens as the constellation Draco.

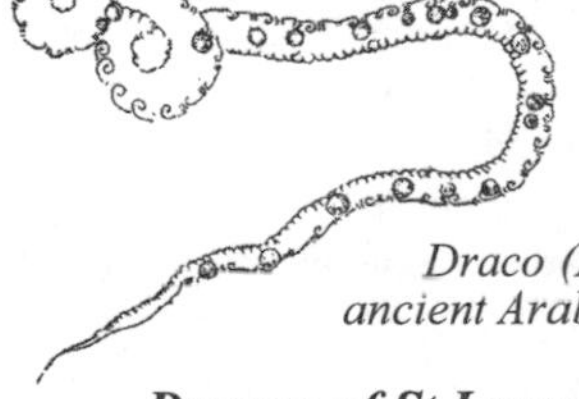

Fig. 6. The Constellation Draco (Al-Thu'ban), from an ancient Arabian manuscript.

Dragon of St Leonard's Forest—A Dragon reported to have ravaged the country around Horsham, in Sussex, England, in 1614.

Dragon of Wantley—According to the manuscript known as *Percy's Relics*, this monstrous Dragon plagued the region of Wantly (present Wharncliffe) in Yorkshire, England. It was vanquished by More of Mere's Hall, who had a special suit of armor made that was studded with sharp spikes. He crept up to the Dragon and gave it a swift kick in the rear, whereupon it attacked him in rage and impaled itself on the spikes. This story is virtually identical to that of the *Lambton Worm* (below), which would seem to be the original version.

Fig. 7. The Dragon of Wantley

Drake—A wingless Dragon or *Lindorm* in Swedish folklore, this term may apply as well to Elemental Dragons, such as Fire-Drakes, Sea-Drakes, Ice-Drakes, and so on. It is also sometimes used for male Dragons.

Fafnir—An evil wingless Dragon of Norse and Teutonic mythology. Starting life as a greedy dwarf, he was metamorphosed into a hideous Dragon to guard his stolen hoard of cursed gold. Fafnir was killed by the hero Sigfreid (or Sigurd), who dug a trench across the Dragon's path, hid within, and thrust his sword up into the monster's heart when Fafnir passed over. Later, cooking the dragon's heart over a fire, the hero's hand was burned by a splash of blood. As

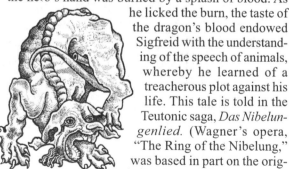

he licked the burn, the taste of the dragon's blood endowed Sigfreid with the understanding of the speech of animals, whereby he learned of a treacherous plot against his life. This tale is told in the Teutonic saga, *Das Nibelungenlied.* (Wagner's opera, "The Ring of the Nibelung," was based in part on the original epic poem.)

Fig. 8. Fafnir

Gargouille (or *Guivre*)—A great Dragon that lived in the marshes of the Seine River and ravaged the countryside around the town of Rouen, France. Associated with woodlands, rivers, streams, and deep wells, it was particularly noted for causing waterspouts and upsetting boats to drown and devour the boaters and fishermen. The Guivre is especially toxic; wherever one dwells so also dwells death and destruction. On an interesting note, the mere sight of a naked human is enough to scare the wits out of the Gargouille. The original Gargouille was slain in the 7th century by St Romain, then Bishop of Rouen. He tied two criminals to stakes to bait the Dragon, and when

Fig. 9. Gargoyle on Notre Dam

it appeared, he transfixed it with his crucifix, tied his bishop's stole around its neck, and led it docilely into Rouen, where it was killed by the townsfolk. From that time on, all monstrous building decorations, antefixes, and waterspouts have been called *Gargoyles.*

Goryschche (from Russian, *gora,* "mountain")—An immense, 12-headed female Dragon of Russian folklore, she stole hundreds of young men and women to feed her monstrous brood. The hero Dobrynya found her lair when the Dragon was out and killed her offspring. Goryschche pursued him, and in the ensuing fight, he cut off 11 of her heads, sparing her life on the promise that she would leave the people alone. This pledge she quickly broke by seizing the princess. Dobrynya returned to the Dragon's cave and slaughtered all the baby Dragons as well as the furious mother upon her return. Finding himself stranded in the midst of a lake of her poisonous blood, he called upon Mother Earth, whereupon a chasm opened and drained the lake. Dobrynya then found the Dragon's treasure hoard and released the captive citizens, including the princess, whom he subsequently married.

Hordeshryde—A mighty, treasure-hoarding Dragon of Norse and English mythology that was slain by the hero Beowulf in the eponymous 8th-century Anglo-Saxon epic. Unfortunately, the Dragon's poison killed Beowulf in return.

Fig. 10. Hordeshryde

Illuyankas (or *Illujanka*)—A vast chaos Dragon in the mythology of the ancient Hittites of Mesopotamia. Its serpentine body sports numerous heads. There are two versions of its defeat and slaughter by the gods.

Koshei the Deathless (or *Kaschchei*; from *kost,* "bone")—A terrible Dragon of Russian folklore, whose soul is hidden in an egg inside a duck within a rabbit on a remote island, rendering him invincible. He is undone, however, when he captures the princess Vasilissa, who persuades him to reveal his secret. She passes this information on to the hero Bulat, who recovers the egg and smashes it on the Dragon's forehead, killing him instantly.

*Fig. 11. The hidden heart
of Koshei the Deathless
by Tracy Swangler*

Kundrav—A gigantic Dragon in ancient Sumerian mythology, so vast that its lower parts can remain in the ocean while its upper parts touch the clouds. The guardian of another and even more terrible Dragon, Kundrav was a destroyer of land and people, but was eventually slain by the hero Keresaspa. A similar story is told in Vedic myth of India, but the Dragon's name is *Gandareva*.

Fig. 12. Kundrav by Tracy Swangler

Lambton Worm—A famous medieval *Orm* from Northumbria, England. According to the legend, the young heir to Lampton Hall, John Lambton, caught a small, glistening black, eel-like creature when he was fishing. He described the catch as having the head of a salamander, with needle-sharp teeth and nine holes along either side of its mouth (a feature unique to lamprey eels). Its skin secreted a viscous, sticky fluid. Lambton tossed the repulsive thing into an ancient well, which thereafter became known as *Worms Well*. Later, while he was off in the Holy Land fighting in the Crusades, the creature grew to enormous size, eventually emerging from the well to ravage the countryside. It coiled around the mound that became known as Worm Hill, forming ridges that remain to this day. When Lambton returned seven years later and discovered the devastation, he vowed to destroy the monster. Upon the advice of a local Witch, he had a special suit of armor made, covered with sharp, double-edged spikes.

Fig. 13. The Lambton Wurm

Wearing this, he confronted the beast, and as the enraged worm coiled around him, the blades sliced it until it was weakened enough for Lambton to kill it.

Lotan (or *Lothan*)—A vast, seven-headed primordial Dragon of chaos in ancient Mesopotamian mythology. Called "the coiling serpent, the fleeing serpent, the powerful with the seven heads," it was slain by the Canaanite god Baal in an epic battle. After the Israelites conquered the region of Palestine in approximately 1000 BCE, they incorporated the legend of the Lotan into their own culture, renaming the beast *Leviathan*. However, the seven heads suggests the same creature known to the Greeks as the *Hydra*, which is certainly based on the giant squid (*Architeuthis*).

*Fig. 14. Lotan
or Mušhuššu*

Mušhuššu (or *Musmahhu*)—A three- or seven-headed Dragon of Sumerian myth, slain by the god Nigirsu. It served under Tiamat in ancient Babylon, and was identified with the constellation *Hydra*.

Paiste (or *Peiste*)—This huge, 11-foot-long Wurm of Irish myth was considered an ancient dragon, in existence since the beginning of the world. He has ram's horns curling around ox-like ears; long fangs full of venom; and ebony, armored scales the size of dinner plates. He was eventually bound to the depths of Loch Foyle by Saint Murrough.

Pisuhand (or *Pukis*, *Pukys*, *Puuk*)—In the folklore of the Baltic states, these are small, serpentine dragons, only 2 feet long, that fiercely guard each house and its treasures. They take the form of cats on the ground, but Dragons when they fly through the air. In Estonia, it is called **Tulihänd**. In some districts it has wings and flies through the air trailing fire.

*Fig. 15. Tulihänd
by Tracy Swangler*

Sea Serpents—Long, sea-dwelling Serpent-Dragons that move with a vertical, rather than horizontal, movement, as true serpents do. They have Dragon-like heads and may or may not have horns. Some Sea-Serpents sport the remnants of flippers.

Serpent of the Reuss—A Serpent-Dragon of Swiss legend, reported in 1566 as having four feet with great claws. It terrorized the countryside around Reuss by attacking and devouring livestock in the fields.

Smok Wawelski—The Dragon of Wawel Hill, on the banks of the Vistula River in Krakow, Poland. It lived in a cave under the hill and ravaged the land unless it was given a monthly sacrifice of a young maiden. When the only maiden left was the King Krak's daughter, Wanda, her father offered her hand

Fig. 16. Smok Wawelski

in marriage to anyone who could vanquish the beast. An apprentice cobbler named Szewczyk Dratewka stuffed a lamb with sulfur and left it by the cave entrance. Upon eating it, the dragon was consumed by thirst, which he slaked in the river. When the water hit the sulfur the dragon exploded, and Szewczyk married the princess.

Tiamet—The great cosmic World-Serpent or Dragon of ancient Mesopotamian mythology, equated with salt water and the Milky Way. She has a vast, invincible body, with two forelegs, two great horns on her head, and an enormous tail. In the Babylonian epic, the *Enuma*

Fig. 17. Tiamet and Marduk

Elish, she and her consort Apsu/Abzu (personifying fresh water) create the heavens and Earth and engender the gods, who rebel against them. Tiamet is slain by Marduk, and her body dismembered to provide lands and stars. Her flowing blood becomes rivers.

Tarasque—A ferocious amphibious River-Dragon of the Rhone Valley in southern France, where it was prone to devouring virgins. Larger than an ox, it had six legs, the head of a lion, the paws of a bear, and a scaly body with a long, serpentine tail ending in a sharp barb. The hard, leathery shell on its back was covered with spikes. Said to be the progeny of *Leviathan* and a *Bonnocon*, it was subdued by St. Martha, who tied her belt around its neck and led it docilely back into the town of Nerlue, where the villagers killed it with stones and spears. Afterward, the town's name was changed to Tarascon, and annual processions continue to commemorate this event to this day. A Spanish derivation, called *Tarasca*, is paraded in effigy on the feast day of Corpus Christi in Redondela, Pontevedra, with small children seated inside it. The

Fig. 18. Tarasque

Tarasque closely resembles an *ankylosaur* or a *glyptodont*. However, Peter Costello suggests that the original animal may have been a crocodile.

Tatzelwurm—A Dragon of the Bavarian, Austrian, and Swiss Alps, its name means "wurm with claws." It is also called *Stollenwurm* or "Hole-Dwelling Wurm." In the French Alps it is called *Arassas*. The Tatzelwurm has the head of a cat, a long, snaky body, and two clawed forepaws. Some accounts give the Tatzelwurm hind limbs, whereas others do not. Likewise, some accounts give it smooth skin, and others feature it having small scales. One of the Tatzelwurm's most interesting abilities is that of

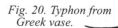

Fig. 19. Arassas by Ian Daniels

being able to jump extremely high and far, earning it the nickname *Springwurm*. Similar such creatures have been reported further south than the Alps. The last reported sighting of a Stollenwurm was in Palermo, Sicily, in 1954. (See Chapter 1: "The Baleful Basilisk.")

Typhon—A giant fire-breathing Dragon of Greek myth, with 9, 50, or 100 snakelike heads whose eyes blazed fire. Typhon was said to be taller than a mountain, with serpentine legs and arms and bird wings. He was eventually overcome by Zeus in the Battle of the Titans and imprisoned in Tartarus, deep beneath Mt. Aetna, where his paroxysms are said to cause typhoons. On *Echinda* he fathered such monsters as *Cerberus*, the *Chimera*, the *Hydra*, the *Sphinx*, the *Nemean Lion*, and the vulture-eagle that ate Prometheus' liver.

Fig. 20. Typhon from Greek vase.

Vishap—A fearsome Dragon of Armenian legend, said to reside at the top of Mt. Ararat. Its blood is so poisonous that any sword or spear dipped into it will render that weapon fatal, even if it makes only the tiniest scratch.

Wode Worm of Linton—A serpentine Dragon or *Orm* in local folklore of northern England. It was vanquished by a hero who thrust a block of burning peat down its throat, thus burning the monster to death from the inside.

EASTERN DRAGONS

Among the Chinese and the Japanese, Dragons are a most potent symbol of the beneficent, rain-giving powers of the gods. They are symbols of power, royalty, and sovereignty. In China, the Dragon is one of the four great protective beasts of the country, along with the Unicorn, the Tortoise, and the Phoenix.

Asian Dragons in general have snaky bodies, horselike heads, and four paws with three to four great curving claws apiece. More elaborate descriptions by the scholar Wang Fu during the Han dynasty (206 BCE–220 CE) add the horns of a stag, the head of a camel, the eyes of a demon, the neck of a

Fig. 21. Eastern Dragon

snake, the belly of a clam, the scales of a carp, the talons of an eagle, the feet of a tiger, and the ears of an ox. Asian Dragons are said to have a total of 117 scales. It is believed that 81 of these scales are imbued with *yang* energy, the active, dominant, masculine force, and the remaining 36 scales are imbued with *yin* energy, the passive, submissive, feminine force. Many Asian Dragons obtain part of their power from a pearl—called a "pearl of wisdom" or "dragon jewel"—that they keep tucked under their chins, under their tongues, or embedded in their foreheads.

Many have the ability to change shape as well, acquiring the form of a human or a more mundane animal, such as a bird or a fish. Dragons turned human or animal are always exquisite specimens of adopted species. Humans and animals may also turn

into Dragons through various means. Mages and sages may spend a lifetime seeking the means to turn into one of these great and wise creatures. The Dragon's Gate, located in the Yellow River, is a place where fish may be changed into Dragons.

Fig. 22. Chinese Dragon

Chinese Dragons (and most other Asian Dragons) live for millennia and undergo many changes throughout their lifetimes. A Chinese Dragon is not considered fully mature until it reaches the age of 3,000 years. A baby Dragon is hatched from a brilliant, gem-like egg that was laid some 1,000 years previously. The newly hatched Dragon resembles a very large water-snake or eel. When it attains the age of 500 years, the hatchling Dragon will gain a head like a carp's. During this stage, the youngling Dragon is known as a *Kiao*. At the age of 1,500 years, the young Dragon will have grown four stubby legs with four claws on each paw, an elongated head and tail, and an abundant beard. At this point it is called *Kiao-lung*. By the time two millennia have passed, the Dragon will have gained horns and a new name, *Kioh-lung*.

During the final millennium it will grow out its wings. Finally, at the age of 3,000 years, the fully grown Dragon is named *Ying-lung*. When most people today think of Chinese (or Japanese) Dragons, these last two forms are the ones that come most readily to mind.

For the most part, Japanese Dragons resemble the Chinese versions in appearance and size. Japanese Dragons tend to be more serpentine, however, and they have only three claws as opposed to the four or five of the Chinese Dragons. Japanese Dragons are the natural enemies of the *Kitsune*, or fox spirits. Many other Asian cultures feature Dragons in their myths and lore. These Dragons tend to be more Western in both nature and appearance than those of Chinese or Japanese myth. They may have four legs, bat-like wings, and a stockier build—a typical Western Dragon—or they may be more like the *Wurms* of the West—giant serpents with gargonesque heads. Following is a sampling of Asian Dragons.

Azhi Dahaki—One of the greatest of the Persian Dragons was Azhi Dahaki (also known as *Az Dahak* or *Azhi Dahaka*). In the Zoroastrian creation myth, this Dragon was created by Angra Mainyu, the "father of lies," in an effort to rid the world of righteousness. Azhi Dahaki is often depicted as a three-headed, winged serpent. His

Fig. 23. Azhi Dahaki

body was thought to be filled with all manner of poisonous creatures, such as spiders, vipers, and scorpions. His three heads represent Pain, Anguish, and Death. Each head has three eyes and three pairs of fangs. His wings are so vast that, when spread, they cover the sky. When the end of the world comes, Azhi Dahaki will break free of the bonds constraining him and will devour a third of all the people and animals that dwell on the Earth before he is finally subdued. Azi Dahaka Dragons make an appearance in the game *Final Fantasy X*.

Barong—A hideous, bug-eyed Dragon with a long, twisted body, featured in Balinese folk drama as the adversary of Ranga the Witch.

Chiao—The supreme Dragon of the Earth in Chinese mythology.

Fig. 24. Barong

Chi Lung Wang ("Fire Engine Dragon-King")—A beneficent celestial Dragon of China, whose duty was to ensure the provision of sufficient household water, especially in case of fire.

Cynoprosopi—These Dragons are akin to the *Ying-Long* of China. They are covered with shaggy fur, and have dog-like heads, muzzles with profuse beards, and bat-like wings.

Dragon-Horse—Dragon-Horses resemble horses but have a dragon's head and scales instead of fur. Although they don't have wings, some of them are able to fly. Most are water dwellers. These creatures were considered divine messengers. A Dragon-Horse was said to have emerged from the Yellow River and given the Emperor the circular diagram representing the Yin-Yang. A Dragon-Horse was also said to have emerged from the River Lao and revealed the eight trigrams of the *I-Ching*. In the anime series *Inuyasha*, the wolf-demon Sesshoumaru travels in a chariot pulled by a two-headed Dragon-Horse.

Fig. 25. *Dragon-Horse*

The Dragon-Kings—The five immortal Chinese Dragon-Kings dwell under the sea in elaborate crystal palaces. One Dragon-King is chief over all, and the other four represent one of the four cardinal directions: North, South, East, and West. Their names are *Ao Ch'in*, *Ao Jun*, *Ao Kuang* and *Ao Shun*. The Dragon-Kings answer to the Jade Emperor, who tells them where to distribute the rains. According to legend, the Dragon-Kings are 3–5 miles long, with shaggy legs and tails and whiskered muzzles. Their slinky, serpentine bodies are covered in golden scales. In the folk legend *Journey to the West*, by Wu Cheng'en, the Great Sage Equaling Heaven (also called Son Goku or the Monkey King) terrorizes the Dragon-Kings before being captured and trapped underneath the Mountain of Five Elements. The Dragon-Kings show up later in the story to assist Goku in his trials, attempting to protect the T'ang Priest Sanzang. In addition to the four ocean-dwelling Dragon-Kings, there are a few others, including *Lung Wang*—the fifth Dragon-King and the master of Fire. *Pai Lung*, yet another of the Dragon-Kings, is unique in that he is all white. A temple on Mount Yang Suchow in Kiangsu contains a tablet recording the legend of his birth.

Fig. 26. *Dragon King*

Fe-lian and ***Shen-yi***—These are rival Dragons. *Fe-lian* is a wind-god who carries a bag of wind. This

Fig. 27. *Falkor*

Fig. 28. *Jurik*

notorious troublemaker is watched over by *Shen-yi*, the Great Archer. Fe-lian and Shen-yi balance one another.

Fuku-Ryu—These are Dragons of luck. They end life in the wingless Kiao-Lung phase, but they can fly nonetheless. Falkor of *The Neverending Story* is a Fuku-Ryu.

Fu-T'sang Lung—Subterranean Dragons that are guardians of great wealth and great wisdom. They are also called *Treasure-Dragons*. The best modern example of these is found in the emblem for the popular *Mortal Kombat* game series (shown here).

Gong-Gong—A huge and terrible black Dragon of Chinese mythology, it nearly destroyed the heavens and the Earth with the mighty horn on its head. In its hatred of the celestial emperor, Yeo, it tore up a mountain, unleashing a world-flooding deluge. Then it ripped open the sky and dimmed the light of the sun and moon. This sounds like a mythologized account of a vast volcanic eruption in ancient times.

Gou Mang and ***Rou Shou***—These are two of China's cosmic Dragons that serve as messengers of the gods. They are *Ti'en-Lung* Dragons (see below). The Dragon of the East, Gou Mang is said to bring good fortune and longevity, and is a herald of the coming of spring. As Dragon of the West, Rou Shou heralds the onset of autumn and presages ill fortune and death.

Jurik—A fire-breathing cosmic Dragon in the folklore of Sunda, Indonesia. It is equated with the meteors and comets that blaze their fiery trails across the night sky.

Ka-Ryu—The Ka-Ryu is among the smallest of the Japanese Dragons. It has fiery red scales and ends its growth in the *Kiao-Lung* phase.

Kiau—A serpentine Dragon living in the marshes along the Chien-Tang River in China. It plagued fishermen until it was killed by a local hero in the year 1129.

Kih Tiau—A Sea-Dragon of Chinese folklore, believed to secrete a substance similar to the ambergris of the sperm whale, which was sold as a preservative in 19th-century markets of Canton and Fouchow.

Leongalli—A Mongolian Dragon with a serpentine body and a leonine head and forequarters.

Li-lung—Benevolent Dragons of earth, wind, and water, they are said to ascend into the heavens in the form of a typhoon or waterspout.

Orochi (also *Eight-Forked Serpent of Koshi, Koshi Dragon, Dragon of Izumo, Yamata Dragon*)—

A vast *Hydra*-esque Japanese Dragon with eight heads and eight tails. According to legend, its gigantic body stretched across eight hills and valleys, and entire forests grew upon its vast back. It terrorized the people of Izumo province for years, kidnapping and eating people along the Koshi Road and demanding an annual sacrifice of a princess. It was finally slain by the hero

Fig. 29. Orochi, Dragon of Koshi

Takehaya Susanowo, who got it drunk on sake (rice beer) and then chopped off each of its heads. He discovered in one of its tails a magnificent enchanted sword, *Ame-no-Murakumo*, which has been passed down ever since as the Imperial Sword of Japan.

P'eng-niao—These Bird-Dragons are rare in Chinese myth. They have the head of a Dragon and the wings and lower body of a bird; or, they may have a completely serpentine body with feathered scales, and birdlike wings, legs, and feet. The Japanese version is called **Tobi-Tatsu** or **Hai-Ryu.**

Fig. 30. Hai-Ryu

Pi-hsi—This chimeric Dragon is Lord of the Rivers. Pi-hsi has the shell of an armored tortoise and the feet, tail, and head of a Dragon. A modern representation of this Dragon shows up in the *Final Fantasy* game series as the giant *Adamantoise* enemies.

Ryo-Wo (or *Ryujin*)—One of the Japanese Dragon-Kings. He is in charge of the Tidal Jewels, which control the tides of the world. He dwells in *Ryugu*, a magickal jeweled palace at the bottom of the sea, from which he controls the tides that flow in and out through his vast mouth. Ryo-Wo is credited with giving the jellyfish its shape. His beautiful daughter was won by the hero Fire Fade, or Prince Hoori, and thus he became the legendary ancestor of the emperors of Japan.

Shin-Lung ("Spiritual Dragon")—The beautiful, multicolored, five-toed Imperial Dragon of China. He brings the wind-borne rains for the benefit of human-

Fig. 31. Shin-Lung

ity. Only the Emperor of China was allowed to wear his image; others were forbidden, under penalty of death.

Tatsu—These Japanese Dragons are said to be descended from a primitive variety of three-toed Chinese Dragon. The Tatsu are more closely linked with the sea than with the rains, as Japan is less likely to suffer from devastating droughts than China. Also a constellation of the Japanese Zodiac, it is associated with the little fish called the Seahorse.

Ti'en-Lung—The *Ti'en-lung* are the guardians and supporters of the celestial palaces of the gods.

Ti-Lung—The celestial Water-Dragon of Chinese mythology, who controls the running waters of rivers and streams.

Fig. 32. Ti'en-Lung

Ukasima Dragon—A great, white-scaled Dragon that dwells in the Ukasima Lake at Yama-shiro, near Kyoto. It is said that every 50 years, the Dragon ascends from the lake and takes the form of a golden songbird or *O-Goa-Cho*. Its mournful songs, reminiscent of the calls of a wolf, bring only sadness and misery to the land. The sight or sound of this creature was a portent of disaster and ill fortune. The Ukasima Dragon was usually a herald for severe drought. The last reported sighting of the O-Goa-Cho was in April of 1834. Widespread famine and an outbreak of the plague followed this last sighting of the Ukasima Dragon.

Yellow Dragon—In Chinese mythology, there are two famous Yellow Dragons. The first is honored for having brought the eight trigrams of the *I-Ching* to humanity. The second is a terrible predator who is vanquished by the hero Lu Tung-pin, one of the eight Immortals. According to the myth, the Yellow Dragon became the Huanghe River in Central China.

Ying-Lung—These Dragons are rather unique in that they have fur instead of scales, and feathered wings instead of the membranous, bat-like wings of most Dragons. They are guardians of the waters of the Earth and the clouds of Heaven. Nall and Ruby from the Playstation games *Lunar: Silver Star Story Complete* and *Lunar 2: Eternal Blue* are good examples of Ying-Lung.

Fig. 33. Ying-Lung

DRAGONS OF THE AMERICAS

What do you think of when you hear the word Dragon? Probably Europe or China? But Dragons occur in the lore and myths of other parts of the world with just as great a frequency as they do in those two cultures. Dragons abound in the stories of the Native cultures of the Americas. Surely you have heard of the Aztec god *Quetzalcoatl*? Quetzalcoatl and his Mayan predecessor, *Kulkulcan*, are types of Dragons similar to the *Amphiteres* of European myth. An even older variation of this feathered Dragon is *Palulukon*.

Dragons of every variety roam the wilds of the Americas. If you live in the U.S., it's likely that you have Dragons in the ancient (or not so ancient) lore of your home state. And if you live in Central or South America, then your local folklore is likely rife with them. Here is a sampling of American Dragons:

The Ancient One—This **Sea-Serpent** of Piute myth dwells in Lake Pyramid. The Ancient One enjoys snagging people from the shore and drowning them. Whenever the Piute see a whirlpool in Lake Pyramid they avoid it, as it means the Ancient One is at large and looking for victims.

Az-I-Wu-Gum-Ki-Mukh-Ti—This Dragon of Inuit myth has black scales, a walrus's head, a dog's body, legs, and feet, and a whale fluke for a tail. This immense beast can sink ships with one blow from its tail and is much feared by the Inuit fishermen.

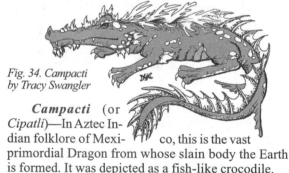

Fig. 34. Campacti by Tracy Swangler

Campacti (or *Cipatli*)—In Aztec Indian folklore of Mexico, this is the vast primordial Dragon from whose slain body the Earth is formed. It was depicted as a fish-like crocodile.

Chac—This Dragon of Mayan myth controls the rains and rules over all the waters. He requires a sacrifice in order that the summer rains might come, but he repays human sacrifices with his own blood. Chac is similar to the Asian Dragons. He has a long, serpentine body covered in fish scales, and catfish whiskers at the end of a tapered snout. Stag horns and deerlike ears adorn his crocodilian head. Chac is often depicted holding his lightning axe in one paw.

Fig. 35. Chac

Fig. 36. Faery Dragon by Tracy Swangler

Faery Dragon—Also called *Fey Dragon* or *Penny Dragon*, this Dragon is prevalent in South America. It ranges from the size of a mouse to up to 1 foot in length. Although Faery Dragons resemble classical Dragons of Europe, there are several important differences between the two. Faery Dragons sport two sets of wings of either the dragonfly or butterfly variety. Also, they have a longer, more tapered snout, large, iridescent eyes, and coloring that blends in with their surroundings in the same manner as certain moths. But if the light hits it just right, the Faery Dragon's hide will shine with a rainbow of colors.

Gaasyendietha—A huge Dragon of Seneca myth believed to have come from a meteorite that fell from the heavens and crashed into the Earth. For this reason it is also known as the *Meteor Dragon*. The Gaasyendietha dwells in rivers and lakes.

Iemisch—This Patagonian Dragon is much like the *Tatzelwurm* of Europe. It has a serpentine body with the forequarters of a fox. The Iemisch uses its body to ensnare victims and crush them as a boa or python does.

Ihuaivulu—This South American Dragon dwells in volcanoes. It has a slinky, serpentine body with burnished copper and red scales. The Ihuaivulu is a South American version of the *Hydra* and sports seven heads. As a volcano dweller, it can breathe fire.

Fig. 37. Piasa

Piasa— The name means "Destroyer." This Dragon is a hodgepodge of animal parts, much like the Asian Dragons. It is said to have the head of a bear, the horns of an elk, the scales of a fish, the legs of a bear, and the claws of an eagle. The Piasa also has a mane around its head and shoulders, and sports a tail that is at least 50 feet long and can wrap around its body three times. The Native Americans call this Dragon *Stormbringer* or *Thunderer*. (See Chapter 7: "Piasa and Manticore.")

Pal-rai-yuk—An Alaskan Dragon that has six legs on a long, snaky body and spikes running along its spine. The Pal-rai-yuk lives in the rivers and waters of Alaska; Inuit peoples would paint its picture on their canoes as a ward against the fearsome beast's attentions.

Palulukon—These Dragons are part of the plumed serpent family of *Amphiteres*, along with the Dragon-gods of Mesoamerica. Although they are powerful Dragons, they are neither good nor bad—they just are. The Palulukon represent the element of water, and are weather-workers in charge of bringing the rains. It is said that the world is carried through the cosmic ocean on the backs of two of these colossal beasts. If mistreated, the Palulukon can wreak much damage by unleashing natural disasters such as droughts and earthquakes.

Fig. 38. Quetzalcoatl

Quetzalcoatl—The Aztec feathered serpent-god, ruler of the winds and rains as well as knowledge and the finer crafts and arts. The Mayans called him *Kulkulkan*, and to the Mixtecs he was known as *Lord Nine Winds*. Quetzalcoatl is credited with creating the calendrical system. Other names for this well-known specimen of the *Amphitere* family are *Ehecatl* and *Lord of the Dawn*. Quetzalcoatl has multicolored scales and feathers. He is often depicted soaring through the sky, creating a rainbow.

The serpent-god was also known to take the form of a human on occasion. It was believed that Quetzalcoatl had departed from this world for the East, traveling on a raft made from serpents, and would one day return. The Aztecs viewed the coming of Cortez and his Spaniards as the return of the Great Plumed One. Thus a mere handful of Spaniards overcame many times their number of Aztec warriors.

DRAGONS OF AFRICA AND OCEANIA

The Dragons of Africa and Oceania tend to be a hodge-podge of all the Dragons previously mentioned, and include *Amphiteres*, *Wurms*, *Drakes*, and *Sea-Serpents*, among others. Here is a sampling of African and Oceanian Dragons:

Bida—A giant *Wurm* of West African Soniniki myth. It circled the city of Wagadu and blessed its inhabitants with gold in exchange for an annual sacrifice of a maiden. She was chosen each year by lottery, until the hero Mamadi Sefe Dekote chopped off its head to rescue his beloved.

Bujanga—A huge protector-Dragon in the folklore of Java and West Malaysia. Dwelling in the jungle, it knows all forest lore and understands the speech of all creatures.

Dragons of Ethiopia (also called *Pa Snakes*)—Great serpentine Dragons, up to 35 feet long, with one or two pairs of wings. They are said to prey on elephants; when they eat one, they do not spit out the bones for three years. They may be derived from the Nile Crocodile (*Crocodylus niloticus*) and the Reticulated Python (*Python reticulatus*), both of which may reach that size (although neither has wings).

Fig. 39. Dragon of Ethiopia

Kongamato—A *Wyvern* of Zambia. It is a small Dragon with a wingspan of only 3–4 feet, and a tapered muzzle full of sharp teeth. It is covered in leathery, reddish-brown skin. Living in the Jiundu swamps, its favorite pastime is swooping down and capsizing boats.

Fig. 40. Kongamato

(See Chapter 24: "Leather Wings")

Nguma-monene—This giant *Wurm* of the Congo has a rigid crest running the length of its back. It is said to make its home in the Dongou-Mataba River.

Scitalis (or *Scytale*; from *scitulus*, "Elegant")—A serpentine winged Dragon with only two front legs, and multicolored scales so beautiful that animals and humans stop to admire it—whereupon the seemingly sluggish reptile strikes them down and devours them. Its poison is so fiery that anyone it bites is consumed in flames. It glows with such inner heat that even in a severe frost it will come out of its den to shed its skin. T.H. White suggests that it may be the "superbly marked" Rhinoceros Viper (*Bitis nasicornis*), found in the forests of West and Central Africa.

LIVING DRAGONS
By Oberon

The Dragon is the primordial and archetypal monster of Western mythology. Dragons dominate each of the four Elements: there are wingless cave Dragons, flying Dragons, sea Dragons and fire-breathing Dragons. Males are called "drakes," and females, "queens." All have been depicted in occidental legend as ancient, ferocious, and terrifying reptiles, symbolic of the raw, untamable, even hostile power of nature. Dragons are intelligent, crafty, cruel, and greedy. They have a passion for collecting vast hoards of treasure: gold, jewels, arms, and fabulous relics. These they pile together and sleep upon, guarding them jealously.

Dragons know the speech of all living creatures, and a drop of Dragon's blood tasted by the Teutonic hero Siegfried enabled him to understand the language of birds and animals. Possessing strong individual personalities, Dragons have distinctive and magickal names that give power to those who learn them. Such names as *Vermithrax*, *Draco*, *Kalessin*, and *Smaug* have been given in stories. But *Velociraptor*, *Tyrannosaurus rex*, *Carnotaurus*, *Deinonychus*, and *Spinosaurus* are other Dragon names in Greek.

Winged Dragons are of two basic types: the four-legged variety, with additional wings like those of bats, or fins supported on extended ribs; and the two-legged *Wyvern*, whose bat-like wings are formed from its forelimbs. These bear such a striking resemblance to prehistoric pterodactyls that they invite speculation as to the survival of such creatures into historic times. There have been some excellent flying Dragons in movies. *Dragonslayer* (1981) depicted a Wyvern, and *Dragonheart* (1996) featured the four-legged variety.

*Fig. 41.
Vermithrax from
the movie Dragonslayer*

Although Dragons are considered to be the quintessential creatures of myth and fantasy, they should not be thought of as purely imaginary. In fact, the legends of Dragons have many firm bases in actual animals, both living and extinct (or at least, commonly presumed so).

Certainly the first true Dragons were the prehistoric monsters that English paleontologist Richard Owen decided in 1842 to call *Dinosaurs* (meaning "terrible reptiles"). He could just as well have chosen the term *Dragons*, as this is what they had been called for millennia—and what they are called today by Chinese paleontologists. Ranging in size from no bigger than a chicken to more than 100 feet long and upward of 100 tons (*Argentosaurus*), they held undisputed reign over the entire Earth for 150 million years, until nearly their entire Order (*Archosauria*—"ruling reptiles") was exterminated in a great cataclysm 65 million years ago. Their immense fossilized bones have provided confirmation, throughout the brief span of human existence, that real Dragons once lived.

Fig. 42. Dinosaur stampede by St. John (from The Lost Warship, 1943)

But such powerful spirits and intelligences that had existed for so long are not simply exterminated overnight. Just as the long-gone Elves and Little People live on as spirit-beings of Faerie, so the souls of Dragons continue their ancient lineage in the Dragonlands of the Dreaming, holding sway, in our collective memories, over the entire span of mammalian existence.[1]

And perhaps some still survive even today. From the time of the earliest European explorations of "darkest Africa," rumors and reports of living dinosaurs have continually trickled out from the vast equatorial swamps of the Congo River basin. Referred to in fearful tones by various local names, monsters such as *Mokêle-M'Bêmbe*, *Chipekwe*, *Emela-Ntouka*, and *Muhuru* are variously described as having thick crocodilian tails, long necks, horns, back plates, and/or fierce teeth and claws. All of these are familiar descriptions of dinosaurs, and natives shown pictures of those ancient beasts readily identify them as their own local monsters. (See Chapter 25: "Living Dinosaurs")

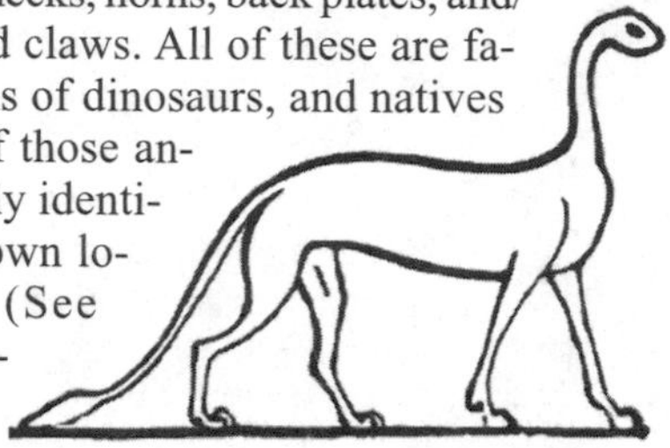

Additional evidence comes

Fig. 43. Sta or Mafadet from Egypt

from some of the earliest depictions of Dragons in ancient civilizations—such as the *Sta* or *Mafadet* of Egypt, and the famed *Sirrush*, or "Dragon of Ishtar," depicted on the Ishtar Gate of ancient Babylon and dating from the reign of Nebuchadnezzar the Great (605–562 BCE). Also called *Mushrush* or *Mušhuššu*, this may very well have been the same "living dragon" featured in the Book of Daniel, who purportedly killed it (Daniel, 14:23–27).

Was this, perhaps, a *Mokêle-M'Bêmbe*,

brought to Babylon as a tribute from an African ruler?

Fig. 44. Sirrush from the Ishtar Gate of Babylon

Although dinosaurs and their fossilized remains certainly provide a solid basis for the existence of true Dragons in the ancient past (and possibly even in some lost world in the swamps of Africa), there is no accounting for the many historical reports of Dragons in European history—such as the Dragon of Wantley, the Lambton Wurm, or the Dragon slain by St. George. I believe that many of these represent true encounters with monstrous invertebrate beasts that today we generically call Lake-Monsters. At least this explanation would fit those accounts in which the Dragon is called a Worm or *Orm*. For a more detailed discussion of such creatures—and my theory on their zoological identification—see Chapter 18: "Lake Monsters."

Fig. 45. Typical lake Monster by Oberon

Although modern representations of Dragons invariably embellish them with great, bat-like wings, this is not how they were depicted throughout most of human history. From ancient times through the Middle Ages, Dragons were most commonly described as either gigantic lizards or enormous serpents—often with little distinction between the two. Indeed, as many of the preceding entries amply attest, virtually any large reptilian creature—aquatic, terrestrial, or amphibious—was automatically considered to be a Dragon by definition.

Certainly the first and most striking example of a living Dragon encountered by European explorers was Egypt's gigantic Nile Crocodile (*Crocodylus niloticus*), which often attains lengths of more than 20 feet. Even bigger is the Estuarine Crocodile (*Crocodylus porosus*), the largest of all living reptiles. Normally confined to Indonesia, they are known to reach 30 feet in length. Some of the classic representations of Dragons are clearly crocodiles.

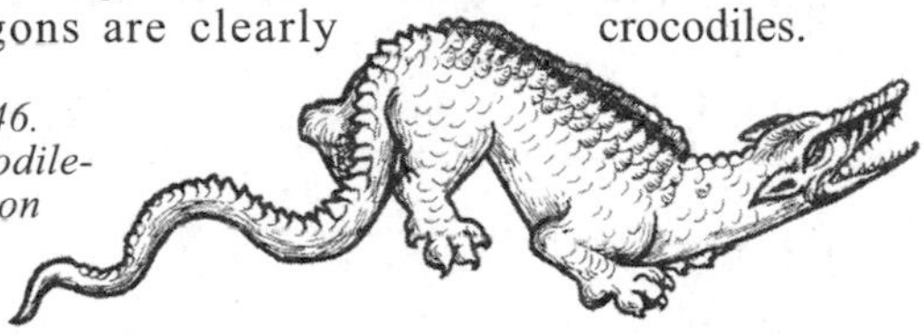

Fig. 46. Crocodile-Dragon

Then there is the famous Komodo Dragon (*Varanus komodoensis*), a giant monitor lizard, also of Indonesia. It attains a length of 6–10 feet and weighs up to 365 pounds, and has a long, yellow, forked tongue that it flickers like a flame. A much larger prehistoric version of this huge reptile was Megalania (*Varanus prisca*), which measured 15–20 feet long and weighed 1,000–1,300 pounds. This is certainly a true living Dragon by anyone's criteria! Although Megalania is believed to have been extinct for 40,000 years, sightings of living specimens are occasionally reported from Australia and New Guinea. In 1979, one was spotted by scientist Frank Gordon, who mistook it for a log before it moved off. Aborigines have legends of a giant lizard called *Mungoongalli*, which is probably the same animal. Recently, part of a Megalania hipbone only 100–200 years old was discovered in a subfossil state.

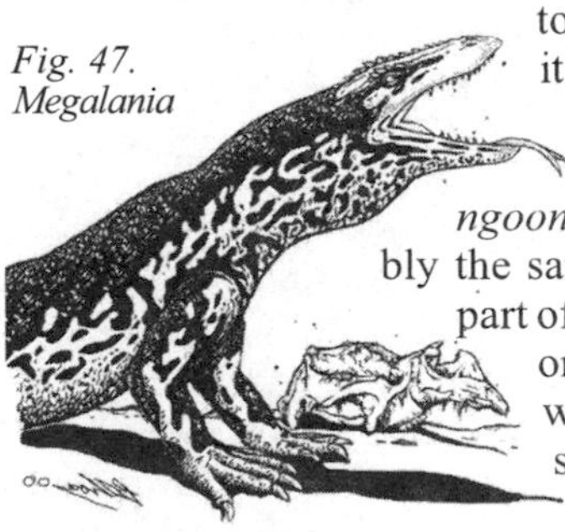

Fig. 47. Megalania

REAL FLYING DRAGONS

As impressive as they are, gigantic lizards and crocodiles don't have wings. So how did our conceptions of Dragons acquire the wings that now seem so integral to their anatomy?

Certainly, there have been mighty leather-winged Dragons in the paleontological record. The first vertebrates to evolve flight, *Pterosaurs* ("winged reptiles") ruled the Mesozoic skies from 228–65 million years ago. They ranged from the size of a sparrow (*Anurognathus*) to giants with wingspans of 40 feet (*Quetzalcoatlus*). In the terminology of medieval Dragonlore, these would be called *Wyverns,* a term for quadrupedal Dragons whose front limbs, like those of bats, supported their wing membranes.

Fig. 48. Wyvern by Oberon

But what then of the hexapod Dragon of popular fantasy—with four legs *and* two bat-like wings? There are no hexapod vertebrates in all of Earth's evolutionary history, so surely such a creature must be impossible, right? Well, don't bet on it.

The Genus *Draco* ("dragon") contains two dozen species of little flying agamid lizards, such as *Draco volens*. Only 7–9 inches long, they are found in the rainforests and rubber plantations of Madagascar, India, Southeast Asia, and throughout Indonesia. They have been recorded gliding up to 164 feet from tree to tree on membranous wings supported by extended movable ribs.

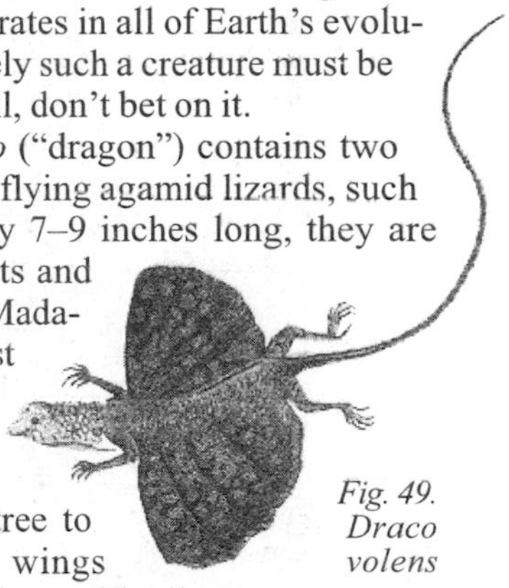

Fig. 49. Draco volens

In the 12th century, the first Europeans began traveling over the ancient Silk Road through Afghanistan to India. They returned with spices, travelers' tales, and small wonders. Among these were the mummified bodies of what traders claimed to be baby Dragons. And surely they could not be doubted as such—for they had fin-like wings growing from their sides. It didn't take much imagination for artists and compilers of bestiaries to envision what the enlarged adults of these "infant"

Fig. 50. Medieval fin-winged dragon by Edward Topsell (1607)

Dragons must look like. And thus was born the image and conception of the winged Dragon so beloved by us to this very day. Take a closer look at many of the early depictions of winged Dragons, and you will see their true origins in these living lizards which bear their name.

In 1960, three teenage boys in New Jersey discovered the fossil of a 7-inch-long flying lizard with ribbed wings with a 10-inch wingspan, in 200-million-year-old deposits of the late Triassic. It was appropriately named *Icarosaurus*, after Icarus of Greek myth, who flew too close to the sun on feathered wings held together with wax. A similar Triassic rib-winged lizard, *Kuehneosaurus*, was about 2 feet long, with a 2-foot wingspan. And a Chinese version, *Xianglong zhaoi*, dates from the lower Cretaceous, 125 million years ago. Like Draco, these ancient anteced-ents could spread their wings for gliding flight, or fold them alongside their bodies. [2]

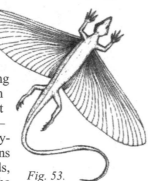

Fig. 52.
Icarosaurus siefkeri

But the most fascinating discovery in the annals of dragonlore was a 250-million-year-old Upper Permian fossil found in a German copper mine in 1910. Its morphology was reinterpreted in 1997 when a complete skeleton was purchased by the Karlsruhe Museum from amateur fossil hunters.[3] The 12-inch-long lizard with a flaring head crest, *Coelurosauravus*, is the oldest known flying vertebrate, with wings unlike those of any other animal. Rather than being support-ed by internal skele-tal elements such as limbs or ribs, its fan-like wing membranes were supported by inde-pendent bony rods extending outward and back from each side of the creature's chest and behind its forelegs— much like the wings of a fly-ing fish. Think of it—millions of years before fishes, birds, pterosaurs, or bats took to the air, the first vertebrate flyers were four-legged reptiles with finlike wings!

Fig. 53.
Coelurosauravus jaekeli

And then in June of 2007, an even more remark-able Triassic flying reptile was discovered in a quarry on the Virginia-North Carolina border. Named *Mech-istotrachelos aperos* ("soaring and long-necked"), the 10-inch-long lizard had fanlike wings like those of *Coelurosauravus*, and also a long neck just as Drag-ons are usually depicted as possessing.[4]

Fig. 54.
Mechistotrachelos aperos

We can easily imagine an alternative paleon-tology where creatures such as Coelurosauravus, Ica-rosaurus, Kuehneosaurus, Xianglong, and Mechisto-trachelos continued to evolve over another 250 mil-lion years, giving rise to larger and larger forms. Surely their descendants would be the very image of our cher-ished conception of flying Dragons. Indeed, this was precisely the premise behind Discovery Channel's delightful 2005 "mockumentary": *Dragon's World: A Fantasy Made Real*.

MONSTER MOVIES: DRAGONS

As the most popular of all fabulous creatures, Drag-ons have probably been featured in more movies than any other mythical monsters. Here is a list-ing of them, in chronological order:

Western Dragons:
The 7ᵗʰ Voyage of Sinbad (1958); *Sleeping Beauty* (animated, 1959); *Goliath and the Dragon* (1960); *The Magic Sword* (1962); *The Hobbit* (animated, 1977); *Pete's Dragon* (animated, 1977); *Dragonslayer* (1981): Wyvern; *Clash of the Titans* (1981): Hydra; *Flight of Dragons* (animated, 1982); *Q—The Winged Serpent* (1981): Amphitere ; *Lair of the White Worm* (1988): Orm; *Dragonworld* (1994); *Willow* (1988): Orm; *Jack the Giant Killer* (1994); *The Pagemaster* (animated 1995); *Dragonheart* (1996); *Hercules* (an-imated, 1997): Hydra; *Quest for Camelot* (animated, 1998); *Dragon World II: The Legend Continues* (1999); *Jason and the Argonauts* (TV, 2000); *Drag-onheart II: A New Beginning* (2000); *Dungeons & Dragons* (2000); *Harry Potter and The Sorcerer's Stone* (2001); *Shrek* (animated, 2001); *Reign of Fire* (2002); *Shrek II* (animated, 2004); *George and the Dragon* (TV, 2004); *Earthsea* (TV, 2004); *Harry Pot-ter and the Goblet of Fire* (2005); *Hercules* (TV, 2005): Hydra; *Dungeons & Dragons II: Wrath of the Dragongod* (2005); *Dragon's World: A Fantasy Made Real* (2005); *King of the Lost World* (2005); *Final Fantasy: Advent Children* (2005); *Eragon* (2007)

Eastern Dragons:
Godzilla (dozens of films from 1954 on); *The Never-ending Story* (1984); *Mulan* (animated 1998); *Drag-onheart II: A New Beginning* (2000); *Saiyuki* (50-episode anime series, 2000–2001); *Spirited Away* (anime, 2001); *Fullmetal Alchemist the Movie: Con-queror of Shamballa* (anime, 2005)

WALBERS
4. THE UNIVERSAL UNICORN

By Oberon and Morning Glory Zell, and Tom Williams

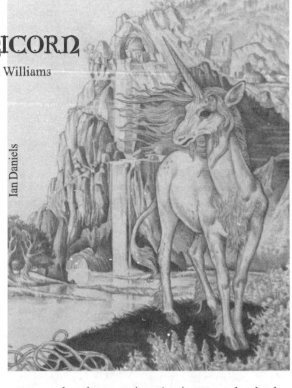

Ian Daniels

Why Unicorns?

Not since the fifteenth century has the unicorn had such an enormous appeal. It is easy to see why. In a world suffering from pollution, the unicorn can purify water with a single dip of its horn. In a world where animals are becoming extinct, the unicorn can never die. In a world where we might literally blow ourselves up at any moment, the unicorn harkens back to another time and a better life. The unicorn symbolizes sensitivity coupled with strength, the lure of sexuality and nature linked with the power of purity and truth. Today, when it is difficult to believe in these things any longer, the unicorn reminds us of a time when good existed—when unicorns existed. In a time when the future is looking bleak, the unicorn is a symbol not just of hope or of strength; it tells us that the unattainable is worth striving for, worth searching for, worth believing in—even if it exists only in our minds. —Nancy Hathaway, *The Unicorn*[1]

EW CREATURES OF FANTASY HAVE SO captured the modern imagination as the Unicorn. The second-best-known of all mythic animals (after the Dragon), it appears in nearly all Occidental and Oriental mythologies, including those of China, Japan, Tibet, Tartary, Malaysia, and Nepal. The contemporary appeal of this gracious medieval beast may derive from its symbolic attributes of purity, strength, and hope—commodities which are in regrettably short supply in our materialistic age. Remarkably, this fabulous beast of legend whose origin is lost in lore and history was reborn in modern times.

In a world become blasé about miracles, such an event must give a moment's pause to even the hardened skeptic—enough at least to generate a quick denial: "Unicorns don't exist. They are nothing but a myth!" Well, the city of Troy was considered to be a mere myth until its excavation in 1871 by Heinrich Schliemann. Like Troy and many other wonders that have become reality, the Unicorn is not just a myth, but a legend. A myth is pure fantasy, whereas a legend has a tiny bit of fact, like the grain of sand at the heart of a pearl.

THE QUEST OF THE UNICORN
By Tom Williams

The origins of the Unicorn have been likened to a great river with many tributaries stretching back into yet unexplored mountains. Ancient travelers' tales from Arabia and Africa told of fabulous one-horned beasts; legends from Persia and India fed the imaginations of medieval Europe with stories that were woven into Christian allegory and magnificent tapestries. And in all the stories, proverbs, relics, and charlatanry there lingered the subliminal certainty that somewhere, in some storied land, the aloof, elusive beast existed as a living animal, and that it could perhaps be captured and presented to the King as a triumph of adventure and faith.

Might it just not really be that one of the many streams that flow into the river of Unicorn lore from those distant, fabled mountains really does spring from the existence of a living Unicorn? If so, what a lure to follow once more those streams of fable in a new quest, a quest that could lead to the discovery of the fierce and gentle beast that has proved such a compelling symbol for the human mind over so many centuries! Such a quest has recently been pursued, but this time it was a quest of scholarship and biology, and its adversaries were cynicism and scientific presuppositions. And this time the adventurers have discovered and returned triumphant with…a living Unicorn.

In the process of separating fact from fiction and extracting legend from the cocoon of myth, misinterpretation, and outright hoax that often surrounds it, it is necessary to adopt a certain attitude—namely, that ancient writers and native peoples are not necessarily fools and liars; that what is scoffed at as superstitious nonsense may seem so because it has been distorted by a cultural and temporal lens to which we are not accustomed. In attempting to view reports from a different historical and cultural perspective, and in also trying to analyze the nature of the distortion, we may often arrive at some very interesting facts.

The legend of the Unicorn is particularly thorny in this regard because it has, over the centuries, become interwoven with religious and romantic fantasies, mystical attributes, and a number of rather disreputable commercial interests, including a once-thriving trade in narwhal tusks. But when authors whose works are otherwise treated as valid and sincere appear to be honestly reporting something as unusual as a Unicorn, it might just do to pay attention. The Unicorn has left many false clues along its trail—attributes which can rightly be traced to one or more of those "logical explanations" so beloved of people who are frightened of the dark. But other aspects of those fabulous tales and depictions have a ring of truth which, when viewed through a lens that corrected for distortions in time and culture, blazed a trail to the living animal.[2]

Fig. 1. Oryx Unicorns
by Karen Jollie

history of the unicorn

According to a popular Biblical tradition (and a catchy little song by Shel Silverstein), the Unicorn is supposed to have become extinct because it missed Noah's ark and drowned in the great Flood. This seems an oddly anachronistic fable, however, as the Unicorn was best-known in the Middle Ages, and the Deluge occurred at least 6,000 years earlier (c. 5150 BCE).

Although the ultimate origin of the Unicorn remains a mystery, it was frequently depicted in the carvings, cylinder seals, and bas-reliefs of the earliest civilizations of Mesopotamia and the Indus valley, more than 4,000 years ago. Only recently have we been able to decipher the inscriptions accompanying these enigmatic images. During the Bronze Age, which was astrologically the Age of Taurus, the Unicorn was commonly represented as a magnificent one-horned bull—a taurine Unicorn. Archaeologists have attempted to explain these representations by saying that the ancient artists were unable to handle perspective, and that they portrayed two-horned animals in profile by showing only one horn. However, there are many bas-reliefs which clearly show both two- and one-horned beasts together in profile, as may be seen in Fig. 2. Other images are fully sculpted, as in Fig. 3, leaving no doubt as to their intended subject.

Fig. 2. Mesopotamian Unicorn (central figure)
on the obelisk of Shalmaneser.

These early civilizations fell victim to the great geological and social upheavals c. 1600 BCE which ended the Bronze Age and ushered in the Age of Iron. This was the time of the eruption of Thera (1628 BCE), the Exodus, the forging of the first iron weapons, the mastery of horseback riding, the Aryan invasion, and other massive changes in the ancient order. The Minoan Period of Crete came to an abrupt end, as did the Middle Kingdom of Egypt and the Harappa culture of the Indus Valley. Amid the fall of these great civilizations, the Unicorn was nearly lost. It became a rare and secret beast, and when it next appeared it had changed its form.

For with the coming of the Iron Age—the astrological Age of Aries—the Unicorn came to be represented as a single-horned ram or antelope. In Egypt, for instance, the species of antelope depicted as Unicorns included gazelles, oryx, and ibex.

The Unicorn's rarity did not reduce its value as a symbol or the accumulation of legends about it. Although the secret of

Fig. 3. 3-inch tall ibex
Unicorn, 2nd cen. BCE.

creating Unicorns was never known in Egypt, tomb paintings and papyri of the New Kingdom depict one-horned antelope being offered as sacrifices at the altars of Isis, goddess of the moon, who was the virgin mother of Horus, the sun-god. These sacrificial "Unicorns" are clearly shown as having one horn sawn off, but they indicate the symbolic significance the Unicorn had attained.

Fig. 4. British Museum papyrus showing chess game of
lion and Unicorn. Antiquity, IV, 1930, p. 433, fig. 11

Perhaps the earliest mention of the Unicorn is by Herodotus (484–425 BCE), who wrote of the "horned ass" of Scythia. By the 5th century BCE, the Unicorn had become a very popular animal in the Western world.[3] Plutarch (45–125 CE) tells of a ram's head with only one horn that was brought to Pericles from his farm as a sign that he would become the single ruler of the Athenian state:

> There is a story, that once Pericles had brought to him from a country farm of his a ram's head with one horn, and that Lampon, the diviner, upon seeing the horn grow strong and solid out of the midst of the forehead, gave it as his judgment, that, there being at that time two potent factions, parties, or interests in the city, the one of Thucydides and the other of Pericles, the government would come about to that one of them in whose ground or estate this token or indication of fate had shown itself.[5]
>
> —Plutarch, Life of Pericles, vii

The prophecy of this arian Unicorn was fulfilled as the warring city-states of mainland Greece united for the first time, and the reign of Pericles (460–429 BCE) became known as the "Golden Age of Greece," during which time brilliant philosophers, playwrights, statesmen, and architects laid the foundations of Western civilization.

From 416 to 398 BCE, the Greek physician Ctesias served Darius II, King of Persia, and his successor, Artaxerxes, as court physician. Although he never traveled to India personally, in his *Indica*, Ctesias offers the earliest known literary attempt to describe the Unicorn: "Among the Indians…there are wild asses as large as horses, some being even larger…. They have a horn on their forehead, a cubit in length (the filings of this horn, if given in a potion, are an antidote to poisonous drugs)."[6] In his *Historia Animalium*, Aristotle (384–322 BCE) includes Ctesias' description of the one-horned "Indian ass."

Fig. 5. Karkadan from Mattaus Merian (1718)

Unfortunately, this contribution to the history of the Unicorn was obviously based entirely upon garbled travelers' accounts of the one-horned Indian rhinoceros. This mistake was made again centuries later by Marco Polo (1254–1324), who was convinced that the rhinoceri he saw on his travels to China were true Unicorns. Certainly they would have seemed fabulous enough in their own right. The rhinoceros Unicorn thus entered the bestiary as the **Karkadan**. It is

described as having the head of a stag, the body of a horse, the feet of an elephant, and the tail of a boar.

Despite the rarity of actual sightings during this period, the legend of the Unicorn spread widely. In China, the Unicorn, or **Ki-Lin,** is said to dwell

Fig. 6. Ki-Lin, the Chinese Unicorn, from an antique Chinese pen drawing.

in heaven and only appear intermittently on Earth, when its appearance signifies the dawning of a new age of harmony and enlightenment. As the Ki-Lin symbolizes good fortune, longevity, grandeur, justice, righteousness, and wise administration, it was believed to appear only during the time of an upright ruler, or immediately preceding the birth or death of a sage.

The first Unicorn in China is said to have appeared almost 5,000 years ago to give Emperor Fu Hsi the secrets of written language. According to Tse-Tchet'tong-kien-kang-mou, in 2697 BCE, another Unicorn was seen in the garden of the Yellow Emperor (Huang Di), which was taken as a prophecy that his reign would be long and peaceful. In the 22nd century BCE, one of the judges of the Emperor Shun possessed a "one-horned goat" called the **Sin-You** that would butt guilty parties but not the innocent. Two Unicorns are also said to have lived during the reign of Emperor Yao, the fourth of the legendary Five Emperors who shaped the world 4,000 years ago. The Chinese Ki-Lin, or "Dragon Horse," is a deerlike or cervine Unicorn, with a branching antler. It is one of the Four Fabulous Creatures of Chinese mythology. One appeared, it is said, before the birth of Confucius in 551 BCE. According to the legend, his pregnant mother encountered a *King* (the male Unicorn; the *Lin* is the female) while she was in the garden skeining yarn. With an engraved tablet of jade in his mouth, the King laid his head in her lap, whereupon she wound some of her yarn among the tines of his horn (Fig. 7). A dithyramb inscription on the tablet praised the great

Fig. 7. Confucius' mother meets the prophetic Ki-Lin

wisdom of her future son. And so it was. The *Analects* of Confucius became the foundation of Chinese culture for all time to come, and dynasties of Emperors ruled according to their precepts, in the hope that their reign would be blessed and sanctioned by the reappearance of the Unicorn.

70 years later, some hunters killed a Ki-Lin. Confucius went to view the body and saw that it still had a bit of yarn wrapped around its horn. He wept, knowing that he would soon die.

Fig. 8. Camphur

An unusual variety of Unicorn called the **Camphur** was said to dwell in the coastal waters off the island of Molucca in Indonesia. It had the body and forelegs of a deer, with the webbed hind feet of a goose.

The Unicorn of the Middle Ages and the Renaissance—from the 3rd to the 16th century CE—is neither bull nor ram nor antelope nor even a rhinoceros, but a pure white buck goat, with cloven hooves, beard, and flowing mane. His uplifted tail is tufted at the end, leading later artists to render him with the tail of the heraldic lion. He is fearless, proud, strong, and beautiful, as well as aloof and unapproachable. He is fierce yet gentle, a protector of other beasts. Physically, he is graceful and fine-boned. The image of the Unicorn is one of manner and behavior as well as of appearance. A typical version of *Physiologus*, the me-

Fig. 9. Salute of the Unicorn, from the 9th-century Bern Physiologus.

dieval bestiary written in the 9th century, describes the Unicorn as "a small animal, like a kid, but exceedingly fierce, with one horn in the middle of his head." This manifestation of the legendary creature is thus identified as a caprine (goatlike) Unicorn.

FACTUAL BASES FOR UNICORNS

Ignoring the rhinoceros as a red herring, all the actual sightings of Unicorns reported by medieval European travelers seem to have come from either Nepal or Ethiopia, the latter being the home of the Kaffir and Dinka tribes who seemed, during this period, to have perfected the production of Unicorns as herd leaders and defenders. Even in the 20th century, it was said that among the herds of these tribes, there may be found males with three, four, and five horns. Odell Shepard quotes another observer as reporting that "the Dinkas, who live just south of the White

Nile, not only manipulate the horns of their cattle as the Dinkas do, but use this practice as a means of marking the leaders of their herds."[7]

Pliny the Elder (23–79 CE), Roman officer and encyclopedist, describes in his *Natural History* a method of manipulating the horns of oxen, which, he says, "are of so pliable a substance and easy to be wrought, that as they grow upon their heads, even whilst the beasts are living, they may be with boiling wax bended and turned every way as a man will."[8] The French traveler François LeVaillant, in his *Travels in Africa*, speaks of a similar method of training the horns of oxen: "As the horns of the young ox sprout, they are trained over the forehead until the points meet. They are then manipulated so as to make them coalesce, and so shoot upwards from the middle of the forehead, like the horn of the fabled unicorn."[9]

It is also a matter of historical record that several Unicorn rams formed part of the large collection of Nepalese animals presented to George V of England when he was Prince of Wales, and that these were exhibited at the London Zoological Gardens in 1906. I have been unable to determine what became of them. A British resident at the court of Nepal was quoted in 1921 as sending reports of unicorned sheep:

> By certain maltreatment ordinary two-horned sheep are converted into a one-horned variety. The process adapted is branding with a red-hot iron the male lambs when about two or three months old on their horns when they are about to sprout. The wounds are treated with a mixture of oil and soot and when they heal, instead of growing at their usual places and spreading, come out as one from the middle of the forehead.[10]

It should be noted, however, that these explanations do not hold up under scientific scrutiny, and can only be the result of conjecture on the part of the reporter, or a tale told to the gullible by natives desiring to guard their secrets. Twisting horns with boiling wax or burning a poor animal's head with a hot poker is not going to produce anything but a mutilated ox or ram.

The legend of the Unicorn gained a new chapter at the beginning of the 13th century,

Fig. 10. Albrecht Durer. From Emperor Maximilian's Prayer Book (1516)

when Mongolian warrior Genghis Khan conquered much of Asia to build a great empire, but the intervention of a Unicorn made him abruptly turn back on the brink of invading India. As the great Khan prepared for what would probably have been an easy victory, a Unicorn "like a deer, with a head like that of a horse, one horn on its forehead, and green hair on its body" approached one of his scouting expeditions and knelt before them, saying, "It is time for your master to return to his own land." When he heard this, Genghis Khan was taken aback, but realizing this was a sign from heaven not to attack, he turned his army away. One of the most ruthless and fearless warriors in history had been "tamed" by a simple Unicorn, and India was saved from invasion.[11]

Fig. 11. By Jörg Breu d.Â. from Ritterlich und Lobwirdig Rayss, *Lewis vartoman (Augsberg, 1515)*

The one of them, which is much higher than the other, yet not much unlike to a coolte of thyrtye moneths of age, in the forehead growth only one horne, in maner right foorth, of the length of three cubits. The other is much younger, of the age of one yeere, and lyke a young Coolte: the horne of this is of the length of foure handfuls. This beast is of the coloure of a horse of weasel coloure, and hath the head lyke an hart, but no long necke, a thynne mane hangynge only on the one side. Theyre legges are thyn and slender, lyke a fawne or hynde. The hoofes of the fore feete are divided in two, much lyke the feet of a Goat. The outwarde part of the hinder feete is very full of heare. This beast doubtlesse seemeth wylde and fierce, yet tempereth that fierceness with a certain comelinesse. These Unicorns one gave to the Soltan of Mecha as a most precious and rare gyfte. They were sent hym out of Ethiope by a kyng of that Countrey, who desired by that present to gratifie the Soltan of Mecha.

—Lewis Vartoman, Itinerario (1576)[13]

The last authentic eyewitness reports of living Unicorns in the classical medieval conception occurred in the 16th century. The most important of these is the account of Lewis Vartoman of Bologna, who traveled through the countries of the Near East in 1503. In his *Itinerario*, Vartoman tells of seeing one-horned cattle in Ethiopia and describes in detail two Markhor (*Capra falconeri*) Unicorns he saw in the private menagerie of the Sultan of Mecca (see box above). Vartoman was followed 60 years later by Vincent Le Blanc, who set out on his travels through the Orient in 1567, at the age of 14. He saw only one of Vartoman's Unicorns, the other having died. But in compensation, he saw two at the Court of Pegu. In his *Les Voyages Fameux du Sieur Vincent le Blanc*, he declared: "I have seen a Unicorn in the seraglio of the Sultan, others in India, and still others at the Escurial."[12] This is our last historical report.

The Unicorn is not a single species, for other than the Chinese Lin, there are no female Unicorns. He is an exemplar or avatar of any of a number of horned ungulate species, and he embodies the highest potential of that species. The single horn grows from the center of his forehead (the "third eye") above the pineal gland—the master gland that ultimately governs the functions of the endocrine glands, such as the pituitary, and also, so the mystics say, the psychic centers of the brain. Therefore, the Unicorn may grow to be larger, more intelligent, and more sensitive than other animals of his ancestral stock. He is a natural herd leader, inevitably rising to dominance. The single perpendicular horn is an invincible weapon compared to the side-swept or backward-curving horns of other horned animals, and it enables the Unicorn to defend his herd even against lions, with which he is often depicted in combat. "The horn that springs from his forehead is terrible to his foe, a defense and a weapon of onslaught"
(Natalis Comes, 1551).[14]

Fig. 12. Lion and Unicorn bull in a Persian frieze.

SYMBOLISM AND ALLEGORY

For these reasons Unicorns developed more than 4,000 years ago, and for these reasons they became symbols of royalty, supremacy, and even divinity. In the Middle Ages, the Unicorn also came to symbolize Christianity, immortality, wisdom, lovers, and marriage.

In astrological symbolism, the Unicorn represents the moon, as the lion does the sun. The contest in which they are so often shown engaged implies an eclipse. Bas-reliefs showing the equation of the horn with the moon go back to prehistoric times, and they appear frequently on cylinder seals from ancient Babylon, Ninevah, Ur, and Persepolis. As the moon waxes and wanes, or is darkened and then lightened during a lunar eclipse, so the Unicorn has been a symbol of rebirth and the triumph of life over death in many cultures throughout the world.

Fig. 13. Illustration from a German translation of Albertus Magnus' Summa de Creaturis *(1545)*

The secret of the Unicorn seems to have been finally lost during the religious upheavals of the 15th and 16th centuries, when the Catholic Inquisition and the Protestant Reformation burned libraries as well as people for anything that could be considered heresy. The Crusades and the Islamic expansion into North Africa destroyed or subjugated the tribal people and farming folk who had perfected various methods of animal husbandry unknown to the Christians and Moslems. When these village shamans vanished, so did their secrets, and the Unicorn as a living animal became even rarer, disappearing altogether by the middle of the 16th century. Although initially heralded by their reappearance, the new light of the Renaissance dawned over a Europe that had no place for Unicorns, and they were seen no more in the flesh.

Their legend survived, however, in allegorical Christian religious art, wherein the Unicorn came to represent the Savior. The medieval and Renaissance depictions of the Madonna, either with the infant Jesus or with a Unicorn representing Christ (and often complete with a crescent moon), are directly descended from the ancient Egyptian portrayals of Isis. In Egyptian art, Isis was commonly shown bare-breasted, suckling the infant Horus on the throne that was her hieroglyph. The earliest versions of the "maiden and Unicorn"

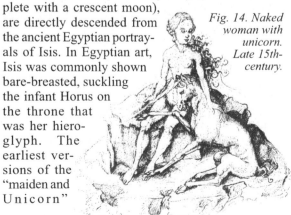

Fig. 14. Naked woman with unicorn. Late 15th-century.

motif show the maiden naked, or at last bare-breasted, and the Unicorn with his head in her lap.

In both European and Oriental traditions, the Unicorn is identified with a Messiah who appears when the world is in its darkest hour, and heralds the dawning of a new and better age. As the alchemical symbol for the Element Earth, he represents Earth consciousness and a reawakening of natural values.

The Hunt of the Unicorn

One of the most popular legends in medieval European lore was the "hunt of the Unicorn." According to the story, the Unicorn is wild, fierce, and wary, and cannot be approached by hunters (presumably to claim his valuable horn). However, he is beguiled and lulled by the innocence of a pure virgin. Accordingly, hunters set a maiden as bait under a tree in the forest and then hide. Because of his own purity, the Unicorn is irresistibly lured to the virgin. He comes to her, lies down beside her, lays his head in her lap, and falls blissfully asleep. Whereupon the hunters spring from the bushes and slaughter him. Lovely story. Strangely, the treacherous virgin in the tale is commonly equated with the Virgin Mary.

Fig. 15. Detail on an Italian miniature, ca. 14th century.

The hunt of the Unicorn is most famously depicted in a series of seven exquisite Unicorn Tapestries dating from 1495–1505. Purchased from the French LaRochefoucauld family in 1922 by John D. Rockefeller, these tapestries now hang in the Cloisters of the New York Metropolitan Museum of Art. Considered by many to be the most beautiful tapestries in the world, they show a group of hunters and richly dressed nobles in pursuit of a Unicorn, which is first encountered purifying the water of a fountain. It is then chased through lush forests, apparently killed, brought back to a castle, resurrected, and chained to a pomegran-

Fig. 16. "Unicorn in Captivity" tapestry.

ate tree enclosed by a little fence. What appear at first to be drops of blood on the Unicorn's white coat turn out upon examination to be pomegranate seeds and juice.

The Unicorn was long identified as a symbol of Christ by Christian writers, who interpreted the Unicorn and his death and resurrection as an allegory for the Passion. But the drops of blood/pomegranate juice also recall the Pagan myth of Persephone and her return from the Underworld.

DISAPPEARANCE AND DISMISSAL

During the 16th and 17th centuries, ground Unicorn horn, called alicorn, was an essential ingredient in European medicine, and was considered a potent palliative against plague and poison. Entire "Unicorn" horns were placed on the tables of political and ecclesiastical rulers and dignitaries in the belief that the horns would sweat in the presence of poisoned food or drink. For the same purpose, royal drinking cups were carved of supposed Unicorn horns. Interestingly, the keratin in natural horn does absorb dissolved arsenic out of a solution, so there is a factual basis for this practice.

With the Age of Enlightenment and the beginning of the founding of the Royal Academy of Science in 1662, belief in Unicorns began to decline, particularly when it became known that most of what had been marketed as true Unicorn horns (unicornum verum) were actually narwhal tusks. This had been a thriving trade in the medieval and Renaissance periods, when alicorn might bring up to 30 times its weight in gold. Later, mammoth and walrus tusks replaced those of narwhals in the apothecaries of wealthy patrons—as did petrified wood, fossil ammonites, and even stalactites—until alicorn was dropped from most pharmacopeias in the mid-18th century. Ironically, narwhal, walrus, and mammoth tusks are composed of ivory, not keratin, and are no help at all in removing poisons. A drinking vessel made out of a regular cow horn would be far more effective!

Unfortunately, Ctesias' ancient identification of the rhinoceros as a Unicorn has resulted, in more recent times, in rhinoceros horn supplanting all previous versions of alicorn in the Orient as a sovereign remedy for many ailments—particularly male impotence. This association has precipitated the near-extermination of both Indian and African rhinos by poachers eager to cash in on such a lucrative market.

Personally, I think it a bit unfair that narwhals were dismissed as true Unicorns. After all, they are the only animal other than the ungainly rhino to naturally sport a single long horn ("uni-cornu"), even if it is technically a tooth. They are exquisitely beautiful creatures, and I love their appropriate French name: la licorne de la mère—"Unicorn of the sea."

Fig. 17. La Licorne de la mère

Only in the last 400 years has the Unicorn come to be drawn as a single-horned horse. Such a creature is purely an invention of artistic fancy, of course, for horses have never had horns. Perhaps the knightly custom of affixing horns to the headgear of jousting chargers contributed to this image. When the real Unicorn was no longer available to grace coronations and other celebrations of royal courts, knights would armor their chargers with Unicorn-styled headgear in imitation of the real thing. But horses have never grown horns and are, in fact, the "false Unicorns."

Even so, the authentic tradition of the Unicorn has managed to persist to the extent that even equine Unicorns are usually portrayed as having cloven hooves and a goatee. Julian Franklin, the foremost authority on heraldry, attempts to clear up this misconception:

> The best known of all fictitious creatures is the Unicorn. Not everyone who knows a Unicorn is quite sure that it is fictitious: further, most people, asked to describe it, would say it is a horse with a spiral horn on its forehead. They are not to blame for this ignorance. It is often so drawn—even when acting as a supporter of the Royal Arms. The Unicorn is in fact based on a goat, has cloven hooves, and a beard…it should be observed that he has an heraldic lion's tail.[15]

Fig. 18.

The Unicorn was considered to have been given his death blow in 1827 by Baron Georges Cuvier, the "father of Paleontology," who declared in 1829 that a cloven-hoofed ruminant with a single horn would be impossible because its frontal bone would be divided and no horn could grow from such a division.[16] There were few in the scientific community who dared challenge such an eminent authority as Cuvier, and this dictum remains in many textbooks even today, despite the fact that it was also Cuvier who, in 1821, said, "There is little hope of discovering new species of large quadrupeds."[17] The subsequent discovery of the Kodiak bear, mountain gorilla, okapi, mountain nyala antelope, pygmy hippopotamus, Andean wolf, kouprey ox, and other large quadrupeds made this statement seem so ludicrous that it is now referred to as "Cuvier's rash dictum" (a phrase coined by cryptozoology founder Bernard Heuvalmans).

For many years scholars have followed Ctesias and Marco Polo in identifying the Unicorn with the rhinoceros, ignoring all the sightings and accounts that could not be so explained or calling them merely tall tales. After all, the experts said that Unicorns could not exist; therefore they did not exist.

ṫhE ḶIVIṄG UṄICORṄ

And now this history of the Unicorn must become personal. My wife and soulmate, Morning Glory, and I tracked the Unicorn down through the centuries, sifting myths, legends, travelers' tales, and anatomical, zoological, and anthropological studies to discover the reality behind the fantastic. We researched numerous texts spanning the ages, and collected artistic representations of Unicorns from all times and cultures. And, in the fall of 1976, we finally found the last piece of the puzzle and uncovered the long-lost secret of the Unicorn.

When we started out, we too assumed, like all the scholars we read, that the Unicorn was merely a distant derivative of the rhinoceros. But as we catalogued all those images, it began to dawn on us that these Unicorns represented not one, but various species, all of which were depicted as ultimate idealizations with only the single horn in common. Another realization was that, other than in modern fantasy novels, there has never been a female Unicorn; even in scenes of the Garden of Eden, where he was said to be the first animal Adam named, he never appears with a mate. When shown with other animals, he is apart, aloof, and acting as a protector or leader.

Fig. 19. Adam naming the Unicorn. From a 15th-century Dutch Bible.

Clearly, then, the Unicorn could never have been a species—not even a mythical one—but was, rather, a phenomenon manifesting as virtually any species of horned animal. Just as albinism occurs in many different species, so does *unicornity* ("one-hornedness"). The difference, however, was that albinism occurs naturally, while unicornity was clearly induced through some lost process of animal husbandry—perhaps comparable with the Japanese art of Bonsai.

In contrast to the assumption that if there had ever been a living Unicorn, it must have had an evolution and a natural history as other species do, we posited unicornity as a multispecies phenomenon, one that perhaps was produced artificially by some lost technique. Any such technique, however, would have to produce not only an animal that fit the description, but also one whose behavior and manner suggested the undeniable insistence of the legends. Such an animal would, in effect, be fundamentally different from its ancestral stock, elevated so profoundly that it would develop as a different animal. Shepard, that unflagging scholar and humanist, nudges exasperatingly close to the answer:

> It seems possible, therefore, that what I may call the Unicorn idea, the notion that one-horned animals exist in Nature, arose from the custom of uniting the horns of various domestic animals by a process which is still in use but still mysterious to the civilized world. Here may be the explanation of the one-horned cows and bulls that Aelian says were to be found in Ethiopia and of the unicorned cattle reported by Pliny as living in the land of the Moors…. The one-horned ram's head sent to Pericles by his farmhands may have been that of the leader of their flock, and so a perfect symbol of that leadership in Athens which, according to Plutarch's interpretation, they wished to prophesy for their master.[18]

The final piece fell into place in 1976 at the University of Oregon in Eugene, where Morning Glory and I were teaching. There I came upon the forgotten work of Dr. Franklin Dove, a biologist at the University of Maine, who, in the 1930s, was experimenting with horn development in cattle. In a 1935 article titled "The Physiology of Horn Growth," he traced various previous efforts at developing a Unicorn and documented his own efforts along those lines. He had made a profound discovery: horns do not, in fact, grow directly out of the bones of the forehead, as had been universally assumed by Cuvier and everyone else. Rather, the *os cornu*, or bony horn spike, originates in special nodes of tissue called "buds," which are imbedded in the loose skin of the forehead and later fuse to the frontal bones of the skull.

Within a few hours after birth, these nodes direct a flow of enzymes down into the bone beneath, which then "influences the tissues below it to change their course of development," stimulating bone to grow upward into the horn core, which becomes correspondingly covered with a horny sheath of keratin. Dove determined through his experiments that if the position of these nodes was shifted immediately after birth, they could cause a horn to grow wherever they were positioned. Of course, the limitation is that the tissue connection cannot at any time be severed, so any rearrangement can extend only so far as a pedicle flap can be moved.

Dove recalled those Nepalese arien Unicorns that had recently been exhibited in London, and became convinced that his experiments could be used to replicate the process by which they had really been created, and furthermore, that this was, in fact, the actual process by which ancient tribes had originally created genuine Unicorns—the real-life basis of the legend.[19]

UNICORNS REBORN
By Tom Williams

In 1933, as an extension of his experiments, Dove manipulated the horn buds of a day-old Ayrshire bull calf to the center of its skull and trimmed their facing edges flat so they would, he hoped, fuse to form a single horn. This is exactly what happened, and the calf grew into a full-sized bull with a single quite formidable horn on its forehead (Fig. 19). The grown animal definitely displayed the one-horned properties and its horn, contrary to Cuvier's opinion, was firmly fused to the frontal bones of the skull. This one-horned bull also turned out to be a Unicorn in ways that even Dove did not expect and though it does not look like the traditional image of a Unicorn, it nonetheless points the way to his creation.

Dove noted that the mere presence of the single horn led to certain conclusions about his behavior which fit the literature about Unicorns. The first was the aristocratic nature inherent in every Unicorn:

> He is always the leader. Quite rightly so, and for reasons quite acceptable to behavioristic interpretation. Any animal fronted with a single horn would learn the advantages of a single well-placed weapon and would, through experience, gain ascendance and leadership over the rest of the herd..... Possession of a single weapon alters the behavior of the animal selected to become a unicorn and indicates that the unicorn's dominant and aristocratic behavior can be brought out as a single behavior factor, unassociated with genetic origin. The dominance of a unicorned animal over the ordinary two-horned beasts of the herd is here offered as a striking instance of the dependence of behavior upon form.[20]

Fig. 19. Dr. Franklin Dove's taurine Unicorn at two years of age

The rationale behind the alleged Unicorn techniques of the Dinka becomes clear, especially when one thinks of what such a weapon might mean to a potential predator such as a lion. In fact, the motif of the lion and the Unicorn as implacable foes is richly interwoven in the Unicorn lore, and has even found its

Fig. 20. Fighting Unicorn by Karen Jollie

way onto the British coat of arms. The Dinka, it seems, were not only creating herd leaders: they were producing some pretty formidable guardians against predators.

With the assimilation of the lore and with the results of Dove's work, the stage was set for the next logical step. Unicorns could be, and probably had been, created by various peoples in the past for very practical reasons. Knowledge of these animals must have come in whatever garbled form to the Europe of the Middle Ages. At some point, roughly 400–500 years ago, the secret was forgotten or lost, and Europeans saw no more living Unicorns. The image of the animal grew distorted, and because it was assumed to be entirely mythical, it took on the incongruous equine qualities of later times. But enough remnants of the image remained to be pieced together in the light of Dove's discovery: the Unicorns of the medieval tapestries had been created from goats.

Oberon and Morning Glory Zell decided that they could resurrect the creation of the medieval Unicorn, so they searched for a type of goat most like the animals in the tapestries. What they finally settled on was a relatively intelligent breed of Angora: white, with a long, silken coat, slender legs, and a beard.

So it was that at the Spring Equinox of 1980, Lancelot was born, and within a few hours of his birth, Oberon performed the operation that would produce a Unicorn. Creation of a Unicorn involves more than the mere manipulation and fusion of horn bud tissue; it is an ongoing process of devotion and training. Due to his dangerous potential, it was decided to shower him with affection in order to "imprint" him to humans. Lancelot and his brother, Bedivere, slept with their creators and had an adopted fawn for a childhood companion.

As in Dove's earlier work, the horn bud tissue attached itself to the skull and began forming the single horn spike. X-rays clearly showed the horn to be contiguous with the skull, forming a definite *boss* (thickening) on the forehead. An unanticipated effect was that the sinuses grew up into the horn, vastly increasing the animal's sense of smell. Lancelot soon discovered the utility of his horn as a tool—and a weapon—during a couple of encounters with dogs, for whom it was fortunate that it was kept dull and that people were present!

Fig. 21. Lancelot, the Living Unicorn. Photo by Ron Kimball

ᴛᑋᴇ RETURN OF ᴛᑋᴇ UNICORNS
By Oberon

Dr. Dove was convinced that his technique was in fact identical to that used by ancient tribes to create the original Unicorns of legend. When Morning Glory and I managed to get hold of Dove's research notes, we also became convinced, and realized that we now knew the secret of the Unicorn, and that it was in our power to resurrect the authentic medieval Unicorn into the modern world.

Well, someone else might just have written a book about it, as we had originally planned to do. But the temptation was irresistible. We just had to give it a try! We moved to the country as caretakers of a 220-acre parcel of undeveloped land which was part of a much larger 5,600-acre homesteading community, to create a Unicorn farm. We built a home, barns, pens, and gardens, and developed the springs, planted trees, raised pet deer, put in a pond, and otherwise devoted ourselves to a life of pioneer homesteading. Meanwhile, we located appropriate breeding stock (Angora goats), studied veterinary medicine and stockbreed-

ing, and embarked upon a truly amazing adventure raising living Unicorns.

As Tom already stated previously, the magick worked, and Lancelot was born at the Spring Equinox of 1980, to be followed two weeks later, at the full moon, by his brother Bedivere (we decided to name them for knights of the round table). They were certainly beautiful. Their coats were iridescent white in the sunlight, with the texture of satin, and their long manes were like cloud fluff.

And we discovered an amazing magickal synchronicity. That spring, for the first time, virtually every gift catalog was highlighting Unicorns. Books, jewelry, T-shirts, figurines, calendars, posters, decorations, greeting cards, teapots, TV cartoons, gimcracks, and tchotchkes—everywhere we looked it was the Year of the Unicorn!

During that first summer, we appeared at the local Renaissance faire, and on countless TV news, talk, and animal shows, both local and national. Our Unicorns were front-page news in every paper in the country, and were featured in many magazines and even a few books. The 1982 *Encyclopædia Britannica Book of the Year* ran a photo of Lancelot over the caption: "Encyclopedia Britannica defines a unicorn as 'a mythological animal resembling a horse or a kid with a single horn on its forehead.' Visitors to Marine World, an amusement complex not far from San Francisco, are sure that Lancelot, a young angora goat, is real. That being the case, Lancelot must be a real mythological unicorn."[21]

A highlight for Morning Glory and I was attending the 1981 Octacon science fiction convention in Santa Rosa, California, with Lancelot, where we won the grand prize in the costume contest as "Molly Grue, Schmendrick the Magician, and the Last Unicorn," from Peter Beagle's 1968 fantasy novel, *The Last Unicorn*. This brought our entire adventure around full circle.

For the next several years, as we continued to produce a couple more Unicorns each year, we appeared at Renaissance faires all over the United States and Canada—sometimes with as many as four separate teams, each with a different Unicorn. Some of them we exhibited on a rotating schedule at Marine World/Africa U.S.A., near San Francisco, where they were featured as billboard attractions on huge signs overlooking the freeway..

In 1984, after a four-year struggle with the U.S. Patent Office, we finally obtained a patent on the operation itself, citing Dove's prior work and many references from various dictionaries and encyclopedias to prove the authenticity of our animals. In this, we had the support of our local livestock veterinarian, Dr. James Madigan.

Finally, our booking agents landed us a four-year exhibition contract with the Ringling Bros. and Barnum & Bailey Circus, and for the rest of the decade, our Unicorns were the stars of the Greatest Show on Earth, seen by millions. We kept several of them at home as our own companions, and placed some for a while at local animal parks. Decades later, we still hear from people whose lives were transformed by their encounter with "the impossible dream" made manifest, and the epiphany that if a Unicorn can be real, then anything is possible!

Fig. 22. Circus poster featuring Lancelot, the Living Unicorn.

So the story of the Unicorn has a modern sequel. Yet another of those ancient rivers has been traced into the mountains of fable and fact, an act that is a testimony both to the dedication of truly scientific curiosity as well as to a devotion to the compelling beauty that has been a part of the Unicorn throughout its long history.

The Unicorn belongs to no one country or continent, nor even to the human race alone. He is a child of peace and a prophet of good fortune.

Fig. 23. The Unicorn misses the Ark. Tobias Stimmer (1576)

"...O golden hoofs, O cataracts of mane,
      O nostrils wide
With high distain, and O the neck
      wave-arched, the lovely pride!
O long shall be the furrows ploughed
      upon the hearts of men
Before it comes to stable and
      to manger once again.
Now dark and crooked all the roads
      in which our race will walk,
And shriveled all their manhood
      like a flower on broken stalk.
Now all the world, O Ham, may curse
      the hour that you were born—
Because of you, the Ark must sail
      without the Unicorn."
                    —N.W., "The Sailing of the Ark,"
                                    from *Punch*, 1948

The Prophecy of the Unicorn

(from the *Codex Unicornis,*
by Magnalucius, founder of the Collegium
Gnosticum, 15th century CE)

The Unicorn is a kindred race, bound to us in love and service. He points the way, he guards the gate, he waits until the end.

Behold! An age shall come when science shall darken everywhere the hopes of men, Chariots of iron shall roll the land, which shall grow hard and barren to bear their weight. The air shall be filled with a clamor of many voices. Unknown plagues and sicknesses shall arise. The sphere of the Moon shall bear the booted heels of Man.

Two mighty kingdoms will contend for all the world, and turn against it, until the soil and the sea shall sicken and the wind become a flux of poisoned vapor. And all men shall be sorely tried, so that at the last, none may escape the choice between Light and darkness.

Then, in the Time of Great Purification, will the Unicorn return in strength, lingering at the margins of our realm, to seed our minds with dreams of a brighter age to come....
(Translated from the Latin by Michael Green)[22]

MONSTER MOVIES: UNICORNS

Fantasia (animated, 1940)
The Last Unicorn (animated, 1982)
Legend (1985)
The Little Unicorn (2001)
Chronicles of Narnia: The Lion, the Witch and the Wardrobe (2005)
Stardust (2007)

5. WONDER HORSES

By Morning Glory Zell

Hast thou given the horse strength?
Hast thou clothed his neck with thunder?
The glory of his nostrils is terrible,
He paweth in the valley and rejoiceth in his strength:
He goeth on to meet the armed men.
He mocketh at fear...neither turneth he back from
*   the sword...*
He swalloweth the ground with fierceness and rage...
And he saith among the trumpets, Ha, ha...
*   —Job 39:19–25*

Ian Daniels

I N OUR MYTHS AND LEGENDS WE IM-mortalize beings of all kinds. Long after the originators have passed on, stories that began as campfire tales gather power as they are retold until they gain the stature of a full-scale myth. Creatures that are powerful and amazing and yet share our lives, as horses do, always seem larger than life. From this simple truth is born the Wonder-Horse. Sometimes the Wonder-Horse acts alone—flying to aid a fallen warrior, speaking prophecy, or doing some dastardly deed. But most often, Wonder-Horses are in partnership, usually with a hero of some sort, even if he or she does not know it yet. Most often it is the horse that understands their conjoined destiny and works to teach it to the human. Sometimes these fantastic equines are immortal, and sometimes they are merely mortal. Often the wonder lies in their journey from Earth to heaven—or hell. They can acquire their immortality by birthright, by association, or by earning it the hard way—by becoming a true legend that outlives the horse and sometimes even the culture that created the tale in the first place. Wonder-Horses start with their hooves on the Earth, but, like a mare's nest, they often end up tangled in our dreams. Every culture shares these horse tales, and it is amazing how so many similarities can occur in cultures separated by many thousands of miles and even years. Horses just can't help but fill us with wonder: their size and power when they stamp their shiny hooves; the way their muscles ripple under their sleek coats when they shake their proud heads and toss their flowing manes; the sheer poetry in their movement; and the electric thrill of the wind rushing past as they run so quickly it seems as though they are flying. Even though they are no longer our primary means of transportation,

Fig. 1. Scythian winged horse on stone palette

they still transport us to magickal realms, and there will always be a place for Wonder-Horses in our hearts.

FLYING HORSES

Imagine flying through the air on a horse with wings! Most kids have had this fantasy and a lot of us never outgrew it. But flying horses… how could such a notion come to be? On the face of it, it seems absurd, but to people unfamiliar with horses and all they are capable of—running, leaping and whirling around with a rider—maybe it wasn't such an impossible idea. The Scythians were some of the world's greatest warriors and horsemen and they lived in the Southern steppes of Russia, north of the world of the Classical Greek and Persian civilizations. They were fantastic artisans in gold work, and it is here that we see the first representations of winged horses. The Scythians created fantastic horse gear out of pounded felt that was elaborately dyed and embroidered, with feathered bridles and tall headdresses. They made protective chaps to cover the rider's legs and the horse's shoulders, and decorated them to look like wings. Imagine being at the village well when these men came galloping into the center of the town in a cloud of dust, carrying spears and bows and mounted on huge fantastic beasts that looked like horses, but some having antlers or horns, some with tall plumes like a giant bird, and others with bright red and white wings. One of the winged stallions leaps over a vegetable cart and the seed of a myth is planted.

Pegasus is the most famous of all the immortal horses of Greek mythology. He was born when drops of blood from the severed head of the Gorgon Medusa fell into the sea and mingled with the sea foam of Poseidon. He has a brother, born at the same time but completely unlike him: *Chrysaor*, a dark-winged boar. Originally described as being red, Pegasus is a shining white steed with huge, soft, swan-like wings that enable him to fly so high into the heavens that he can reach the realm of the gods. When he flew back to Earth and first struck the ground, a spring (the

Fig. 2. Birth of Pegasus

Hippocrene, shaped like a hoof print) gushed forth. Its waters inspire poetry. Pegasus was captured by the hero Bellerophon by means of a magick bridle given to him by the goddess Athena. He then rode the great flying steed to slay the monster Chimera (grandchild of Pegasus's brother Chrysaor) that was plaguing the countryside. But afterward, Bellerophon flew higher and higher on Pegasus until he reached the edge of the gods' heavenly kingdom. This intrusion by a human mortal offended Zeus, who cast a thunderbolt, unhorsing Belleraphon so that he fell to Earth and broke his hip. Pegasus flew free, and from that time on lives on Olympus, occasionally helping Eos bring the dawn and carrying lightning bolts to Zeus. He acquired a mate, Euippe, and sired two foals, Melanippe and Celeris. He was given a constellation in his honor, and an entire group of flying horses—the Pegasi—came to be named after him.

Arion is a lesser-known, but possibly even more amazing, stallion from Greek mythology with two origin stories. In the first one, Arion is the first horse—an immortal, dark-maned stallion brought out of the earth when Poseidon strikes it with his trident. In the second origin story, Arion is the child of a union of the god Poseidon, in the body of a stallion, and the goddess Demeter, in the body of a mare. Arion's right legs have feet similar to human hands, but his left legs have hooves. He speaks with a melodious human voice, which can be as loud as a trumpet, and he flies so swiftly that he cannot be seen. Poseidon gives him

to Heracles, who later gives him to the hero Adrastos. In the Battle of the Seven Against Thebes, Arion saves Adrastos with his

Fig. 3. Celestial Horse

quick-witted action and advice, and weeps like a person at the death of a child. As the poet Propertius tells us, "Adrastos' horse, Arion, victory crowned / Grieved at Archemorus' grave with human sounds."[1]

From Hindu mythology comes the wonderful *Dadhikravan*, the luminous, cosmic white horse with eagle's wings. He flies across the night sky as the embodiment of the new moon, vanquishing the enemies of the celestial realms. The *Celestial Horse* of China is an ancient magickal equine. The earliest ancestral horse is *Tiansi*. Because he is located in the constellation Fang (the Azure Dragon), Celestial Horses eventually came to be associated with Dragons. In its earliest representations, this heavenly courser looks somewhat similar to the Luck Dragon from the movie *The Neverending Story*. It also sweats red resin (possibly cinnabar), which resembles blood. It was begotten by a Lake-Dragon and a wild mare from the Pamir mountains. Later, in equine form, the Celestial Horse became one of the animals of the Chinese Zodiac.

The *Seven-Colored Horse* from Spanish fairy tales is a pony whose coat has seven ever-changing colors. The pony speaks, flies, and grants wishes to those who can capture it. He helps the hero gain his bride and his heart's desire. The wish-granting horse that flies in order to achieve the hero's goals is a common fixture in fairy tales.

Fig. 4. The Seven-Colored Horse

Tipaka, the steed of the legendary King Sison, is the beautiful magickal horse in the mythology of Thailand. He flies so fast that he arrives at his destination even as it is being named. *Beligen* is the celestial flying bay horse of Geser, the Mongolian Buryat hero/savior. Beligen's hooves never slip, his legs do not get cold, and his eyes flash lightning bolts.

Many of the gods and goddesses of ancient Greece—including Hera, Hades, Helios, and the twin Dioskouroi—drive chariots pulled by flying horses. The *Anemoi* are the gods of the four winds who, in

Fig. 5.
Aurora,
Goddess of
the dawn

the guise of horses, draw the chariot of Zeus. The golden mares of Demeter race so lightly over the tops of the cornstalks that they do not bend.

Many Norse gods and goddesses also fly about on magickal equines, sometimes on horseback and sometimes in chariots. Odin, Sunna and Mani, Gna, Nott, and others fly the northern skies from Asgard to Bifrost to visit the realms of the giants. Others, such as the Valkyries, sweep down to Earth to reclaim the souls of heroic mortals.

There are many heavenly horses in the Hindu Pantheon as well. Recounted in the Vedas and later sacred scriptures, Rudra, Brahma, Vishnu, Shiva, Soma, and Suraya all ride or drive flying horses. Some, such as Suraya and Vishnu, take equine forms themselves at times. The *Naras* are the beautiful winged chariot horses that transport Kubera, the Hindu god of wealth, on his journeys across the sky.

FAERY HORSES

Ears cocked to hear the slightest rustle, nostrils quivering to catch an elusive scent, skin quivering and muscles tensed to spring into flight, horses seem to sense a world that we cannot perceive with our own limited senses. Is it any wonder that we have always thought of them as being not quite of this world? With their beauty and their flighty nature they seem akin to Faeries. Indeed, what is a fairy tale without the Magick Horse? Some of the most famous horses of this variety come from Celtic legends and medieval lore.

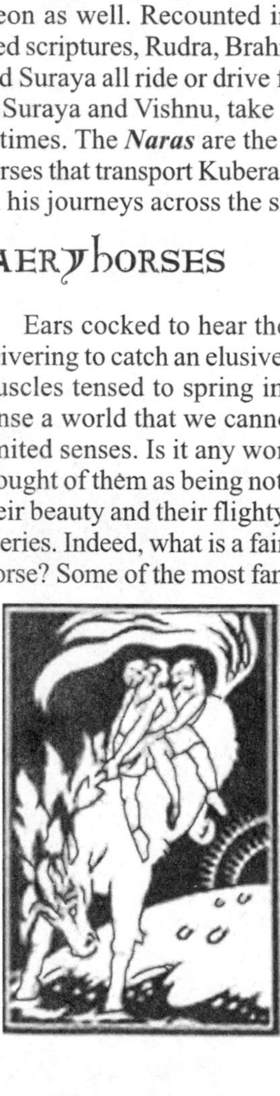

The *Tanglecoated Horse* is an Irish tale in which the Celtic Chieftain Fionn encounters a wild, gigantic, and unlovely horse—the Tangle-Coated Horse—while out hunting. The horse is befriended by Cunnaun, who climbs up on his shaggy back. Then Fionn and all the

Fig. 6. The Tanglecoated Horse

rest of his men join Cunnaun on the animal, whose back stretches to fit them all. Then the horse carries them over the land and into the sea. There, under the waves, the horse bears them to a magickal realm of Sea Faeries. The name of the Tangle-Coated Horse is *Earthshaker*, and when he hears his name spoken, he transforms into a noble and graceful steed with a beautiful silver coat shining with Faery light. The band mount Earthshaker for the return journey through the sea (as long as the men keep hold of the horse they can breathe under water). Yet, when he leaves the Faery realm, Earthshaker turns back into the shaggy, homely Tangle-Coated Horse again. However, anytime Fionn and his men wish to visit the realm of Under Wave, Earthshaker will take them back.

Fig. 7. The Faery Reid by Scott Fray

In other classic fireside stories you may hear of the *Horses of the Faery Reid*. These magickal steeds are ridden by Faery folk from their hollow mounds to their gatherings. Some horses are silver grey, some satin black, some fiery golden chestnut, and others snowy white. All are heartbreakingly beautiful, adorned in green and with gold and silver bridles trimmed with ribbons and bells. Sometimes a mortal manages to sneak into the procession and mount one of these fantastically graceful and ethereal creatures. The horse carries the mortal until he does something to offend the Faery folk, at which point the steed pitches the offending mortal headfirst into a ditch.

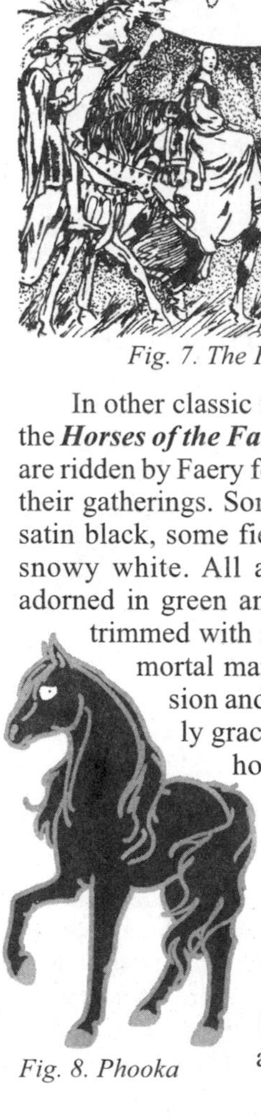

A similar creature, though a little darker in nature, is the Irish *Phooka*. This mostly harmless but mischievous spirit can appear in the shape of many dif-

Fig. 8. Phooka

ferent creatures. But his favorite form is a pitch-black horse with fiery eyes. He likes to disguise himself as an apparently tame and shaggy pony and let some weary traveler climb up on his back for a ride. But as soon as the traveler mounts him, he is off like a shot through marshes and thorn bushes for a hell ride. Finally, his terrified passenger is thrown into a ditch or pool of mud, and when he cleans the muck out of his ears he can hear the chuckling of the Phooka as he regains his Faery shape and gallops away.

Often the heroic knight of a fairy tale encounters a horse that will lead him into an adventure—for example Ogier, a Prince of Denmark, encounters the Faery horse **Papillon**, a glorious creature famed for his wise discourse, his strength, and his magickal powers. Papillon can talk as well as fly, and walk between the worlds. The Faery steed leads Ogier into a flowering meadow where he meets the Faery Morgana, who takes him to Avalon. Papillon graciously takes Ogier back and forth between the realm of mortals and Avalon, where they eventually remain.

Fig. 9. Ogier and Papillon

Sometimes the hero of the tale must do battle to gain the horse. **Sir Osbert's Phantom Courser** is a large, beautiful, black steed won in a battle with a mysterious knight errant, whom Sir Osbert encounters on a moonlit plain surrounded by ancient ruins. Triumphant though wounded, Osbert leads the fiery-eyed sable courser back to his stable where it remains until the cock crows, at which point it rears with flashing eyes, spurns the ground, and vanishes.[2]

Many of our heroes stray from this world into the world of myth and fairy tale, and there they remain with their mighty steeds. In the depths of a lost mountain cavern lies the last kingdom of a great warrior king and his knights. They are all mounted on their favorite bold steeds that have led them to glory in a former time and place. There they sleep suspended in the Dreaming awaiting the call of their country's greatest need, when they will awake and ride forth to glorious victory. Most of the national heroes from ancient and medieval times have a spiritual existence in this magickal cavern, together with their faithful mounts.

Fig. 10. The Little Humpbacked Horse

But sometime the hero is not a powerful knight at all, but just a simple peasant boy, such as Ivan of Russia, who meets the **Wish-Fulfilling Horse**, known sometimes as the **Humpbacked Horse** (*konyok-gobunok*), the **Little Magic Horse**, or the **Golden-Maned Horse**. This little horse appears as modest and unassuming as Ivan, and yet it has wondrous Faerie powers that enable it to grant wishes and transform the peasant boy into a hero who brings the beautiful magic Firebird to the Tsar and marries his love, Princess Yelena the Beautiful.

ANGEL HORSES

The galloping Angel-Horses come sweeping down from the clouds like cloudy visions themselves. Angels are often thought of as the good guys; certainly they are the companions and helpers of the gods, their avatars, and their prophets. The wise and shining white horse named **Kantaki** bore Siddartha Gautama on his journeys leading to enlightenment as the Buddha.

In the *Mahaburata*, the first created horse was **Uccaihcravas** ("he with ears held high"), who became the king of all horses. Luminous white with a black tail, Uccaihcravas was swift as thought and flew through the air to follow the path of the sun. He became one of the horses of Indras.

Fig. 11. Siddhartha Gautama and Kantaki

In the Old Testament, Zachariah records two visions of horses that appear to be guardian angels of the world. In the first vision, an angel rides a red horse and is followed by many red and speckled horses; they go to and fro throughout the Earth and report that all is well. In

Fig. 12. Zachariahs's vision

the second vision, four chariots are pulled by angelic horses: the first chariot has red horses that go to the West; the second chariot has black horses that go to the North; the third chariot has grizzled (grey or blue roan) steeds that go to the South; and the forth chariot has white horses that go to the East. There are also some bay horses that are keen to head out on their own.

The prophet Mohammed had many horses, the most famous of which was **Al Borak**, a stallion

Fig. 13. Al Borak

whose name means "the lightning." Given to the Prophet by the Archangel Gabriel, it was upon the back of this fiery angelic horse that the Prophet ascended into heaven. There are two different descriptions of Borak. In the first one his face is like a man's but his cheeks are like a horse's, and his eyes are the color of jacinths (hyacinth flowers) and as brilliant as stars. He has wings like those of an eagle, speaks with the voice of a man, and glitters all over with radiant light. In the second glowing (but slightly more prosaic) description from *Croquemitaine*, II. 9, Al Borak is characterized as a tall, strong, and clean-limbed steed, whose saffron-golden coat is as glossy as marble. Both his eyes and nostrils are large and full of fire. He has a white star on his forehead, a long, silky mane hangs from his high, arched neck, and his thick tail sweeps the ground.[3] Despite his

Fig. 14. Valkrie

mutable appearance, Borak was one of the few animals to be admitted into Paradise.

In the icy realm of the Norse Heavens lived the **Horses of the Valkyries**. Originally, "horses of the Valkyries" meant the wolves and ravens that gathered around a battle, but in later tales, they became nine cloudy white horses with great swan wings. They flew over the land, enabling the Valkyries to choose and gather the slain from the battlefield; or over the sea, lifting the dead out of the longships or the sea itself. Their manes and tails dripped dew and frost, lightning came from their hooves and from the swords of the battle-maidens, and the flickering aurora borealis was reflected in both the shields and the horse-armor.

DEMON HORSES

Everything must have its opposite, and so we must also have Demon-Horses. If you have ever had to ride an angry horse on a stormy night, you too would probably have a tale or two to tell afterward! Yet it is interesting that as much as we love a thing, we often fear it even more. Thus we have many more stories of demonic equines than we have of the angelic variety, though one or two are definitely borderline cases. The original meaning of the word *hobgoblin* is a Demon-Horse. Its derivation is *hob*, from the Middle English word *hoby*, meaning "a small horse." and *goblin*, meaning a demon

Fig. 15. Brag by Dana Keyes

licious fairy. Appearing as a shapen black horse, the spectral steed known as **Brag** might be seen on lonely moors and roads of England's northern counties, where it would lure wanderers to their death.

You would rather not encounter the **Horse of Gwyn ap Nudd**, for it is the courser of the Wild Huntsman of Wales. The Huntsman comes astride a Demon Horse of blackest hue, whose name means "the torment of battle." He hunts not the deer, but the souls of humanity, for he is the lord of the Celtic Underworld. In Mecklinburg, Germany, another phantasmal Wild Hunt is sometimes seen, in which the **White Horse of Frau Wode** charges through the wooded hillsides. This apparition of an archaic goddess on her spirited white palfrey is accompanied by white hounds and ghostly wild beasts, and yet her appearance is seen as benign and a harbinger of good fortune and a bountiful harvest.

The **Yellow Horse of Loch Lundie** is sometimes considered the devil in disguise. It appears as a golden yellow pony to folks breaking the Sabbath to go fishing in the Loch. Anyone who tries to mount the horse they immediately stick to it and cannot get free.

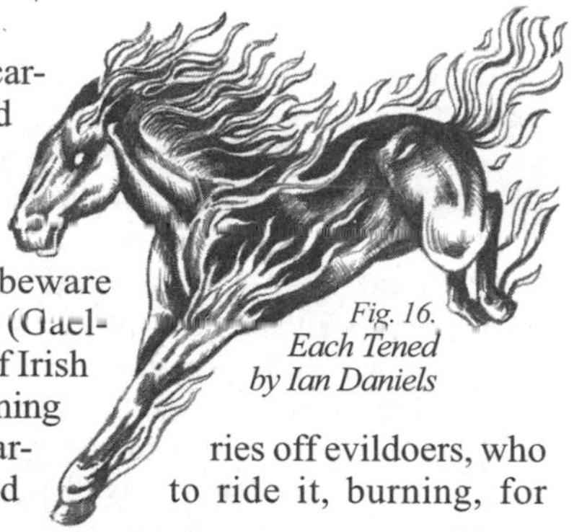

The horse then carries them off and they are never seen again. Even more flagrant scoundrels must beware the *Each Tened* (Gaelic, "fire horse") of Irish folklore. This flaming phantom horse carries off evildoers, who are then compelled to ride it, burning, for eternity.

Fig. 16.
Each Tened
by Ian Daniels

Out of Asia come other equine terror horses. The *Bai-Ma* ("white horse") was a strange albino horse with a tail like that of an ox and a voice like the roar of a tiger. It lived in the Bai Ma Valley of China, between the Sichuan and Gansu provinces. In Persian mythology, the *Conopenii* was a giant fire-breathing horse with the head of an ass. *Keshi* (Sanskrit, "long-haired") was a giant, vicious, long-maned horse in Hindu myth that attacked humans until the god Vishnu choked it to death by shoving his arm down its throat. The Rigvedas also mention the *Yatudhanas*, a horse-headed monster with huge claws that fed on both human and horse flesh and drank cow milk. Agni, the god of fire, cut off its head.

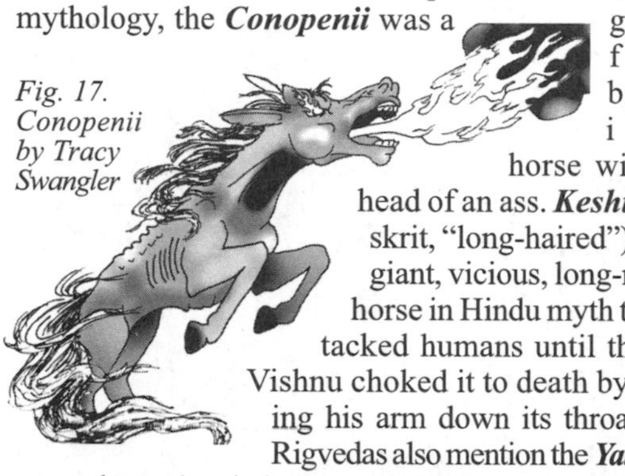

Fig. 17.
Conopenii
by Tracy
Swangler

Even in the United States you find such demon steeds lurking. The tale of *Sam Hart and the Devil's Mare* is an American folk-legend of a farmer who loves to race, and who is challenged by a stranger riding a spirited black mare smelling of brimstone. Sam wins the race on his plow horse, Betsy, by detouring through a churchyard where the Devil's Mare can't follow. His reward for winning the race is the black mare herself. The Demon Mare wins every race Sam enters and makes him wealthy, but he becomes mean and greedy, losing his wife, his faithful horse, and dying an alcoholic.[4]

Such legends predate Christian times. The ancient *Horses of the Wild Hunt* are as dark as pitch or pale

Fig. 18. *The Wild Hunt*

and windblown with fiery eyes and eerie neighing. They ride the stormy night skies to the sound of thunderous hoofbeats and the crash of falling tree branches. Various gods and goddesses are associated with this hunt, including Odin, Hel, Herne, Frau Holde, Gwen ap Nudd, and Arawn. They are accompanied by a huge pack of baying black or white hounds, as well as thunder and lightning. In some areas, to hear the passing of the hunt was a good omen, but in others, it foretold a dire event. Eventually the "hunters" became identified with malevolent Faery folk, cruel or greedy nobles, and finally—predictably—with the devil himself. The horses can fly like the wind, and appear and disappear at will. They sometimes leave their hoofprints in stone.

Fig. 19. *The Morrigan in her chariot*

The *Horses of the Morrigan and the Cailleach* are the steeds of warrior goddesses; ridden into battle, they carry off the souls of warriors fated to die. In many ways they are similar to the angelic horses of the Valkyries. They are black or as red as blood, with glowing eyes. They fly over the battlefield in the company of crows and ravens and smell the scent of death on a man even before he falls. The sound of their unearthly whinnies and the call of ravens are the last sounds a fallen warrior ever hears. Then, swooping down, they bear away his soul between the worlds and into the Summerland, where all is green and there is no more war. The Morrigan sat astride a horse with one leg when she rode to meet Cuchulain in the *Tain bo Regamna*.[5]

From out of the pages of the Book of Revelation in the Bible comes the image of a tall white or pale grey horse ridden by a skeletal figure in a black hooded robe and carrying a scythe. It is the *Pale Horse of Death*. "And I looked, and behold a pale horse: and his name that sat on him was

Fig. 20. *Death Tarot card*
by Pamela Coleman Smith

Death, and Hell followed with him. And power was given unto them over the fourth part of the earth, to kill with sword, and with hunger, and with death, and with the beasts of the earth." (Rev. 6:8) From this beginning, a millennium of folklore has been spun about Death's Pale Horse. His perfect expression is seen in the white horse of the Death card in the Tarot. The Horse of Death can fly, go under the water, and walk through walls or through fire—in short, anywhere death occurs and souls need releasing. In a more modern interpretation, he has become less of a demon and more of a bringer of the compassionate grace stroke. This point of view is typified by **Binky**, Death's horse in Terry Pratchett's *Discworld* novels.

Fig. 21. Hades abducting Kore

Hades' Horses, though not properly demonic, are the four horses that pull the chariot of the Lord of the Underworld in Greek myth, and are certainly considered to be creatures of the dark. Their names are **Abatos** ("inaccessible"), **Abaster** ("away from the stars"), **A'eton** ("swift as an eagle"), and **Nonios**. They are black as coal, with eyes that shine like bright jewels. Their manes are long and loose, and they can surround themselves with a cloud of smoky darkness that hides them entirely from view. Where they strike the earth with their hooves, it cracks open to make caverns. Thus did the Dark God carry away Koré in his golden chariot to become his Queen of the Dead.

According to the Romans, every horse had a piece of black flesh upon its lips (called *hippomanes* by the Greeks). It was thought that a mare would refuse to suckle a colt afflicted with this demonic parasite, though sometimes the mother herself would eat it. Theokritos mentions the hippomanes as coming from Arcadia, "where it maddened colts and swift mares." Also from Greek mythology come the **Mares of Diomedes**. This team of four gigantic, maneating mares was owned by the Thracian King of the Bistones in ancient Greece. Sometimes depicted as winged, the horses were related to the Gorgons and Harpies. Their names were **Deinos** ("terrible"), **Lampon** ("bright"), **Xanthos** ("yellow"), and **Podarkes** ("swift-foot"). Diomedes fed his mares on the flesh of newcomers to his kingdom, but Heracles tamed these mares as his eighth Labor: "He controlled with bit those mares who greedily champed their bloody food at gory mangers with unbridled jaws...." Then the mighty hero fed Diomedes to his own horses and drove the now replete

Fig. 22. The man-eating Mares of Diomedes

and docile mares to Mycenae, where he dedicated them to the goddess Hera. Their descendants were said to still be around at the time of Alexander the Great (356–323 BCE); indeed, his charger **Bucephalus** was said to be one of them.

A thousand years later, Native Americans also had their share of man-eating, troublesome nags. Shoshone Indians tell legends of a **Black Devil**, a jet black stallion with fiery red eyes and sharp teeth said to stalk and eat humans.

But all of these dark horses are eclipsed by the grandmother of them all. She is one of the oldest shadows haunting our subconscious mind, galloping off the limestone walls from the time of the caves. I mean, of course, the **NightMare**. Of all the Demon-Horses mentioned, she is the most familiar and ubiquitous.

The NightMare is an archetypal being composed of scraps of myth and folklore from many cultures. She is the red horse of Ereshkigal, Sumerian goddess of the Underworld; the shadowy horse of Greek Hecate at the crossroads of sleep and death; the icy skeletal steed of Hel in Norse legend; the vampiric Saxon *Mare* or *Mara*; and the clacking, biting skull on a pole called the *Mari Lludd* in Wales. She is even joked about in popular culture as the horse of Casper the friendly ghost. Most of the high and holy images of her have weathered down, but are kept alive by the experience of the NightMare itself. These elements have fused together and given shape to something that has the power to follow us into our own dreams.

The NightMare is a succubus that sits on sleepers' chests, sending them enticing and erotic dreams which slowly become more and more horrifying. The weight of the NightMare makes it difficult to breathe

Fig. 23. Nightmare by Stephanie Hahn-Synnabar

as she feeds on the fear and agony of the sleepers. She slowly draws their souls out of their bodies until they either awaken or expire in their sleep. Death can, in fact, occur as a result of a visitation of Mare. Modern science talks about sleep paralysis and offers their own potions and remedies, but still must acknowledge the mysterious and deathly power of the NightMare.

She dwells in a mare's nest of tangled weeds, bones, feathers and junk that often hides some sort of treasure trove. The best methods of keeping her at bay are to hang a horseshoe over the bedroom door, hammer horseshoe nails into the bed itself, or hang a holy stone (a stone with a hole) around the neck of the sleeper. Various herbs in the artemesia family are also efficacious. To keep Mare away from horses, an iron key is hung on a cotton thread in the stalls or

Fig. 24. Micheal Scott

attached to the halters. Keys are the symbol of the goddess Hecate, and thus the horse is placed under the protection of a more powerful entity. Night-Mare is a truly ancient being that can hold us all in her power. May we awaken to find ourselves safe in our beds.

Yet sometimes the demonic horse can be working for you instead of against you. The **Wizard Michael Scott's Demon-Horse** comes from a 16th-century legend telling of this Wizard who conjured a fiend in the shape of a huge black horse with silver hooves and incredible powers. He flew over the ocean from Scotland to Paris and conversed in human speech, attempting to trick his rider into mentioning holy names in order to get free. When the Wizard confronted the king of France, the Demon-Horse stamped three times: at the first stamp all the bells on the steeples rang, and at the second stamp three of the palace's towers fell down. The king capitulated before the horse stamped a third time.

From medieval *chansons de geste* comes the Demon-Horse **Bayard**, whose name means "bright bay colored." Led from hell by the sorcerer Malagigi, he was given to Aymon of Dordogne. This magickal steed had many amazing powers: he was swifter than any other horse, he could understand human language, and he could grow larger or smaller at will. He was inherited by Reynaud, the son of Aymon,

Fig. 25. Bayard

and though he served the son as well as he had the father (even winning a golden crown from Charlemagne in a race), he fell victim to that emperor's rage and jealousy. Charlemagne conquered the sons of Aymon and had Bayard weighted with a millstone and thrown into the Seine. Some say he drowned, but some say the steed used his demon-spawned magick to free himself. For centuries, farmers in the Ardennes Forest saw his tracks, and heard his hoofbeats and neighing at the full moon. According to tradition, one of the hoofprints may still be seen in the forest of Soignes, and another on a rock near Dinant.

DIVINE AND IMMORTAL HORSES

Now the winged horses and the charioteers of the gods are all of them noble and of noble descent...and there the charioteer putting up his horses at the stall, gives them ambrosia to eat and nectar to drink. —Plato, *Phaedrus*, 246

Some horses achieve divinity all on their own; certainly Pegasus is one, as well as many other noble steeds mentioned previously. Other horses, however, gain their status by association, such as the chariot horses of the various gods. Because horses are accorded status mostly in connection with their relationship to a rider, it is sometimes difficult to separate the equine member of that team from its human partner in this regard. Nevertheless, we have to find ourselves wondering where the Lone Ranger would have been without Silver? Of course, the answer is "on foot."

The Greek list of **Hippoi Athanatoi** ("deathless horses") could go on for pages.[6] Though many of the gods had chariots drawn by their totem creatures—for example, Aphrodite's shell-shaped chariot drawn by gigantic swans—most of the Olympians had their favorite horses, whether riding in a chariot or astride. Zeus, Hera, Ares, Nike, Demeter, Poseidon, and Hades all had chariots pulled by teams of mighty winged stallions, or mares fed on nectar and ambrosia, the elixir of immortality.

Fig. 26. The Dioskouroi

The *Dioskouroi*, Castor (called the "horse tamer") and Pollux, were the divine twins. Both of them put together a team of the most marvelous divine horses imaginable to race their chariots through the clouds and over the Earth. *Harpagos*, *Kyllaros*, *Phlogeus*, and *Xanthos* comprised one of the teams. When the Romans were battling the Latins at Lake Regillus, the heavenly champions fought at the head of their legions. These *Hippoi Athanatoi* carried news of the victory with lightning speed to Rome. At the fountain of Inturna, the divine twins watered their lathered steeds, and the grateful people built a temple there in their honor. On the volcanic rock at Lake Regillus, marks in the shape of horses' hooves were believed to have been left by the celestial chargers.

The *Immortal Mares of Laomedon* were given to Tros by Zeus in compensation for the abduction of Ganymede. They could run over water and the heads of standing grain. They were sold to Laomedon, the king of Troy, who offered them to Heracles for rescuing his daughter Hesione from a Sea-Monster. When Laomedon reneged on the agreement, Heracles sacked Troy in order to claim these fabulous creatures.

Fig. 27. Sleipnir and Odin

The Norse are most remembered for their dragon ships, but horses were a very important part of the culture, both as mounts and as sacrifices. Each day the Aesir rode over Bifrost (the rainbow bridge) to visit other realms, so of course the gods and goddesses of this pantheon had their favorite equine supporters—the most famous of which is *Sleipnir* ("slipper," as in smoothly gliding). This magickal horse was the eight-legged steed of Odin, the great Norse All-Father. Sleipnir could run faster than the wind, traveling in the air, over all the land and sea, and down into the regions of the goddess Hel—all in only nine days. The eight legs symbolize the points of the compass. There is a riddle about him and his master:

> *Who are the two who ride to the Thing?*
> *Three eyes they have together,*
> *Ten feet and one tail.*[7]

Odin of course has only one eye, having sacrificed the other to gain ultimate wisdom.

Sleipnir was grey like a cloudy Nordic sky, and he gained immortality (until Ragnarok) by feeding upon the great World Tree, Yggdrasil. Odin inscribed

the runes he won through his great sacrifice on the teeth of Sleipnir, which granted the horse the boon of supernatural wisdom. He was considered by the Norse people to be the greatest of all horses. The other horses of the Aesir are *Gladr*, *Gyllir*, *Glaer*, *Skeidbrimir*, *Silfrintoppr*, *Synir*, *Gils*, *Falhofnir*, *Gulltoppr*, and *Lettfeti*.

Another famous Norse horse was *Svadilfari* ("he who makes an unfortunate journey"). He was a huge magickal horse belonging to the giant Hrimthurse, who agreed to erect a defensive wall around Asgard, home of the Aesir gods, in return for the sun and the moon—and also the goddess Freya. Persuaded by Loki, the gods accepted and set a deadline of one winter, which they were certain Hrimthurse would be unable to meet. But the gigantic stallion Svadilfari had the strength of 100 mortal horses, and with his help the wall was nearly completed by the eve of the last day. The desperate gods demanded that Loki do something to stop the giant from winning, whereupon Loki transformed himself into a beautiful white mare in heat, seducing Svadilfari away and compelling Hrimthurse to abandon the wall in order to chase his horse. Of this union was born the eight-legged steed Sleipnir, after which Loki returned to his own form.

In the Celtic pantheon, horses were very important, as evidenced by their appearance in artwork—most especially the huge horses cut into the chalk hillsides. But most of the divine equines were under the guardianship of one or more of the horse goddesses: Epona, Rhiannon, and the Morrigan. Because these goddesses rode horses and changed into horses at will, their mutable forms made it difficult to discern who or what they really were. However, one divine Celtic horse that has come down to us in his own right is *Aonbarr* ("unique supremacy"). This magnificent stallion of the Irish god of the sea, Mannan Mac Lir, could cross any sur-

Fig. 28. Aonbarr and Mannanan

face, be it mountain, plain, or ocean, and could even dive beneath the waves. He was loaned to the god Lugh on his quest for the sword of light.

Sometimes divinity comes about in a very odd or even backward way. For instance, take the story of *El Morzillo*, the favorite mount of Hernando Cortez. Morzillo was a shiny black stallion with a reddish luster. He injured his foot and had to be left behind in the village of Peten Lake. There, the Indians, who had never seen a horse before, worshipped him as a god. When he died of their dietary excesses, his image was carved in stone, replacing the image of their previous

Fig. 29.
El Morzillo

rain-god. Priests who came back later were horrified, but El Morzillo became the only horse from the Spanish Conquest of the New World whose name we know: the horse who became an Aztec God.

HORSES OF THE SUN THE MOON THE WIND, AND THE NIGHT

Look! His horses mount so high,
Good of limb and stout and strong.
In the forehead of the sky,
Runs their course the heavens along.
—*The Rig Vedas* (trans. R.T. Griffith)[8]

The Sun

The **Chariot Horses of Helios**, the Greek sun-god, are immortal and wildly strong. Sometimes white with flaming golden-red manes and tails, they fly through the heavens pulling the great burning chariot that is the sun. Once, they ran away with Phaeton, the mortal son of Helios, and almost burned up the Earth until Zeus stopped them. His team of seven are: **Bronte** ("thunder"), **Eos** ("dawning"), **Ethiops** ("flashing"), **Ethon** ("flam-ing"), **Erythreios** ("red-producing"), **Philogea** ("earth-loving"), and **Py-rois** ("fiery"). His alternate team of four are: **Actaeon** ("brilliance"), **Phlegon** ("burning"), as well as Eos and Pyrois. Actaeon is the most strong-willed and headstrong; Eos is the slowest witted; Pyrois is the gentlest and most easily handled; but Phlegon is the favorite.

Fig. 30. Helios and his sun-chariot

The Greek goddess of dawn, Eos, drives a smaller chariot than that of the sun-god. She has a team of two of the immortal flying horses: **Lampos** ("shining") and **Phaethon** ("gleaming")—the latter named after the unfortunate son of Helios.

Surya, the Hindu sun-god, also drives a team of beautiful flying horses called the **Seven Harits**, all of which are mares. They pull his golden chariot through the skies of India. The Seven Harits are: **Gayatri**, **Brhati**, **Usnik**, **Jagati**, **Tristup**, **Anustup**, and **Pankti**. Seven **Gandarvas**, who are demigods of nature, follow in the form of stallions to accompany his flight. Sometimes, Surya appears as an avatar in the form of horse named **Tarkshya**.

In ancient Armenian mythology, **Enik**, **Menik**, **Benik**, and **Senik** were the names of the horses of the sun, and are the source of the children's choosing rhyme, "eenie, meenie, miney, moe."

The Norse sun-deity is a goddess called Sunna or Sol, and she drives a team of two giant, shining horses: **Alsvid** ("all-swift") and **Arvakur** ("early wak-

Fig. 31. Sunna's chariot of the sun.

er"). The Norse personification of the day, Dagur, has a beautiful flying horse, **Skinfaxi** ("shining mane"), whose mane lights up the Earth and sky.

Though horses came later to the Native Americans, they took to them and learned to love them and ride them like no one else. The Navaho sun-father, **Tsohanoai**, had the most beautiful and swiftest horses in all the many levels of being. There were five horses for the different times of the day: an albino for dawn, a blue roan for noon, a red chestnut for sunset, and a dapple grey or dark bay for twilight. The Night-Horse was a coal black steed named **Nightaway**, and he was the favorite of Tsohanoai's right-handed son. Nightaway was a sleek, long-maned black stallion

Fig. 32. Tsohanoi's son and Nightaway

whose fine coat was flecked with tiny silver flecks of mica. He could outrun a comet, leap the tail of a shooting star, and dance in the circle of the rainbow. Tsohanoai's right-hand son rode his father's most powerful horse to Earth. Nightaway ran away with the boy, ripping the reins from his hands, snorting fire, and plunging through the starry midnight sky unchecked, but the boy, whose manhood rite had made him a god, recaptured the reins and rode Nightaway into the dawn. Nightaway became the ancestor of all Navaho horses.[8]

The Moon

To many people, the moon was a goddess or a god carried through the skies on **Lunar Horses**. The Greek Titaness of the moon, Selene, drove a silver chariot with two milk-white steeds, or rode bareback on a single white mare with a silver bridle. You can see her image carved in the marble of the Parthenon. The Norse moon-god was Mani, and his horse was **Alsvider** ("all swift"), and there are tales of Mani mounted on Alsvider pursuing the chariot of Sunna the sun-goddess. When he caught her there was an eclipse of the sun. **Arva**, the winged silver horse of Soma, the Hindu moon-god, flew over the Earth, illuminating it with his brilliance. In Lithuania, the horse of Menulis, the moon-god, has many names. He is called **Kumeliuku Aukso Pasagom**, "the foal with the golden shoes," or **Laukas Arklys**, "the horse with the shining white muzzle" or "horse of the fields." This shining white horse is sent by Menulis to the aid of young heroes in order to help them find the maidens for whom they are searching.

Fig. 33. Selene

The Wind

Allah said to the south wind, "I want to make a creature out of you. Condense." And the wind condensed. He then said to the newly created horse, "I will make you peerless and preferred above all the other animals. You alone shall fly without wings, for all the blessings of the world shall be placed between your eyes and happiness shall hang from your forelock."[9]

On blustery days, horses in a pasture will "get the wind up" and run around wildly with their tales raised, shaking their heads, and snorting and bucking just as though they were challenging the wind to a race. Galloping over the earth with the sound of their

Fig. 35.
Banat al Rih

hooves like rolling thunder and the wind at their backs blowing their manes into a tangle, no wonder so many folktales connect horses with the wind. In Sanskrit, the expression *vatacvas* means "wind horse," and it is still commonly used to describe the swiftest horses. The **Banat al Rih** ("daughters of the wind") are the archetypal pureblood Arabian horses.

In an apocryphal tale, the prophet Mohammed had a stable of 100 of the fastest and most beautiful horses and decided to test them for loyalty. He penned them up for three days until they were mad with thirst. Then he let them go to the water, but blew a battle horn to summon them. Only five mares answered the call; they became his favorite horses, and their foals alone were honored with the name *asil*—"purest blood."

The Greeks might try tracing their racehorses back to the **12 Mares of Erichtonius**, sired by Boreas, the north wind, with a herd of mares belonging to the king of Dardania. The resulting 12 fillies born could run over the heads of grain in a field of wheat and not bend them, or race along the top of the ocean and gallop on the crests of the breakers.

In Hindu myth, the **Dappled Mares of the Maruts** are the horses formed of grey storm clouds ridden by the storm-gods. In Norse mythology, Gna was a handmaiden to Frigg, and she rode a horse whose magickal powers allowed him to move through the air and over the water, running errands for Odin's wife. His name was **Hofvarpnir,** meaning "hoof-thrower."

Native American people of the Choctaw tribe have a story of the love and self-sacrifice of the **Choctaw Wind-Horse**. The last of an archetypal race of free horses with all the powers of nature, Wind-Horse could run through the air and he felt no fear. He was the fastest, kindest, and gentlest of all his kindred. Wind Horse would carry any Indian in distress to safety, but once, out of love, he carried a small wounded boy all the way to the Happy Hunting Ground even though he knew he could not return. The Indian people lost Wind-Horse, but the Great Spirit sent everyday horses to them to be their friends.[10]

Night-Horses

Not all Night-Horses are Night-Mares. We have many positive images of the horses of the night. The ***Vedic Cosmic Horse*** symbolizes the night sky where the Pitris "adorn the black horse with pearls."

Fig. 36. Nott and Hrimfaxi

In Navaho tales, the sun-father's favorite horse was the midnight black ***Nightaway***, who became the progenitor of all horses.

Hrimfaxi ("frost mane") is the horse of Nott, the Norse goddess of night. He was coal black with a scattering of white hairs. His mane and tail were white, and dew-drops dripped from them and from the champing of his bit. These drops, similar to the ambrosia dropped by the horses of the Vedic God Indra, fertilize the Earth.

Fig. 37. The chariot horses of Nyx

The ***Chariot Horses of Nyx***, the Greek goddess of night, are described by many of the later Greek poets. She was sometimes seen as a dark-haired goddess wearing a misty black veil and seated in a black chariot pulled by sable horses, scattering stars in their wake. As she yokes her horses at sunset, the stars come out to be her attendants.

Ancient memories of these nocturnal equines extraordinaire persist in modern narratives. Dr. Clarissa Pinkola Estés tells us: "The old people in my family say as meteors flash through the night sky, it is the Sky Smithy hammering on the iron anvil. *She* is shaping raw silver buckles for the saddle straps of the Night-Horses. They are the ones that pull the sun up from under the dark earth every night."[11]

bEROIC AND WAR bORSES

Much of the history of humanity's partnership with horses is related to warfare. The term "war horse" is synonymous with courage, loyalty, and stoicism in the face of desperate odds. It's no wonder that legends have arisen around these heroic chargers, because nowhere does the line between the real and the fantastic blur as strongly as on the battlefield. As a motif in folklore, a Hero Horse will only allow a true hero to ride it. In a Russian fairy tale, Little Tom tries to pass himself off as a hero, but when he tries to ride the horse of a true fallen hero, the Hero Horse knows he is a fake and will not permit him to mount. In addition, the Hero Horse can speak, and often warns his master or gives good advice. The Hero Horse has compassion as well as wisdom, and weeps for the fate of his master. Even after death, the bones of a Hero Horse contain the strength of the horse itself.

Perhaps the strangest of all the Hero Horse myths comes from Hungary, in the form of tales about the ***Tatos***. The Tatos is born deformed. It bursts out of a black pentagonal egg on an Ash Wednesday, after the hero has carried it for seven summers and seven winters under his arm. It is fed upon golden oats from a silver field. The day it is born the Tatos colt grows half as high as a tree and its mane turns shining silver. On the second day it is higher than the tree and its coat turns a rich gold. And on the third day all its blemishes are removed; it becomes as high as the heavens and can bear the hero on their journeys.[12]

In the Iranian epic, the *Shanamah*, the gigantic hero Rustam chooses ***Raksh***, a huge, red-speckled young stallion, as his steed. The charger is such a determined partner in warfare that he goes out and fights the monsters while his master sleeps. He is also wise and sensitive, communicating with Rustam about impending danger. In the heat of battle, Rustam ignors Raksh's warning, thinking him afraid. He commands Raksh to go forward and applies the whip; Raksh plunges forward and into a hidden trap, and they are impaled on buried stakes.[13]

Another attribute of the Hero Horse is that it will often avenge its master's death. ***Abjer*** is the incomparably brilliant and loyal horse of Antar, one of the greatest desert warriors of Arab folklore. A stallion blacker than night and faster than the wind, Antar purchases him at the cost of everything he owns. When Antar is killed in battle, Abjer goes mad and avenges him by killing every single one of the enemies except the leader—who is deliberately left eyeless and maimed in the

Fig. 38. Rustam and Raksh

Fig. 39. Antar and Abjer

desert to suffer.

Often the hero and his horse have to overcome a handicap, either physical or spiritual. **Sivushko** is the fantastic coal-black steed of the medieval Russian *bogatyr* (knight), Ilya Muromets. The stallion is also called Barushka, Matushka, or Kosmatushka. The most beautiful horse in all of Russia, he is capable of taking 33-mile-long strides and clearing whole mountain ranges in a single leap. Both horse and hero are born lame, but are healed by a mysterious monk. Together they kill a monster called the Nightingale Robber, and single-handedly defend the city of Chernigov from invasion.

Fig. 40. Sivushko by Vastnetsov, 1914

Oftentimes, real heroes and their horses can become legends long after they have gone on to the pastures in the sky. Krali Marko was a Bulgarian war hero who lived around 1350 CE and fought the Ottoman Empire, and **Shar-koliya** was his mighty horse. Legend, however, is eternal: Marko was adopted by a *vila* (a forest nymph), and he was so strong that he chose the only horse he could not throw over his shoulder. Sharkoliya was a piebald stallion that could leap over mountains, snort fire, and drink wine mixed with blood. Though they were killed in battle, it is believed that they sleep in a cave, waiting for times when they are needed to inspire their

Fig. 41. Sharkoliya and Krali Marko

countrymen to victory. The most recent sighting occurred during World War I at the siege of Castle Marko. Likewise, **Hengroen** and **Llamrei**—King Arthur's favorite stallion and mare—are said to be interred with him in a secret cave near

Badbury Rings, and will emerge when Britain's last battle is fought.

One of the most famous warhorses of all time, **Bucephalus**, was the wild and unruly stallion that no one could ride until the young Alexander of Macedon climbed on his back. He turned the horse's head toward the sun so he would not be afraid of his shadow. His name means "bull's head," and it is said that he had horns like those a bull. Alexander the Great is said to have fed the huge black charger on the flesh of conquered enemies, à la Diomedes, and given him wine mixed with bull's blood to drink. Bucephalus carried Alexander on his conquest of the world and died fighting war elephants in India, carrying his master to safety before expiring. Alexander built a city on the spot where Bucephalus was buried and named it after him.

Fig. 42. Alexander the Great and Bucephalus

Although Alexander himself was considered a god in certain regions, Bucephalus was considered to be a mortal, if magickal, creature. However, the Roman emperor Caligula declared his horse **Incitus** to be a god, adorned him with jewels, and then rode him into the halls of the Roman senate, naming him as consul. Caligula explained that his horse was far more intelligent than those men who tried to run the empire. Another Roman emperor with a strange horse was Julius Caesar, whose horse supposedly had toes instead of regular hoofs. This polydactylic equine was said to portend Caesar's world conquest.

On the other hand, the divine coursers of Ares, the god of war, were the very archetypes of savage warhorses and needed no mere emperor's declaration to confirm this. Born of the north wind, Boreas, and one of the *Erinnyes* (Furies), their names were: **Aithon** ("red fire"), **Phlogeus** ("flame"), **Phobos** ("panic"), and **Konobos** ("tumult"). They breathed fire, dried up rivers, and the Earth herself trembled beneath their hooves.

In the German epic poem, the *Nibelungenleid*, Brynhilde the Valkyrie had a magickal white horse named **Grane**. He could fly, and had the power to carry his rider through any battle unscathed. He was given to the hero Siegfried as a love gift from Brynhilde, and when Siegfried was killed, Grane carried Brynhilde into his flaming funeral pyre.

phantom horses

The White Horse of Uffington is the most famous and impressive

Fig. 43. The White Horse of Uffington

hillside carving in Britain. It dates from around 1000 BCE and is incised through the green turf and into the underlying white chalk. It is difficult to see the entire animal from the ground; the best views are from the air. There is a small hillock with a circular depression in the center, called the manger. Folklore says that the horse sometimes comes alive during the full moon and eats from the manger. Many people leave gifts for the horse, asking it to ride into their dreams and bring them fertility, prosperity, and healing.[14]

In the Shetland Islands you might encounter ***Neugles***. Once dangerous kelpies, these are now benevolent Horse Phantoms that will rise up out of the bogs or around moors and help lost travelers find their way back home safely. They leave round hoofprints beside *burns* (streams), where they take off to jump over the water. Neugles are small ponies, but they have hoofs the size of dinner plates.

Fig. 44. Neugle by Oberon

At midnight in the Ilmington Hills, an apparition known as the ***Gloucester Night Coach*** haunts the lonely roads. A coach drawn by six dark horses passes over places where no mortal can drive. Throughout Britain, ***Headless Phantom Horses*** abound. It is simply amazing how many of these truncated ghosts haunt the scenes of their former activities. Headless Nick from the *Harry Potter* book series is not the only one of his kind. From Lanreath in Cornwall come headless horses pulling a carriage. Sir Thomas Boleyn, the father of Anne Boleyn ("Anne of the Thousand Days"), can be seen with his daughter riding through the countryside in their coaches with headless horses. Even in the United States, areas of New England are haunted by several genuine versions of the nemesis of Ichabod Crane and his boney old cob. A 1999 movie popularized the tale all over again, embellishing it with a Hessian mercenary and his huge, wild-eyed Friesian steed.

White Spirit-Horses can be both harbingers of magick and otherworldly apparitions. When the Lakota Sioux Indians see a white horse, they know that it brings a message from the spirit world. When the Navajo see a white horse, they know that it brings a gift from the sun-father. The milk-white charger of the prairies was so fast that he could never be caught,

and so smart and canny he could hide anywhere and evade any trouble. "Behold a white horse: and he that sat on him had a bow…" From the Lone Ranger's Silver to the wild white mustang stallion only glimpsed but never captured, the mystical mystery horse is the phantasmic apparition tantamount to the Native American's White Buffalo.

talking and prophetic horses

To Horses beyond all mortal creatures cunning Nature has given a subtle mind and heart. …Ere now in battle a horse, Xanthos, has burst the bonds of silence and overleapt the ordinance of Nature and taken a human voice and a tongue like that of man. Arion too, had such powers of speech and could run with light feet over the corn-ears and brake them not.—Oppian, *Cynegetica*[15]

The most renowned of all their kind in classical history are ***Balios*** and ***Xanthos***. This pair of immortal horses, a dappled grey and a golden bay, were born to the harpy Podarge, and sired by Zephyrus, the west wind. Poseidon gave them to King Peleus at his wedding to the sea-goddess, Thetis. In turn, Peleus gave them to his son, Achilles, who took them into the Trojan War. They pulled his war chariot and helped to make him invincible. He loaned them to his beloved friend Patroklos, and when he was slain by Hector, the horses grieved so much by his body that they would not leave until commanded personally by Zeus. When Achilles rebuked them for allowing Patroklos to be killed, Xanthos answered him, "We will keep you safe for this

Fig. 46. Balios and Xanthos

time, O hard Achilles, but the day of your death is near. Yet we are not the ones to blame. Know instead that it is a great god and a powerful Destiny."[16]

Arion, the magickal flying horse, also spoke and warned his master Adrastos not to go to battle in Thebes, lest he be defeated. Adrastos would not listen and yet, out of the famous "Seven against Thebes," Adrastos was the only one saved, by his horse Arion.

Germans, Slavs, and Persians all had ***Equimantic Horses***. Tacitus tells us that the ancient Germans practiced a kind of augury with sacred horses, listening to their neighing and interpreting it as the messages of the gods. The primary god of ancient Slavic

Paganism was Svantevit, who had a sacred white horse that he rode in battle and which was kept in his temple. The behavior of the horse was read by priests and used to predict the future. In Persia, around 500 BCE, the custom for choosing a king was that the competitors would meet at an agreed-upon spot at an agreed-upon time, and he whose horse whinnied first would be named king. Darius's groom ensured his succession by taking his stallion to that place the night before and showing him a mare in heat. The next day, when the stud arrived, he whinnied for the mare and won Darius the throne.

Similar to the stories of the Russian Humpbacked Pony and the Five-Colored Horse of Spain, the Chinese story of the **Good Luck/Bad Luck Horse** concerns a crooked little grey horse with no eyes originally created by a lonely boy with the help of a compassionate Wizard. The wish-fulfilling equine is granted a charm of unfathomable goodness. Originally called **Bad Luck Horse**, he is ridden, together with his mate, **No Good Mare**, by his best friend, Wa Tung, to the beginning of a war. Then, as the horses on both sides of the river line up for the big battle, the odd little horse transforms into a beautiful flying white steed with rainbow hoofs and soars across the river, where he negotiates with the enemy's horses. Next, he flies back across to negotiate with his own side's horses. All the horses on both sides bolt, carrying their riders into the river and 'round and 'round until the whole thing becomes such a mess that everyone, even the leaders, burst out laughing and the war is called off.[17]

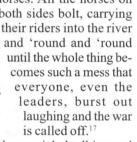

Fig. 36. Good Luck Horse

Kourkig of Sasun was the magickal talking and flying marine horse that originally came from a kingdom at the bottom of a lake and assisted his divine riders—Sanasar, Mher, and David, three generations of primal Armenian heroes. Kourkig carried his riders in their quests to slay Dragons and retrieve magick gemstones, as well as other feats, and he advised the grandson, David, to drink from the milk fountain of his father when he was wandering and delirious. The milk was *soma*, the drink of the gods, and David's power was restored.

Sometimes horses don't have to talk as Mr. Ed or Francis the Mule do in order to change the future. **Doomstead** is a magickal grey horse that transports the veiled maiden Skuld, the norn of the future, on her rides with the Valkyries. Doomstead, who is named for the home of the norns, aids Skuld's choice of heroes to claim. The Prophetic **Horses from Revelation** were described by St. John in his biblical vision

representing the future. The **Red Horse** represents war, the **Black Horse** represents famine, the **Pale Horse** is death, and the **White Horse** is conquest. There are also several monstrous horse hybrids—locust-scorpion-horses and fire-breathing lion-horses—that emerge from the pit to terrorize the future world.

Fig. 37. The Four Horsemen of the Apocalypse

The point of so many of these divine—or divining—horse tales is not so much that the animals spoke. Rather, it was that they were so much more intelligent and sensible than their owners and all the other people around them. If only Achilles had listened to Xanthos…

MONSTER MOVIES: WONDER-HORSES

Fantasia (animated-1940)—Pegasi ; *Francis the Talking Mule* movie series (1948-52); *Darby O'Gill and the Little People* (1959)—Phooka, Spectral coach horses; *Clash of the Titans* (1981)—Pegasus; *High Spirits* (1988)—Phooka; *The Adventures of Baron Munchauen* (1989)—Heroic Horse; *Wyrd Sisters* (animated-BBC-1996)—Death's Pale Horse (*Binky*); *Soul Music* (animated-BBC-1997)—Death's Pale Horse; *Sleepy Hollow* (1999)—Demon Horse; *Lord of the Rings: The Two Towers* (2002)—Heroic Horse; *Lord of the Rings: Return of the King* (2003)—Heroic Horse; *Harry Potter and the Goblet of Fire* (2007)—Pegasi; *Hogfather* (BBC-2006)—Death's Pale Horse; *Harry Potter and the Order of the Phoenix* (2007)—Spectral coach horses (*Thestrals*)

6. holy cows and sacred bulls

By Oberon Zell-Ravenheart

*An old cowpoke went ridin' out
  one dark and windy day,
Upon a ridge he rested as
  he went along his way,
When all at once a mighty herd
  of red-eyed cows he saw,
Plowin' through the ragged skies
  and up a cloudy draw.
Their brands were still on fire and
  their hooves were made of steel,
Their horns were black and shiny
  and ther hot breath he could feel.
A bolt of fear went through him
  as they thundered through the sky,
For he saw the riders comin' hard
  and heard their mournful cry:
Yippee-yi-ay-ay, yippee-yi-yo-oh!
  Ghost riders in the sky!*
    —Johnny Cash, *Ghost Riders in the Sky*

Ian Daniels

ATTLE WERE FIRST DOMESTICATED IN the early Neolithic Age, around 9,000 years ago, becoming the first animals to be raised for food. The earliest known cattle ranchers were the Anatolians of Asia Minor (now Turkey). Herds of cattle soon became equated with wealth, and they are still so regarded throughout the world. Indeed, the very term *cattle* comes from Latin *caput* ("head"), and originally meant "unit of livestock," which is why we still refer to so many "head" of cattle. Other terms deriving from this root are *chattel* (property) and *capital* (wealth).

Fig. 1. Bull heads excavated from Çatal hüyük in the Museum of Anatolian Civilizations in Ankara.

Adult female cattle are called *cows*, and adult males are *bulls*. The young are *calves*. These terms also apply to other animals, such as buffalo, elephants, and whales. A young female before she has calved is a *heifer*. A young male is a *bullock*, which, along with *steer*, is also the term for a castrated male. A steer used as a draft animal (as in pulling a plough or cart) is called an *ox* (plural *oxen*). If it was castrated as an adult, however, it is called a *stag*. The adjective that applies to cattle is *bovine*, from Latin *bovis*.[1] But along with domestic cattle, the biological subfamily *Bovinae* includes two dozen species of medium-to-large

ungulates, including Bison, Water Buffalo, Yaks, and four-horned and spiral-horned antelopes.[2]

But with all this terminology, there is a remarkable omission: there is no common, non-gender-specific, singular term for the animal itself. For instance, we have equivalent terms for equines: a male is a *stallion*, a female is a *mare*, a castrated male is a *gelding,* and so on. But generically we can still refer to a horse. For cattle, there is no equivalent to "horse."

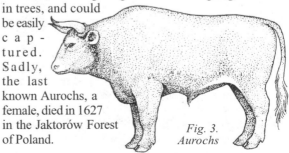
Fig. 2. Domestic cow

The progenitor of all domestic cattle was the mighty European Aurochs (*Bos primigenius*). It is called the *Urus* in medieval bestiaries, where it is described as an ox-like animal the size of a large bull, having huge, saw-tooth horns with which it cuts down trees. When the Urus drank seawater, it became disoriented, stabbing the ground or entangling its horns in trees, and could be easily captured. Sadly, the last known Aurochs, a female, died in 1627 in the Jaktorów Forest of Poland.

Fig. 3. Aurochs

Biblical scriptures and legends often refer to a gigantic wild ox called the *Re'em*. There was said to be only one pair at a time, living at opposite ends of the Earth. After 70 years apart, they would come together for one day, and after mating, the female would kill the male. After 12 years of gestation, the female would bear twins, a male and a female, herself dying in childbirth. And then the cycle would repeat. The Re'em is mentioned nine times in the Old Testament: in Job 39:9-10; Deuteronomy 33:17; Numbers 23:22, 24:8; Psalms 22:21, 29:6, 92:10; and Isaiah 34:7. Although this word was mistranslated as "Unicorn" in the *King James Bible*, the animal intended was, of course, the Aurochs.

Cattle became supremely important to the emergence of Bronze Age civilizations in Anatolia, India, Crete, Egypt, and the British Isles. These cultures venerated sacred bulls and cows, and even adopted the social model of their livestock, with powerful men accumulating large harems of women and even larger numbers of castrated eunuchs. In the book of Exodus, an idol of a golden calf (representing the Apis Bull of Egypt) leads to the first recorded massacre of heretics, as Moses orders the slaughter of its worshippers. Interestingly, the Bronze Age of cattle prominence was also the Zodiacal Age of Taurus the Bull. And an ox also appears as one of the 12 signs of the Chinese Zodiac, which otherwise bears no resemblance to the Western version.

COSMIC COWS

In Hinduism, cows are considered to be particularly sacred. The cow symbolizes abundance, the sanctity of all life, and the bountiful Mother Earth, who gives much while asking nothing in return. Hindus respect the cow as a maternal figure both for her gentleness and for providing nurturing milk and milk products for a basically vegetarian diet. Hindus do not exactly worship cows, yet these placid animals hold an honored place in their society, and few Hindus eat beef.[1]

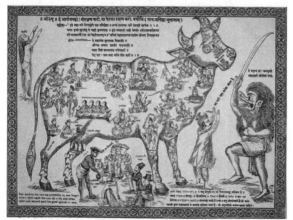

Fig. 4. Nagpur Cow Protection League (1890)

In Hindu mythology, *Aditi* or *Surabhi* ("Fragrant Rain") is the primordial cosmic cow that brings forth and nourishes every living thing. It is her milk in the great Sea of Milk (the Milky Way) that is churned by the gods to create the world. *Kama-Dhenu,* the great Cosmic Cow of Plenty, is a child of the sun-goddess Rohini. She was born during the Churning of the Ocean of Milk, from which many things were created in the manner of butter. Her great udders produce an endless supply of milk that nourishes all beings. She also grants wishes. And the world itself is supported upon the enormous horns of an immense white cosmic cow named *Dhol* (or *Dhaul*).

Fig. 5. Vishnu Churning the Ocean of Milk

As in India, cows often figure in creation myths as bringing forth gods, humans, and other creatures—and nourishing them with their abundant milk. In Egyptian mythology, *Mehturt* or *Mehet-Weret* ("Great Flood") is the primoridial cosmic cow-goddess and mother of Ra, the sun-god. She represents the heavenly river (the Milky Way) upon which the solar barque sails across the sky.

In Persian mythology, *Gush Urvan* (also *Gosh, GMshkurkn,* or *GMshkurvan*) is a vast cosmic cow that contains the seeds of all plants and animals. She grazes upon the barren Earth for 3,000 years, until she is killed by Mithra. From her body emerges a pair of cattle plus 282 pairs of other animals, and from her legs arise 65 species of vegetation. In one later version of the myth, however, she is a bull.

And in the Norse creation myth, an immense cow named *Audumbla* is the second being after the giant Ymir to appear from the melting ice of Niflheim. Her milk feeds Ymir, and her licking of the ice reveals the first gods.

Fig. 6. Audumbla licking Odin free of the ice (Tracy Swagler)

Glas Ghaibhlann (or *Glass Ghaighlaann,* "grey, white-loined cow") is a great magickal cow of Scottish and Irish folklore. Owned by the smith god Goibniu, she is pale grey with green spots, and gives an endless supply of milk. She often stays with poor families to assist them, until a fool strikes her, or she is milked into a leaky bucket, at which point she departs. When speaking of a particularly fertile field, it is still sometimes said that "the Grey Cow slept here."

Dun (brown) cows figure prominently in a number of legends and folktales of the British Isles. The **Dun Cow of Warwick** is an enormous magickal cow from 10th-century Shropshire. The stone circle on Staple Hill was used as a corral for her, and she provided perpetual milk for local giants and others. But a skeptical old crone produced a sieve to test her, and, furious at this insult, the cow became a rampaging monster and was eventually killed on Dunsmore Heath by Sir Guy of Warwick. One of the cow's alleged horns was displayed at Warwick Castle for generations, but was probably the tusk of an elephant or fossil mammoth.

Another Dun Cow features in *Book of the Dun Cow*, a 7th-century collection of tales of the Irish epic hero Cuchulainn.

The legend of the founding of Durham Cathedral in County Durham, northeast England, also involves a Dun Cow. As the story goes, a band of monks was fleeing Viking incursions in 995 CE, transporting the sacred remains of the 7th-century saint, Cuthbert of Lindisfarne, in search of a safe haven. It is said that they followed two milkmaids who were searching for their lost Dun Cow. The trail led onto a peninsula formed by a loop in the River Wear, and there was the cow, lying down. The monks set down Cuthbert's coffin and were unable to lift it again. This was taken as sign that the new shrine should be built on that very spot.[1]

Fig. 7. Legend of the Dun Cow of Durham

SACRED BULLS

The sacred bull of the Hattians, whose elaborate standards were found at Alaca Höyük alongside those of the sacred stag, survived in the Hurrian and Hittite mythologies as *Seri* and *Hurri* ("Day" and "Night")—the bulls who carried the weather god Teshub on their backs or in his chariot, and who grazed on the ruins of cities.[3]

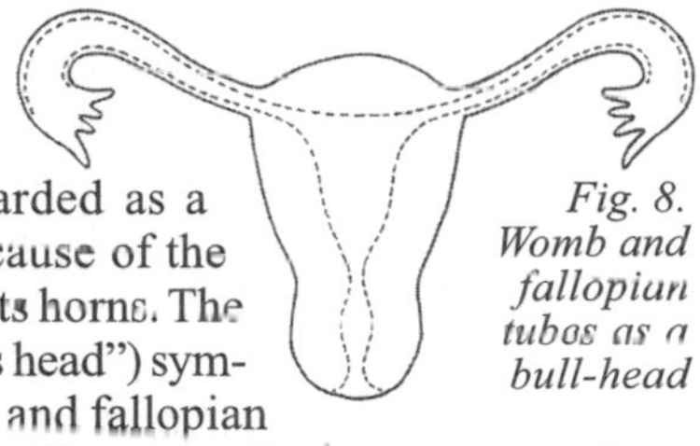

Fig. 8. Womb and fallopian tubes as a bull-head

In ancient Mesopotamia, the bull was regarded as a lunar creature because of the crescent shape of its horns. The *bucranium* ("bull's head") symbolized the womb and fallopian tubes, which were often inscribed upon its surface. (Fig. 8) Indeed, the Egyptian word for bull, *ka*, also means the life-force or soul. Bull skulls were prominently displayed in temples and on altars throughout the Middle East—sometimes covered with clay in a semblance of flesh. Neolithic sanctuaries in Çatalhöyük in eastern Anatolia (Turkey), Crete, and Cyprus featured bull-horned stone altars, and masks made of bull skulls were worn in fertility rites. The legend of the Cretan Minotaur may very well have been inspired by these ritual costumes.

In Greek myth, the **Minotaur** ("Bull of Minos") is a ferocious monster with the body of a powerful man and the head of a carnivorous bull. Called *Asterion*, he is the hideous, cannibalistic offspring of Crete's Queen Pasiphaë and a beautiful white bull that King Minos refuses to sacrifice to Zeus. The queen's unnatural lust for the bull is inflicted as divine punishment for the offense. Minos keeps Asterion in an underground maze called the *labyrinth*, designed by the brilliant architect Daedalus (best known for fabricating wax and feather wings for himself and his son, Icarus) specifically to imprison the beast. Minos feeds Asterion on tributory sacrifices of Athenian youths (seven boys and seven girls every nine years) until the hero Theseus (aided by princess Ariadne, who gives him a ball of thread to lay down as a trail) enters the labyrinth and slays the monster.

But even before he faces the fearsome bull-man, Theseus must capture the ancient and sacred *Marathonian Bull*, 26 miles outside of Athens. And famous

Fig. 9. Minotaur by Joe Butt

Fig. 10. Bull-leaping fresco from Knossos, Crete

frescoes adorning the walls of Crete's Knossos necropolis depict athletic youths of both sexes catapulting over charging bulls by grasping their horns. (Fig. 10)

Crete is also the place where all-father Zeus, in the guise of a magnificent white bull, brings the Phoenician princess Europa, after arising from the sea and abducting her from her homeland across the waves. Their children become the Europeans, and the constellation of Taurus the Bull commemorates this myth.

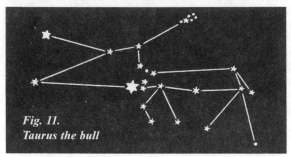

**Fig. 11.
Taurus the bull**

In the ancient Sumerian *Epic of Gilgamesh, **Gugalana*** (or *Gudanna*) is Anu's monstrous Bull of Heaven. Gugalana is the first husband of the Goddess of the Underworld, Ereshkigal, and his poisonous breath can kill 200 warriors. Anu sends him to plague the city of Uruk as punishment for King Gilgamesh having rejected the advances of his daughter, the goddess Inanna. Gilgamesh and his companion, Enkidu the wild man, fight and butcher him, but in retaliation Anu causes Enkidu to sicken and die. This is another reference to the constellation Taurus and the precession of the Equinoxes.

*Fig. 12. Gilgamesh
and the Bull of Heaven*

A similar myth involving the slaying of the great Bull of Heaven (the constellation Taurus) forms the basis of Mithraism—a widespread cult throughout the Roman Empire that was the primary competition for early Christianity in the 2nd–4th centuries CE. A representation of the *tauroctony* ("killing of the bull") was depicted in every *Mithraeum* (temple). This is another reference to the precession of the Equinoxes and the transition of the vernal equinoctial sun from Taurus to Aries around 2300 BCE.[4] Some historians have suggested that the sport of bullfighting in Spain and southern France originated in this cult.

In the depiction [of the tauroctony], Mithras, wearing a Phrygian cap and pants, slays the bull from above. A serpent that symbolizes the earth and a dog drink from the bull's open wound, and a scorpion attacks the bull's testicles sapping the bull for strength. Typically, a raven or crow is also present, and sometimes also a goblet and small lion. Cautes and Cautopates, the celestial twins of light and darkness, are torch-bearers, standing on either side with their legs crossed, Cautes with his brand pointing up and Cautopates with his turned down. Above Mithras, the symbols for Sol and Luna are present in the starry night sky.

The scene seems to be astrological in nature. It has been proposed by David Ulansey that the tauroctony is a symbolic representation of the constellations…the bull is Taurus, the snake Hydra, the dog Canis Major, the crow or raven Corvus, the goblet Crater, the lion Leo, and the wheatblood for the [red] star Spica. The torch-bearers may represent the two equinoxes.... Mithras himself could also be associated with Perseus, whose constellation is above that of the bull.[5]

*Fig. 13. Mithras
slaying the Bull of
Heaven. Marble
group in the
British Museum.*

Egyptian mythology includes several sacred bulls. Most important is certainly ***Apis*** (also *Hap*, or Greek, *Epaphus*), a gigantic black bull sacred to the creator-god Ptah. He was shown bearing a solar disk between his horns, with a white square or triangle on his face, a *scarab* under his tongue, and a white eagle upon his back. As the embodiment of Ptah and later Osiris, Apis was represented in Memphis by a living bull that bore certain sacred markings, and whose mother had been struck by lightning. The bull was housed in the temple for its lifetime, and, upon death, was mummified and entombed in a giant sarcophagus at Zaqqara, city of the dead.

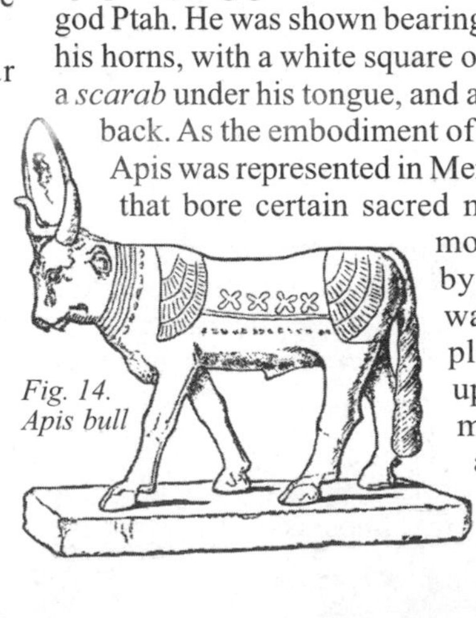

*Fig. 14.
Apis bull*

Another Egyptian sacred bull is **Merwer** (also *Mnevis*, Greek, *Menius*, or "Bull of Meroe"), herald and avatar of the sun god Atum-Ra. Similar to Apis, he was represented at Heliopolis by a magnificent living bull that was mummified upon its death.

Fig. 15. Merwer

Buchis (Greek, "Bull"; also *Bukhe, Bukhe See*) is another great bull in Egyptian mythology, sacred to the god Menthu at his temple at Hermonthis. His hair grows backwards, and changes color every hour of the day.

OTHER MYTHIC BULLS

Aatxe—A terrifying red bull in the Basque folklore of Spain. Dwelling among the canyons, caves, and gorges of the Pyrences Mountains, he comes out on stormy nights to harass travelers. His younger self is called *Aatxegorri*. He is the nemesis of all Unicorns in Peter Beagle's fantasy novel and movie, *The Last Unicorn* (1968). His mate is *Beigorri*, a crimson cow.

Apres—A Heraldic bull with a short tail similar to that of a bear.

Fig. 16 Apres

Donn of Cuálgne (also *Donn Tarbh*, "Brown Bull")—The gigantic, magickal bull of the Irish national epic, the *Tain bó Cuáilgne* ("The Cattle Raid of Cooley"), in which it is said that: "50 youths engaged in games on his fine back, finding room every evening to play draughts and engage in riotous dancing." He screened 100 warriors "from heat and cold under his shadow and shelter," and "his musical lowing every evening as he returned to his shed and byre was music enough and delight enough for a man in the north and south and in the west and in the middle of the cantered of Cooley." His lowing alone was enough to put all the cows that heard him in calf.

HadhayMsh (also *Hadhayoshi* or *Sarsaok*)—A mighty ox in the Zoroastrian mythology of ancient Persia, that carried the first humans over the primal ocean. At the time of the *Frashkart*—the ending of all things—its fat will be used to create an elixir of immortality, called *haoma*, for the resurrection of the righteous.

Itharther—In the mythology of the Kabyl people of Algeria, a titanic, primal buffalo whose seed engenders all the wild animals of the Earth.

Kudan—A kind of inverted Minotaur, Kudan is a human-headed bull from Japanese folklore, with three eyes on each side of its body and horns down its back. He always speaks truth and is sought out as an oracle of things to come.

Fig. 17. Kudan

Kujata—The vast and mighty bull in Moslem myth that sits astride the cosmic fish **Baharmut**. On his back, Kujata bears a gigantic, glowing ruby as well as the angel who carries the Earth on his shoulders. Kujata is said to have 4,000 eyes, 4,000 ears, 4,000 mouths, 4,000 nostrils, and 4,000 legs!

Nandi—In Hindu mythology, a gigantic, milk-white bull that is the steed of the god Shiva, the leader of the Ganas, and the protector of all animals. His consort is the cow *Nandini*.

Fig. 18. Nandi bull

And finally, we must include **Babe**, the giant ox companion of legendary logger Paul Bunyan. Babe was born white, but he turned blue under the snow of the Winter of Blue Snows. He was 93 hands high, and Minnesota's 10,000 lakes were created when his huge footprints filled up with water. Babe would eat 30 bales of hay as a snack (with baling wire intact!). But he died after eating all the pancakes in camp—including the burning stove they were being grilled on. The Dakota Badlands are the mound that Paul raised over his grave.

MONSTER MOVIES: TAURINES

The Last Unicorn (animated—1968): The Red Bull; *Time Bandits* (1981): Minotaur; *Tall Tale* (1994): Babe the Blue Ox; *Hercules in the Maze of the Minotaur* (TV—1994); *Chronicles of Narnia: The Lion, the Witch and the Wardrobe* (2005): Minotaur; *Minotaur* (2006).

7. THE PIASA AND THE MANTICORE

By Oberon Zell-Ravenheart

The Manticore is equally appealing,
He jumps about and has a prickly tail.
Three rows of teeth and two superb mustaches,
You'll find him leaping over hill and dale.
　　　　　—Barbara Wersba (1932–)
　　　　　The Land of Forgotten Beasts

THE PIASA

ALLED "ONE OF THE MOST HAUNTED towns in America," Alton, Illinois, is about 12 miles north of St. Louis, situated between the mouths of the Missouri and Illinois Rivers, on the east bank of the mighty Mississippi featured in the stories of Tom Sawyer and Huckleberry Finn. But Alton is also the home of a deeper and more ancient legend—and an intriguing monster of mystery.

Writing in 1836, Professor John Russell of Bluffdale, Illinois, described the perpendicular bluffs and cliffs, rising to a height of 100 feet, that bordered the river's edge:

> In descending the river to Alton, the traveler will observe, between that town and the mouth of the Illinois, a narrow ravine through which a small stream discharges its waters into the Mississippi. This stream is the Piasa (pronounced Pi-a-saw). Its name is Indian, and signifies, in the Illini language, "The bird which devours men." Near the mouth of this stream, on the smooth and perpendicular face of the bluff, at an elevation which no human art can reach, is cut the figure of an enormous bird, with its wings extended. The animal which the figure represents was called by the Indians the Piasa. From this is derived the name of the stream.[1]

This now-famous petrograph had been first reported in 1673 by Father Jacques Marquette, who was recording his famous journey down the Mississippi River with Louis Joliet. Here is the entry from Fr. Marquette's diary:

While Skirting some rocks, which by Their height and length inspired awe, We saw upon one of them two painted monsters which at first made Us afraid, and upon Which the boldest savages dare not Long rest their eyes. They are as large As a calf; they have Horns on their heads Like those of a deer, a horrible look, red eyes, a beard Like a tiger's, a face somewhat like a man's, a body

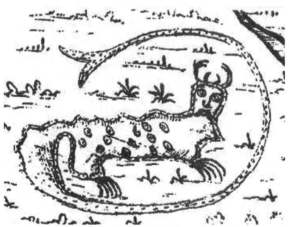

Fig. 1.
"The Manticora
Monster of Tartary," 17th century

Covered with scales, and so Long A tail that it winds all around the Body, passing above the head and going back between the legs, ending in a Fish's tail. Green, red, and black are the three Colors composing the Picture. Moreover, these 2 monsters are so well painted that we cannot believe that any savage is their author; for good painters in France would find it difficult to reach that place Conveniently to paint them. Here is approximately The shape of these monsters, As we have faithfully Copied It.[2]

Fig. 2. Piasa from Fr. Marquette's diary

Interestingly, the creature depicted by Fr. Marquette is wingless. Created long before the arrival of any European explorers in that area, the so-called Piasa petroglyph was probably actually a representation of the **Underwater Panther**, a powerful and usually malevolent creature appearing in the mythology of several native traditions, particularly in the Great Lakes region. These monsters combine features of several animals: the body and tail of a mountain lion, the horns of a deer or bison, scales of a snake, feathers of a bird, and other parts as well. One variant, *Michi-Pichoux*, figured in the folklore of the Cree Indians of eastern Canada, where it dwelled among the islands

of the St. Lawrence River. It was described by French priest Fr. Louis Nicholas in his *Histoire Naturelle* (1675) as a hairy, tiger-like beast more than 18 feet long, with huge, clawed feet and a paddle tail like a beaver's. Its enormous head had fangs more than 2 feet long, and it preyed upon humans, especially children.

Fig. 3. Underwater Panther   (Ojibwa petrograph), from Lake Superior Provincial Park, Ontario, Canada

Moreover, it seems that the term *Piasa* is actually from the Miami-Illinois word *páyiihsa*—supernatural dwarfs that attack travelers—and has no meaning of "man-eating bird."[3]

The petrograph was noted subsequently by LaSalle and other 17th-century French explorers. Additional sightings were reported in the early 19th century, and a sketch was made in 1825 by William Dennis, who labeled it as a "Flying Dragon." In 1841 the "Piasa Bird" was included in a lithograph by John Casper Wild, and in 1846, the petrograph was sketched by Henry Lewis for a collection of lithographs published in 1854. In 1847, Swiss artist Rudolf Friederick Kurz described the image as "a colossal eagle."[4]

In his 1836 article titled "The Bird That Devours Men," Russell referred to the "Piasa Bird" for the first time. He also related a legend, much of which he apparently invented, which became the widely accepted explanation of the petrograph.

The legend of the Piasa, according to Russell, is that long, long ago there lived a terrible bird so vast that he could carry off grown men, swooping down upon them unexpectedly and bearing them off to his inaccessible caves in the cliff to be devoured. Hundreds of warriors attempted to vanquish him, but without success. His depredations depopulated entire villages, and all the tribes were in woe.

Finally, following a vision from the Great Spirit, Ouatogo, the great chief of the Illini, selected 20 of his bravest warriors and concealed them in ambush. Standing in open view as a willing sacrifice for his people, Ouatago chanted the death chant as the great bird plunged toward its victim. But moments before the deadly claws could strike, 20 arrows were shot into the monster's body. Uttering a fearful scream of pain and rage, the mighty raptor died without touching the courageous chief.

To commemorate this great victory, the image of the Piasa was carved and painted upon the face of the bluff, below the caves where the bird had taken his victims. And forever after, every Indian passing by that spot in his canoe would fire arrows (and later, guns) at the effigy. Indeed, in 1836, Russell said, "The marks of the balls on the rock are almost innumerable."

Fig. 4. The Piasa on the cliff face, by Henry Lewis, 1846

In March of that year, led by "an intelligent guide, who carried a spade," Russell claimed to have made the arduous climb over the perpendicular face of the 150-foot cliff to reach a cave, about 50 feet above the surface of the river, which was attributed in legend to be one of those where the Piasa had carried his victims. Clambering with great difficulty through the opening, he found himself in a cavern about 20 by 30 feet wide, with a vaulted ceiling at least 20 feet high. Astonished, he said that "the floor of the cavern throughout its whole extent was one mass of human bones. Skulls and other bones were mingled in the utmost confusion. To what depth they extended I was unable to decide; but we dug to the depth of 3 or 4 feet in every part of the cavern, and still we found only bones. The remains of thousands must have been deposited there."[5]

Tragically, the entire cliff, petrographs, cavern, and alleged bones were dynamited into oblivion only 11 years later in 1847, when the property was purchased by a limestone quarry. In 1882, although he had never seen the original image, Professor William McAdams, an Illinois State geologist, drew an imaginative illustration of the Piasa Bird. Based on this drawing, a full-color life-size reconstruction of the image of the Piasa was eventually created, and it may be seen today hanging on a wall of the old quarry near its original location. The site has become a place of annual pilgrimage by local Indians in ceremonial costume.[6]

Fig. 5. The Piasa by William McAdams

However, there is something odd about this modern image, which we are supposed to believe is a replica of the original. It does not particularly resemble either the original drawing in Fr. Marquette's diary, or even the later renderings by Henry Lewis and others. Rather, it calls to mind a pen drawing from a 17th-century bestiary manuscript, titled "The Manticora Monster of Tartary" (see Fig. 1), which would seem to be the original prototype from which McAdams' popular Piasa image was derived. Oddly enough, no one else seems to have noticed this uncanny resemblance, and this may be the first place this connection has been brought to anyone's attention.

The Manticore

Which, of course, leads us directly into the next subject of this investigation—the malevolent *Manticore*. Also called *Martikhora, Martiora, Manticore, Mantichora, Manticory, Manticoras, Mantiquera, Mantiserra, Mancomorion, Memecoleous, Satyral*, this is a ferocious, red, lion-like creature of India with the face of a man, mane of a lion, tail and stinger of a scorpion, three rows of iron teeth, and a beautiful musical voice like a trumpet or flute. Its name, in all these variations, comes from Persian *Mard-khor*, and means "man-eater."

The earliest historical reference to this horrific monster comes from the indefatigable Ctesias, a 5th-century BCE Greek physician who served for 17 years in the Persian court of Darius II and Artexerxes Memnon. During that time he compiled histories and geographies of Persia and India (he never actually visited India), which formed the basis for virtually all subsequent bestiary accounts through the ages.

Fig. 6. Royal Bengal Tiger (Panthera tigris tigris) by Glenn Gore

Ctesias' **Martikhora** (changed by Aristotle to *Manticora*, and corrupted by later writers into other variations) is certainly based upon the Royal Bengal Tiger (*Panthera tigris tigris*), but it also seems to include elements of the Porcupine (*Hystrix leucura*). Here is his account, in full, from *Indica* (as preserved by Aelian):

He [Ctesias] describes an animal called the martikhora, found in India. Its face is like a man's—it is about as big as a lion, and in colour red like cinnabar. It has three rows of teeth—ears like the human—eyes of a pale-blue like the human and a tail like that of the land scorpion, armed with a sting and more than a cubit long. It has besides stings on each side of its tail, and like the scorpion, is armed with an additional sting on the crown of its head, wherewith it stings any one who goes near it, the wound in all cases proving mortal. If attacked from a distance it defends itself both in front and in rear—in front with its tail, by uplifting it and darting out the stings, like shafts from a bow, and in rear by straightening it out. It can strike to the distance of a hundred feet, and no creature can survive the wound it inflicts save only the elephant. The stings are about a foot in length and not thicker than the finest thread. The name martikora means in Greek "man-eater," and it is so called because it carries off men and devours them, though it no doubt preys upon other animals as well. In fighting it uses not only its stings but also its claws. Fresh stings grow up to replace those shot away in fighting. These animals are numerous in India, and are killed by the natives who hunt them with elephants, from the backs of which they attack them with darts.[7]

Drawing on Ctesias (whose writings survived only as fragments in the works of others writers, and extracts compiled in the 9th century CE by Photius, Patriarch of Constantinople), various other authors added their own comments and elaborations to the mythology, carrying the legend of the monstrous Manticore far from its origin in the reality of the Indian tiger. In Haitian Voodoo folklore, for example, the **Cigouave** is a predatory monster with the body of a lion or panther and a human head; it was derived from 16th-century missionary descriptions of the Indian Manticore.

Depictions of this creature also became more and more fantastic, until some scarcely resembled

Fig. 7. Phrygian-capped Manticora from a 12th-century bestiary

any living beast at all. Later artists even added horns, udders, draconic wings, and, most curiously, a Phrygian cap (Fig. 7). A heraldic version became known as the **Lympago** (also *Mantygr, Man-Tiger, Montegre,* or *Satyral*). It has the body of a lion or tiger, the head of an old man, and horns. Sometimes the horns resemble those of an ox, and the feet are more like a dragon's.

Fig. 8. Heraldic Lympago

The culmination of this artistic evolution is the truly bizarre representation described at the beginning of this chapter—which seems to have leapt the oceans to become finally affixed in stone in the center of America as the supposedly indigenous Piasa.

"There are," replied Apollonius, "tall stories current which I cannot believe; for they say that the creature has four feet, and that his head resembles that of a man, but that in size it is comparable to a lion; while the tail of this animal puts out hairs a cubit long and sharp as thorns, which it shoots like arrows at those who hunt it"
— Philostratus (170–245 CE)
The Life of Apollonius of Tyana[8]

Another maner of bestes there is in Ynde that ben callyd manticora; and hath visage of a man, and thre huge grete teeth in his throte. He hath eyen lyke a ghoot and body of a lyon, tayll of a Scorpyon and voys of a serpente, in such wyse that by his sweet songe he draweth to hym the peple and deuoureth them. And is more delyuerer to goo than is fowle to flee.
—Willam Caxton (1422–1491)
The Mirrour of the World[9]

Fig. 9. The terrible Manticora monster, caught in the year 1530 in the Hauberg Forest, Saxonia.

From Konrad Gesner's De Quadrupedobus Vivipari, *Basle, 16th century.*

I saw some manthicores, a strange sort of beast: the body a lion's, the coat red, face and ears like a man's, and three rows of teeth closed together, like joined hands with fingers interlocked. Their tails secreted a sting like a scorpion's; their voices were very melodious.
—François Rabelais (1495–1553)
Gargantua and Pantagruel[10]

The Manticora, (or, according to the Persians, Mantiora) a Devourer, is bred among the Indians; having a triple Row of Teeth beneath and above, and in bigness and roughness like a Lion's; as are also his Feet; Face and Ears like a Man's; his Tail like a scorpion's, armed with a Sting, and sharp-pointed Quills. His Voice is like a small trumpet, or Pipe. He is so wild, that 'tis very difficult to tame him; and as swift as an Hart. With his Tail he wounds the Hunters, whether they come before or behind him. When the Indians take a Whelp of this Beast, they bruise its Buttocks and Tail, to prevent its bearing the sharp Quills; then it is tamed without danger.
—Thomas Boreman (fl.–1744)
A Description of Three Hundred Animals[11]

Fig. 10. The man-dragon Manticora, used as a device by the printer Busdrago, Lucca, Tuscany, 1551.

The spiky tail of the Manticore can probably be attributed to a confusion with the porcupine, which was (and still is) popularly believed to be able to shoot its tail quills like arrows. Perhaps more likely, one can easily imagine the appearance of a tiger whose tail has had an unfortunate encounter with a porcupine! However, it was also a common belief in India that tigers' whiskers were poisonous quills, and natives routinely plucked them from slain specimens to prevent accidents.

But one feature that remains consistent from its very earliest description by Ctesias seems inexplicable—namely, the scorpion sting with which the monster's tail was said to terminate. However, in 1884, the Irish scholar Valentine Ball published a paper on the Manticora, which addressed this apparent anomaly. Having worked for years as a geologist in India, and later becoming director of the National Museum in Dublin, Ball's research convinced him that nearly everything the Greek physician had reported had a factual basis.[12]

For example, it is true that in India, tigers were hunted by princes from the backs of elephants—a custom that persisted into the 20th century. They are also notorious and feared man-eaters. And Ball attributed the "triple rows of teeth" to the distinctive three-lobed carnivore molars of tigers. As for the scorpion-like tail stinger, Ball asserted that "at the extremity of the tail of the tiger, as well as other Felidae, there is a little horny-dermal structure like a claw or nail, which I doubt not, the natives regard as analogous to the sting of the scorpion."[13]

One of the greatest publishing achievements of the mid-16th century was the massive four volume *Historia Animalum* (1555) by Swiss naturalist Konrad Gesner (1516–1565), which included hundreds of original woodcut illustrations. Considered to be the foundation of modern zoology, this comprehensive documentation of the animal world also included a number of fabulous creatures, including the Manticore. In 1607, Edward Topsell (1572–1625) compiled an English version of Gesner's work, which he titled *The Historie of Foure-Footed Beastes.* Topsell's image of the Manticore has remained the best known and most often reproduced; and his text entry on this beast introduced yet another element into the myth—an equation with the Leucrocota, or Hyaena:

Fig. 11. Topsell's Manticora (1607)

This beast or rather monster (as Ctesias writeth) is bred among the Indians, having a treble row of teeth beneath and above, whose greatness, roughness, and feet are like Lyons, his face and ears like unto a man, his eyes gray, and colour red, his tail like the tail of a Scorpion, of the earth, armed with a sting, casting forth sharp pointed quills…. This also is the same beast which is called Leucrocuta about the bigness of a wilde Ass, being in legs and Hoofs like a Hart, having his mouth reaching both sides to his ears, and the head and face of a female like unto a Badger. It is called also Martiora, which in the Persian tongue signifieth a devourer of men; and thus we conclude the story of the Hyena for her description, and her several kinds.

—Edward Topsell (1572–1625)
The Historie of Foure-Footed Beastes[14]

The **Leucrocota** (Greek, "White Wolf-Dog") that Topsell mentions was an Ethiopian animal first described by Pliny the El-

Fig. 12. Leucrocota by Merian (1718)

der in his *Historia Naturalis* (77 CE). He said it was the size of a donkey, "with cloven hooves, the haunches of a stag, the neck and tail of a lion, the head of a badger, and a mouth that extends to the ears; it imitates the sound of the human voice." Later writers called it *Crocotta, Corocotta, Crocotte, Crocuta, Curcrocute, Cynolycus, Leucrota, Rosomacha, Akabo, Alazbo, Zabo,* and *Lupus Vesperitinus*. It was said to be an ass-sized dog-wolf of India with a leonine body, deerlike legs with cloven hooves, and a human-like voice with which it lured its victims. Instead of teeth, it had bony jaws to crush its prey, which it then swallowed whole. It had to turn its entire head to focus its immobile eyes. Ctesias had referred to this creature as the *Cynolycus,* "Dog-Wolf." Also called *Yena, Akabo, Alzabo, Zabo, Ana,* and many other names, it is the animal we know as the Hyaena (*Crocuta crocuta*), but confused with elements of the antelope.

We can see the entire story come full circle in the description of the **Rompo**, a nocturnal scavenger beast from India and Africa that feeds on human corpses. It was said to have a long body and tail, the head of a hare, the ears of a man, a mane of hair, the forefeet of a badger, and the hind feet of a bear. These habits and the description clearly identify it as the hyaena, and yet some are also reminiscent of the Manticore. I believe the final connection between these two animals may be found in the Striped Hyena (*Hyaena hyaena*), whose distinctive coat patterns are similar to those of the tiger.

Fig. 13. Striped Hyaena

There is one last footnote to this fascinating history. Peter Costello reports that André Thévet, writing in 1571, described a personal encounter with a Manticore: "When I traveled on the Red Sea, some Indians arrived from the mainland…and they brought along a monster of the size and proportions of a tiger without a tail, but the face was that of a well-formed man."[15] Costello suggests that this "Manticore" was probably an anthropoid ape, but none of the great apes or baboons are indigenous to India, and it is impossible to determine from this description what species it may have been.

FLYERS
8. THE FIERY PHOENIX

By Oberon Zell-Ravenheart

How many creatures walking on this earth
Have their first being in another form?
Yet one exists that is itself forever,
Reborn in ageless likeness through the years.
It is that bird Assyrians call the Phoenix,
Nor does she eat the common seeds and grasses,
But drinks the juice of rare, sweet-smelling herbs.
When she has done five hundred years of living
She winds her nest high up a swaying palm—
And delicate dainty claws prepare her bed
Of bark and spices, myrrh and cinnamon—
And dies while incense lifts her soul away.
Then from her breast—or so the legend runs—
A little Phoenix rises over her,
To live, they say, the next five hundred years.
When she is old enough, in hardihood,
She lifts her crib (which is her mother's tomb)
Midair above the tall palm wavering there
And journeys toward the City of the Sun,
Where in Sun's temple shines the Phoenix nest.
—Ovid (43 BCE–17 CE), *The Metamorphoses*

Ian Daniels

HE LEGEND OF THE PHOENIX HAS GIVen rise to one of the most powerful and empowering metaphors in all of human history—that of miraculous resurrection or rebirth following total destruction. The phrase "rising from the ashes" is applied to everything from the rebuilding of cities that have been leveled by war or natural calamities, to personal recovery from a devastating tragedy or illness. Even sports teams that achieve victory after a season of defeats are said to rise from the ashes. In medieval times, the Phoenix was adopted by Christians as a symbol of the resurrection and immortality of the soul, and the eternal-life-after-death of Jesus Christ.

The Phoenix was a heraldic badge of Queen Elizabeth I (1533–1603). It appears also on the city flags and seals of the American cities of Atlanta, Georgia (torched in the Civil War), Lawrence, Kansas (burnt by Confederate raiders), San Francisco, California (destroyed by earthquake and fire in 1906), and Portland, Maine (destroyed four times by fire), to symbolize these cities' rebirths from the ashes. It is

Fig. 1. Phoenix crest of the University of Chicago

also the seal of Phoenix, Arizona, the 5th largest city in the U.S., and which sits atop the ruins of the former Hohokam city.

The Phoenix was also said to regenerate when hurt or wounded by a foe, thus making it invincible and virtually immortal—an appropriate symbol of fire and divinity. In a Greek version of the myth, the Phoenix lived in Arabia next to a well. At dawn, she bathed in the water of the well, and the Greek sun-god, Apollo, stopped his chariot (the sun) in order to listen to her song.[1]

Fig. 2. The Phoenix emblem attached to the eight trams built in Brisbane Australia, from material salvaged from trams destroyed in the Paddington tram depot fire.

In alchemical symbolism, the Phoenix corresponds to the color red, the regeneration of universal life, and the successful completion of a process. According to the Stoics, the universe itself is born in fire, dies in fire, and is reborn in an eternal cycle. The Phoenix is but a microcosmic reflection of this cosmology.

HISTORY OF THE LEGEND

The word *phoenix* (often spelled *fenix* in medieval bestiaries) means "purple or crimson one," from the Greek *phoeniceus*, meaning "reddish-purple." In various depictions, she resembles a flame-colored synthesis of an eagle, a peacock, and a pheasant. Her legend was spread by the ancient Phoenician traders (taking their name from the distinctive royal purple dye which they derived from the purple murex snails, *Murex brandaris* and *Murex trunculus*), who sailed throughout the world for centuries before their defeat by the Romans during the Punic Wars, with the *coup de grace* delivered by Julius Caesar in 50 BCE.

The earliest known mention of the Phoenix is by the Greek poet Hesiod (8th century BCE), who implies that the Phoenix is already very well-known, and that it lives for a very long time.[2] Ionian historian Hecataeus of Miletus (6th–5th century BCE) also described the fabled bird, but unfortunately only fragments survive of his *Periegesis* ("A Journey Around the World"). The most detailed early account comes from the Greek historian Herodotus (484–425 BCE), who claimed to have received it from Egyptian priests in Heliopolis. In the second book of his *History*, he notes that he did not see the bird himself, and is skeptical of the story. He states that "its size and appearance, if it is like the pictures, are as follows: The plumage is partly red, partly golden, while the general make and size are almost exactly like that of the eagle."[3]

Fig. 3. Classic Phoenix

In his *Natural History*, Pliny the Elder (23 BCE–79 CE) says the Phoenix "is as big as an eagle, and has a gleam of gold around its neck and all the rest of it is purple, but the tail which is blue picked out with rose-colored feathers and the throat picked out with tufts, and a feathered crest adorning its head."

According to the legend, the Phoenix (of which there is only ever one) comes from Ethiopia, where every 500 years, at the end of her life-cycle, she lays a single egg in a nest she builds of cinnamon and frankincense atop the tallest Date Palm tree (*Phoenix dactylifera*). Then she sits upon the egg and sings a song of indescribable beauty at the dawn of the day. As the burning rays of the rising sun heat the flammable nest, she fans it with her wings until it bursts into flames, consuming her in self-immolation. Nine days later, when the egg, warmed by the glowing embers, hatches, she is reborn amid the ashes. Manius Manilius (Roman Consul, 149 BCE) dispenses with the egg, avowing that the reincarnated bird miraculously coalesces out of the ashes, appearing at first like a little caterpillar, which then metamorphoses into an adult bird.[5]

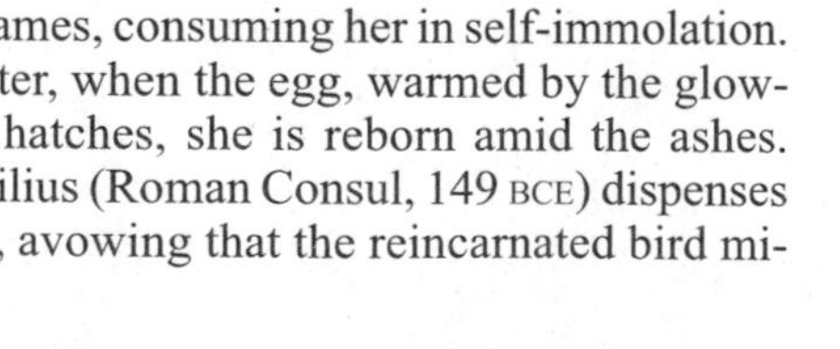

Fig. 4. Phoenix

Fig. 5. Phoenix from Lycothenes' Prodigiorum as Ostentorum Chronicon

When she attains her full plumage, the resurrected Phoenix gathers up the ashen remains of her parent and former incarnation, plasters them into a hollowed-out ball of myrrh, and wraps the whole thing into an egg-shaped bundle tightly bound in aromatic leaves. She flies with this packet to Egypt, followed at a respectful distance by a contingent of other birds. There she deposits it on the altar of Ra, the sun-god, in his temple at Heliopolis ("City of the Sun"). This event was celebrated in Egypt with major festivities, and was heralded as the beginning of a new era.

Like the Phoenix, the Arabian *Cynamolgus*, or "Cinnamon Bird," was also said to bring cinnamon from afar to built its fragrant nest at the top of a tall palm tree, where spice gatherers would then shoot it down with leaden arrows. It was claimed that this was how cinnamon was obtained.

CYCLES OF RESURRECTION

Manilius stated that the period of the 540-year-long astronomical Great Year coincided with the life cycle of the Phoenix, with its last appearance in 215 AUC (*Anno urbis conditae*—"year of the founding of the city," that is, Rome—traditionally set in 753 BCE). By our present reckoning, then, that appearance would have been in 538 BCE.

Cornelius Tacitus (55–120 CE) says in *The Annals* that Phoenixes flew into Heliopolis successively during the reigns of Pharaohs Sesostris, Amasis, and Ptolemy III of the Macedonian dynasty, but he does not give specific years. He notes, however, that the interval between the last two appearances was less than the traditional 500 years, and suspects that the last sighting was spurious:[6]

Sesostris III (Khakhaure) ruled Egypt from 1878 to 1843 BCE.

Amasis reigned from 570 to 526 BCE (right on the mark for the 538 BCE appearance, but 1,300 years after Sesostris, not 500).

Ptolemy III held the throne from 246 to 221 BCE (only 300 years after Amasis).

Although 500 years is the period given by Herodotus, and 540 by Manilius, other accounts indicate cycles of 1,000, 1,461, 1,700, or even 12,994 years. Using 538 BCE as a starting point, past and future appearances can be shown in the following chart:

500 yrs	540 yrs	1,000 yrs	1,461 yrs	1,700 yrs
1038	1078	1538	1999	2238
538 BCE	538 BCE	538 BCE	538 BCE	538 BCE
462 CE	2 CE	462 CE	923 CE	1162 CE
962	542	1462	2384*	2862*
1462	1082	2462*		
1962	1622			
2462*	2162*			

So if you are wondering when the Phoenix is next due to reappear on the Earth, you can take your pick of the years marked with an asterisk. Personally, having been there, I'd opt for 1962 as the "Year of the Phoenix." Or, we can conclude from the historical record that the schedule isn't all that precise, and the Phoenix is due any moment!

The Phoenix in Other Lands

The Orient has its own Phoenix, known in China as the *Fêng Huang* ("Red Bird"). Frequently depicted in oriental art, the *Fêng* is male and the *Huang* is female; together the pair symbolizes everlasting love, high virtue, yin and yang, and the primordial force of the heavens. This beautiful bird is said to stand about nine feet tall. It has the breast and sinuous neck of a swan, the head and comb of a pheasant, the face of a swallow, the back of a tortoise, and the 12-feathered tail of a peacock. This descriptions fits remarkably well the rare Ocellated Pheasant, or Rheinart's Crested Argus (*Rheinarta ocellata*), found in central Vietnam and the Malayan peninsula. Its resplendent tail feathers may attain six feet in length![7]

The form of the Fêng Huang represents the six celestial bodies, and its shimmering striped plumage displays the five fundamental colors (yellow, green, red, black, and white). Originating in the sun, it will not eat any living thing, including plants. It is one of the *Ssu Ling*, the Four Spiritual Creatures of China, along with the *Lung Wang* (Dragon), the *Gui Xian* (Tortoise), and the *Ki-Lin* (Unicorn). It stands at the South, and symbolizes the season of summer and the Element of Fire. Representing the Empress, its rare and auspicious appearance heralds good fortune, peace, and prosperity; but calamity occurs upon its departure.[8]

Fig. 7.
Fêng Huang

In Japan, the same creature is known as *Ho-Oo*—the *Ho* being the male aspect and the *Oo* being the female. Said to be the embodiment of the sun, its appearance heralds the dawn of a new era. It comes to Earth as a messenger of goodness and to do good deeds for people, after which it ascends back to heaven to await the next cycle. Like the Feng-Huang, the Ho-Oo has been adopted as a symbol of the royal family, particularly the Empress. It is supposed to represent the sun, justice, fidelity, and obedience.

From Russia comes the legend of the *Zshar-Ptitsa*, or *Firebird*, with its shining feathers of gold and silver and sparkling crystal eyes. Pearls fall from its beak when it sings, and its song can heal the sick and cure blindness. A single fiery tail feather can light an entire room. It grazes in the garden of its owner, Czar Dalmet, but at night it sometimes sneaks into the nearby orchard of Czar Vyslav Anronovich to steal his golden apples of youth, beauty, and immortality. The fabled Firebird is the subject of the famous 1910 ballet score by Igor Stravinsky.[9]

Fig. 9. Firebird
by Ian Daniels

The *Kerkes* of Turkish tradition lives 1,000 years and then consumes itself by fire, arising renewed to live another millennium. This cycle will repeat 7 times 7, or 49 times, until the Day of Judgment comes. The mystical tree *Ababel*—the "Father Tree" in the Quran—shoots out new branches and vegetation at every resurrection of the Kerkes.

According to the Jewish Talmud, the *Milcham* was the only animal not to eat from the Tree of Knowledge in the Garden of Eden, and was rewarded with the gift of immortality from the Tree of Life. It lived in a walled city for 1,000 years, at the end of which time it was consumed by fire, leaving an egg to begin a new cycle.

Persian and Hindu mythology tells of the *Huma*, a bird of paradise that dwells in the heavens and never touches the Earth. The Huma joins both the male and female natures together in one body, each having a wing and a leg. Like the *Phoenix*, it consumes itself in fire every few hundred years, only to rise renewed from the ashes. A compassionate bird, it avoids killing for food, preferring instead to feed on carrion. Great blessings and good fortune come to any who see or touch it—especially if its shadow falls on them.

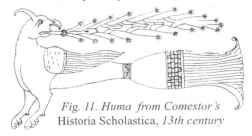

Fig. 11. Huma from Comestor's
Historia Scholastica, *13th century*

Some of the fab-
ulous birds associat-
ed with the legend of the
Phoenix are gigantic,
similar to the *Roc*
of Madagascar.
For example, the
Angka, an enor-
mous Arabian
bird, was said to
be large enough to car-
ry off an elephant. After living for 1,700 years, it
burned itself to ashes and rose again. The Arabs believed that the Angka was originally created as a perfect bird, but eventually it came to devour all the animals on Earth and carry off children. The people appealed to God, who then prevented the Angka from
multiplying; thus it eventually became extinct.[10]

Fig. 12.
Angka

The *Simurgh* (meaning "30 Birds") is the magnificent King of the Birds in Arabian legend, representing divine unity. Its beautiful feathers are prized
for their healing properties. Like the Angka, it is so
huge that it can carry off an elephant or a camel, but it
is also known to take human children into its nest to
foster them. It dwells in the mountains of Alberz in
northern Persia. Like the Phoenix, this wise and peaceful bird lives for either 1,700 or 2,000 years. Some
accounts claim it is immortal, nesting in the Tree of
Knowledge. It is
said to be so old that
it has seen the de-
struction of the
world three times
over. A bird of the
same name attended the
Queen of Sheba. It had metallic orange feathers, a silver
head, a human face, four
wings, a vulture's talons, and a peacock's tail.[11]

Fig. 13.
Simurgh

Nicolo de Conti (ca.1395–1469), a Venetian merchant who traveled for either 25 or 36 years through
India, Asia, and Africa, brought back the legend of
the *Sevienda*, which had a beak full of holes. Like the
Phoenix, it was consumed by fire and then regenerated from the ashes as a little worm or caterpillar.

Appearing in the Hindu epic the *Ramayana*,
Garuda is the mystical Firebird that serves as the
mount of the god Vishnu. Garuda appears as the coat
of arms of the Republic of Indonesia (Garuda Pan-
casila).[12]

SOURCES OF THE LEGEND

Was there ever a real Phoenix—or at least a living bird that gave rise to the legend? As with many
other mythological creatures, the legend of the Phoenix is not a simple matter of identifying a single source
or species. A number of mythic birds became absorbed

into the legend as it grew, and it in turn also contributed
to the legends of totally different birds in other lands.

Perhaps the oldest source of the Phoenix legend
is the Egyptian *Benu*, a heron-like bird with red legs
and a crest of long feathers sweeping back from the
crown of its head. The word *Benu* in Egyptian means
both Purple Heron (*Ardea purpurea*) and date palm
tree. The legendary Benu comes from the Isle of Fire
in the Underworld and brings the *Hike*, the vital essence of all life. It was said
to rise from its burning
tree with such melodious song
that even the gods were enthralled. Known from *The Book of
the Dead* and other Egyptian texts as
one of the sacred symbols of worship at
Heliopolis, the Benu was associated
with the rising sun and the sun-god,
Ra, who was reborn each morning in
the fiery dawn. It was also identified with Osiris because of its
ability to resurrect itself from death.[13]

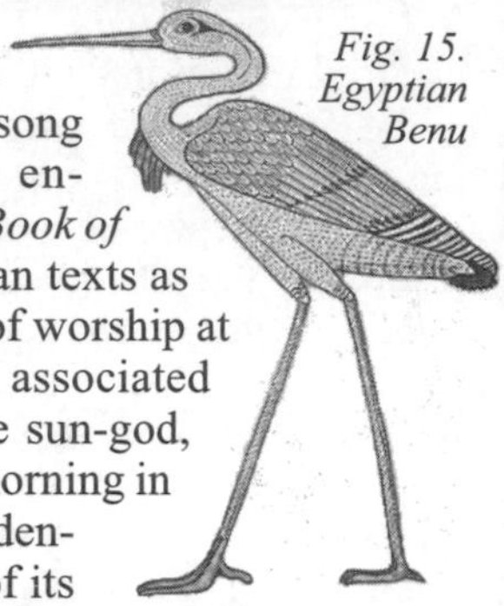

Fig. 15.
Egyptian
Benu

An East African desert bird —possibly a Sand-
grouse (*Pteroclidae*)—has also been suggested as inspiration for the Egyptian Phoenix. Said to nest on
salt flats that are too hot for its eggs or chicks to
survive, it builds a mound several inches tall, laying a
single egg atop that marginally cooler pedestal. The
convection currents around these mounds may have
resembled the turbulence of a flame.[14]

Another suggested inspiration for the Phoenix,
and other mythical birds closely associated with the
sun, is the total solar eclipse, when the sun's blazing
corona often displays a distinctly birdlike form that
almost certainly inspired the winged sun-disk symbols of ancient Egypt and Mesopotamia.[15]

And yet another frequently noted source of the
legend of the Phoenix may be found in the strange
avian behavior called "anting" by Professor Erwin
Stresemann of Berlin in 1935. Various perching birds
will pick up ants with their beaks and rub them under
their wings and over their plumage, evidently enjoy-
ing an intoxicating effect from the formic acid. In 1957,
Maurice Burton undertook a study of this behavior
and learned that aromatics and fire smoke were equally
effective intoxicants. But the most remarkable behavior involved a tame rook named Niger, who "disport-
ed himself in a heap of burning straw":

> With flames enveloping the lower part of his body
> and smoke drifting all around him, he flapped his
> wings, snatched at burning embers with his beak,
> and appeared to be trying to put them under his
> wings…. Every now and then he would pose amid
> the flames with his wings outstretched and his
> head turned to one side, looking exactly like the
> traditional picture of the Phoenix.[16]

Fig. 17. Niger rises, Phoenix-like, from the flames

The most important component of the legend may be found in the trade of *Bird of Paradise* skins from New Guinea, dating from 1000 BCE, when the island was first discovered by Phoenician seafarers. The most flamboyantly plumaged and abundant species, and therefore the most commonly exported, was Count Raggi's Bird of Paradise (*Paradisea raggiana*), the male of which sports profuse sprays of brilliant scarlet feathers under his wings. These are activated and agitated in his courtship dance, during which it looks as though he is dancing amid flames.[17]

What makes this magnificent bird particularly fascinating as a source of the Phoenix legend is not just its spectacular physical appearance, but also the manner in which it was brought to Western attention in ancient Egypt and other civilizations along the Phoenician trading routes. In order to preserve the delicate skins of Birds of Paradise for their transport by sea all the way to Egypt, Phoenicia, and elsewhere, the tribespeople of New Guinea carefully embalmed them in myrrh that was molded into an egg-shaped parcel, which they then sealed in a wrapping of charred banana leaves—exactly as Herodotus described. No doubt the delivery of these precious packages to the temples in places such as Heliopolis and Tyre was also attended by considerable pomp and ceremony, heralding the return of the sacred Phoenician bird.[18]

Fig. 18. Count Raggi's Bird of Paradise

ᚦhe ONCE ᚪND FUᚦURE phOENIX

I suspect that there is another element of this wondrous bird that has not yet been considered—namely, an actual living creature that bears the appearance of those iconic images. Because the Phoenix, like the Unicorn, is not a continuous presence on the Earth, but only appears intermittently, a reasonable assumption is that it might have been produced artificially. The most likely prospect is a sterile hybrid of two living birds whose separate features would combine into the classic archetype.

Leaving aside the various species of Birds of Paradise (see above), the *Galliformes* fowl are eminently suitable prospects for such a hybrid. This order of birds contains the turkeys, grouse, quails, chickens, peafowl, and pheasants, of which there are about 256 species worldwide. The entire order exhibits enormous diversity, and is distinguished by flamboyant plumage among the males, which are notoriously polygamous. The ranges of most species overlap considerably throughout Asia, and many have been domesticated for millennia. Although radically different courtship behaviors normally keep the various species from hybridizing, spontaneous hybrids are not unknown in close captivity, and intentional hybridization by breeders has produced many unique varieties.[19]

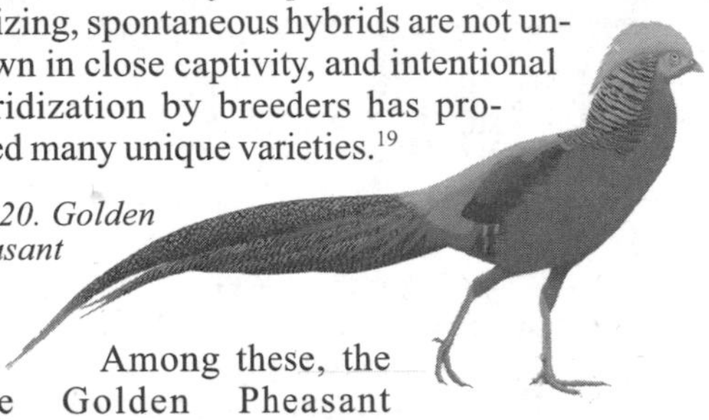

Fig. 20. Golden Pheasant

Among these, the male Golden Pheasant (*Chrysolophus pictus*) has the correct colors: iridescent flaming reds and golds. The peafowl, on the other hand, has approximately the right body shape and size, including the long neck, the head crest, and the tail feathers with their distinctive "eyes."

Whereas the iridescent colors of peacocks are at the opposite end of the spectrum—blues, greens, and violets—a color mutation of the Indian Blue Peafowl (*Pavo cristatus*) is pure white (not an albino, as many assume). A hybrid derived from a golden pheasant cock and a white peahen might just result in a progeny that looks exactly like the Russian Firebird.

Perhaps it is time for the fabled Phoenix to return in the flesh.

Now I will believe
That there are unicorns; that in Arabia
There is one tree, the phoenix' throne; one phoenix
At this hour reigning there.
       —Shakespeare, *The Tempest* (III.iii.27)

MONSᚦER MOVIES: ᚦhE phOENIX

The immensely popular *Harry Potter* books and movies feature prominently a Phoenix named Fawkes belonging to Albus Dumbledore, the Headmaster of Hogwarts School of Witchcraft and Wizardry. In the film *Harry Potter and the Chamber of Secrets* (2002), the process of immolation and resurrection is dramatically shown. *Harry Potter and the Half-Blood Prince* (2008) also features Fawkes. And in the 2005 movie *The Chronicles of Narnia: The Lion, the Witch and the Wardrobe*, based on the book by C.S. Lewis, a Phoenix bursts into flame and flies low over the grass in front of the Snow Queen's lines, creating a wall of fire to guard Peter's retreat.

9. Gryphons and Hippogriffs

By Ash "LeopardDancer" DeKirk and Oberon Zell-Ravenheart

Gryphus significat sapientiam jungendam fortitudini, sed sapientiam debere praeire, fortitudinem sequi.
(The griffin represents wisdom joined to fortitude, but wisdom should lead, and fortitude follow.)
—Chassaneus

ERHAPS SOME OF THE MOST UNUSUAL and captivating creatures of the mythic world are the **Gryphon** and the **Hippogriff**. Like the Dragon, Unicorn, and Phoenix, they are beloved elements of universal myth and folklore. These are *chimeric* creatures, comprised of parts from several different animals. The Gryphon has the hind body and tail of a lion, and the head, wings, and front claws of a mighty eagle. It is usually depicted with feathery, horselike ears, or feathered "horns" like those of a great horned owl. Some Gryphons have serpents in place of the tufted lion tail, much like the traditional Chimera does. Others have a lion tail with a fan of feathers at the end. The Hippogriff has the same eagle forequarters, but with the hindquarters of a horse.

Ian Daniels

astrological iconography, they are shown pulling the chariot of the sun.

Fig. 2. Oldest known representation of a Gryphon, from a cylinder seal found at Susa, Western Iran, 3,000 BCE.

Fig. 1. Gryphon by Matthaus Merian (1718)

The mythological history of the Gryphon goes back more than 5,000 years, and there are many variations on its name. The word *Gryphon*, in every language in which it appears (French *Griffon*, Italian *Grifo,* German *Greyff,* English *Griffin*), derives from the Greek *grypos* ("hooked") because of its large predatory beak. One alternate spelling, *Griffin*, means "to seize." Other names include *Gryph*, *Gryphus*, and *Epimacus*; also *Gryps* or *Grypes*, meaning "curved, having a hooked beak." A Japanese version of the Gryphon is called a *Kirni*.

The Gryphon figures prominently in the art and legends of the ancient Sumerians, Assyrians, Babylonians, Chaldeans, Egyptians, Mycenaeans, Indo-Iranians, Syrians, Scythians, and Greeks. In medieval European heraldry, Gryphons are frequently represented as a symbol of eternal vigilance, and in ancient

Some of the earliest accounts of Gryphons come from the Egyptians. Egyptian Gryphons were portrayed with a lion's body and a falcon's head. Egyptian deities depicted as Gryphons included Sefer and Axex. Ancient Elamite statuary often featured Gryphons, as they considered them to be sacred beasts. In Persia, Gryphons called *Homa* were featured in statuary and as symbols of royalty. The Homa were considered guardians of light.

Fig. 3. Assyrian Gryphon, a stone carving in the Nimrod Palace at Nineveh.

Fig. 4. Gryphon as Greek akrotrion (apex statuette)

The Grecian Gryphons were even more chimeric, having the front half of an eagle and back half of a lion. They were said to build their nests within caves, laying within them three eggs roughly the size of ostrich eggs. Typically a Gryphon's eggs resemble those of an eagle, but in some accounts the eggs resemble sapphires. And in other accounts they are actual sapphires, or even made of agate. Sometimes the mother Gryphon will place agate in the nests to protect the eggs and young.

Fig. 5. Babylonian Gryphon from the Ishtar Gate

Masters of sky and Earth, Gryphons were said to have made their homes upon the Scythian Steppes, a region stretching from the modern Ukraine area all the way into Central Asia. According to the Greek historian Herodotus, writing in the 5th century BCE, Gryphons lived in an area between the *Hyperboreans*, the north-wind people of Mongolia, and the *Arimaspians*, a one-eyed tribe of Scythian horsemen. The latter were named for the stream Arimaspias, from which Gryphons were said to take gold. The favorite prey of the Gryphon was horses, and its greatest enemies were the equestrian Arimaspians, who were continually trying to capture the vast hoard of gold guarded by the Gryphons. Both the Greek Cyclops and the Gryphons' hatred of horses may have been derived from this legendary tribe.

In the late 5th century BCE, Ctesias relocated Herodotus' "gold-guarding Griffins" to the "high-towering mountains" of India, where they became four-footed birds more like the later conception we know today. In his *Indica*, Ctesias said the Griffins "are about as large as wolves, having legs and claws like those of the lion, and covered all over the body with black feathers except only on the breast where they are red."[1]

The Roman rhetorician Claudius Aelianus, or Aelian (170–235 CE), compiled a popular compendium of anecdotal animal lore, called *On Animals*. Here is what he has to say about Gryphons:

> I have heard that the Indian animal the Gryphon is a quadruped like a lion; that it has claws of enormous strength and that they resemble those of a lion. Men commonly report that it is winged and that the feathers along its back are white, and those on its front are red, while the actual wings are neither but are white. And Ctesias records that its neck is variegated with feathers of a dark blue; that it has a beak like an eagle's, and a head too, just as artists portray it in pictures and sculptures. Its eyes, he says, are like fire. It builds its lair among the mountains, and although it is not possible to capture the full-grown animal, they do take the young ones. And the people of Bactria, who are neighbors of the Indians, say that the Gryphons guard the gold in those parts; that they dig it up and build their nests with it, and that the Indians carry off any that falls from them…while the Gryphons fearing for their young ones fight with the invaders. They engage too with other beasts and overcome them without difficulty, but they will not face the lion or the elephant.[2]

Gryphons were considered monogamous animals that mated for life. If their mate died, the other would remain solitary for the rest of its life, a trait that later made it a prime target for the Church as a symbolic warning against remarriage.

These magnificent animals are associated with the sun and are often depicted pulling the chariot of the sun. The Gryphon is traditionally a guardian of gold, treasure, and wisdom, much like the Dragon (especially Asian dragons, in terms of wisdom). If a person dared to attempt gathering the Gryphon's treasure, he or she would be torn to bits. Gryphon talons were supposed to be capable of detecting poison, and many alleged specimens were brought back to Europe by crusaders. These invariably turned out to be antelope horns, sold to the gullible crusaders by enterprising African traders. Giant bones from the steppes, said to be "Griffen" bones, were most likely dinosaur fossils, a possibility that makes them no less impressive.

Fig. 6. Gryphon statant

Fig. 7. Gryphon seal of
Count Fredrich von
Brene, Germany (1208)

The Gryphon was depicted quite extensively in pottery, coinage, and statuary around the world. In ancient Greek art, bronze cauldrons were cast or molded showing stylized Gryphon heads with upright ears and gaping beaks. Some modern depictions of stone Gryphons show them with the horned heads of big cats rather than the more traditional eagle head, though they still have wings and eagle forelimbs.

Gryphons were also widely used in heraldry. The heraldic Gryphon resembles the Grecian Gryphon in form (the ears distinguish it from the heraldic eagle). Heraldic Gryphons are usually shown *sergeant*—a term similar to rampant but used solely for Gryphons— that is, rearing up with one leg and

Fig. 8.
Gryphon sergeant

both front claws raised. One of the earliest recorded heraldic Gryphons is that of Richard De Redvers, Earl of Exeter, and dates back to the early 1100s.

Fig. 9. Kerythong

A **Keythong** is a male Gryphon, represented in heraldic symbolism with spikes or jets of flame springing from its shoulders in place of wings. The **Heliodromos** is a fusion of Gryphon and vulture in medieval European lore and heraldry. It is known today as the Griffin Vulture (*Gryps fulvus*), found throughout southern Asia and South Africa.

Similar to the heraldic Gryphon is the **Opinicus**, a creature found only in the world of heraldry. The Opinicus, or "False Gryphon," looks much like the Gryphon except that it lacks a Gryphon's distinctive ears. In addition, it has the forepaws of a lion, and the tail of a camel.

Fig. 10.
*Heliodromos
by Ian
Daniels*

Fig. 11. Opinicus

The horse is generally regarded as the enemy of the Gryphon, but tales have been told of bizarre and forbidden couplings that led to the **Hippogriff** (or *Hippogryph*; Greek, "horse-gryphon"), a beast part Gryphon, part horse—the result of the impossible breeding of a mare with a male Gryphon (whose favorite food is horse-flesh). The unlikely nature of this union led to the phrase "to cross Gryphons with horses," which meant essentially the same thing as the more well-known phrase "when pigs fly," referring to something virtually impossible. A Hippogriff has the head, wings, breast, and claws of an eagle, but the hind parts of a horse instead of a lion. Hippogriffs were able to be tamed and are featured in tales of Charlemagne, often as steeds for noble knights. A large and powerful beast that can fly faster than lightning, it appears in Ludovicio Ariosto's epic saga *Orlando Furioso* (1516) as a mount for the Wizard Atlantes. Harry Potter's godfather Sirius Black has one named "Buckbeak."

Fig. 12.
Hippogriff

STRANGE TALES AND TRUE
By Oberon

The Gryphon, however, is no mere creation of fantasy, but is actually based on the Lämmergeier (*Gypaetus barbatus*, "bearded vulture"), which measures 4 feet in length with a 10-foot wingspan. A "mane" of long, ragged feathers around the bird's head and neck has given it the popular name of "lion eagle," an appellation which gave rise to the common depiction. The largest and most powerful of all raptors, it was the eagle of Zeus.

Fig. 13. Lämmergeier—head

The only member of the genus *Gypaetus*, the lämmergeier is intermediate between eagles and vultures. Its German name means "lamb stealer," from its habit of carrying off lambs. The powerful but rarely seen raptor inhabits high mountain ridges in southern Europe, Africa, India, and Tibet. It nests on mountain crags, laying one or two eggs in mid-winter which hatch at the beginning of spring.

Unlike carrion vultures, the lämmergeier disdains rotting meat, living on a diet of 90 percent bone marrow. To get at this delicacy, it will drop large bones from a height to break them into smaller pieces, which earned it the old name of *Ossifrage* ("bone crusher"). In similar fashion, lämmergeiers will drop live tortoises onto rocks to crack them open.[3]

Fig. 14. Lämmergeier, or lion-eagle; the true Gryphon

An ironic historical connection involves the Greek playwright Aeschylus (525–456 BCE), author of *Prometheus Bound*, in which the rebel Titan is tortured daily by having his liver devoured by the eagle of Zeus (that is, a lämmergeier). In 458, Aeschylus traveled to Sicily, staying in the city of Gela. One day, as he was pacing in his courtyard lecturing students, a lämmergeyer flew high overhead, carrying a large tortoise in its claws. Mistaking the old man's shiny bald pate for a rock, the mighty bird dropped the tortoise on it. Thus the great playwright met his death by the very creature he had cast as the bane of his hero.

And there is yet a final note to be added to the natural history of this seemingly supernatural monster. In 1991, Dr. Adrienne Mayor, a classical scholar from Princeton, New Jersey, noted that the Altai Mountains of central Asia, famous for their rich gold deposits and the locality of many ancient Gryphon legends, also contain the fossilized skeletons and eggs of a lion-sized quadrupedal dinosaur called *Protoceratops* ("first horn-face"), whose most distinctive feature is its strikingly eagle-like beak and head. Dating from the Cretaceous Period (136 million to 64 million years ago), if its remains had been encountered by early gold prospectors many centuries before the correct identity of dinosaurs was recognized, how would they have been explained by such people? Surely (and accurately) as the skeletons of four-footed, eagle-headed

Fig. 12. Protoceratops andrewski by Bob Giuliani

monsters—or, as we call them today, Gryphons.[4]

But perhaps the most remarkable coincidence that supports this dinosaurian identity for the legendary "lion-eagle" is the fact that we now understand that dinosaurs were not sluggish, lizard-like reptiles, as had been commonly believed, but active, warm-blooded creatures whose modern descendants are birds. Recently discovered, exquisitely preserved fossils from China indicate that many of them were feathered—including, quite possibly, Protoceratops!

MONSTER MOVIES: GRYPHONS AND HIPPOGRIFFS

Merlin, 1998 (TV) (Gryphon)
Quest for Camelot, 1998 (Gryphon)
Harry Potter and the Prisoner of Azkaban, 2004 (Hippogriff)
Chronicles of Narnia: The Lion, The Witch and The Wardrobe, 2005 (Gryphon)
Gryphon, 2007 (TV) (Gryphon)

Fig. 6. John Tenniel's Gryphon, from Alice in Wonderland

BOOKS FEATURING GRYPHONS AND HIPPOGRIFFS

Alice in Wonderland by Lewis Carroll (Gryphon)
Beyond the North Wind by Gillian Bradshaw (Gryphon)
Chronicles of Narnia by C.S. Lewis (Gryphon)
The Crystal Gryphon by Andre Norton (Gryphon)
Divine Comedy by Dante (Gryphon)
Dragons of Autumn Twilight by Margaret Wies and Tracy Hickman (Gryphon)
The Gryphon King by Tom Deitz (Gryphon)
Harry Potter and the Prisoner of Azkaban by J.K. Rowling (Hippogriff)
Mage War trilogy by Mercedes Lackey and Larry Dixon (Gryphon)
Orlando Furioso by Ludovico Ariosto (Hippogriff)
The Once and Future King by T.H. White (Gryphon)
Princess of Babylon by Voltaire (Gryphon)
Source of Magic by Piers Anthony (Gryphon)
Wizard's Heir by Daniel Hood (Gryphon)

SWIMMERS
10. MERFOLK

By Oberon Zell-Ravenheart & Tom Willams

Ian Daniels

*My gentle Puck, come hither. Thou rememb'rest
Since once I sat upon a promontory,
And heard a mermaid on a dolphin's back
Uttering such dulcet and harmonious breath,
That the rude sea grew civil at her song,
And certain stars shot madly from their spheres,
To hear the sea-maid's music.*
— Shakespeare, *A Midsummer Night's Dream*
(2.1:148-154—Oberon to Puck)

HE MERMAID (FROM LATIN *MER*, "sea"), an alluringly beautiful woman from the waist up, and a fish from the waist down, has always been a favorite creature of legend and romance. She personifies the beauty, romance, and treachery of the sea, and especially the coastal shoals and rocks upon which many a ship is wrecked. There has never been a time or place in nautical history when mariners have not told of Mermaids they encountered. Bare-breasted Mermaids are often shown sitting on rocks combing their long, green hair to entice sailors to a watery doom. They have been confused with Sirens, even giving that name to a class of marine mammals (*Sirenia*). However, the original Sirens of Greek mythology were not aquatic at all, but birds with the heads and breasts of women.

Sirenomelia, also called "mermaid syndrome," is a rare congenital disorder in which a child is born with his or her legs fused together and the genitalia reduced. This condition is usually fatal within a day or two of birth because of kidney and bladder complications. There are three known survivors of this disorder alive today.

The folklore of Mer-people is ancient and widespread, crossing cultures, continents, and centuries. They have been called by diverse names—*Abgal, Adaro, Sirens, Selchies, Tritons, Undines, Melusines, Morgans, Korrigans, Lorelei, Rusulki, Nixies, Nereids, Naiads*, and *Ningyos*. Inhabiting splendorous undersea kingdoms of coral castles, they are said to be as soulless as water, but they may acquire a coveted soul by marrying a human. Symbolizing eloquence in speech, the heraldic Mermaid is common-

*Fig. 1.
Heraldic Mermaid*

ly shown with a comb and a mirror, and described as a "mermaid in her vanity." (Fig. 1) The mirror also represents the moon, ruler of the tides.

MERFOLK OF HISTORY

The earliest recorded Merman of legend was *Ea*, or *Oannes* in Greek. He was an Akkadian deity originating around 5,000 BCE, who was later adopted by the Babylonians. An account by Berossus, a Chaldean priest of Bel in Babylon, was preserved by Alexander Polyhistor of Greece:

> In the first year [of Babylon] there made its appearance from a part of the Erythrean Sea, an animal with reason, who was called Oannes. The whole body of the animal was like a fish; and had under the fish's head another head, and also feet below, similar to those of a man, subjoined to the fish's tail. His voice, too, and language were articulate and human; and a representation of him is preserved to this day. This Being in the daytime used to converse with men; but took no food at that season, and he gave them an insight into letters and sciences, and every kind of art.[1]

At sunset, Oannes would return to the sea, where he remained until dawn. The following figure shows a human apparently wearing a fish headdress and cape—probably a costume worn by his priests. Later, he came to be depicted as a typical Merman, with a human torso and a fish's tail.

*Fig. 2. Oannes by
Manly Palmer Hall*

Ea/Oannes seems to be related to the *Abgal* or *Apkallu* of even earlier Sumerian myth. With the head of a man and the lower body of a fish, they were regarded as guardians and patrons of society, and teachers of the arts and sciences. It is thought that they are derived from the *Apsu* of the entourage of Enki, the god of wisdom who taught irrigation. In Philistine-Assyrian myth, their king is *Dagon*, god of earth and agriculture.

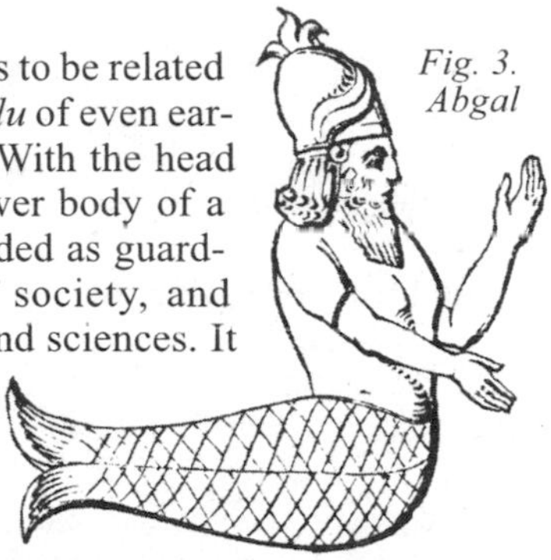

Fig. 3. Abgal

Kul or *Kulili* are freshwater Merfolk of ancient Assyrian myth, with the typical upper body of a human and lower body of a fish. *Kulullu* are the males and *Kuliltu*, the females. Generally hostile to humans, they dwell in lakes, pools, and wells, which they stir up and pollute to render the waters undrinkable. They can be mollified by music, and singing a paean to them will secure their lifetime friendship.

Countless other varieties of Merfolk appear down through the ages, in the mythologies and mariner's tales of many seafaring peoples. Although most dwell in the seas, there are plenty of freshwater analogs—such as *Naiads*, *Nixies*, and *Undines*—said to inhabit various lakes and rivers. Although both Mermen and Mermaids are mentioned, most of the legends focus on the females of the species.

Fig. 4. Japanese Mermaid

Although some of the Merfolk—such as the German *Hakenmann*, the Tsimshian *Hakulaq*, the Inuit *Ikalu Nappa*, the *Margygr* of Greenland, and the Brazilian *Igpupiara*—are described as hideously ugly, the Mermaid of tradition is beautiful, seductive, and dangerous. Her long hair is said to be composed of seaweed. For a sailor, to see a Mermaid is almost always a portent of disaster—storm, shipwreck, drowning. Merfolk are said to dwell in a kingdom ruled by Neptune on the bottom of the sea, and they entice sailors to leap into the water to join them with seductive singing and music. However, Mermaids do sometimes rescue a drowning sailor.

The Mermaid was believed to be real by both natural historians and explorers, who have reported many sightings and encounters over the centuries. Pliny the Elder (23–79 CE) was the first naturalist to record one in detail, in his monumental *Natural History* (77 CE):

> And as for the Meremaids called Nereides, it is no fabulous tale that goeth of them: for looke how painters draw them, so they are indeed: only their bodie is rough and scaled all over, even in those parts wherein they resemble women.[2]

But the classic form of the Mermaid was provided by the influential 5th-century bestiary, the *Physiologus*, which describes the mermaid as "a beast of the sea wonderfully shapen as a maid from the navel upward and a fish from the navel downward, and this beast is glad and merry in tempest, and sad and heavy in fair weather."[3]

By the mid-13th century, the legend of the Mermaid was fully defined. In *De Propietatibus Rerum*, Bartholomew Angelicus describes her as a lethal seductress who charms sailors through sweet music: "But the truth is that they are strong whores [who lead men] to poverty and to mischief." Typically, a Mermaid would lull a crew to sleep, kidnap a sailor, and take him to "a dry place" for sex. If he resisted, "then she slayeth him and eateth his flesh."[4]

TRITONS AND MONKFISH

Tritons are Mermen of Greek lore, but not nearly as attractive as some of their kin in other parts of the world. Children of the Greek god of the sea, Poseidon (Roman, Neptune), they have forked fishtails and a mouthful of sharp teeth, as well as green hair, gills, and pointy ears. They are commonly shown bearing a trident, and blowing a "Triton's trumpet" seashell (*Charonia tritonis*). Male Tritons delight in playing malicious tricks on hapless sailors, earning them a reputation for lasciviousness and deceit. Ambroise Pare (1517–1590), in his *On Monsters and Marvels*, reports that a male and female Triton were sighted around that time in the Nile River of Egypt. The 2nd-century Greek philosopher Pausanias described a famous pickled "Triton" exhibited in the temple of Dionysos in Tanagra, Boiotia, Greece, where it was said to have been captured in the local river:

> On their heads they have hair like that of marsh frogs not only in color, but also in the impossibility of separating one hair from another. The rest of their body is rough with fine scales just as in the shark. Under their ears they have gills and a man's nose, but the mouth is broader and the teeth are those of a beast. Their eyes seem to me blue, and they have hands, fingers, and nails like the shells of the murex. Under the breast and belly is a tail like a dolphin's instead of feet.[5]

Fig. 5. Preserved "Triton"

Both of these accounts are certainly descriptions of Angel Sharks (*Squatina*), an unusual group of sharks with flattened bodies and broad pectoral fins similar to those of rays. (Fig. 7) According to J.W. Buel, "it is frequently called Monk-Fish on account of its rounded head, which seems to be enveloped in a hood, and also because of a habit it has of rolling its eyes in a kind of reverential and supplicatory manner."[6] In the 13th century, one was captured in the Baltic Sea and taken to the King of Poland. Upon being shown to some Bishops of the Church, its rolling eyes were taken as a plea for release, and so it was. Another was caught off the coast of Germany in 1531, but it refused food and died after three days. In the Orient, these peculiar fish are called the *Sea Bonze*, or *Sea Buddhist Priest*.

Fig. 6. Angel Shark from Buel

Likewise, Bishop Erik Pontopiddan, in his *Natural History of Norway* (1752), describes the *Marmaele* as small Merfolk, human in the upper part and fishlike below the waist. Thought to be the progeny of Mermaids and Mermen, they vary in size, from "the bignesse of an infant of half a year old" to a child of three. Local fishermen sometimes caught them: "They tell us that these creatures then roll their eyes about strangely, as if out of curiosity, or surprise, to see what they had not seen before." Some were brought home and fed on milk, in hope of a foretelling of the future; but they were always returned to the sea within a day. Again, the detail of the rolling eyes strongly suggests the angel shark.

JENNY HANIVERS

Fig. 7. Sea-Monk (L) and Sea-Bishop (R) from J. Sluper's Omnium fere gentian, *1572*

For centuries it has been a common taxidermy practice to creatively cut up and cobble together preserved rays and other sea life into weird "creatures." Not only Tritons, but Monkfish, Bishop Fish, and Mermaids were created in this fashion, often using parts of different animals, and mummified expertly enough to appear quite real on the surface. For reasons long forgotten, these artificial monsters became known as *Jenny Hanivers*. The term is said to be derived from Anvers (modern Antwerp) in Belgium, which was supposedly a center for their creation. But most were manufactured by Japanese fishermen as curiosities and souvenirs for travelers. Each came with an individual story of its capture, and some sold for thousands of dollars.[7] In the mid-19th century, such preserved specimens became popular spectacles in Victorian London, and most people accepted them as authentic. The most famous was the *Feejee Mermaid*, first shown in a Lon-

Fig. 8. Feejee Mermaid

don coffeehouse and brought to Broadway in 1842 by P.T. Barnum. It was composed of the torso of a female orangutan grafted to the body of a salmon.

A similar composite "Mermaid" appeared in a 1717 book on the sea life of the Molucca Islands of Indonesia. The engravings were done by Samuel Fallour, from specimens collected by Van der Stell, governor of Amboine Island. One of these was labeled a "Sea-Wyfe," but it has become famous as the *Mermaid of Amboine*. The text describes her as "a monster resembling a Siren…. It was 59-inches long, and in proportion like an eel. It lived on land, in a vat full of water, during four days seven hours. From time to time it uttered little cries like those of a mouse…."[8] The color picture shows her as olive green, with webbed fingers and an orange and blue fringe around her waist. Her elongated lower body has green fins along the back and tail. Clearly this is a Jenny Haniver, comprised of the body of a fish—probably a Dorado (*Coryphaena hippurus*)—awkwardly grafted to the torso of a female monkey.

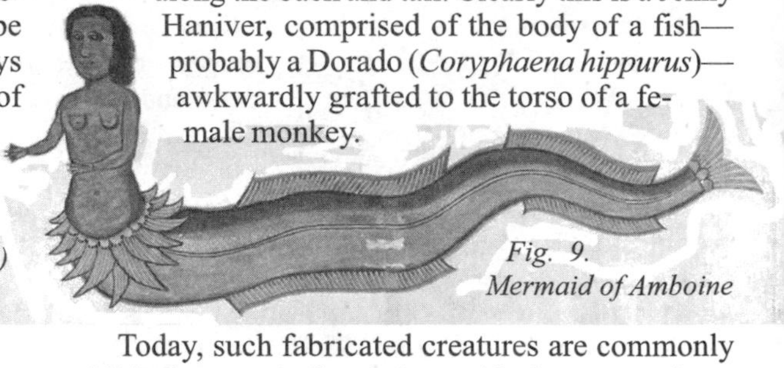

Fig. 9. Mermaid of Amboine

Today, such fabricated creatures are commonly exhibited as carnival and circus sideshow attractions, where they are known in the trade as *gaffs*.

UGLY MERMAIDS

However, there have been countless sightings and reports through the ages of living Merfolk. The universality and vitality of the Mermaid legend suggests a substratum of fact: an actual animal that may appear Mermaid-like from a distance. Possible candi-

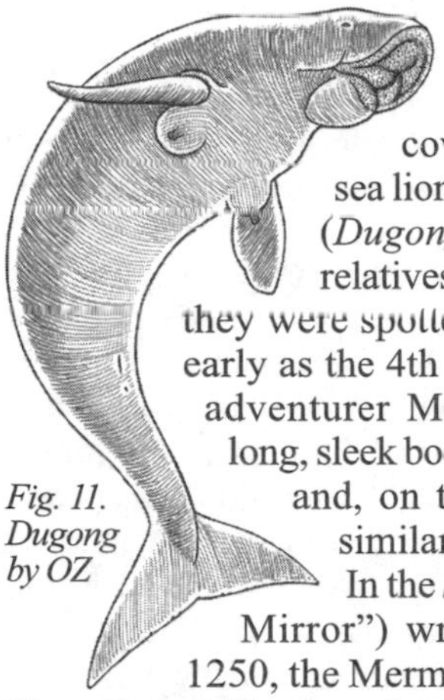

Fig. 11. Dugong by OZ

dates are *sirenians* (manatees, dugongs, and sea-cows) and *pinnipeds* (seals, sea lions, and walruses). Dugongs (*Dugong dugon*) are Indonesian relatives of the American manatee; they were spotted in the Indian Ocean as early as the 4th century BCE by the Greek adventurer Megasthenes.[12] They have long, sleek bodies, large, whale-like tails, and, on the females, breasts very similar to those of women.

In the *Speculum Regale* ("King's Mirror") written in Norway around 1250, the Mermaid is described more as a Neanderthal-like throwback than a beautiful woman:

> Another prodigy called mermaid has also been seen there. This appears to have the form of a woman from the waist upward, for it has large nipples on its breast like a woman, long hands and heavy hair, and its neck and head are formed in every respect like those of a human being. The monster is said to have large hands and its fingers are not parted but bound together by a web like that which joins the toes of water fowls. Below the waist line it has the shape of a fish with scales and tail and fins.... The monster is described as having a large and terrifying face, a sloping forehead and wide brows, a large mouth and wrinkled cheeks.[9]

In all likelihood—especially considering the geographical context—this is a description of a female Walrus (*Odobenus rosmarus*). In Greenland folklore, it was called *Margygr*. In the folklore of northern Germany, the *Hakenmann* ("Hook Man") was a vicious predatory sea-monster with a humanoid torso, and the head and lower body of a gigantic fish. The fearsome "hook" would be the tusks possessed by both sexes.

Fig. 12. Walruses

On January 4, 1493, on his first voyage to the Americas, Christopher Columbus reported seeing three Mermaids frolicking in the ocean just off of Haiti. He recorded in his log that the female forms "rose high out of the sea, but were not as beautiful as they are represented."[10]

Captain John Smith also saw a Mermaid in the West Indies. She swam gracefully as he observed her, and as he "was about to lose his heart the lady turned over, revealing below the tail of a fish."[11]

These could only have been Caribbean Manatees (*Trichechus manatus*).

Fig. 13. Manatee from Buel, 1887

Other Mermaids based on manatees include the Brazilian *Igpupiara* or *Hipupiara* ("Dweller in the Water"), which has a humanoid torso and a fishlike lower body and tail. Its head is said to resemble that of a seal, and its five fingers are webbed. This is probably the Amazon Manatee (*Trichechus inunguis*).

Another creature contributing to sightings and legends of Merfolk in Artic waters was the giant sirenian known as the Stellar's Sea-Cow (*Hydrodamalis gigas*). Living only in the vicinity of Siberia's remote Commander Islands, adults weighed up to 8,000 pounds and measured up to 35 feet in length, with a 20-foot girth that tapered to whale-like flukes. Instead of front flippers, they had stumpy, elephantine feet, with which the placid creatures pulled themselves along the bottom as they grazed in the coastal shallows. Like other sirenians, the females had two humanlike breasts on their upper chests, and nursed their young sitting upright in the water. First discovered officially in 1741 by a Russian expedition commanded by Dane Vitus Bering, successive explorers killed and ate every one over the next 27 years, resulting in their extinction by 1768.

Fig. 14. Stellar's Sea-Cow

Inuit legends of the giant Merfolk they called *Ikalu Nappa* surely referred to sea-cows. The sea-cow is probably also the basis of the *Hakulaq*, a huge female sea-monster in the folklore of the coastal Tsimshian Indians of America's Pacific Northwest. She was said to use her progeny as bait; if humans tried to take her baby from the water, she would follow and swamp their boat with stormy waves. The Micmac Indians of eastern Canada tell of the *Halfway People*, whose upper bodies are humanoid and their lower parts are those of huge fish. They sing to warn people of approaching storms, but if shown disrespect, they invoke terrible tempests and turbulence. Similarly, the Norwegian *Havfine* ("Sea-Woman"), with the torso of a woman and the tail of a fish, was said to be a wave herder. When the storm waves were driven like fleecy sheep upon the shore, any sailors still at sea were in danger of shipwreck. The Welsh *Gwenhidwy* was also said to be a shepherdess of the waves. The sight of her was said to bring good fortune.

SELBIES AND ROANE

Another group of Mermaid legends is associated with seals. The *Auvekoejak*, found in the waters around Greenland, was described by the Inuit as similar to Merfolk, but covered in fur rather than scales. The same creature was called *Havstrambe* by the Norse of Iceland and Scandinavia. It has been equated with the Northern Fur Seal (*Callorhinus ursinus*). In 1608, the English navigator Henry Hudson was skirting the polar ice off the arctic coast of Russia in his second attempt to find a northeast passage to the spice markets of China. Near the coast of Nova Zembla, Hudson made this log entry of 15 June: [12]

> This morning, one of our companie looking over board saw a mermaid, and calling up some of the companie to see her, one more came up, and by that time shee was close to the ship's side, looking earnestly upon the men: a little after, a Sea came and overturned her: From the Navill upward, her backe and breasts were like a woman's…her body as big as one of us; her skin very white; and long haire hanging down behinde, of colour blacke; in her going down they saw her tayle, which was like the tayle of a Porposse, and speckled like a Macrell.

Ben-Varry and *Dinny-Marra* (Manx, "man of the sea") are seal-like Merfolk said to dwell around the Isle of Man. Ben-Varrey are the females, who delight in enchanting sailors with their beautiful songs, then luring them to their deaths. The males, who tend to be friendly and easy to get along with, are called Dinny-Marra. In Danish folklore, the females are called *Havfrue* or *Havfinë* ("sea-woman"), and the males are *Havmand* or *Havman* ("sea-man"). They have blue skin and green or black hair, and tend to be very unpredictable—one moment kind, the next vicious. It is considered very unlucky to see one. Able to shift from fish tail to human legs, they can live in either salt or fresh water.

In Scotland's Orkney Isles, the *Fin People* bask on the shore during the summer near Eynhallow village. According to legend, the people of Eynhallow were once in communion with the Fin People of *Finfolkaheen*, a mirror village beneath the waves. If any of the Fin People could succeed in seducing a human, they would lose their fish tail and live on land. Likewise, the Shetland Island *Sea Trow* is able to shift from a fish's tail to legs and feet. Hans Christian Anderson's story of *The Little Mermaid* is based on such creatures, as was the 1984 hit movie *Splash!* and the 2006 teen chick-flick, *Aquamarine*.

Fig. 15. Daryl Hannah in Splash!

But the quintessential mythology of Merfolk that can become human is found in the legends of the *Roane* and *Selchies* (Orcadian, "seal") from the Orkney and Shetland islands of Scotland, Ireland, and Britain. Rather than sporting fish tails and human bodies, the shy Selkies and Roane appear as Grey Seals (*Halichoerus grypus*) while in the water. However, they can remove the sealskins if they wish and walk upon land as humans. Of the two, the Scottish Roane are the more gentle-natured. Angered Selkies can raise fierce storms to sink the boats of seal hunters or any others who offend them. Both can be captured by taking their skins and hiding them. If a Selkie or Roan thus captured is forced into a marriage, it will be a faithful and loyal spouse, albeit somewhat sad. But if ever it should recover its sealskin it will return to the ocean and never look back. This legend is hauntingly told in the movie *The Secret of Roan Inish* (1994). People born with webbed hands or feet are said to be "Selkie-born."

Fig. 16. Selchie removing seal-skin

Virtually all other claimed sightings of living Merfolk that provide enough descriptive information can be identified with known pinnipeds or sirenia. However, there is another very intriguing possibility.

AQUATIC APES

In 1960, British marine biologist Sir Alister Hardy outlined a radical new theory of human origins. [13] He suggested that our apelike proto-hominid ancestors might have spent a period of their evolutionary history in the sea, living much like sea otters. Foraging along the shores of the shallow tropical sea, covering what is now the Afar Peninsula, they would have had access to a rich diet of crabs, mussels, fish, and seaweed while the rest of Africa was suffering from the 3-million-year drought of the Pliocene Era.

Groping around the rocks and tide pools, these littoral apes would have moved out gradually to greater depths, becoming more and more erect and bipedal as they held their heads above the water, and eventually becoming swimmers. Following the evolutionary adaptations of other marine mammals, they would have lost their body hair, retaining only a cap on their heads as protection against the sun.

Interestingly, the fossil remains of "Lucy," widely hailed as one of our earliest ancestors, were found in an aquatic environment, along with turtles and seashells.

Just as sea otters use rocks to bash open mussels, the aquatic apes would have learned to use stones and other implements to crack shells and winkle out snails. As the long drought came to an end, they would have returned to the land with tool-using skills, bipedality, and hairless skin. Unique among apes, but in common with all other sea mammals, they would have developed layers of subcutaneous fatty tissue as insulation, as well as the ability to hold their breath underwater and cry salty tears.

Concerned about his academic reputation, Hardy never developed this controversial thesis further. But it came to the attention of Elaine Morgan, who presented and championed it for a popular audience in her 1972 book, *The Descent of Woman*,[14] and in several subsequent books and articles.

The aquatic ape theory does seem to account for virtually all of the otherwise inexplicable ways in which humans differ physically from all other apes—especially because all of these features are endemic to marine mammals. It explains why human babies swim naturally immediately after birth; why humans so enjoy swimming and water activities; why we have webbing between our fingers and toes; why women's buoyant breasts, like those of sirenia, are designed to float so that babies can suckle at the surface without drowning; why our uniquely downward-opening nostrils trap air when we submerge; and perhaps most indicative of all, because this appears in the fetal stage, why the hair tracks on our bodies are aligned with

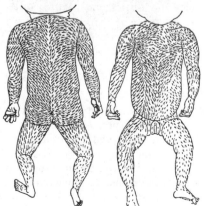

Fig. 18. Hair tracks on human fetus, from F.W. Jones, Man's Place among the Mammals.

Fig. 17. Lucy

the flow of water for swimming—completely different from those of terrestrial apes. (Fig.18)

Two million years ago, the long drought of the Pliocene era finally came to an end. Forests and grasslands spread across equatorial Africa, and diverse populations of animals soon followed. At the same time, sea levels dropped hundreds of feet, exposing vast territories of continental shelves as the northern latitudes succumbed to the glaciations of the Pleistocene. And along those newly expanded coastal plains, early humans emigrated from Mother Africa and spread throughout the world.

But why should all of the aquatic apes have given up their idyllic existence at the seashore to brave a more difficult life on land, in competition with tougher apes and ferocious predators? Clearly some did return to the land, or we wouldn't be here now. But surely others would have remained in the sea and continued evolving further aquatic adaptations, just like the cetaceans, sirenia, and pinnipeds did before them. Given those examples, it would be expected that eventually, their hind legs would diminish into flippers like those of a seal, or would disappear altogether to be replaced with a fluked tail like that of a dolphin. But the arms would very likely remain humanlike, as the grasping fingers and opposable thumbs had become far too useful to abandon.

These are the very reasonable speculations that make the existence of marine primates resembling our traditional descriptions of Merfolk seem plausible.

THE FAR SIDE/GARY LARSON

Early Pleistocene mermaids

ṭḅE ḅunṭinɢ oꝫ ṭḅE RI

In July of 1983, off the coast of New Ireland, 300 miles northeast of New Guinea, Dr. Roy Wagner, head of the Department of Anthropology at the University of Virginia at Charlottesville, and cryptozoologist Richard Greenwell observed an unknown sea mammal that Wagner had heard about four years earlier.[15] Local natives called it a *Ri* or *Ilkai*, describing it as having a fishlike lower body and a humanoid head and torso, with prominent breasts on the females. In other words, a Mermaid! This identification was reinforced by its Pidgin name: *Pishmeri* ("fish-woman"), and confirmed by the natives' pointing to the Mermaid depicted on cans of tuna (R) as being the same creature.

The animal flexed its back sharply, waved its wide, fluked tail high in the air when diving, and stayed underwater for periods of about 10 minutes, surfacing for only two seconds. Although dugongs are known in the area, experts on dugong behavior report average durations of submergence at one minute. Although unable to approach closer than 50 feet away in a small dinghy, Wagner got a few murky photos of a rolling back and an uplifted tail. The field report, published in *Cryptozoology,* concluded that

> Having considered all the possibilities, the authors have not been able to identify the Ri or Ilkai as part of the known inventory of zoology. None of the marine mammalogists consulted so far are convinced that the animal we observed and photographed is one they are acquainted with. We are therefore left with the tantalizing possibility that the animal we observed is indeed new to science. [16]

This report became an immediate sensation, resulting in other articles appearing in *Science,*[17] *Omni, Weekly World News,* and various other journals.

In February of 1985, irresistibly intrigued by the ISC report, I assembled and led a 13-person diving expedition to New Ireland to identify and videotape the Ri. This expedition was sponsored jointly by the Ecosophical Research Association (ERA) and the International Society of Cryptozoology (ISC), and funded by the lease of our living Unicorns to the circus (see Chapter 4: "The Universal Unicorn"). We all became SCUBA certified, and several of us learned Pidgin to enable us to communicate with the native people. We chartered a 65-foot Australian dive boat called the Reef Explorer, and set out from Port Moresby, Papua New Guinea, steaming to New Ireland by way of the Trobriand Islands. Our destination was Nokon Bay, a small lagoon on the north side of the island where Wagner and Greenwell had sighted the Ri/Ilkai two years before.

Oberon Zell

"There must be a Ri!" the Spellman cried,
As he conjured his crew with care;
Encouraging each with excitement and pride
Or a finger entwined in their hair.[18]

RI EXPEDITION MEMBER TOM WILLIAMS REPORTS

Even in Port Moresby, we began to hear stories of "mermaids." While the ship was being fueled, a native by the name of Alphonse Bouhoudumu told us of a creature he had seen in 1970 in Manus after it had been brought ashore by Japanese fishermen. The "woman fish" had a fish-like tail instead of legs and long hair. The local doctor had been asked to operate to see if he could find any legs, but had said there was nothing he could do. The creature was subsequently released back into the sea.

The Reef Explorer arrived at Nokon on Feb. 11th, and dropped anchor at 1:45 p.m. Almost immediately, two expedition members, Morning Glory Zell and Rich Bergero, sighted the flukes of an animal above the water on the south side of the bay. Observations were made from 2:00 p.m. until about 5:30, both from the surface and once from under water. Surface observation revealed flukes or a rolling back, often with a head visible. In addition, another, distinctly small individual was sighted.

About that time, a native called Tom Omar came up in a rowboat. When asked about the Ilkai, he pointed to a tail that was just breaking surface and exclaimed, "Ilkai, ilkai, em I stap!" ("There it is!"). He then went on to describe the female as having a woman's face, hair, hands, and breasts, saying that there was a family living in the bay: a male, a female, and a child ("Em i man, na meri, na pikinini."). All the while, the animal was displaying the rolling back and tail activity described by Wagner and others who were on the previous ISC expedition.

A much more spectacular observation was made under water by the captain of the Reef Explorer, Kerry Piesch. At about 3:30 p.m., he set out from the boat with fins and snorkel and a small underwater camera. Shortly thereafter, he signaled that he had observed and photographed the animal under water.

Its length was approximately 5 feet and the color appeared a greenish-grey underwater. A distinct head was joined to the body with

Fig. 19: Underwater photo of Ilkai by Capt. Kerry Piesch

no discernable neck. The forelimbs were short and paddle-shaped, but the face could not be seen clearly from the observer's position. The hindquarters tapered off in a very streamlined shape ending in the wide-fluked tail seen from the surface.

The morning of Feb. 15th brought an abrupt end to activities at Nokon. Early in the morning some villagers were observed pulling a large animal out of the water onto the beach. When expedition members Oberon Zell and Tom Williams swam to the beach from the Reef Explorer, they discovered that the animal was an adult female dugong. She had apparently been killed by a single wound, slightly behind the right flipper. Subsequent autopsy by Oberon revealed that she had been shot by a high-powered rifle. The night before, another boat, named the "Cuddles" had anchored in the bay. The next morning it was gone. We could only conclude that the creature had been shot by someone on that boat.

There can now be little doubt that the animal variously known as the *Ri* or *Ilkai*, and associated with stories of Merfolk and possible marine primates is in reality the Indo-Pacific Dugong (*Dugong dugon*). The combination of visual sighting, both above and under water, along with photographic evidence and, tragically, the death of an animal at about the same time and place make this conclusion inescapable.

One of the lingering questions is how the myths of Merfolk can arise and persist in the face of the obvious reality of the dugong. The statements of Tom Omar are a case in point. There is apparently a kind of belief system at work whose nature transcends the strict discipline of zoology and spills over into the realm of anthropology and psychology. Whatever the original source of the stories, they appear to persist as some sort of self-perpetuating male fantasy.

Oberon Zell

Their guest, he looked pensive and stared out to sea—
Then he smiled all the while he declaimed:
"Oyo mama!" he whistled most suggestively—
"Yu should see em, tasol!" he exclaimed.[20]

The structure or mechanism of such a male fantasy became apparent in conversations with various individuals. Whatever the actual facts behind various reported sightings and incidents, there appeared to be a certain prestige associated with having had an encounter with a *Ri* or *Ilkai*. Thus, when one male of the tribe gained that prestige through telling his tale, others felt they, too, needed to have stories in order to gain recognition from their peers. When another man had a story and gained equal footing with the first teller, the cycle would repeat. Pretty soon a sort of tacit "club" formed consisting of those who had tales to tell. Now, each might know the truth or falseness of his own tale, but could never be quite sure of that of the next fellow. In fact, it was tacitly unac-

ceptable to question the tales of others lest one's own tale be called into question. By this route, an actual "belief" in the existence of the *Ri* or *Ilkai* arose because those who did not have their own experience tended to accept the tales of those who so claimed. This made for a form of social interaction for the menfolk of the tribe allowing them to engage in what in our culture might be called "bull sessions" sharing tales, much as men do in bars all over the world. The only members of the tribe who seemed unimpressed with this entire structure of storytelling were the women.

Oberon Zell

MONSTER MOVIES: MERMAIDS

Many popular fantasy movies have featured Mermaids. *Mr. Peabody and the Mermaid* (1948) is told by a psychiatrist whose patient claims to have caught a Mermaid which he is keeping in his bathtub. In *Miranda* (1948), a comely Mermaid marries a London doctor and bears a fish-tailed baby. A sequel, *Mad About Men*, was released in 1954. In *The Mermaids of Tiburon* (1962), beautiful Mermaids aid a diver in his search for sunken treasure. *Beach Blanket Bingo* (1965) also includes a human-Mermaid romance. In *Splash* (1984), Daryl Hannah plays a Mermaid who falls in love with a man. She can walk on land as a woman, but if water touches her legs, they revert to a fish tail. In the German film, *Ondine* (1991), a freshwater Mermaid, or *Undine*, is saved from a developer who wants to destroy her lake for a ski resort. Disney's *The Little Mermaid* (1989), is based on the Hans Christian Anderson story of a Mermaid who sacrifices her tail and voice to gain legs for a human lover. *She Creature* (2001) features a villainous Mermaid with a taste for human flesh. *Aquanoids* (2003) was about siren-like sea-creatures. In *Aquamarine* (2006), two 12-year-old girls befriend a sassy teenage Mermaid with the ability to change her tail into legs when on land. In *Heart's Atlantis* (2006), a grieving boy finds solace with a Mermaid in his backyard pool. *Lady in the Water* (2006) features a *Narf*, or water-Nymph, who appears in the swimming pool of an apartment building. Mermaids also appear briefly in all the *Peter Pan* movies, in *Narnia* (2005), and in *Harry Potter and the Goblet of Fire* (2005).

11. The Braßen

By Tom Williams

The Kraken

Below the thunders of the upper deep;
Far far beneath in the abysmal sea,
His ancient, dreamless, uninvaded sleep
The Kraken sleepeth: faintest sunlights flee
About his shadowy sides; above him swell
Huge sponges of millennial growth and height;
And far away into the sickly light,
From many a wondrous grot and secret cell
Unnumber'd and enormous polypi
Winnow with giant arms the slumbering green.
There hath he lain for ages, and will lie
Battening upon huge seaworms in his sleep,
Until the latter fire shall heat the deep;
Then once by man and angels to be seen,
In roaring he shall rise and on the surface die.

—Alfred, Lord Tennyson, 1830

Ian Daniels

 HAT IS THE SEA? SUPERFICIALLY, IT IS the layer of saline water covering 70 percent of our planet. Yet on a deeper level it has influenced the cultures and psyches of countless societies throughout history. It has provided food and sustenance, served as a route for trade and exploration, borne military fleets on voyages of conquest, served as a barrier against marauders, evoked mystery and poetry from bards and singers—and represented some of humanity's deepest fears. The sea represents to this very day a frontier of the unknown—a place of darkness and discovery, harboring strange and beautiful creatures as well as devouring monsters that haunt our dreams and the deepest recesses of our imaginations.

It is from the realm of the sea and its darkest depths that the engrossing legend of the Kraken rises—the Kraken, universally depicted as an all-devouring monster with arms that draw its victims inexorably and inescapably to an implacable, consuming maw that shreds and consumes the very being. The Kraken—the creature that lurks in the darkness and sometimes emerges on the surface to wrap its tentacles around a hapless vessel to draw it beneath the waves. From earliest times, it is represented with multiple arms or heads on stalks, often with a mouth or beak at the center that rends and bites and consumes the flesh—and in many cases the soul—of its prey.

Of all the frightening beasts of legend, it is seldom that there has been such a direct correspondence between the mythical image and the actual animal. For the Kraken is real, as real as a whale or a turtle or a gull skimming the waves. The real animal, a taxonomically identifiable organism as plainly a part of the grand march of evolution as any other creature, embodies most of the horrific attributes associated with the Kraken in the most fanciful legends and seamen's tales. In its largest and most incredible manifestation, the real animal could very well convince us of the reality behind the most fantastic metaphysical horrors and tortured fantasies of crazed authors of fiction.

Fig. 1. Attack of the Giant Squid in 20,000 Leagues Under the Sea

The Kraken is the giant squid—and its more recently discovered cousin, the colossal squid. Yet having said that, how do we approach this realization? Simply being handed the solution to what started as some sort of cryptozoological investigation does not do justice to the reality or to the legend that preceded it. For a good long time, the question of the giant squid really was a cryptozoological issue. There were reports, a sampling of which we will review in this chapter, dating from the early days of seafaring. There were the legends of Scylla and Charybdis; there were the tales of Jules Verne; there were questions such as, "Did such a thing really exist, and, if so, how big could it really be?" As we shall see, we have now answered most of those questions. Still, the mind-boggling question remains: "If this thing really does exist as a living creature, how to we *deal* with that fact?"

I am proposing that the reality of the Kraken highlights one of those rare instances in which the metaphysical world of our legends, fears, and archetypal fantasies overlaps with the real, biological, physical world on a continuing basis. But the Kraken has several characteristics that arise from and feed our deepest fears—and which can be identified as well in the living animal. Among these characteristics is that of implacability; despite all attempts to slay or stop the beast, it just keeps coming. It seems that wounding it simply makes it attack all the more. Consider the most ancient legend that can be identified with the multi-armed monster we know as the giant squid—namely, that of the Hydra.

ⳠE HᙁORA

The Hydra was a monster living in the swamps near the city of Lerna in Argolis (in ancient Greece). It was the offspring of Echidna (half maiden, half serpent), and Typhon, who had 100 heads. The Hydra had the body of a serpent

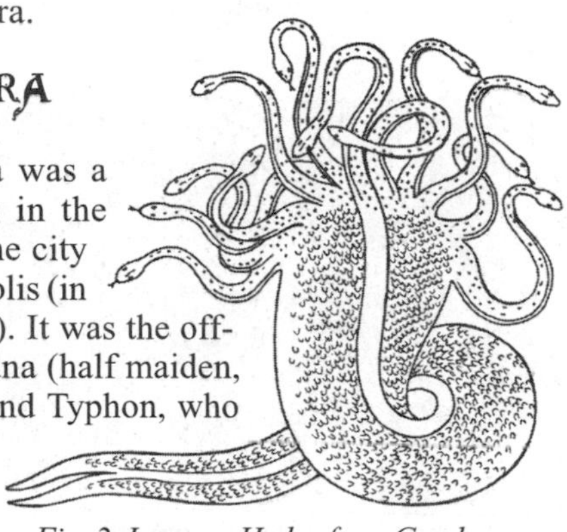

Fig. 2. Lernean Hydra from Greek vase

and many heads. In some versions of the legend they numbered nine, and in others, 100. The point here is that the multiple heads probably refer to semi-independent attacking arms belonging to the same creature. One of these heads was impervious to any weapon, and the others, if cut off, simply regrew. In some versions, two regrow for every one cut off. Its breath had a stench that could kill as well. The Hydra was known for attacking herds of cattle and whole villages, which it devoured with its many heads.

The hero Heracles came to do battle with the Hydra, bringing his nephew and charioteer, Iolaus. Heracles defeated the Hydra by bending the rules a bit: Realizing that simply cutting off heads was a losing proposition, he instructed Iolaus to cauterize each wound from a severed head with his torch to keep them from growing back. The final head, which was said to be immune from every weapon, Heracles simply bashed with his club, tore it off with his bare hands, and buried it. Now, a club is technically a weapon, so Heracles appears to have been given a pass here.

But let's look at some of the relevant details. The thing lives in the swamp, which, while not the ocean, is still a place of the dark unknown which may swallow the unwary wanderer. It is the deep even if it is not the ocean. The Hydra's many heads are depicted as being on long, flexible necks, which enables them to come at its opponents from different directions. There is what appears to be a central head, the invincible one that all the others serve and protect. Attempts to slay the beast only result in making matters worse. It just keeps coming.

SCᙁLLA

Now, there is not a lot of evidence that the ancient Greeks had any direct experience with giant

Fig. 3. Scylla, by Hal Foster

squid…or is there? Scylla is the name of a monster living under a huge rock in the Straight of Messina. She is a nymph who was transformed by the wrath of Circe into a monster with twelve feet and six heads. When a passing ship comes within range, each one of her heads plucks a hapless sailor from the deck and devours him. Still, there is no direct (or indirect) evidence that a cephalopod is at the basis of the Scylla myth. No large squid are known to inhabit the Mediterranean, and small octopus species are more prized as delicacies than feared as monsters.

It is more likely that Scylla, and her companion horror, Charybdis, are mythical embodiments of a deep human fear of being drawn into the abyss and devoured. Charybdis is the daughter of Poseidon and Gaia, whom Zeus had turned into a monster for stealing Helios' cattle. Sucking in and spewing out large amounts of water, and sucking under whole ships with their crews, Charybdis also embodies the consuming horror of the deep. Ulysses steers clear of Charybdis, opting to have six of his shipmates grabbed and eaten by Scylla rather than lose the whole ship to Charybdis. Still, the association with cephalopods is hard to deny. Part of the Odyssey's description of Scylla reads, "Her legs, and there are twelve, are like great tentacles, unjointed, and upon her serpent necks are joined six heads…." As for a direct connection between the myths of seamonsters and great squid among the ancient Greeks, however, we must be content with speculation.

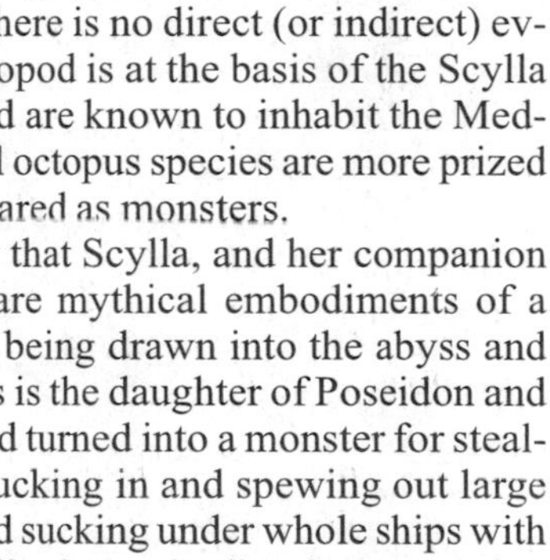

Fig. 4. Charybis

MARINERS' TALES

In the post-Classical era, however, the picture is quite different. Here we have not simply stories set in some mythical past, but reports of actual sightings and incidents, told by sailors who claimed to base them on real experience, however much they may have embellished the retelling. We also have drawings either taken from the descriptions or done by the actual witnesses. It is here that the connection to real cephalopods becomes unmistakable.

When Europeans first ventured beyond the Gates of Hercules they hugged the coasts of Europe and Africa. The vastness of the Atlantic must have appeared as a huge unknown, and quite naturally would have harbored monsters both real and imagined. Tales, of course, abounded, as the appearance of the great whales, such as the blue whale or the sperm whale, would certainly have qualified as the sighting of a monster.

The literature contains a fairly large number of reports that could quite easily be identified as sightings of giant squid, but others are more of a stretch. These reports, which range roughly from about 1000 CE to the early 20th century, constitute an interesting mixture of tales. Some later authors and investigators have rightly concluded that there is a squid at the bottom of some of them, whereas others simply projected their own preconceived notions about the anatomy of squids into the descriptions of sightings, and asked themselves what part of a squid's anatomy seen from which perspective could have given rise to those descriptions.

An exhaustive recounting of these tales is not appropriate in this contribution, but a few examples certainly are. One of the more noteworthy is a description of "monstrous fish" by Olaus Magnus, who was the Catholic archbishop of Sweden. Part of that description (circa 1555) reads, "Their forms are horrible, their heads square, all set about with prickles and they have a sharp horn round about like a tree rooted up by the roots…."

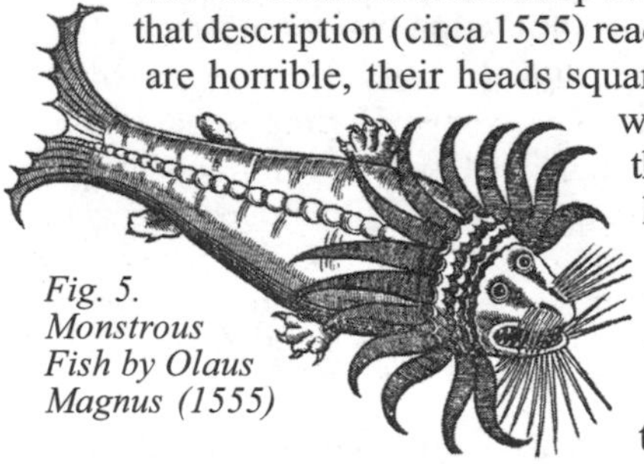

Fig. 6. W.C. Coup (1882)

What is interesting in the Magnus account is the description of it resembling an uprooted tree, which brings us to the topic of the word *Kraken*. Around 1000 CE, King Severre of Norway first used *Kraken* to describe a sea-monster, and the word occurs again in another work by a Norwegian, Bishop Erik Ludvigsen Pontoppidian, in his *The Natural History of Norway* (1755). Apparently, the association of the word Kraken with an uprooted tree is a tenuous connection at best. *Kraken* is actually the plural of the word *krake*, which simply means "sea-monster."

*Fig. 5.
Monstrous
Fish by Olaus
Magnus (1555)*

There are a few remarkable illustrations of sightings that are unmistakably giant squid. Even the ones that look more like octopuses are surely based on squid.

Sorting out exactly how factual the accounts behind these engravings are is not so much the point as is the anatomical similarity between the drawings and the actual animal. Everything we know today about large squid—be they giant or colossal—tells us that none of them is large enough to actually drag a ship down to Davy Jones's Locker. That doesn't mean they are not big and dangerous, mind you—just not *that* big.

Fig. 7. Kraken attack on a sailing ship

A recent and more realistic account came in 1861 from the French corvette *Alecton*, whose crew reported the killing and capture of a giant squid. The crew was able to bring only a portion of the body aboard because it broke apart while being hoisted out of the water. The *Alecton* report and the accompanying illustrations appear in the light of today's knowledge to be quite realistic, yet the captain and crew were denounced as liars.

The eyes were described as the size of dinner plates, and the mouth as being 18 inches across. In addition, the crew mentions a horrible stench. In a freshly caught animal, this would not be the result of putrification but the normal characteristic of the giant squid—that is, the ability to secrete ammonia. We know now that both the giant and the colossal squid lack swim bladders like those of fish, but

Fig. 8. The Alecton encounter[3]

can adjust their buoyancy by secreting ammonia into their tissues, thus changing their specific gravity. This results in the smell, and renders the flesh completely incdible. The *Alecton* incident appears to be a reliable and factual account of an encounter with a giant squid.

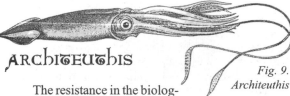

ARCHITEUTHIS

Fig. 9.
Architeuthis

The resistance in the biological community to accepting the existence of this species as well as its size remained intense until the late 20th century, when it could no longer be denied. One is tempted to attribute this to the normal skepticism of the scientific community, but one must factor in an additional element—the archetypal horror of the all-consuming Kraken of our deep, existential fears. This, then, leads us to the question of just how big and aggressive can these monsters be—for monsters they truly are.

When we talk about the Kraken, we are actually speaking of two distinct species that are now (albeit after much convincing) recognized by science: the Giant Squid, *Architeuthis dux*, and the Colossal Squid, *Mesonychiteuthis hamiltoni*. For some time, it was speculated that *Architeuthis* was a passive feeder, hanging inverted in a chosen temperature layer deep in the ocean, seizing passing prey with its long tentacles, and then drawing the prey to its beak with its eight shorter arms. We now know that *Architeuthis* is an aggressive predator. Like all squid, it has two long appendages called "tentacles" that are elastic and can be shot out to seize prey with the club-like pods on the end of each. Then it has eight shorter arms that grab and draw the prey to the savage beak, which shreds and devours it. In the case of giant squid, the suckers on both tentacles and arms arc ringed with sharp tooth-like hooks.

The first *Architeuthis* caught live (in December of 2006, by a team of Japanese researchers) actively attacked the bait and fought being hauled in, losing the pod of one tentacle, which writhed for some time with its toothed sucker cups on the deck of the ship. The squid itself did not survive the capture, but was the first example of *Architeuthis* to be photographed live.

As to the aggressive nature of large squid in general, we can look at a more familiar example, the Humboldt squid, *Dosidicus gigas*. Unlike the two giant species, the Humboldt squid is edible—but then it has the same attitude toward those who would try to capture it. Growing up to six feet long, including the arms (but not the tentacles), and weighing about 100 pounds, the Humboldt squid inhabits the Sea of Cortez and from the tip of Baja, California, to, most recently, the Central California coast. They move in schools of up to 1200 individuals and can swim at up to 13 knots,

often coming up at night from depths of around 2,000 feet to feed.

Local fishermen fear them because a significant number of them have been attacked and badly bitten, and some have been dragged down to their doom by groups of squid that were trying to eat the victim and each other. Humboldt squid have toothed suckers like those of the giant varieties. Their reputation as aggressive hunters is not in doubt, and, given the observed behavior of the one living *Architeuthis*, can probably be assumed to be the case with the two giant species. Both the giant and colossal squid have toothed suckers on their arms. The *Architeuthis* has toothed suckers on the pods of its tentacles, whereas *Mesonychoteuthis* has swiveled hooks.

Fig. 10. Architeuthis *club (a) compared with* Mesonychoteuthis *club (b)*

The question of how big is a thornier one. Extrapolations of *Architeuthis* attaining 150 feet in length are just not credible. Also, statements about the length of giant squid tend to be confusing in general. Measurements—inflated to sound more sensational—include the arms, as well as the two elastic tentacles with wider clubs on the ends used to grab prey. At least in the case of *Architeuthis*, the length of these tentacles can vary widely, sometimes depending on how far they have been stretched by those doing the measurements. Then there are the eight arms, which typically have a length proportional to that of the particular specimen. The head, arms and tentacles extend from the front of the mantle, whose length is the standard used for comparing the relative sizes of giant and colossal squid.

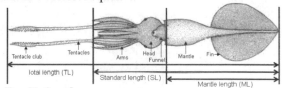

Fig. 11. Squid measurements

By now we have a fairly large sample of specimens of *Architeuthis*, and it is not known to attain a mantle length greater than 7.4 feet, which would result in a length with the arms (not the tentacles) of no more than about 16.5 feet. To those among us who may be disappointed with these sizes, that is a very large and *dangerous* animal. But it's just not capable of pulling under a vessel or impeding the progress of a 19th-century submarine.

MESONYCHOTEUTHIS

Mesonychoteuthis is a somewhat different matter. Colossal is quite the appropriate word for it. We know for a fact that it exists on the basis of at least two specimens, one of which was captured live in February of 2007 and brought, completely intact, aboard the fishing vessel that caught it, but died in the process of being hauled in. Unlike the *Alecton*, the fishing vessel was able to freeze the creature until it could be brought in for study. This creature, a mature male, weighed 992 pounds and was supposedly 39 feet long. Early reports neglected to specify which measurement this was. *Mesonychoteuthis* is considerably stockier and heavier than *Architeuthis*, in addition to being longer. The only other intact specimen was an immature female with a mantle length of 7.5 feet. Based on the estimates of female to male size, it is quite possible that a mature female could reach a mantle length of 13 feet or a little more. The weight, however, would approach a ton. Again, the beak is enormous, as can be seen in the photo of the captured male (Fig. 12).

Fig. 12. Captured male colossal squid (AP 2/22/07)[1]

Estimates of squid size have been done by comparing beaks taken from the stomachs of sperm whales, which is the giant and colossal squids' only natural predator. Some of the extrapolation has been done by examining fragments of tentacles and using their diameter to estimate the overall length. Because the *Mesonychoteuthis* is proportionally more heavy-set than *Architeuthis*, mistaking a colossal squid arm for that of a giant squid could lead to wildly different length estimates.

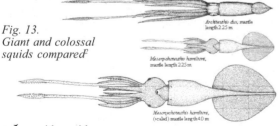

Fig. 13. Giant and colossal squids compared[2]

Architeuthis dux, mantle length 2.25 m

Mesonychoteuthis hamiltoni, mantle length 2.25 m

Mesonychoteuthis hamiltoni, (scaled) mantle length 4.0 m

ᴛʜᴇ ʙʀᴀʙᴇɴ

So now we know our monster. It is real. It is an implacable hunter, aggressive and deadly in its element—the deep ocean. Yet it rarely if ever has been known to attack humans. There was one incident off the coast of Nova Scotia in which a young boy in a small boat beat back an attacking squid while two adults cowered against the gunwales, but that is the only verified incident. Yet this image populates some of our deepest fears. It lurks in realms of mystery and nightmare. What has made it so compelling?

Written when he was only 21, "The Kraken" by Tennyson contains evocative elements that foreshadow the Cthulhu mythos, begun in the early 20th century by H.P. Lovecraft and continued by other authors including Robert Bloch, August Derleth, Robert E. Howard and others. Among these elements are a mysterious great being slumbering beneath the depths of the sea, images of great age and murkiness, and the prospect that it will awaken and rise in the midst of some unnamed catastrophe. Just what moved Tennyson to write such a thing at such a tender age will never be known, except that he might have tapped into some archetypal imagery that would resonate and be reprised by others. Nor is it known whether Lovecraft or his circle were aware of this poem.

As an author, H.P. Lovecraft was an admirer of such writers as Edgar Allan Poe, Lord Dunsany, and Arthur Machen. In terms of the literary craft, he never rose to the level of Poe, but his work influenced a good number of writers in the fantasy and horror genre. The Cthulhu mythos became a sort of shared world to which many contributed, but which was under no single author's control.

ɢʀᴇᴀᴛ ᴄᴛʜᴜʟʜᴜ

Fig. 14. Great Cthulhu

The Cthulhu mythos revolves around a race (or races) of alien beings who came to this planet untold ages ago—the chief among these being the Great Cthulhu—but who are now mostly dormant. Cthulhu lies dead but undead in the sunken city of R'lyeh in the depths of the Pacific. He is described as a large, green creature with bat wings, huge talons, and the head of a squid—that is, with tentacles below the eyes. Every so often, R'lyeh rises from the depths and the Great Old Ones hold sway until it sinks again. The myth holds that someday, when the "stars are right," the sunken city will rise and the Old Ones led by Cthulhu will reign supreme over the Earth.

As Cthulhu dreams in his slumbers, his thoughts influence certain sensitive persons who form cults to him, portray his image and perform deeds supposedly dedicated to him. The Cthulhu Mythos is populated by a number of other gods and beings such as "the crawling chaos that is Nyarlathotep," a nebulous devouring being named Yog Sottoth (the "eater of souls"), and others. Yog Sottoth is instructive in that it exemplifies the all-devouring nature of an eater of souls—again, here is the image of implacably drawing in and consuming, linked to the clacking beak of a huge squid. The horror here is that one is not simply swallowed, but rapidly picked to pieces, bite by bite, and consumed most horribly.[3]

The slumbering beneath the sea seems to tie in with the fact that great squid dwell at incredible depths and thus are rarely seen on the surface—usually only when they are sick or dying. However, the sight of the emergence of a hungry, deadly Humboldt squid from the depths of the ocean—or, in the case of the Great Cthulhu, from a place beyond space—can give rise to an implacable horror of the sightless deep, as well as the hapless victim's fear of being dragged into the creature's alien world. Even a very bad 2006 HBO movie, *Kraken: Tentacles of the Deep*, depicted a giant squid recently woken from its long slumber and eating everybody (except, of course, the beautiful blonde leading marine biologist).

It is a commonplace in Lovecraft stories that certain realities would better be left unknown. In *The Call of Cthulhu*, he writes, "The most merciful thing in the world, I think, is the inability of the human mind to correlate all its contents. We live on a placid island of ignorance in the midst of black seas of infinity, and it was not meant that we should voyage far. The sciences, each straining in its own direction, have hitherto harmed us little; but some day the piecing together of dissociated knowledge will open such terrifying vistas of reality, and of our own frightful position therein, that we shall either go mad from the revelation or flee from the deadly light into the peace and safety of a new dark age."[4]

One of the elements of *The Call of Cthulhu* is the existence of a cult, depicted by Lovecraft in his ingrained, racist way as made up of squat, swarthy men influenced by the thoughts of dreaming Cthulhu to do his bidding. They celebrate unspeakable rites and do dastardly things in their efforts to waken Cthulhu from his slumbers. Interestingly, something analogous to these cults may exist in the real world that involves the giant and colossal squid. Given that the only natural predator of both is the sperm whale,

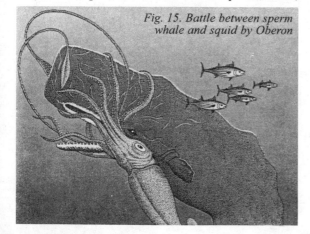

Fig. 15. Battle between sperm whale and squid by Oberon

would not Great Cthulhu wish to free his "children" by doing away with this nasty menace?

Sperm whales and giant squid do tremendous battles in the depths, with the whale usually coming out ahead of the game and eating the squid. If there were fewer whales, there could be more and larger squid. Now, despite the international pressure to ban or at least limit whaling, there are several nations that defy the International Whaling Commission and continue to slaughter whales all over the world. Could it be that these whalers are consciously or unconsciously doing the bidding of a dreaming Cthulhu by killing off the enemies of his minions?

It has not escaped attention that there have been more *Architeuthis* brought out of the ocean depths in recent years than in all previous history. Even more recently, we have observed the recovery of at least two *Mesonychoteuthis* and can expect more. On the one hand, these developments have finally convinced a skeptical scientific community that these creatures do, indeed, exist. On the other hand, the increase in numbers could strike one as disturbing.

Of course, such creatures as giant and colossal squid are just biological creatures that evolved in tune with their environment like all other forms of life, aren't they? How then does humankind appear to have had a notion of their form before it became known in photos and specimens? How is it that there is a creature living today that appears to embody some of our most basic fears regarding our own existence and the integrity of our being? Are their numbers really increasing, or does the proof of their existence simply lend itself to the recognition of existing numbers? In other words, are there more or does it just seem as though there are more?

If there truly are more, what is behind that increase? Is it possibly another effect of climate change, or is some other agency at work—buried behind a wall of dreams and lost in a realm of strange angles and dark shades? If you found yourself confronted with such a creature in its own realm, would it matter what the answer is? The horror is far away from our daily "placid island of ignorance," as Lovecraft puts it. But it is real. It lurks in the sightless depths, its beak shredding toothfish and marlin with an intractable indifference to the fate of either. And, just occasionally, but perhaps more frequently, it reaches up above the waves to remind us of some of our most deeply seated and repressed fears.

ADDENDUM BY OBERON...

Like Tom, I too have always been fascinated with cephalopods in general, and giant squids in particular. I was enthralled by Jules Verne's *20,000 Leagues Under the Sea* as a kid, and, in 1954, I eagerly awaited Disney's terrific movie version, wherein my favorite scene was the battle with the giant squid. I grew up near Chicago, where I spent many happy weekends exploring the wonderful museums of the windy city. The indelible image that has remained in my mind these 50 years later is the full-size model of a giant squid that hung from the ceiling of the Field Museum of Natural History. Starting with Bernard Heuvelman's classic *Le Kraken et le Poulpe Colossal* (1958), I have read every book and article on these creatures I could get my hands on, saved every news clipping on beached carcasses, and recorded every TV special on the current quest to film and obtain a live specimen.

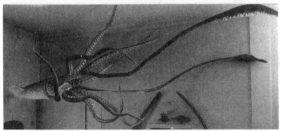

Fig. 16. Giant squid, life-size model, Natural History Museum[5]

I consider cephalopods to be among the most fascinating creatures on Earth. They belong to the order of *Mollusca*, which first appeared in the mysterious "Cambrian Explosion" 542 million years ago, along with every other order of multicellular life forms (including a couple dozen that were never seen again). They are undoubtedly the first animals to have developed intelligence. Laboratory studies of common reef octopuses indicate they are as smart as dogs. Unlike vertebrates, whose brains cannot outgrow their rigid skulls, the brains of cephalopods continue growing throughout their lives, just as the animal itself does. For an octopus, however, that isn't a very long time. Even the giant Pacific Octopus lives no longer than six years, and the females of all octopi die after hatching their eggs. So whatever degree of intelligence they attain must be developed during a period of time corresponding to our own early childhoods. How smart were you at six, compared to now?

Octopi are solitary hunters, and associate only briefly to mate. Therefore, other than territorial and mating signals, they have no need to develop any sophisticated form of communication with each other. It is pretty well considered axiomatic that the greatest intellectual development among all creatures occurs as a factor of intercommunication among the members of social species (for example, cetaceans, primates, wolves, elephants, and probably velociraptors), so the solitary existence of octopi, along with their short life span, would also limit how intelligent they can become.

Neither of these limitations applies to giant squid. Although the largest remains found washed up on beaches have been in the very impressive neighbor-

hood of up to 60 feet long from tail to tentacle tip, sucker scars on the skins of the adult male sperm whales that eat them, and undigested beaks found in the bellies of such whales, indicate the probable existence of truly colossal giants—possibly twice that size. Although no live specimen of *Architeuthis* has ever been obtained for study, experiments with other common species of squid—with brains the size of marbles—have indicated intelligence equivalent to that of octopi. There is no reason to assume less for their enormous cousins, whose donut-shaped brains surround their esophagi at the front of their heads.

The confirmation of giant squids up to 60 feet long—and the probable existence of far larger specimens in the abyssal depths of the oceans—indicates that giant squids, like anacondas, great white sharks, and some dinosaurs, probably continue growing throughout their life. And, like all other cephalopods, their brains continue growing larger along with their bodies. What we don't yet know, however, is their life span. Is it short, like that of other cephalopods, or long?

Unlike octopi, squid are social hunters, often aggregating in vast schools. Indeed, early sonar developed during World War II often returned "false bottom" soundings, which were later thought to have been caused by extensive shoals of giant squids. The near-simultaneous coordinated movements of schools of small squid which have been extensively filmed implies a sophisticated degree of communication—probably effected through subtle shifts in the coloration patterns made possible by the uniquely sensitive chromatophores possessed by all cephalopods. Squid have the greatest eye-to-body size ratio of any living creatures, and giant squid possess the largest eyes on Earth.

Given large brains, coordinated social predation, and possible longevity, it is not much of a stretch to hypothesize a considerable intelligence for *Architeuthis* and *Mesonychiteuthis*. We are, of course, familiar with the nature of vertebrate intelligence (based largely on vocal/auditory communication), as it is our own. And we are somewhat aware of the nature (or at least the existence) of arthropod intelligence, in the form of "hive minds" among the social insects, which communicate primarily by scent. We are only lately beginning to study cephalopod intelligence; and as yet we have no idea how it may manifest in these monstrous squid.

And thus, out of paleontology and marine biology, I offer my own contribution to the Cthulhu mythos:

542 million years ago, the Great Old Ones came to Earth, manifesting in many bizarre forms (see the Burgess Shale[6]). Most of those original orders killed each other off during the early millennia, and others (such as coelenterates, sponges, echinoderms, and worms) retreated into mindlessness and even sessility. Successful active hunters included the arthropod eurypterids and giant trilobites, but they never devel-

oped significant intelligence. Cephalopods—the Spawn of Cthulhu—first appeared as organisms with shells in the form of ammonites and nautiloids, some of which grew to more than 15 feet. And, they became intelligent.

They ruled the oceans of this world unopposed for 200 million years, until a rival intelligence finally arose in the form of vertebrates—the first of which were armored like tanks to ward off beaks, claws, and suckers. From the 30-foot-long *Dinicthys* of the Upper Devonian, the 50-foot-long Icthyosaurs and Kronosaurs of the Cretaceous, and the Archaeocetae of the Eocene, to the 60-foot-long sperm whales of today, calamari has been a favorite food of many oceanic hunters specifically evolved to eat them (a real challenge for *Architeuthis,* whose body fluids are ammonia- rather than water-based!). And the bigger the squid, the bigger the hunters. We grew up together and in opposition to one another, each species stimulating the evolution—and intelligence—of the other.

Fig. 17. Cretaceous Giant Squid and Mosasaur

And for the past 350 million years, these three emerging orders of intelligence have been locked in ceaseless and savage warfare—in the seas and, eventually, on land. In the seas, cephalopods hunt and eat arthropod crustaceans and vertebrate fish; in turn, both are hunted and eaten by vertebrates: fish, marine reptiles, and marine mammals. And on land, where cephalopods have never emerged, the battle still rages between arthropod insects and all land vertebrates.

Throughout human history, rare encounters with the Spawn of Cthulhu have given rise to horrific legends: the Hydra (from the Labors of Heracles); Scylla (from the *Odyssey*); the Centimani ("hundred-handed") of the *Titanomachia*; the Norwegian Kraken; "Le Poulpe Colossal"; Bishop Olaus Magnus's "monsterous fish"; Charles Douglas's "Stoor worms"; and so on. Deep beneath the ocean waves, in the sunken land called R'lyeh, the collective soul of Great Cthulhu resides in a mon-

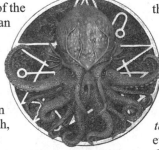

Fig. 18. Cthulhu by Oberon

strous entity—like the termite queen in the foundation of the hive. He waits, hates, and dreams...

And his malevolent dreams have seeped out into the nightmares of humanity. He is at war; he has always been at war, for 350 million years: at war with all vertebrate life, but particularly with his greatest adversary, the mighty sperm whale—the only creature on Earth that can defeat him in physical battle.

And so Cthulhu has fostered a cult among humanity dedicated to destroying his ancient enemy: the worldwide whaling industry. In my fevered fantasies, I imagine secret temples hidden somewhere in the bowels of the whaling companies, with shrines to Great Cthulhu, where the whaling lords pay homage to their true master...

> *That is not dead which can eternal lie,*
> *And with strange aeons even death may die.*
> —Abdul Alhazred, *Al Azif*

MONSTER MOVIES: The Kraken and the Hydra

The earliest attempt to create an animated cephalopod on film was a 1916 silent adaptation of Jules Verne's *20,000 Leagues Under the Sea*. A far more successful version was produced by Disney in 1954, and remains an all-time classic. Although Ray Harryhausen's monstrous 6-tentacled cephalopod in *It Came from Beneath the Sea* (1955) was depicted as a gigantic octopus, it was certainly meant to be a Kraken. And in that same year, *Ulysses* portrayed the multiheaded Scylla. A 1960 Italian film titled *Hercules vs. the Hydra* featured that beast. Harryhausen's 1961 adaptation of Verne's *Mysterious Island* had Captain Nemo's divers attacked by a giant prehistoric nautilus. Harryhausen's finest film, *Jason and the Argonauts* (1963) had a Hydra guarding the Golden Fleece. In the marvelous *7 Faces of Dr. Lao* (1964), the Loch Ness Monster becomes a multiheaded Hydra. In 1981, Harryhausen included both the Kraken and the Hydra in *Clash of the Titans. Cast a Deadly Spell* (TV, 1991) featured Great Cthulhu. Peter Benchley's *The Beast* (1996) was a quite realistic giant squid. Scylla appears in the 1997 TV miniseries of *The Odyssey*, and that same year, Disney's animated *Hercules* included the Hydra. Peter Jackson's superb adaptation of *Lord of the Rings: Fellowship of the Ring* (2001) presented the "Watcher in the Water" as a kind of freshwater Kraken. Disney's animated *Atlantis: The Lost Empire* (2001) again featured a Kraken. The Hydra was also portrayed in a very good TV miniseries simply called *Hercules* (2005). In 2006, the Sci Fi Channel premiered *Kraken: Tentacles of the Deep*. But the most spectacular Kraken ever created on screen was in Disney's *Pirates of the Caribbean: Dead Man's Chest* (2006).

12. hippocampus:
the seahorse and the waterhorse

By Oberon and Morning Glory Zell

O under the ocean waves
I gallop the seaweed lanes,
I jump the coral reef,
And all with no saddle or reins.
I haven't a flowing mane,
I've only this horsy face,
But under the ocean waves
I'm king of the steeplechase.
　　　　　　—Blake Morrison

Ian Daniels, from a sculpture by Oberon Zell

T IS AN AXIOM IN THE MEDIEVAL BES-tiary, the *Physiologus*, that the surface of the water is like Alice's looking glass, with the world beneath being a kind of distorted reflection of the one above. Therefore it was believed that all creatures of the land had their aquatic counterparts in the sea, often distinguished by little more than fins instead of legs. Thus our fantastic menagerie is enriched by such wonders as Mermaids and Mermen (meaning "Sea-maids" and "Sea-men"), Sea-Lions, Sea-Unicorns (Narwhals), Sea-Cows (dugongs and manatees), Sea-Dogs, Sea-Cats (catfish), Sea-Bats, Sea-Anemones, Sea-Cucumbers, Sea-Hares, Sea-Goats (Capricorn), Sea- Gryphons, Sea-Monks, Bishop-Fish, Angel-Fish, Devil-Fish, Ichthyocentaurs ("Fish-Centaurs"), Cock-Fish, Falcon-Fish, Elephant-Fish, Sea-Serpents, Sea-Stags, Sea Wolves—and Sea-Horses.

Nearly all of these creatures actually exist, though our naturalistic modern depictions may seem sadly prosaic compared to their fabulous medieval anteced-ents. Remarkably, however, apart from a matter of scale, the zoological seahorse more exactly resembles its mythical counterpart than any other fabled sea-monster.

Fig. 1. Hippocampus by Konrad Gesner (1558)

the seahorse

The mythical Sea-Horse or ***Hippocampus*** ("horselike water-monster"; from Greek *hippos*, meaning "horse," and *kampos*, meaning "sea-mon-ster") is an equine aquatic beast in classical Greco-Roman mythology, with the head and forelegs of a horse and the body and tail of a fanciful fish. Its equine forefeet terminate in flippers rather than hooves. It is also known as the *Hydrippus* ("water-horse") or Horse-Eel, and was a favorite art subject in Greco-Roman times, especially in Roman baths, where it is frequently found depicted in mosaic. In Roman lore, the Hippocampus was said to be the fastest creature in the ocean. It is thus the favorite steed of Poseidon (Roman Neptune), King of the Sea, and a team of them draw his chariot.

Fig. 2. Poseidon on Hippocampus

These beautiful white horses of the sea are a perfect metaphor for the plunging waves have given rise to many stories involving their exploits. They have been known to save drowning sailors, to pull ships through difficult passages and to do battle with various dread monsters of the deeps. In the ancient Phoenician and Etruscan fashion, they are sometimes depicted with wings like the statues at the famous Trevi Fountain in Rome. Poseidon's favorite Hippocampoi was a stallion named ***Skylla*** and a mare named ***Sthenios***.

Enbarr of the Flowing Mane was the steed of the Irish Sea God, Manannan Mac Lir. A personifica-tion of the waves, Enbarr could travel swifter than the cold, naked wind of Spring over the sea as easily as over land. He also ferried the souls through the Western Gate to the Blessed Isles. No one could be killed or seen if they did not want to be seen when mounted on his back, he had a magick bridle which had the property of causing an image of anyone work-ing evil magick to appear in a pail of water, nevertheless Mannanan gave him to his foster-son Lugh who was a sun god.

In China, little seahorses were once thought to be baby sea dragons. This name has been given to the Leafy Sea Dragon (*Phycodurus eques*) (shown) and the Weedy Sea Dragon (*Phyllopteryx taeniolatus*), charming little fishes related to the common Seahorse (*Hippocampus*), which are decorated with leafy projections to camouflage them among seaweed. The Sea-Dragon is also a heraldic beast with the foreparts of a dragon and a fish's tail.

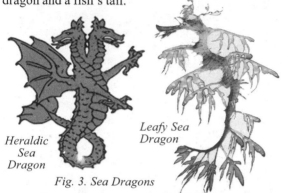

Heraldic Sea Dragon

Leafy Sea Dragon

Fig. 3. Sea Dragons

Among the Seri Indians of northwestern Mexico, there is a legend of a man who fled into the sea to escape his pursuers, tucking his sandals into the back of his shirt above his belt. Once in the water he was transformed into a seahorse, thus explaining the origin of that animal.

The Sea-Horse appears in European heraldry as the *Hippocampus*, with webbed feet in place of hooves, and a long dorsal fin down its back. A Hippocampus is the right-hand supporter of the Isle of Wight arms, the supporters (on either side) of the crest of the city of Newcastle upon Tyne, and also the arms of the University of Newcastle, Australia. A Hippocampus is also prominent in the logo of Waterford Crystal, and is the logotype of illustrator W. W. Denslow.[1]

Fig. 4. Heraldic Sea-Horse, or Hippocampus

The *Havhest* ("sea-horse") is a gigantic Sea-Serpent of Scandinavian folklore, with a horselike head and a double-lobed tail like that of a fish. It has glittering yellow eyes, a long mane down its back, and forelimbs like a seal's. Its double row of fangs may grow to 6 feet long. On top of all this, it also breathes fire! This sinker of ships has only been seen a few times since the 19th century.

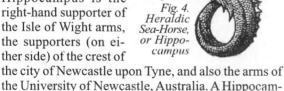

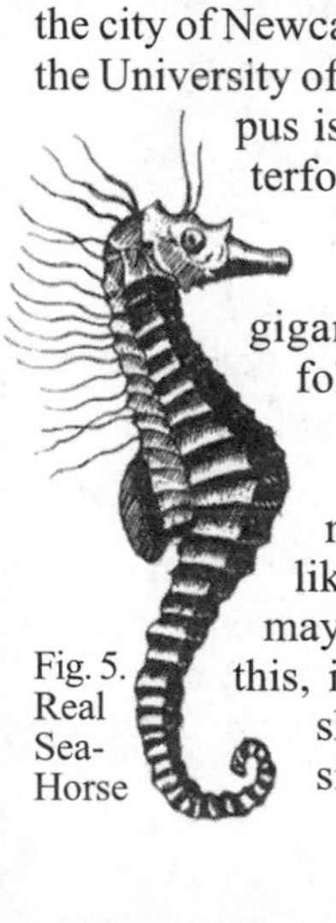

Fig. 5. Real Sea-Horse

Such a malevolent Sea-Horse is also said to inhabit Britain's Shetland and Orkney Islands. Called the *Tangie* (Danish, "seaweed"), it resembles a scruffy pony with a long, shaggy mane of sea wrack; or, it may appear as a Merman. It terrorizes lone travelers along the

Fig. 6. Horse-headed Sea-Monster by Olaus Magnus (1555)

lochs at night—especially young women, whom it abducts and devours. And on the Isle of Man, fishermen fear a horse-headed Sea-Monster they call **Yn Beisht Kione** ("the beast with the black head").

The Mosquitos tribe of the Caraibes Indians of Honduras, Central America, tell tales of the **Wihwin**, a horselike Sea-Monster with huge fangs. During the hot, dry months, the Wihwin leaves the ocean and prowls the land seeking human prey. It returns to the sea when the rains come.

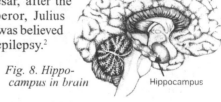

Fig. 7. Wihwin

Hippocampus is now the scientific name given to the curious little fish commonly known as the seahorse (Fig. 5). Looking very much like the mythic beast, the largest species is only 14 inches long. This name has also been given to a part of the brain that is shaped somewhat like a seahorse. Because the cerebral hippocampus is resistant to damage from epileptic seizures, the National Society for Epilepsy chose the seahorse for its mascot. They named it Cesar, after the Roman emperor, Julius Caesar, who was believed to have had epilepsy.[2]

Fig. 8. Hippocampus in brain

Hippocampus

THE ROSMARINE

Although the name "seahorse" has been given to little fishes that look remarkably similar to the mythic Hippocampus, the original Sea-Horse of legend was undoubtedly a walrus.

Fig. 9. Walruses

Although it may seem odd to us that anyone could have equated the ungainly walrus with the graceful horse, keep in mind that *hippopotamus* means "river horse" in Greek. Ancient peoples did not have as wide an acquaintance with large, four-footed animals as we do, so their basis for descriptive comparisons was limited. If you are encountering a large beast for the first time and trying to describe it to someone else, you have to do so in terms the other will understand. Now, if I'd been in that position, I think I'd have likened the hippo to a giant pig—which would have been more zoologically correct. But per-

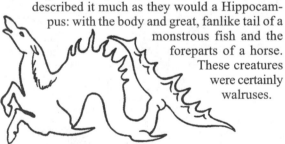

haps horses were more familiar to whoever assigned that name to the hippopotamus, and so we've been stuck with it ever since.

Fig. 10.
Hippopotamus—"river horse"

It is a similar situation with the Sea-Horse, Merhorse, or *Morse*. In British and Scandinavian folklore, this is described as a giant fish having the head, mane, and foreparts of a horse, and cloven hooves. Equally at home on land or sea, it was often seen basking on ice floes. And early English explorers of northern Canada reported a beast they called *Equus Bipes* (Latin, "two-footed horse"). They described it much as they would a Hippocampus: with the body and great, fanlike tail of a monstrous fish and the foreparts of a horse. These creatures were certainly walruses.

Fig. 11. *Equus Bipes (4th century Roman amphora)*

Medieval sailors told of a huge, scaly fish they called the *Sea Hog*, *Marine Boar*, or *Marine Sow*. According to naturalist Ambroise Paré (1517–1590), one was seen in the North Sea in 1537. It had the body and head of a huge boar, with a fishlike tail and reptilian forelegs. It also had prominent tusks, which clearly identify it as a walrus. A heraldic version of this tusked beast—with a quarter moon behind its horned head, Dragon's feet, eyes on its sides, and a fish tail—was called the *Wonderful Pig of the Ocean*.

Fig. 12.
Wonderful Pig of the Ocean

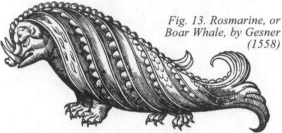

Fig. 13. *Rosmarine, or Boar Whale, by Gesner (1558)*

The *Rosmarine* (also called *Rosmarus* or *Rosmer*; all meaning "horse of the sea") was a fantastical depiction of the walrus, shown with tusks pointing upward rather than downward as they are in reality. In Norwegian waters the same giant sea-monster was called *Roshwalr* ("horse-whale"), *Ruszor*, or *Cetus Dentatus* ("toothed whale"), and described as having a bulky, smooth body like a whale's and the head of a horse. A severed head was sent to Pope Leo X in 1520; it was drawn at the time and later described by Paré. It has been clearly identified as a walrus, which has therefore been given the scientific name of *Odobenus rosmarus*.

Tursus is a marine monster of Finnish legend, described as having the body and head of a walrus with a humanoid torso and arms. It derived its name from the *Thursir* (frost giants) of Norse myth.

WATERHORSES

Water-Horses are amphibious beasts with horse-like heads, believed to lurk in the depths of many rivers, lakes, swamps, and pools throughout the world. In the British Isles they are often described as grey or black horses whose hooves point backward. They are said to be able to change shape at will. It is said that if one mates with an ordinary horse, its progeny will always lie down in the water when crossing fords. Their temperament ranges from relatively docile to voraciously carnivorous. A friendly Water-Horse may allow a human to ride it over a river, but if he should mention the name of Christ, the beast will drop him into the water.

In Scotland the Water-Horse is called the **Kelpie**. It lurks in freshwater lochs, marshes, and rivers, preferring torrid rapids to placid pools. Normally it is an ugly black beast, part horse and part bull with two sharp horns, but it can also shapeshift into the form of a beautiful white horse. The Kelpie operates much like the Phooka, in that it lures travelers onto its back and then rides into the sea or the loch to drown and then eat the rider. The main difference is that the Phooka is

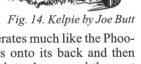

Fig. 14. *Kelpie by Joe Butt*

Fig. 15. Aughisky by Ian Daniels

more playful about the business whereas the Kelpie often intends to eat his passengers. Occasionally, however, the Kelpie might help a miller by keeping the mill wheel turning at night.

In Ireland the same creature is known as the **Peiste** or the **Aughisky**. It inhabits seas and lochs and is very dangerous. Appearing as a tame horse, it is easy to catch and invites weary travelers to mount it, whereupon it plunges into the nearest water and drowns them, devouring everything but their livers. As long as riders keep the Aughisky away from water there is no danger, but any sight or scent of the sea means certain doom because it will bolt and dive in, dragging the rider down. It sometimes appears human, except for its horselike ears.

But the **Each Usige,** a Highland water horse, is the fiercest of all its kin. It appears like a sleek and desirable horse but if you even touch its skin you will stick fast and be dragged off into the deeps where the Usige will drown you but devour just your liver.

In northern Wales, local legends tell of the **Ceffyll-Dwr** ("water horse"), a glowing, grey, horselike monster haunting waterfalls and mountain pools. It was said that anyone brave enough to attack and kill this evil creature would find no solid body but only an amorphous, fatty mass floating on the water.

Fig. 16. Afanc on old Pictish stone carving

The **Afanc** is another evil water-beast of Welsh folklore resembling the Hippocampus or Water-Horse, sometimes with elements of a crocodile or beaver. It is also called *Adang, Abhac, Abac, Addanc, Addane, Adanc,* or *Avanc.* Lurking for prey in river pools near Brynberian Bridge, Afanc would pull in those who were unlucky enough to wander too close, and would also cause random flash floods in the surrounding areas. Other locations where it was seen include Llyn Llion, Llyn Barfog, and Llyn yr Afanc. The Afanc was eventually destroyed, some say by King Arthur himself.

It is very likely that this is the same beast known in Irish folklore as the **Dobhar-Chú** (Gaelic, "water hound"; also *Dorraghow, King of the Lakes, Dhuragoo, Dorraghowor, Dobarcu, Anchu*). A voracious, man-eating, otter-like creature, it is considered the father of all otters. Reported back at least to 1684, it is described as being "half wolfdog and half fish," 6–8 feet long, with short, white fur and a dark brown cross on its back. Some, however, say it is hairless with slimy

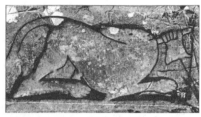

Fig. 17. Dobhar-Chú on old stone carving

black skin. Because of its ferocity, locals call it the "Irish crocodile."

Loch Oich, Scotland, is a narrow stretch of fresh water feeding directly into Loch Lochy (home of *Lizzie*) and separated from Loch Ness by the Caledonian Canal. Sightings of an enormous beast known as the **Oich Monster** date back to the 19th century. It is described as an equine- or dog-headed serpent, with black skin, two humps, and a snakelike neck with a long, horselike mane.

Scalloway in the Shetland Islands north of Scotland has its own Water-Horse. Variously called **Neugle**, *Nogle, Noggle, Nuggle, Nuggie,* or *Nygel*, it resembles a horse, with a green mane and a peculiar tail similar to a wheel

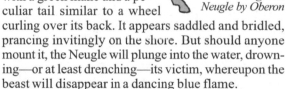

Fig. 18. Neugle by Oberon

curling over its back. It appears saddled and bridled, prancing invitingly on the shore. But should anyone mount it, the Neugle will plunge into the water, drowning—or at least drenching—its victim, whereupon the beast will disappear in a dancing blue flame.

The Isle of Man is home to a ferocious freshwater monster called the **Cabyll-Uisge** ("water-horse") or *Each Uisce* ("water monster"). Similar to other Water-Horses, it lures its victims into the water, where it tears them apart and devours them. The **Glashtyn** can also appear as a handsome young man to entice fair maidens to their undoing, but his horse ears are a dead giveaway.

Fig. 19. Cabyll-Uisge by Dana Keyes

In the Hebrides, the **Biasd na Srognig** ("beast of the lowering horn") is a huge, ungainly Water-Horse with very long legs and a single horn protruding from the top of its head, similar to an aquatic Unicorn. It lives only in small lochs on the Isle of Skye.

And the **Buckland Shag** is a Water-Horse in the folklore of Buckland, Devon County, England, where red stains on a large rock were said to be the blood of its victims. Few dared venture into its territory for fear of being trampled to death.

Freshwater Hippocampi are not, however, confined to the British Isles. The **Cheval Bayard** is a supernatural Water-Horse said to haunt the banks of rivers, pools, and swamps in Normandy, France. As is typical with such creatures, it entices unwary humans onto its back and then plunges with them into the water, where it devours them.

The **Näcken** is a water-monster of Scandinavian and Icelandic folklore. Also called *Bäckahäst, Näkki, Nikke, Nicker, Nickur, Nicor, Nickel, Ninnir, Nikyr, Nykur, Nykkjen, Nøkk, Nøkke, Nøkken,* and *Haikur,* it is usually described as

Fig. 20. Näcken by Dana Keyes

a great white Water-Horse, similar to the Scottish Kelpie, with its hooves facing backward. But should anyone attempt to ride it, the Näcken will plunge into the water, drowning its victim. When it emerges onto land at dawn or dusk, it may appear as a Centaur-like creature. It may also take the form of a golden-haired boy wearing a red cap, or an old man with a dripping green beard. In Estonia it is associated with the whirlpools that suck down boats and devour their crews.

The **Endrop** is a Romanian Lake-Monster described as a Water-Horse. Like a Scottish Kelpie, it entices wayfarers to mount it, then plunges with them into the water to drown and devour them. Lake Maggiore in Italy is also inhabited by a monster. As is typical of such creatures, it is described as having a serpentine body and a horselike head.

And in North America, **Champ** is the affectionate appellation for a horned Lake-Monster reported for at least 400 years to inhabit Lake Champlain, on the border between Quebec and Vermont. The Abenaki Iroquois Indians call it *Tatosok.* It is said to be 20–30 feet long, with a barrel-shaped body and a horselike head. There have been many sightings and even some photographs.

Fig. 21. Photo of Champ, taken in July 1977 by Sandra Mansi

Even far-off India has a dreaded Water-Horse called **Jala-Turga** that attacks travelers along lonely waterways. And Argentina has the **Piranu**—a Water-Monster in the form of a great black fish, with the head of a horse and large eyes. It lives in deep rivers and overturns boats that intrude upon its territory.

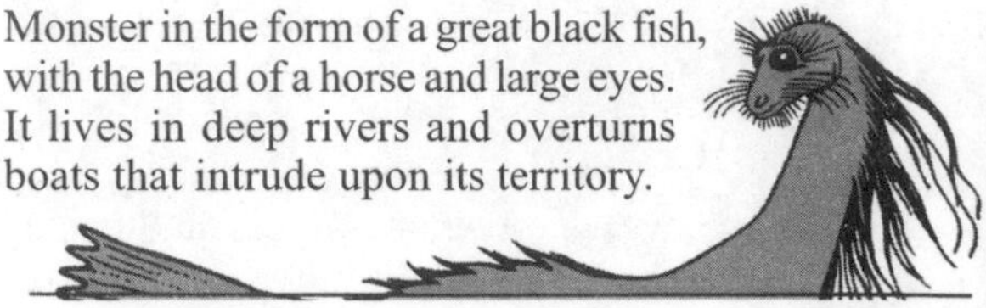

Fig. 22. Merhorse by Oberon (after Heuvelmans)

All these Water-Horses may be equated with the legendary Loch Ness Monster and its relatives—essentially all the Lake-Monsters and Sea-Serpents that have been reported in dozens of locations throughout the world. (See Chapter 18. "Lake Monsters," and 19. "Sea Serpents") Often referred to by eyewitnesses as Water-Horses, Horse-Eels, or Horse-Heads, these elusive monsters are commonly described as immense, undulating, serpentine creatures with a head and neck proportioned similarly to that of a horse, complete with "ears." Some witnesses, however, describe these appendages as horns, so the same animals may also be called Water-Bulls or Horned Serpents. Sometimes they are said to have glowing red or yellow eyes, great fangs, and even the ability to breathe fire. Small ones, which are sometimes reported in marshes and peat bogs, are sometimes called Bog-Dogs.

The **Phooka** (or *Pooka, Puka;* Welsh *Pwca;* Cornish *Bucca;* Manx *Buggane*) is a mischievous, shape-shifting Water-Horse in Irish folklore. It may even serve as a House-Elf, or Brownie. Interestingly, Irish children call snails pookas, and exhort them to extend their horns in a nursery rhyme, thus alluding to the true mollusk identity of all these creatures.

OTHER AQUATIC EQUINES

Farasi Bahari (or *Sabgarifya*) are fabulous emerald-green horses that live in the Indian Ocean. On certain nights of the year, the stallions graze on an island off the coast of Africa, where horse breeders leave their mares in hopes that a mating will produce mighty green foals with incredible endurance which is strangely attributed to a lack of lungs.

But the worst of all the aqua-equi-demons surely is the **Samvarta**. One of seven gigantic sea mares in Hindu legend with churning fires in their bellies, they inhabit each of the seven seas. At Doomsday, they will arise from the waters and their fire will spread over all the lands, consuming everything.

MONSTER MOVIES: HIPPOCAMPUS

The only movie in which I can recall having seen a Sea-Horse was Disney's cute animated version of the famous Hans Christian Anderson story, *The Little Mermaid* (1989). However, a film called *The Water Horse* is scheduled for release at Christmas, 2007.

human-animal hybrids
13. the enigmatic sphinx

By Oberon Zell-Ravenheart

Ian Daniels

From Egypt we, long since, with all our peers,
Accustomed were to reign a thousand years.
If for our place your reverence be won,
We rule for you the days of Moon and Sun.
We sit before the Pyramids
For the judgment of the Races,
Inundation, War, and Peace,—
With eternal changeless faces.

—Goethe, *Faust*
"The Beasts of Walpurgis-Night"
speech of the Sphinx[1]

HE *SPHINX* IS AN IMPOSING COMPOS-
ite monster of classical tradition,
depicted with a lion's body and
paws, and the head of some other animal or a human. Sometimes
it has the hindquarters of a bull,
and in many versions, eagle's
wings sprout from its shoulders. It originated with
the Egyptians of the Old Kingdom (2686–2134 BCE),
from whence it was imported into Assyrian and Greek
mythology, appearing famously in the tragedy of Oedipus Rex. The Asian Sphinxes appear to have originated independently.

The name Sphinx comes from the Greek verb
sphingo, meaning "to strangle." Another possible derivation has been claimed from the Egyptian *shesep
ankh*, meaning "living statues." Because its form en-
compasses both human and animal elements, the
Sphinx symbolizes the union of body, mind, and soul;
or physical, mental, and spiritual attributes. The human head represents intellect and knowledge, the lion's claws connote daring and action, the bull's loins
symbolize stamina and perseverance, and the eagle's
wings connote silence. Thus composed of three animals and a human, the Sphinx is a symbol of the four
Pythagorean Elements: Earth, Air, Fire, and Water.

*Fig. 1.
Babylonian
Sphinx
(Lamassu),
from an
antique stone
carving at the
Palace of
Nimrud,
Nineveh.*

In ancient As-
syria and Phoenicia,
winged lions with human heads appeared as symbols
of rulership and guardians of temples and palaces.
They were called *Lamassu*, and they were commonly
paired with similar creatures called *Shedu*, which had
human heads on the bodies of winged bulls.

With the sole exception of the cruel, riddling
Greek Sphinx of Thebes (the only one capable of
speech), all other Sphinxes were friendly and benevolent guardians of sacred Mysteries; and their image
universally symbolized enigma, mystic wisdom, and
secret-keeping silence. In Egypt, the Sphinx was the
guardian of arcane magick and occult wisdom, and
was endowed with the four powers of the magi: to
know, to dare, to will, and to keep silent.[2]

Sphinx composed of a man's head and chest, an
eagle's wings, a bull's hindquarters, and a lion's
forequarters, became symbols of the Biblical Tetramorph and the four creatures of Revelation.
[Ezek. 1:5–14; Rev. 4:6–8] These in turn represent the Cherubim; the four Evangelists and their
Gospels (Matthew, Mark, Luke, and John); the
four kings of the created world: the Lion (king of
the jungle), the Eagle (king of the air), the Bull
(king of the farm), and Man (king of creation);
and, according to St. Jerome, Christ's Incarnation (the man), His Passion (the bull), His Resurrection (the Lion), and His Ascension (the eagle).[3]

The Tetramorph appears twice in the Tarot cards,
on The Wheel of Fortune and The World. In the
former, the Sphinx sits atop the Wheel to represent

Fig. 2. Wheel of Fortune Tarot card by Pamela Coleman Smith

equilibrium within a perpetually fluidic universe.[4]

The later Roman Sphinx was a simple solar symbol. To astrologers, it is a calendar beast, with the female head representing Virgo, and the lion's body, Leo. The version with a human head, bull's body, lion's legs and claws, and eagle's wings symbolizes, respectively, the fixed signs of the Zodiac: Aquarius, Taurus, Leo, and Scorpio. And the Druids included a many-breasted female Sphinx among their fertility and maternal symbols.

With their rich symbolism, Sphinxes were popular creatures in ancient art. They were often inscribed upon gravestones of teenage boys, and they commonly appeared with lions and Sirens in beast processions on Greek vases.

ᛏᚺᛖ ᛖᚷᛁᛈᛏᛁᚨᚾ sᛈᚺᛁᚾᚷ

Three types of Sphinxes appear as guardians in Egyptian statuary, all with the wingless bodies of crouching lions. Herodotus distinguished them as the *Criosphinx*, the *Hieracosphinx*, and the *Androsphinx*. The Egyptian Sphinx was only rarely portrayed as having the head of a woman. In such cases, the *Gynosphinx* symbolized the Goddess Isis or Hathor, and/or the reigning queen. In Egypt, it was believed that the creature's intellectual faculties, represented by the human head, ennobled and balanced its bestial attributes, represented by the lion's body.

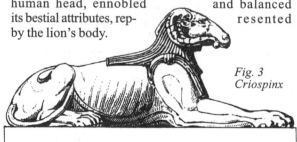

Fig. 3 Criospinx

The ***Criosphinx***—Guardian and container of the soul of the creator-god, Amun (whose title was "Father of the Gods"), the Criosphinx is a great lion with the head of a ram. With magnificent spiraling horns, it was usually shown lying down with head erect and alert, as a guardian's should be. In the city of Thebes, there were originally about 900 Criosphinx statues, and the great Temple of Karnak at Luxor was approached by an avenue flanked by them.

Fig. 4. Avenue of Criosphinxes at Karnak in Luxor

The ***Hieracosphinx***—A representation of the Egyptian sun-god, Horus, it has the body of a lion and the head of a falcon.

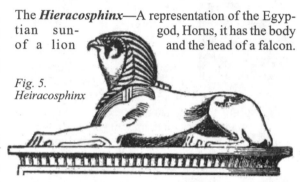

Fig. 5. Heiracosphinx

The ***Androsphinx***—This Sphinx had the head of a man—specifically, that of the reigning Pharaoh who ordered its construction. It was intended to symbolize the divine power and wisdom with which he ruled and protected his people. Representing abundance, power, secrets, truth, unity, wisdom, and the Mysteries, the Androsphinx guarded pyramids, tombs, and sacred highways. Sometimes a pair of Androsphinxes was portrayed in conjunction with the Tree of Life as symbols of fertility and conception.

> As a solar symbol, the Androsphinx was associated with the sun god Ra; Horus on the Horizon; and Harmakhis, the Lord of the Two Horizons, representing the rising and setting sun, rebirth, and resurrection. ... As Lord of the Two Horizons, the Androsphinx's dual nature came in Christian mythology to reflect the dual nature of Christ, who was both human and divine. Like many other solar symbols, an image of the Androsphinx was placed in or near early Christian graves as a representation of the divine Light of the World.[5]

ᛏᚺᛖ ᚷᚱᛖᚨᛏ sᛈᚺᛁᚾᚷ ᛟᚠ ᚷᛁᛉᚨ

The largest and most famous ancient statue, and

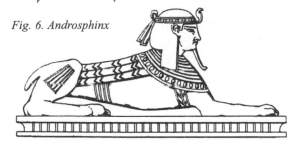

Fig. 6. Androsphinx

one of the Seven Wonders of the World, *Sesheps*, the Great Sphinx of Giza, is 240 feet long and 66 feet high, with a small Roman temple and stele between its outstretched paws. Situated on the Giza Plateau on the west bank of the Nile near the Great Pyramids, it faces due east.

The face of the Great Sphinx is generally thought to be a portrait of the Pharaoh Khafra, or possibly of his brother, the Pharaoh Djedefra. This would date its carving to the Fourth Dynasty (2723–2563 BCE).

Fig. 7. The Great Sphinx of Giza

Some think that the Great Sphinx is more than 12,000 years old, and that it was originally a complete crouching lion intended to represent the constellation Leo—long before its head was resculpted into that of a Pharaoh. The vertical patterns of erosion on its flanks seem to indicate centuries of rain, rather than the horizontal markings that would result from windblown sands of the desert which now surrounds it. Legends claim that a tunnel runs from beneath the Sphinx into the Great Pyramid, and that other secret passageways and chambers remain hidden under the Giza sands. Recently a few narrow tunnels have indeed been discovered around the statue, and ground-based sonar has indicated the existence of a chamber beneath it.

The granite stele set between the paws of the Great Sphinx gives the following account: One day young Prince Thutmose was out hunting when he lay down for a nap in the shadow of the Sphinx's head—which was all that protruded from the entombing desert sands. The Sphinx appeared to him in his dream and prophesied that he would sit on the throne of

Egypt if he promised to clear away the sands of time from around the great figure. As Thumose was the younger son, this seemed unlikely. But soon thereafter his elder brother was killed in a hunting accident, and Thutmose unexpectedly became Pharaoh—the fourth with that name, reigning from 1425–1417 BCE.

The new ruler immediately ordered the excavation of the statue, placing the Dream Stele between its paws to commemorate the incident and to honor the sun-god, Harmakhis, who had spoken to him through the Sphinx. On the stele, Thutmose IV inscribed three names of the sun: *Kheperi*, *Re*, and *Atum*. However, it is not known what name the original sculptors gave to the figure itself. The Greeks called it the Sphinx, and its Arabic name, *Abu al-Hôl*, means "father of terror."[6]

Perhaps due to the legendary dream of Thutmose, pilgrims once sought the oracular advice of the Sphinx by placing an ear to its lips. Due to its enigmatic history, the great monument has become an icon for all who seek wisdom.

THE GREEK SPHINX

The Greek version, of which there was only one, had the head and breasts of a woman, with eagle's wings. Sometimes it was depicted with the body of a bull or dog, the legs of a lion, and the tail of a serpent. It had a human voice and spoke in riddles. In contrast to the aristocratic Egyptian Sphinx, she was regarded as a demon of death, destruction, and ill fortune. In Greek mythology, the bestial elements were believed to have warped her mind and spirit, and she was portrayed as a grim and miserable monster, a symbol of the "wicked mother," and an evil perversion of the intellect, of womanhood, and of power.[7]

Fig. 8. Theban, or Greek Sphinx

According to Hesiod's *Theogony* (c. 700 BCE), "the deadly Sphinx which destroyed the Cameans" was a daughter of Echidna and her son Orthus, the hound of Geryones. Her brother was the Nemean Lion, "which Hera, the good wife of Zeus, brought up and made to haunt the hills of Nemea, a plague to men." Like many other fabulous beasts, the Sphinx was believed to inhabit the mountains of Ethiopia.

The Sphinx was sent from her Ethiopian homeland into Boiotia by Hera, who was angry with the

Thebans for not having punished King Laios, who had carried off Khrysippos from Pisa. The grim creature now sat upon a crag on Mount Phikion, overlooking the road to Thebes, where she challenged all travelers with a riddle she had learned from the Mousai. In Sophocles' *Oedipus Tyrannus*, the riddle is stated as follows: "What goes on four legs, on two and then three; but the more legs it goes on the weaker it be?" If they replied correctly, they would be allowed to pass; but if they failed—as all did—she would strangle and devour them. Oedipus, who had fled to Thebes in a futile effort to escape from a prophesy that he would kill his father and marry his mother, was accosted by the Sphinx, who demanded an answer. "Man," replied Oedipus. "He crawls on all fours as an infant, then walks on two feet as a child and adult, and finally, leans on a cane in old age." Thereupon the mortified monster leapt from the precipice to her death on the rocks below (evidently the wings were just for show!).[8]

Fig. 9. "Oedipus and the Sphinx" on Greek plate

ᴛʜᴇ ᴀѕɪᴀɴ ѕᴘʜɪɴx

Sphinx-like, human-headed lions are common figures in the mythology and art of India, China, and Southeast Asia. Some of these date from as early as the 3rd century BCE, indicating independent origin from the Western Sphinx, which originated in Egypt.

The *Purushamriga* ("human-beast") of India is believed to take away the sins of devotees when they enter a temple, and to ward off evil in general. It is therefore usually strategically positioned on the temple gateway or near the entrance to the inner sanctum. Also called *Naravirala* ("man-cat"), images of them decorate lamps used in the lamp ceremony, as well as in various other iconography.

The Sphinx of Sri Lanka is called *Narasimha* ("man-lion"). It is a Buddhist guardian of the North, and is often depicted on banners. In common with all

Fig. 10. Purushamriga or Indian Sphinx depicted on the Shri Varadaraja Perumal temple in Tribhuvana, India

other Sphinxes, it has a human head on a leonine body. However, it bears the same name as, and is thus easily confused with, *Narasimha,* the fourth incarnation of the god *Mahavishnu,* who has the head of a lion on a human body.

Fig. 11. Indian Sphinx from Rajasthan

In Myanmar, or Burma, the Sphinx is called *Manusiha.* According to legend, it was created by Buddhist monks to protect a newborn royal infant from fierce ogresses who wished to devour the child. Images of Manusiha as a guardian may be seen today on the corners of Buddhist temples.

The Sphinx of Thailand, which is also a protector, is known as *Nora Nair* or *Thep Norasingh.* It has the lower body of a lion or deer, and the upper body of a human. It is always shown walking upright, often in male/female pairs. They are listed among the fantastic creatures that dwell upon the sacred mountain, Himapan.[9]

The Sphinx appears in China as well, as in this example from the *San Li T'u* (ca.1661–1723). It is one of three ceremonial targets to be used by officials of different ranks in military examinations. These tests required that arrows be fired upward from a distance, with the goal of landing them in the barrel behind the figure.[10]

Fig. 12. Chinese Sphinx, from the San Li T'u

ѕᴘʜɪɴxᴇѕ ɪɴ ᴀʀᴛ

Mannerism is a period of European architecture and decorative arts which lasted from the end of the Italian Renaissance around 1520 until the dawn of the Baroque period around 1600. The typical Mannerist Sphinx is sometimes called the French Sphinx. Her elaborately-coiffed head is held proudly erect, and she has the bust of a pretty young woman. She wears pearls and eardrops, and her lioness body is rendered realistically. Such images attained popularity in the enthusiasm for the 15th-century excavations of the treasures of Nero's Golden House in Rome, and they were incorporated into the new fashion of classical decorative motifs and Arabesque designs that spread throughout Europe during the 16th and 17th centuries. The Mannerist Sphinx first appeared in the School of Fontainebleau in the 1520s to the 30s, and she lasted into the Late Baroque style of the French Régence (1715–1723)[11]

Fig. 13. French Sphinx

But Sphinxes passed out of fashion in the flamboyant Rococo period and were not seen again until the 19th century, when the Romantic and later Symbolist schools revived them once again. As with the Mannerist Sphinx, these schools drew more of their inspiration from the Greek than the Egyptian model—particularly in their depictions of the feminine. However, they were generally presented as wingless.

Fig. 14. Cheetah Sphinx by Ferdnand Khnopff

SPHINXES AS APES

Pliny the Elder mentions Sphinxes, saying they are common, "with a brown duskish hair, having dugs in their breast." Clearly, he considered the Sphinx to be a kind of ape—specifically, a baboon. Indeed, the Guinea Baboon (*Papio papio*) is still called a Sphinx. Baboons in particular seem to combine human and leonine features. They are quadrupeds, as lions are, but they have humanlike bodies, arms, legs, and hands. Their heads and faces are very doglike, with fierce, sharp teeth, but the males of several species have great manes like those of lions. These include the Olive Baboon (*Papio cynocephalus anubis*), the Gelada (*Theropithecus gelada*), and the Hamadryas (*Papio hamadryas*).

The Olive Baboon, also called the *Anubis Baboon* for its doglike head, is the most widely distributed of all baboons. Dwellers of savannahs, steppes, and forests, they are found throughout northern Africa, from Mali south to Ethiopia and Tanzania. Isolat-

Fig. 15. Ape Sphinx by Ashton

ed populations even inhabit some mountainous regions of the Sahara Desert. They were domesticated in ancient Egypt and trained to pick fruit for harvest.

The Gelada is found only in the highlands of Ethiopia and Eritrea, with large populations in the Semien Mountains. Its Latin name, *Theropithecus*, means "beast-ape."

Hamadryads are the northernmost of all the baboons, their range extending from the Red Sea in Egypt south to Ethiopia and Somalia. The Hamadryad was sacred to the ancient Egyptians as the attendant of the scribe god Thoth, and therefore is also called the Sacred Baboon. Colonies live in semi-deserts, savannas, and rocky areas, requiring cliffs for sleeping and access to drinking water.[12]

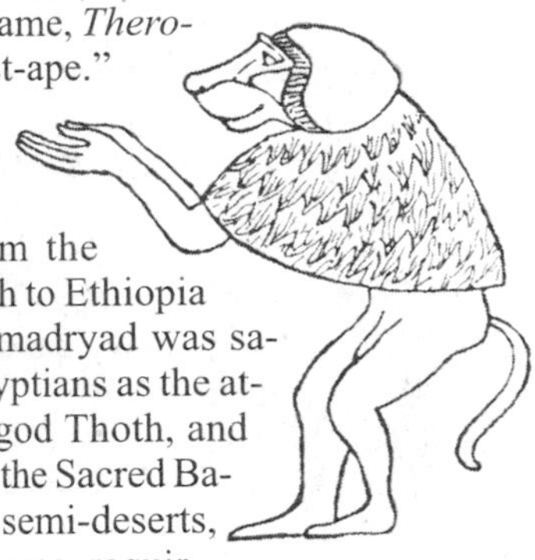

Fig. 16.
Olive baboon

Cynocephali (Greek, "dog-headed") are Sphinx-like creatures said to be very common in Ethiopia. They are described as having a black, hairy, humanoid body and the head of a dog. Because of these attributes, they are associated with the Egyptian god Anubis. These ferocious creatures have been identified as Olive Baboons, as indicated in their Latin name, *cynocephalus*. However, the 3-foot-tall Indris Lemur (*Indri indri*) of Madagascar also looks very much like a short, dog-headed human, especially as it often stands or sits upright.

MONSTER MOVIES: THE SPHINX

Only one movie to date has featured the Sphinx: *The Neverending Story* (1984), from the book by Michael Ende. A pair of gigantic golden Sphinx statues guard access to the Southern Oracle, and they incinerate any unworthy pilgrims who pass between them.

Fig. 17. Guardians of the Southern Oracle
from The Neverending Story (1984)

14. HOOF AND HORN:
CENTAURS, SATYRS, AND FAUNS

By Ash "LeopardDancer" DeKirk

The Satyrs are manikins with upturned noses; they have horns on their foreheads, and are goat-footed, such as the one St. Anthony saw in the desert.

—Isidore of Seville

ALF HORSE AND HALF GOAT DEMIHU-mans abound in world mythology, from the Centaur and Satyr to the Betikhan and Sileni. These creatures have fascinated and captivated us, coming into play in both Pagan pantheons and classical mythology. For who has not heard of Pan, of Puck, of Cernunnos? And who has not read of Herakles' deadly encounter with Nessus, or of the wise and self-sacrificing Centaur Chiron, tutor of heroes?

CENTAURS AND OTHER HORSEMEN

Centaurs are mostly known from Greek mythology, but they are a part of the lore and myth of areas all over the world, particularly in the Middle/Near East. They are believed to be derived from garbled descriptions of early horsemen by people who had never before seen horses being ridden. Half man and half horse, the Centaur was originally envisioned as a full human with the hindquarters and rear legs of a horse growing from his back. Later, it came to be depicted with the man's torso grafted onto the horse's shoulders (properly, a *Hippocentaur*). Centaurs have been noted in sculpture and other art since the time of great Babylon, where they are prominent on seals and stamps. These Centaurs sometimes sported scorpion stings for tails and often were depicted holding clubs or bows. Even the peoples of Asia have legends and tales of horse-men.

The Greek Centaurs dwelled primarily in Arcadia and Thessaly, and were renowned for their skills in magick. Some Centaurs were hostile to humans,

Fig. 1.
Chiron

Ian Daniels

whereas others were helpful and friendly, such as the healer Chiron—a kind and wise teacher who tutored Aesclepius, Jason, and Achilles, and freed Prometheus by relinquishing his own immortality in return. Zeus placed him in the heavens as the constellation Sagittarius. The benevolent Centaurs (including Chiron) were said to be the descendants of Centaurus, who fathered the first Centaurs through congress with the Magnesian mares.

Another group of Centaurs are said to be descended from Cronus and Philyra. These are as different

Fig. 2. Centaur

from Chiron's "people" as the Satyrs are different from the Fauns. These Centaurs dwelled on Mount Pelion in Thessaly, northern Greece, and were lecherous and cruel to humans. After a particularly noxious episode at the wedding of Hippodameia and Pirithous, king of the Lapiths, where they got drunk and attempted to abduct the bride, they were driven from Thessaly in a famous battle. Nessus, the Centaur that Heracles encountered, was one of this variety. Nessus was the ultimate cause of the great hero's death, when Heracles donned a turnic sent to him by his beloved wife, Deianara. The tunic had formerly been given to Deianara by Nessus as he died from arrows shot by Heracles which had been dipped in the venomous blood

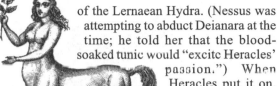

Fig. 3. Centauress (Heraldic)

of the Lernaean Hydra. (Nessus was attempting to abduct Deianara at the time; he told her that the blood-soaked tunic would "excite Heracles' passion.") When Heracles put it on, he died in excruciating agony from the poison.

Centaurs later became popular in European heraldry. They were usually male and almost always held a bow. One of the most famous Centaur coat-of-arms is that of King Stephen. The image of the Centaur with a drawn bow is today most often associated with the Zodiac sign of Sagittarius, the Archer.

In the mid 1980s, Professor William Wallers of the University of Wisconsin (re)constructed a Centaur burial in an attempt to get people to think about biological possibilities, mythological realities, and how myth is transmitted, among other things. Wallers's Centaur skeleton now resides in the library of the University of Tennessee.

Fig. 4. Wallers's Centaur burial

The **Gandharvas** of India were demigods depicted with the body of a man and the head of a horse. They were deities of air and rain as well as medicine and healing. They also have a connection with reincarnation and musical skills, and were often the patrons of skilled singers and musicians.

As described in the *Physiologus*, *the **Ichthyocentaur*** (Greek, "fish-centaur") is an aquatic variation of the Centaur, with the torso, arms, and head of a man, the forelegs of a horse (or sometimes a lion), and, similar to the Hippocampus, the lower body and tail of a dolphin or fish. It symbolizes fertility.

Fig. 5.
Ichthyocentaur by OZ

SATYRS FAUNS AND OTHER GOATMEN

Fig. 6. Satyr by Ian Daniels

Satyrs are beings of the forest and of wild, untamed nature. Also called *Silvani* ("forest people"), they are most often associated with the god Pan, also called the goat-foot god. Satyrs are depicted as having shaggy legs and the cloven hooves of goats, with goatlike ears and small horns. They are usually shown with slanted eyes and snubbed noses. These demihumans are considered to be the embodiment of wild passion. They are fond of dancing, music, wine, and women—be they human or nymph. They are mischief-makers prone to drunken vandalism and scaring lone travelers out late at night. Satyrs live in the deep woods of Arcadia and Thessaly, where they enjoy dancing to the flute music of the *syrinx,* or Panflute. Satyrs from Roman lands and Ireland are also known.

Satyr plays were a form of Greek tragicomedy that featured a chorus of Satyrs and focused on themes of drunkenness, overt sexuality, mischievousness, and merriment. These parodies were called *satires*. The only Satyr play known to have survived in a complete form is Euripides' *Cyclops.*

Roman Satyrs were more mild-mannered than their Greek cousins and less inclined to force unwanted sexual attention upon fair maidens. In addition to the goat-legged version, Roman Satyrs were also depicted as men with fluted ears and small horns upon their brows. They are usually dressed in panther skins and carry small flutes.

Saint Jerome writes of the capture of a Satyr, which was later displayed in Greece. After its death, the captive Satyr was preserved in salt and taken to the Emperor Constantine. This was probably an ape of some sort, as Satyrs have been particularly identified with anthropoid apes, such as Orangutans (named by Linnaeus *Simia satyrus*, "satyr monkey") and Chimpanzees (*Pan troglodytes*). Medieval Christian artists used their images of Satyrs to represent devils and demons. Clinically obsessive hypersexuality in men is called *satyriasis.*

Fauns are similar to the Satyrs in appearance, save for their curling ram's horns. Some descriptions give them the lower body of a deer rather than a goat. In addition, they tend toward the more passive and gentle side. These demihumans are the children and companions of the animal god Faunus, "the kindly one," and dwell in the deep woods where they, like their cousin Satyrs, may be found playing the flute and dancing. Although they were said to cause nightmares, Fauns were considered the embodiment of the gentler side of Nature. They enjoy enticing humans to share in their woodland revels, but do not force what is not wanted. They are also associated with Silvanus, a woodland god of Roman Britain, and with Cernunnos, the Horned One—a Celtic deity depicted with a stag's or deer's lower body and antlers. The charming Faun Tumnus is an important character in C.S. Lewis's *Narnia* books.

In India, Fauns are called *Betikhan*. They are said to live in the forests around Neilgherry Hill, hunting animals for food. The *Sileni* ("forest people"), also known to the Greeks, were demihumans with the body of a human and the ears

Fig. 7. Betikhan by Ash

and tail of a horse. They were said to live in Phrygia and were led by their father, Silenus. The Sileni followed the god Dionysos. In northern Greece and Crete, they are referred to collectively as *Callicantzari*, and are popularly portrayed by costumed mummers during the 12 days following Christmas.

A true-life encounter by Oberon

Many years ago, in the Summer of 1981, Morning Glory and I were on Chautauqua with one of our living Unicorns—traveling around the Pacific Northwest with other performers from the Oregon Country Faire. One place we stopped was a big Hippie commune up in Washington. It was sometime in mid July, and there was a full eclipse of the moon that night. That evening, a woman and her young daughter approached us outside in the silver moonlight. The mother said: "You have a magickal creature. My daughter is also a magickal creature, and she would like you to know." Whereupon the little girl turned around and shyly lifted up the back of her dress to show us a long, beautiful tail—not a monkey-like tail, but more like a horse's tail, with silky blond hair reaching down below her knees. Where is she now?

Another hoofed being of English lore is *Puck*, also called *Pooka*, who is a shapeshifter sometimes depicted with the lower body of a goat and upper body of a man. Puck is mischievous and likes to lead travelers astray, but is not likely to ravish women as the Satyrs were known to do. He plays a willow flute and likes to dance under the moon. Puck is

Fig. 8. Puck or Robin Goodfellow

benevolent toward people and may help them, so long as they appreciate the help and are willing to acknowledge that he exists. William Shakespeare secured Puck a prime place in our modern world in his timeless classic, *A Midsummer Night's Dream*, in which the sprite also goes by the name of Robin Goodfellow.

In Germanic countries, beings called *Kornbockes* were goat-men who would help farmers with corn and grain crops, though they would destroy the crops if upset. *Leshy*, woodland beings of Russia and other Slavic areas, are often described as having the lower body of a goat, as well as horns and fluted ears. These guardians of the forests are not prone to harming people, but who do enjoy getting travelers lost in the woods.

And finally, a malevolent goat-human hybrid creature has been reported around the United States. Some witnesses say it is a man with a goat's head, others say he looks more like a Satyr, and some reports combine the two. Dubbed *Goatman*, its reported height varies from 6 to 12 feet. He has attacked pets and even cars— sometimes with an ax.

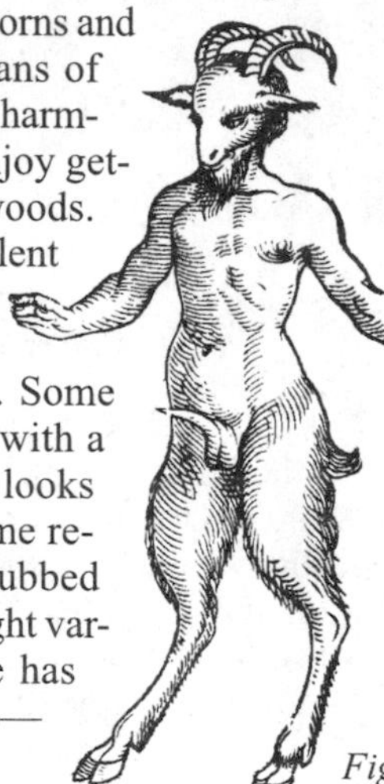

Fig. 9. Goatman

MONSTER MOVIES: CENTAURS, SATYRS, AND FAUNS

Fantasia (animated-1940)—Centaurs, Fauns
The 7 Faces of Dr. Lao (1964)—Pan
The Chronicles of Narnia: The Lion, the Witch and the Wardrobe (BBC TV-1988)—Faun
Hercules (animated-1997)—Satyr, Centaur
Harry Potter & The Sorcerer's Stone (2001)—Centaur
Chronicles of Narnia: The Lion, the Witch and the Wardrobe (2005)—Faun, Centaurs, Goat-men
Hercules (TV-2005)—Centaur
Pan's Labyrinth (2007)—Faun
Harry Potter & Order of the Phoenix (2007)—Centaurs

ANIMATE PLANTS
15. PLANTIMALS

By Oberon Zell-Ravenheart

The slender delicate palpi, with the fury of starved serpents, quivered a moment over her head, then as if instinct with demoniac intelligence fastened upon her in sudden coils round and round her neck and arms; then while her awful screams and yet more awful laughter rose wildly to be instantly strangled down again into a gurgling moan, the tendrils one after another, like great green serpents, with brutal energy and infernal rapidity, rose, retracted themselves, and wrapped her about in fold after fold, ever tightening with cruel swiftness and savage tenacity of anacondas fastening upon their prey.

—Carl Liche, *South Australian Register*, 1881,
regarding the fabled
Man-Eating Tree of Madagascar[1]

Ent by Ian Daniels

ODAY WE TEND TO THINK OF THE DEmarcation between the plant and animal kingdoms—flora and fauna—as quite distinct. However, it has not always been so. Medieval bestiaries contained a number of creatures that straddled the borderline, possessing features and qualities of both plants and animals. We call these "animate plants," "vegetable animals," or "Plantimals."

Russian biologist Dr. Dmitri Bayanov has pointed out that there is no botanical equivalent of cryptozoology, because plants cannot actively hide themselves, as animals can.[2] Nevertheless, as the following items will attest, there are a goodly number of legendary and mythical plants reported throughout the world that have not yet been brought into the light of scientific scrutiny. I believe that cryptobotany deserves to be elevated to a sister discipline, and that its subjects demand inclusion in any compilation of fabled organisms.

CARNIVOROUS PLANTS AND MAN-EATING TREES

The first Venus Flytraps (*Dionaea muscipula*) were received with incredulity when they were first presented to botanists in the 1760s. The idea that a plant could move to catch and devour insects seemed inconceivable. But, once the reality of the known carnivorous plants was accepted by the scientific community—especially in regards to those plants that actually move to trap or enfold their prey, such as flytraps and Sundews (*Drosera*)—the possi-

bility of larger-scale versions became plausible.

Although flytraps, with their blood-red fanged maws and hair-trigger reaction time, are certainly famed as the most dramatic of carnivorous plants, they are quite rare, and occur naturally only in the meteorite-gouged oval bogs called the Carolina Bays, around Wilmington, North Carolina. And, like vampires, they must be bedded in their native soil if they are to survive elsewhere. These facts certainly raise the question of a possible extraterrestrial origin for these unique little plants!

Fig. 1. Venus Fly Trap (Dionaea muscipula)

But I think that the tentacled Sundews, of which more than 170 species are known worldwide, are really the most fascinating of the botanical carnivores. All species are able to move their tiny glandular tentacles, which are tipped with sticky secretions, upon contact with prey. This response to touch is called *thigmotropism*, and it can be quite rapid in some species. The outer "snap tentacles" of *D. burmannii* and *D.*

Fig. 2. Cape Sundew (Drosera capensis)

sessilifolia can bend inward toward prey within seconds after contact, and *D. glanduligera* can do this in mere tenths of a second! In addition to tentacle movement, some species, such as the Cape Sundew (*D. capensis*), are able to curl their long thin leaves, or *laminae*, completely around prey in order to maximize contact.[3]

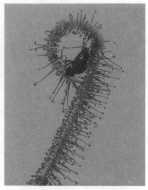

Fig. 3. Lamina of Cape Sundew enfolding an insect

Given the reality of such carnivorous plants, it doesn't seem to be too far a stretch to imagine larger versions existing in some far-off jungle or undiscovered island—large enough, perhaps, to attack and consume human prey. But no such plant is known to exist; the carnivorous plant with the largest traps is the Giant Malaysian Pitcher Plant (*Nepenthes rajah*) of Borneo, which produces pitchers up to 14 inches tall and consumes small mammals, reptiles, and birds if they happen to fall in.[4] This is most likely the basis of the Indian Mouse-Eating Plant, a specimen of which, according to Chase Salmon Osborne, was supposedly exhibited at the London Horticultural Hall in the 1920's.[5]

The *Tepe*, or **Man-Eating Tree of Madagascar** (*Crinoida*) is a fantastic carnivorous plant first reported in 1878 by one Carle Liche, who said that it resembled a fossil *crinoid*, or sea-lily, and claimed to have witnessed the sacrifice of a native girl to it by members of the Pygmy Mkodo tribe. The trunk, he said, was like an 8-foot-tall pineapple topped with eight long. broad leaves 11–12 feet long that drooped to the ground. In the center of these was a liquid-filled hollow, surrounded by "a series of long hairy green tendrils" 7–8 feet long, tapering from 4 inches to one-half an inch in diameter. Above these, "six white almost transparent palpi reared themselves towards the sky, twirling and twisting with a marvelous incessant motion" to a length of 5–6 feet. Liche reported that the sacrificial victim was forced to climb the tree and drink from the hollow, whereupon the tentacles and then the leaves enveloped and crushed her.[6]

The legend was firmly established by Chase Salmon Osborn, former Governor of Michigan, in his 1924 book, *Madagascar, Land of the Man-eating Tree*. He reprinted the Liche report, and added that both tribes and missionaries on Madagascar knew of this monstrous tree. However, in his

Fig. 4. Crinoid by Ernst Haeckel (1904)

1955 book *Salamanders and other Wonders*, science author Willy Ley determined that the "Mkodo tribe," Carle Liche, and the Madagascar man-eating tree itself all appeared to be fabrications.[7]

However, in a 1998 letter to Karl Shuker, Ivan Mackerle, the Czech explorer/cryptozoologist, reported from his own Madagascar expedition: "We found the killer tree 'Kumanga,' which is poisonous when it has flowers. We took gas-masks for protecting ourselves, but the tree did not blossom at that time. We had seen a skeleton of a dead bird and a dead turtle under the tree. The tree grows only in one place in Madagascar and it is rare today. It was difficult to find it."[8]

Shuker adds that the New Brunswick *Watchman* of May 29, 1995, claimed to have discovered an account of the Man-Eating Tree dating back to 1875—three years earlier than the Liche report. This account placed the legendary tree in New Guinea rather than Madagascar.

Similar carnivorous trees have been reported in Central America, South America, Mexico, and elsewhere. Like the Tepe, the vampiric **Ya-te-veo** ("I can see you") of Central America is also said to have multiple squid-like tentacles, or shoots, atop its short, thick trunk, with which it captures prey in the same manner as a sea anemone. Edged with sharp teeth, the shoots hang down to the ground, appearing immobile until prey steps within range. Then, the tenta-

Fig. 5. Ya-Te-Veo Tree, from Sea and Land (1887)

cles spring into action, wrapping around the victim as a constrictor does and pressing him or her to the trunk, where his or her body is pierced by the dagger-like thorns and drained of blood, which is absorbed by the tree. The name of this plant supposedly derives from the hissing noise made by the agitated rasping of its toothy tendrils against each other.[9]

The **Brazilian Devil Tree**, or "Octopod Tree," was described by Harold T. Wilkins in 1952:[10] "Native to the Matto Grosso, it is said to be as big as a willow, but hides its branches deep in the earth or the surrounding undergrowth. Should anything (or anyone) go near to it or trip over its concealed branches, however, this diabolical plant will stealthily draw them out from under the soil or bushes and snare its unwary victim in the grip of their ever-tightening tendrils."[11]

The **Nicaraguan Dog-Devouring Tree** is yet another example of this legend. As reported by naturalist Dr. Andrew Wilson in the *Illustrated London News,* Auguse 27, 1892, this "plant or vine seemed composed entirely of bare, interlacing stems, resembling more than anything else the branches of a weeping willow denuded of its foliage, but of a dark, nearly black hue, and covered with a thick, viscid gum that exuded from the pores." As with other such plants, it entraps prey with its mobile tendrils and drains all the fluids from their bodies.[12]

Wilson also described the **Mexican Snake Tree**, which has movable, sucker-covered branches of a "slimy, snaky appearance." Allegedly found in the Sierra Madres, it was said to seize birds that landed on its branches and absorb their blood via the suckers. An apparently identical "Vampire Plant" was reported in 1933 by the French explorer Baron Byron Khun de Prorok, from the Chiapas jungles of southern Mexico. De Prorock claimed to have witnessed its capture of a bird: "The poor creature had alighted on one of the leaves, which had promptly closed, its thorns penetrating the body of the little victim, which endeavored vainly to escape, screaming meanwhile in agony and terror."[13]

In his *Carnivorous Plants* (1974),[14] Randall Schwartz reports on the **Brazilian Monkey-Trap Tree**, which lures its victims with an attractive scent

Fig. 6. Nicaraguan Dog-Devouring Tree

and then envelops them with its leaves. After three days, the leaves open, dropping the fleshless bones to the ground.

Although it is not entirely impossible that some such large-scale predatory plants may eventually be brought to light, it seems likely that at least some of these fabulous carnivores with their octopoid tentacles may have been inspired by Africa's weird-looking but harmless *Welwitschia mirabilis*, named after Dr. Friedrich Welwitsch, who discovered it in 1860 prior to the above accounts. Living 2,000 years or more, Welwitschia's two broad, sprawling leaves continue to grow throughout its life, eventually reaching 13 feet long or more, and splitting into several strap-like sections surrounding a wide central bowl on a short, thick trunk.

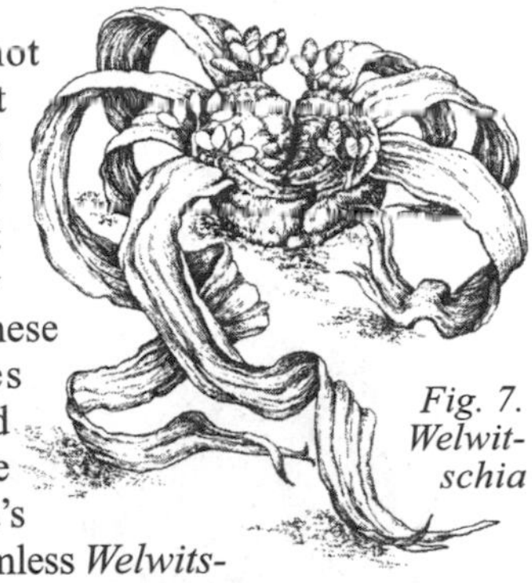

Fig. 7. Welwitschia

More passive than the tentacled predatory plants described above is the legendary **Death Flower of the South Pacific**. According to Captain Arkright, a 1581 explorer, it dwelt on an island called El Banoor ("Island of Death") amid an archipelago of coral atolls. The huge flower exuded a narcotic fragrance that seduced unwary victims to lie down to rest upon its great, rainbow-hued petals. But none would awaken from this drugged sleep, for the petals would then close over the victim and digest him with acidic juices. Cryptozoologist Roy Mackal has suggested that this could be a distorted account of the Sumatran *Rafflesia arnoldii*, the largest flower in the world. At least 3 feet in diameter, its blood-red, cream-speckled petals are leathery in texture, and surround a spiny central bowl containing several pints of dirty water.[15] However, the nauseating rotting-flesh stench of the Rafflesia—popularly called "Corpse Flower"—is so revolting that it is inconceivable that any human would be drawn to it! Its carrion aroma is actually designed to attract scavenging blowflies, its pollinators.

An equally sinister sleep-inducing predatory plant is called **el Juy-Juy** by the Indians of the Chaco forest bordering Argentina and Bolivia. Wilkins says its soporific perfume lulls humans and large animals to sleep in its shade, whereupon "the floral canopy overhead sends down masses of lovely blossoms, each flower of which is armed with a powerful sucker, which draws from the body all its blood and juices, leaving not even a fragment to tempt the vulture to shoot down from the skies to gorge on a bare skeleton."[16]

And finally, the **Upas Tree**, or "Tree of Death" is a poisonous tree of Java, said to be so deadly that any creature approaching it would be killed by its noxious exudations. The region around it is said to be desolate for miles, and the ground littered with skeletons. Also called *Mancenillier*, *Manchineel*, or *Manzanilla*, in actuality this is the Arrow Poison Tree (*Antiaris toxicara*), whose sap is used in making poison arrows. But the deadly emanations attributed to it are actually carbon dioxide emissions from volcanic fissures on this island. A similar poisonous tree, *Hippomane mancenilla*, grows in the West Indies, where its sap is also used for poison arrows.[17]

Fig. 7. The Upas, or poison-tree of Java, with a Rafflesia flower in the foreground.

plant-animal hybrids

A **Mandragora** (also called *Mandragore* or *Mandrake*) is a humanoid effigy formed from the Mandrake plant (*Mandragora officinarum*), which is a member of the psychotropic Nightshade family (*Solanaceae*). White mandrakes are considered male, and black ones, female. The leaves are used as a narcotic, as a laxative, and for magick. It was said that in order to conceive, the female elephant must eat some mandrake root. Mandrakes are said to grow only beneath gibbets, deriving nourishment from the gory and seminal exudations of hanged men, and that this is what gave the plant its aphrodisiac potency when ground

Fig. 8. Mandragores— male and female

into powder and used as a philter. Dioscorides called this an anthropomorphic powder, meaning a man-shaped natural object that has been ground up.

Fig. 9. Mandrake with natural root

This is how a Mandragore is made: Early in the plant's development (at about two months), the magician must dig it up carefully and modify its branching root to resemble a human figure, pinching a constriction a little below the top to form a head and neck, removing all but two of the upper branches, which are left as arms, and leaving the lower two branchings as legs. The semblance can even be improved with a bit of judicious carving. Then the mandrake is replanted until it grows to full size and produces fruit, at which time it is harvested.

The mature Mandragore is said to shriek in pain when it is finally pulled from the ground, and this hideous shriek can deafen, madden, or even kill an unprotected person. Flavius Josephus (c. 37–100 CE) gives the following instructions for harvesting it safely: "A furrow must be dug around the root until its lower part is exposed, then a dog is tied to it, after which the person tying the dog must get away. The dog then endeavours to follow him, and so easily pulls up the root, but dies suddenly instead of his master. After this the root can be handled without fear." (Modern mages would sensibly just wear earplugs!)

The **Barliate**, also known as *Annes de la mer*, *Barchad*, *Barnacha*, *Bernekke*, *Bernaca*, *Bernicle*, *Barnacle Goose*, *Tree Goose*, or *Boumgan*, is a type of goose that was believed to begin life as a fruit growing from trees or attached to driftwood. It is based upon actual Goose-neck Barnacles (*Lepas anatifera*).[18]

There is quite a history behind this legend, for the Barnacle Goose (*Branta leucopsis*) is a real bird, common along the north-western coasts of the British

Fig. 10. Barnacle Goose

isles. However, it nests far away in Novaya Zemlya—an archipelago in the Arctic Ocean north of Russia—and therefore its eggs and young were never seen, giving rise to speculation as to their true origins.

However, pieces of driftwood occasionally washed up on northern shores with clusters of gooseneck barnacles attached to them. These bear an uncanny resemblance to miniature geese, even down to the feathery gills within the outer shells, which resemble embryonic wings. (Fig. 11) Thus was born the widespread belief in a species of tree in a remote land which produced avian fruit just as other trees produced apples or plums. These goose-trees were believed to grow along the coast, where this fruit, falling into the sea, would continue to develop into adult geese. Storms would sometimes break off branches with the strange fruit still attached, and the currents would carry them to foreign shores.

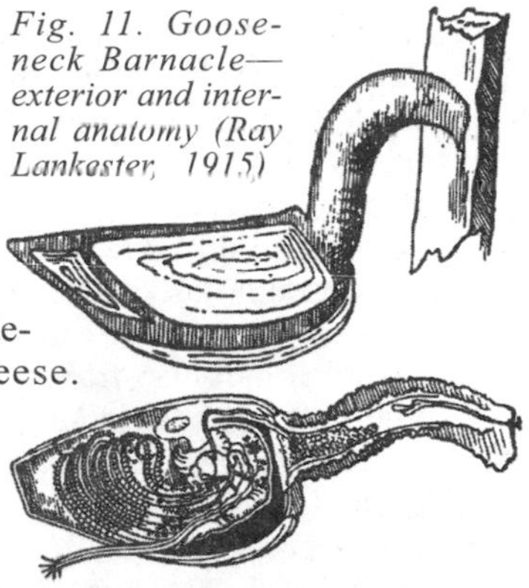

Fig. 11. Goose-neck Barnacle—exterior and internal anatomy (Ray Lankester, 1915)

The earliest recorded account of the Barnacle Goose dates from the year 1186, in Gerald de Barri's *Topography of Ireland*, where he refers to it as *Bernacae*, and recounts its development in some detail—though omitting the tree (that part of the story first appeared in the widely read encyclopedia of Vincent of Beavais, c.1190–1264) and merely stating that "they are produced from fir timber tossed along the sea, and are at first like gum." Because of their supposed botanical origin, these birds were deemed not to be "flesh," and were thereby permissible to eat during Lent and other Church-designated fasting times. It should also be noted that *bernacae* is the Celtic term for barnacles, which are, of course, mollusks.

Fig. 12. Barnacle Goose tree, from Aberdeen Bestiary (12th cent.)

Interestingly, Heinrich Schliemann's excavations of the ancient Greek city of Mycenae in the 1870s turned up a number of objects with depictions of what Ray Lankester, in his *Diversions of a Naturalist* (1915), later called "barnaculised geese." Note in his illustration the odd leg of this creature—which is actually the seminal duct of the barnacle, as shown in Fig. 11.

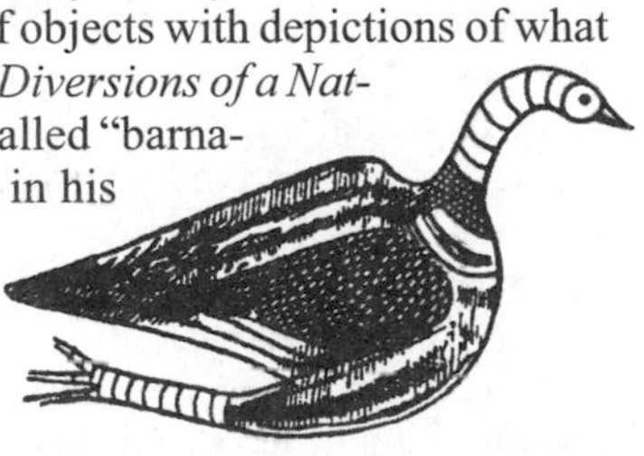

Fig. 13. Barnaculised goose from Mycenaean pot (from Schliemann)

While the Barnacle Goose (*Branta leucopsis*) is the bird specifically identified with this legend, ancient writers did not distinguish it from the Brent Goose, which has, in fact, been given the scientific name of *Branta bernicla*. Peter Costello recounts this entire fascinating tale in great detail in his marvelous book, *The Magic Zoo* (1979).[19]

The **Barometz** (Tartar, "little lamb") is also called the *Tartary Lamb, Barbary Lamb, Scythian Lamb*, or *Vegetable Lamb*, (*Lycopodium*). In Hebrew legend, this is a wool-bearing sheep-like creature from the Middle East that is half vegetable. Formally called *Agnus scythicus* or *Planta Tartarica Barometz*, they are produced from small gourds, which ripen and open to reveal tiny

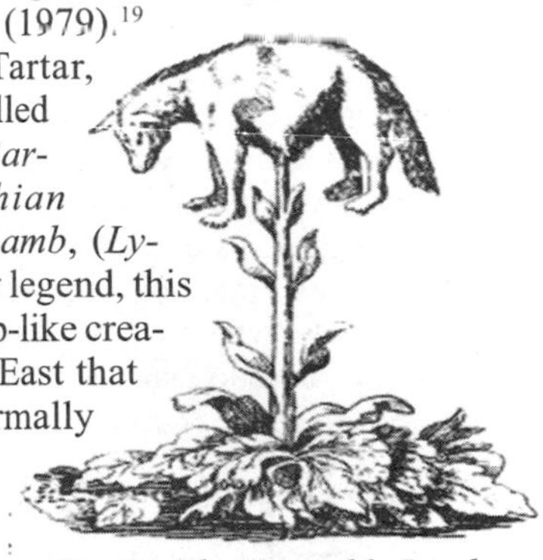

Fig. 14. The Vegetable Lamb of Tartary, from The Travels of Sir John Mandeville

lambs inside. These remain attached to their shrubs by very short stems, allowing them to graze around the plant. Once they have consumed all the grass within reach, both the lamb and the plant die of starvation. Barometz was considered a delicacy, as its meat supposedly tastes like crab, and its blood, like honey. Its bones were used in rituals to give the power of prophecy.

The legend of the Vegetable Lamb originated in the popular 14th-century book *The Travels of Sir John Mandeville*: "There groweth a manner of fruit as it were gourds, and when it is ripe men cut it a sonder, and men fynde therein a beast as it were of flesh and bone and blood, as it were a lyttle lambe without wolle, and men eat the beast and fruit also, and sure it seemeth very strange."[15]

Fig. 15. The Barometz

This marvelous plant is generally assumed to be the cotton shrub (*Gossypium*), and this is probably the most likely basis for the legend. But it has also been explained as a Wooly Fern (*Cibotium barometz*) that grows in the Middle East and is used as a styptic. But a better candidate is *Polypodium barometz*, an Asian fern with thick roots growing along the surface of the ground, which are covered in a dense wool, and when cut, ooze a blood-red fluid. In China and Indonesia, these roots were commonly fashioned into the

Fig. 16. Toy dog from China, made of Polypodium Barometz (Costello)

form of little toy dogs, called *Caw-tieh* and *Kew-tsi* (perhaps "cutsie"?).[20]

The **Jidra** is a voracious plant-animal hybrid mentioned in *Zoology des Talmuds*, by L. Lewysohn (1858), as well as in various medieval travelers' tales and folklore of the Middle East. Growing on a long vine from roots implanted in the ground, the Jidra is a kind of human-shaped gourd, with magickal bones prized as an aphrodisiac when powdered and added to wine. It devours anything it can reach within the radius of its vine, but if the umbilical vine is severed, the creature will die screaming, with blood spurting from the severed ends. The similarity to the legend of the Mandragore is worth noting.

OTHER PECULIAR PLANTS OF MYTH AND LEGEND

Peridexion Tree (Latin, *Peridixion*; also *Circa dexteram*, *Environ destre*, *Paradixion*, *Pendens*, *Perindens*)—A tree growing in India that attracts doves, which gather in its branches because they like its sweet fruit. There they are safe from the Dragon, who would eat the doves if he could. But he fears the shadow of the tree and stays on the sunny side of it. Doves that remain in the shadow are safe, but any who leave it are caught and eaten by the Dragon.

Fig. 18. Peridexion Tree, from Aberdeen Bestiary *(12th century)*

Leontophontes—As described in the *Physiologus*, these are "certain creatures of moderate size" that people burn in order to sprinkle their poisonous ash onto meat to kill lions, "should the lions eat the least little bit of it." These may actually be plants rather than animals, as Arnica is also known as Leopard's Bane, and Dandelion belongs to the genus *Leontodon*.

Solar Complexus Americanus—heat-generating plants supposedly imported from Venezuela. The Scandinavian botanist responsible for discovering these hot-air producers was said to be Professor Olaf Lipro (an anagram of "April Fool"). A news report of this "discovery" was an April Fool's Day joke launched by the *Glasgow Herald* in 1995.[21]

Other mythical plants include:
- **Austras Koks**—a tree in Latvian mythology which grows from the start of the sun's daily journey across the sky.
- **Ents** (Anglo-Saxon, "Giant")—Historically referring to any number of large, roughly humanoid creatures,

Ents are best known today as the ambulatory, humanoid trees from J.R.R. Tolkien's fantasy world of Middle-Earth. A wise and ancient race, they appear to have been inspired by the talking trees found in folklore throughout the world. Their appearance and size varies according to the species of trees they shepherd. The long-lost females are called *Entwives*.
- **Lotus tree**—a tree described in *The Odyssey* as bearing a narcotic fruit that causes a pleasant drowsiness. It may have actually been a type of Jujube—perhaps *Ziziphus lotus*—or possibly even the Date Palm.
- **Moly**—a magic herb of Greek myth with a black root and white blossoms. In *The Odyssey,* Hermes gives it to Odysseus, thus enabling him to resist the enchantments of Circe.
- **Raskovnik**—a magic plant in Serbian mythology which can open any lock.
- **Yggdrasil**—the mighty World Tree of Norse mythology. Its three main branches support the nine realms of the Gods, and its three roots delve deep into the Underworld.[22]

MONSTER MOVIES: PLANTIMALS

After the hostile animated apple trees of *The Wizard of Oz* (1939), the next plant monster to appear on screen was *The Thing from Another World* (1951). Unfortunately, it looked just like a human. *Invasion of the Body Snatchers* (1956, and the 1978 remake) featured Jidra-like pod-people. Audrey Jr. was the ever-growing, man-eating plant in the 1960 black comedy film *The Little Shop of Horrors*. *Day of the Triffids* (1962), from the 1951 novel by John Wyndham, featured ambulatory carnivorous plants with whip-like, poisonous stingers. The 1963 Japanese film *Matango, Fungus of Terror* (released in America as *Attack of the Mushroom People*) featured mutated mushroom-people. Another giant carnivorous houseplant starred in the 1977 comedy *Adele Hasn't Had Her Dinner Yet*. *The Mutations* (1974) featured mutated plant-people. *John Carpenter's The Thing* (1982) was a remake of the 1951 film, with much more impressive special effects. *The Dark Crystal* (1982) included several animate plants. 1986 saw a remake of *Little Shop of Horrors* as a campy musical. Also that year, *Troll* had a teenage magick-user named Harry Potter, Jr. battling vine-grown pod-people. The 1989 Japanese movie *Godzilla vs. Biollante* featured a monstrous, mobile mutant plant. *Harry Potter and the Chamber of Secrets* (2002) introduced Mandrakes and the aggressive Whomping Willow, which latter appeared again in *Harry Potter and the Prisoner of Azkaban* (2004). And who can forget the marvelous Ents of *Lord of the Rings: The Two Towers* (2002) and *Return of the King* (2003)? *Pan's Labyrinth* (2007) also included a Mandragore.

ꜰʟɪɢʜꜱ ꝏꜰ ꜰᴀɴꜱᴀꜱꝩ
16. ᴏʀɪᴇɴꜱᴀʟ ꜱᴘɪʀꜱ-ᴄʀᴇᴀꜱᴜʀᴇꜱ

By Ash "LeopardDancer" DeKirk and Oberon Zell

Hunter of the Still Waters

Flash of silvery scale, clack of sharp beak,
sight and sound of the rarest of river hunters,
dragging its quarry beneath the waves-
such is the kappa, a most masterful predator.

Sight and sound of the rarest of breeds,
the briefest and most fleeting of glimpses.
Then the kappa is gone,
leaving behind only ripples in the faint water.
> —Ash "LeopardDancer" DeKirk

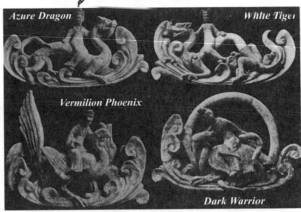

Chinese pottery decorations from the Six Dynasties period (221-581 CE), showing goddesses riding on the Ssu Ling—the sacred animals of the four directions.

ROM ITS VERY BEGINNINGS, IN THE writings of Pliny, Herodotus, and Ctesias, the now-familiar European bestiary was comprised largely of strange creatures reported to be dwelling in far-off places such as Egypt, India, Ethiopia, Asia, and Madagascar. These reports were based on travelers' tales told by adventurers such as the Argonauts; soldiers in the armies of Alexander and Caesar sent to expand the frontiers of the Empire; crusaders fighting to liberate the Holy Land; and merchants who plied their trades on the Silk Road to far-off Cathay, and who later sailed the seven seas to the Indies and the Americas. Europeans were familiar with the animals in their forests and fens and they encountered few unknowns, save the elusive beasts lurking in the dark depths of various lakes and lochs. However, when returning travelers told of mountainous monsters with ears like vast fans and noses like huge serpents; thundering armored beasts with massive, single horns; towering, long-legged, long-necked, spotted "camel-leopards" that browsed the tops of trees; birds that laid gigantic eggs, and whose downy, flightless chicks stood at twice the height of a man; immense and mighty serpents; and huge, lumbering reptiles with enormous jaws that could take down and devour a horse and rider, well, how could imagination conjure anything more fantastic than the reality? For, of course, all those creatures really existed—but only far, far away. Could Gryphons, Unicorns, Perytons, Mermaids, and Hippocampi seem any more unbelievable than elephants, rhinos, giraffes, elephant birds, pythons, and crocodiles? So, all of these beasties—both actual and imaginary—became mixed together in the delightful cryptozoological compilations called bestiaries.

But the strange creatures that figure so prominently in the mythologies of the Orient are quite different. These are not denizens of some far-off lands, recounted in dubious travelers' tales. The cultures of the Far East were much more insular than those of the West, and they didn't send explorers to faraway countries to return with tales of fantastic fauna. The mythical menageries of China, Japan, and Korea are comprised of spirit-beings (*Kami*, in Japanese), which seldom have a basis in real animals. (If they do, they are usually presumed to be shape-shifters that only appear to be, say, an ordinary fox or raccoon dog.)

Following are some interesting spirit-creatures of the Orient. Note that we are omitting all the Oriental Dragons (*Lung,* in Chinese), as well as Unicorns (*Ki-Lin* in Chinese, and *Kirien* in Japanese), as these creatures are discussed in great detail in our chapters on Dragons and Unicorns. —OZ

cbɪɴᴀ

By Ash "LeopardDancer" DeKirk

Dogs of Fo

These are guardian beasts with the broad head of a hound, the body of a lion, and a feathery tail. Some Dogs of Fo sport a horn in the middle of the forehead, and some have wings. In classical depictions, male Dogs of Fo are shown with one paw resting atop a globe, "feeling the pulse of the world." Females are depicted with a puppy between their front paws. These celestial hounds are always depicted in pairs, especially in the art and sculpture of the Imperial periods. Statues are usually placed in front of gates or temple entrances for protection. It is believed that the statues would come alive at night and roam the grounds as spirit guardians. Males guarded the grounds while females guarded the inhabitants. These beasties were first noted in the myth and architecture of the Han Dynasty (around 206 BCE). They are also known as Celestial Dogs, Fu-Dog, Foo Dog, Lion-dog. In Tibet they are known as Snow Lions, and in China they are called *Rui-shi* or *Shi.*

These statues greatly resemble the snub-nosed Oriental dogs such as the Pekingese, Shih Tzu, and Lhasa Apso. Temples and palaces often kept small guard dogs to keep the area clean of vermin. These little guard dogs

Fig. 1. Dogs of Fo

were also believed to be able to chase away evil spirits. Dogs were bred for loyalty and courage, but also for smallness in size. It is believed that the Chinese were breeding small dogs that resembled a beast they thought existed in the spirit realm—the Dogs of Fo.

Ssu Ling

These are the four sacred "auspicious animals," or spiritual creatures, that grew from the dead Phan-ku and stand at the four corners of the Earth in Chinese mythology. Also representing seasons of the year and constellations of the Chinese Zodiac, they have been portrayed in many historical Chinese stories, as well as modern Japanese manga comics and animé.

- The *Lung Wang* (Azure Dragon) in the East (spring); his element is Wood, he brings the regenerating rains, embodies the positive *yang* principle, and represents the Emperor.
- The *Fêng Huang* (Vermilion Phoenix or Red Bird) rules the South (summer); its element is Fire, it brings drought, embodies the negative *yin* principle, and represents the Empress.
- The *Ki-Lin* (Unicorn; also *Baihu,* the White Tiger) governs the West (autumn); its element is Metal, the key to sovereignty.
- And the *Gui Xian* (Black Tortoise, also called Dark Warrior) rules the North (winter); its element is Water. The Black Tortoise is usually depicted as both a tortoise and

Fig. 2. Gui Xian

a snake, with the snake coiling around the tortoise.

Sun Wukong (also *Sun Wu-Kung, Sun Hou-Zi,* or *Son Goku*)

The clever, magickal monkey of Chinese mythology—the "Handsome Monkey King"—hatched from an egg impregnated by the wind. Ruling over an island of monkeys, he sets out on a quest for eternal life. Along the way, he becomes a master of martial arts, learns the art of shapeshifting, and manages to eat some Peaches of Immortality. Sun Wukong claims the outrageous title of "Great Sage Equaling Heaven." His mischievous ways cause the Buddha to imprison him beneath the Mountain of Five Elements, where he stays for 500 years until the Bodhisatva Kuan Yin sets him free with the charge

Fig. 3. The Monkey King

to protect Priest Sanzang on his journey west. After many adventures, developing more skills and tricks, and overcoming all manner of adversities, he eventually becomes the "Buddha of Victory Through Strife." Derived from the legend of *Hanuman,* the monkey hero from the Hindu *Ramayana,* Sun Wukong's adventures are told in the epic story, *Journey to the West.*

Kapila (Hundred-Heads)

This monstrous, allegorical fish is recorded in a Chinese biography of the Buddha. According to the legend, the Buddha once met some fishermen who caught in their nets a huge fish with 100 heads, each of a different creature: ape, bull, dog, fox, horse, pig, tiger, and so on. The Buddha explained that the fish had, in a former incarnation, been a monk named Kapila who had berated his students by calling them names, such as pig-head, bull-head, and so on. The karma of those insults resulted in his rebirth as a sea monster bearing the all the heads he had verbally bestowed upon others.

OTHER CHINESE SPIRIT-CREATURES

Bixie—A kind of Chinese *Chimera,* the Bixie is a winged lion with horns.

Bo—A voracious, horse-like creature with the razor-sharp teeth and claws of a tiger, and a

Fig. 4. Bixie (Ash)

Fig. 5. Bo

single horn atop its head, similar to that of a Unicorn. It is impervious to all man-made weapons, and can emit a thunderous roar similar to the sound of rolling drums.

Celestial Horse—A creature resembling a white dog with a black head, it has fleshy wings with which it can fly.

Celestial Stag—A deer of legend that is capable of human speech. Dwelling in the Heavens and beneath the Earth, it guided lost miners to veins of precious ores and gems. But if it ever touched the surface of the Earth, it would dissolve into jelly.

Fig. 7. Celestial Stag

Chan—An immense clam whose exhalations form wondrous undersea palaces of coral. Very likely this is a description of the giant clam (*Tridacna gigas*) that inhabits coral reefs of the South Pacific and Indian oceans. These can weigh more than 400 pounds and measure as much as 5 feet across.

Chiang Liang—A monster with the body of a panther, the head of a tiger, and the face of a human. It has long legs and hooves, and is often shown with a snake in its mouth.

Ch'ou-T'i—A composite creature described as having a head at each end, similar to an *Amphisbaena* or Dr. Doolittle's Pushmi-Pullyu. It lives in the country west of the Red Water.

Fei Lian (or *Feng Bo,* meaning "Wind Lord")—A celestial monster with the body and legs of a stag, the spots of a leopard, and the tail of a serpent. Its head is similar to a sparrow's, with bull's horns. It controls the fierce storm winds, releasing them from a bag at its whim.

Fig. 8. Fei Lian (Ian Daniels)

Heavenly Cock (or Bird of Dawn) —A golden-plumed, three-legged rooster that crows three times a day—at dawn, noon, and sunset. From his perch in the vast *fu-sang* tree, the first crowing stirs the heavens and awakens all creatures. He lays eggs from which hatch red-combed chicks from which all the roosters of Earth are descended.

Fig. 9. Heavenly Cock

Hua-Hu-Tiao—A monstrous, supernatural white elephant with immense wings, in the mythology of Chinese Buddhism. From time to time it would break free of its confinement and wreak havoc upon the world, killing and eating all creatures and people. It was eventually killed by the warrior hero Yang Ching, who, after being swallowed, hacked it to death from the inside.

Hui—A giant dog with a human head. It is fleet-footed, able to leap all obstacles, and unafraid of humans. Its appearance forebodes a typhoon.

I-Mu Kuo Yan—An anthropomorphic bird-creature with a feather-covered body of a human, and bird wings in place of arms. These creatures are shy and avoid human contact.

Kw'ên—An immense fish, miles in length, that dwelt in the North China Sea. Eventually it metamorphosed into a truly vast bird called the *P'êng*.

Lwan (also *Luan* or *Lwan Shui*)—A majestic, gigantic pheasant, the Lwan can change the color of its feathers. When it does so, it gains a different name: A Lwan with black feathers is called *Yin Chu*, one with a red head crest and red wings is called *Fung,* a pure white Lwan is a *Hwa Yih*, one with sapphire-blue feathers is a *Yu Siang,* and one with golden feathers is known as *To Fu*.

P'êng (or *Pyong*)—An enormous bird that is the metamorphosed form of the huge fish called *Kw'ên*. Its outspread wings cover the sky from horizon to horizon. It lives in the north, but each year it rises thousands of feet into the air and flies toward the south, bringing the typhoon season.

Shachihoko—A water monster with the body of a carp and the head of a tiger. Covered all over with poisonous spines when it is in the sea, it can transform into a tiger on land. It became a popular form of Gargoyle on medieval Japanese buildings.

*Fig. 10. **Shachihoko***

Shang Yung (also *Shang Yang,* meaning "rainbird")—A fabulous, one-legged bird that can change its height. It heralds the return of the rainy season and warns of floods. It draws water into its beak from rivers and seas, and blows it out in the form of rain onto the thirsty land. For this reason it is often petitioned in time of drought. Children hop about, hunched over on one foot, chanting: "It will thunder, it will rain, because the Shang Yang's here again!"

Song-Sseu—A bird with the body of a hen pheasant and the head of a woman. The first mating call of the pheasant was a signal for young people to come out and dance, so its image was embroidered on the ceremonial dance gowns of marriageable princesses.

Fig. 11. Song-Sseu (Tam Songdog)

T'ao T'ieh ("Glutton")—One of the oldest known Chinese mon- sters, with one head and set of forelimbs and two hugely fat-bellied bodies, each with its own hind limbs and tail. These can be based on any of several animals as well as humans. Its head is disproportionately large, with a cavernous mouth lined with rows of pointy teeth. This six-legged beast represents gluttony, and it is painted on dishes as a subtle admonition against overindulgence at the dinner table. T'ao T'ieh is one of the creatures featured in the PS2 game, Culdcept.

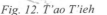

Fig. 12. T'ao T'ieh

T'ien Kou—An enormous

celestial dog with a fiery plumed tail similar to a comet. Mentioned in the legend of the Monkey King, *Sun Hou-Zi,* he descends to the Earth at night in search of unwatched small children to eat. If he can't find any, he kills adults and devours their livers. Failing Earthly sustenance, he returns to the Heavens to consume the moon (thus explaining lunar phases and eclipses). Then the Celestial Archer, *Hou I,* shoots down the great dog. But the T'ien Kou is always resurrected each morning to start the cycle all over again.

Too Jou Shen—An animal with a leonine body and head, cloven hooves, and a short, blunt horn projecting from the center of its forehead. Two pairs of these form a portion of the avenue of stone figures leading up to the Ming tombs, about 80 miles north of Peking.

Fig. 13. Too Jou Shen

Xian Yao—A disgusting and hideous monster with a serpentine body and nine human heads. It is the companion of *Gong-Gong,* the Black Dragon. The two of them go about fouling lakes and rivers with their excrement, turning them into fetid swamps.

Yu Lung ("Fish Dragon")—A Dragon with a fish head and fins. Originally a celestial carp, it was transformed after leaping the Dragon's Gate waterfall and flying to Heaven. It represents high aspirations and success in examinations.

JAPAN
By Ash "LeopardDancer" DeKirk

Kitsune

Kitsune are the trickster fox spirits of Japan. These mischievous little creatures can turn into an exact copy of *any* person they so choose, which can, of course, lead to many problems for humans! Kitsune often live amongst humans, with the humans none the wiser. Other Kitsune live in the wilds, and are thought of as nothing more than ordinary foxes until they reveal their powers. Not only can Kitsune take the shape of a human, but they can possess a human as well. Indeed, this belief is still around today. Asahara Shoko, the leader of *Aum Shinrikyo*—one of Japan's newer religions, and the group responsible for the 1995 Tokyo subway disaster—was accused of forcing followers to become possessed by fox spirits.

Kitsune are associated with the Japanese goddess *Inari*, and are often considered her spirit messengers. White foxes and white fox Kitsune are especially sacred to Inari. The fox spirits are said to live for hundreds of years, with some living to be 1,000 years old! As they grow older, the Kitsune increase their powers, such that the older ones become godlike themselves. According to legend, Kitsune came under Inari's protection and rulership after a family of

them sought shelter in one of Inari's shrines. Inari granted them shelter so long as they served her. The family took oaths binding them to the goddess, and the Kitsune have served Inari ever since. Kitsune are such popular figures that sub-shrines within Inari

Fig. 14 Kitsune by Ash

shrines have been devoted to the white fox Kitsune.

Japan has two native subspecies of foxes: the Hokkaido fox (*Kita Kitsune*) and the Japanese red fox (*Hondo Kitsune*). If you know what to look for, there are several ways to distinguish a Kitsune from an ordinary fox. Kitsune often have multiple tails, and sometimes they retain a tail in their human forms. Kitsune in human form may cast a fox shadow and, similar to the vampire legends of Europe, will reflect their fox part in the mirror. Some legends say that a Kitsune gains a tail for every century lived, and others say that they attain all 9 at the time they turn 900 years old. Kitsune are portrayed most often with one, five, or 9 tails. Their pelt changes color as well, turning to white, then silver, and then finally to gold. All of these themes are very popular in Japanese art.

There are several types of Kitsune in Japanese myth and legend. Celestial Kitsune, called *Tenko,* are the white Kitsune that primarily serve Inari. Dark Kitsune, or *Reiko,* are black fox spirits that serve Inari. *Kuko Kitsune* are wind foxes. These Kitsune are regarded as evil. Often, they appeared as spectral forms created from fog, mist, or whirlwinds. *Kiko Kitsune*, the "demon foxes," were also regarded as creatures of evil intent.

Fig. 15. Kitsune

In actuality, the Kitsune are neither "good" nor "evil"; they are amoral creatures, carving their own path between the two extremes. They are Trickster figures, akin to *Coyote* in Native American myth. Kitsune are mercurial creatures: If you adhere to what the fox spirit considers "right," then it will be helpful, polite, and considerate. But offend the fox at your own risk! They will easily turn on you, becoming malicious and disruptive. If a Kitsune regards you as immoral, they may play tricks and confuse your sense of being, leading you down a path of self-destruction. On the other hand, the fox spirits tend to help those they regard as noble or moral, though they will still play small tricks on them, usually to help them learn lessons that need learning. Despite their trickster natures, Kitsune are honorable and will keep their words. If you manage to befriend a fox spirit, you will have a loyal and trustworthy friend for life. On the other hand, if you manage to anger a Kitsune, expect to have a vengeful enemy for life.

Fig. 16. Kitsune disguised as a woman

Kitsune have the ability to possess people, though usually this process involves permission of the person being possessed. A Kitsune possession usually does not last terribly long either—just long enough for the Kitsune to carry out its business or pass along information. When the Kitsune departs, the person will have no memory of what has transpired. It some cases, a fox spirit will take over a person's body by force. When that happens, the fox usually means to stay. A Kitsune may also try to take possession of an unborn child. In doing so, the mother will weaken and grow sick. When the child is finally born, it also will be weak and sickly. If the Kitsune does not succeed in fully taking over the child, or if it chooses not to leave, then the child will eventually perish. If the fox spirit does succeed, then it will grow up with the new human form, gradually attaining its powers as the body matures. Kitsune are not limited to taking possession of only humans; they can do so with any creatures they choose.

Kitsune possess many other abilities besides being able to possess people. The most well-known, especially in their role as tricksters, is their ability to create elaborate illusions, which for them are reality. Kitsune can create small "pocket" realities where time passes faster or slower than in the real world. Size is also manipulated in these pocket realities; for example, they can turn a small hole into a huge house on the inside. Kitsune can also create foxfire, an illusory light source that is usually green in color. They can also breathe fire over a short distance.

Fox spirits can change shape, but they are not limited to taking fox or human forms. A Kitsune can change into anything it wishes, from a rock to a bird. Similar to a Dragon and its dragon pearl, the Kitsune

Fig. 17. Kitsune

keep a "fox ball" with them. This ball often looks like a simple child's toy, but it really contains either a piece of the fox's soul or a portion of its power. If a person can get his or her hands on a fox ball, then he or she can make a Kitsune do just about anything. With all of these strengths must come some weakness. A Kitsune's weakness lies in religion: Those who possess religious faith cannot be fooled by Kitsune illusion, and if they touch one of these illusions it will shatter—a very traumatic experience for a Kitsune!

Kitsune are quite prevalent in modern Japanese media. In the popular anime series *Inuyasha,* the character of Shippo is a young, orphaned Kitsune who often helps out the group with his illusory magic. Kitsune make an appearance in the popular children's game/anime *Pokemon,* in the form of the five-tailed fox, Vulpix, and its nine-tailed evolution called (ironically enough), Nine-Tales. In the Sega game *Sonic the Hedgehog,* Sonic's pal, Tails, is a two-tailed Kitsune. These devious fox spirits also show up in a great many fantasy novels. Fr example, a young, female Kitsune is one of the main characters in Neil Gaiman's *The Dream Hunters.* Kitsune also make an appearance in Mercedes Lackey's *Serrated Edge* series.

Kappa

Fig. 19. Mito Kappa

These malicious creatures dwell in lakes, rivers, and ponds. They have a monkey-like body, with green, blue, or yellowish-brown scales and a turtle shell on their backs. Some are depicted with simian faces with long hair, and some with turtle beaks or duck bills. Kappa have depressions in their heads filled with a fluid which maintains their life force and physical strength. If you bow to a Kappa, it will bow back—and spill the fluid, rendering it helpless. Pouring water into the hollow restores the Kappa's power. Similar to other reptiles, Kappas become sluggish in cold weather and hibernate during the winter. There are two distinct species: those that dwell in lowland waters, and others, called *Yamawaro,* that live in mountain streams.

Kappa like to play jokes and tend to be troublesome creatures. They will ruin or steal crops, kidnap children, and eat both adults and children if given the chance. Kappa can be befriended by people, though, if provided with suitable gifts and offerings. They are naturally curious creatures and find men interesting as well as tasty. A good offering for befriending Kappa is cucumbers, as they live on blood and cucumbers, and fly through the air on enchanted cucumbers with dragonfly wings. They can also be tricked into helping a human and if you can extract a promise from one, he will honor it. Kappa have been known to aid in irrigation and are quite knowledgeable in the area of medicine, particularly when working with bones.

Several possibilities have been put forth as to what the Kappa actually is. One is that they originated from the act of floating stillborn fetuses down rivers. Another is as a mere scare tactic to keep children away from waterways ("nursery bogies"). Yet another is that the Kappa are rare, as-yet-unstudied, water-dwelling creatures. More modern speculation is that they may be aliens! A Kappa was reportedly captured along Mito Beach in 1801. A drawing of the Mito Kappa depicts a simian creature scaled in blue-grey, with webbed feet, a shelled back and long, sharp teeth.

Tanuki

A mischievious shape-shifter akin to the Kitsune, though they are often gullible and absent-minded. Similar to the Kitsune, this beastie is also a real creature, some-times called a raccoon or a badger, though it is neither. Rather, it is a species of dog, the raccoon-dog (*Nyctereutes procyonoides*) that

Fig. 20. Tanuki

resembles the fox. *Tanuki* are often depicted as being chubby with large testes. They wear leaf hats and often carry sake jugs. Tanuki statues are often placed outside of bars to beckon customers inside. Another name for the Tanuki is *Mujina*.

Tanuki can transform themselves into anything, animate or inanimate. They love to disguise themselves as anything from traveling monks to tea kettles in order to play tricks on unsuspecting humans. They can also use illusion to turn leaves into money and grass into a delicious meal. The leaf on the Tanuki's head, often a lotus leaf, is used for the Tanuki's transformations, and the Tanuki must also chant incantations to effect the changes. In the video game series *Super Mario Bros.*, if Mario gets a leaf he can put it on his head and gain the ears and tail of the Tanuki. Mario can also acquire a "Tanooki" suit, in which he and the Tanuki become virtually indistinguishable.

You may ask yourself why many Tanuki are depicted as being very well-endowed. Tanuki are not fertility beings, and the giant testes are regarded as symbols of good luck rather than overt symbols of masculine prowess and fertility. These are called *kintama*, or "golden balls," and are likely a reference to the real Tanuki's extremely large genitalia.

Tengu

These are Japanese *Youkai,* or spirit beings. *Tengu* are part human and part bird, with glowing eyes and large, beak-like noses. There are several varieties. Most commonly they are portrayed as people with avian features, with the low-ranking *Karasu Tengu* and *Ko-Tengu* (or *Konoha Tengu*) being the most bird-like. These sport a bird head with human ears, and human hands at the end of thin, tapered wings. Tengu have faces that may be red, green, or black, and often they have human ears and hair. Their beaks are some-times lined with sharp teeth, and they have clawed, birdlike hands and feet. Their wings and tails are feathered, as may be their entire body. They are generally depicted with red clothing, hair, or skin. The Karasu Tengu preys upon humans, which it is big enough to carry off.

Tengu are associated with the ascetic *Yamabushi* priests, and are often garbed in their raiment. Residing in a fortress on Mount Kurama, north of Kyoto, Tengu sometimes carry ring-topped staffs called *shakujo* used for fighting and warding off evil magic. Other Tengu carry feather fans that they use to stir up great winds. These Tengu are believed to be derived from the Hindu eagle god, *Garuda.* Garuda and Tengu appear in the video game Culdcept as the bird-demon, *Gouda.*

Earlier Tengu were canine creatures that preyed on humans. These were also called Heavenly Dogs, and resembled a thunderous shooting star. These Tengu were heralds of war, and are believed to be inspired by actual comet sightings or meteor impacts.

Fig. 21. Tengu

Tengu may be benevolent or malevolent, with just as many protecting people as there are seeking to destroy them. They have great magickal powers and can transform into any animal. They have also been known to possess people, though once the Tengu leaves the human host has no memory of the possession. Tengu are skilled in martial arts and are often associated with them. Tengu are also forest guardians capable of causing terrible storms to drive people away from their woods.

OTHER JAPANESE BAMI-CRITTERS

Akuma—Also called *Toori Akuma,* or *Ma,* this demonic monster is terrifying and evil. With an enormous flaming head and eyes like coals, it flies through the air brandishing a sword. It brings bad luck to anyone who sees it.

Amikiri—Small flying creatures with crab claws and long, serpentine tails. They cut up mosquito nets, fishing nets, and laundry hung out to dry.

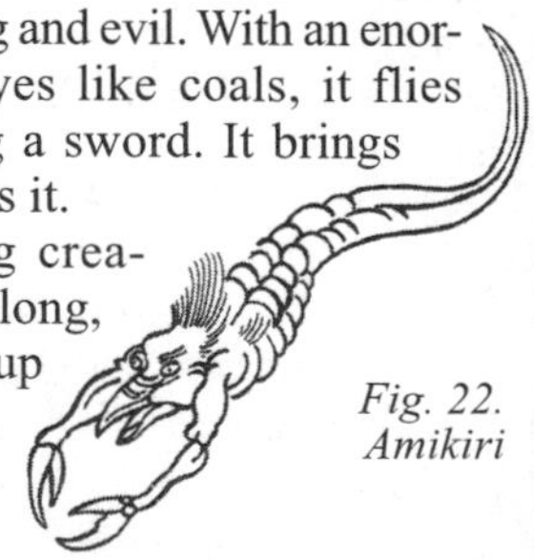

Fig. 22. Amikiri

Baku—Called the Eater of Dreams, this chimerical creature is a benevolent being. It has the body of a tapir, the head of an elephant, the mane of a lion, the tail of an ox, and the legs and paws of a tiger. It is invoked

Fig. 25. Baku

upon first awakening by saying, "Oh Baku, eat my dreams," and it gobbles up any lingering nightmares so that the dreamer may have a peaceful day. The Baku appears in many Japanese fantasy tales, especially in anime and manga. It also plays a big part in Neil Gaiman's *The Dream Hunters.*

Hiyakudori—A mythical, two-headed bird. Resembling the bird of paradise, it symbolizes the union of two famous lovers.

Jinshin-Mushi ("earthquake beetle")—A bizarre, bug-like creature whose burrowings are said to cause earthquakes in Kyoto, in southern Japan. Its immense, scaly body has 10 hairy spider's legs and a Dragon's head.

Jinshin-Uwo ("earthquake fish")—This 700-mile-long eel carries all the Japanese islands on its back. Its head lies beneath the city of Kyoto, and a massive rivet driven into the ground in the temple gardens of Kashima secures the country to its back. The lashing of its mighty tail causes earthquakes.

Kamaitachi ("sickle weasel")—Vicious, weasel-like creatures that move too quickly to be seen. They always hunt in packs of three: the first one knocks the prey down, the second slashes its throat, and the third heals the wound so they can repeat the process until the victim is dead.

Fig. 26. Kamaitachi

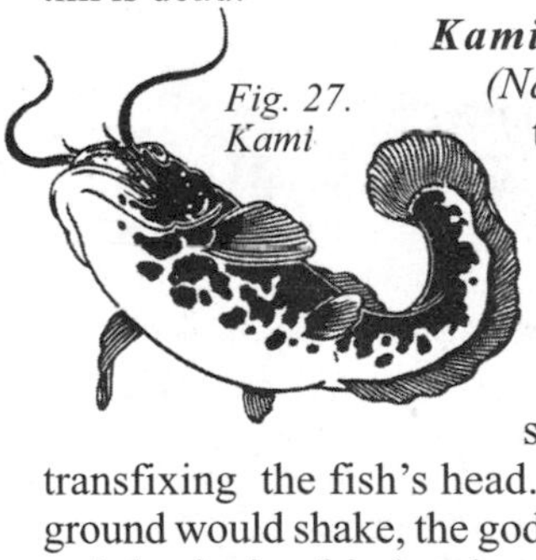

Kami—A gigantic catfish *(Namazu)* dwelling beneath the Japanese islands, and thought to be responsible for causing earthquakes. According to legend, the god of Deer Island thrust his mighty sword through the Earth,

Fig. 27. Kami

transfixing the fish's head. From then on, when the ground would shake, the god would quiet it by laying his hand on the granite hilt, which still protrudes near the shrine of Kashima. Kami is also the name given to Japanese Shinto Nature Spirits.

Kamakiri ("sickle-cutter")—A Shinto nature-spirit identified with the praying mantis (*Cottus kazika*).

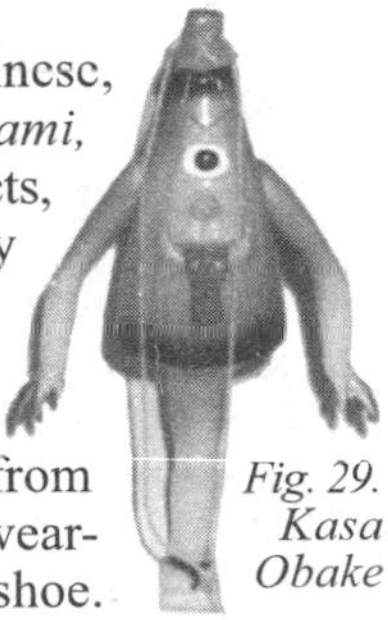

Fig. 28. Kamakiri

Kasa Obake ("umbrella"; Chinese, *Karakasa*)—A type of *Tsukumogami*, Japanese spirits that were once objects, which became animate when they reached 100 years of age. Kasa Obake are spirits of century-old umbrellas. They are portrayed with one eye, a long tongue protruding from an open mouth, and a single foot wearing a *geta*, a Japanese clog shoe.

Fig. 29. Kasa Obake

Kudan—A human-headed bull with three eyes on each side of its body and horns down its back. It always spoke truth, and was sought out as an oracle of things to come.

Fig. 30. Kudan

Moshiriikkwechep ("world backbone trout")—A vast fish that lies in the mud beneath the ocean and supports the world on its back. Its periodic wriggling causes earthquakes and tsunamis.

Nue (or Japanese chimera)—A hybrid creature with the body of a *Tanuki*, the head of a monkey, the legs of a tiger, and a snake for a tail. A bringer of misfortune and illness, it can also transform into a black cloud and fly around.

Nupperabo—The flabby, dough-like guardian of *Jingoku*, the underground hell of Japanese folklore.

Fig. 31. Nue by Kuniyoshi Utagawa, 1852

Nure-Onna ("getting wet woman")—A serpentine enchantress typically seen by the shore, washing her long, long hair. Her snaky body is said to be 900 feet long, and she moves extremely fast through the water. She has long fingers with claws, along with a snake's eyes, forked tongue, and fangs. Some stories say she feeds on people, but others say she merely resents being disturbed when she's washing her precious hair. It is also said she can suck the blood from a victim at a distance.

Fig. 32. Nure-Onna

Pheng—A bird so gigantic that it eclipses the sun and can carry off and eat a camel. Very similar to the *Roc* of Arabian myth.

Raichô ("thunder bird")—A fabulous giant rook or crow-like bird. He lives in a tall pine tree, and his raucous calls summon the storms. This is also the name of a real bird—*Lagopus mutus*—a kind of ptarmigan.

Raiju ("thunder animal")—The pet of Raijin, the Shinto god of lightning, this demonic little creature has the body of a cat or weasel, the agility of a monkey, and the sharp claws of a *Tanuki*. Composed of fire, he is the animal manifestation of the phenomenon of ball lightning. He becomes frenzied during

Fig. 33. Raiju

storms, leaping about in trees, fields, and even buildings in frantic terror, and making a cry like thunder. A tree marked by lightning is said to have been scratched by Raiju. He tries to hide by digging into human navels, so it is best to sleep on your stomach during a thunderstorm!

Samebito ("shark-man")—A sea monster that is half-human and half-shark, with a black body, big, glowing green eyes, and a pointy little beard. Samebito inhabit a vast underwater kingdom and have little contact with humans. If you find one on land, it is usually in some sort of trouble. But they are honest creatures and will repay any kindness offered them. A Samebito is featured in the tale of the noble hero Totaro, who invites the exiled monster to live in a lake near Totaro's castle and feeds him. When Totaro falls in love with Tamana, whose greedy father demands 10,000 jewels for her dowry, Samebito's tears of sympathy become precious gems, thus enabling the couple to wed.

Fig. 34. Samebito by Tam

Takujui—A monster similar to the *Kudan,* having a human head on the body of a beast, with eyes on its flanks and spiny projections down its back. It is an auspicious creature, appearing only in times of wise government.

Fig. 35. Tsuchi-Gumo

Tsuchi-Gumo—A monstrous, invincible spider. It preyed upon the populace until it was finally trapped in its cave with a steel net and then roasted to death in a fire. Similar giant spiders are often featured in Japanese folktales, as they also appear in the fantasies of J.R.R. Tolkein and J.K. Rowling. In these stories, travelers and heroes exploring ancient castles, dank caverns, or dark forests will come upon passages strung with great webs in which they get caught, and from which they must free themselves by killing the spider.

Uwabami—A monstrous flying serpent, sometimes portrayed with wings

Fig. 36. Uwabami

and sometimes without. It would fly down and scoop up human victims in its enormous jaws, until it was slain by the hero Yegara-no-Heida.

Yata Garasu—An immense, three-legged crow that serves as a divine messenger between humans and the gods.

Borean Creatures

Fig. 39. Haetae

Haetae—A leonine creature of stone. It feeds on fire, and therefore guards against it and all other forms of disruptive or violent change. It can bite the sun or moon, create an eclipse, and even challenge time itself. The Haetae also symbolizes water and justice. Statues of Haetae were installed at the gate outside the Kyongbok palace to protect the royal line and the nation.

Kumiho—A cruel, supernatural, vampiric, nine-tailed fox, it is what an ordinary fox becomes after living 1,000 years. Similar to the Japanese *Kitsune,* it can metamorphose into a beautiful woman—sometimes even a bride—in which form it seduces men and kills them. But, unlike the Kitsune, the Kumiho is always malevolent and predatory towards humans.

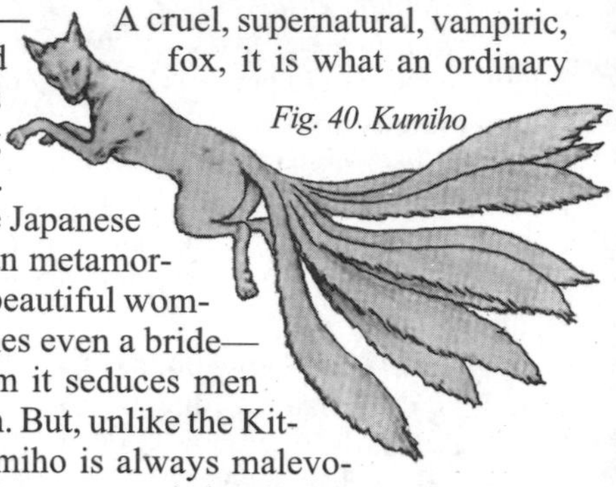

Fig. 40. Kumiho

Kyeryong—A creature of South Korean folklore that resembles a cross between a chicken and a Dragon (similar to a *Cockatrice*). There is a mountain by this name, in which is a pool where the female Kyeryong dwells. Women shamans bathe in this pool to obtain magickal powers. *Alyeong,* the first queen of Shilla, was said to the child of a Kyeryong.

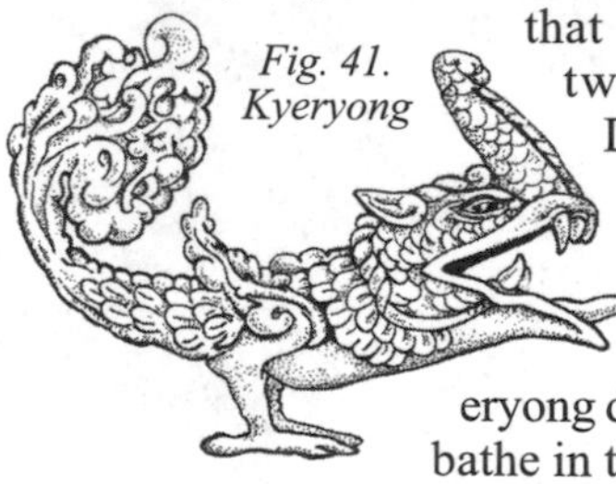

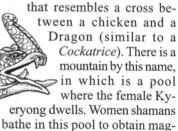

Fig. 41. Kyeryong

Monster Movies: Oriental Spirit-Creatures

Alakazam the Great (anime—1961): Monkey-King
Akira Kurosawa's Dreams (anime—1990): Kitsune
Pom Poko (anime—1994): Tanuki
Gensomaden Saiyuki (anime—1996): Kappa
Saiyuki: Reload (anime—1998): Kappa
Saiyuki: Requiem (anime—1998): Kappa
Saiyuki Reload:Gunlock (anime—1999): Kappa
Pokemon (anime—1999): Kitsune, Kappa, Tanuki
Spirited Away (anime—2001): Kappa
Inuyasha (anime—2001): Kitsune/Tanuki
Naruto (anime—2004): Kitsune/Tanuki
Princess Raccoon (anime—2005): Tanuki
The Great Youkai War (anime—2005): Tengu
Hellboy: Sword of Storms (anime—2006): Kappa, Kitsune

17. FEARSOME CRITTERS
OF LUMBERJACK CAMPFIRE TALES
By Oberon Zell-Ravenheart

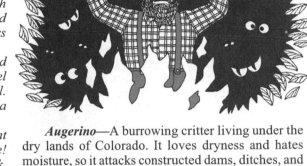

As a tenderfoot who has just joined the logging crew, this is your first night sitting around the camp-fire with these burly and boisterous men who have been living in these timber woods and felling these trees for a long time. They laugh and joke easily with one another as they pass the whiskey bottle around the fire. Some of their stories would scare the hairs off a razorback hog!

After a pot of beans, a few shots of whiskey, and a couple of cups of strong and bitter coffee, you feel the urge to go water the shrubbery or enrich the soil. But as you get up to leave, a thick-bearded giant of a man delivers a warning from across the campfire:

"Now, don't you go gettin' too far from the light of the fire! There's some fearsome critters out there! They'll sneak up on you from behind outta the dark. Why, ain't you never heerd of the...."

—Oberon Zell

EARSOME CRITTERS IS A TERM coined by 19th-century American and Canadian lumberjacks to encompass an endless and entertaining assortment of imaginary animals with colorful names, which were claimed to inhabit the vast timber woods of North America. Invented as preposterous explanations for the unknown dangers and difficulties that sometimes claimed the lives of loggers, these wacky beasts were created out of whole cloth in tall tales and practical jokes to tease and impress gullible tourists and newcomers to the logging camps. Fearsome Critters ranged from downright silly to bizarre and terrifying. Other regions and countries have similar traditions, such as the French *Dahu*, the Scottish *Wild Haggis*, and the Australian *Drop Bears* and *Bunyips*. Their countless stories have been collected and compiled by folklore enthusiasts. Here are but a few of the more famous examples:

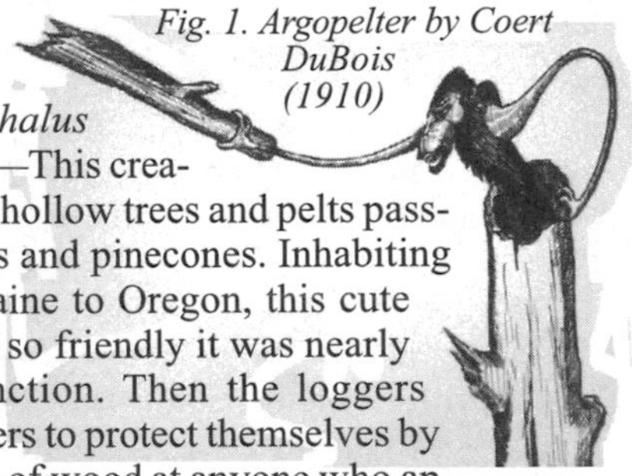

Argopelter **or *Forest Monkey*** (*Anthrocephalus craniofractens*)—This creature lives inside hollow trees and pelts passersby with twigs and pinecones. Inhabiting forests from Maine to Oregon, this cute little critter was so friendly it was nearly hunted to extinction. Then the loggers taught Argopelters to protect themselves by throwing pieces of wood at anyone who approached their trees.[1]

Fig. 1. Argopelter by Coert DuBois (1910)

Augerino—A burrowing critter living under the dry lands of Colorado. It loves dryness and hates moisture, so it attacks constructed dams, ditches, and watercourses, releasing the water. As it lives underground, it has never been seen, and therefore cannot be described.

Axhandle Hound—It has a long, thin body in the shape of—you guessed it!—an ax handle, with its head resembling the axhead. This odd body is supported by four stubby legs, bringing to mind images of Dachshunds. It is said to eat the handles of any axes left unattended.

Fig. 2. Axhandle Hound

Billdad (*Saltipiscator falcorostratus*)—An odd critter from Maine, roughly the size of a beaver. It has a hooked beak like a hawk's, webbed feet, and powerful, kangaroo-like hind legs that allow it to jump up to 60 yards. It dwells near rivers and streams and lives on a diet of fish, which it stuns with a slap of its heavy, flat tail.[2]

Fig. 3. Billdad by DuBois

Cactus Cat (*Cactifelinus inebrius*; also *Gysacutus*)—The Cactus Cat is the size of the average housecat and covered with prickly spines like those on a hedgehog. Even the ears are covered in spikes. The spines of the legs and tail are particularly long and sharp. The Cactus Cat enjoys drinking the fermented juice of cacti, upon which it gets royally drunk.

Fig. 4. Cactus Cat by DuBois

Dahu (*Rupicapra vacca montanus*)—A French critter similar to the American *Gyascutus*. It looks much like a deer or chamois, except that the legs on one side of its body are much shorter than those on the other, thus enabling it to walk along the steep

Fig. 5. Dahu

slopes of its mountainous environment. Of course, it can only walk around the mountain in one direction. There are two subspecies, which seldom interbreed: the *Laevogyrous dahu* (which have shorter legs on the left side), and the *Dextrogyre dahu* (with shorter right legs).[3]

Drop Bears—Unusually large, vicious, carnivorous koalas that inhabit eucalyptus trees in the Australian Outback and attack their prey by dropping onto their heads from above. It is said that sticking forks in your hair or spreading Vegemite or toothpaste behind your ears will deter the critters. To find out whether there is a Drop Bear in a tree, lie down on your back under the tree and spit upward. If a Drop Bear is in the tree, it will spit back at you.[4]

Fig. 6. Drop Bear by Stale Cracker

Interestingly, the Drop Bear myth may have its origins with the carnivorous *Phascolarctos involus*, or perhaps *Thylacoleo carnifex*—prehistoric marsupials about twice the size of modern koalas. *Thylacoleo* is thought to have been an arboreal predator that may well have ambushed prey by dropping on it from overhead branches.

Fig. 7. Terrashots by DuBois

Funeral Mountain Terrashot (*Funericorpus displosissumum*)—A strange critter inhabiting California's Funeral Mountains, which were named for it. It has a shell-encased, casket-like body, 6–8 feet long, and four spindly legs upon which it wobbles uncertainly. It lives in meadows in the high range, multiplying until it is seized by a desire to migrate. Forming a long procession, the Terrashots march out of the mountains into the desert. When they encounter the hot sands they explode one after the other, leaving grave-shaped holes.[5]

Gillygaloo—A bird that nested on the slopes of Paul Bunyan's famous Pyramid Forty Acres, laying square eggs to keep them from rolling down the steep incline and breaking. Lumberjacks hard-boiled these eggs and used them for dice.[6]

Glawackus—A ferocious critter said to resemble a hybrid of a bear, a panther, and a lion. Native to New England, it was allegedly sighted in 1939 in Glastonbury, Connecticut, and in 1944 in Frizzelburg, Massachusetts.

Goofang—A fish that swims backward to keep the water from irritating its highly sensitive eyes. It has been described as being "about the size of a sunfish, only much bigger."[7]

Goofus Bird—A bird that builds its nest upside down and flies backward, not caring where it's going but only where it's been.[8]

Gumberoo (*Melagaster repercussus*)—Found in the Pacific Northwest, this critter hides out in the bases of large, burned-out cedar trees, which turn it charcoal black. It resembles a black bear, but is nearly hairless. When it emerges it is always hungry, and devours anything it can find. It can eat an entire horse at one sitting, which distends its belly greatly. Its tough, rubbery hide is extremely flammable, and in a forest fire it burns with explosive force, leaving a smell similar to burning rubber. It is derived from the European *Gulon*.[9]

Fig. 8. Gumberoo, DuBois

Gyascutus (also called *Sidehill Dodge Hodag*, *Sidehill Gouger*, or *Sidehill Dianther*)—A quadruped living in the Rocky Mountains whose legs are longer on one side than the other to facilitate living on hillsides, around which it can only go one way. Around the size of a white-tailed deer, it has a spiked tail and eats rocks. It is certainly related to the European *Dahu*. A similar critter in Vermont is known as the *Wampahoofus*, and the American Southwest has the peccary-like *Rackabore*.

Fig. 9. Gyascutus

Haggis (*Haggis Scotticus*)— Native to the Scottish Highlands, this is a three-legged bird with vestigial wings and fierce fangs. Each leg is a different length, one short and two long, which allows it to run rapidly around the mountains and hillsides of its natural habitat. However, once it reaches the top of a hill, it loses its balance and tumbles into the valley below. Males run only clockwise and females, only counterclockwise. A group of Haggis is known as a heap. Haggis meat is a local delicacy.[10]

Fig. 10. Haggis by OZ

Hidebehind—A critter that you may spot in the corner of your eye, but it is so fast that it can hide behind the nearest tree before you can turn around. Nobody knows what it looks like because no one has ever seen one clearly. Hidebehinds are aggressive and deadly, attacking and eating anyone who intrudes upon their territory.

Hodag—Several varieties are known, of which the largest is the **Shovel-Nosed Hodag** (*Nasobatilus hystrivoratus*). Said to be very intelligent, it is the size of a rhinoceros, with a hairless body suggestive of the patterns on Mackinaw clothing. On its nose, instead of a horn, there is a large, spade-shaped bony growth.

Fig. 11. Shovel-Nosed Hodag, DuBois

This is used for cutting the roots of trees and knocking them over in order to get to its favorite food, porcupines, which it then devours head first. It is found only in Wisconsin and Minnesota.[11]

The **Black Hodag** (*Bovinus spiritualis*), is the second largest and most ferocious of the three, 7 feet or more in length, 3 feet high at the shoulder, and weighing approximately 185 pounds. It is covered with black fur, and has two horns on its head and spikes along its back.

Smallest of all, the **Cave Hodag** seems to be a slight modification or evolutionary successor of the Sidehill Dodge Hodag, or *Gyascutus*, with three glowing eyes which enable it to see in limestone caves throughout the United States.

Hoop Snake— Referred to in the Pecos Bill stories, a Hoop Snake can grasp its tail in its jaws and roll as a wheel does after its prey. At the last second, the snake straightens out and skewers its victim with its venomous tail. The only escape is to hide behind a tree, which receives the deadly blow instead and promptly dies from the poison. The basis of this critter is the Mud Snake (*Farancia abacura*), popularly called Hoop Snake or Stinging Snake, for the sharply pointed tail with which it prods its prey.

Fig. 12. Hoop Snake

Hugag (*Rythmopes inarticulatus*)—Found from Hudson Bay down to Wisconsin and Minnesota, this critter is the size of a moose, with jointless legs and a long upper lip which prevents it from grazing, lest it trample its lip into the dirt. Because it cannot lie down, it must lean against a tree to sleep. Hunters notch likely trees, and when the Hugag leans against them, both tree and beast fall over, whereupon it is easily dispatched. In European bestiaries, this animal is known as the *Achlis*.[12]

Fig. 13. Hugag by DuBois

Joint Snake—A snake that can break itself, or be cut, into pieces and then reassemble itself. It was used as a symbol in the American Revolution, along with the motto, "Join, or die." The myth is based on the 2 to 3-foot-long, legless Glass Snake Lizard (*Ophisaurus*) that can regenerate its tail after it is broken off. Such lizards are, in fact, often called joint snakes.

Pinnacle Grouse— This odd bird has only a single wing, which allows it fly in one direction only around the top of a conical hill. The color of its plumage varies according to the season and the condition of the observer.[13]

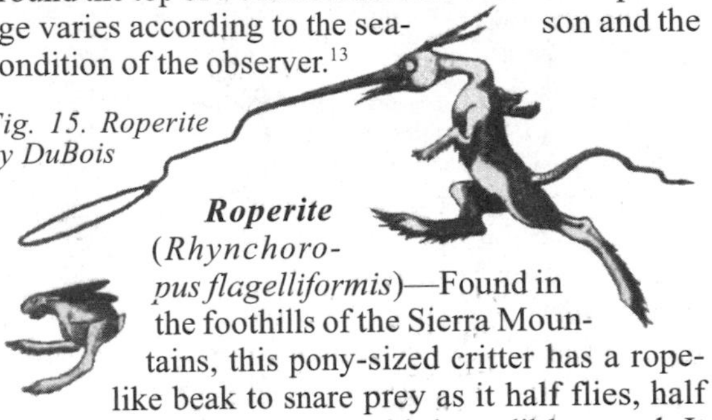

Fig. 14. "Join, or die"

Fig. 15. Roperite by DuBois

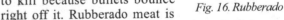

Roperite (*Rhynchoropus flagelliformis*)—Found in the foothills of the Sierra Mountains, this pony-sized critter has a rope-like beak to snare prey as it half flies, half bounds across the country with incredible speed. It has a large set of rattles on its tail which it vibrates as a rattlesnake does when in pursuit of game. Its leathery skin and horny feet are impervious to injury.[14]

Rubberado (or *Bouncing Porcupine*)—A North American critter with rubbery flesh and a spherical, prickly body. Instead of walking or crawling, it bounces from place to place. Every time it bounces it laughs. It is difficult to kill because bullets bounce right off it. Rubberado meat is quite tasty, but you'll find yourself bouncing around and laughing for a couple of days after eating it.[15]

Fig. 16. Rubberado

Shagamaw (*Bipedester delusissimus*)—This bipedal critter follows logging roads and trails through the woods, its tracks changing every quarter mile from those of a moose to a bear. This because its back feet are like those of a moose, but its front feet are just like a bear's. It walks exactly 440 steps on its hind legs, then flips over to walk on its forelegs, leaving very confusing trails.[16]

Fig. 17. Shagamaw, DuBois

Slide-Rock Bolter (*Macrostoma saxiperrumptus*)—Living on Colorado mountain slopes that exceed a 45-degree incline, this huge, whale-like critter has a tail with grab hooks

Fig. 19. Slide-Rock Bolter by DuBois

which it fastens over the edge of a ridge. When it sights tourists, it releases its tail and toboggans down the slope, aided by drooling skid grease. It scoops up its victims in its enormous, wide maw and continues its slide up the opposite slope, where it again hooks its tail into place and awaits its next meal.[17]

Snoligaster
(*Dorsohastatus caudirotula*)— This monstrous critter from Lake Okeechobee,

Fig. 20. Snoligaster by DuBois

Florida, resembles a gigantic crocodile, and is covered with long, glossy fur. It has no legs or fins, but one long spike protrudes from its back. At the end of its tail are three bony plates that can rotate like a propeller, driving it through the muddy water like a torpedo. It tosses its human victims onto its back, impaling them on the spike. It later rolls over and scrapes them off to be eaten. It is derived from the *Snallygaster*, a pterodactyl-like monster said to inhabit the Blue Ridge Mountains of Maryland.[18]

Fig. 21. Wasset, DuBois

Snow Wasset (*Mustelinopsis subtivorax*)—This creature dwells in the most northerly parts of Canada. When it hibernates in the summer it sprouts rudimentary legs, its hair turns green, and it curls up in a cranberry bush. But in the winter, it turns white and sheds its legs, swimming through the snow like a snake to snatch and devour prey —sometimes even wolves, for it is four times as big and 40 times as active as they are.

Splintercat (*Felynx arbordiffusus*)—A ferocious nocturnal feline found east of the Rockies, from the Great Lakes to the Gulf. It flies through the air with terrific speed; when it hits a large tree it knocks off the branches, withers the trunk, and

Fig. 22. Splintercat, DuBois

leaves a dead snag standing. It does this to expose bees and the honey that it loves to eat. However, smashing into trees with its head gives it a constant headache, which always put it in a foul mood. Therefore, one should never approach a Splintercat.[19]

Squonk (*Lacrimacorpus dissolvens*)—A pathetic little critter living in the hemlock forests of northern Pennsylvania. Because its ill-fitting skin is cov-

Fig. 23. Squonk

ered with warts and other blemishes, the Squonk stays in hiding and weeps constantly in misery over its own ugliness. When cornered, it dissolves completely from embarrassment into a pool of tears and bubbles.[20]

Teaketteler—Native to Minnesota and Wisconsin, it resembles a small, stubby-legged dog with the ears of a cat. It always walks backward, issuing steam from its mouth as it whistles. It is named for the sound it makes, which is similar to a boiling teakettle. It is very shy, but if a whistling kettle is heard and nowhere to be found, it is sure to be a Teaketteler.[21]

Tripodero (*Collapsofemuris geocatapeltes*)—This Californian critter has two telescoping legs and a tail like a kangaroo's. These enable it to raise itself to a great height and see over the chaparral, or lower to a compact form to move through the underbrush. When it sights game, it adjusts the angle of

Fig. 24. Tripodero, DuBois

its tripod, takes aim with its huge snout, and blows a quid of dried clay, knocking its victim senseless.[22]

Upland Trout—A species of flying fish that is afraid of water and lives on land, preferring to build its nests high in trees. It has a delicious flavor, and experienced campers will often send newcomers out into the woods to search for nests.[7]

Wapaloosie (*Geometrigradus cilioretractus*)—Found from the Pacific coast to Idaho, this squirrel-sized critter lives on shelf fungus on high trees. Its feet and toes are like those of a woodpecker, and it "humps" along like a measuring-worm caterpillar. Its tail is spiked at the end to provide good anchorage as it climbs.[23]

Fig. 25. Wapaloosie by DuBois

Whintosser (*Cephalovertens semperambulatus*)—A mean and vicious critter that lives in an area ranging from Central America to the California Coast Range. Its head and tail can swivel and rotate at the rate of hundreds of rpm. Its body is long and triangular, and its three

Fig. 27. Whintosser by DuBois

sets of legs enable it to always land right side up—a useful ability in earthquake country.[25]

Whirling Whimpus (*Turbinoccissus nebuloides*)

—A bloodthirsty, gorilla-like critter from Tennessee with enormous hands. Stationing itself at a bend in a trail, it stands upon its small legs and whirls rapidly, making a droning sound, until it becomes invisible. Any unsuspecting creature or person coming along the path is smashed to jelly by the whirling massive paws.[24]

Fig. 26. Whimpus

III. MONSTERS OF MYSTERY

AQUATIC ENIGMAS
18. LAKE MONSTERS

By Oberon Zell-Ravenheart

Ian Daniels, from a sculpture by Oberon Zell

On another occasion, when the blessed man was living in the province of the Picts, he was obliged to cross the river Nesa (the Ness); and when he reached the bank of the river, he saw some of the inhabitants burying an unfortunate man, who was a short time before seized, as he was swimming, and bitten most severely by a monster that lived in the water. The blessed man, on hearing this, was so far from being dismayed, that he directed one of his companions to swim over and row across the coble that was moored at the farther bank. But the monster, which, so far from being satiated, was only roused for more prey, was lying at the bottom of the stream, and when it felt the water disturbed above by the man swimming, suddenly rushed out, and, giving an awful roar, darted after him, with its mouth wide open. Then the blessed man observing this, raised his holy hand and, invoking the name of God, formed the saving sign of the

cross in the air, and commanded the ferocious monster, saying, "Thou shalt go no further, nor touch the man; go back with all speed." Then at the voice of the saint, the monster was terrified, and fled more quickly than if it had been pulled back with ropes....

Fig. 1. St. Columba vs. Nessie

—From "How an Aquatic Monster was driven off by virtue of the blessed man's prayer."
Life of Saint Columba, Founder of Hy. by Adamnan, Ninth Abbot of that Monastery, 1874[1]

ARGE AND AS-YET-UNIDENTIFIED creatures inhabiting the murky depths of Loch Ness, Loch Morar, and around 250–300 other peat-filled lakes, lochs, swamps, and bogs of Scotland, Ireland, Canada, and other countries throughout the world have aroused both curiosity and controversy since 565 CE, when St. Columba

of Iona (521–597), the first Christian missionary to Scotland, had a legendary encounter with "a certaine water monster" on the banks of Loch Ness.

But even earlier, at the time of St Patrick (390–474 CE), a female Lake-Monster called the *Caoránach* and her demonic brood terrorized Donegal in Ireland. The saint banished her to the depths of Lough Derg, where she is said to remain still.

Nearly all of the bodies of water said to be inhabited by monsters are extraordinarily deep and icy cold, which seems to contradict the popular assumption that these creatures are reptilian. These lakes were also connected at one time with the sea during the last glacial epoch, and are on the spawning routes of fish such as salmon and eels.

Here we will consider only freshwater monsters, although the classic long-necked variety is similar enough to many reported Sea- Serpents to suggest a very close relationship (Chapter 19. "Sea Serpents."). Several distinct types of monstrous, lake-dwelling creatures have been described by eyewitnesses. Some of these are unusual due only to size, such as gigantic sturgeons, eels, and catfish. Others are within the accepted range of size for their species, but are reported from locations where such creatures should not be found, such as marine cetaceans in freshwater lakes, or tropical crocodiles in temperate regions. And still others would be perfectly normal in size and in their appropriate location—35–70 million years ago!

THE UNUSUAL SUSPECTS

Super Sturgeon (*Acipenser*), a prehistoric-looking, toothless ganoid fish with large boney plates, or scutes, forming a serrated ridge along its back. One of the oldest genera of fish in existence, with 21 known species, they are found in all waters of the Northern Hemisphere. Some individuals have been known to live for more than 200 years. Sturgeons ranging from 8 to 11 feet in length are not unusual, and some species grow much bigger. The Beluga Sturgeon (*A. Huso Huso*) of the Caspian and Black seas is one of the largest species, reaching enormous lengths of more than 16 feet and weights of more than 2,000 pounds. But the record belongs to a 27-foot-long Lake Sturgeon (*A. fulvescens*) caught in Russia. Sturgeons stir up the soft bottom mud with their projecting, wedge-shaped snouts, and with their sensitive whiskers, or barbels, they detect the mollusks, crustaceans, and small fish upon which they feed. Most species are now considered to be at least vulnerable, if not critically endangered, so sightings are rare but unforgettable.[2]

Among the Lake-Monsters that may reasonably be identified as super sturgeons is the ***Flathead Lake-Monster***—an enormous whale-like creature inhabiting a 28-mile-long, 300-foot-deep lake in the state of Montana. It was first reported in 1889. Witnesses say it is 15–20 feet long and steel-grey in color, with a roundish head and up to three humps. Most accounts describe it as resembling a White Sturgeon (*A. transmontanus*).

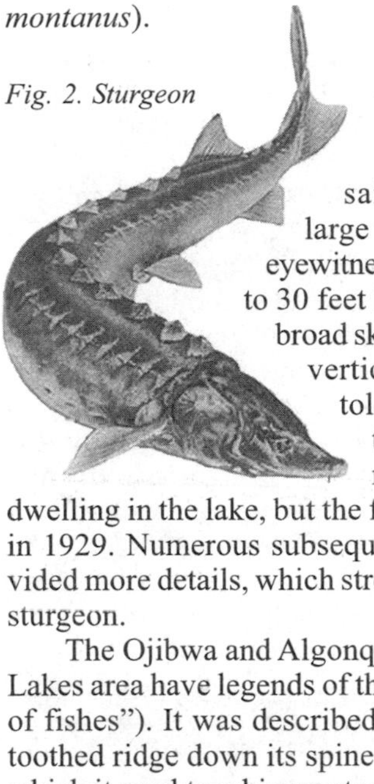

Fig. 2. Sturgeon

The frigid waters of Alaska's vast Lake Illiamna, in the Katmai National Preserve, are said to be inhabited by large unknown creatures that eyewitnesses describe as being up to 30 feet long, with grayish skin, broad skulls, slender bodies, and vertical tails. Aleut Indians told the first Russian settlers about a colony of man-eating monsters dwelling in the lake, but the first official report came in 1929. Numerous subsequent sightings have provided more details, which strongly suggest a gigantic sturgeon.

The Ojibwa and Algonquin Indians of the Great Lakes area have legends of the ***Mishipizhiw*** ("master of fishes"). It was described as catlike, with a saw-toothed ridge down its spine and a long, sinuous tail which it used to whip up storms and whirlpools.

In the folklore of the Alaskan Inuits, the ***Pal-Rai-Yuk*** are very long creatures with two heads, six legs, three stomachs, two tails, and a saw-toothed ridge down their backs. They inhabit creeks and river estuaries. All of these features suggest mating sturgeons.

And certainly we would expect Russia to have monstrous sturgeons, such as ***Brosnie***, a 16-foot-long, bioluminescent aquatic reptile with a serpentine head that inspires terror in the fishing communities around Russia's Lake Brosno and along the Volga River.

Enormous Eels (*Anguilla*) can reach as much as 30 feet in length. Although the common European Eel (*A. anguilla*) seldom exceeds 5 feet in length, Africa's *A. mossambica* and *A. marmorata* can both

reach about 6 feet. And the Conger Eel (*Conger conger*) can grow to more than 10 feet long. But much larger specimens have been reported since ancient times. In the 1890s, a gigantic eel was caught in a deep landlocked pool on the island of Reunion, near Mauritius, from which "steaks as thick as a man's thigh were cut."[3] Eels will sometimes swim on their sides at the surface of the water, thus producing the vertical undulations so often associated with Lake-Monsters.

Fig. 3. Eel swimming on side

For centuries, gigantic eels have been said to dwell in Scotland's Loch Awe. One of the few written accounts of these creatures comes to us from Timothy Pont (c.1562–1614), who described them as "big as ane horse with incredible length," and said they had frightened most of the fishermen away from the loch.

In 765-foot-deep Lake Ikeda, a volcanic crater lake on Japan's Kyushu Island, a 30-foot-long, humped creature called ***Issie*** has been seen and even photographed by numerous witnesses. Interestingly enough, the lake is also the home of humongous eels, some of which weigh as much as 33 pounds and measure 6 feet in length.

Newfoundland's Crescent Lake is said to be inhabited by a 5 to 15-foot-long, eel-like monster called ***Cressie***. Mysterious holes that appear in the winter ice are attributed to these creatures, and a couple of scuba divers searching for a plane that had fallen into the lake in the mid-1980s said they found themselves surrounded by a school of gigantic eels "as thick as a man's thigh," which attacked them viciously.

St. Cronan Mochua, who founded the Church and Abbey of Balla, in County Meath, Ireland, in 616 CE, first chronicled the ***Beast of Lough Ree*** after a group of hunters refused to pursue a stag that fled into the lake, for fear of the vicious monster that dwelled therein. Three priests encountered it in 1960, when a large,

Fig. 4 Lough Ree Monster

Fig. 6. Wels Catfish

black, eel-shaped animal reared its head not 300 feet from shore. According to their report, "it went down under the water and came up again in the form of a loop. The length from the end of the coil to the head was 6 feet…about 18 inches of head and neck [was] over the water. The head and neck were narrow in comparison to the thickness of a good-sized salmon. It was getting its propulsion from underneath the water, and we did not see all of it."[4]

Legends of a large, serpent-like monster dwelling in the muddy waters of Cayuga Lake, near Ithaca, New York, date back to the early 1800s. In 1929, people began reporting two animals, approximately 12–15 feet long, cavorting simultaneously along the lake's eastern shoreline. In the summer of 1974, teenager Steven Griffen was attacked while swimming by an "eel-like" creature whose powerful jaws broke his arm. In the spring of 1979, Jack Marshall, owner of J.T. Marshall Professional Diving Service, was boating with some friends on the lake when they nearly collided with a 30 to 35-foot "creature" that submerged before their astonished eyes. The creature has been nicknamed "Old Greeny."

Eel-like monsters have also been reported from the Zambales region of the Philippine island of Luzon, where as many as five huge, black serpentine creatures have been seen swimming in the Tikis River. Local Aetas insist that these animals are unlike any eels, fish, or snakes with which they are familiar. The first reported sighting was on November 5, 2002, when an Aleta boy mistook one for a floating log until it moved. Two months later, several witnesses observed a 7-foot-long, 3-foot-wide, black creature undulating silently down the river.

Colossal Catfish are named for
their prominent barbels, which resemble cat whiskers, Catfish (*Siluriformes*) are a diverse group of fish found primarily in freshwater environments on every continent except Antarctica. There are armor-plated as well as naked species, but none of them has scales. They include the toothless Mekong Giant Catfish (*Pangasianodon gigas*), indigenous to the Mekong basin in Southeast Asia. This very bulky fish has attained reported lengths of more than 16 feet, and is believed to be the world's largest freshwater fish.[5]

Fig. 5. Mekong Giant Catfish

The **Lukwata** is a carnivorous cryptid reported from Africa's Lake Victoria, which borders Uganda, Kenya and Tanzania. It is most commonly described as having a square head and a brownish body resembling that of a dolphin, with a white underbelly. Many local natives maintain that the Lukwata is a colossal 12-foot-long catfish, possibly a Wels (*Silurus glanis*), which is known to reach 10 feet in length and weigh 330 pounds. These fish are voracious predators, able to secrete a powerful acidic substance from their barbels to help digest large prey. Natives claim that the Lukwata often fights with crocodiles, their primary natural enemy.

Cetaceans and **crocodiles** have often been proposed as candidates for Lake-Monsters. Certainly these creatures are normally quite big enough to match the sizes described. Estuarine Crocodiles (*Crocodylus porosus*) are the largest of all living reptiles. Normally confined to Indonesia, they are known to reach 30 feet in length. A cetacean proposed by Antoon Cornelis Oudemans (1858–1943),[6] and favored by Roy Mackal and many other cryptozologists, is the prehistoric *Archaeocetid* ("ancient whale") named **Zeuglodon** or, erroneously, **Basilosaurus** ("king lizard") —an elongated, serpentine whale of the Eocene period, 37–40 million years ago.

Fig. 7. Zeuglodon (Basilosaurus)

Aquatic creatures with prominent dorsal fins can only be fish or cetaceans. An example is the monster of Lake Labynkr, Russia. It was first reported in 1964 by some hunters whose dog had chased a deer into the lake. Abruptly, both animals disappeared beneath the surface. Suddenly the placid water began to froth, and up came a large, black monster with a prominent dorsal fin, which emitted a horrible shriek before resubmerging. Later that year, a Soviet research team sighted three large objects about 900 feet from shore. These appeared to submerge and resurface simultaneously, suggesting they were all parts of the same animal.

In July of 1953, renowned geologist V.A. Tverdokhlebov sighted a monster in isolated Lake Vorota, in the Sordongnokh tablelands of Siberia. He described it as being approximately 30 feet long and 6 feet wide. Its head bore a pair of strange, light-colored markings, and it had a prominent dorsal fin that appeared to be facing backward. Swimming with vertical, porpoise-like undulations, it leapt from the water—making a tremendous splash—before submerging. This sounds very much like an Orca or Killer Whale (*Orcinus orca*), but how could one have gotten into this lake?

Fig. 8. Lake Vorota Beast

And then there is the presumably mated pair of monsters living in the depths of Lake Kariba, located in the Mashonaland West Province of Zimbabwe, Africa, near the southwestern border of Zambia. They also occasionally venture into the Zambenzi River. For centuries these creatures have been worshiped as gods by the Tonga, who call them the *Nyaminyami*. They are described by natives as scaly, serpentine creatures with fishlike heads, whereas others have reported sightings of gigantic, humpbacked, almost whale-like animals. Some claim that at least one of the Nyaminyami has reached a length of 120 feet!

A monster dubbed "Slimy Slim" is said to inhabit the depths of Lake Payette in Idaho. It has a serpentine body at least 36 feet long and a head like a crocodile's. And the Kiowa Indians of America's southern plains tell of a great, alligator-like beast with two horns on its head, which are considered powerful medicine for healing as well a poison.

Plesiosaurs (Greek, "near lizard") are long-necked, aquatic reptiles contemporary with the dinosaurs. Ranging in size from 15 to 50 feet long, they had squat, flattened bodies, short tails, and four flippers. Although they were supposedly exterminated 65 million years ago along with the dinosaurs, creatures said to resemble them continue to be reported worldwide as Sea-Serpents and Lake- Monsters. In most cases, these reports are based only on the sight of a longish neck, but in 1955, naturalist Alexander Laime reported seeing three such creatures sunning themselves on rocks at the summit of the Auyan-tepui River in Venezuela, the location of Arthur Conan Doyle's "Lost World." Two French explorers to the same area claimed to have seen a similar animal in 1990.

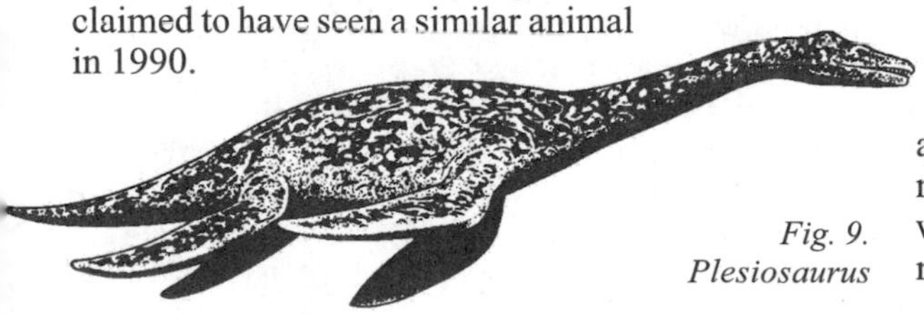

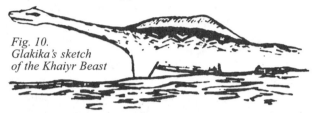

Fig. 9. Plesiosaurus

A monster dwelling in the actively volcanic Lake Khaiyr in the remote Yanski area of Yakutsk, eastern Siberia, has been dubbed the ***Khaiyr Beast***. It was first reported by a Russian mineralogist, Mr. Gladkika, who was in the region to sample rare mineral deposits. As he sat on the lake shore, a jet-black, long-necked, small-headed animal resembling a plesiosaur emerged from the water to graze on the long grass growing on the bank. (Fig. 11) A few days later, the expedition chief and two of his assistants observed the creature in the center of the lake. Their description matched Gladkika's, but they added a prominent dorsal fin—a feature normally found only in fish and cetaceans. All witnesses agreed that the monster's skin was so black as to appear almost blue.

Fig. 10. Glakika's sketch of the Khaiyr Beast

An immense, plesiosaur-like creature with a long, tapering neck and a donkey-like body with flippers is said to lurk in the dense papyrus swamps around Lake No in south-central Sudan, east Africa. It emits a cry like the trumpeting of elephants. Bristling tendrils protrude from the animal's muzzle that aid it in snaring prey. Called the ***Lau***, it was brought to international attention in 1914 when a group of Shilluk natives killed a specimen in the swamps of Addar to use its bones in protective amulets.

Another African "plesiosaur" is the ***Inkanyamba***, said to dwell in the deep pools and caverns beneath South Africa's Howick Falls. Affectionately dubbed "Howie," it is described as a gigantic, plesiosaur-like creature, up to 24 feet long, with skin like a crocodile's, a finned mane, large fore flippers, red eyes, and a nasty disposition. Such beasts are depicted in 2,000-year-old Aboriginal petroglyphs throughout the KwaZulu-Natal area, where they have been feared by the Zulu and Xhosa natives for millennia.

Fig. 11. Inkanyamba

LONGNECKED "ORMS"

Now we come to the most frequently reported and enigmatic of all mysterious creatures: the long-necked Lake-Monster, or ***Orm***. Despite countless eyewitness reports spanning many centuries and even a number of photographs, no actual specimen or other substantive evidence of its existence has yet been produced. It is commonly described as an immense, serpentine creature with a head and neck proportioned similarly to that of a horse or camel, complete with ears. Some witnesses, however, identify these appendages as horns, so the same animals may also be called Horse-Eels, Water-Horses, Horse-Heads, Water-Bulls, Sea-Goats, or Horned Serpents. Sometimes they are said to have glowing red or yellow eyes, great fangs, or even the ability to breathe fire.

They move in vertical undulations, and often show several keeled humps above the water. A single hump looks very much like an overturned boat. They normally range in size between 15 and 30 feet long, but specimens more than twice that size have been reported in a few instances. Small front flippers have sometimes been seen, rarely rear ones or tails.

The poster child of this class is the famous monster affectionately referred to as **Nessie**, inhabiting the murky 755-foot depths of 23-mile-long Loch Ness in the Scottish Highlands. Its bulky, undulating body has been reported as being up to 30 feet long, sometimes showing several humps above the surface. Its head and neck are proportioned similarly to those of a horse or giraffe, and are topped with small, hornlike projections. The earliest recorded appearances were in 565 and 690 CE, and continued sporadically through the centuries. But the number of sightings increased dramatically after the construction of a public motorway along the Loch in 1933.

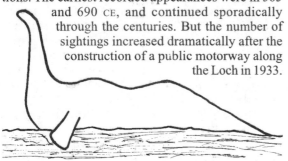

Fig. 12. Sketch by Margaret Munroe of the animal she saw on Borham Beach, Loch Ness, on 6/3/34.

Lake-Monsters of this description have been reported in at least 265 bodies of water around the world. These include virtually every loch in Scotland, as well as countless other similar habitats across all of northern Europe, Russia, Asia, Canada, and even further afield, including sub-Saharan Africa and the United States. Here are a few typical examples:

Arkaig Monster—A long-necked, wide-bodied, Lake-Monster with four flippers, similar to the famous Loch Ness Monster, and said to inhabit Loch Arkaig, Scotland. Sightings have been reported since the mid-1800s.

Ashuaps—A Nessie-like Water-Monster that lives in Lac Saint-Jean, in Canada. Ashuaps is about 60 feet long with a black hide. The first recorded sighting was in 1950, and it has been seen many times since.

Beast of Bynoe—A plesiosaur-like animal reputed to haunt Bynoe Bay near Darwin, Australia, and supposedly depicted in a series of Aborigine cave paintings.

Bruckee—An enormous, four-footed Lake-Monster said to inhabit the Lough of Shandangan in Ireland.

Caoránach— (or *Keeronagh*) A female Lake Monster and her demonic brood that terrorized Donegal in Ireland, at the time of St Patrick (390-474 CE). The Saint banished her to the depths of Lough Derg, where she is said to remain still.

Champ—A horned monster reported for at least 400 years to inhabit Lake Champlain, on the border between Quebec and Vermont. The Abenaki Iroquois Indians call it *Tatosok*. It is 20–30 feet long, with a barrel-shaped body and horselike head. There have been many sightings and even photographs.

Fig. 13. "Champ." Photo taken July 1977 by Sandra Mansi

Elbst—A serpentine Lake-Monster reported from 1584 to 1926 as dwelling in the depths of the Selisbergsee near Lucerne, Switzerland. It is described as dragon-like, the size of two upturned boats, with four clawed feet and a huge, porcine head.

Gryttie—A monster reported to be dwelling in the frigid depths of Lake Gryttjen in central Sweden. Described alternately as being serpentine or large and round, this animal has been sighted numerous times since the 1980s.

Heavenly Lake Monster—A mysterious creature reported for more than a century to be dwelling in China's deep, volcanically formed Lake Chang bai shan Tianchi, near the border of North Korea. First brought to public attention in 1968, it is described as being approximately 30 feet long, grayish-black, with a head like that of a horse or dog and two small horns.

Igopogo—A seldom-seen monster dwelling in circular Lake Simcoe, just north of Toronto, Ontaria, Canada. It has been described as having a neck resembling a stove pipe, crowned by an emphatically doglike head.

Leelanau—A monster inhabiting Lake Leelanau in Michigan. It is described as having a long neck, an equally long tail, and two large eyes. It first appeared after a dam was built in the late 1800s, which raised the water level 10–12 feet and created a marshy environment where the creature was said to thrive. In the summer of 1910, a teenager named William Gauthier attempted to tie his rowboat to what appeared to be one of several dead tree stumps jutting out of the water. He chose a tree that was approximately 5 feet tall and 6 inches thick, but when the rope touched the snag, two eyes suddenly popped open right in front of the horrified boy's face. After staring at each other for a few moments, the animal dove beneath the boat. Gauthier claimed that the creature was so long that its submerged head appeared on the far side of the boat while its tail remained in front of him. It has been many years since the last reported sighting.[7]

Lizzie—A monster reported to be dwelling in the depths of the Great Glen's Loch Lochy in Scotland (which is separated from Loch Ness only by Loch Oich). First spotted near Spean Bridge in 1929 by two game wardens, Lizzie is described as 35 feet long with three distinct humps running along its back. Many subsequent sightings were chronicled in 1933 by the monks of Fort Augustus Abbey. In July of 1960, Eric Robinson, his family, and nine other witnesses observed a creature they estimated to be 30–40 feet in length, with a dark back and pale underbelly. As they watched, it rolled in the water, exposing a huge flipper, before disappearing below the surface. And in 1996, Alastair Stevenson had a terrifying encounter while fishing on the loch. An animal approximately 18 feet long and shaped like an overturned rowboat snatched his bait and began pulling his boat until the line snapped. Later that year, an expedition to Loch Lochy of the Official Loch Ness Monster Fan Club had a sonar hit of an object 18–20 feet long moving at a depth of 160 feet toward the center of the loch, which is more than 300 feet deep.[8]

Lough Fadda Beast—A long-necked monster inhabiting Ireland's Lough (Lake) Fadda. The first report came in 1954, when Georgina Carberry and several companions encountered a "long-necked monstrosity" which suddenly thrust its head out of the water and bore toward their boat. "The head was about 3 feet out of the water, in a long curve," and its mouth was wide open, revealing whiteness within. At the last moment, the creature dove beneath the boat and then reemerged on the other side, displaying two distinct humps on its back. In 1965, inspired by this encounter, members of the Loch Ness Investigation Bureau detonated 5 pounds of gelignite in the same location as the Carberry encounter. Within seconds of the explosion, a large, dark object rose to the surface. The creature thrashed so wildly that it was difficult to make out any details, but all witnesses agreed that it resembled no other known animal.[9]

Manipogo—A monster reported by many witnesses in Canada's Lake Manitoba, as well as in nearby Lake Winnipeg, Lake Winnipegosis, Lake Dauphin, Lake Cedar, and Dirty Lake. Known by local Indians since they first settled the area, the creature is described as being 12–24 feet long and dark green or muddy-brown in color, and resembling a giant eel or snake with a single hump in the middle of its elongated body. Its head resembles that of a snake or a sheep. On August 10, 1960, three were seen swimming together, and two years later one was photographed.[10]

Fig. 15. Photo taken on Aug. 12, 1962 by Richard Vincent

Mjosa—A typical long-necked Lake-Monster reported for centuries in Norway's Lake Mjosa, near Lillehammer. The fjord lake is Norway's largest body of fresh water, nearly 100 miles long, more than 1,400 feet deep, and with a surface area of 400 square miles.

Monster of Brompton—A typical Lake-Monster sighted during the 1970s in Lake Brompton, Lycoming County, Pennsylvania. It was grey-green in color, with a three-humped back extending about 8 feet above the surface. It had a horselike head with bristles around its mouth. Its rapid passage left a 250-foot-long wake in the murky waters, frightening fishermen trying to avoid it.

Morag—A monster dwelling in the 1,000-foot depths of Loch Morar, Scotland. Numerous witnesses during the 19th and 20th centuries described a green or brown serpentine creature around 25–30 feet long with multiple humps. These humps, called "funeral boats," are often seen gliding across the Loch, and are said to herald the death of a clan member. In 1969, Morag even attacked a boat, and was beaten off with oars and rifles.

Nahuelito—A monster reported to be inhabiting Argentina's Lago (lake) Nahuel Huapi. For centuries, local Indians have told of a gigantic creature dwelling in the lake. They described the beast as having no head, legs, or tail. George Garrett, who saw it in 1910, said it "appeared to be 15 or 20 feet in diameter, and perhaps 6 feet above the water." In 1922, American gold prospector Martin Sheffield reported seeing an aquatic animal that moved like a crocodile, but bore an extended, swanlike neck. And in 1994, a number of tourists witnessed what they described as a headless whale with a humped back and small fins along its side frolicking in the water.

Fig. 16. Nahuelito

Ogopogo—A Lake-Monster inhabiting Lake Okanagan in British Columbia, Canada. The Shushwap Indians called it *Naitaka* ("long fish"). Said to dwell in a cave under an island in the middle of the lake, it was depicted in rock paintings and given effi-

Fig. 17. Ogopogo

gy offerings of propitiation. Many sightings have been recorded since it first received international coverage in the 1850s. In 1975, it was observed churning the lake waters and smashing up through the winter ice. Eyewitness reports are inconsistent at best. Some tell of an enormous log, 15–20 feet long and 1–2 feet in diameter, with a horse- or goat-like head; some, an undulating, serpentine form with several humps; others, a creature with saw-toothed ridges on its back like those on a sturgeon; and still others, a smooth back with several fins. In 1914, a group of Indians found a decomposing carcass on Rattlesnake Island. The bluish-gray body was about 5–6 feet long, and appeared to weigh about 400 pounds. It bore four distinct flippers and a long tail, but there was no sign of a head.[11]

Fig. 18. Naitaka–Shushwap petroglyph

Oich Monster—An enormous beast living in Loch Oich, Scotland, a narrow stretch of fresh water feeding directly into Loch Lochy (home of Lizzie) and separated from Loch Ness by the Caledonian Canal. Sightings date back to the 19th century. It is described as an horse- or dog-headed serpent, with black skin, two humps, and a long, horselike mane.[21]

Ponik—A monster inhabiting Lake Pohenegamook in Quebec, Canada. According to eyewitnesses, it resembles an overturned canoe about 36–40 feet long, with a ridge down its back, a head like a horse's or cow's, no ears, and long, catfish-like whiskers. Some witnesses have reported three humps and two large flippers.

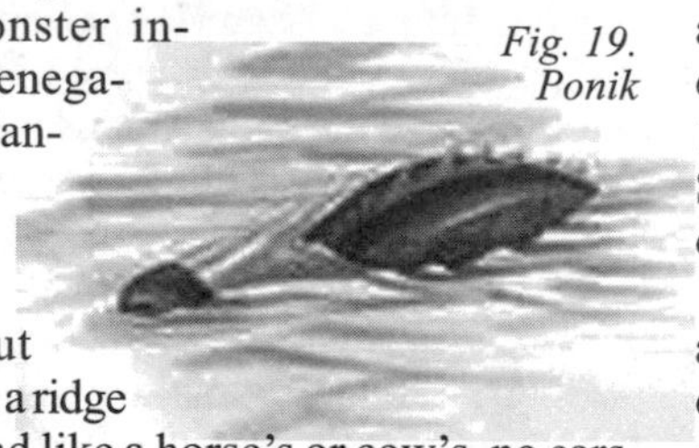

Fig. 19. Ponik

Seljordsorm (or *Selma*)—A Lake-Monster dwelling in 12-mile-long Lake Seljordsvatnet, near Telemark, Norway. First sighted in 1750 by Gunleik Andersson, it has been seen more than 100 times since. It is usually described as serpentine, about 30 feet long, with a snakelike head and several humps on its back. In 1880, an unnamed woman managed to cut one of the animals in half. The lower portion squirmed back into the lake, but the front part of the beast remained on shore, where it rotted away without any tissue samples being taken. In 1986, Aasmund Skori described it as resembling a black bow lying on the calm lake surface. It was 6 feet long and very thick, and the water around it was frothing and foaming.[12]

Shielagh—A monster lurking in Scotland's 17-mile-long Loch Shiel, just south of Loch Morar (home of Morag). It is described as a 70-foot-long beast with three large humps along its back. The earliest recorded sightings go back to 1874, and continued through the turn of the 20th century. Then the animal was not seen again until 1997 or '98, when a new spate of sightings was reported, including one in which four creatures were seen simultaneously.

Storsjöodjuret ("great lake monster"; or *Storsie*)—A horned or long-eared monster said to inhabit Lake Storsjön, in the province of Jämtland, Sweden. Reported since 1635, descriptions

have varied over the years, leading some to speculate that there is more than one. Some witnesses have described it

Fig. 20. Storsjöodjuret cartoon by Karl Iwar

as serpentine, with multiple humps, a feline or canine head, and grayish skin. Others have claimed that the creature is short and fat, with a rounded head. Many have compared it to a crocodile, and others have likened it to an eel or otter. Some witnesses have noted large flippers, whereas others describe strong back legs and short forelimbs. Almost all agree that it is 20–30 feet in length, with large eyes and a gaping mouth. Whatever it is, in 1986, it was officially listed as a protected species. But the most remarkable evidence is the discovery on the lakeshore, on June 18, 1984, of a small carcass that is believed to be a Storsjöodjuret embryo. This preserved carcass now occupies a glass jar in the Museum of Jämtland.[13]

Tahoe Tessie—Reported to inhabit Lake Tahoe, a 22-mile-long, 12-mile-wide, 1,645-foot-deep lake on the California-Nevada border, Tessie is usually described as more than 60 feet long, with an undulating, serpentine body, dark skin, and reptilian features. Some witnesses say it resembles a gigantic sturgeon. Legends of this creature date from the mid-1800s, when Washoe and Paiute Indians told Caucasian settlers about the "monster" dwelling in the lake. In the mid-1970's, renowned French oceanographer Jacques Cousteau led an expedition to explore the depths of Lake Tahoe. Cousteau encountered something so ter-

Fig. 21. Tahoe Tessie (photo montage)

rifying that he refused to reveal what it was, and never released any of his film. He was quoted as saying: "The world wasn't ready for what was down there!"[14]

Wallowa Lake Monster—Reported to be dwelling in a deep glacial lake in Oregon, this horned amphibious beast has terrified local Nez Perce Indians for generations. It has been described by some eyewitnesses as being 75 feet long with seven humps along its back. Other witnesses, however, insist that there are two distinctly different species living in the lake: The first is 12 long, with a serpentine, dragon-like body, and a head like a hog's fused with a shark's. The second animal is only about 8 feet long, with a head like a buffalo's and eyes 14 inches apart. Other witnesses claim the creature bears a large, rhinoceros-like horn.[15]

Fig. 22. Wallowa Lake Monster

hoaxes

Unfortunately, as with so many so-called fringe phenomena, the history of Lake-Monsters has been plagued with notorious hoaxes that have seriously damaged the credibility of all witnesses, and embarrassed and discouraged serious investigators. In December of 1933, big-game hunter Marmaduke Wetherell discovered enormous tracks on the shore of Loch Ness leading down to the water. Investigators from the Natural History Museum determined that these had been made with a dried hippopotamus foot, such as were popular at the time as umbrella stands. Humiliated, Wetherell struck back: A few months later, on April 19, 1934, a highly respectable British surgeon, Colonel Robert Wilson, snapped the famous photo that became the iconic image of Nessie for the next 60 years.

But in 1994, just before his death at the age of 90, Christian Spurling, the last living conspirator, revealed that, at the request of Wetherell, he had rigged

Fig. 23. "The Surgeon's Photo" of Loch Ness Monster, taken April 19, 1934

a toy submarine with a carved monster head. This was taken to Loch Ness, photographed in the water, and the photo given to Wilson as a credible witness to present it to the world.[16]

oBay, what is this REALLy?

Popular conceptions of the phylogenetic identity of Nessie and other Lake-Monsters of her ilk have invariably been based on plesiosaurs. But any similarity between reports and photos of modern Lake-Monsters and fossil forms is superficial at best. It seems to me that researchers attempting to identify these creatures with known vertebrates are just not taking all the observations into account. I would like to attempt to apply some simple logic in hopes of unraveling this mystery, and propose an identification which, if not yet provable by an actual specimen, at least makes zoological sense.

Fig. 24. Typical Lake-Monster in silhouette by Oberon

First and most obvious, these creatures must breathe under water, because surface appearances are extremely rare—years apart in many cases. This ability is restricted to all fish, some amphibians, and many invertebrates. Any reptiles or mammals would have to appear frequently at the surface to breathe, as with marine iguanas, crocodiles, seals, otters, sirenia, and whales. Plesiosaurs were marine reptiles, living much as sea lions do, which some of them resembled. A colony of them would hardly be inconspicuous. Likewise, ancient whales (*archaeoceti*) would be as prominent at the surface as modern whales or dolphins. The very rarity of sightings argues irrefutably against Lake-Monsters being air-breathing animals.

Second, all the long-necked Lake-Monsters are invariably reported to move in vertical, rather than horizontal, undulations. This is crucial. Among vertebrates, only mammals and birds are capable of vertical flexion of their bodies. This is why cetaceans and sirenia have horizontal tail flukes, as opposed to the vertical fins of fishes. Again, plesiosaurs were reptiles, and their bodies, like those of crocodiles, moved side to side, not up and down.

Third, the long neck for which these creatures are noted precludes gills, which are an integral part of the skull and jaw structures of fish and amphibians; no gilled vertebrate has ever had a neck. This feature also eliminates whales, including the Eocene archaeocetid *Zeuglodon* or *Basilosaurus*, as all cetaceans—even prehistoric ones—lack necks. Some ancient reptiles, such as sauropods and plesiosaurs, did have long necks, which is, of course, why they have so often been proposed as candidates. But their horizontal flexion and need to breathe air disqualify all reptiles. Al-

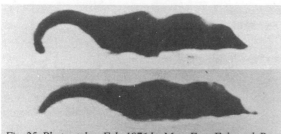

Fig. 25. Photos taken Feb. 1976 by Mary F. on Falmouth Bay, Cornwall. She described the creature as 15-18" long.

though all mammals have only seven cervical vertebrae, a few, such as the giraffe, do have long necks. Indeed, the "horse-head" profile so often described seems very mammalian. And mammals have vertical flexion, another point in their favor. But unfortunately for their case, all mammals must breathe air, and thus aquatic mammals are highly visible at the surface.

This leaves birds, which have both vertical flexion and long necks. Many are quite aquatic, and some, such as loons (*Gavia*) and cormorants (*Phalacrocorax*), both of which sit very low in the water, have been proposed as monster candidates, albeit on a very small scale. Some reports (see Nahuelito) have even described the necks of Lake Monsters as "swan-like." And the Cretaceous *Hesperornis* reached lengths of 5 feet. But birds breathe air, and none is known to even remotely approach the average reported 15- to 30-foot lengths of Lake Monsters, let alone the much larger individuals occasionally sighted.

So let's review the relevant features of all aquatic vertebrates (marine and extinct species are included, and maximum sizes given are generous):

Animal	Flexion	Neck	Breathes	Max. Size
Monster	**Vertical**	**Long**	**Water**	**30–70 ft.**
Fish	Horizontal	None	Water	30–50 ft.
Amphibian	Horizontal	None	Water/air	6–9 ft.
Reptile	Horizontal	Short/Long	Air	5–50 ft.
Mammal	Vertical	None/Short	Air	5–120 ft.
Bird	Vertical	Short/Long	Air	5 ft.

It should now be abundantly clear that no vertebrates, extant or extinct, could account for the reported sightings of long-necked Lake-Monsters. So what is left? In the words of Sherlock Holmes, "when you have eliminated the impossible, whatever remains, however improbable, must be the truth" (Sir Arthur Conan Doyle, *Sherlock Holmes*). In the case of the Loch Ness Monster and similar creatures around the world, the only remaining possibility is that they are some sort of gigantic invertebrate. But which kind?

ᛏᚢᛚᛚɪ'ꜱ ᛗᚩᚾꜱᛏᛖᚱ

In 1968, F.W. "Ted" Holiday proposed a radical theory regarding the zoological identification of the

Loch Ness Monster—and by extension, similar creatures worldwide. In his brilliant and insightful *The Great Orm of Loch Ness*,[17] he subjected all the sightings and photos collected to date to comparative analysis above. He was one of the first to conclude that the data rules out any possibility of a vertebrate identification, and that therefore these creatures must be some sort of gigantic, worm-like invertebrates. Holiday considered the *Opisthobranchia* (sea slugs) as possible candidates, but favored instead a bizarre ancient fossil named for its discoverer, Francis Tully: *Tullimonstrum gregarium* ("Tully's monster, common").

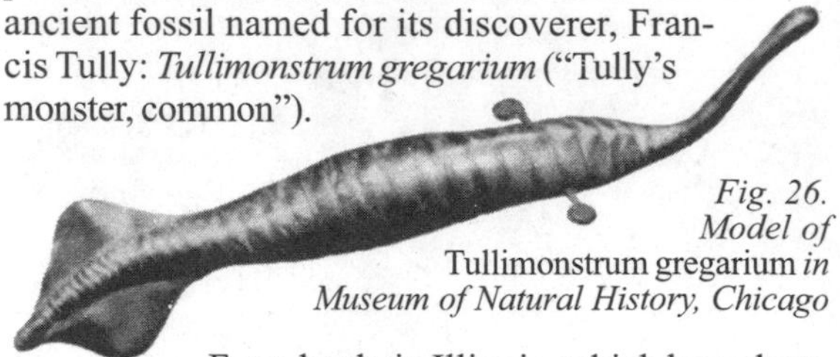

Fig. 26. Model of Tullimonstrum gregarium in Museum of Natural History, Chicago

Found only in Illinois, which has adopted the creature as its official state fossil, Tully's Monster was a fairly common sea animal during the Pennsylvanian Period, 300 million years ago. But that was a long time ago, and no examples have been found in more recent strata.

While the general morphology of *Tullimonstrum* initially seemed to match very closely with that of the generic Lake-Monster, subsequent analysis has cast doubt on this relationship. What had originally been thought to be a long neck with a small head on the end has turned out instead to be an elongated snout or pharynx culminating in toothed jaws. What had seemed initially to be two little fins at the base of the "neck" turn out instead to be eyes on stalks. Moreover, of the dozens of fossil specimens found, their sizes ranged only from 2 to 14 inches long. A current description is somewhat less convincing.

> The Tully Monster had an elongate, segmented body that tapered at both ends. At the front was a long snout ending in a "jaw" with eight tiny "teeth." At the other end was a tail and two fins. Two eyes on stalks projected out sideways near the front of the body. Judging from the streamlined shape, flexible body, and maneuverable fins, it's likely the Tully Monster was an active swimmer. Perhaps, like a modern squid, it hovered near the sea bottom. The Tully Monsters' "jaws" and apparent swimming abilities suggest that they attacked other marine animals such as jellyfish and shrimp, perhaps piercing their prey with their "teeth" and sucking out the juices.[18]

ᛏʜᛖ ᚩᛏʜᛖᚱ ᚩᚱᛗ

The only remaining possibility among known invertebrates is a phylum that includes what may be the largest animals on Earth: the *Mollusca*, of which some representatives—for example, the Giant Squid (*Mesonychoteuthis*)—may reach lengths of more than 100 feet, and thus easily encompass the reported dimensions of Lake-Monsters.

In studying accounts of Lake-Monster sightings, especially close-up encounters, it is striking how often the creatures are described as wormy, slimy, and/or repulsive. Of the creature she saw swimming up Logh Fadda in 1954, Georgina Carberry reported that it was "wormy. You know—creepy. The body seemed to have movement all over it all the time."[19] George Spicer, who, with his wife, saw the Loch Ness Monster crossing the road on July 22, 1933, said the animal was "horrible—an abomination." Its skin was a "terrible, dark elephant grey, of a loathsome texture, reminiscent of a snail."[20] Regarding his sighting of creature on shore of Loch Ness, on September 30, 1974, Dick Jenkyns said: "I felt that the beast was obscene. This feeling of obscenity still persists and the whole thing put me in mind of a gigantic stomach with a long writhing gut attached." Spicer said it had "an undulating sort of neck, a little thicker than an elephant's trunk," which was contorted into half-loops, and that it looked like "a huge snail with a long neck."[21]

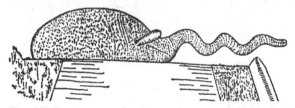

Fig. 27. Creature seen by George Spicer on July 22, 1933

Engineer-commander Richard Meicklem, who had a clear, 3-minute view of its hump on August 5 of that year, described the skin as "knobbly and warted," and certainly granulated. Tim Dinsdale notes that "those who have had a close sighting have generally agreed that it is rough, or warted like the skin of a great toad."[22]

The ancient name for these creatures was, in fact, "worm," or *orm*—a term widely applied to Dragons. Ancient and medieval Dragonlore frequently mentions that the bodies of slain orms "melted away," leaving nothing but the teeth, which would

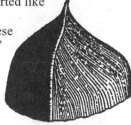

Fig. 28. Commander Meicklem's "hump"

explain the lack of fossils or bones in the lochs or elsewhere. In northern Wales, local legends tell of the **Ceffyll-Dwr** ("water horse"), a glowing, grey Lake-Monster that haunts waterfalls and mountain pools. It was said that anyone brave enough to attack and kill this evil creature would find no solid body, but only an amorphous, fatty mass floating on the water.

Another feature that becomes apparent upon examination of many reports and drawings is the rubbery elasticity of the neck and body, which may extend to become long and thin, or contract to become short and stubby. The length of the neck, in particular, may vary "from two or three feet to as much as ten feet in length, and a foot in diameter."[23] Rare sightings of the creatures on land often describe their movements as "caterpillar-like." During the night of September 30, 1965, two motorists independently saw a 20-foot-long creature "humped like a giant caterpillar" moving slowly on the road verge, not far from the River Tay on the A85 road between Perth and Dundee in Scotland.[24]

Fig 29. Drawing by Torquil MacLeod of his sighting on February 28, 1960

This flexibility is clearly apparent from the series of drawings made by Torquil MacLeod based on his sighting through binoculars of the creature, which was partially out of the water upon the opposite shore of Loch Ness, on February 28, 1960.[25] (Fig. 29) Similar proportions and apparent flexibility can be seen in one of the few unambiguously authentic photos of Nessie, taken by Hugh Gray in November of 1933.

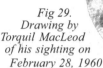

Fig 30. Drawing based on photo of Loch Ness Monster taken by Hugh Gray, November 1933.

Also, both eyewitness reports and photos of the head (Fig. 32) have indicated extensible, hornlike antennae similar to those of snails and slugs. (Fig. 31) Indeed, Tim Dinsdale notes that "sometimes, on top of the head two small projections are seen like 'the horns on a snail,' and the eyes (which are not often seen) are like 'slits in a darning needle,' and they are 'bright and glittering.'"[26] Regarding a sighting of February 22, 1968, in beat bog called Lough Nahooin in Connemara, Ire-

Fig 31. Face of a snail

land: "Both Mr and Mrs. [Stephen] Coyne agreed that the creature was about 12 feet long and both agreed that they saw no eyes. Mrs. Coyne told us that she noticed two horn-like projections on top of the head." Regarding a sighting in Loch Ness on November 17, 1976, which he photographed, Cornish Wizard Tony "Doc" Shiels noted: "The head had horns, stumpy little things… the head was extremely ugly, like a big snail's head with those odd little stalks."[27]

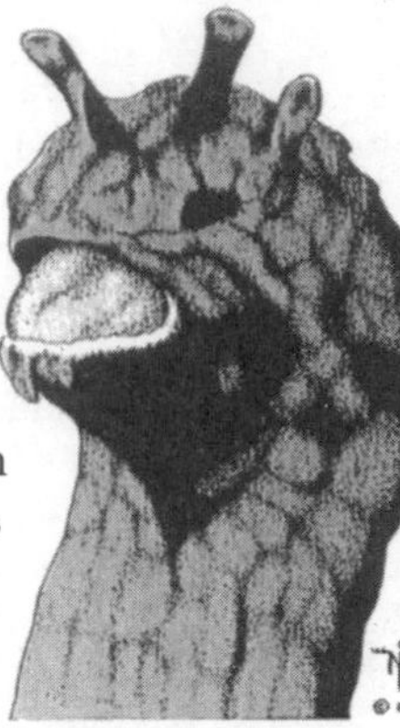

Fig 32. Head of "Nessie"? From underwater photo taken August 9, 1972, by the Academy of Applied Science.

Interestingly, the ancient Egyptian heiratic glyph for "man" and also the sound of the letter "F," which is generally regarded as a representation of a "horned viper," looks exactly like our monster:

Fig. 33. Lake Monster in Egyptian heiroglyph?

And perhaps most telling of all, a Welsh legend of a local *Wyvern* first translated into English in 1921, states: "At times one could see it creeping with hateful, stealthy movements, here and there upon the fertile slopes of Moel Offrum, jerking its cumbersome form into uncanny humps as it made its way in quest of food, and leaving a *slimy trail* behind it."[28] Such slimy trails are uniquely characteristic of snails and slugs.

For these reasons, I conclude that Nessie, Chessie, Champ, Morag, and the like, with their long necks and two "horns" like those of a garden snail, are probably giant aquatic slugs, perhaps with several subspecies to account for the reported variations.

The *Opisthobranchia* (sea slugs) are a highly evolved order of gastropods with hundreds of radically diverse species, of which only marine forms are currently recognized. They have small eyes and several sensitive, hornlike feelers at the fronts of their heads, used for orientation and olfaction. The sides of the foot have evolved into fleshy, wing-like outgrowths called *parapodia*. In several suborders, such as the *Thecosomata* and *Gymnosomata*, these are used as fins to move in a swimming motion.[29]

Here is a comparison of the relevant features of these invertebrates with those reported of Lake-Monsters:

Animal	Flexion	Neck	"Horns"	Breathes	Size
Monster	**Vertical**	**Long**	**Yes**	**Water**	**30-70 ft**
Tullimonstrum	Vertical	Long	No	Water	14 in.
Opisthobranch	Vertical	Extensible	Yes	Water	30 in.-?

In 1975, based upon underwater photos obtained in 1972 by the Academy of Applied Science (Fig. 34), the official name of *Nessiteras rhombopteryx* ("Ness wonder with diamond-shaped fins") was bestowed upon the Loch Ness Monster by Sir Peter Scott. Interestingly, the Greek word *pteras* ("fin") also means "wing," suggesting a basis for legends of winged Dragons. But if these creatures are actually aquatic mollusks, as I believe them to be, the highly-positioned diamond-shaped fin for which they are named is probably an *operculum* (Latin, "little lid")—a flap covering the gill opening, which in sea slugs is located below the neck and just behind the heart, rather than behind the head as in fish and amphibians. This is exactly the position indicated in the photos, drawings, and eyewitness reports.

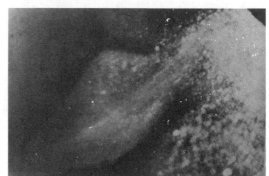

Fig. 34. Nessie "fin" underwater photo taken August 9, 1972, by the Academy of Applied Science.

A RECONSTRUCTION

In 1987, I sculpted a model of the Loch Ness Monster based on a synthesis of all recorded descriptions and drawings. (See opening graphic.) I believe it to be as accurate a representation as possible until we can manage to obtain a physical specimen. Furthermore, I believe that the erroneous assumption that these creatures are vertebrates (in particular, plesiosaurs) has misdirected previous attempts at capture. Future efforts might search for larval stages more productively by dredging the bottom muck of the lochs—or even better, some of the many Irish bogs and marshes rumored to harbor smaller and probably related Bog-dogs, Horse-eels, or Kelpies. (See Chapter 12. "The Hippocampus") This is the approach currently being undertaken by marine biologist Steven O'Shea in his successful search for Giant Squid (*Architeuthis*) larvae amid the oceanic zooplankton.

Fig. 35. Nessie in full-figure by Oberon Zell (1987)

Assuming that these creatures are actually gigantic freshwater aquatic slugs, what other correlations can be made with historical traditions and accounts of Orms? One of these characteristics is the Orm's vile toxicity, which is said to burn the skin and poison wells, springs, pools, and the very ground beneath it. The slimy skin of many opisthobranchs contains distasteful and sometimes toxic chemicals as a defense against predation. Others have special stinging cells or toxic glands, which in some cases are used to paralyze their prey.[30]

A recurring theme in myths is that of "Dragon's teeth"—seemingly the only recoverable remains of an Orm or Dragon, as no skull, skin, or other expected trophy has ever been exhibited. A slug's teeth—its only hard parts—are not set in jaws, as they are in vertebrates, but on a flexible tongue, or *radula*, which is a ribbon of precisely arranged teeth, like those on a rasp, used for scraping or grasping its food.[31] A dead slug simply dissolves into a pool of goo, and only the teeth remain.

The keeled humps reported in virtually all sightings of Lake-Monsters are particularly interesting in this context. (Fig. 28) The number of these varies with the length of the animal, as there seems to be a maximum length of about 5 feet for each hump. "Most peculiar of all, people have actually reported the humps changing shape."[32] Because the creatures are commonly reported to rise and sink vertically, these humps are most likely gas-filled flotation chambers, much like the swim bladders of fish (see diagram). In fish, these closed organs are precursors of lungs, and are filled with respiratory air extracted from the water. But in gigantic, muck-dwelling aquatic slugs, the gas that fills such chambers would more likely be derived from the digestive process, and would therefore consist of methane, or marsh gas. And, as everyone knows, this gas is highly flammable. In order to sink vertically, the creature would have to evacuate gas; the most logical orifice for this purpose would be the mouth, which is not used for breathing. And if these creatures happen to possess bioelectrical faculties similar to those found in certain eels and other fish that inhabit murky waters (which utilize electrical discharges both to navigate and to stun prey), then electric sparks could be used to ignite the expelled gas, and we would have fire-breathing Dragons. What an impressive defense mechanism *that* would make!

And finally, when the gas-filled humps are evacuated, they would flatten into the apparent dorsal "fin" occasionally reported, as in the monster of Lake Khaiyr, Russia. (Fig. 10)

EDINBURGH, Scotland (AP) — On May 26, 2007, an amateur scientist captured what Loch Ness Monster watchers say is among the finest footage ever taken of the elusive mythical creature reputed to swim beneath the waters of Scotland's most mysterious lake. "I couldn't believe my eyes when I saw this jet black thing, about 45 feet long, moving fairly fast in the water," said Gordon Holmes, the 55-year-old lab technician from Shipley, Yorkshire, who took the video. He said it moved at about 6 mph and kept a fairly straight course.[33]

MONSTER MOVIES: LAKE-MONSTERS

Several movies have been inspired by the mystery of the Loch Ness Monster, beginning with *The Secret of the Loch* (1934), right after the construction of a public motorway along the Loch in 1933 resulted in a flurry of sightings. The monster puts in a rather spectacular showing in *The 7 Faces of Dr. Lao* (1964), and also appears briefly in *The Private Life of Sherlock Holmes* (1970), in which it is sighted by Dr. Watson. *The Crater Lake Monster* (1977) is hatched from an egg heated by a meteorite. *Loch Ness Horror* (1981) involves the monster's egg, a mad scientist, and a sunken Nazi plane. *Loch Ness* (1996) is a charming fantasy starring Ian Holm, who protects the monsters from exploitation. In *Beneath Loch Ness* (2001), a scientific expedition discovers the body of an enormous creature washed up on the loch's shore. *Incident at Loch Ness* (2004) involves competing film crews making documentaries about the mysterious monsters. In *Mee-Shee: The Water Giant* (2005), a teenage boy befriends an endearing Lake-Monster in a remote Canadian lake. And *The Water Horse: Legend of the Deep* is scheduled for release at Christmas of 2007. Unfortunately, all of these films presume that the creatures are plesiosaurs. However, *The Monster that Challenged the World* (1957) features giant snails, and there was also *Attack of the Giant Leeches* (1959).

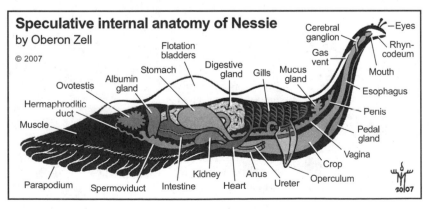

Speculative internal anatomy of Nessie
by Oberon Zell
© 2007

Cerebral ganglion — Eyes
Gas vent — Rhyncodeum
Mouth
Gills
Mucus gland
Esophagus
Flotation bladders
Digestive gland
Stomach
Albumin gland
Ovotestis
Hermaphroditic duct
Muscle
Penis
Pedal gland
Vagina
Crop
Operculum
Parapodium
Spermoviduct
Intestine
Kidney
Heart
Anus
Ureter
20|07

19. SEA-SERPENTS

By Oberon Zell-Ravenheart

Canst thou draw out Leviathan with a fishhook,
or run a line around his tongue?
Canst thou put a ring through his nose,
or pierce his jaw with a hook? ...
Is he to be sold by the fishmongers,
and filleted on the block in the market? ...
Who can unloose the front of his coat,
or piece the double armor of his breastplate?
Who can open the gates of his mouth?
Terror dwells in those rows of teeth! ...
He maketh the deep to boil like a cauldron,
and the sea to fume like a censer....
He hath no equal upon the Earth...
of all the sons of pride he is the king.

—Job 40:25–32; 41:1–26

Ian Daniels

A S LONG AS MEN HAVE BEEN GOING down to the sea in ships, they have reported encounters with gigantic marine monsters that have been universally referred to as Sea-Serpents. Cryptozoologist Bruce Champagne estimates that there have been 1,200 or more sightings throughout the seven seas, which have been recorded in the annals of maritime history.[1] The creatures have been seen from shore as well as ship, and many sightings have involved dozens or even hundreds of witnesses observing them, sometimes over the course of several hours. Witnesses have included people from all walks of life, from sailors to professional scientists. Sightings continue to this day, with recent reports coming in from California and the Pacific Northwest. Such encounters have been well-documented in newspapers, although many preceded the invention of photography.

Descriptions of Sea-Serpents, however, do not present a single image. Some appear to be gigantic snakes, enormous eels, oversized seals, huge crocodilians, or even prehistoric creatures such as long-necked plesiosaurs. In his monumental work, *In the Wake of the Sea Serpents* (1968), Bernard Heuvalmans (1916–2001), the father of cryptozoology, distinguished seven varieties based on consistent descriptions. These are: Long-Necked, Merhorse, Many-Humped, Many-Finned, Super-Otter, Super-Eel, and Marine Saurian. But, despite many sightings, no confirmed specimens of truly unknown animals have yet been retrieved.

SEA-SERPENTS IN NORSE LEGEND

The earliest recorded accounts of Sea-Serpents come from the sailors of the North Sea known as the Vikings, who inhabited the countries now called Norway, Sweden, Denmark, and Iceland. 1,000 years ago, these bold Norse seafarers carved the prows of their oceangoing longships into images of a type of Sea-Serpent they called Wave-Thrasher (*Ythgewinnes* in Old English). The purpose was to ward off real Dragons.

The **Stoorworm** ("great serpent") is an immense Sea-Serpent that once dwelt in the area now known as the North Sea. It was so vast that its body could cover all of northern Europe. It threatened to flood all the lands of Britain unless it was appeased by human sacrifices. When the King's daughter was slated to be next, her father offered half his kingdom to whomever would slay the Dragon. A youth named Assipattle volunteered. He shoveled slow-burn-

Fig. 1. Dragon-prowed Viking longship

Fig. 2. Stoorworm

ing peat into the worm's mouth, which burned it up from inside. Its death throes cut the Skaggerak Sea between Denmark, Norway, and Sweden, and its teeth became the Faroe, Orkney, and Shetland Islands. Its ever-burning body remains as volcanic Iceland. This story may represent a memory of the submergence of all the lowlands between Britain, Scandinavia, and Europe, which occurred 10,500 years ago at the end of the Ice Age, when the glacial ice melted and sea levels rose 400–600 feet.

In Icelandic folklore, the **Skrimsl** is a gigantic Sea-Serpent that inhabited the sea around Lagarfljot, where it was seen during the Middle Ages and into the 18th century. However, it was considered harmless, as its power had been bound by St. Gudmund until Doomsday. In recent years, however, a bizarre, wormlike Lake-Monster has been reported in Iceland's Lake Lögurinn (20.5 miles long and 367 feet deep), which some believe to be a reincarnation of the legendary Skrimsl.

The **Great Norway Serpent** is an enormous Sea-Serpent reportedly dwelling in the North Sea. Black and scaly, with a long mane of hair, it is said to be 200 feet long and 20 feet thick. It inhabits coastal caves, emerging onto the land on summer nights to feast on livestock. Other gigantic Sea-Serpents of Norwegian legend are the **Sjøorm** ("sea-worms"). They are hatched on land as little snakes, but grow bigger and bigger as they eat ever-larger prey, until the land can no longer support their vast bulk and they retreat to the sea, where they continue to grow.

Fig. 3. Norwegian Sjøorm

In his *Carta Marina* ("map of the sea"), printed in Venice in 1539, Swedish ecclesiastic and writer Olaus Magnus (1490–1557) depicted many marine monsters of varied forms, including an immense Sea-Serpent attacking a ship and devouring a crewman. In his 1555 work, *History of the Northern Peoples*, Magnus provides the following description of the Great Norwegian Sea-Serpent:

> Those who sail up along the coast of Norway to trade or to fish, all tell the remarkable story of how a serpent of fearsome size, 200 feet long and 20 feet wide, resides in rifts and caves outside Bergen. On bright summer nights this serpent leaves the caves to eat calves, lambs and pigs, or it fares out to the sea and feeds on sea nettles, crabs and similar marine animals. It has ell-long [45 inches] hair hanging from its neck, sharp black scales and flaming red eyes. It attacks vessels, grabs and swallows people, as it lifts itself up like a column from the water.[2]

Fig. 4. Great Norwegian Sea-Serpent by Olaus Magnus

LEGENDARY SEA-SERPENTS OF OTHER LANDS

Hedammu is the name of a vast, all-devouring Sea-Serpent in the mythology of the Hurrians of ancient Mesopotamia. Similarly, **Tannin** is an enormous and powerful Sea-Serpent of Hebrew legend, mentioned in the Bible. Referred to as a Dragon of primal chaos, it is probably a version of Leviathan or Rahab.

In Scottish folklore, **Cîrein Cròin** (Gaelic, "grey crest") is the most enormous Sea-Serpent that ever existed, able to swallow entire whales in a single gulp. Also called *Curtag Mhòr a' Chuain* ("great whirlpool of the ocean"), *Mial Mhòr a' Chuain* ("great beast of the ocean") and *Uile Bhéisd a' Chuain* ("monster of the ocean"), this is very likely a reference to the Corryvreckan whirlpool located between the islands of Scarba and Jura in Argyll and Bute. At its wildest, this maelstrom forms a vast swirling cauldron 300 feet wide and 100 feet deep, and has been known to suck ships to their doom.

Fig. 5. Cîrein Cròin by Dana Keyes

The Bella Coola, Haida, and Kwakiutl Indians of Canada's Pacific coast tell of the monstrous **Sisiutl**, variously described as a salmon-serpent, a horned serpent, or even as a two-headed serpent. Sometimes it is depicted with fins, four legs, and huge fangs, often with two serpentine bodies emerging from either side of an enormous head. Anyone who meets its gaze will be turned to stone. Sisiutl is an assistant to Winalagilis, the war-god, and its powers are sought by warriors.

Fig. 6. Sisiutl

Unhcegila is a huge female Water-Serpent with flaming eyes in the folklore of the Lakota Indians. Her scales were flint and her heart was a quartz crystal. She lived in the sea but periodically swam up into Nebraska, bringing tidal waves that turned the water brackish and unfit to drink. She was eventually slain by two heroes.

Raja Naga ("serpent king") is an immense Sea-Serpent in the folklore of West Malasia. Greatest of all the Sea-Dragons, he dwells in a splendid palace beneath the waves, called the *Pusat Tasik*.

Ryujin is one of the Dragon-kings in Japanese mythology. He dwells in a magickal jeweled palace at the bottom of the sea, from which he controls the tides passing through his vast mouth. His beautiful daughter is won by the hero Fire Fade, or Prince Hoori, and thus he becomes the legendary ancestor of the emperors of Japan.

Fig. 7. Ryujin

Also in Japan, ***Yofune-Nushi*** was a gigantic Sea-Serpent that, for decades, terrorized the fishing villages of Oki Island. Once a year, on the night of June 13, the monster had to be offered a maiden, lest it raise up a terrible storm and destroy the fishing fleet. One year, a young girl named

Tokoyo volunteered for the sacrifice. But when the beast arose from the foam to devour her, the courageous girl pulled a long knife and slashed out its eyes. As the serpent reared back in pain and confusion, Tokoyo impaled its exposed throat, thus ending its reign of terror.

Fig. 8. Yofune-Nushi by Rebecca Carr

TYPES OF SEA-SERPENTS

The enormous variation in the descriptions of creatures reported as Sea-Serpents has always cast doubt on the credibility of witnesses, and few scientists have deigned to take such reports seriously. But starting around 200 years ago, a few researchers have attempted to compile and categorize reports of different sightings and create systems of classification. The story of the Sea-Serpent cannot be told without mentioning these pioneers in the field.

Rafinesque

Constantin Samuel Rafinesque-Schmaltz (1783–1840) was the first naturalist to attempt to classify Sea-Serpents. In the November 1819 issue of *Philosophical Magazine,* he published an article titled "Dissertation on Water-Snakes, Sea Snakes, and Sea Serpents." In addition to discussing numerous known species, he also categorized four different types of Sea-Serpent. These were each based on single sightings, and have been superseded by more extensive surveys. But at least this was a start.[3]

Oudemans

Dutch scientist Antoon Cornelis Oudemans (1858–1943) was a doctor of zoology and director of the Royal Zoological Gardens at The Hague. In *The Great Sea Serpent* (1892), a study of 166 Sea-Serpent reports, many of high quality, Oudemans concluded that such sightings might be of a single previously unknown, enormous, sea-lion-like creature with a long neck and long tail, which he dubbed *Megophias megophias* ("great serpent"). He also considered the possibility of an ancient whale called *Zeuglodon plesiosauroids*, but later changed his mind. Although he ignored many features and reports that did not fit these interpretations, Oudemans's suggestions that Sea-Serpents might be mammalian rather than reptilian had a great influence on later researchers. Indeed, Heuvelmans maintained that *The Great Sea Serpent* laid the foundational framework for all of modern cryptozoology.

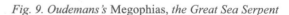

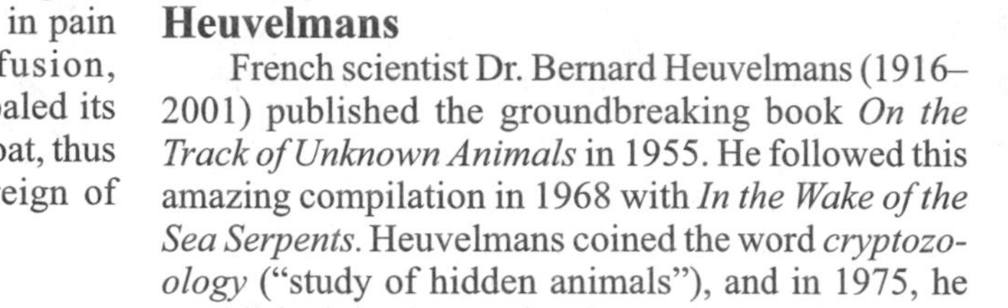

Fig. 9. Oudemans's Megophias, *the Great Sea Serpent*

Heuvelmans

French scientist Dr. Bernard Heuvelmans (1916–2001) published the groundbreaking book *On the Track of Unknown Animals* in 1955. He followed this amazing compilation in 1968 with *In the Wake of the Sea Serpents.* Heuvelmans coined the word *cryptozoology* ("study of hidden animals"), and in 1975, he established the Center for Cryptozoology in France. In 1982 he helped found the International Society for Cryptozoology, serving as its first president. For these reasons, he is justly regarded as the father of cryptozoology.

Here are the categories of Sea-Serpents proposed by Heuvelmans, incorporating some more recent analyses by Loren Coleman, Patrick Huyghe, and Bruce Champagne.[4] The illustrations are mostly based on those of Heuvelmans:[5]

1. Long-Necked or *Megalotaria longicollis* ("giant sea lion with a long neck") — A 15- to 65-foot-long, plesiosaur-like creature with a long neck, several humps, and the ability to move in vertical undulations. The head has a distinctive horse-like or "cameloid" appearance, and hair and whiskers have been reported. Believed to be a long-necked, short-tailed sea lion. Seen worldwide, with 82 reported sightings.

2. Merhorse or *Halshippus olai-magni* ("sea-horse of Olaus Magnus")—A 30- to 60-foot-long, medium-necked, large-eyed, horse-headed pinniped. Often has whiskers. Only the males have manes, but females appear to have snorkels. In some reports, their eyes are rather small. They have been sighted in both salt and fresh water. Seen worldwide, with 71 reported sightings.

3. Many-Humped or *Plurigibbosus novae-angliae* ("many-humped thing from New England")—A 15- to 65-foot-long, medium-necked, long-bodied *archeocetacean* (ancient whale) such as *Zueglodon* (*Basilosaurus*). Found only in the North Atlantic, it has a series of humps or a crest along the spine like that of a sperm or grey whale. 82 reported sightings.

4. Super Otter or *Hyperhydra egedei* ("Egedi's super otter") —A 60- to 100-foot-long, medium-necked, long-bodied archeocete resembling an otter. It moves in six to seven vertical undulations. Once reported near Norway and Greenland, but now presumed to be extinct. 28 reported sightings.

5. Many-Finned or *Cetioscolpenda aelani* ("Aelian's cetacean centipede")—An elongated creature up to 70 feet long, with the appearance of segments and many lateral projections that resemble dorsal fins, but turned backwards. Found in the western Atlantic, Indian, and Pacific oceans, this creature is also known as the Great Sea Centipede. It may be an invertebrate. 26 reported sightings.

6. Super Eels—A group of large and possibly unrelated eels. Partially based on the *Leptocephalus giganteus* larvae, later found to be normal sized. Heuvelmans theorized eel, *synbranchid*, and *elasmobranch* identities as possibilities. Seen worldwide, with 23 reported sightings.

7. Marine Saurian—A 50- to 60-foot-long crocodile or crocodile-like animal (*Mosasaur*, *Pliosaur*, and so on). Found in the northern Atlantic Ocean and Mediterranean Sea. Possibly an Estuarine Crocodile (*Crocodylus porosus*) a long way from its Indonesian and Northern Australian habitat. Nine reported sightings.

Ian Daniels

SIGHTINGS ACCORDING TO CATEGORIES

Long-Necked

Sailing off the west coast of Africa in 1893, the steamship *Umfuli* had a famous encounter with a long-necked Sea-Serpent. According to Mate C.A.W. Powell's entry in the ship's log, it was "of the Serpent shape, about 80 feet long with slimy skin and short fins about 20 feet apart on the back and in circumference about the same dimension of a full sized whale. I distinctly saw the fish's mouth open [and] shut with my glasses. The jaw appeared to me about 7 feet long with large teeth. In shape it was just like a Conger Eel." Captain R.J. Cringle added: "I saw full 15 feet of its head and neck on three several occasions.... The body, from which the neck sprang, was much thicker than the neck itself, and I should not, therefore, call it a serpent."[6]

Fig. 10. Umfuli Sea-Serpent, 1893, by Robert T Gould

"Colossal Claude" is the local name given to a Sea-Serpent first seen in 1934, cavorting near the mouth of the Columbia River in Oregon. According to L.A. Larson, mate of the Columbia River lightship, "It was about 40 feet long. It had a neck some 8 feet long, a big round body, a mean looking tail and an evil, snaky look to its head." Over the years Claude has been sighted by other lightship crewmen and fishermen. In 1937, skipper Charles E. Graham of the trawler *Viv* sighted a "long, hairy, tan-colored creature, with the head of an overgrown horse, about 40 feet long, and with a 4 foot waist measure." Captain Chris Anderson of the schooner *Arpo* said he said he got a close look at Claude: "His head was like a camel's. His fur was coarse and gray. He had glassy eyes and a bent snout that he used to push a 20-pound halibut off our lines and into his mouth."[7]

Similar Oregonian Sea-Monsters have been sighted off Bandon, Delake, Empire, Nelscott, Newport, and Waldport; and also in Crescent and Crater lakes. They come in several varieties and sizes. Some are shiny and some have scales. Some reportedly have coarse fur. Their most common feature is the shape of their heads, usually said to resemble that of a camel or horse. Some of these blend into the next category.

Merhorse

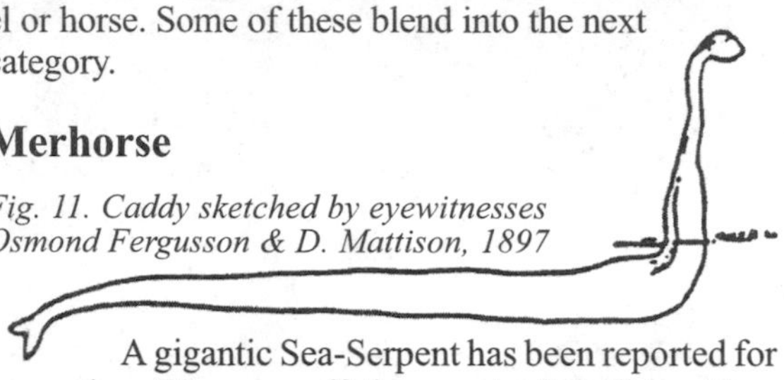

Fig. 11. Caddy sketched by eyewitnesses Osmond Fergusson & D. Mattison, 1897

A gigantic Sea-Serpent has been reported for more than 70 years off the coast of Cadboro Bay, British Colombia, Canada. The first reported sighting was in 1933, by a Victoria lawyer and his wife cruising in their yacht. It is consistently described as a long, serpent-like beast with flippers, a horselike mane, and a camel-like head. It ranges from 40 to 70 feet in length. In 1933, two fishermen saw two monsters in the bay, one about 60 feet long and the other half that size. Another sighting was made by two hunters trying to recover their wounded duck. The monster rose out of the water, swallowed the duck, snapped at some gulls, and then submerged. They noted a 6-foot-long head with saw-like teeth. Following in the tradition of Nessie, locals affectionately dubbed their local monster *Cadborosaurus Willsi*, or "Caddy."[8]

Many-Humped

The first American Sea-Serpent was reported from Cape Ann, Massachusetts, in 1639. A similar creature, reported from 1777 into the 1950s, was the Casco Bay Sea-Serpent of Maine, affectionately dubbed "Cassie."

From 1817 to 1918, an enormous, serpentine marine animal was reported in the harbor off Gloucester, Massachusetts, by numerous eyewitnesses.

Fig. 12. Gloucester Sea-Serpent, 1817-1818

Described as being 80–100 feet in length, with a broad, horselike head and a hornlike appendage jutting from its skull, this scaly monstrosity was said by some to resemble a "row of casks" upon the water. It became known as the Gloucester Sea-Serpent or the Great New England Sea-Serpent, and was officially named *Scoliophis atlanticus*.

A great many-humped Sea-Serpent was sighted off of Cape Cod on July 29, 1826, according to the Boston *Zion's Herald*, August 2, 1826:

> Captain Holdredge, of the ship *Silas Richard*, which arrived yesterday from Liverpool, says that in passing George's Banks five days since, he had a fair view of the Serpent. It was about ten rods [175 feet] from the ship, the sea was perfectly calm, and that part which appeared out of water was about 60 feet in length. The head and protuberances of the Serpent were similar to the representations which have frequently been given of him by persons who had seen him. He was visible about seven minutes to the passengers and crew, who were on deck at the time. A certificate has been drawn up and signed by the passengers which, with a drawing made by one of the gentlemen, gives a minute description of the Serpent as seen by them. The number and credibility of the witnesses place beyond all doubt the existence of such an animal.

Many-Finned

On July 8, 1856, the *Princess,* sailing off the cape of Africa, encountered a "very large fish, with a head like a walrus, and 12 fins, similar to those in a black fish, but turned the contrary way. The back was from 20 to 30 feet long; also a great length of tail." (Captain A.R.N. Tremearne). The good captain's drawing was published in the *Illustrated London News:*

Fig. 13. Princess Sea Serpent, 1865, by Capt. Tremearne

In 1883, Tan Van Con discovered an enormous, centipede-like creature washed up on the coast of Along Bay, Vietnam. Called *Con Rit* ("centipede"), it was 60 feet long and 3 feet wide, dark brown on top and yellow underneath, and had a segmented body comprised of 3-by-2-foot chitinous hexagonal segments. Filaments 28 inches long protruded from both sides of each segment. Nothing else like it has ever been found, and its zoological identity remains a mystery. Cryptozoologist Karl Shuker believes that the

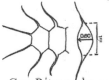

Fig. 14. Con Rit segments (1883) and reconstruction of Arthropleura

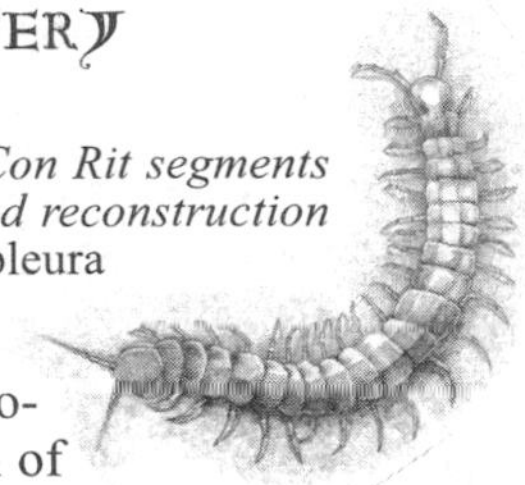

Con Rit may be a gigantic isopod or an undiscovered form of aquatic *chilopoda* (centipede).[9] The largest known centipede of all time was the 11-foot-long *Arthropleura* of the Carboniferous era. The biggest known living species is the Amazonian Giant Centipede (*Scolopendra gigantea*), which attains 14 inches in length.

Super Eels

An enormous, eel-like Sea-Serpent was seen by the crew of the British frigate *Daedalus* on her passage from the East Indies through the Cape of Good Hope in the year 1848. About 300 miles off the coast of what is now Namibia, a Sea-Serpent passed just 100 yards from the ship. In his log, Captain M'Quhae described it thus:

> An enormous serpent, with head and shoulders kept about four feet constantly above the surface of the sea, and as nearly as we could approximate it comparing with the length our maintopsail yard would show in the water, there was at the very least 60 feet of the animal *á fleur d'eau,* no portion of which was, to our perception, used in propelling it through the water…. The diameter of the serpent was about 15 or 16 inches behind the head, which was, without any doubt, that of a snake…its colour a dark brown, with yellowish white about the throat.

Fig. 15. Daedalus Sea-Serpent 1848

In August of 1880, a 35-foot-long, eel-shaped fish was captured by Captain S.W. Hanna off the coast of New Harbor, Maine. Called the New Harbor Sea-Serpent, its elongated body was only 10 inches wide, and it had a pair of small fins behind its flat head. The upper portion of the skull extended over its narrow mouth, which contained two rows of sharp teeth. It had three sets of uncovered gills, a small, triangular dorsal fin, and an eel-like tail. Its entire body was covered with skin like a shark's. Unfortunately, these amazing remains were inexplicably discarded.

According to eminent ichthyologist Spencer Baird, the description of this fish closely resembles the serpentine Frilled Shark (*Chlamydoselachus Angui-neus,* "snake-like shark

Fig. 16. Oarfish

with frills").[10] However, the largest recorded specimen of a frilled shark came to only 7 feet long. A more likely candidate might be the ribbon-like Oarfish (*Regalecus glesne*), of which specimens up to 56 feet long have been reported.

In 1930, a 6-foot-long eel larva (*leptocephalus*) was caught off the Cape of Good Hope, South Africa, by a trawler called the *Dana*. For a long time, this find was believed to be the larval form of a Sea-Serpent. The leptocephalus of a common eel (genus: *Anguilla*) measures only 3 inches long, and matures at about 4 feet long. Because this leptocephalus was 24 times larger than that of n anguilla, estimates of its adult length ranged from 20 to 180 feet long. How-

Fig. 17. Giant leptocephalus caught by Dana, 1930

ever, several similarly-shaped leptocephali belong to the group called Spiny Eels (*Notacanths* and *Halosaurs*). These larvae—called *Leptocephalus giganteus*—have been witnessed transforming into their adult stages, during which they gain very little length compared to true eels. The *Dana* larvae is still bigger than any of the known ones; however, this specimen also had an abnormally large number of vertebrae in its spine, a number which only a Snipe Eel (*Nemichthyidae*) can match. Because snipe eels reach only 5 feet in length, the *Dana* larvae was probably a post-larval snipe eel of unusually large proportions.[11]

Marine Saurian

A reptilian Sea-Serpent was reportedly encountered by a German submarine, the *U-28 Schmidt,* on July 30, 1915. After torpedoing the British steamer *Iberian* in the North Atlantic, the submarine crew saw a gigantic unknown aquatic animal thrown up by the explosion. According to Commander Freiherr Georg Günther von Forstner, "this wonder of the seas, which was writhing and struggling among the debris…resembled an aquatic crocodile, which was about 60 feet long, with four limbs resembling large webbed feet, a long, pointed tail and a head which also tapered to a point."

Fig. 18. U-28 abomination, 1915 (after Richard Hennig)

CURIOUS CARCASSES

Part of what has contributed to the legend of Sea-Serpents over the centuries has been the physical evidence of monstrous carcasses occasionally discovered washed up on beaches. Invariably in an advanced state of decay, they have appeared to resemble no known living animal. Many seem to have the long thin necks, wide bodies, and four flippers of Cretaceous-era *plesiosaurs*, thus supporting such a popular identification for sightings of both long-necked Sea-Serpents and Lake-Monsters.

Unfortunately for proponents of the plesiosaur hypothesis, the vast majority of such carcasses have turned out to be the remains of common Basking Sharks (*Cetorhinus maximus*), of which the largest ever caught (in 1851) measured 40 feet long, although much larger ones have been reported. When a basking shark decays, its enormous jaws and gills drop away, leaving the relatively tiny skull at the end of what appears to be a long neck. The cartilage-supported lateral fins and upper tail remain, but the dorsal fin and ventral tail lobe break up into hair-like fibers. The final result does uncannily resemble the form of a plesiosaur, and it is easy to see how these could cause such confusion.

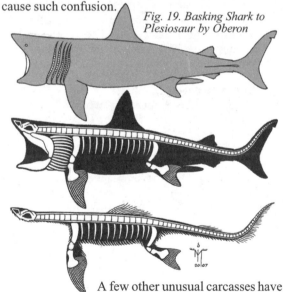

Fig. 19. Basking Shark to Plesiosaur by Oberon

A few other unusual carcasses have been identified as various species of beaked whales, such as the Giant Beaked Whale (*Ziphiidae Berardius*), which is known to reach 43 feet in length, or the rare Baird's Beaked Whale (*Berardius bairdi*).

Here are a few famous "curious carcasses:"

Stronsa Beast—A strange carcass discovered washed up on the rocky shores of Stronsa Island, one of the Orkney Islands off northern Scotland, on September 26, 1808. The serpentine remains measured 55 feet long, with a 15-foot-long neck, a slightly broader torso, and a horselike mane along its spine. It also appeared to have three sets of legs, each with five to six

Fig. 20.
Stronsa Beast

toes. Local farmer George Sherar measured the carcass, and preserved a section of skin, a few vertebrae, and the skull. News of this discovery soon reached Patrick Neill, secretary of Edinburgh's Wernerian Natural History Society, who presented the Stronsay Beast with the scientific name *Halsydrus pontoppidani* ("Pontoppidan's water snake of the sea"). But in 1811, Society member Dr. John Barclay, who had examined the remains in Orkney, published a paper describing them in which he noted that the so-called legs of the carcass had been misidentified, and were only fins. This paper attracted the attention of renowned naturalist Sir Everard Home, who had just completed a detailed study of basking sharks and was able to identify the Stronsa Beast as one of these great fish.[12]

Suwarrow Island Devilfish—A gigantic carcass discovered by natives on the south Pacific atoll called Suwarrow Island, in the 19th century. An English trading steamer, the *Emu*, made a brief stop on the island, and the crew decided to investigate. The carcass was approximately 60 feet long and covered with brown hair. The captain estimated the creature's weight at around 70 tons, and described the animal's head as horselike, with two tusks at the end of its lower jaw. The captain had the 3-foot-long skull removed and stored in the ship's hold. Upon reaching Australia, he presented the find to the Australian Museum, where it was determined that the skull belonged to a Giant Beaked Whale (*Ziphiidae Berardius*).[13]

Fig. 21. Giant Beaked Whale (Ziphiidae Berardius)

Trunko—A bizarre, 45-foot-long carcass that washed ashore on November 1, 1922, on Margate Beach in KwaZulu-Natal, South Africa, after several people had witnessed an epic battle the previous evening between three gigantic Sea-Monsters. Two of these beasts were readily identified as whales, but the third was utterly unclassifiable. The carcass that washed ashore that evening bore a 5-foot-long headless neck or trunk (hence the name), as well as a 10-foot-long, prawn-like tail, all of it covered with a coat of 8-inch-long, snow-white hair. After rotting for 10 days with no scientific investigation, the carcass was washed back out to sea, never to be seen again. This was certainly a rotting basking shark carcass, and the witnesses had probably observed it being torn apart by Orcas.

Fig. 22. Trunko, as popularly reconstructed

Zuiyo-Maru Carcass—The badly decayed remains of a Sea-Monster hauled aboard in the nets of the Japanese fishing boat *Zuiyo-Maru,* on April 25, 1977, while trawling off the coast of New Zealand. Although the 33-foot-long, 4,000-pound carcass was widely and famously reported to be that of a *plesiosaur,* subsequent tissue analysis determined that it was just another decomposed basking shark.[14]

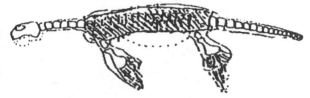

Fig. 23. Sketch of Zuiyo-Maru carcass, 1977

Masbate Plesiosaur—Remains of an unidentified animal discovered on the beach of one of the Masbate Islands in the Philippines in the mid-1990s. It was reported as being approximately 40 feet in length, with dark and possibly scaly flesh, a long tail, and four flippers. The natives who discovered it sold the rotting carcass to a local butcher, who later described it on TV as being a cross between a small plesiosaur and a large tortoise pried from its shell. But of course it turned out to be yet one more decayed basking shark.[15]

IDENTIFICATIONS

In 1892, when Oudemans conducted his analysis of 166 Sea-Serpent sightings, the sciences of both paleontology and marine biology were in their infancies, and many creatures now well-known had not yet been officially discovered or recognized by science. Some of these may be significant contributors to reports of then-unknown monsters, and I believe it is time to reevaluate some of these early categories and propose new identifications.

After we have done with the rotting carcasses, several likely contenders for the real identity or identities of Sea-Serpents are: seaweed masses; giant squids; oarfish; frilled sharks; huge crocodiles and lizards; and seals. But before we examine these possibilities, we have to address the matter of scale. Many written descriptions and drawings of Sea-Serpents match the proportions of known creatures, except for one glaring factor—their immense size. Witnesses often report creatures resembling eels, seals, or otters, but at exaggerated sizes many times greater than that which such animals are known to attain. How can we account for this discrepancy of scale?

In February of 1985, as our dive boat, the *Reef Explorer,* was crossing the Solomon Trench on the way from Australia to New Guinea in search of Mermaids (see Chapter 10. "Merfolk"), we encountered a true monster of the deep. A huge whale shark ap-

peared right beside our boat, just beneath the surface. I was the first to dive into the water and swim alongside this giant fish, until it eventually descended beyond my range, seeming to simply grow smaller and smaller in the crystal-clear water until it appeared to be but a tiny minnow. Back on the boat, we all compared impressions. There was no doubt in most of our minds that the immense creature must have been at least 40 feet long. Our skipper, however, had a bit more experience with such matters. He had noted the length of the shark in comparison to the boat, and he confirmed that it had been "only" about 20 feet long.

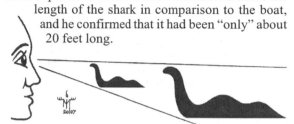

Fig. 24. Size perceived according to estimated distance

There are two perceptual factors at work here, I believe. The first is pretty straightforward: In the open ocean, as in the sky, there is little objective basis for comparison. Binocular vision only works over short distances. A creature flying overhead could, for all you know, be 100 feet above and have a 5-foot wingspan; or, it could be 1,00 feet above and have a 50-foot wingspan. If the air is clear, there is almost no way to know. The same thing is true on the ocean. In the absence of some object of known dimensions at the same distance, a shape in the water could be of any size, depending on how far away you estimate it to be. Moreover, a swimming creature may leave a long wake, which would create the added semblance of a greatly extended tail.

The second factor is even more interesting, in that it has more to do with our emotional reactions than to what we actually see. It seems we have a kind of built-in "zoom lens" in our brains that automatically responds to anything visually alarming or potentially threatening by zooming in to enlarge it, and simultaneously blanking out everything else. The effect of this tunnel vision is that such things are suddenly perceived as being much bigger than their actual size. I used to encounter this all the time when I lived in a wilderness homesteading community. Rattlesnakes were fairly common on the land, and whenever there was one spotted in an area where children might encounter it, someone would call me to come and remove it, as I knew how to handle them safely. Every time, I would be told about some "huge snake—at least 6 feet long!"—only to discover it was just a little guy, at most half that size. In fact, the snakes even grew larger with each retelling of the story, which greatly enhanced my reputation as a snake handler!

This is just the way our minds work, after millions of years of evolution, to draw our attention to anything that might threaten our survival. And I am certain that the same perceptual distortion plays a large part in reported sightings of oversize monsters.

With such considerations in mind, let's now consider these candidates in order.

Seaweed Masses

It may seem unlikely, but long masses of seaweed certainly account for some important sightings, especially of incredibly long "serpents" 100–300 feet in length. As the following report attests, these masses can be uncannily convincing. In 1848, a "Mr. Smith" was making a voyage in his father's ship, the *Pekin*, when he recorded this remarkable encounter:

> When near Moulmein [Burma], in calm weather I saw at a certain distance something extraordinary, balancing itself on the waves, and which appeared to be an animal of immeasurable length. With our telescopes we could perfectly distinguish an enormous head, and a neck of monstrous size covered with a mane, which alternately appeared and disappeared. This appearance was likewise seen by all our crew, and everybody agreed that it must be the great sea-serpent. I…immediately ordered a boat to be lowered…the monster did not seem to be disturbed by their approach…. I saw them busily uncoiling the rope with which they were provided, while the monster continued to raise its head and unfold its enormous length…

Fig. 25. The great Sea-Serpent as it appeared

> In less than half an hour the formidable monster was hauled on board. The body appeared to be endowed with a certain suppleness so long as it remained suspended. But it was so covered with marine parasites of every species that it was not until some time had elapsed we arrived at the discovery that this terrible animal was neither more nor less than a monstrous algae, upwards of one hundred feet long and four feet in diameter, whose root at a distance had represented its head, while the motion communicated to it by the waves had given it the semblance of life.

Fig. 26. The gigantic seaweed serpent

Immediately after my arrival in London, the Daedalus reported its encounter with the great serpent in nearly the same parts, and I cannot doubt but that it was only the floating wreck of the algae whose history I have just related. Nevertheless, the illusion is rendered so justifiable by the appearance of the object, that if I had been unable to dispatch the boat at the *moment* I did, I should have remained all my life in the conviction that I had seen the great serpent of the sea.[16]

Giant Squids

Although the form of a Giant Squid (*Architeuthis*) may not seem particularly serpentine, there is little doubt that many early sightings of Sea-Serpents can be so identified. While this true monster of the deep seems well-documented today, it was not always so. As recently as 1958, when Heuvelmans wrote *The Kraken and the Giant Squid*, the very existence of this mythic beast was considered highly controversial. Numerous old drawings, supposedly depicting huge Sea-Serpents in pitched battles to the death with Sperm Whales (*Physeter macrocephalus*), fairly accurately illustrate the feeding of such whales upon giant squid.

Fig. 28. Pauline Sea-Serpent , 1875, after Rev. Penny

Another classic image in the annals of Sea-Serpent sightings is based on a report by Norwegian missionary Hans Egede (1696–1758). On a voyage to Greenland, he reported a personal encounter in July of 1734:

> On the 6th appeared a very terrible Monster of so huge a Size, that coming out of the Water, its Head reached above our Mast-Head; its Body was as bulky as the Ship, and three or four times as long. It had a long pointed Snout and spouted like a

Whale-fish; great broad Flappers, and the Body seemed covered with shell-work, its skin very rugged and uneven. The under Part of its Body was shaped like an enormous huge Serpent, and when it dived again under Water, it plunged backwards into the Sea, and so raised its tail aloft, which seemed a whole Ship's Length distant from the bulkiest part of its Body.[17]

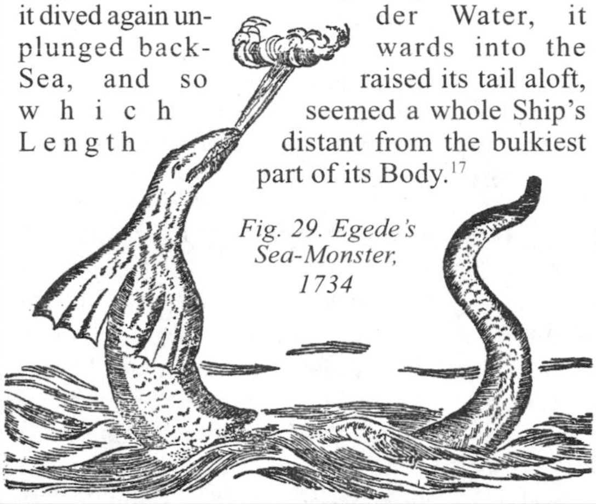

Fig. 29. Egede's Sea-Monster, 1734

Cryptozoologists have remarked that the accompanying illustration, drawn from this description by one of Egede's fellow missionaries, bears too great a resemblance to the thrashing back and tail of a giant squid, along with one of its waving tentacles, for it be a coincidence. This resemblance was first noted by Henry Lee, curator of the Brighton Aquarium, in his *Sea Monsters Unmasked* (1883). (Fig. 30). I concur that this seems the likeliest identification, and it demonstrates that, as with an iceberg, what may be observed above the surface does not necessarily give an accurate impression of what lies beneath and out of view.

Fig. 30. Egede's Sea-Monster, interpreted as a giant squid, after Henry Lee

Oarfish

A likely candidate for many sightings of long serpentine Sea-Monsters is the Oarfish (*Regalecus glesne*, also called the Ribbonfish)—the longest living bony fish. In 1808, a 56-foot-long specimen washed ashore in Scotland. With their bright silvery bodies, dramatic, scarlet, cockatoo-like head crests, attenuated, paddle-tipped pectoral fins, and long dorsal fin, they seem to me to qualify perfectly well as genuine Sea-Serpents, with no embellishments needed whatsoever.

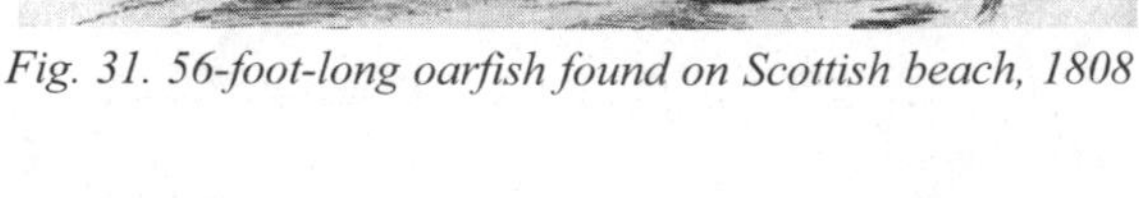

Fig. 31. 56-foot-long oarfish found on Scottish beach, 1808

Frilled Shark

Often called a "living fossil" because its characteristics have changed very little in 350 million years, the Frilled Shark (*Chlamydoselachus anguineus*) is long and slender like an eel, and takes its name from its six pairs of fringed gills, one set more than most sharks. It has 25 rows of sharp teeth, some of which protrude from the sides of its jaws like those of a crocodile. It was discovered in Japanese waters in the 19th century. On January 23, 2007, a specimen was captured alive off the coast of Japan, but it died shortly thereafter from the change of pressure. Sometimes caught in the nets of trawlers, their range is worldwide, but they dwell at depths of 2,000–3,300 feet, where they are the only predators of giant squids, other than sperm whales.[18] Although none of those caught has been more than 7 feet long, it is possible that much larger specimens may exist in the abyssal depths. If so, these would certainly account for reports of Sea-Monsters resembling *zueglodons*, as they closely match the common reconstructions of *archaeoceti*.

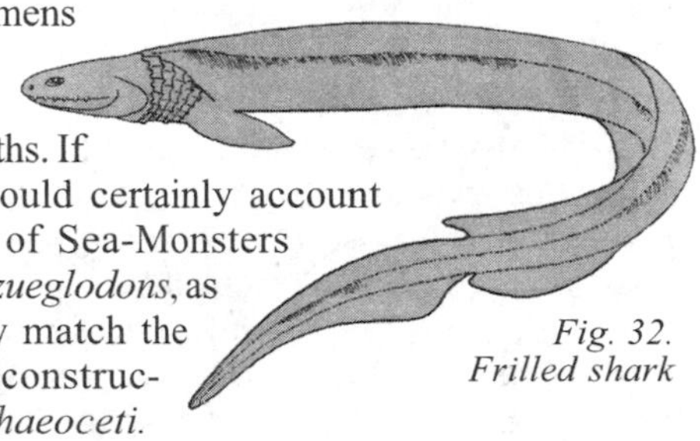

Fig. 32. Frilled shark

Crocodiles and Giant Lizards

Heuvelmans' Marine Saurians have been reported only 9 times, and I think that so few sightings can surely be accounted for by known reptiles. The Estuarine Crocodile (*Crocodylus porosus*) of Indonesia and northern Australia is the largest of all living reptiles. Also called marine crocodiles for their penchant for swimming freely in the open sea, they are known to reach 30 feet in length. Even larger specimens have been reported, if not confirmed.

The same region is the habitat of the largest lizards on Earth—the Komodo dragons, which grow up to 10 feet long and have been seen swimming between islands. But a prehistoric cousin, Megalania (*Varanus prisca*), was much larger, attaining lengths of 15–20 feet and weighing 1,000–1,300 pounds. Although believed to have been extinct for 40,000 years, sightings of living specimens are occasionally reported from Australia and New Guinea. Recently, part of a Megalania hipbone only 100–200 years old was discovered in a subfossil state.

Leopard Seals

Even though the *Daedalus* sighting (see above) is traditionally listed as a ***Super-Eel***, I am certain that this creature was a Leopard Seal (*Hydrurga leptonyx*), especially as it was encountered near Antarctic waters. A ferocious and terrifying predator, the leopard seal is characterized by its long streamlined body, a long neck, and a massive, almost reptilian, head with a flat forehead. The nostrils are positioned on top of the muzzle, and the animal has a heavy lower jaw with a huge gape. Males can be as long as 10 feet and weigh 1,000 pounds. These seals are silvery dark-grey on top and somewhat lighter on the bottom, with speckled counter-shading. They have long fore flippers (about one-third of their body length), and their hind flippers resemble double fish tails.[19]

Fig. 33. Leopard seal with swimming waterline indicated

They inhabit Antarctic waters, feeding on fish and penguins. Swimming at the surface, leopard seals hold their heads high and parallel to the surface, with their long, straight backs showing; sometimes front or rear flippers may be seen. As it is in all mammals, their spinal flexion is vertical. At times their insulating blubber undulates in the rolling waves, giving the appearance of moving humps along their bodies.

It seems to me very likely that leopard seals might also account for other sightings as well. Compare the image of a leopard seal with the 1848 Daedalu sighting (Fig. 15) and Heuvelman's drawing of the many-humped Sea-Serpent with the right flipper raised out of the water (a common thermoregulatory behavior for seals and sea lions, called flipper fanning.)

Fig. 34. Many-humped Sea-Serpent drawn by Heuvelmans

Other Seals

Descriptions and depictions of the **Merhorse**, with its mammalian whiskers and large, friendly eyes, can be matched with only one known class of animals: seals and sea lions—particularly the Common Seal

Fig. 35. Seal in "periscope" position

(*Phoca vitulina*) and the Grey Seal (*Halichoerus grypus*). These animals frequently adopt a distinctive "periscope" posture, in which they rise vertically as far as possible out of the water, holding their front flippers tightly against their sides and keeping their heads at a 90-degree angle so as to obtain a maximum view over the waves. The effect looks uncannily like the head and neck of a horse, dominated by

the enormous eyes of these pinnipeds. The analogy is further enhanced when the animal rises up through a mat of seaweed, which then falls about its head and neck like the mane of a horse (or the hair of a Mermaid…).

However, it would be imprudent to consign all sightings of "horse-headed" monsters of seas, lakes, lochs, or bogs to sightings of seals. Many of these— especially when they are accompanied by humps— appear to be something else entirely, and are thus more properly referred to as long-necked Sea-Serpents (or Lake-Monsters).

ThE GREAT MYSTERY REMAINS

Although I believe that the categories of living animals enumerated above may satisfactorily account for many sightings of the great Sea-Serpent, they do serve to clear the decks for the remaining true unknown monster of the sea—namely, the long-necked Sea- Serpent. I cannot accept the proposal by Oudemans and Heuvelmans, and the other cryptozoologists who have followed them, that these creatures are some sort of gigantic, long-necked, benthic pinnipeds. Although I too found the idea appealing when I first read *In the Wake of the Sea-Serpents* more than 35 years ago, I eventually had to conclude that this explanation really didn't work. After all, pinnipeds are air-breathers that spend a good part of their lives out of the water. Unlike cetaceans or even sirenians, which are fully adapted to an aquatic life and cannot return to land, all pinnipeds congregate in coastal colonies to bask, breed, and nurse their young on rocky shores and beaches. Thus, no species of pinniped could remain hidden today.

I have come to believe that long-necked Sea-Serpents are not mammals at all, nor plesiosaurs, nor even vertebrates. Despite his charming reconstruction of a long-necked seal, Heuvelmans' own silhouette drawings based on actual eyewitness descriptiona—especially that of the remarkable *Cuba* sighting in July of 1934, in which the animal leapt from the water (Fig. 36)—do not exhibit the proportions of his model, nor do they support his pinniped hypothesis, any more than they resemble a plesiosaur; against which identification all the arguments in the previous paragraph also apply.[20]

Fig. 36.

The Cuba sea-serpent, after Capt. P. Maguerez

Rather, the common description of the reported Long-Necked Sea-Serpents seems exactly similar to that of the classic Lake-Monsters I examined in the previous chapter, and I believe them to be a larger marine variant of these same creatures. That is, some sort of enormous aquatic slug, characterized by a long, extensible neck with diamond-shaped fins at its base, and a large, bulky body topped with a series of keeled humps, whose number increases with the size of the animal itself. The proportions of the head and neck are similar to those of a horse, camel, or giraffe, and the hornlike projections atop the head are certainly the eyes and feelers common to all snails and slugs. The rear parts and tail are seldom seen, and thus are poorly described. Probably there are *parapodia*— fleshy growths resembling wings that are used as fins in swimming. These appendages occur in several known Opisthobranch suborders, such as the *Thecosomata* and *Gymnosomata*, and would seem to fit the few observations of the hind parts of Long-Necked Sea-Serpents.

Fig. 37.

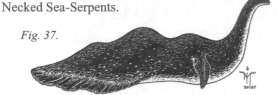

Sea-Serpent as giant marine slug, by Oberon Zell

I think that the best evidence in favor of this hypothesis is the remarkable pair of photographs of Morgawr, the Cornish Sea-Serpent, taken by "Mary F." in February of 1976, from Rosemullion Head near Falmouth Bay. (Fig. 42) In her letter to the *Falmouth Packet*, which published the photos, Mary F. said that the monster was only visible for a few seconds, and that the part she could see was about 15–18 feet long: "It looked like an elephant waving its trunk, but the trunk was a long neck with a small head on the end, like a snake's head. It had humps on the back which moved in a funny way. The color was black or very dark brown, and the skin seemed to be like a sealion's…the animal frightened me. I would not like to see it any closer. I do not like the way it moved when swimming."[21]

Fig. 38. Morgawr, photographed by "Mary F." in February, 1976, from Rosemullion Head near Falmouth Bay

As I write this in December of 2006, the first giant squid has just been captured alive and videotaped as it thrashed about at the surface.[22] Prior to this moment, no living specimen of the legendary Kraken has been witnessed in modern times, and all we knew of them was from rotting carcasses washed up on beaches. Perhaps someday a living long-necked Sea-Serpent will also be captured in a net or on video, and we'll finally know for certain what they are.

Meanwhile, it's good to know that there still remain some unsolved mysteries of the deep.

POSTSCRIPT

Shortly after I completed this chapter, I received information that my wish for a breakthrough may have come true: On March 27, 2007, on a dolphin-watching cruise off the coast of South Africa, 13 crew members of the Ocean Safari vessel *Dolphin* and volunteers from the Centre for Dolphin Studies took numerous photographs (Fig. 39) of an unknown marine invertebrate, which to me looks exactly like a small version of the long-necked sea slug I have postulated. Miss Gwenith Penry posted photos and a detailed description to teuthiologist Steve O'Shea's *TONMO.com* (The Octopus News Magazine Online).[23]

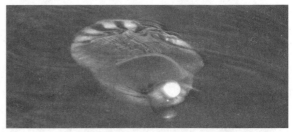

Fig. 39: Unidentified sea-creature photographed by Gwenith Penry on March 27, 2007

Penry reported that the creature was 12–16 inches long. At its anterior end was a "very distinctive 'nose'/ trunk like protrusion which appeared to be able to move independently of the rest of the body…. There was a notable inflation of the 'melon' as the animal surfaced and this then deflated as it dived." There appeared to be a membranous "skirt," or parapodia, "on the posterior end of the body, mostly grey but with banding around the edges…. This looks like a thin layer of 'skin' that 'flaps' like a ray. The banded area looks like two separate appendages that do not join, but the ends meet." It was "first spotted just below the surface (~30 cm), it then surfaced and swam towards the boat, stopped and lifted the 'nose' towards us as if sensing something in front of it."

In the four excellent photos Penry posted, the extensible neck, inflatable hump, and parapodia are clearly visible. After the posting, heated discussion ensued, but ultimately, no conclusive identification could be made. I believe it was a very young long-necked Sea-Serpent, and I eagerly await further sightings.

MONSTER MOVIES: SEA-SERPENTS

The only movie I know of that featured a Sea-Serpent was Terry Jones's *Erik the Viking* (1989), which was inspired by his children's book, *The Saga of Erik the Viking* (1983).

20. TITANIC TURTLES, FANTASTIC FISH, AND LEGENDARY LIZARDS

By Oberon Zell-Ravenheart

My sons, do not be afraid. God has revealed to me during the night in a vision the secret of this affair. Where we were was not an island, but a fish—the foremost of all that swim in the ocean. He is always trying to bring his tail to meet his head, but he cannot because of his length. His name is Jasconius.
—*The Voyage of St. Brendan* (9th century)[1]

THE ISLAND-BEAST

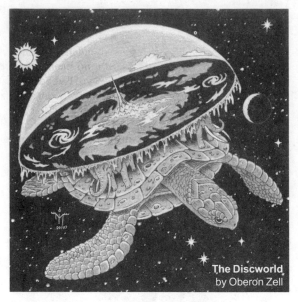

The Discworld
by Oberon Zell

NE OF THE MOST FASCINATING MONsters of mariners' lore is the great Island-Beast or Devil-Whale—a Sea-Monster of such immensity that when it is basking on the surface of the water, sailors mistake its back for an island and land on it. When they build a fire, however, the living "island" plunges into the depths, dragging the ship and crew to a watery doom. Various tales describe it as a titanic turtle, a prodigious whale, or even a colossal cephalopod such as the Kraken. Often depicted on maps among other fabulous Sea-Monsters, it is invariably shown with a ship anchored to it and a landing party building a fire on its back. European sailors told many tales of its existence and sightings.

Fig. 1. Aspidochelone by Konrad Gesner (1563)

In Greco-Roman times, the Island-Beast was called **Aspidochelone** (Latin, "shield turtle"). This name became corrupted in later medieval bestiaries to *Aspidodelone* or *Aspidoicholon* ("asp turtle"). The *Physiologus*, dating from the 2nd century BCE, refers to this monster as **Fastitocalon** ("floater on ocean streams"). It is described as a stony-skinned Sea-Monster the size of a whale, resembling a small rocky island fringed with sand and seaweed. It was said to be very dangerous, luring ships' crews to disembark for shore leave, then plunging with them into the depths to devour them. In the absence of any potential human victims, it emits a sweet perfume from its mouth that lured shoals of fishes within, swallowing them by the thousands.

Arabian writers called the Island-Beast the **Zaratan**, and described it as a gigantic turtle, adding the detail that its vast back is festooned with rocks and crevices overgrown with trees, grass, and shrubbery. In Scheherazade's *1,001 Arabian Nights*, Sinbad the Sailor encounters this monster on the first of his seven legendary voyages.

Fig. 2. Zaratan

Such a great Sea-Monster was said to have been encountered by the Irish monk St. Brendan (484–578 CE) during his legendary seven-year voyage to the promised land of the saints. Disembarking onto a stony island to celebrate Easter mass, the monks were stoking a fire to boil a pot when the island began to move under them like a wave. As they all rushed back to their boat, the "island" swam away. Then Brendan told them (somewhat belatedly, it seems) that God had revealed to him in a dream that the supposed island was in reality a monstrous fish, "the foremost of all that swim in the ocean. He is always trying to bring his tail to meet his head, but he cannot because of his length. His name is **Jasconius**" (Latinized Irish, "fish").[2]

Fig. 3. Jasconius

The Inuit natives of Greenland tell of an Island-Monster they call **Imap Umassoursa**. It would rise up underneath boats and capsize them into the frigid waters.

Fig. 4
Imap Úmassoursa by Xander

The Island-Beast is also linked to the Biblical account of Jonah and the great fish, which finds an echo in the story of Pinocchio, the runaway marionette, being swallowed by Monstro the Whale. A particularly spectacular version of this beast is found in the fabulous adventures of Baron Munchausen (1720–1797), first collected and published by an anonymous author in 1781, and made into several extravagant movies in the 20th century. In Munchausen's tale, the monster is so enormous that entire ships and their crews repose within its cavernous belly, swallowed but undigested.

Fig. 5. Jonah and the great fish

COSMIC WORLD-TURTLES

Many cultures throughout history have thought of the land as being carried on the back of a giant fish or turtle swimming through an infinite sea. This is why North America is sometimes referred to as Great Turtle Island by its native peoples. In the Hindu mythology of India, the disc of the Earth was thought to be supported on the backs of four, eight, or 16 colossal elephants; they, in turn, were thought to be standing on the shell of a gigantic cosmic turtle named **Ak-upara**, swimming eternally through space.

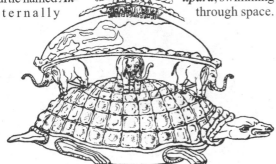

Fig. 6. Akupara, the Hindu world-turtle

Fantasy author and parody master Terry Pratchett has written dozens of delightful satirical novels set on such a world, which he calls the *Discworld*. These books are favorites among magickal people (they feature some memorable Wizards and Witches), and several have already been made into movies. In these stories, the great world-turtle is named Atuan, and she is seeking a place to lay her eggs. (See my opening graphic at the beginning of this chapter.)

Kurma is the name of the vast cosmic turtle of Hindu mythology. Its carapace forms the vault of the heavens, while its plastron is the foundation of the Earth—particularly the Indian subcontinent. When the Hindu gods churn the ocean of milk (the Milky Way) to create many things and beings, they ask Kurma to dive to the bottom to support the mountain they used for a dash, with the great serpent *Sesha-Naga* as a rope.

OTHER MONSTROUS TURTLES

The **Father of All Turtles** is an enormous sea-turtle of Sumatran legend, and one of several varieties of Sea-Serpents distinguished by Bernard Heuvalmans (1916–2001), the father of cryptozoology. There have been four recorded sightings of such a creature in different oceans. An example is the 30-foot-long monster sighted by Captain P. Merlees of the steamer *Hanoi* in June of 1908.

Fig. 7. The Hanoi sea-monster, by Capt. Merlees, 1808

Ikaki is a supernatural tortoise in the mythology of the Kalabari natives of Nigeria, West Africa. He loves to dance and sing, but each time he lifts one of his legs, everyone on that side falls down dead—no doubt from his terrible flatulence. A ritual dance called the tortoise masquerade is still widely performed, in which a dancer with a tortoise shell helmet imitates Ikaki's movements, which convey powerful magick.

Kappa are river-dwelling Japanese creatures of Shinto mythology. They have the body of a tortoise, long scaly limbs, the head of a monkey, and long hair. They live on blood and cucumbers, and they fly through the air on enchanted cucumbers with dragonfly wings. If treated with courtesy, the Kappa is friendly. However, if it is ill-treated, it will eat its tormentor.

Fig. 8. Kappa

Skahnowa is a monstrous turtle in the folklore of the Seneca Indians of the northeastern United States. It aids the horned serpent Doonongaes in hunting human and animal prey.

Bosco (or Oscar, beast of 'Busco) is the affectionate appellation of a gigantic turtle reported to be dwelling near Churubusco, Indiana. It has been spotted several times since 1950, when several swamps were drained in order to create more farmland. Witnesses have described Bosco as weighing between 100 and 500 pounds, with a shell 4 feet wide. In 1937, an enormous Alligator Snapping Turtle (*Macrochelys temminckii*) was in fact captured at the Neosho River in Kansas. It weighed a whopping 403 pounds.

Fig. 9.
Alligator
snapping turtle

Archelon ("old turtle") was the largest turtle that has ever lived, living during the Upper Cretaceous period 65–99 million years ago, when the shallow waters of the Niobrara Sea covered the central portion of North America. The biggest *Archelon* fossil, found in the Pierre Shale of South Dakota, measures nearly 14 feet long, and is 16 feet wide from flipper to flipper. The live weight of an *Archelon* is estimated to have been more than 4,500 pounds.

Fig. 10. Archelon skeleton

Another huge prehistoric sea turtle was **Protostega** ("first roof"). Reaching 10 feet in length, it is the second-largest turtle that has ever existed.

Archelon and *Prostega* were related to the present-day Leatherback Sea Turtle (*Dermochelys coriacea*). At 9 feet long, this is the largest living turtle. Similar to the modern leatherback, the shells of *Archelon* and *Prostega* had no scutes, making them weaker but also lighter. They probably fed on shellfish and slow-moving jellyfish.[3]

Fig. 11. Leatherback sea turtle
by Heuvelmans

The largest land turtle known to have ever existed was *Testudo atlas* ("atlas tortoise"), also known as **Colossochelys** ("colossal turtle"). At 8 feet long and 6 feet high, it probably weighed around 4 tons. Looking much like a modern Galapagos tortoise, this giant chelonian herbivore lived in the Pleistocene period—1.5–2 million years ago. Similar to its modern relatives, *T. atlas* could probably retract its legs and head into its shell when threatened.[4]

Legendary Lizards

Monstrous lizards figure prominently in the legends of Dragonlore. Although no such creatures are known to have existed in Europe in human times, the discovery of giant, 10-foot-long, 300-pound lizards on the Indonesian island of Komodo in 1910 created a worldwide sensation. They were immediately dubbed Komodo Dragons (*Varanus komodoensis*). A legendary 1926 expedition led by W. Douglas Burden and sponsored by the American Museum of Natural History brought back two live dragons and 12 preserved bodies. Two of these skins were mounted and can still be seen today in the museum's Hall of Amphibians and Reptiles. Burden recounted his adventure to an island of prehistoric reptiles to movie producer Merian C. Cooper. Inspired, Cooper changed the subject of the quest from a giant lizard to a giant ape and added a beautiful heroine to produce the classic 1933 film *King Kong*.[5] The gigantic lizards weren't forgotten, however, for they became dinosaurs in the movie version.

Fig. 12.
Komodo dragon

A much larger prehistoric version of the Komodo dragon was **Megalania** (*Varanus prisca*), which was 15–20 feet long and weighed 1,000–1,300 pounds. Although it is believed to have been extinct for 40,000 years, sightings of living specimens are occasionally reported from Australia and New Guinea. In early 1890, residents of Euroa, Australia, claimed that their vil-

Fig. 13. *Megalania*

lage was being terrorized by a 30-foot-long, unidentifiable reptilian monster. A representative of the Melbourne Zoological Gardens, equipped with a big net, organized a search party of 40 trackers. They discovered a set of huge footprints, but these unfortunately terminated before the creature could be found.

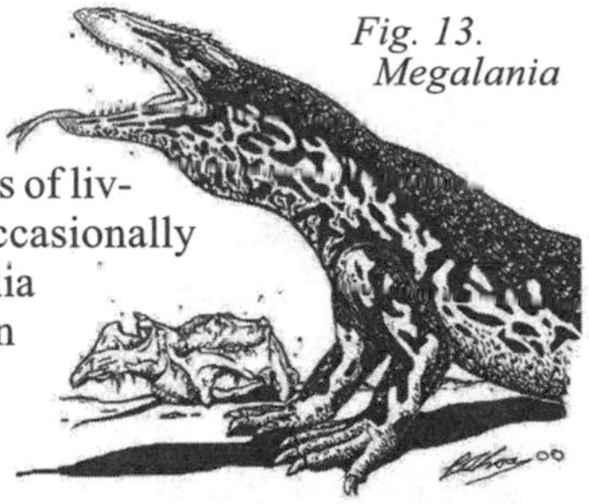

Whowhie is a monstrous lizard in the legends of the Aboriginal people of Australia's Murray River area. It terrorized the region, devouring many people—especially children. After a particularly devastating raid on a village, the people tracked the monster to its lair in a cave, where it was sleeping off its meal. They burned brushwood at the entrance, fanning smoke into the cave for seven days, until Whowhie finally emerged, coughing and blinded—whereupon the people rushed it, clubbing and spearing it until it was dead. This tale suggests an actual encounter with the gigantic Pleistocene *Megalania*.

Kurrea was a monstrous, swamp-dwelling reptile of the Australian Aborigine Dreamtime, with a voracious appetite. It threatened to eat everyone, so the hero Toola was sent to kill it. But his spears just bounced off its armored back, and it then turned to pursue him, burrowing through earth and rocks as easily as water. As it closed on him, Toola led it to his mother-in-law, Bumble Tree. Kurrea took one look at her, screamed in terror, and dove into the earth, leaving a great hole. It never returned to bother people again. Could this story possibly reflect another memory of *Megalania*?

Fig.14. *Tuatara*

The *Tanihwa* are gigantic guardian reptiles in the traditions of the Maori natives of New Zealand. They are said to live in deep pools of rivers, dark caves, or the ocean—especially where there are dangerous currents or breakers. Some can tunnel through the earth, causing landslides and uprooting trees in the process. Others are said to have created harbors by carving out channels to the sea. In the ocean they usually resemble a large shark or whale, but in inland waters they resemble a giant Tuatara (*Sphenodon*), with a row of spines down their back. They are protectors of their respective tribespeople, attacking any others on sight.

The Taniwha *Horomatangi*, a gigantic aquatic lizard, does not prey on people, and sometimes even helps them. But he often attacks canoes and other boats, especially modern powerboats. He created the great Karapiti blowhole. *Hotu-Puku*, on the other hand, hunted and devoured people, and it was so strong and fast that none could escape it. Eventually it was killed by a party of hunters who laid a net across the entrance to its cave and taunted it to come running out into the snare, where it was speared until dead. If an *Ihu-Mataotao* is killed and its belly cut open, its victims will emerge undigested. And *Parata* sucks in and spews out the waters of the oceans with its cavernous mouth, thus accounting for the tides. Scientists have named a fossil mosasaur *Taniwhasaurus oweni*, in honour of the Taniwha.

Fig. 15. Mosasaur by Zdenek Burian (1905-1981)

Gurangatch is an immense lizard-fish Water-Monster from the Dreamtime lore of the Aborigines of New South Wales, Australia. It can tunnel through solid rock from pool to pool, causing rivers to overflow their banks.

While traveling through Africa's Kasai valley in 1932, a Swedish plantation owner named Johnson and his native servant witnessed a gigantic reptile attack and devour a rhinoceros. He described it as a 40-foot-long lizard with a long, thick tail, leonine legs, and long, sharp teeth in huge jaws. It was dark red, with vertical black stripes like a tiger's down its neck, back, and tail. This monstrous lizard has been dubbed *Kasai Rex*.

Fillyloo (also *Gowrow*, *Golligog*, or *Gollygog*) is a giant lizard-monster or Dragon in the Native American legends of the Ozark mountains, which it was reported to frequent in the 19th century. As described by V. Randolf in 1951, it was said to be at least 20 feet long, with boar-like tusks. Another lizard-like monster in the native folklore of the Ozarks is called *Moogie*.

And the legends of the Araucanian Indians of Chile tell of *Lampalugua*—a gigantic predatory lizard with enormous claws. It devours both cattle and people.

A large, lizard-like creature was sighted in the early 1960s in the Nith River, which flows through New Hamburg, Ontario, Canada. Many witnesses described it as weighing about 50 pounds, greenish-brown in color, with four legs and a scaly tail. But this relatively small creature seems likely to have been just an alligator that someone released into the river.

COLOSSAL CROCS

Medieval bestiaries include a creature called the **Cocodryllus** or *Corkendril*. Though often bizarrely depicted, this is just a monstrous, 30-foot-long version of the crocodile, with vivid crocus or saffron hues. The Nile Crocodile (*Crocodylus niloticus*) of Egypt and the Estuarine Crocodile (*Crocodylus porosus*) of Indonesia and northern Australia can both grow to this size, but they are basically grey in color, with yellowish underbellies. Amusingly, it seems to have been considered essential to the décor of any proper medieval Wizard's sanctum or alchemist's laboratory to have a stuffed "Corkendril" hanging from the ceiling!

*Fig. 16.
Medieval
Cocodryllus*

During the Cretaceous era (141–65 million years ago), a truly monstrous crocodile called *Phobosuchus* ("fearsome crocodile") haunted the world's shorelines. The giant predator was about 50 feet long; its head alone measured 6 feet long, and its teeth, 4 inches!

A gigantic crocodilian, called **Mahamba** by locals, has been reported from the Lake Likouala swamp region of central Africa's Republic of the Congo. It is said to reach an impressive 50 feet in length, and devour entire rafts and canoes along with their occupants. Natives insist that the animal is a unique species, quite distinct from the familiar Nile crocodile. Could this possibly be a surviving example of Phobosuchus?

*Fig. 17. Nile
Crocodile*

Tompondrano is a gigantic Sea-Monster of Madagascar, covered with armored plates like those on a crocodile. Its phosphorescent head can be seen under the water, as was reported by some fishermen in 1926. This is certainly an Estuarine Crocodile (*Crocodylus porosus*), the largest of all living reptiles. Normally confined to Indonesia, it is known to reach 30 feet in length. The reported phosphorescence is created by any disturbance of bioluminescent plankton, which this author has personally observed at night

in the Coral Sea.

Orobon is a ferocious, fish-like predator said by the Arabs of Mount Mazovan to inhabit the region of the Red Sea. It was described in medieval bestiaries as being about 10 feet long, with a head like that of a catfish, webbed, clawed feet, and a hide like that of a crocodile—which is most likely what it was based upon. However, considering the description of the head, it may have been a Wels Catfish (*Silurus glanis*), which is known to reach 10 feet in length and weigh 330 pounds. Perhaps what we are dealing with is a confusion of two separate animals.

*Fig. 18.
Orobon*

Slimy Slim is the local name for a Lake-Monster inhabiting the depths of Lake Payette, Idaho. It is said to have a serpentine body at least 36 feet long, and a head like that of a crocodile.

MONSTER MOVIES: GIANT FISH, TURTLES, LIZARDS, AND CROCS

(Author's note: I am omitting the "giant lizards" of cheap dinosaur movies that used ordinary lizards on miniature sets to represent what were supposed to be dinosaurs. These are called *slurpasaurs*, and are distained by all true dino film aficionados. -OZ)

Pinocchio (animated, 1940)—Fastitocalon
The Giant Gila Monster (1959)—giant lizard
The Fabulous Baron Munchausen (1962)—
    Fastitocalon
One Million Years B.C. (1966)—giant turtle
The Neverending Story (1984)—giant turtle
The Adventures of Baron Munchausen (1988)—
    Fastitocalon
Pinocchio (animated, 1992)—Fastitocalon
The Adventures of Pinocchio (1996)—Fastitocalon
Aladdin and the King of Thieves (animated, 1996)—
    Zaratan
Wyrd Sisters (animated-TV, 1996)—world-turtle
Soul Music (animated-TV, 1997)—world turtle
Godzilla (1998)—giant lizard
Komodo (TV, 1999)—Megalania
Lake Placid (1999)—gigantic crocodile
Blood Surf a.k.a. *Krocodylus* (2000)—
    giant crocodile
Hogfather (TV, 2006)—world-turtle
Lake Placid 2 (TV, 2007)—gigantic crocodile

21. OCCULT OCTOPUSES

By Oberon Zell-Ravenheart

Ian Daniels

Frodo felt something seize him by the ankle, and he fell with a cry…. The others swung around and saw the waters of the lake seething, as if a host of snakes were swimming up from the southern end. Out from the water a long sinuous tentacle had crawled; it was pale-green and luminous and wet. Its fingered end had hold of Frodo's foot, and was dragging him into the water. Sam on his knees was now slashing at it with a knife. The arm let go of Frodo, and Sam pulled him away, crying out for help. Twenty other arms came rippling out. The dark water boiled, and there was a hideous stench.

　　—J.R.R. Tolkien, "The Watcher in the Water" from *The Fellowship of the Ring*, 1954

EVERAL TYPES OF MYSTERIOUS, tentacled aquatic creatures have been reported for centuries to be lurking in the deeps. The *Kraken*—based on the real animal we now more commonly call the Giant Squid (*Architeuthis*)—is certainly the most storied in myth and legend, and is discussed fully in another chapter. But many cryptic cephalopods appear not to be squids, but rather octopuses, which are quite different beasts. The two categories I would like to discuss here are those said to dwell in freshwater lakes and rivers; and gigantic species believed to dwell in the oceans. I use the term "occult" not in the sense of "supernatural," but rather in the original sense of the Latin *occultus*, meaning "hidden, concealed, secret."

ᴛʜᴇ ʟᴜʀᴋᴇʀ ɪɴ ᴛʜᴇ ʟᴀᴋᴇ

Although there are no known species of cephalopods able to live in fresh water, there have been numerous reports over the past couple of centuries of octopus-like creatures inhabiting lakes in Indiana, Kentucky, Oklahoma, and West Virginia, as well as the monster-infested Ohio River. They are always described as being ugly, grey in color, and about 3 feet long. They appear to be similar to *Octopus burryi* and *Octopus filosus/hummelinki*. With over 300 species of octopus catalogued to date, it is not inconceivable that a freshwater variant might turn up,

Fig. 1. Octopus burryi

though probably not as impressive as Tolkein's "Watcher in the Water."

Such a tentacled creature is said to be lurking in the depths of Oklahoma's Thunderbird, Oolagah, and Tenkiller lakes. Long feared by the local Indians, who likened it to a leech, this animal has been described as roughly the size of a horse, with a leathery, reddish-brown skin, small beady eyes, and multiple tentacles. It is said to be a voracious predator and violently territorial.

A similar monster is said to inhabit the deep, cold, salty water of mist-shrouded Devil's Lake, in Sauk County, Wisconsin. The local Lakota Indians have stories of this creature going back centuries, of which one of the earliest

Fig. 2. Devil's Lake Monster

recounts a fatal attack on a canoe full of warriors by something with many tentacles, such as a Kraken.

South America seems to be a particularly favored locale for freshwater cephalopods. The most famous of these is *El Cuero* (Spanish, "the cowhide"), also called *El Trelquehuecuve*, or *El Bien Peinado* ("the smooth-headed one"). Reported to be lurking in the glacial waters of Lago (Lake) Lacar, in the southern Andes province of Neuquen, it is a large and dangerous Water-Monster described as a flat skin resembling a cowhide, with clawed tentacles and multiple eyes. According to legend, it originated from a donkey's hide that fell into the water and came to life, engulfing every

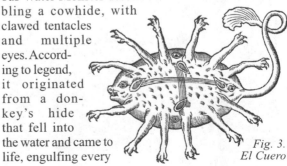

Fig. 3. El Cuero

living thing it encountered by folding around them. It suns itself on the rocks and causes windstorms. Elsewhere the same creature is called *Hueke Hueku* ("the leather"). A dreaded creature inhabiting lakes and rivers, natives say that when it floats on the surface of the water it resembles a stretched animal skin.[1]

This sounds very like a giant octopus, but one that lives in fresh water.

The ***Glyryvilu*** or *Guirivulu* is a freshwater monster dwelling in Chile's Andean Mountains. In some districts it is known as ***Vulpangue*** ("fox-serpent"), and is described as a fox-headed snake or a puma with the head of a fox. Its long tail terminates in a vicious claw, with which it seizes its victims. (Fig. 4) As it swallows them whole, its mouth and belly extend like those of a snake.

Elsewhere, it is said to be a gigantic fish or Dragon. But another version—more relevant to our present inquiry—claims it is flat and disc-shaped, like a ray, but with tentacles like those of an octopus and eyes around its perimeter.

Fig. 4. Vulpangue

West central Africa is also said to be home to a freshwater cephalopod. Known as the ***Migas***, it is reported to dwell in the upper reaches of the Congo River. Similar to *El Cuero*, it is described as a huge, flat creature with long tentacles. All of these creatures would seem to be some kind of octopus, but no species of freshwater cephalopod is currently known to science. However, a marine animal that matches the descriptions of El Cuero, Glyryvilu, and Migas quite well is the Japanese Pancake Devilfish (*Opisthoteuthis depressa*). (Fig. 5.) Could a similar species have adapted to fresh water, just as other mollusks (clams, snails, and slugs) have?

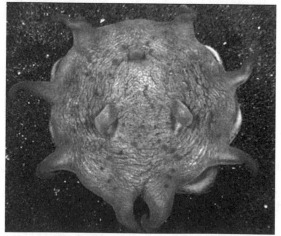

Fig. 5. Japanese pancake devilfish

OCTOPUS GIGANTEUS

Fig. 6. Lusca

A gargantuan octopus is reported to be dwelling in the crystal waters of the Bahamas islands off the coast of Florida. It is variously called the ***Lusca,*** the *Giant Scuttle,* or *Him of the Hairy Hands*. Normally living in very deep water, this creature is said to inhabit large limestone marine caves, called "blue holes," off the coast of the mysterious, mangrove-choked island of Andros. Similar tentacled monsters are said to inhabit the island's "banana holes"—deep, brackish pools and small lakes. Divers have reported attacks by "many-armed animals resembling giant octopuses."[2] One native guide maintained that the arms of the Giant Scuttle were about 75 feet long, but they are not dangerous to fishermen unless they can grip the ocean floor and the boat at the same time.

> The legendary Lusca is either octopus or squid-like, but it often combines elements of a dragon-like creature. There are some assorted tales of very large creatures stealing bait from fishing boats, although it is not certain that they all were cephalopods. Of additional interest is a photograph taken by the Cousteau team of one of those mysterious animals, although it just shows unidentifiable brown flesh. Cuba also has some legends of a giant octopus, except that they often have phosphorescent eyes and other parts. In addition, there was at least one non-ambiguous giant octopus sighting from Florida.[3]

This as-yet-unconfirmed cephalopod has been assigned the scientific name of *Octopus giganteus*.

Tales of giant octopuses are not limited to the Caribbean. In the folklore of Chiloc, Chile, a gigantic Sea-Monster called the ***Manta*** is the marine equivalent of the freshwater *Cuero* ("hide"). It is described as resembling a flayed cowhide with clawed tentacles and tail, and eyes all around the edges and four more on top. Although the name would seemingly refer to the giant Manta Ray (*Manta birostris*), which is certainly flat, and can measure up to 25 feet long and weigh up to 6,600 pounds, the tentacles indicate it may be a cephalopod, such as the Pacific Giant Octopus (*Enteroctopus dofleini*), which may grow to more than 30 feet long and weigh more than 100 pounds. Mantas were said to sometimes climb out on land to sun themselves, and cause violent gales upon their return to the sea. This suggests carcasses washed ashore after a storm, which would account for the appearance of a stretched cowhide. However, it has been ingeniously suggested by Karl Shuker[4] that the Manta may be a gigantic jellyfish, such as the Nomu-

ra's jellyfish (*Echizen kurage*), which can be 6 feet across and weigh 450 pounds. Lately, populations of these huge creatures have been exploding in many fishing waters—particularly around Japan, wherre they are considered a devastating plague.

Fig. 7. Echizen kurage

J.W. Buel described a huge and powerful Sea-Monster having "eight long arms attached to a broad, flat body, in the center of which are its leering eyes and cavernous mouth, around which are several horny spines."[5] He called this creature the ***Devil Fish*** (also known as the *Sea Devil* or *Sea Bat*). (Fig. 8) These names and eyewitness reports clearly identify it as the giant Manta Ray (*Manta birostris*), the largest known specimen of which had a 25-foot-wide "wingspan" and weighed 6,600 pounds. However, these fish do not have tentacles, which makes the description a bit puzzling, as it seems to conflate the manta ray with a cephalopod. A creature that does fit the description, however, is the aforementioned Japanese Pancake Devilfish (*Opisthoteuthis depressa*).

Fig. 8. Manta or Devil-Fish, from J. W. Buel

In addition to the freshwater reports from North America, Chile, and Africa, Hawaii also has had many reported sightings. And Tahitian folklore tells of an immense spotted octopus called *Tumu-Ra'i-Fuena*, whose prodigious tentacles permeate and hold together every part of the Earth and the Heavens.[6]

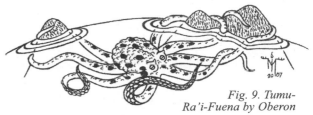

Fig. 9. Tumu-Ra'i-Fuena by Oberon

BLOBS AND GLOBSTERS

Many moundlike, amorphous carcasses have been found washed up on ocean beaches of Florida, Bermuda, New Zealand, and Tasmania. Called Globsters or Blobs, they are roughly cylindrical in shape, with a flattened underside. They vary in size from 8 to 30 feet long. Virtually unidentifiable masses of fibrous collagen, they have no internal skeleton—neither bone nor cartilage—and their rubbery skin is as tough as a car tire and often covered in thin hair. Some appear to have gill-like slits, small mouths, and long fleshy lobes or tentacles along the sides, but no eyes have been reported. Although considered by many to be storm-ravaged carcasses of the as-yet-unconfirmed *Octopus giganteus*, it has recently been determined that these are the boneless remains of decomposed Sperm Whales (*Physeter macrocephalus*), consisting of the huge mas of blubber above the head and shoulders, and strips of blubber from between the ribs.

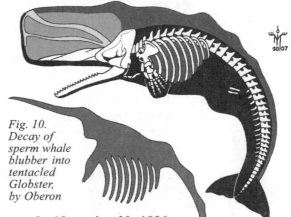

Fig. 10. Decay of sperm whale blubber into tentacled Globster, by Oberon

On November 30, 1896, an enormous carcass was found partial-ly buried in the sandy beaches of Anastasia Island, off the coast of St. Augustine, Florida. Dubbed the *St Augustine Phenomenon*, the exposed portion was 7 feet tall, 23 feet long, and 18 feet across. Excavation revealed multiple tentacles up to 30 feet long. (Fig. 11) Renowned marine biologist A.E. Verill—who was instrumental in the discovery of the giant squid—became involved in the study of the remains. Confirming that it was an octopus and not a squid, he named the creature *Octopus giganteus verill*, and estimated its total length to be in excess of 100 feet. The carcass soon washed back out to sea, but in 1957, some original tissue samples were located and reexamined. Sadly, the results

*Fig. 11. The Sea-Monster that came ashore
on the Florida coast (1896)*

were inconclusive due to cellular decay from the prolonged storage.[7]

In May of 1988, Teddy Tucker found a peculiar blob washed up on the beach of Mangrove Bay, Bermuda. Called the *Bermuda Blob*, it was approximately 8 feet long and 3 feet wide, extremely pale and fibrous, and with no apparent bones, cartilage, or visible openings. It seemed to have five arms or legs, the effect of which Tucker described as being akin to a disfigured star. (Fig. 12)[8]

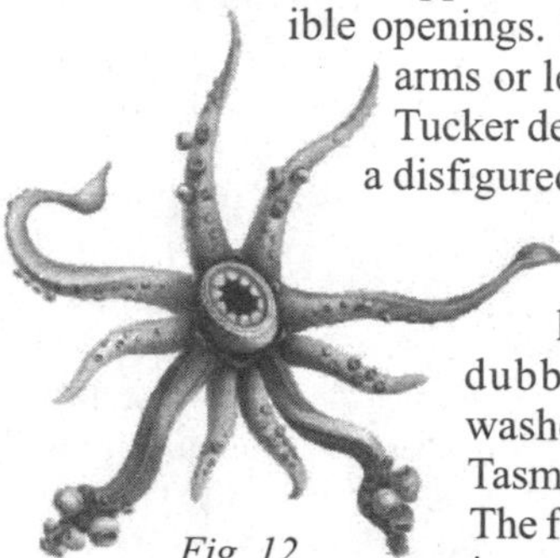

Several huge mysterious blobs of boneless flesh—popularly dubbed Globsters—have washed up on the beaches of Tasmania, south of Australia. The first discovery to become internationally known occurred on August, 1960, when a couple of ranchers stumbled across a huge carcass on the bank of the Interview River near Hobart. The corpse measured 20 feet long and 18 feet wide, with a 4-foot-high hump in the center. Its weight was estimated at 4–10 tons. It had a layer of fine, greasy hair like sheep's wool, and its flesh was hard and rubbery. In March of 1962, these remains were revisited and examined more thoroughly. Five to six gill-like slits were discovered running down either side of the creature's anterior. The investigators also found four large hanging lobes on what they assumed must be its head. Between the center pair was a smooth orifice resembling a gullet. No eyes were found.[9]

*Fig. 12.
The Bermuda Blob*

Fig. 13. The Tasmanian Globster

In 1970, a second Globster washed ashore a few miles south of Sandy Cape. This humped carcass was approximately 8 feet long and much fresher than the 1960 specimen. And in 1997, yet another curious carcass was discovered washed up on a stretch of Tasmanian coast known as Four Mile Beach. Named the Four-Mile Blobster, this amorphous creature had pad-

dle-shaped flippers, strands of white hair like spaghetti, and six long, fleshy lobes along its sides. The corpse was 15 feet long, 6 feet wide, and weighed approximately 4 tons. As with other Globsters, it seems to have been made up primarily of fibrous collagen.[10]

In March of 1965, a 30-foot-long, 8-foot-tall Globster washed up on Muriwai Beach, New Zealand. The carcass was described as having 4- to 6-inch-long long wooly hair over a tough, one-quarter-inch thick hide. Beneath this was a layer of fat, then solid meat. According to investigator J. Robb, the blob was covered not with hair, but with fibrous connective tissue. The "creature" turned out to be just a hunk of decomposing whale blubber.[11]

MONSTER MOVIES: DEADLY OCTOPUSES

Fig. 14. Coiled nautiloid from Mysterious Island, 1961

Reserving movies featuring the giant squid for the chapter on the Kraken, other monstrous cephalopods have also appeared in films, from the giant octopus shown in the 1929 silent film adaptation of Jules Vern's *Mysterious Island* to the absurd rubber octopus in Ed Wood's *Plan 9 from Outer Space* (1959), generally considered the worst movie ever made. *It Came from Beneath the Sea* (1955) features an immense, six-tentacled giant octopus by stop-motion legend Ray Harryhausen. A six-tentacled giant nautiloid by Harryhausen attacks Captain Nemo's divers in *Mysterious Island* (1961). The 1970 Japanese film, *Space Amoeba* (released in America as *Yog, Monster From Space*) features a giant cuttlefish called "Gezora." *Tentacles* (1977) is a horror film about a giant octopus. Ralph Bakshi's animated version of Tolkein's *The Lord of the Rings* (1978) includes the Watcher in the Water. *The Goonies* (1985) includes a giant octopus in a scene that was deleted from the theatrical release, but included on the DVD. *Octopus* (2000) and its sequel, *Octopus 2: River of Fear* (2002), also feature giant octopuses. But by far the best octopus-like monster ever created onscreen is the "Watcher in the Water" in Peter Jackson's *Lord of the Rings: The Fellowship of the Ring* (2001).

22. THE BUNYIP OF THE BILLABONG

By Oberon Zell-Ravenheart and Anna Fox

What have we here? a man or a fish?
Dead or alive? A fish: he smells like a fish;
A very ancient and fish-like smell...
I shall laugh myself to death at this
Puppy-headed monster. A most scurvy monster!
A most ridiculous monster,
To make a wonder of a poor drunkard!
A howling monster: a drunken monster!
　　　　　　　—Shakespeare, Trinculo's speech,
　　　　　　　　　　　　　The Tempest, 2:2

J. MacFarlane, 1890, Illustrated Australian News

HE MOST FAMOUS OF AUSTRALIA'S Mystery Monsters is undoubtedly the ***Bunyip*** ("evil spirit" in the Aboriginal language). Also called *Moolgewanke, Tuntabah, Tunatpan,* and *Wee-Waa*, this fierce, bellowing Water-Monster is said to dwell at the bottom of still swamps, lakes, rivers, creeks, water holes, and *billabongs* (stagnant oxbow pools attached to waterways) of the Australian Outback. Their blood-curdling cries may be heard at night as they attack and devour any poor creatures that venture near their watery abodes. Generally described as being about the size of a calf, and resembling a dark, hairy seal or hippo—sometimes with long arms and enormous claws—the Bunyip has also been depicted with walrus-like tusks, fins, scales, flippers, wings, a long, horselike tail, and/or feathers. In Tasmania, it is called the Universal Eye, and is portrayed as a snake. Natives fear it greatly as a man-eater.

During the early European settlement of Australia, when its unique creatures were still being discovered, it was generally assumed that the Bunyip was just another unknown but or-

Fig. 1. "The Bunyip of Aboriginal Legend," Australian postage stamp by Toogarr Morrison

dinary animal. Unfamiliar and unidentifiable nocturnal cries were attributed to the Bunyip. In 1846, the discovery of a bizarre skull on the banks of Murrumbidgee River in New South Wales—an area associated with such Bunyip calls—seemed to provide tangible evidence of the Bunyip's existence. Several experts rashly concluded that it was something unknown to science, and in 1847, the alleged "Bunyip skull" was exhibited in the Australian Museum in Sydney. Unfortunately, the mysterious skull was later identi-

fied as that of a deformed horse or calf.[1]

Today, however, the word "Bunyip" is used much as "Bogey" is—to refer to some weird and spooky unknown critter that is slightly silly and probably imaginary. Depictions of these critters have become increasingly bizarre and preposterous over the years. The Rev. George Taplin described the Bunyip of Lake Alexandra as being half man and half fish, with hair resembling a wig of water weeds. It roared like a cannon and gave people rheumatism.[2]

Unfortunately, these associations have made the legendary creature a perfect subject of hoaxes, practical jokes, and bogus reports. It has entered the category of "Fearsome Critters (Chapter 17). Anyone claiming to have seen a Bunyip is assumed to be lying or drunk, and gets treated about as seriously as if he or she had claimed to have seen a Purple People-Eater. The expression, "Why search for the Bunyip?" (meaning that a proposed course of action is futile) arose from repeated but fruitless attempts to spot or capture the elusive creature.

Fix. 2. "Bunyip" (1935), artist unknown, from the National Library of Australia digital collections

history
By Anna Fox

Fig. 3. "The Nature Spirit Bunyip," Australian postage stamp by David Lancashire

The earliest report in the strange history of the Bunyip is not of a sighting, but of a sound. In June of 1801, French explorers in the crew of the *Géographie* made their way inland along the Swan River from the bay on the southwestern tip of the Australian continent, which they had named after their vessel. Suddenly a terrible roar, louder than a bull's bellow, rang out from the reeds along the riverside. The terrified explorers beat a hasty retreat, convinced that they had been threatened by some horrible Water-Monster.[3]

The first white person to sight the Bunyip was an escaped convict named William Buckley, who lived with the Aborigines in Victoria from 1803 to 1835. He reported seeing a Bunyip from the back more than once, and even tried to kill it with a spear. According to Buckley, the Bunyip was covered in grey feathers and was about the size of a full-grown calf.[4]

Fig. 4. "The Bunyip of Natural History," Australian postage stamp by Marg Towt

English explorer Hamilton Hume reported seeing an animal like a manatee or hippopotamus in Lake Bathurst, on the opposite side of the continent. Members of the Philosophical Society of Australasia immediately offered to pay all his expenses if he could obtain a specimen or the remains of this creature. Hume claimed to have found large bones in 1818 which could have belonged to a Bunyip, but he was never able to produce the bones for scientific study. Nevertheless, throughout the 19th century, it was common for the Australian newspapers to report Bunyip sightings, and many tales were invented by parents to discourage children from wandering off into the bush.[5]

In 1848, a creature identified as a Bunyip was sighted in Victoria's Eumeralla River. It was described as a large brown animal with a long neck, a hairy mane, and a head like a kangaroo's. Witnesses claimed it had an enormous mouth.[6] The long neck and kangaroo-like head sounds much like a typical Lake-Monster, which is described in other lands as having a head like that of either a horse, a bull, a deer, a camel, or a giraffe. The heads and necks of all these creatures are remarkably similar in profile, suggesting that a real animal is involved.

A similarly-described Lake-Monster seen in the Port Phillip area was called the *Tunatpan*: "It was as big as a bullock, with an emu's head and neck, a horse's mane, and seal's flippers, which laid turtle's eggs in a platypus' nest, and ate blackfellows when it was tired of a crayfish diet."[7] Reports of such long-necked Bunyips have come only from New South Wales

Fig. 5. Long-necked Bunyip by Alisa Stern

The Greta Bunyip was said to dwell in the swamps of the Greta area, in Victoria. Locals often heard a loud booming sound coming from the swamps, yet no search parties were able to locate its source. When the swamps were drained, the night noises ceased. Some thought that the Bunyip had moved on, but others believed it had died when its habitat was destroyed.[8]

ABORIGINAL TALES
By Anna Fox

According to Aboriginal legend, Bunyip was originally a man who disobeyed the Rainbow Serpent by eating one of his own totem animals. He was banished from his tribe, and so decided to take on a spirit form and terrorize his people. He became the evil spirit known as the Bunyip.

The Aboriginal people feared the Bunyip, and their folklore is full of legends of the Bunyip stealing tribe members near waterways at night. They rarely drew the Bunyip, possibly fearing that the image would attract the beast. But sometime during the Dreaming, a strange creature thought to be the Bunyip died by a creek in Victoria, so they stuck spears around the outline of the creature and later removed the turf within. This became a sacred site. The outline was maintained for many years, and was still there in 1840 when white settlers arrived to the area. By this time, the outline was about 30 feet long and had a shape that resembled a large seal (or the Loch Ness Monster). Eventually the outline faded.[9]

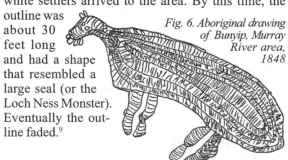

Fig. 6. Aboriginal drawing of Bunyip, Murray River area, 1848

IDENTIFYING THE BUNYIP

In 1872, a possible Bunyip appeared and was described as a "puppy-headed monster." The animal, which was also likened to "a big retriever dog, with a round head and hardly any ears," came so close to a boater in Lake Corangamite that the terrified man capsized his boat.[10] This sounds exactly like a seal, as do many of the sightings reported since. However, the Indo-Pacific Dugong (*Dugong dugong*) has also been proposed as a candidate, even though they are marine animals and not known to enter fresh water.

Fig. 7. Dugong

A creature sighted in a lagoon near Narrandera in 1872 or '73 was also compared to a retriever. This one was half the size, however, and covered in long, shiny, black hair. Another seal-headed beast was seen emerging from the water near Dalby in Queensland. This one had an asymmetrical double tail fin, which could be accounted for by an injury to a rear flipper.[11]

Similar aquatic creatures have also been sighted quite often in several Tasmanian lakes from the mid-19th century into the 20th century, with the most recent report in 1932 near a large hydroelectric dam. Their length is always between 3 and 4 feet, and they have a rounded head similar to that of a bulldog. They have two little fins in front resembling small wings, and they move at speeds up to 30 miles per hour. Frequently they splash water up to 10 feet into the air.[12]

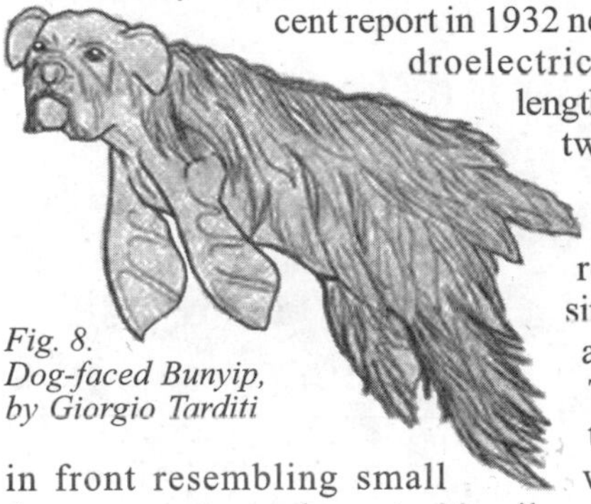

Fig. 8. Dog-faced Bunyip, by Giorgio Tarditi

Other than those that bear a striking similarity to long-necked Lake-Monsters, sightings of dog-faced Bunyips are described with remarkable consensus. Inhabiting waterways in New South Wales, Victoria, Tasmania, and the Australian Capital Territory, it is commonly said to be a shaggy animal the size of a sheepdog or retriever, with a doglike head, very tiny or nonexistent ears, two front flippers, and a fluked tail. Its long hair is usually said to be jet-black, but one sighted in 1886 in a river near Canberra had a white coat.

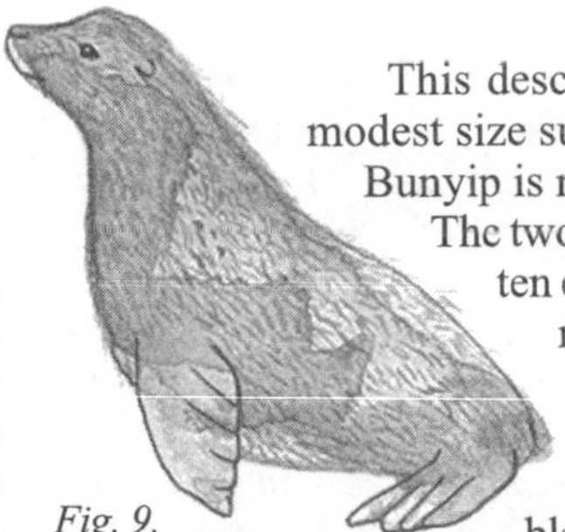

Fig. 9. Australian fur seal by Louise Jennison

This description and the animal's modest size suggest that the legendary Bunyip is nothing more than a seal. The two families of pinnipeds often exhibit extreme sexual dimorphism (with the males usually being twice the size of females) and sometimes even resemble entirely different species, especially in the case of elephant seals. Eleven known species of seals frequent Australian and Tasmanian waters—more than in any other area on Earth.

Species of seals found in Australian waters

Otariidae (Eared Seals)

Arctocephalus forsteri, New Zealand Fur Seal (M 8 ft., 408 lbs.; F 4 ft., 154 lbs.)
Arctocephalus gazella, Antarctic Fur Seal (M 6 ft., 293 lbs.; F 4 ft., 75 lbs.)
Arctocephalus pusillus, Australian Fur Seal (M 7.7 ft., 154 lbs.; F 6 ft., 270 lbs.)
Arctocephalus tropicalis, Subantarctic Fur Seal (M 6 ft., 364 lbs.; F 4.75 ft., 120 lbs.)
Neophoca cinerea, Australian Sea Lion (M 6.7 ft., 660 lbs.; F 5 ft., 250 lbs.)
Phocarctos hookeri, New Zealand Sea Lion (M 7.25 ft., 880 lbs.; F 6 ft., 507 lbs.)

Phocidae (True or Hair Seals)

Hydrurga leptonyx, Leopard Seal (M 9 ft., 720 lbs.; F 9.8 ft., 815 lbs.)
Leptonychotes weddelli, Weddell Seal (M 8 ft., 860 lbs.; F 8.8 ft., 992 lbs.)
Lobodon carcinophagus, Crabeater Seal (M 7.7 ft., 485 lbs.; F 7.7 ft., 485 lbs.)
Mirounga leonina, Southern Elephant Seal (M 16 ft., 5,290 lbs.; F 9.8 ft., 1,500 lbs.)
Ommatophoca rossi, Ross Seal (M 6.7 ft., 395 lbs.; F 6.7 ft., 395 lbs.)[13]

Fig. 10. Elephant seals

Readers might question the presence of seals in freshwater lakes and rivers far from the sea. However, this is not unusual. Many seals are known to travel far inland up tributaries, and one species, the Baikal

Seal (*Phoca siberica*), lives only in the fresh waters of Siberia's huge Lake Baikal (also, interestingly, the home of the legendary Baikal Lake-Monster). Australian fur seals have been known to swim up rivers during times of flood and become trapped within the river system once the flooding recedes. Dozens of these seals have been killed or captured as far north as Canberra—coincidentally, in areas where alleged Bunyips have been sighted. Other seals and sea lions have been seen in the great drainage basin of the Murray and Darling rivers.[14]

> Dr. Charles Fenner mentions a seal killed at Conargo, 900 miles from the mouth of the Murrumbidgee. A sea leopard [leopard seal] was killed in the Shoalhaven River in 1870. When it was cut open an adult platypus was found in its stomach. As [Gilbert Whitely of the Australian Museum] remarked, "Surely a bunyip within a bunyip!"[15]

Fig. 11. Leopard seal

Personally, I'll never forget my eyeball-to-eyeball encounter with an adult male leopard seal at the Taronga Zoo in Sydney, Australia. With a massive toothy head like a mammalian T-Rex, it glared back at me with uncanny predatory intelligence. Even now, a quarter of a century later, the recollection still raises the hair on the back of my neck. Encountering such a beast in a river or billabong in the wild Outback would definitely be an unnerving experience!

Some cryptozoologists, however, have postulated that the Bunyip may have originally been *Diprotodon australis*, a gigantic Pleistocene wombat the size of a rhinoceros. It was depicted in rock paintings by the early Aborigines, who evidently hunted it to extinction about 10,000 years ago.

Fig. 12. Aboriginal petrograph of Diprotodon, believed to be 10,000 years old.

These petrographs accurately include the characteristic large incisors that give the animal its scientific name, which means "two teeth in front."

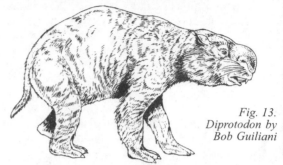

Fig. 13. Diprotodon by Bob Guiliani

Says Dr. Karl Shuker: "As far back as 1924, Dr C.W. Anderson of the Australian Museum had suggested that stories of the Bunyip could derive from aboriginal legends of the extinct diprodonts—a view repeated much more recently in Kadimakara (1985) by Australian zoologists Drs. Tim Flannery and Michael Archer, who nominated the palorchestids as plausible candidates."

The problem with this popular identification of *Diprotodon* with the legendary Bunyip is that there is no indication that the giant herbivore was amphibious and every reason to believe that it was not, because, as all indigenous Australian mammals are, it was a marsupial. There are no known amphibious or aquatic marsupials, extant or extinct, for the very good reason that they carry their babies in an open pouch on their bellies. Were such creatures to submerge, their babies would drown, effectively terminating their evolutionary lineage.

OTHER CONTRIBUTORS TO THE LEGEND

Children of the night —shut up!

The raucous night cries of possums and koalas could understandably be mistaken for those of the Bunyip, as most people cannot imagine that these small, timid creatures are capable of making such

Fig. 14. Brown Bittern

loud racket. The Barking Owl (*Ninox connivens*), a nocturnal bird that lives around swamps and billabongs, may also be credited for making Bunyip noises. Its call can easily be taken for the cries of a woman or child. The booming call of the Brown Bittern (*Botaurus poiciloptilus*) has earned it the nickname of the "Murray Bull." And Bush-Stone Curlews (*Burhinus grallarius*) emit blood-curdling shrieks that have often been attributed to Bunyips.[16]

Jolly Swagmen

It has been proposed that many sightings of supposed Bunyips from the 1890s through the 1930s were of nothing more than fugitives hiding from the law in the inhospitable swamps and billabongs. Along with transient workers, these outlaws were called swagmen or "swaggies," for their canvas bedroll of belongings, or "swag."

Fig. 15. Swagman

Whenever they heard someone coming, they would take cover by ducking under the water. When they thought the coast was clear, they would emerge covered in muck and weeds. Any passerby would certainly have been frightened by this apparition and run off.[17]

BUNYIPS IN POPULAR CULTURE

Bunyip on the stage

By the middle of the 19th century, the Bunyip had become an obvious element to add local color to a play or pantomime. For Christmas of 1916, one of the most popular pantomimes ever presented in Australia was *The Bunyip*, by Ella Airlie. An elaborate and expensive production, the plot involved the Fairy Princess being turned into a Bunyip by an evil Gnome. In Sydney alone, *The Bunyip* was seen by 150,000 people. Among its more memorable scenes was one in which real Aborigines threw boomerangs out over the heads of the audience.[18]

Fig. 16. "The Bunyip" playbill (1916)

Bunyips commemorated

In 1994, the Australian Postal Service issued a series of four highly popular stamps featuring different concepts of the Bunyip. Aboriginal artist Toogarr Morrison depicted his Bunyip as the traditional guardian of the waterholes in his homeland of Western Australia. It has a flat, beaver-like tail, which it uses to slap the water and lure victims to their doom. Marg Towt's depiction is based on the reports of 19th-century settlers whose strange encounters in the Australian Outback convinced many that Bunyips were real animals. David Lancashire drew his Bunyip as a grotesque, winged creature similar to the medieval European Gargoyle. And Ron Brooks's illustration from his 1973 children's book, *The Bunyip of Berkeley's Creek*, is an image beloved by generations of Australian children. Peering into a mirror, an endearing Bunyip asks, "What am I?"[19]

Fig. 17. "The Bunyip of Berkeley's Creek" Australian postage stamp by Ron Brooks

MONSTER MOVIES: THE BUNYIP

During the 1950s and '60s, a children's show called *Bertie the Bunyip*, created by Australian Lee Dexter, was aired in Philadelphia, Pennsylvania. *Dot and the Kangaroo* (1977), an animated musical short from Australia, showed an aboriginal painting of the dreaded Bunyip during a song about the creature, and 10 years later, in the movie *Dot and the Smugglers* (1987), Dot tries to rescue the Bunyip along with other native animals. During the 1980s, Australian children's books and TV featured Michael Salmon's friendly "Alexander Bunyip." On the Australian children's show, *Hi-5*, Kellie Hoggart took a journey to "Bunyip Island." In the children's show *Mona the Vampire*, a Bunyip appears as a large, brown, rabbit-like creature. In the 1986 Australian film *Frog Dreaming*, a Bunyip known as "Donkegin" is reputed to haunt a quarry. And on the TV series *Charmed*, the Bunyip is one of many demonic creatures the charmed ones must battle. In the show's *Book of Shadows*, its depiction resembles a Tauntaun from the second *Star Wars* movie.[20]

Fig. 18. Bunyip from The Book of Shadows on Charmed

Arial Anomalies
23. Thunderbirds, Rocs,
and Other Awesome Avians

By Ash DeKirk and Oberon Zell-Ravenheart

The people of the island [of Madagascar] report that at a certain season of the year, an extraordinary kind of bird which they call a Rukh, makes its appearance from the southern region. In form it is said to resemble the eagle but it is incomparably greater in size; being so large and strong as to seize an elephant with its talons, and to lift it into the air, from whence it lets it fall to the ground, in order that when dead it may prey upon the carcass. Persons who have seen this bird assert that when the wings are spread they measure sixteen paces in extent, from point to point; and that the feathers are eight paces in length, and thick in proportion. —Marco Polo, *Travels* (III, 36)

HE SKY DARKENS SUDDENLY, THE shadow of huge wings sweeping the ground. A crack of thunder as the Roc dives, then it is gone again, an elephant clutched in massive claws. Giant birds have held sway over our imaginations since perhaps as long as humanity has existed—perhaps longer. In his book, *An Instinct for Dragons,* author David Jones proposes that Dragons are an amalgamation of the three great predators of our earliest ancestors: the big cats, the serpents, and the raptors—the birds of prey. He suggests that our earliest primate ancestors were hunted by these predators and, through what Jung might call the "world mind," we have retained these memories even until today.[1] If this be true, such memories might account for many of our mythic creatures, be they Dragon, Gryphon, or giant birds. Even so, the Roc and the Thunderbird are awe-inspiring figures, symbolically representing storms, wind, thunder, and lightning.

Watch for Falling Rocs

The **Roc** (Persian, *Rukh* or *Rucke*) is a bird of immense size found in Persian and Indian myth. It lived on the island of Madagascar, and was said to be large enough to carry off elephants to feed its gigantic chicks. In the "Voyages of Sinbad," found within the famous Arabian *Thousand Nights and a Night*, or *Arabian Nights* (compiled ca. 800–900 CE), a Roc attacks Sinbad and destroys some of his ships in retaliation for the destruction of one of its eggs. In another story out of the same book, Rocs drop boulders upon the ships of Abdal al-Rahman in retaliation for his sailors killing a Roc chick.

Stories of the Roc can be traced back to the Greek Historian Herodotus (484–424 BCE), who was told by Egyptian priests of birds so huge they could carry off a person. The story recounted in the *Arabian Nights* first appeared in the Jatakas of India, a great compendium of folktales dating from at least the 4th century BCE. However, the great bird is not named as a Roc. Crusaders brought the story back to Europe in the Middle Ages, and in the 13th century, Marco Polo described the Roc in some detail.[2]

Early accounts do not specify if the Roc is actually a raptor or not, but today it is universally regarded as such. Some myths say that the Roc never lands on Earth but only on the mountain known as Qaf, in

Fig. 1. Roc attacking Abdal al-Rahman's ship

Ian Daniels

the center of the world. The Roc was said to have a wingspan of some 48 feet and its feathers alone could measure up to 24 feet long. In the mid-1200s, gigantic feathers said to be from the Roc were presented to Kublai Khan, grandson of Emperor Genghis Khan. These, however, were actually dried fronds of the Raffia Palm (*Raphia*), the longest leaves in the plant kingdom, which reach an impressive 80 feet.

Fig. 2. The gigantic egg of the Roc

The origin of the legend of the Roc may be found in Madagascar's enormous, flightless Elephant Bird or *Vouron Patra (Aepyornis maximus)*, which reached 11 feet in height and weighed 1,100 pounds. Its 3-foot-circumference eggs had a liquid capacity of 2.35 gallons. Bigger than any dinosaur eggs, these were the largest single cells to have ever existed on Earth. This awesome avian was exterminated by humans in the 16th century. Because Vourons had insignificant wings, and black, down-like pilli rather than true feathers, they were thought to be only the chicks of truly colossal flying adults. Consider that two of the four *Arabian Nights* tales involving the Roc focus on its enormous eggs and chicks. Sinbad found a Roc's egg to be as large as 148 hen's eggs; the egg of *Aepyornis maximus* actually had a volume about 160 times greater than that of a chicken.[3]

Malcolm South has suggested that tales of the Roc may have been created to explain meteorites, as several of the stories have the giant birds dropping huge stones, particularly on ships. This would also seem to be a pos-

Fig. 3. 11-ft. tall Elephant Bird or Vouron Patra

sible origin for the tale of the *Ababil*. According to the Quran, these were huge birds that saved the city of Mecca in the year of Mohammed's birth (571 CE) by dropping bricks on an attacking army of elephants. Ababil is now a local name for the common Barn Swallow (*Hirundo rustica*).[4]

And Peter Costello suggests that the huge Wandering Albatross (*Diomeda exultans*) could have also contributed to the legend of the Roc. It holds the record as having the largest wingspan of any living bird—some reported as large as 17.5 feet across.

Fig. 4. Wandering albatross

Thunderbirds

The Native American equivalent of the Roc, the *Thunderbird* is said to carry off bison or even whales. Its feathers are as long as canoe paddles, and when it flaps its wings, thunder sounds, the wind roars, and lightning flashes from its eyes. The Thunderbird is often described as a giant, condor-like creature, though sometimes it resembles a more hawk-like raptor. They were said to have been sent from the gods to protect humanity from evil. In other cases, they are regarded as shapeshifters, and are believed to take a human form at times and intermarry with people.

In some Native American myths, the Thunderbird is the enemy of the killer whale. In others, it is the enemy of giant, horned Water-Dragons, the *Unktehi* (see the book *Dragonlore* for a recounting of this tale, called "The Tlanuhwa and the Uktena"). The *Tlanuhwa* resembles a Red-Tailed Hawk (*Buteo jamaicensis*) of gigantic proportions, and is believed to have been the progenitor of this magnificent predator. There are caves along the Tennessee River where the Tlanuhwa were said to have once dwelt.

Fig. 5. Thunderbird - Kwakiutl

Thunderbirds are known by various local names among different tribes. In Iroquois tradition, the chief of the Thunderbirds is *Keneun*, the guardian of the sacred fire. To the Kwakiutl it is *Jojo*, its Nootka name is *Kw-Uhnx-Wa*, and the Ojibwa word for it is *Animikii*. Its Alaskan Inuit name is *Tinmiukpuk*, an immense eagle that carries off caribou and lone humans in its mighty talons and takes them back to its mountain nest to be devoured.

Wuchowsen is a colossal bird in the folklore of the Maliseet-Passamaquoddy of New England. It sits still on its rock at the northernmost point of the world, and the slightest rustling of its feathers sends winds across the entire Earth. The same bird is called **Bmola** in the mythology of the Western Abanaki. It is also known as the Wind Bird, as it is associated with the frigid winds that sweep down from the frozen North in winter.

Kaneakeluh is a great cosmic bird in the mythology of the Kwaiutl of British Columbia, Canada; it brought fire to humanity.

The Lakota call the Thunderbirds *Wakinyan* or *Waukkeon*, and identify four types that can be distinguished in part by the brilliant colors of their feathers: blue Wakinyan

Fig. 6. Thunderbird - Lakota

have no eyes or ears, black ones have huge beaks, and yellow ones have no beak at all. Red Wakinyan are like great, scarlet eagles.

Oshädagea ("dew eagle" or "big eagle of the dew") is a rather unusual Thunderbird in the mythology of the northeastern Woodlands Iroquois. He dwells in the western sky and carries a lake of dew in a hollow on his back, which he sprinkles over the land each morning to keep it fertile. When there is a forest fire caused by evil demons, he scoops water from the sea to douse the flames and routs the demons.

Fig. 7. Wakinyan - Lakota

Nihniknoovi is a monstrous predatory bird in the folklore of the Kawaiisu Tubatulabal of the Southwest. It hunts humans, carrying his victims in its great talons to a waterhole where it drains their blood before eating the corpses.

Thunderbirds have been sighted throughout the United States, but mostly in the West and Midwest. One of the most famous encounters was reported in 1890 in Arizona. Two cowboys supposedly shot and killed an enormous, birdlike creature with a whopping 160-foot-wide wingspan, far outstripping the wingspans of more recent Thunderbird sightings and vastly outreaching the wingspans of any known bird species.

Although that report is generally considered a hoax, a more modest, but still quite large, specimen of a condor-like bird with a 20- to 30-foot-wide wingspan was said to have been killed sometime in the late 1800s. Although a photo of the bird "strung up with outstretched wings against a barn, with six men with outstretched arms fingertip to fingertip, to show its size"[5] was said to have been published in the Tombstone *Epitaph*, all trace of it has disappeared, though

Fig. 8. Thunderbird shot in late 1800s

it has been redrawn from memory (Fig. 8). In all likelihood, this was a California Condor (*Gymnogyps californianus*), though this bird generally attains a wingspan no wider than 9 feet.

Thunderbirds are commonly identified with the California Condor or even the Andean Condor (*Vultur gryphus*), which is known to reach a wingspan of more than 15 feet. Some cryptozoologists have proposed that the original Thunderbird may have been the giant Pleistocene raptor *Aiolornis incredibilis*, which had a wingspan of 17 feet. This huge bird of prey has also been called a giant condor, though it is not related to modern condors. Even the smaller Ice-Age *Teratornis merriami* of California, with its 12-foot wingspan, may have contributed to the legends. And recently, fossils have been found of an Argentine teratorn which stood 5 feet tall and had an astonishing wingspan of 24 feet!

Though Thunderbirds are usually likened to condors or other raptor birds, there is some

Fig. 9. Pteranodon by Bob Giuliani

speculation that they may represent relic specimens of pterosaurs—a theory based either on fossils or on continuing reports of live sightings. As Thunderbirds are often portrayed with long crests at the backs of their heads, they have often been equated with the great crested *Pteranodon*, which attained a wingspan of 27 feet. The largest of the known flying reptiles, however, was *Quetzalcoatlus northropi*, which boasted a wingspan of some 40-50 feet.

Though it is now believed that many dinosaurs actually had feathers, pterosaurs were not dinosaurs, and were hairy, like bats. The 1890 Arizona specimen was said to be featherless, with skin wing flaps instead, and an elongated head and beak some 8 feet in length. Was it a relic pterosaur or not? We may never know. (For more information on possible living pterosaurs see Chapter 24. "Leather Wings.")

There is also the possibility that the Thunderbird myth originated with *Titanis walleri,* North America's only (thus far) recorded *phorusrhacid,* or "terror bird." Some sources say that *Titanis* did not become extinct until as recently as 15,000 years ago, though others claim it died out at least 1.8 million years ago. Fossil remains have been found in Texas and Florida, indicating the wide range of these awesome birds, and they would certainly have impressed any Indians who came upon them. All terror birds are giant, flightless, predatory birds with heavy, hooked beaks the size of a horse's head. Most species have been recorded in South America and Mesoamerica. *Titanis* stood up to 10 feet tall and may, like the elephant bird, have been regarded as the chick of a much larger raptor.

Fig. 11. Titanis wallleri

In 1838, a 5-year-old girl named Marie Delex was playing with a friend on a mountainside in the Valais, Switzerland. Suddenly a gigantic eagle swooped out of the sky and carried her off, despite the screams of her companion. Searchers found only one of her shoes on the edge of a precipice. The great bird's nest was located, and inside it were two eaglets surrounded by heaps of goat and sheep remains; of little Marie there was no sign. Two months later a shepherd discovered her mutilated corpse lying on a rock a mile and a half from where she had been seized.[6]

The only known bird this could have been is the Lammergeier (*Gypaetus barbatus*). Also called lion eagle or bearded vulture, it is the basis of the legend of the Gryphon. The world's mightiest raptor, its German name means "lamb stealer," which is what it is known for. But it is not believed to be capable of carrying off prey as large as a child. (See Chapter 9. "Gryphons and Hippogriffs.")

Fig. 12. Marie Delex carried off by an "eagle" in the Swiss Alps, 1838

In 1868, an 8-year-old boy named Jemmie Kenney was snatched from a schoolyard in Tippah County, Missouri, by an enormous eagle, which bore him aloft. In response to shouts, the monstrous bird dropped the boy, but he died from the cruel talons and the fall.

In July of 1977, a Thunderbird was sighted in Lawndale, Illinois. Around 9:00 p.m. on the 25th, three young boys were playing in their yard when they were attacked by a giant bird. One of the boys suffered scratches on his shoulder when the bird grabbed him and carried him for a distance of roughly 2 feet before dropping him. The boys said the bird was black with a white ruff, which fits the description of a condor.[7]

As recently as June and July of 2001, Thunderbird sightings were reported from Pennsylvania. Witnesses say the bird had a wingspan of about 15 feet and a head roughly 3 feet in length. It was described as being grayish-black in color with a long, thin beak. More sightings occurred in late September of the same year. One of the most recent sightings occurred in 2002 off the coast of Alaska, but it is believed that this may have been a wayward Stellar's Sea Eagle (*Haliaeetus pelagicus*). At 26 pounds, and with a wingspan up to 8 feet, this is the largest eagle in North America

OTHER GIANT BIRDS OF NOTE

Ai Tojon—A great, two-headed eagle of Siberian myth, the Ai Tojon lives at the very top of the World Tree, from which he shines forth light over all the world.

Fig. 13. Ai Tojon by Ash

Angka—An enormous Arabian bird large enough to carry off an elephant. Much like the Phoenix, it lives 1,700 years, at the end of which time it burns itself to ashes and rises again. Because of its great size, it has also been associated with the Roc. The Arabs believed that they were originally created as perfect birds, but that, over time, they eventually devoured all the animals on Earth and started carrying off children. The people appealed to God, who prevented the Anka from multiplying; thus it eventually became extinct.[8]

Fig. 14. Angka

Anzu (or *Zû*)—A gigantic storm-bird in ancient Mesopotamian mythology. Like a *Gryphon*, it has a lion's body and the head of an eagle with a saw-like beak, though it was sometimes said to have the body of an eagle and the head and torso of a bearded man. It is the attendant of Tiamet, the great, primordial serpent-Dragon.

Bar Juchne (or *Bar Yacre*)—In Talmudic Jewish legend, this is an enormous bird, similar to the

Roc, whose wingspan can eclipse even the sun. It preys on cattle and even humans. It was said that, once upon a time, an egg fell from a Bar Juchne nest, shattering 300 trees and flooding 60 villages.

Crocho—An immense bird said to dwell on Cape Daib (Cape Corrientes) at the tip of Africa. It was said to be 60 paces from wing tip to wing tip, and able to carry off elephants. According to Fra Mauro (1459), in 1420, an Indian junk putting in at the coast discovered an egg of this bird that was "as big as a butt" (a butt is a large cask holding a volume of 126 gallons).

Garuda (or *Taraswin,* "swift one")—A gigantic, man-like bird of Hindu mythology who is the celestial mount of the god Vishnu. He has the body, wings, talons, and head of an eagle-vulture (*lammergeier*), but with a human face and limbs. His colors are gold, scarlet, and green. He is the sworn enemy of the snakelike Nagas. Emblemizing royalty throughout Southeast Asia, he is also the symbol of the Indonesian Garuda Airlines. In Thailand he is called *Galon* or *Khrut*.[9]

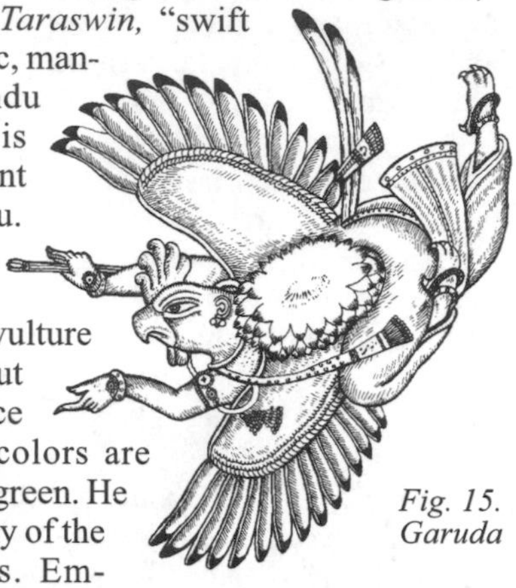

Fig. 15. Garuda

Hraesvelg ("corpse-eater"; or Windmaker)—A vast, eagle-like bird of Norse mythology that nests upon the icy peaks of the frozen North. Her eaglets are the frigid winds blasted forth by the flapping of her mighty wings.

Kreutzet—A vast eagle of the folklore of northwestern Russia.

Kusa Kap—A gigantic hornbill bird inhabiting one of the many tiny islands in the Torres Strait, which separates New Guinea from the northern tip of Queensland, Australia. With a 22-foot wingspan, this avian prodigy is said to carry dugongs aloft in its mighty claws, much as the fabled Roc is said to carry off elephants. The sound of its wings in flight is said to resemble the roar of a steam engine—a characteristic feature of the Rhinoceros Hornbill (*Buceros rhinoceros*) (shown), which attains a length of 4 feet and a wingspan of 5 feet.[10]

Fig. 16. Kusa Kap

Naui—A giant bird of Russian folklore resembling a Dragon, with the head and talons of an eagle.

Ngani-vatu (or *Ngutu-lei*)—A gigantic predatory bird in the folklore of the island of Fiji. Its vast body eclipses the sun, and the flapping of its mighty wings causes great storms. It preyed upon the ani-

mals and people of the Pacific Islands until it was destroyed by the hero Okova and his brother-in-law, Kokoua.

Fig. 17. Crowned eagle

The **Ngoima**—An enormous eagle said by local natives to be dwelling in the forests of the African Congo. With a wingspan of 9–13 feet, it preys upon monkeys and goats. Its plumage is dark brown above and paler beneath. Its legs and talons are as large as a man's forearms and hands. This is certainly an exaggerated description of the rarely seen Crowned Eagle (*Stephanoaetus coronatus*), the most powerful eagle in Africa, whose diet consists of monkeys and even small antelopes. There have even been reports of the remains of a human child having been found in the nest of a crowned eagle, though the eagle may have found the child as carrion rather than actually having killed it. The Martial Eagle (*Polemaetus bellicosus*), Africa's largest eagle species, is also known to attack impala and duikers.

Recently, subfossils were found of the Crowned Hawk-Eagle (*Stephanoaetus mahery*), the largest and strongest bird of prey of prehistoric Madagascar, which only became extinct after people settled on the island. It was a giant variant within the *Stephanoaetus* raptor family, which also includes the crowned eagle.

P'êng (or *Pyong*)—A vast bird of Chinese legend that is the metamorphosed form of the huge fish called *Kw'ên*. Its outspread wings cover the sky from horizon to horizon. It lives in the north, but each year it rises thousands of feet into the air and flies toward the south, bringing the typhoon season.[11]

Pheng—A bird from Japanese legend that is so gigantic it eclipses the sun and can carry off and eat a camel, much like the Roc of Arabian myth.

Fig. 18. Pheng

Pouakai (or *Pouki*)—A monstrous predatory bird of Maori legend. It hunted livestock and people until the last one was trapped in a great net and stabbed to death by the hero Hau-o-Tawera. This was a real creature, the giant Haast's or Harpagornis Eagle (*Harpagornis moorei*), that once lived on the South Island of New Zealand. Exterminated only 600 years

Fig. 19. Pouakai (Haast's eagle) attacking a moa

ago, it was the largest eagle to have ever lived. A female weighed 22–30 pounds and stood 4 feet tall, with a wingspan of 8–10 feet. [12]

Raichô ("thunder bird")—A fabulous giant rook or crow-like bird in Japanese folklore. He lives in a tall pine tree, and his raucous calls summon the storms. This is also the name of a real bird, *Lagopus mutus*, a kind of ptarmigan or grouse.

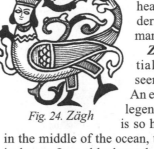

Fig. 20. Raicho

Sampati—A giant human-headed bird in Hindu mythology that was the offspring of the great *Garuda*. In the *Râmâyana*, Hanuman, the monkey-god, asks Sampati to help find the goddess Sita, who has been abducted to Ravana by the demon king who killed Sampati's brother, Jataya. Sampati flies to Sri Lanka and locates Sita, returning to inform Hanuman and his army how to destroy Ravana and effect Sita's rescue. And thus Sampati avenges his brother's death. [13]

Fig. 21. Sampati

Simurgh (or *Sîna-Mrû, Simarghu, Simurg, Sumargh*: "30 birds")—The magnificent king of the birds in Arabian legend, representing divine unity. Its beautiful feathers are prized for their healing properties. Similar to the *Roc*, it is so huge that it can carry off an elephant or a camel, but it is also known to take human children into its nest to foster them. Derived from the Senmurv, it dwells in the mountains of Alberz in northern Persia. As the Phoenix does, this wise and peaceful bird lives for either 1,700 or 2,000 years. Some accounts claim it is immortal, nesting in the Tree of Knowledge. It is said to be so old that it has seen the destruction of the world three times over. A bird of the same name attended the queen of Sheba. It had brass feathers, a silver head, a human face, four wings, a vulture's talons, and a peacock's tail. [14]

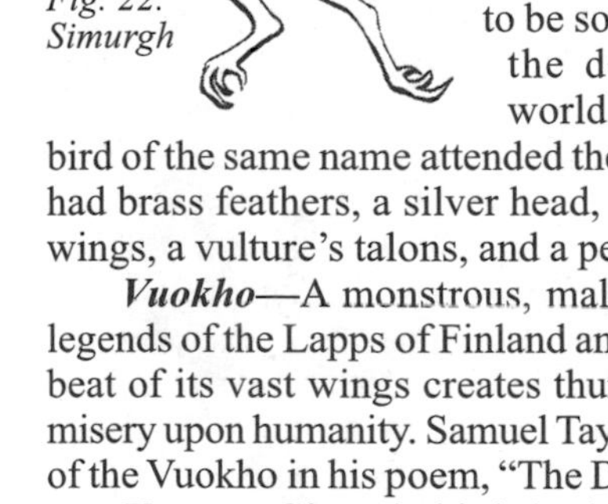

Fig. 22. Simurgh

Vuokho—A monstrous, malevolent bird in the legends of the Lapps of Finland and Scandinavia. The beat of its vast wings creates thunder, and it inflicts misery upon humanity. Samuel Taylor Coleridge wrote of the Vuokho in his poem, "The Destiny of Nations."

Xexeu—Gigantic birds in the mythology of the Cashmawa Indians of South America. Similar to the North American ***Thunderbirds***, they are responsible for bringing the clouds together to create huge storms. Most likely these creatures derive from the magnificent Andean Condor (*Vultur gryphus*), with its 10-foot-wide wingspan.

Fig. 23. Xexeu

Yata Garasu—A three-legged crow of immense proportions. In Japanese mythology, the Yata Garasu serves as a divine messenger. It makes a more modern appearance in the popular card game *Yu-Gi-Oh!*

Zägh—A gigantic bird of Islamic legend, it has a human head and the ability to understand and speak all human languages.

Ziz (also *Renanim*, "celestial singer"; *Sekwi*, "the seer"; "Son of the Nest")—An enormous bird of Hebrew legend, much like the ***Roc***. It is so huge that when it stands in the middle of the ocean, the water comes only to its knees. It can block out the sun with its vast wings and has incredible strength. Once upon a time an addled egg broke, washing away 300 cedar trees and drowning 60 villages. Equated with the Persian *Chamrosh*, the Ziz was said to have been created to protect all the small birds, which would have otherwise died out long ago. According to rabbinical tradition, the meat of this bird will be served, along with that of the Behemoth and the Leviathan, at a great victory feast at the end of the world. Corresponding to the giant archetypal creatures of Persian mythology, the trio of the Behemoth, Leviathan, and Ziz was traditionally a favorite decorative motif for rabbis living in Germany. [15]

Fig. 24. Zägh

Fig. 25. Ziz

Monster Movies: Giant Birds

The Giant Claw a.k.a. *Mark of the Claw* (1957)— Giant Buzzard
The 7th Voyage of Sinbad (1958)—Roc
Mysterious Island (1961)—Phorusrhacos
Food of the Gods (1976)—Giant Chicken
The Hobbit (animated, 1977) Giant Eagles
The Rescuers Down Under (animated, 1990)— Thunderbird
LOTR: Fellowship of the Ring (2001)—Giant Eagle
LOTR: Return of the King (2003)—Giant Eagles

24. LEATHER WINGS

By Oberon Zell-Ravenheart

Professor Challenger, who with the two local Indians was in the van of the party, stopped suddenly and pointed excitedly to the right. As he did so we saw, at the distance of a mile or so, something which appeared to be a huge gray bird flap slowly up from the ground and skim smoothly off, flying very low and straight, until it was lost among the tree-ferns.

"Did you see it?" cried Challenger, in exultation. "Summerlee, did you see it?"

His colleague was staring at the spot where the creature had disappeared. "What do you claim that it was?" he asked.

"To the best of my belief, a pterodactyl."

—Sir Arthur Conan Doyle
The Lost World, Chapter 8; 1912[1]

Ian Daniels

 T'S HARD TO IMAGINE A SCENE OF DInosaurs without great Pterosaurs soaring overhead. It used to be thought that they were mere gliders, incapable of flapping their vast wings for sustained flight. They were envisioned hanging upside-down from cliff faces, like bats, and dropping into a gliding swoop. But it is now the consensus that the smaller ones flew as well as birds, and the truly huge ones, such as *Pteranodon* (with a 27-ft wingspan) and *Quetzalcoatlus* (with a wingspan of forty feet!) could take off as easily as a kite into a light breeze, and soar aloft for days, scarcely moving their mighty wings, much like albatrosses. Evidence has emerged that some of them migrated across entire oceans to reach their nesting grounds.

The first vertebrates to evolve true flight, *Pterosaurs* ("winged lizards") were flying reptiles with their front limbs modified into wings of webbed skin like the wings of bats. Since the wing is supported by an enormously elongated little finger, they are also called *Pterodactyls* ("wing-finger"). They were furry, evidently warm-blooded, with large and sophisticated brains. They ruled the Mesozoic skies from 228-65 million years ago. In the terminology of Medieval Dragonlore, they would be called *Wyverns.*

Fig. 1. Rhamphorynchus—early reconstruction

The **Wyvern** (or *Wivern*) is a kind of flying serpentine Dragon with bat-like wings, two avian hind legs with eagle talons, and a long barbed tail. Basically, it is a Pterosaur, like *ramphorhynchus.*

Variants include the *Sea-Wyvern,* which has a fish-like tail. Wyverns have been described as the largest form of Dragon, able to prey on such huge creatures as elephants and rhinos. In Heraldry, the Wyvern symbolizes war, pestilence, envy and viciousness. The default coloration of a Heraldic Wyvern is green with a red chest, belly and under-wings.

Fig. 2. Heraldic Wyvern

LIVING PTEROSAURS?

Although they are supposed to have been extinct for 65 million years, sightings of apparent living Pterosaurs are still reported from time to time.

Snallygaster (or *Snollygoster*) was a Pterosaur-like beast said to inhabit the Blue Ridge Mountains near Braddock Heights, Maryland, USA. The first German settlers in the 1730s were terrorized by a monster they called *Schnellgeiste* ("quick spirit"). It was described as half-reptile, half-bird, with a metallic beak and razor-sharp teeth. It swooped silently from the sky to carry off its victims and suck their blood. Seven-pointed stars to keep the Snallygaster at bay can still be painted on local barns.

Fig. 3. Snallygaster

In *The Illustrated London News* (February 9, 1856, page 166) it was reported that workmen cutting a tunnel for a railway line, between Saint-Dizier and Nancy, in France, were blasting through Jurassic limestone when a bizarre winged creature tumbled out of a cavity. It fluttered its wings, made a hoarse croaking noise, and dropped dead. According to the workers, the creature had oily black leathery skin, a 10-ft.-7-in. wingspan, and four long legs with "crooked talons," joined by a membrane. The size of "a large goose," it had a long neck, and a mouth full of sharp teeth. The body was brought to Gray, where, a paleontology student identified the animal as a *Pterodactyl anas* ["wing-fingered duck"—a made-up species][2]

Fig. 4. Pterodactyls on ground

This incredible story is simply a hoax. At the time, many exquisite fossils were being extracted from Bavaria's Solnhofen Limestone (which would later yield the famed *Archaeopteryx*). Each of these discoveries was triumphantly announced by German paleontologists. The tunnel in question was through limestone of similar age to the Solnhofen beds, so some French wags decided to do the Germans one better.[3]

In April of 1890, two cowboys in Arizona allegedly killed an enormous bird-like creature with smooth skin and featherless leathery wings like a bat. Its head resembled that of an alligator. They said they had come upon it in the desert, and it was apparently sick or wounded. The animal managed to take off and fly about half a mile before sinking to the ground again, where the cowboys finished it off with rifles.

Fig. 5. Cowboy wrestling Pteranodon (Valley of the Gwangi)

Harry McClure was a young man living in Lordsburg, New Mexico in 1910 when the two cowboys came to town, telling of their encounter 20 years earlier. 60 years later, in a letter to the Summer 1970 issue of *Old West Magazine,* McClure recalled their description of the creature: *"Its eyes were like saucers; its two legs and feet up at the front part of its body were the size of those of a horse; its hide was leathery, instead of feathery. It lit on the ground once at a safe distance from the two cowboys, but it took to the air again soon afterwards only to come down again a second time..."*[4]

According to the account published in the April 26 edition of Arizona's *Tombstone Epitaph*, the cowboys paced off the dimensions of their monster as an astonishing 92-ft long, with a wingspan of 160-ft! The cowboys cut off a wingtip and took it into the town of Tombstone. Plans were made to skin the creature for a museum, but nothing further was ever reported.[5]

But another version of the story is that they dragged the entire carcass back to town, where it was pinned, wings outstretched, across the entire side of a barn. This time, its wingspan was said to be "only" 20-30 ft. This account—supposedly with a photo—was reprinted in 1969, but no one now seems to be able to track down a copy, and the hunt for the elusive photo has itself become a cryptozoological quest. I suspect that this case (and photo) has become confused with a different story involving an alleged frontier snapshot of a dead "Thunderbird" held up with 20-30 ft wings outstretched, with six men standing behind it to demonstrate its size. (See Chapter 23. "Thunderbirds")

Another mysterious photo claims to show a dead Pterosaur surrounded by Civil War soldiers, but no further information on it seems to be available:

Fig. 5. Photo of trophy Pteronodon killed in Civil War

In Feb.-Mar. 1909, residents of Braddock Heights, Maryland (previous haunt of the legendary Snallygaster) reported sightings of a creature with "enormous wings, a long pointed bill, claws like steel hooks, and an eye in the center of its forehead." It screeched "like a locomotive whistle." The Smithsonian Institute offered a reward for the hide, and President Theodore Roosevelt considered postponing an African safari to personally hunt for the beast. But after the initial flurry, nothing more was heard of it.

From late 1975 through early 1976, people along the lower Rio Grande valley between Texas and Mexico reported a wave of "big bird" sightings. The avian anomalies were described as impossibly huge, with membranous wings like bats, and often cat-like faces.

In January 1976, two sisters, Libby and Deanie Ford, saw a large strange "bird" standing by a pond outside of Brownsville, Texas. They said it was as tall as a person, all black, with a face like a cat. Later, they identified it from a book as being a *pteranodon.* Given their description, this seems like a very odd identification indeed; a pteranodon's head looks like a pickax, not a cat!

A few days later, southwest of San Antonio, Texas, three schoolteachers were driving to work when a large flying creature swooped low over the highway at about the height of the phone poles. It cast a shadow across the width of the road, and by that the women estimated its wingspan as 15-20 ft. They said they could see the bones of the bat-like wings through the grey membrane that covered them. Later, at school, they pored through encyclopedias and found a picture of what they had seen. It was a *pteranodon.* This story was reported in the *San Antonio Light,* Feb. 26, 1976.[6]

Fig. 6.
Pteranodon
(Bob Giulani)

Throughout the year, other residents of the Rio Grande Valley were terrorized by a five-foot-tall, gorilla-faced creature, with blood-red eyes and bat-like wings. It became known as "Big Bird." But no sightings have been reported since. Interestingly, Fortean investigators Jerome Clark and Loren Coleman found similar reports in that region tracing back over 30 years; and even earlier, local Indian folklore included legends of such creatures.

On the other side of the country, in Woodbine, Maryland, another pterosaur-creature was sighted in 1980. Recalling the local legend of the Snallygaster, it was six feet tall, brownish-grey, and stood on two legs like a man. It flapped its wings as it flew away. This, however, seems certainly to have been a Great Blue Heron (*Ardea herodias*). This magnificent bird stands five feet tall, with a wingspan of seven feet. It really does look much like a pteranodon in flight, even to having a swept-back plume of feathers on its head like the bony crest of that pterosaur.

Fig. 7. Great Blue Heron

And finally, a bizarre, bat-winged nocturnal primate is said to dwell in the dense forests surrounding Mt. Saint Helens in the state of Washington, USA. Dubbed **Batsquatch,** it has purple skin, red eyes, and a simian head with bat-like features. Some cryptozoologists speculate that it may be an unknown species of fruit bat. But none of these fructivorous chiroptera are known to be indigenous to North America.

SOUTH AMERICAN PTEROSAURS

Legends of giant flying creatures in South America predate the arrival of the Conquistadores, and continue into modern times. Indeed, some of these were surely an inspiration to Arthur Conan Doyle for setting the locale of his "Lost World" in Venezuela.

In April of 1868, mine workers in Copiapo, Chile, were preparing for supper when they sighted *"a gigantic bird, which at first we took for one of the clouds then partially darkening the atmosphere, supposing it to have been separated from the rest by the wind."* As it flew over their heads, they could see that its immense wings were not feathered, but webbed in skin like those of a bat. This story was reported in the July, 1968 issue of *The Zoologist.*[7]

In February of 1947, Mr. J. Harrison of Liverpool, England, was navigating an estuary of the Amazon when he and others observed a flight of five huge "birds" flying down the river in a V formation. In an unpublished letter to the *Fortean Times,* Harrison said: *"The wingspan must have been at least twelve feet from tip to tip. They were brown in colour like brown leather, with no visible signs of feathers. The head was flat on top, with a long beak and a long neck. The wings were ribbed...just like those large prehistoric birds."*[8] Here is the drawing he enclosed with his letter:

Fig. 8. J. Harrison's drawing of a "prehistoric bird" he saw over the Amazon in 1947

And in 1992, the Australian weekly magazine *People* reported a close encounter between a small commuter airplane and a huge flying reptile over the mountains of Brazil. The creature appeared alongside as the plane was preparing to land, and the pilot had to veer away to avoid a collision. Stewardess Maya Cabon said: *"Here was this giant monster flying right next to the plane. He was only a few feet from the window—and he looked right at me. I thought we were all going to die."* U.S. anthropologist Dr. George Biles, one of the 24 passengers aboard, elaborated: *"This was a classic case of a white pterodactyl with a giant wingspan. Of course, I've heard the rumors for many years that these prehistoric creatures still roamed the Amazon. But I was skeptical like everybody else. But that wasn't an airplane of a UFO flying beside us. It was a pterodactyl."*[9]

AFRICAN PTEROSAURS

From swampy regions of Zambia, Congo, Angola, and Kenya come reports of **Kongamato** ("Overwhelmer of Boats"). Numerous reported sightings of these large, leathery-winged flying creatures have led cryptozoologists to speculate that there may be a relic population of Pterodactyls still living in Africa. They are colored black or red, and are named for their proclivity of capsizing canoes. Frank H. Mellon, in his *In Witchbound Africa* (1923),[10] described them as smooth-skinned, with toothy beaks and wingspans of 4-7 ft. Another witness said the wings made a loud thunderous noise when flapped. When they are shown pictures of pterosaurs, all witnesses immediately identify them as Kongamoto. It is far more likely, however, that these creatures are actually Hammerhead Bats (*Hypsignathus monstrosus*), Africa's largest bat species. They are dark gray with black wings spanning three feet, and have elongated, dog-like snouts.

Fig. 9. Kongamato attack, by William M. Rebsamen

In 1925, southern Rhodesia produced reports of a Kongamato attack on a man in a swamp, and reports issued from Africa in 1928, 1942, the 1950s, up through modern times, including a colleague of cryptozoologist Roy Mackal's who saw one in 1988.[11]

Either the same or another gigantic black pterodactyl-like creature was encountered in 1932 in the Assumbo Mountains of the African Cameroons by zoologist Ivan T. Sanderson and naturalist Gerald Russell in 1932. As they were crossing a river, it dived at them, then flew away. Apparently the size of an eagle, it had "pointed white teeth set about their own width apart from each other" and "Dracula-like wings." They saw it again that evening. Locals called the creature *Olitiau.* Sanderson later speculated that the beast was probably an exceptionally large specimen of the Hammerhead Bat. But there's a huge gap between the 3-ft wingspan of the Hammerhead, and the 12-ft span Sanderson estimated for the Olitiau!

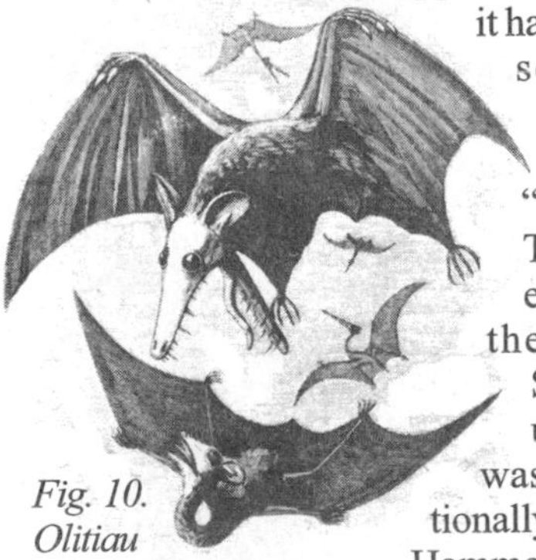

Fig. 10. Olitiau as Hammerhead bats

Guiafairo is a great grey flying creature reported from West Africa, where it hides in caves and hollow trees during the day, emerging only at night. It has clawed feet and a human-like head. Cryptozoologists speculate that it may be an unknown species of giant bat, or another example of the Hammerhead Bat.

Fig. 11. Guiafairo by Ian D.

NEW GUINEA FLYERS

Gigantic flying predators have also been reported in Papua New Guinea. Called **Duah,** they have a 24-foot leathery wingspan, a long, toothless beak and a large head crest, precisely matching the image of a *Pteranodon.* Likewise, they are oceanic fish-eaters, though there are reports of vicious and fatal attacks on humans.

Another Pterodactyl-like creature has been reported from the jungles of New Guinea since the 1950s. The *Ropen* ("Demon Flyer") lives in caves along the islands of New Britain and Umboi, and flies only at night. It has leathery wings spanning 3-4 ft, a narrow, tooth-filled beak, a head crest, webbed feet, and a long tail culminating in a diamond-shaped flange. It is said to feast on decaying flesh, harassing funerals to attack the corpse. The description sounds uncannily like a *Rhamphorynchus,* believed to have been extinct for 65 million years. I have personally visited several of those islands, climbed their cliffs, and explored their caves. Alas, I found no pterodactyls, only fruit bats.

Fig. 12. Ropen by Garth Guessman & Jonathan Whitcomb

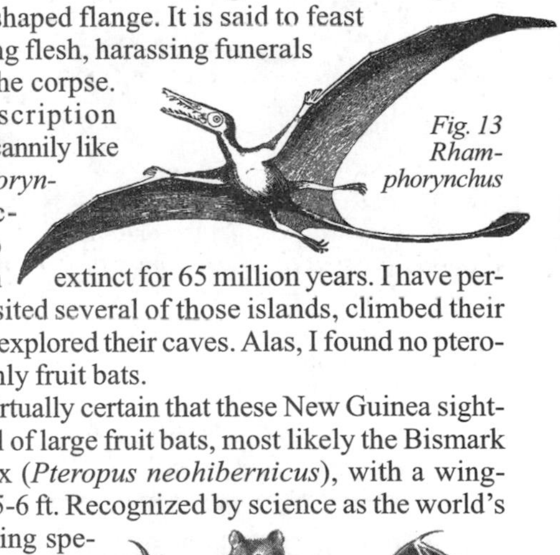

Fig. 13 Rhamphorynchus

It is virtually certain that these New Guinea sightings are all of large fruit bats, most likely the Bismark Flying Fox (*Pteropus neohibernicus*), with a wingspan of 5.5-6 ft. Recognized by science as the world's largest living species of bat, it is native to New Guinea and the Bismark Archipelago.

Fig. 14. Flying Fox

EYEWITNESS ACCOUNT

Here is a fascinating eyewitness account of a sighting of living Pterosaurs in Cuba in March of 1971. The witness, Eskin Kuhn, was a Marine. His report was accompanied by his own excellent drawings:

> It was a beautiful, clear Summer day. I was looking in the direction of the ocean when I saw an incredible sight. It mesmerized me!
>
> I saw 2 Pterosaurs flying together at low altitude, perhaps 100 feet, very close in range from where I was standing, so that I had a perfectly clear view of them.
>
> The rhythm of their large wings was very graceful, slow; and yet they were flying and not merely gliding, like turkey vultures do here in Ohio. The rate of their wings was more like that of crows, perhaps a little slower; but very graceful.
>
> The structure and the texture of the wings appeared to be very similar to that of bats: particularly in that the struts of the wings emanated from a "hand" as fingers would ; except that a couple of the fingers were short (as for grasping) and the other ran out to the tip of the wing, others back to the trailing edge of the wing to stretch the wing membrane as a kite would.
>
> The Pterosaurs I saw had the short hind legs attached to the rearwardmost part of the wing, and they had a long tail trailing behind with a tuft of hair at the end.

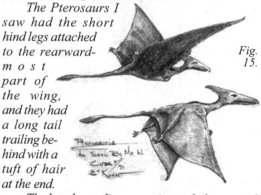

Fig. 15.

> The head was disproportionately large, with a long crest at the back, long bill, long neck with a crook in it. The chest of the creatures was similarly prominent, protruding forward like the prow of an old ship.
>
> The vertebrae of their backs was noticeable, mostly between the shoulders. I would estimate their wingspan to be roughly 10 feet.[12]

With all due respect to the young Marine, however, I find his description and drawings to be a close match to the flying appeance of great blue herons. What Kuhn took to be a long tail with a "tuft of hair at the end" (which he drew as a flange like that of a rhamphorynchus) is actually the long legs of the bird, which it extends stiffly behind in flight. The graceful rythmn of the wings, the crest behind the head (actually feathers), the crooked neck, and the chest "protruding forward like the prow of an old ship," are all characteristic of these impressive birds. At a distance of 100 feet, this is exactly what would be observed.

FLYING MONKEYS

Hsigo— (or *Hsiao*) These Chinese creatures are exactly like the flying monkeys from *The Wizard of Oz*. They have apelike bodies with a dog's tail, a birdlike head, a human face, and wings. They are probably based on fruit bats, or "flying foxes," of India, Asia, Indonesia and Australia. These monkey-size

Fig. 16. Hsigo

bats are not related to the other insectivorous bats, but are genetically closer to primates, and thus really are a kind of "Flying Monkey."

Ahool— Reported from Java and Vietnam, these are giant bats of an unidentified species. Named for their cry, they are said to be the size of a year-old child, dark grey, with a head like a monkey. These would certainly seem to be large fruit bats. The Ahool, however, is said to be a fish-eater which, if true, would mean it has to be something else.

Alan— Mischievous half-human, half-bird creatures from the forests of the Philippines. With extended fingers on their backwards-facing feet and stubby toes on their hands, they spend much of their time hanging upside down from trees. They are often very helpful toward humans and have served as foster parents to several legendary heroes whom they found

Fig. 17. Flying fox

lost in the forest as babies. This description, and the locale, strongly suggest a large fruit bat, such as the Malayan Flying Fox.

Orang-Bati— ("Men with wings") Predatory nocturnal flying primates from the obscure Indonesian island of Ceram—the second largest island in the Moluccas group. The natives of Ceram describe these soaring simians as approximately five feet tall, with black leathery wings, blood-red skin, and a long thin tail. Emitting a "mournful wail," they are said to abduct infants and small children. During the day they retreat into a network of caves in an extinct volcano, Mount Kairatu. This description, and the locale, strongly

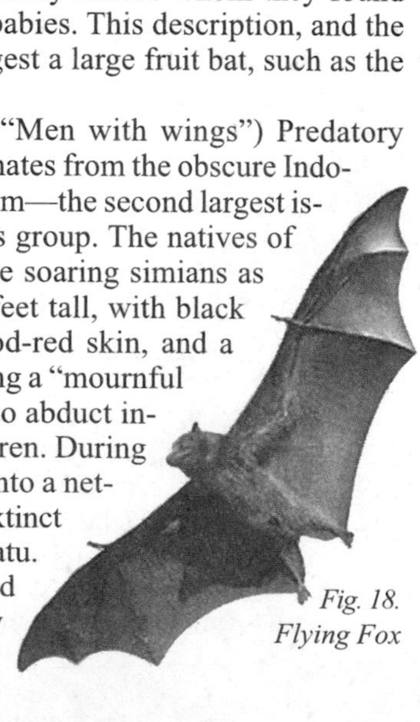

Fig. 18. Flying Fox

suggests a giant fruit bat—probably, again, the Malayan Flying Fox.

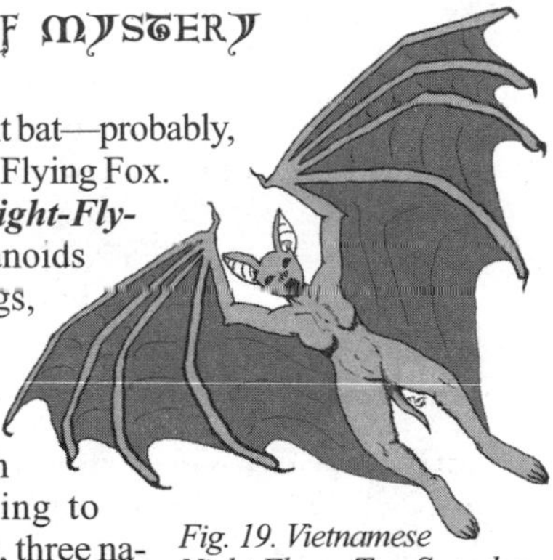

Vietnamese Night-Flyers— Flying humanoids with bat-like wings, sighted by three U.S. Marines in 1969, near Da Nang, South Vietnam. According to the soldiers' report, three naked, hair-covered, feminine

Fig. 19. Vietnamese Night-Flyer; Tam Songdog

figures, all approximately five feet in height, flew over their post in the dead of night. The Marines claimed they could hear the flapping of their leathery black wings. These were certainly Malayan Flying Foxes, of which the females (which have two thoracic breasts like humans) can have wingspans of six feet, although they weigh only up to 3.3-lbs.

Fig. 20. Hammerhead bat

Sassabonsum is a huge evil fruit bat in the folklore of Ghana, West Africa. With red hair, hooked wings, and backwards-pointing feet, it swoops upon people and carries them off at the bidding of the Mmoatia, or pygmy sorcerers. As with the Kongamoto, Olititau and Guiafairo, this is probably the Hammerhead Bat.

However, in his 1972 book, *Investigating the Unexplained,* Ivan Sanderson suggested another possible identification for these oversized bat-like creatures; that they may represent a hitherto-unknown enormous species of *microbat* (*Microchiroptera*), commonly referred to as "insectivorous bats," "echolocating bats," "small bats," or "true bats."[13]

In contrast to the doglike snouts of fruit bats, or *megabats* (*Megachiroptera*), microbats have the flattened monkey-like faces described as characteristic of all the above "flying monkeys." While most of them are insectivorous, some of the larger species hunt birds, lizards, frogs, or even fish—behavior that is often mentioned in regard to these cryptic creatures, and does not occur among any of the megabats. Even vampire microbats exist, though only, as far as we know, in South America.

Fig. 21. Vampire bat

According to native witnesses, when Ahools are seen on the ground, or perched like a bird on a tree branch, they fold their wings at their sides like a bird, as do all microbats. Megabats, on the other hand, wrap their wings around their bodies like a cloak. Ahools are also said to be able to stand upright on two legs, and

in doing so their feet point backwards. Again, only microbats can stand erect (though they seldom do so); megabats can stand only on all fours, or hang upside down from tree branches. But it is true that the hind feet of all bats point backwards.[14]

The difficulty with this hypothesis is that microbats are well-named. They are all quite tiny, with the largest, the Big Brown Bat (*Eptesicus fuscus*), attaining a wingspan of only 13 inches. A microbat with a 6-12 foot wingspan seems like an incredible stretch, with nothing in between. However, I have had personal experience which may help put this matter into perspective, so to speak.

One night when we were lying outside watching a meteor shower, a pale ghostly shape swooped down out of the sky, circled our blanket, and then soared off. In the light of our candle, it seemed huge—at least a three-foot wingspan! Even though we knew it had to be a bat, we all agreed that our first impression was of a pterodactyl! So I immediately went to my library and looked up local bats, and lo and behold, there it was: a Pallid Bat (*Antrozous pallidus*). They eat ground-dwelling crickets and scorpions, so they swoop rather than flitter.

But the thing is—they have a wingspan of no more than 12 inches. So how come it appeared so immensely large to us? Well, as I explained in the chapter on Sea Serpents, in the sky, as in the open ocean, there is no objective basis of comparison against which to measure an

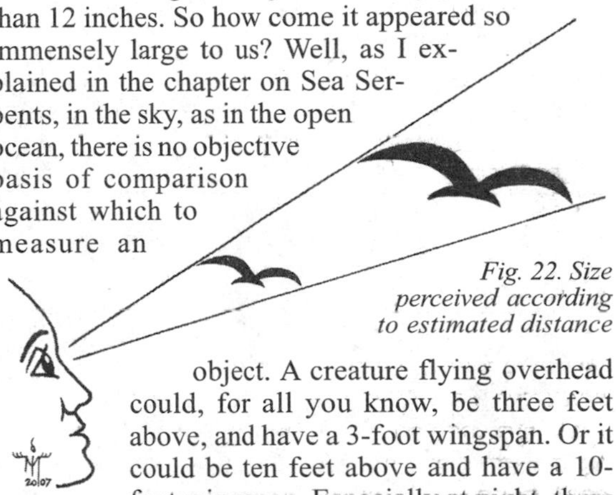

Fig. 22. Size perceived according to estimated distance

object. A creature flying overhead could, for all you know, be three feet above, and have a 3-foot wingspan. Or it could be ten feet above and have a 10-foot wingspan. Especially at night, there is no way to know. So, like the fisherman whose catch got away, we declare for the largest size. The pallid bat is nearly white on the underside, and it reflected so much illumination from the candle that it appeared to be much closer than it really was.

In addition, as I also mentioned in the Sea Serpent chapter, there is the factor of the automatic "zoom lens" mode that our brain goes into when we see something highly alarming. This evolutionarily adaptive mechanism creates an exaggeration of size in our mind's eye, just as it does in a camera when we use the zoom lens. And thus are creatures of ordinary size transformed into giants.

As much as I would love to know that somewhere on Earth, pterodactyls still ride the skies, I'm afraid I will just have to settle for extra-large bats.

MONSTER MOVIES: PTEROSAURS
By Oberon Zell and Seth Tyrssen

Pterosaurs and Wyverns have been featured in many movies, in both prehistoric settings of the "Lost World" genre, and as flying Dragons. Pterosaurs are routinely included among dinosaurs, although there have been a few films where they appear in modern times—often hatching in the heart of a volcano from long-dormant eggs. As pterosaurs really were ancient "flying dragons," it is perfectly reasonable that the appearance of some film dragons should be based on their anatomy, rather than on the less-justifiable model in which two bat-like wings are affixed to the body of a quadruped reptile. Excellent examples of such "Wyvern" dragons appear in *Dragonslayer* (1981) and *Dragon Storm* (2004).

Rodan (or *Radon*) is a well-known fictional Pterosaur, introduced in *Rodan*, a 1956 movie from Toho Studios, which created the Godzilla series. Like Godzilla, Rodan was also modeled after a real prehistoric reptile. The Japanese name *Radon* is a contraction of "pte**ra**no**don**" and also suggests radiation. Radon is referred to as *Rodan* in the U.S., possibly to avoid confusion with the atomic element Radon. He was initially portrayed as an enemy of Godzilla, but they later became allies against more dangerous monsters.[15]

Fig. 23. Rodan

Here are a number of films featuring living Pterosaurs, Wyverns, and Bat-monsters—omitting those which take place during the Mesozoic Age, or on other planets. The following is by Seth Tyrssen:

The Lost World (silent -1925) This is the original version of the famous story, and it still holds its own today. The then-new art of stop-motion animation brought a variety of prehistoric beasties to life, including some very life-like "flying lizards." *King Kong* (1933) saw the art of stop-motion animation carried to new heights, and one of its best scenes shows the great ape battling a pteranodon at his mountain retreat, as the hapless heroine Fay Wray looks on…screaming, of course. *Rodan* (1956) was one of Eijii Tsubaraya's early works. Japanese animation, as seen in this and a whole slew of Godzilla movies, will never win any awards for realism, but Rodan (like all

the others) is amusing because it's so bad, it's good. Rodan appears to be a basic pteranodon, more or less. *The Land Unknown* (1957) and *The Lost World* (1960) join the ranks of several other bad remakes.

One Million Years BC (1966) is actually a remake of the earlier *1,000,000 BC* but featured Raquel Welch in her first major role. The pterosaurs and other monsters are credibly done. *The Valley of Gwangi* (1969) featured the work of Ray Harryhausen, and in spite of a silly premise, is actually quite good. Harryhausen's realistic Allosaurus shares space with some well-done pterosaurs, and even an Eohippus, the first tiny horse. *The Land That Time Forgot* (1974) is more notable for lovely Caroline Munroe than for its creatures, clearly not up to the standards set by Harryhausen, but that was probably due to the obviously low budget. *Dragonslayer* (1981) gave us the first really impressive dragon since Disney's animated "Sleeping Beauty," complete with an engrossing plot.

In *The Lost World* (1992), John Rhys-Davies and David Warner are wonderful, as the philosophically sparring Professors Challenger and Summerlee, respectively. Though the story was seriously altered for "political correctness," it's a tolerable version, with tolerable–though not great–critter-animation. *Jurassic Park II: the Lost World* (1997) Like its predecessor, this one had pterosaurs that looked incredibly real. The special effects folks really did their homework on these films. *Jurassic Park III* (2001) continues the excellent standards set by the first two films, with a whole host of realistic creatures. *The Lost World* (BBC-TV, 2001) At last, a worthy remake! Bob Hoskins (of "Roger Rabbit" fame) is teamed with James Fox, and a wide variety of well-done dinos. In this one, his pterosaur escapes into London, never to be seen again. One of the few remakes worth watching. *Dinotopia* (TV, 2004) was a beautiful miniseries based on the exquisitely-illustrated books by James Gurney.

Lord of the Rings: The Two Towers (2002) and *Lord of the Rings: Return of the King* (2003) magnificently capture Tolkien's fantasy-world, with striking realism. The "pterosaurs" in this case are more dragon-like, as they carry the dread Nazgul warriors on their backs. *Dragon Storm* (TV, 2004) has John Rhys-Davies as a rather nasty and treacherous king; the dragons are well done, and carry a lame plot fairly well. *King Kong* (2005), directed by Peter Jackson of *Lord of the Rings* fame, is, if possible, even better than the original. Infinitely better than the sorry attempt years earlier, that brought Jessica Lange to stardom. Its excellence extends to the dino-critters of all types. *Pterodactyl* (TV-2005) was a brutal made-for-TV production involving a flock of unkillable man-eating pteranodons hatching today in a remote mountain wilderness and hunting down students and military commandos. The critters were quite realistic, even if the plot wasn't.

pREhISTORIC pUZZLES
25. LIVINg DINOSAURS?

By Oberon Zell-Ravenheart

*I say that Mr. Waldron is very wrong in suppos-
ing that because he has never himself seen a so-called
prehistoric animal, therefore these creatures no longer
exist. They are indeed, as he has said, our ancestors,
but they are, if I may use the expression, our contemporary ancestors, who can still be found with all their
hideous and formidable characteristics if one has but
the energy and hardihood to seek their haunts. Creatures which were supposed to be Jurassic, monsters
who would hunt down and devour our largest and
fiercest mammals, still exist. How do I know, you ask
me? I know because I have visited their secret haunts.
I know because I have seen some of them."*[1]

—Prof. Challenger, from Chapter 5 of
The Lost World, by Sir Arthur Conan Doyle

Ian Daniels

VER SINCE THE REMAINS OF GIGAN-
tic prehistoric "dragons" were officially identified by science as *dinosaurs,* these Mesozoic monsters have fascinated us with their
gargantuan proportions and astonishing diversity. Speculations
continue regarding their actual appearance and behavior in life, as well as the mystery of their global
extermination 65 million years ago.

Although dinosaur fos-
sils have been known
for millennia, various

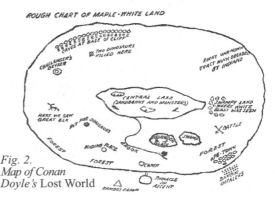

*Fig. 1.
Megalosaurus
by Bob Guiliani*

explanations have been
offered for their exist-
ence. In Europe, they
were generally believed
to be the remains of gi-
ants drowned by the biblical Deluge. The Chinese, on
the other hand, considered them to be Dragon bones,
and gave them the name *konglong* ("terrible dragon").
The first dinosaur to be formally described by science
was *megalosaurus* ("great lizard"), after part of a bone
was recovered in 1676 from a limestone quarry near
Oxford, England.

It was English paleontologist Richard Owen who,
in 1842, formally bequeathed the taxon of *Dinosauria* to these ancient animals, as "a distinct tribe or
sub-order of Saurian Reptiles."[2] The term is derived
from the Greek words *deinos,* meaning "terrible,"
"fearsome," or "formidable," and *saura,* meaning "liz-

ard" or "reptile." At first, this term was applied not
only to animals belonging to the orders of *saurischia*
and *ornithischia,* but to all fossil megafauna, including those we no longer consider to be true dinosauria
at all—such as archaeocetaceans (ancient whales), pterosaurs, ichthyosaurs, plesiosaurs, mosasaurs, and so on.

Today, the proper dinosaurs have been reevalu-
ated and grouped under *Archosauria,* which also includes birds and crocodilians. They are now believed
to have been active, warm-blooded, and supremely
successful. Far more birdlike than lizard-like, the bipedal predators we collectively call "raptors" were
quite intelligent, and evidently adorned with feathers.
Had they not been exterminated eons ago, their evolved
descendants would surely rule the galaxy by now!

LOST WORLDS OF FANTASY

Victorian fascination with the newly recognized
dinosaurs gave rise to an entire literature of adventure fiction involving lost lands somewhere on Earth
where remnant populations of dinosaurs still survived.
The first and classic story of this genre is, of course,

ROUGH CHART OF MAPLE-WHITE LAND

*Fig. 2.
Map of Conan
Doyle's* Lost World

The Lost World, by Sir Author Conan Doyle (1859–1930). Written in 1912, it inspired the first monster movie of the same name—a silent film released in 1925 that included remarkably realistic model dinosaurs built and animated by Willis O'Brien (best remembered for the perfection of his art in the 1933 *King Kong*—another tale of a lost world of prehistoric monsters). Interestingly, a later movie version of *The Lost World* (1962) sets Conan Doyle's story in Africa.

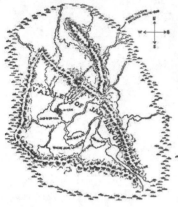

Fig. 3. Burroughs' Pal-ul-don

Whereas Conan Doyle set his lost world atop an actual immense and inaccessible plateau in Venezuela (the 9,000-foot-high Tepui Monte Roraima), and Kong's Skull Island was placed in the Indian Ocean, southwest of Sumatra, another popular adventure writer, Edgar Rice Burroughs, envisioned a hidden valley called *Pal-ul-don* ("land of men") deep within the impenetrable jungles of central Africa, where it is discovered by Tarzan of the Apes in *Tarzan the Terrible* (1921). Pal-ul-don is inhabited by humans with tails, and dinosaurs, including the savage and carnivorous triceratops-like *Gryfs*.[3]

If ever there was a place on Earth where a remnant population of dinosaurs could have escaped the extinction of their kind so long ago, it would have to be central Africa, especially in the vast and largely uninhabitable marshes of the Congo River basin—an area evidently hardly affected by the many Earth changes of the past 65 million years. Off the coast of Africa living *Coelacanths* were discovered in 1938. These large prehistoric fish with limb-like paddles were thought to have died out 70 million years ago. And a number of large African animals have been discovered only in the last century—including the okapi and the mountain gorilla. What other beasts still remain undiscovered?

Fig. 4. "The gryf issued his hideous challenging bellow and charged the warriors" (Tarzan the Terrible-1921)

DINOSAURS IN THE BIBLE?

There are several interesting images of dinosaur-like creatures depicted in ancient Egypt and Babylon—and possibly even described in the Old Testament, for example in this passage from the Book of Job (40:15–18): "Behold now behemoth, which I made with thee; he eateth grass as an ox. Lo now, his strength is in his loins, and his force is in the navel of his belly. He moveth his tail like a cedar: the sinews of his thighs are wrapped together. His bones are as strong pieces of brass; his bones are like bars of iron." Behemoth is normally assumed to be the hippopotamus; but what are we to make of "a tail like a cedar"? Hippos have small, pig-like tails, but a tree trunk is certainly an apt analogy for the tail of a sauropod dinosaur.

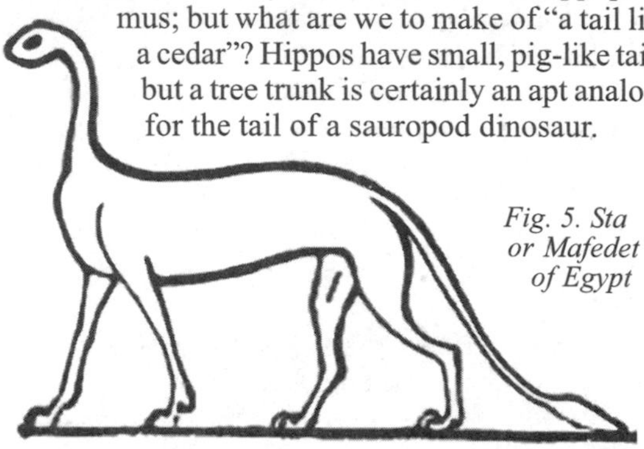

Fig. 5. Sta or Mafedet of Egypt

The *Sta* or *Mafedet* is a creature often depicted in Egyptian art, with the neck and head of an asp on a quadruped's body (Fig. 5). Similar creatures also appear in Roman art, such as this 2nd-century mosaic of two sauropod-like creatures with entwined necks (Fig. 6). Called the "Beasts of Nodens," they are in the ancient Roman camp of Lydney Park, Gloucester, England.

Fig. 6. Dinosaur-like creatures in a Roman mosaic

But the most famous example is sculpted in bas-relief on the great Ishtar Gate of ancient Babylon. Called the *Sirrush*, this draconic reptile has a serpentine head and neck, with the forefeet of a cat and bird claws for hind feet. It is covered with scales and has a long tail. Atop its head sits a crest, frill, or possibly a horn. The bas-reliefs were apparently intended to represent an actual animal. (Fig. 7)

In Babylonian mythology, Sirrush is one of the Dragons attendant upon the great Dragon-serpent-mother, *Tiamet*. At the time the Ishtar Gate was erected, Nebuchadnezzar the Great was King of Babylo-

Fig. 7. Sirrush from the Ishtar Gate of Babylon

nia. Reigning from 605 to 562 BCE, he is famous for his conquests of Judah and Jerusalem, his monumental building within his capital of Babylon, and his construction of the legendary hanging gardens. Nebuchadnezzar is featured in the Book of Daniel, wherein it is mentioned that his priests kept a "living dragon" in the temple of Ishtar, which they worshipped and which Daniel killed. This may have been the very creature depicted on the Ishtar Gate:

> There was a great dragon in Babylon, which was worshipped. The king said to Daniel, "You are not going to tell me that this is no more than bronze? Look, it is alive; it eats and drinks; you cannot deny that this is a living god; worship it, then." Daniel replied, "I worship the Lord my God; he is the living God. With your permission, O king, without using either sword or club, I will kill this serpent." "You have my permission," said the king. Whereupon Daniel took some pitch, some fat and some hair and boiled them up together, rolled the mixture into balls and fed them to the dragon; the dragon swallowed them and burst. Daniel said, "Now look at the sort of thing you worship!" (Book of Daniel, 14:23–27)

AFRICAN DINOSAURS?

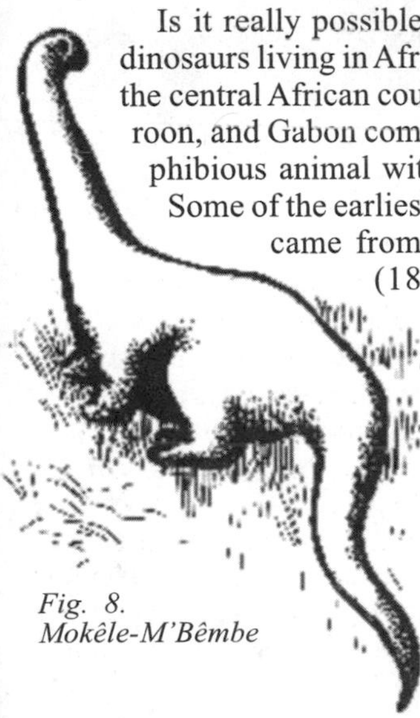

Is it really possible that there may still be dinosaurs living in Africa? From the jungles of the central African countries of Congo, Cameroon, and Gabon come reports of a bulky amphibious animal with a long neck and tail. Some of the earliest and most colorful tales came from Alfred Aloysius Horn (1854–1927), a traveler, trader, and adventurer. He told of a creature living in the swamps and rivers that was called *Jago-Nini*, meaning "giant diver." Though Horn never saw the creature himself, he did see a footprint that was "about the size of

Fig. 8. Mokêle-M'Bêmbe

a good frying pan in circumference and three claws instead o' five" (Fig. 9) He was told that it "comes out of the water and devours people."[4]

People of the Likouala swamp region call it *Mokêle-M'Bêmbe*, meaning "one who stops the flow of rivers" in Lingala, the language of the Pygmy natives of the Congo Basin; and this is the name which has become best-known in the West. In other districts, a creature of the same description is called *Iriz Ima, Dingonek, Ol-umaina,* or *N'yamala.* Reports have been recorded since 1776, when European explorers first penetrated into the mysterious jungles of west-central "darkest Africa."

Fig. 9. Track of Mokêle-M'Bêmbe

Fig. 10. Mokêle-M'Bêmbe

Also depicted in ancient rock paintings, Mokêle-M'Bêmbe's body size is said to be somewhere between that of a hippopotamus and an elephant. It has been reported to be 15–30 feet long, with the neck and tail each being 5–10 feet long. But sightings from Cameroon have reported such creatures to be up to 75 feet in length. The hairless, leathery skin is predominately reddish-brown ranging to grey. It has short legs with three-clawed feet, a reptilian head atop a long, flexible neck, and a long, muscular tail similar to that of an alligator. Some witnesses have described a frill on the back of its head like the comb of a rooster, and others mention a single tooth or horn. These details are certainly suggestive of the Sirrush.

When natives draw a representation of Mokêle-M'Bêmbe in the dirt it resembles a *sauropod* dinosaur. Then, when they are shown a picture of a sauropod dinosaur, they say that is Mokêle-M'Bêmbe. They claim that it lurks in the area of Lake Tele, and that its lairs are in the deep, partly submerged caves that line the banks.

Natives claim the creature is herbivorous, subsisting primarily on the *malombo* plants (*Landolphia mannii* and *Landolphia owariensis*) along the shores of the Likoula-aux-Herbes River. But it is also aggressive, and ferociously attacks and kills hippos and people. Tribespeople tell of hunters and fishermen whose boats have been capsized by Mokêle-M'Bêmbe and the people held under water by its massive tail. Corpses of these victims have later washed ashore, crushed but not eaten. There have been numerous sightings by local villagers and explorers since 1913, and one was even killed by natives around 1959. But all those who ate of its flesh died, and the village was subsequently afflicted with a plague of house fires, illnesses, and deaths.

Texan herpetologist James Powell led the first cryptozoological expedition to the area in 1979. His report included tales of a strange animal called *N'yamala*, which resembled the *Diplodocus*, living in the swamps of Gabon.

Fig. 11. Nyamala

A local witch doctor claimed to have seen one around 1946. It was more than 30 feet long, with a long neck and tail, and weighed at least as much as an elephant. In the Belgian Congo in 1912, an Ituri native told Colonel Alex Godart, a Belgian hero of World War I, that the *Nyama* was "a very big beast like a hippopotamus, but with a little head with feathers— and a crest like a cock's comb." He said it "makes the earth shake when it comes out of the water."[5]

One of the best eyewitness accounts came from zoologist Marcellin Agnaga of the Brassaville Zoo, who led a Congolese-sponsored expedition to Lake Tele in April of 1983. Only 800 feet from where they stood on the shore, a Mokêle-M'Bêmbe raised its head and neck in clear view of the team. Agnaga reported that it had a narrow, reddish head, large, oval crocodilian eyes, and thin nose. It was clearly reptilian, but of no known type.[6]

Much earlier, in 1932, legendary American cryptozoologist Ivan T. Sanderson came upon a set of "vast hippo-like tracks" on the Upper Cross River above Mamfe Pool, where no hippos are known to exist. Later, he saw a huge body slip beneath the water while he was boating near his camp. His native guides called

Fig. 12. Tracking the Mokele-M'Bembe

the creature *Mgbulu-e M'bembe*.[7]

In 1980 and 1981, Dr. Roy Mackal of the University of Chicago led ISC-sponsored expeditions into Lake Tele and the Likouala swamps. Although he collected several stories he never actually saw a Mokêle-M'Bêmbe. The closest he came was hearing a loud "plop" as some heavy body entered the river, and seeing a large wake splash up on the far bank.[8]

A somewhat different large amphibious creature is said to dwell in the Likouala swamps of the Congo, in Lake Banweolo, Cameroons, and in other swamps of the West African coast. It is called *Emela-Ntouka* (Lingala, "killer of elephants"), *Chipekwe*, or *Groot Slang*. It is described as slightly smaller than a hippo, which it kills and feeds upon. It has a smooth dark green, grey, or brown body without bristles, a crocodile-like tail, and a single ivory horn on its nose like that of a rhino, with which it is said to disembowel elephants.[9] Like Mokêle-M'Bêmbe, its elephantine footprints show three-toed claw marks. One was killed

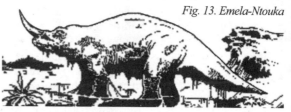

Fig. 13. Emela-Ntouka

in 1934, but no scientific study was done. Some cryptozoologists have noted the similarity of this description to the Cretaceous ceratopsian, *Monoclonius,* but of course those animals were herbivores. Indeed, this creature actually sounds more like the carnivorous *Gryfs* of Pal-ul-don! Is it possible that Burroughs had heard these tales, and was thus inspired to include such beasts in *Tarzan the Terrible?*

Fig. 14. Triceratops

A similar creature called *Ngoubou* is described as having a large head-shield and "tusks" (horns?), much like a ceratopsian dinosaur. Unlike the solitary Emela-Ntouokas, these are said to live in herds and contend with elephants over territory.

Another possible living dinosaur is reported to be dwelling in the jungles of Kenya, West Africa. Called *Muhuru*, it is described by eyewitnesses as a heavily armored reptilian beast, with large bony plates jutting out of its spine and an intimidating spiked or club-like tail. A similar creature of the Congo is *Mbielu-Mbielu-Mbielu* ("one with planks growing out of their back"). Pygmy fishermen have reported seeing it half submerged in water with algae growing on its back, which is said to have several flat "planks" projecting from the skin. No one has ever seen the full body,

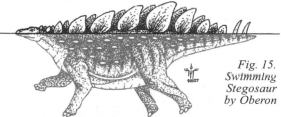

Fig. 15. Swimming Stegosaur by Oberon

legs, and tail of the creature, but they claim that it is peaceful and herbivorous. The "planks" suggest the back plates of a *Stegosaurus* ("roofed-lizard"). An African version was *Kentrosaurus* ("pointed lizard"). But these Jurassic ornithiscian dinosaurs are not believed to have been amphibious.

Kasai rex is yet another of the supposed living dinosaurs reported from the jungles of Central Africa. In 1932, a Swedish plantation owner named Johnson and his native servant were tra-ve-ling through the Kasai valley when they

Fig. 16. Kasai rex

witnessed one attack and devour a rhinoceros. He described it as a 40-foot-long lizard, with a long, thick tail and leonine legs, and long sharp teeth in huge jaws. It was dark red, with vertical black stripes like a tiger's down its neck, back, and tail. It is unclear from the description whether this animal was bipedal with tiny arms, as the name suggests, or just a gigantic lizard—in which case it would not be a dinosaur.

In addition to dinosaurs, other

Fig. 17. Spinosaurus by Bob Giuliani

Mesozoic monsters have been reported from Africa. The Great Rift Valley of Kenya is said to be home to a large, sail-backed reptile whose description matches that of the Cretaceous African carnosaur, *Spinosaurus.*

The *Lau* is an immense plesiosaur-like creature with a long tapering neck, a donkey-like body, and flippers, said to lurk in the dense papyrus swamps around Lake No in south-central Sudan, East Africa. Bristling tendrils protrude from the animal's muzzle, aiding it in snaring prey. It was brought to interna-

Fig. 18 Lau

tional attention in 1914 when a group of Shilluk natives killed a specimen in the swamps of Addar to use its bones in protective amulets.

OTHER "LOST WORLDS" OF MESOZOIC MONSTERS

Because Conan Doyle's "Lost World" was located not in Africa but in South America, we should not be surprised that reports of dinosaurs have also emanated from the green mansions of the Emerald Forest, such as this one of the *Madidi Monster:*

In 1907 Lieutenant-Colonel Percy Fawcett of the British Army was sent to mark the boundaries between Brazil and Peru. He was an officer in the Royal Engineers and was well known as a meticulous recorder of facts. In the Beni Swamps of Madre de Dios Colonel P. H. Fawcett saw an animal he believed to be Diplodocus.... The Diplodocus story is confirmed by many of the tribes east of the Ucayali....

(*The Rivers Ran East*, by Leonard Clark, 1953)[10]

Fig. 19. Diplodocus by Bob Giuliani

And in 1955, naturalist Alexander Laime claimed to have seen three plesiosaurs sunning themselves fully on rocks at the summit of the Auyan-tepui River in Venezuela. Two French explorers to the same area saw a similar animal as recently as 1990. Even today, natives living in the vicinity of the Roraima tepui describe large pterosaurs flying over their villages from the plateau high above—just as Conan Doyle described.

The huge island of New Guinea—still largely unexplored by outsiders—is home to quite a variety of legendary monsters, including the *Pish-meri*, or Mermaids (see Chapter 10. "Merfolk"). Among these is a "dinosaur-like reptile" first reported in 1999 from the 100-mile-long Lake Murray in Papua New Guinea. Described by eyewitnesses as being "as long as a dump truck," it is a bipedal, amphibious animal, approximately 6 feet wide, with two short forelimbs,

Fig. 20. Carno-taurus

legs "as wide as palm tree trunks," a long neck, and a slender tail. Its head resembles that of a bull, with large eyes and teeth as long as a man's fingers. Its back is said to have "largish triangular scoops," and its skin resembles that of a crocodile. This description sounds very much like a theropod dinosaur. The bull-like head is suggestive of *Carnotaurus*, but the "largish triangular scoops" are characteristic of stegosaurs.

POSSIBILITIES

Of course, what we are all hoping for is that there really *is* a Lost World, a Skull Island, a Land That Time Forgot, or a Lost Land of Pal-ul-don somewhere out there with real live dinosaurs—perhaps in South America, New Guinea, or, even more likely, in Africa. But although hope will launch expeditions, hope alone will not manifest a modern-day Jurassic Park. As Professor Challenger did, we will need to bring back something a bit more conclusive than second-hand reports of eyewitness accounts and out-of-focus photographs.

I have little doubt that Mokêle-M'Bêmbe is "real" in the sense that there is some actual animal behind the sightings and reports. Just what that animal may be, however, is another matter, as I learned personally from the Mermaid Expedition of 1985 (see Chapter 10. "Merfolk"). It is natural for us to project our own interpretations to fill in the blanks according to our desires and preconceptions. The Mermaid story is an excellent case in point, and a cautionary one.

A small head atop a long neck and a large bulky body is certainly descriptive of a sauropod dinosaur. But, as I discussed in Chapter 18, "Lake Monsters," witnesses have also attributed such sightings to plesiosaurs, which would look very different if we saw the part beneath the surface. On the other hand, Oudemans and Heuvelmans believed the great Sea-Serpent to be a kind of long-necked seal. As I have argued elsewhere, I don't accept any vertebrate identification for long-necked Lake-Monsters and Sea-Serpents, and feel that the best fit for the recorded observations is with a gigantic, slug-like mollusk.

But besides the long neck, two noted features distinguish Mokêle-M'Bêmbe from those other mystery

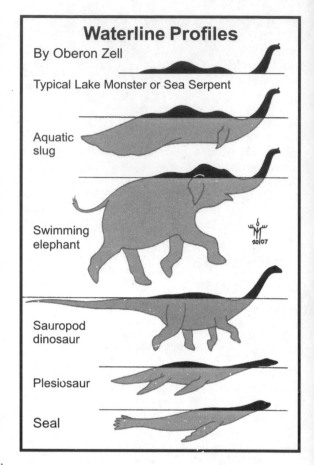

Fig.21. Forest elephant compared with savannah elephant, by B. Heuvelmans

monsters of lochs and seas. These are the elephantine legs, which leave round, 3-clawed footprints, and the long, thick, reptilian tail, likened to that of a crocodile. If all these elements do, in fact, belong to the same animal, the only known candidate would have to be a sauropod dinosaur. And I truly hope this proves to be the case.

However, in all honesty, it must be noted that the African Congo is also home to the Forest Elephant (*Loxodonta africana cyclotis*), a smaller subspecies than the far better-known Savanna or Bush Elephant (*Loxodonta africana africana*). Its size is, in fact, precisely that which is ascribed to Mokêle-M'Bêmbe. Several specimens of an even smaller dwarf elephant have been collected from the Congo region and exhibited in zoos in Africa, Europe, and the United States. Its height is no more than 6.5 feet, and its color has a decided reddish cast. But, although it has been bequeathed the scientific name of *Loxodonta pumilio*, this animal's claim to species or subspecies status is not universally accepted by all zoologists.

Both the forest elephant and the dwarf variety inhabit the Congo basin's dense swamps and marshes, rather than the open savannas favored by the bush elephant. In this regard, they are even more amphibious than other pachyderms—all of which are known

to love bathing and swimming. A swimming elephant with its snorkel trunk held high looks uncannily like the classic image of a Lake-Monster.[11] The tops of its ears even resemble the "fins." (Fig. 22) And all of the recorded sightings of Mokêle-M'Bêmbe by Westerners have been in the water, where its body was submerged with only the back and neck visible.

Fig. 22. Photo of swimming elephant taken by Admiral R. Kadirgama off the coast of Sri Lanka. From New Scientist, Aug. 2, 1979.

Interestingly, an aquatic elephant-monster called the Water Elephant has also been reported to be dwelling in the Congolese jungles. But elephants have five toes on each foot, not three, and their ropelike tails bear no resemblance to those of crocodiles or sauropods. So, until a successful expedition returns with full-body photos, videos, or an actual specimen, the jury is still out on *Mokêle-M'Bêmbe*, *Iriz Ima*, or *N'yamala*.

Likewise the nose-horned, carnivorous *Emela-Ntouka*, *Chipekwe*, or *Groot Slang*. Probably it is just a briefly glimpsed rhino enhanced by wishful thinking. But rhinos aren't carnivorous, and they don't have crocodilian tails—perhaps it really *is* a Gryf!

And perhaps the *Muhuru* or the *Mbielu-Mbielu-Mbielu* really is a *Stegosaurus*. The only way to know for sure is to go find one!

MONSTER MOVIES: LIVING DINOSAURS IN THE MODERN WORLD

Dinosaurs have always been immensely popular subjects of fantasy films. Here are some that featured living Dinosaurs in the modern world and inhabiting forgotten lands or remote islands. *The Lost World* (1925) is a silent film adaptation of the Arthur Conan Doyle novel, with quite realistic dinosaurs by Willis O'Brian that even fooled the great Houdini. In 1933, *King Kong* presented living dinosaurs and a gigantic ape on an uncharted island, with more animated monsters by O'Brian. *The Land Unknown* (1957) takes place in the heart of Antarctica. In *The Lost World* (1960), an inferior adaptation of the Conan Doyle novel, the "dinosaurs" are just blown-up lizards (referred to in Hollywood as *slurpasaurs*). In *Dinosaurus!* (1960), undersea explosions near a Caribbean island release prehistoric creatures, including a *T-Rex* and a *Brontosaurus*. *One Million Years B.C.* (1966), *When Dinosaurs Ruled the Earth* (1970), and the 1981 comedy *Caveman* are all supposedly set in the time of dinosaurs, but because they all included more modern-looking cave people, I am including them here. *The Valley of Gwangi* (1969) is hidden in the American Southwest, where cowboys rope dinosaurs. *The Land That Time Forgot* (1974) is based on the 1914 novel by Edgar Rice Burroughs. *Baby—Secret of the Lost Legend* (1985) is a Disney film about Mokêle-M'Bêmbe. *The Lost World* and its sequel, *Return to the Lost World*, both in 1992, move Conan Doyle's tale to Africa. *Jurassic Park* (1993), from the novel by Michael Crichton, features cloned dinosaurs in a high-tech theme park. In *Jurassic Park II: The Lost World* (1997), the sequel to the 1993 movie, a cloned *T-Rex* is captured from a second experimental island and brought to Los Angeles, with predictable consequences. In 1998, a really awful version of *The Lost World* inexplicably moves the location to Mongolia. *Jurassic Park III* (2001) requires a return to the second island to rescue a boy from ferocious raptors, pteranodons, and a *Spinosaurus* that has swallowed a cell phone which keeps ringing. *The Lost World* (2001) is an excellent BBC-TV adaptation of Conan Doyle's novel, with very realistic CGI dinosaurs. Peter Jackson's *King Kong* (2005) once again features living dinosaurs on an uncharted island in the 1930s, this time with wonderful CGI creatures. But my personal favorite is *Dinotopia* (2002), a TV miniseries based on the lovely books by James Gurney, which tell of an island utopia where humans and intelligent dinosaurs have built a magnificent society.[11]

Fig. 23. Movie poster from the original Lost World (1925)

26. hairy hominids & mystery monkeys

By Oberon Zell-Ravenheart

These huge creatures walk constantly upon their hind feet, and never yet were taken alive; they watch the actions of men, and imitate them as nearly as possible.... They build huts nearly in the shape of those of men, but live on the outside; and when one of their children dies, the mother carries it in her arms until it falls to pieces; one blow of their paw will kill a man, and nothing can exceed their ferocity.

—Mr. and Mrs. Bowditch, in the late 1800s, describing the *Ingheena* of Africa[1]

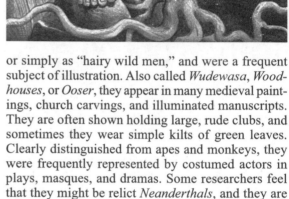

Ian Daniels, from a model by Oberon Zell

THIS IS BY FAR THE MOST DIFFICULt chapter to write. The sheer volume of information available is mind-boggling—as are the numbers of reported sightings and the diversity of the creatures described. Dozens of entire books have been devoted to this subject, as well as numerous organizations, Websites, TV documentaries, and periodical publications. A number of researchers have dedicated their lives to the quest for this elusive quarry. Living in the redwood country of Northern California, I myself was involved in the investigation for several years in the late 1970s, with Peter Byrne of the Oregon Dalles Bigfoot Research Center and *The Bigfoot News*. In this brief space, I can offer only a cursory overview of the subject.

Although reports of giant, hairy, manlike creatures have occurred worldwide throughout much of recorded history, the great majority of contemporary sightings come from America's Pacific Northwest, an unexplored wilderness extending more than 125,000 square miles. In this vast territory, these creatures are commonly known as Bigfoot or *Sasquatch*. Similar, perhaps even identical, beings are called *Kaptar* in the Russian Caucasus, *Chuhuna* in northeast Siberia, *Almas* in Mongolia, *Kangmi* in Tibet, *Yowies* in Australia, and *Yeti* in Nepal.

In medieval Europe they were known as *Wodwoses* (Anglo-Saxon for "wood man"),

Fig. 1. Hairy wild man-medieval

or simply as "hairy wild men," and were a frequent subject of illustration. Also called *Wudewasa*, *Woodhouses*, or *Ooser*, they appear in many medieval paintings, church carvings, and illuminated manuscripts. They are often shown holding large, rude clubs, and sometimes they wear simple kilts of green leaves. Clearly distinguished from apes and monkeys, they were frequently represented by costumed actors in plays, masques, and dramas. Some researchers feel that they might be relict *Neanderthals*, and they are very likely the basis of legends of giant Trolls and Ogres.

There are even legends of giant apes in the British Isles, where they were greatly feared. The *Ferla Mohr* (Gaelic, "big grey man") was an aggressive grey ape supposedly living in mountainous areas of Scotland. It was said to stand 20 feet tall.

Similar creatures collectively referred to as Giant Monkeys have been reported throughout the globe, and probably involve several species. They range from 4 to 6 feet tall, with barrel chests, thick arms, powerful legs, and bushy tails. Smaller ones are said to resemble kangaroos. They have fierce-looking, baboon-like faces and pointy ears. Their fur may be short to shaggy, and can vary from red to black. Their three-toed tracks are 12-15 inches long, with the larger ones being thinner. American versions are often called Devil Monkeys.

BIGFOOT

The Bigfoot of the Pacific Northwest seems to average about 8 feet tall, and leave footprints about 18 inches long. The color of its hair ranges from reddish-brown to grey to black. Males, females, and infants have been reported, often in family groups, and they usually display shy, benign curiosity in contact with humans. They also seem to be basically nocturnal, for which they have been designated *Homo nocturnus* ("night man"), a name originally set aside by Carolus Linnaeus (1707 1778) for just such a creature. By all accounts, they seem to have no language, do not make or use tools, and have no mastery of fire—the very qualities that distinguish humans from all other animals. The designation "Bigfoot" first appeared to the public in an article in the October 5, 1958 issue of the *Humboldt Times* by columnist and editor Andrew Genzoli, and was based on enormous, 16-by-7-inch footprints discovered at a construction

site in Bluff Creek Valley in Northern California. Interestingly, this is the same area as the famous Roger Patterson sighting and brief film of a large and distinctly female Bigfoot nearly a decade later, on October 20, 1967.[2]

Bigfoot seems pretty straightforward as a cryptid, or "hidden animal."

Fig. 2. Female Bigfoot--frame from Patterson film, 1967

We have many sightings, with consistent descriptions of all aspects of its appearance. Countless eponymous footprints have been found, cast, collected, and analyzed. Really clear ones obtained from smooth river mud show unique dermal ridges, depth impressions consistent with expected weight distribution for such a large bipedal hominid, and particularly nonhuman features such as a double-balled big toe and extended talus. The spacing of prints indicate a reasonable walking stride for the reported leg lengths, as does the flexion of the foot with each step. Although not without controversy, several blurry photos and some film footage have also been taken, and these precisely match the descriptions of eyewitnesses. Hair samples have been retrieved from branches where the creatures have passed, and subjected for DNA analysis. This has indicated anthropoid origin, but of no identifiable species. Feces have been examined and found to contain unknown parasites.

ᴛʜᴇ ᴍɪɴɴᴇꜱᴏᴛᴀ ɪᴄᴇᴍᴀɴ

The record even includes a detailed examination of an alleged frozen corpse, viewed in 1968 by Ivan T. Sanderson (then president of the Society for the Investigation of the Unexplained) and Dr. Bernard Heuvelmans (president of the French Center of Cryptozoology). Sanderson's drawings and Heuvelmans' photographs of the so-called Iceman have been widely published.

Fig. 3. Iceman photo by Bernard Heuvelmans and drawing by Ivan Sanderson

Shortly after this examination, however, the specimen was withdrawn from public display, and has since vanished. Cryptozoologist Loren Coleman says:

> The original body disappeared, and a model, apparently made in California, replaced it, with various Hollywood makeup artists claiming to have created the Iceman. But Sanderson and Heuvelmans knew of at least fifteen technical differences between the original and the replacement, thanks to photographs of the traveling exhibit taken by Mark A. Hall and Loren Coleman. When the Smithsonian Institution and the FBI got involved, Hansen explained that the creature was owned by a millionaire and declined to have it further examined."[3]

In 1981, at a County Fair in northern California, I saw what appeared to be the mummified body of an 8-foot-tall female Bigfoot exhibited as a carnival sideshow attraction by John Strong Jr. of the John Strong Family Circus. In writing this chapter, I contacted John for more details. He confirmed that it was a fake, and filled me in a bit on the history of Bigfoot *gaffs* (manufactured exhibits) that have become staples of such sideshows. Showman Rick West tells me: "Yep, I had two Bigfoot creatures. One I bought from Jerry Malone that was built by Johnny Chambers and one that a friend and I built in 1969. Had the Bigfoot on the road for 5 or 6 years. I knew Frank Hansen, owner of the Iceman, since 1967. I was the last showman to visit him before he died. I took photos during my last visit, of Frank and the creature. Have heard a new Bigfoot Show is being framed to tour this summer."

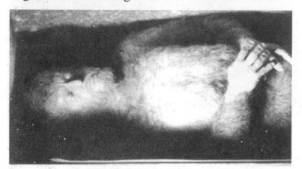

Fig. 4. Rick West's Bigfoot gaff

I asked Rick for more details on the Minnesota Iceman, and he replied:

> I first met Frank Hansen in 1967 at the fair in Peoria, Illinois (I was showing a Giant Steer). It was the first year out for the "Iceman." In the 1970's Frank framed the creature so it could be displayed in malls (the '67 display was in a semi-trailer). The creature was encased in a REAL block of ice!
>
> I visited Frank in Nov. 2002. (He died early spring 2003) He explained that the creature was designed and built by Howard Ball and his son Kenneth helped. Wax figure artists, Peter and Mary Corral put in the hair. Frank told me another person worked on the creature also but he could not remember his name at our Nov. meeting. The idea was to capitalize on the Bigfoot craze but not call his creature a Bigfoot.
>
> The creature I designed and built with a friend in '69 was pretty much a copy of Frank's creature although mine had greater detail.The Jerry Malone creature was on a small trailer with lots of chrome. It was displayed as "What is it?" and was basically another copy of Frank's show but without the ice. The creature was cast in plaster,

Fig. 5. Jerry Malone's Bigfoot gaff exhibit

I believe. It was heavy and hard. The hair was on the surface and not inserted into the body like Frank's and my creature's hair.After I bought it I changed the signage to "Bigfoot." I sold the Bigfoot show back to Rick Owens.

Many people believe there was/are two Hansen creatures, one being REAL. The idea played well for Frank. People will always believe there were two, but the timeline will not support it. Sanderson and Heuvelmans thought they found the Holy Grail! They had been waiting for this moment their whole life. After they wrote their articles saying the creature was real, it would have been hard to admit they had been taken in. When they were up at Frank's it was winter. The creature was in the closed-up trailer, in ice. They said they smelled rotting flesh. It just so happens that rotting latex has a similar smell. But Sanderson and Heuvelmans wanted/needed to BELIEVE. The Smithsonian Institute was interested in the creature, but backed out of the deal after talking to the California artists.

(——Rick West, Dr. West's Traveling Sideshows and Animal Menagerie; personal e-mail correspondence, April 2007)

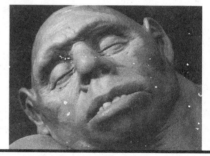

Fig. 6. Bigfoot gaff before insertion of hair

CANADIAN MAN-APES

Canada also claims another hairy hominid similar to Bigfoot, but this one is considered by the local Indians to be quite different—and far more dangerous, as it preys on humans. It is called **Wendigo**; also *Windigo, Windago, Wiendigo, Witigo, Witiko,* or *Wee-Tee-Go.* The most feared creature in Inuit and Algonkian folklore, it is described as a lanky, 15-foot-tall "man-beast" covered in matted fur, with glowing eyes, long, yellow canine teeth, and a hyperextended tongue. Some eyewitnesses insist that the creature is hairless, with sallow, almost jaundiced skin. Popularized by Algernon Blackwood's short story, *The Wendigo* (1907), legends of this beast date back centuries. This name is also applied to an alligator-like monster said to inhabit Berens Lake, Ontario, where it tears up fishing nets.

But with everyone carrying digital cameras these days, it seems only a matter of time before more con-

Fig. 7. Wendigo

crete evidence is obtained in the form of indisputable images or—the holy grail of all monster-hunters—a physical specimen. Even a corpse or skeletal remains would provide the long-awaited proof necessary for scientific recognition. Indeed, given the history and frequency of sightings, it seems incredible that such a creature could have eluded pursuit for so long. But we have to keep in mind that Bigfoot's territory is vast—hundreds of thousands of square miles of dense and ancient forest blanketing not only the Pacific Northwest, but most of Canada as well. New animals are still being discovered in much smaller habitats, such as Cambodia (the Forest Ox or Kouprey, *Bos sauveli*), Vietnam (the Saola or Vu Quang Ox, *Pseudoryx nghetinhensis*), the Philippines, New Guinea, and pockets of equatorial Africa, and a reasonably intelligent hominid that didn't want to be found could certainly remain hidden indefinitely.

In fact, large hairy hominids have been known for centuries by the native peoples of North America's northern states and provinces, such as California's hairy big man, *Oh-mah*. The popular name **Sasquatch** was coined in the 1920s by teacher J.W. Burns, who conflated several native Canadian words, such as the Salish *se'sxac*, meaning "wild man." This is only one of more than 150 local names for a giant hairy hominid reported by local Indians for centuries to be inhabiting the forests from Alaska down through British Columbia. It is even featured in native folklore and iconography, such as these 19th-century masks.

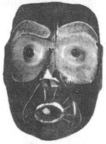

Fig. 8. Salish (L) and Tlingit (R) Sasquatch masks

Legends of the Nootka and Salish Indians of the Pacific Northwest tell of a massive hairy hominid covered in black bristles. Called *Matlose* or Caliban of the Nootka (after the monstrous character in Shakespeare's *The Tempest*), it has ferocious teeth and claws like a bear. Its terrible cry paralyzes its prey.

Haunting the folklore of the Tanaina Indians of subarctic Alaska is a giant biped they call the Hairy Man. Dwelling in the mountains, he is covered in long grey hair, and his eyes are said to have no pupils. He is not aggressive to humans unless they threaten him.

Smaller monkey-like creatures are also described in the traditions of the Ojibwa and Cree Indians of Minnesota. Called *Memegwicio* ("men of the wilderness"), they are said to be the size of 12-year-old children, with hair-covered faces.

Canada's Sasquatch was first seen by white men in 1811, and since then hundreds of sightings and encounters have been reported. It is anywhere from 6 to 12 feet tall, weighs 600–900 pounds, and is covered with shaggy black or reddish-brown hair. It has long arms, and an apelike face with a flat nose. Walking upright as a human does, it leaves humanlike footprints up to 20 inches long. It also has a distinct and very foul odor, similar to a combination of skunk and wet dog.

There is every reason to think that Bigfoot, Sasquatch, Matlose, Wendigo, and all the other names by which these creatures are known represent a single species, which probably includes at least one variety of the Himalayan *Yeti*. The burning question seems to be this: is it human, or ape?

YETI AND OTHER ASIAN ANTHROPOIDS

As North America has its Bigfoot, Asia is home to the even more famous **Yeti**. Also known as *Ginsung*, *Metoh-kangmi*, *Nyalmo*, *Rakshi Bompo*, *Rimi*, *Thloh-Mung*, the Wildman of the Himalayas, or, famously though erroneously, the Abominable Snowman, this snow-dwelling man-ape is said to live high up in the cold, desolate Himalayan mountains of Tibet and Nepal. It is described by eyewitnesses as 7–10 feet tall and covered in long, coarse hair—silver-white in the snowy mountains and orange-brown in the lower forests. As with its American cousin, the only evidence for its existence consists of a few hair samples, footprints, and questionable sightings. Upon examination, however, the "yeti scalps" preserved in lamaseries have turned out to be ritual objects fabricated from the skin of the goat-like serow, and the mummified "yeti hands" were those of langur monkeys.

According to the Sherpas, there are actually four types of *Yeti*, all distinguished by size,

Fig. 9.

Yeti, by Heuvelmans

with the *teh* in the name of each implying a flesh-and-blood animal. The largest (13–16 feet tall) is the *Nyalmo* or **Dzu-Teh** ("big thing"); the medium-sized one (7–9 feet) is the *Rimi* or **Meh-Teh** ("manlike thing"); and the smaller (man-sized) and best-known is the *Rakshi Bompo* or **Yeh-Teh** ("that thing there"). Many believe that the Yeh-Teh is simply the Nepal Gray Langur Monkey (*Semnopithecus schistaceus*), which is fairly common in the higher plains of the Himalayas, and that the Dzu-Teh is really a Himalayan Black Bear (*Ursus thibetanus*). Then there is the *Teh-Lma* ("that there little thing"), the least known, said to be 3–4 feet tall and covered in reddish-grey hair, with hunched shoulders and a pointy head. It eats frogs and other small animals.

West of the Himalayas, in eastern Afghanistan, as well as in the Shishi Kuh valley in the Chitral region of Northern Pakistan, there dwells a shaggy hominid called **Barmanu** ("big hairy one"). Similar to the American *Skunk Ape*, it is noted for its revolting stench.

Although the only recognized ape outside of Africa is the Orangutan (*Pongo*), a remarkable number of other unknown apelike creatures are continually being reported throughout Asia and Indonesia. Although there seem to be far too many distinct species for these reports to be credible, locals insist that they really exist, and are awaiting discovery by modern science.

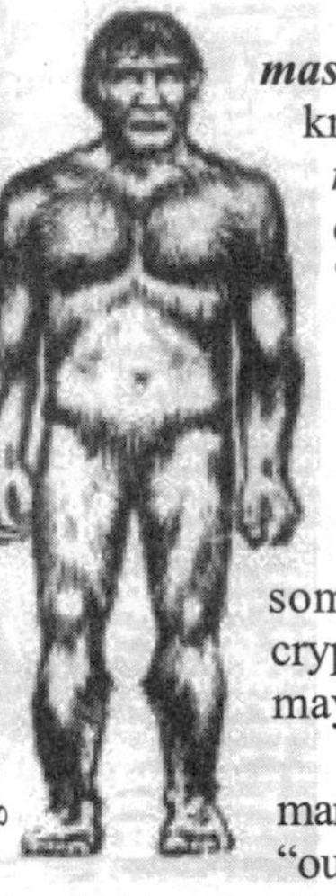

Most famous perhaps are the **Almas**, or Mongolian Wild Men. Also known by the names *Albasty, Abnuaaya, Almasti,* they are said to dwell in the Altai Mountains near Tien Shan in the province of Sinkiang, Mongolia. These wild people live as animals do, and are covered with hair except on their hands and faces. Although this description would seem to describe some sort of unknown ape, some cryptozoologists have suggested they may be remnant *Neanderthals*.

Fig. 10. Almas

In Siberia, hairy hominids or man-apes called **Chuchunaa** (Tungus, "outcasts") have been seen clothed in animal skins, leading some researchers to speculate that they may represent a relic population of *neanderthals*. Also known as *Mulen*, Bandit, or Siberian Snowman, they have been described by eyewitnesses as being tall and humanlike, with broad shoulders, protruding brows, long, matted hair, and occasionally unusual fur coloration. These may be the same as the Almas.

Further west, in the Volga region of Russia, a hairy hominid called *Ova*, with backward-pointing feet, is said to menace travelers by tickling them to death. But touching its vulnerable spot—a hole under its left armpit—renders it helpless. Perhaps by the time the stories traveled that far from either Europe or Asia, they were beginning to get a bit strange.

Large hairy hominids are also said to inhabit the forests and mountains of China's remote Hubei province. Called **Yìrén** ("wild person"), they are typically reported to be covered in reddish-brown hair, although some white individuals have also been sighted. Their height is estimated at 5–7 feet, although some colossal specimens more than 10 feet tall have been reported. They are known by many other names, including *Yiren, Yeh Ren, Sangui, Hsing-hsing, Fei-fei*, Chinese Wildman, Wildman of Shennongjia, Man-Monkey, or *Ren Xiong* ("man-bear"). In a Chinese dictionary compiled in 200 BCE during the Chou dynasty, the Fei-fei was described as a 10-foot-tall hairy cross between a human and an orangutan, with an appetite for human flesh.

Fig. 11. Chuchunaa by Xander

Fig. 12. Yeren

Some think that the Yìrén or Fei-fei may be a surviving *Gigantopithecus*, and others suggest it may be a relict population of mainland Orangutans (*Pongo pygmaeus*), supposedly extinct in China since the Pleistocene.

In the small country of Bhutan, on the eastern side of the Himalayas, locals describe a tall, hairy creature they call the **Migyur**. It stands 9 feet tall, with long arms and a nose like those of an ape.

In April, 2001, DNA tests performed on Migyur hair samples indicated that they belong to an unidentified creature completely unknown to science. Bryan Sykes, professor of human genetics at the Oxford Institute of Molecular Medicine, and one of the world's leading experts on DNA analysis, examined the hair. "We found some DNA in it, but we don't know what it is. It's not a human, not a bear not anything else we have so far been able to identify. It's a mystery and I never thought this would end in a mystery. We have never encountered DNA that we couldn't recognize before."[4]

Japanese folklore also includes tales of a huge hairy hominid called Mountain Man. Said to dwell in mountain forests, he is seldom seen, but fearful locals leave offerings to appease him.

The foul-smelling **Hibagon** is a smaller Japanese hominid. One was sighted in Hiwa in 1972. Looking much like a gorilla, it was about 5 feet tall, with a bristle-covered face, glaring eyes, and a snub nose.

Fig. 13. Hibagon (stamp)

Hibagon footprints can be as much as 10 inches long and 6 inches wide.

THE STORY OF ZANA

In Abkazia, in the Western Caucasus, large hairy hominids are called *Abnauaayu*. In the early 19th century, a female was captured. Named "Zana," she was passed through several hands, eventually coming into the possession of a nobleman, Edgi Genaba, who took her to his estate in the village of Tkhina on the Mokva River, where she lived for many years until her death in the 1880s or '90s. Over years of captivity in a strong enclosure, Zana gradually became tame enough to be allowed the freedom of the estate. But she always returned for meals, and to sleep in a hole she made under an awning near the house.

Her skin was black, or dark grey, and her whole body covered with reddish-black hair. The hair on her head was tousled and thick, hanging mane-like down her back.

…Over decades that she lived with people, Zana did not learn a single Abkhaz word; she only made inarticulate sounds and mutterings, and cries when irritated. But she…carried out commands given by her master…She was very tall, massive and broad, with huge breasts and buttocks, muscular arms and legs, and fingers that were longer and thicker than human fingers. She could splay her toes widely and move apart the big toe.

…Her face was terrifying: broad, with high cheekbones, flat nose, turned out nostrils, muzzle-like jaws, wide mouth with large teeth, low forehead, and eyes of a reddish hue. But the most frightening feature was her expression which was purely animal, not human. …[Her teeth] were so strong that she easily cracked the hardest walnuts.

She lived for many years without showing any change: no grey hair, no falling teeth, keeping strong and fit as ever. Her athletic prowess was enormous. She would outrun a horse, and swim across the wild Mokva River even when it rose in violent high tide. Seemingly without effort she lifted with one hand an 80-kilo sack of flour and carried it uphill from the water-mill to the village.

…She took swims the year around, and preferred to walk naked even in winter, tearing dresses that she was given into shreds.

Zana became pregnant several times by various men of the village. But the half-breed babies didn't survive her cold-water ablutions, until the villagers took four of them—two boys and two girls—from her and raised them as their own. Other than being powerfully built and strong, with dark skins, these offspring seemed entirely human, and possessed full speech and reasoning.

After several fruitless attempts in the 1970s to locate and excavate Zana's grave, Russian archaeologist Boris Porshnev was able to find and exhume the skeleton of her younger son, Khwit, who died at the age of 65-70. Porshnev brought the skull to Moscow, where it was examined by physical anthropologists, with the study published in 1987. The skull (Fig. 15) clearly exhibits primitive features, resembling that of a Neanderthal.

Fig. 14. Exhumed skull of Zana's son, Khwit

APEMEN OF THE INDIES

The thousands of islands comprising the East Indies are the remnants of a once-great mountainous region called Sunderland, which extended southward from present-day Indochina. Similarly, dry land once connected all the Philippines, and New Guinea was part of Australia. All the low-lying areas, however, were drowned by the South China Sea when the ocean levels rose at the end of the last Ice Age 10,500 years ago. The conversion of highlands into islands isolated populations of people and animals from each other and from the rest of the world.

The largest islands of Indonesia are Borneo and Sumatra, respective homes to the two known species of orangutan. This name derives from the Malay and Indonesian phrase *orang hutan*, meaning "person of the forest."[6] But from the Malay Peninsula throughout the many islands of this region, apelike creatures continue to be reported which have not yet been firmly identified by science. These may eventually prove to be nothing more than orangutans, but it is possible

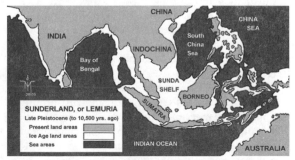

Fig. 15. Map of Ice-Age Sunderland by Oberon Zell

that some may yet turn out to be previously unknown primate species. Here is a sampling:

Orang Dalam—Hairy hominids of Malaysia, said to be 6–9 feet tall, with red eyes. Males have much hair about their head, chest, arms, and legs. They give off a powerful odor likened to monkey urine. At first contact they appear friendly, making overtures and approaching slowly.

Fig. 16. Orangutan

Then they invariably become frightened and flee into the jungle. This is certainly the Bornean Orangutan (*Pongo pygmaeus*), called *Mias-Pappan* in Borneo.

Stinking Ones—Malodorous, white-skinned hairy hominids occasionally seen and smelled in the jungles of Malaysia.

Batutut—A small, red, apelike creature reported to dwell in the rainforest of the Malaysian state of Sabah. It is thought to be related to the little frog-eating hairy hominid known as the **Teh-Ma** (in Vietnamese, the **Nguoi-Rung**). Perhaps this is a pygmy species of orangutan.

Ebu Gogu—Small, hairy, inarticulate cave dwellers first reported by Portuguese sailors visiting the Indonesian island of Flores in the 16th century. Sightings continued well into the 19th century. Then, in 2003, the subfossil remains of seven diminutive hominids were discovered on the tiny island. Officially designated *Homo floresiensis* ("man of Flores"), they were immediately dubbed hobbits in the popular press. Ranging in height from 3 to 4 feet, they appear to have been a dwarf race of *Homo erectus*.

Orang Pendek (or *Sedapa*, *Batutut*)—A hairy hominid reported to be dwelling in the millions of acres of rain forests on the island of Sumatra. Standing 3–5 feet tall, its brownish skin is covered with short black or brown hair, and it has a long black mane. It has no tail, and its arms are shorter than an ape's. It walks mostly on the ground, and its footprints are very similar to a human's. The creature eats primarily fruit and small animals, and is seen fairly often by locals, who say it has a rudimentary language, although the Sumatrans cannot understand it. It's possible that this is the Sumatran Orangutan (*Pongo abelii*), the smaller and rarer of the two known species of orangutans. However, some

Fig. 17. Orang Pendek by Heuvelmans

researchers have proposed that the so-called hobbits of nearby Flores are also likely candidates.

Kapre—Giant hairy hominids in the folklore of the Philippine Islands, they are said to be 7–9 feet tall and covered in long, shaggy brown hair. The Kapre lives in groves of bamboo, acacia, and mango, and may be encountered sitting under a tree smoking a pipe of tobacco. He is usually friendly and helpful to humans, especially women, but he also has a mischievous side, often leading travelers astray in the forest.

AUSTRALIAN APEMEN

An Australian hairy hominid, similar to the Yeti or Bigfoot, is described as 6–14 feet tall, more human than ape, with broad shoulders and no neck. Popularly known as **Yowie**, it is covered in longish hair ranging from black or dark brown to shades of red, tan, and almost white. Dark brown or reddish are the most common colors. It leaves footprints up to 16 inches long and 8 inches wide. The first report from European settlers

Fig. 18. Bombala Yowie seen by Charles Harper in southeast Australia in 1912 (FPL)

dates to 1881, but the Aborigines had always known of them, calling them *Youree*. The settlers initially named them *Yahoos*, after a subhuman race in Jonathan Swift's *Gulliver's Travels* (1727). These terms eventually combined into *Yowie*.

Like most hairy hominids worldwide, Yowies are said to have an overpowering stench. The smaller individuals, probably juveniles, are quite shy, whereas the taller ones are bolder and often aggressive. In fact, there is such a difference between the two groups in behavior, size, and coloration that some researchers think they are two species—or at least sexually dimorphic ones. Some even think they may represent a relict population of *Homo erectus*, known to have inhabited Sunderland.

Maori natives on the South Island of New

Fig. 19. Moehau

Zealand tell of a large hairy hominid with bony fingers that they call **Moehau**, *Moeroero, or Maero.* These are solitary creatures, but will kidnap people if given the chance. Those living in the mountains are called *Moeroero,* and those in the interior are called *Maero.* Said to be strong and aggressive, they are described as resembling a man covered over with hair, but smaller and with long claws; they inhabit trees and live on birds. Sightings have been reported since the 1840s.

AFRICAN APEMEN

No, this isn't about Tarzan. But it might be about his foster people, the *Mangani,* or Great Grey Apes. Many have assumed these creatures to be gorillas, but Edgar Rice Burroughs, author of the *Tarzan* series, clearly distinguished between them, referring to gorillas as *Bolgani.* Because there is no mention of chimpanzees per se in the Tarzan books, I had always thought that the Mangani must be chimps. But it now seems more likely that they were bonobos, or even the recently discovered Bili Apes.

Fig. 20. Ingheena (from Buel)

Accounts of African apemen should really begin with the *Ingheena*—a *quadrumana* (four-handed animal) reported by travelers Mr. and Mrs. Bowditch in the late 1800s, from the vicinity of the Gaboon River. They had not seen it themselves, but according to the natives, "these huge creatures walk constantly upon their hind feet, and never yet were taken alive...one blow of their paw will kill a man, and nothing can exceed their ferocity."[7]

These were, of course, Lowland Gorillas (*Gorilla gorilla*), considered mythical at that time, when it was believed that all great apes were orangutans. It took a while for gorillas and chimpanzees to become recognized by science, even though there were many reports of them. The Mountain Gorilla (*Gorilla beringei*) was acknowledged only in 1901, and Bonobos (*Pan paniscus*), identified in 1928 by American anatomist Harold Coolidge from a skull in Belgium's Tervuren Musem, were simply called pygmy chimpanzees until recently. Indeed, their status

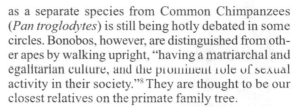

Fig. 21.
Bonobo

as a separate species from Common Chimpanzees (*Pan troglodytes*) is still being hotly debated in some circles. Bonobos, however, are distinguished from other apes by walking upright, "having a matriarchal and egalitarian culture, and the prominent role of sexual activity in their society."[8] They are thought to be our closest relatives on the primate family tree.

On August 14, 2003, the Associated Press reported the discovery of a possible new species of anthropoid ape in the northern part of Africa's Republic of Congo. The Bili Apes, which stand up to 6 feet tall and have feet nearly 14 inches long, were first documented in 2002 by primatologist Shelly Williams. According to a *National Geographic* report, "The apes nest on the ground like gorillas but have a diet and features characteristic of chimpanzees."[9] Preliminary genetic testing with non-nuclear DNA, however, indicates a close relationship with a subspecies of Common Chimpanzees (*Pan troglodytes schweinfurthii*).[10]

Fig. 22.
Bili Ape

A shaggy, black-haired, bipedal, apelike creature was sighted by an entomologist in Guinea, West Africa, in November of 1992. Local natives call it *Fating'ho,* and they claim it is neither a chimpanzee nor a gorilla. It has not been identified by science.

Small furry hominids have been reported from Tanzania, East Africa, as well. They are known as *Agogwe* (*Kakundakri* in Zimbabwe, or *Sehit* on the Ivory Coast). They were first reported in the early 1900s by big game hunter Captain William Hitchens, who encountered two of them on a lion-hunting safari in East Africa. In 1927, while traveling along the coast of Portuguese Africa, Mr. and Mrs. Cuthbert Burgoyne saw two apparently identical creatures walking peaceably among a troop of baboons without causing a stir. But none of these diminutive anthropoids have been seen since, and they may now be extinct.

With grotesque features and aggressive behavior, Agogwe are 3–4 feet tall, bipedal, long-armed, and covered with a scraggly coat of thick, russet hair over reddish-yellow skin. This description does not match that of any known apes, and Bernard Heuvelmans suggested that they may be remnant *Australopithecines.*[11]

The Canary Islands (from Latin *Insularia Canaria,* "island of the dogs") are an archipelago of seven volcanic islands in the Atlantic Ocean off Morocco, along the northwest coast of Africa. A shaggy man-ape called **Hirguan** is said to dwell on the island of La Gomera. Probably this is an isolated population of the Barbary Macaque (*Macaca sylvanus*), a large, ape-like, tailless monkey found in the Atlas Mountains of Algeria and Morocco, as well as (famously) on the Rock of Gibraltar.

SOUTH AMERICAN APES

According to science, indigenous apes are entirely unknown in the Western Hemisphere. Interestingly, however, in *Sea and Land* (1887), J.W. Buel reports that "Dr. Lund has furnished us with descriptions of the Brazilian orang outan, which he calls the Caypore, obtained principally from the legends of the natives."

And in the early 19th century, German naturalist Alexander von Humboldt heard stories from the Orinoco about furry, humanlike creatures called *Salvaje* ("wild"). These were said to build huts, capture women, and eat human flesh. All apelike creatures reported in South America are collectively dubbed *Mono Grande* ("large monkey").

Such a creature—one of a pair—was shot, killed, and photographed in 1920 by Swiss geologist François de Loys, during an expedition to the jungles of Venezuela. In 1929, Dr. George Montadon named it *Ameranthropoides loysi* ("Loys' American anthropoid"). It is commonly referred to as the De Loys ape. Skeptics have dismissed the unique photo as nothing more than a Spider Mon-key (*Simia paniscus*), although it has an adult body length of only 20 inches. But recently, fossilized remains have been found of a giant prehistoric howler-spider monkey, which, if still living, could account for this specimen.

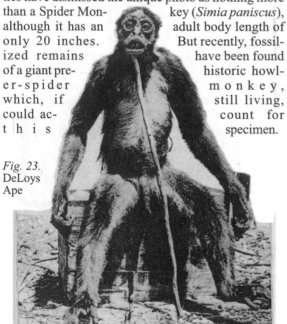

Fig. 23. DeLoys Ape

AMERICAN ANTHROPOIDS

Even though there seem to be entirely too many species of unknown apes to be accounted for, at least most of the above seem to represent physical animals, and hopefully, more of them will be officially discovered over time and take their places in the zoological catalogues.

But when we turn to the United States, reports begin to get decidedly weird. Far from the traditional northwestern haunts of Bigfoot or Sasquatch, sightings of somewhat similar but distinctly different hairy hominids have proliferated during the 20th century. To distinguish them from the others, researcher Loren Coleman coined the term *Napes*—an acronym for **N**orth **A**merican **Apes**. Invariably dubbed with colorful local names, these large primates have been reported mostly from the forests and swamplands of the southeastern and midwestern United States.

Skunk Ape (or *Southern Bigfoot*)—A large hairy hominid reported in Florida, with more than 100 sightings during the 1970s and 80s. However, the earliest published report is from 1942, in Suwannee County, by a man who claimed the creature rode on his running board for half a mile. Their presence is announced by a revolting stench similar to rotting cabbage. Eye-

Fig. 24. Skunk Ape

witnesses usually describe them as having reddish-brown fur, but their color can range from black to white. Albino specimens commonly have bald heads and nostrils the size of half dollars. They have long, dangling, apelike arms with clawed fingers, and they tend to snort. Tracks suggest that there are two species: the larger has three toes and an aggressive disposition, while the smaller 5-toed variety is shy and harmless. The mention of red fur has led some researchers to speculate that an escaped Orangutan (*Pongo*) may be the basis of the sightings. But the 3-toed footprints cast doubt on this identification.

Marked Hominids—Hairy hominids resembling Bigfoot, but smaller and more human in build. They are smelly, social creatures that live in forests and mountains of the frozen north. Sturdy, muscular creatures with large eyes and big bellies, they are nocturnal and omnivorous. Some, such as Old Yellow Top, have light-colored manes; others have patches of light fur surrounded by darker fur; and

Fig. 25. Marked Hominid

some appear to be nearly albino.

A large hairy hominid sighted in Ohio several times over the past century was named Old Yellow Top for its mane of yellow hair. Otherwise mostly black, it is said to be about 7 feet tall. It was seen in 1906, 1923, 1946, and 1970, when it nearly caused a bus to crash. An apparently identical creature had also been reported in the mining district around Cobalt, Ontario, Canada, since September of 1906. Its large body was covered with long, dark hair, but the fur on its head was light yellow. It, too, was named Yellow Top.

Fig. 26. Honey Island

Swamp-Monster

Honey Island Swamp-Monster—A 7-foot-tall, Bigfoot-like creature reported for centuries to be dwelling in the Honey Island Swamp, near New Orleans, Louisiana. Covered with dingy grey hair, its weight has been estimated by witnesses to be 400–500 pounds. But most memorable are its sickly yellow eyes, set far apart, and its horrific stench of death. Indians called this creature the *Letiche*, a carnivorous aquatic humanoid, which they believed was once an abandoned child who was raised by alligators. Cajuns call the beast the *Loup Carou*—similar to *Loup Garou*, a term for "werewolf." It has been blamed for the numerous human and livestock deaths that have plagued the area for decades.

Devil Monkeys—Strange baboon-like creatures with powerful kangaroo-like legs have been reported throughout the American Midwest and as far north as Alaska. One was even sighted in downtown Chicago! They seem to be extremely aggressive, attacking people and even moving cars. Some researchers have speculated that they may be a remnant species of an ancient family of primates called *Tarsiids* or *Simopithecus*.[12]

Momo (abbreviation of *Missouri Monster*)—A large, stinky, hairy hominid reported from the backwoods of Missouri. It has so much fur that you cannot see its face.

Murphysboro Mud Monster—A shrieking, 7-foot-tall, white-haired, apelike monster reported on May 25, 1972, by more than 200 witnesses around Murphysboro, in central Illinois.

Myakka Ape—A hairy hominid reported to be dwelling in the swamps around Sarasota, Florida. It is described as a chimp- or orangutan-like animal.

Fig. 27. Momo

Booger—A large, apelike creature sighted in the area around Clanton, Alabama, in the fall of 1960. It made cries like a woman screaming, and left big footprints in the sand along a creek.

El Campo Ape Man—In 2004, residents of El Campo in Matagorda County, Texas, reported bizarre encounters with what one eyewitness described as a 5-foot tall, grayish animal that resembled a large monkey.

Fouke Monster—A large, hairy man-ape reportedly stalking the backwoods and creeks of Miller County in Arkansas. It has been known to attack and kill animals. One three-toed footprint that was cast in plaster measured 13.5 inches long. In October 2003, witnesses throughout northwest Arkansas reported sighting a large, apelike creature, which they compared to Florida's Skunk Ape.

Fig. 28. Man-Ape

Orange Eyes—A huge hairy hominid reported since 1959 near the Charles Mill Reservoir outside of Mansfield, Ohio, from which has also been reported a bizarre, armless, amphibious humanoid known as the Mill Lake Monster (see Chapter 30. "Monsters of Mystery"). Orange Eyes is estimated to be 11 feet tall, and weigh 1,000 pounds. The most recent reported encounter with this creature was in June of 1991.

There is also a Mexican version of the North American Bigfoot, called ***El Hombre y el Oso*** ("bearman"). It has been sighted in wilderness areas across the land, from the western desert of Chihuahua to Veracruz on the Gulf Coast.

EL HOMBRE Y EL OSO

Fig. 29. El Hombre y el Oso

THEORIES: MONSTER, MAN, OR MYTH?

When I first met Peter Byrne in 1978 at his Bigfoot Research center in the Oregon Dalles, I inquired about his theory regarding the zoological classification of these creatures. His response has remained a guide to me over the three decades since, though I have not always followed it myself: "Theories," said Peter, "are a true researcher's worst enemy. When you have a theory, you will only see evidence that supports your theory, and you'll miss or ignore evidence that doesn't. So I try not to hold a theory; I just seek to follow the evidence."

Keeping this wise admonition in mind, here are several theories that have been proposed and passionately advocated over the years—specifically regarding the large hairy hominid commonly referred to as Bigfoot.

Hoaxes

Unfortunately, there have been many hoaxes associated with Bigfoot that have muddied investigations and diminished credibility of the phenomenon among establishment scientists. These hoaxes have included men dressing up in gorilla suits to be filmed and photographed in wilderness settings, as well as bogus footprints created with oversized wooden shoes or even replicas of genuine plaster footprint casts. One gruesomely determined hoaxer apparently went so far as to stretch the flayed skin of a butchered gorilla foot over a carved wooden mold. Several oft-cited photos and sightings have been admitted as hoaxes by people who claim to have participated in the deception, while other witnesses just as fervently continue to maintain their authenticity. The frequency of revealed hoaxes, however, has certainly necessitated the critical examination of all evidence, which is to the good.

In this regard we must certainly include the several artificial Bigfoot mummies and stuffed carcasses that have toured in carnival sideshows since the original Minnesota Iceman was examined by Sanderson and Heuvelmans in 1968. Such *gaffs,* as they are called by showmen, are a thriving art form created by ingenious taxidermists who are rather proud of their work, and pleased that so many are fooled.

Escapees

Although this theory would not seem applicable to the 6- to 9-foot-tall shaggy bipeds we are primarily concerned with here, nonetheless many skeptics insist that sightings must be of known apes, such as orangutans, gorillas, or chimpanzees—possibly escapees from a zoo, circus, or animal park. And to give them credit, some of the American reports—such as those of the Myakka Ape and the El Campo Ape Man—may be examples of this, especially in the swampy regions of Florida and Louisiana. Certainly, known apes would seem to account for most of the creatures sighted in Asia, Indonesia, and Africa.

Gigantopithecus

Bigfoot researcher Grover Krantz (1931–2002) was the major proponent of the theory that the North American Bigfoot—and probably the Himalayan *Nyal-*

Fig. 30. Gigantopithecus blacki —*life-size model by Bill Munns*

mo or *Dzu-Teh* Yeti as well—represents a relic population of the presumed extinct Ice Age anthropoid called *Gigantopithecus,* which is believed to have lived from 5 million to as recently as 100 thousand years ago. Only a few teeth and mandibles of this prodigious primate have been recovered, mostly from caves in Southeast Asia. These bear similarities to both humans and apes, but unfortunately, they provide little information as to the proportions and stance of the living animal. Nonetheless, paleontologists estimate that an adult *Gigantopithecus* would have stood more than 10 feet tall, and weighed about 1,200 pounds. It may have resembled a modern gorilla or orangutan, and many scientists think it was probably quadrupedal. But Kranz has pointed out that the very few jawbones found are U-shaped and widen towards the rear—providing space for the windpipe within the jaw, and allowing the skull to sit squarely upon a fully-erect spine like humans, rather than projecting in front of it, like great apes. It is on this basis that great ape sculptor Bill Munns designed this model (Fig. 33).[13]

Paranthropoids

When I first began studying the Bigfoot phenomenon upon moving to the Pacific Northwest in the mid-1970s, I was struck by the similarity of Bigfoot photos, descriptions, and drawings to reconstructions of a large Pleistocene proto-human called *Paranthropus robustus* (also called *Australopithecus robustus* or *Australopithecus boisei*). Dwelling in South Africa between 2 and 1.2 million years ago, this hominid was nearly twice

Fig. 31. Paranthropus

the size of the little *Australopithecus africanus* believed to have been our own ancestor. The length of its limbs and the proportions of its massive pelvis are quite unlike those of either humans or apes. Another significant feature is the prominent saggital crest atop the skulls of both *Paranthropus* and Bigfoot.[14]

The single feature of Bigfoot that we have been able to study extensively is its eponymous footprint. One aspect of those prints cannot be overlooked by even the most casual observer: the forward position of the big toe is not that of an ape, but of a human. There are enough significant differences between these prints and ours that their species cannot be *Homo sapiens*. But they could be *Paranthropus* ("the other man").

In 1971, crypto-anthropologist Gordon Strasenburgh first proposed the scientific name *Paranthropus eldurelli* for the Bigfoot of the Pacific Northwest. Today, this identification is gaining credence among serious investigators, and it is the one I, too, find most convincing.[15]

We are so used to thinking of humans as the only species of our genus, *Homo*, that we tend to overlook the fact that it was not always so. Just as there are several species of each of the great apes, early hominids also exhibited species diversity. Perhaps some of our presumed-extinct cousins still survive, undiscovered out there in the vast northern forests.

Missing Links

Since Darwin, just about every discovery of a primitive hominid has been hailed in the popular press as a missing link between modern humans and our anthropoid ancestors. It has seemed only too obvious to draw the same conclusion regarding sightings of hairy hominids, and many have done so, assuming these creatures to be surviving examples of our proto-human progenitors. Given the distinctly humanoid appearance of their footprints, this is not an unreasonable conclusion, nor is it a far stretch from the *Paranthropus* hypothesis. It is an especially credible proposition for African hominids presumed to be still surviving in their (and our) original homeland, along with several other species of known and unknown apes, most of which have been discovered only in the last century.

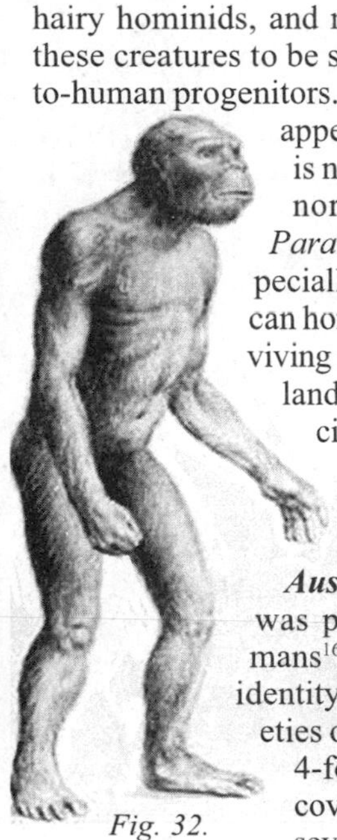

Australopithecus ("southern ape") was proposed by Bernard Heuvelmans[16] as a likely contender for the identity of several of the smaller varieties of ape-men, especially the 3- to 4-foot-tall African Agogwe. Discovered by Raymond Dart in 1924, several species lived in Africa dur-

Fig. 32.
Australopithecus

ing the Pliocene era, 4 to 2.4 million years ago. The famous "Lucy" was a representative of the older *A. afarensis*. She and the later *A. africanus* were slenderly built, or gracile, and are believed to have been the direct ancestors of modern humans.

Unfortunately, the last sighting of an Agogwe was in 1927, and if they did exist at that time, they may not any longer. Under present conditions of warfare and poaching, gorillas and chimps are severely endangered. Indeed, "when the bough (on the Tree of Life) breaks, the cradle (of Life) must fall."

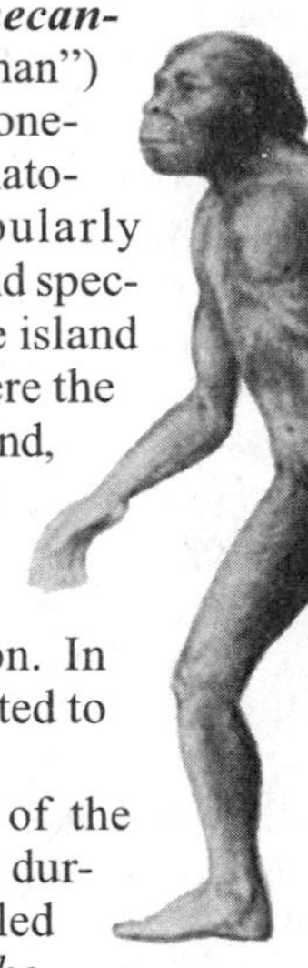

The first fossils of ***Pithecanthropus erectus*** ("erect ape man") were discovered in Java, Indonesia, in 1891 by the Dutch anatomist Eugène Dubois. Popularly known as "Java Man," a second specimen was located on the same island in 1936. At the time, these were the oldest hominid remains yet found, and many referred to them as the missing link between humans and apes predicted by Darwin's theory of evolution. In turn, the remains were then cited to validate Darwin's theory.

Fig. 33.
Homo erectus

Subsequent discoveries of the same creatures in East Africa during the 1950s and 70s have led to a reclassification, and *Pithecanthropus* has now been absorbed into the broader species of ***Homo erectus*** ("erect man"). They became the first hominids to leave Africa around 2 million years ago, when lowered sea levels of the Pleistocene era permitted extended migrations along the exposed continental shelf around Arabia, India, and into Sunderland (now Indonesia). They also appear to have been the first to master fire. Various sightings of mystery hominids throughout Indonesia have been evidenced as possible survivals.

Neanderthals

Homo sapiens neanderthalensis is now believed to have been of the same species as our own—*sapiens*—but of a different subspecies. Inhabiting Europe from 130,000 to 24,000 years ago, they had 99.5 percent of the same genes we have, but little if any of their genetic heritage survives among modern humans. Famous for enduring much of the Ice Age through their invention of clothing (made from tanned hides stitched together using sinews and bone needles), neanderthals used to be depicted as hulking, hairy, brutish figures—the archetypical "caveman" of popular conception. More recent discoveries have mitigated that image, as it was learned that the first specimens discovered suffered from severe arthritis and rickets owing to chronic vitamin D deficiency.

Dr. Myra Shackley, a world expert on neanderthals, has proposed that the Almas of Mongolia and the Chuchunaa of Siberia may represent relic populations of neanderthals, surviving into the 20th century. In her 1983 book, *Still Living? Yeti, Sasquatch and the Neanderthal Enigma*, she also provides an analysis of the medieval European Wildmen, or Woodwoses, tracing them back to the Satyrs, Fauns, and *Silvestres* of classical lore. But she concludes disappointingly that these are entirely creatures of myth, and do not represent relic survivals—an assumption that seems unwarranted to me.[17]

Fig. 34. Neanderthal

Hobbits

In 2003, the subfossil remains of seven diminutive hominids were discovered on the tiny Indonesian island of Flores. Officially designated *Homo floresiensis* ("man of Flores"), they were immediately dubbed hobbits by the media, due to the popularity of Peter Jackson's *Lord of the Rings* movies. Only 3–4 feet tall, with skulls the size of a grapefruit, they appear to have been a dwarf island-race of *Homo erectus*. Stone tools associated with the remains indicate that they existed from 18,000 to as recently as 12,000 years ago—

Fig. 35. Homo floresiensis

well into the time period of modern humans in the area. It is believed that they and other unique animals on the island were exterminated by a volcanic eruption about 12,000 years ago. However, Portuguese sailors visiting Flores in the 16th century heard native descriptions of small, hairy, inarticulate cave-dwellers they called *Ebu Gogo*. Sightings of these creatures continued into the 19th century. And some researchers have proposed that Sumatra's Orang Pendek may also be surviving Flores men.[18]

Humanzee

Also known as the *Chuman*, or *Manpanzee*, this is a hypothetical chimpanzee/human hybrid. Chimpanzees and humans are very closely related, having in common 95 percent of DNA sequences, and 99 percent of coding DNA sequences.[19] Numerous claims have been made over the

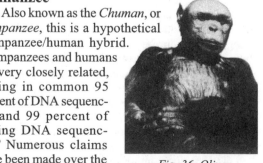

Fig. 36. Oliver

years for experimental or feral hybrids, most famously in the case of one named "Oliver." But when the candidates were subjected to DNA tests, no such hybrid specimen has ever been confirmed. Oliver turned out to be pure chimp, albeit with very little hair.

Aliens?

This may seem like an absurd notion to introduce, but it cannot be ignored. Particularly in the American South and Midwest, many sightings of large, hairy hominids include aspects of Fortean weirdness. Some of these creatures seem to have no facial features, some have long claws rather than fingers, and others leave three-toed tracks. And quite a few appear incomplete, as if they are holographic projections and part of them is invisible. Such sightings are often accompanied by reports of UFO activity in the vicinity. There is really no way to integrate these sorts of anomalies into any coherent theory of biological evolution and natural history, and I deem it wise to not even try. Reports of this nature, I submit, can only be relegated to investigators' "X-files."

MONSTER MOVIES: HAIRY HOMINIDS

Willis O'Brien's seminal *King Kong* (1933) introduced the world to the eponymous giant gorilla. It was followed by many sequels and imitations, beginning immediately with O'Brien's own *Son of Kong* (1933), and his later *Mighty Joe Young* (1949). *The Snow Creature* (1954) and *The Abominable Snowman of the Himalayas* (1957) both feature the legendary Yeti, which also made a brief cameo appearance in *The 7 Faces of Dr. Lao* (1964). *Konga* (1961) is an obvious Kong rip-off, shortly followed by more films that continued the saga of the mighty Kong: *King Kong vs. Godzilla* (1962), *King Kong Escapes* (1967), and *Kong Island* (1968). The 1976 *King Kong* is an updated remake of the original, but without the dinosaurs. The abysmal *Queen Kong* (1976) and *Mighty Peking Man* (1977) followed hot on its heels. *Quest for Fire* (1981) pits *Homo erectus* against neanderthals. *King Kong Lives* (1986) resurrected everyone's favorite giant ape. *Harry and the Hendersons* (1987) is a family film featuring an endearing Bigfoot, and was turned into a TV sitcom of 72 episodes over three seasons. It was followed by a moving remake of *Mighty Joe Young* (1998). *Wendigo* (2001) is a brooding horror film of the Canadian legend. In 2005, Peter Jackson reprised the original story of *King Kong* with a special effects extravaganza remake. On the DVD, a bonus mockumentary has Kong descended from *Gigantopithecus*. *King of the Lost World* (2005) is a forgettable return to the land of the giant gorilla. *Abominable* (2006) features the Yeti, and *Tenacious D in the Pick of Destiny* (2006) includes a Sasquatch.

MODERN MYSTERIES

27. DEMONIC DOGS

By Ash "LeopardDancer" DeKirk

Mauthe Dhoog

Standing over Hugo, and plucking at his throat, there stood a foul thing, a great, black beast, shaped like a hound, yet larger than any hound that ever mortal eye has rested upon. And even as they looked the thing tore the throat out of Hugo Baskerville, on which, as it turned its blazing eyes and dripping jaws upon them, the three shrieked with fear and rode for dear life, still screaming, across the moor. One, it is said, died that very night of what he had seen, and the other twain were but broken men for the rest of their days.

—Sir Arthur Conan Doyle,
The Hound of the Baskervilles

LACK *DOGS* ARE A WHOLE CLASS OF monstrous, canine apparitions prevalent in European folklore, showing up quite frequently in English and Scottish lore. These beasties, also called Hellhounds, are said to be huge dogs, roughly the size of a calf (though some as big as horses have been reported), covered in thick, shaggy, black fur, and with glowing red eyes. Despite their name, these creatures are not necessarily black, as there have been reports of white, spotted, yellow, and brown ones. Sometimes, though very rarely, there are reports of Cerberean Black Dogs sporting two or three heads. The Hellhound's canine teeth are often described as longer than average, and, to many people, they seem to be grinning at some hidden knowledge, rather like a canine Cheshire Cat. Black Dogs may be benevolent, they may be malicious, or they may be neither.

These apparitions appear at places that serve as transition archetypes—places such as lonely county rounds, ancient highways, bridges, crossroads, and shadowed entrances. Some Hellhounds guard treasures or sacred places. More often than not, if you leave a Black Dog alone, it will not bother you; but if you should attempt to harm one, you are the one who will suffer. Black Dogs can inflict frightful wounds that may prove fatal. Indeed, in much of the folklore that describes these creatures, to see one is a portent of death, though there have been purported instances of Black Dogs guiding lost travelers to safety. Black Dogs are also associated with fire—specifically, the flames surrounding the hound, and the presence of scorched earth and/or claw marks burned into wood or metal left in the beast's wake.

LOCAL VARIANTS

The names for the Black Dog are many and varied: In Scotland they are the *Cu Sith,* in Wales they are known as *Gwiyllgi,* on the Isle of Man they are called *Mauthe Dhoog,* and in Ireland they are the *Coinn Iotair.* Other names include *Black Shuck, Barghest, Ki Du, Gytrash, Padfoot, Rongeur d'Os, Saidhthe, Skirker, Suaraighe,* and *Trash.*

Here is an alphabetical listing of a number of important Black Dogs:

Barghest (also *Barguest, Barvest,* or *Boguest;* from German, *Bahrgeist,* "Spirit of the Bier")—One of the many Black Dogs of English and European myth, the Barghest can be as small as a bull mastiff or

Fig. 1. Faust confronts a Black Dog in his study.

as big as a bear. Covered in shaggy black fur, it has long fangs, claws, horns, a tail, and fiery red eyes. Seen around the northern English counties of Yorkshire, Durham, and Northumberland, it only appears at night in specific locations, primarily fishing villages and churchyards. It is also sometimes described as a huge bear, a headless man or woman, or even a white rabbit similar to the one Alice followed. The Barghest drags a clanking chain behind it, sometimes wrapping its body in it. The sighting of a Barghest is a guaranteed portent of disaster and misfortune.

Fig. 2. Barghest by Sam Wood

Cu Sith (Gaelic, "Fairy Dog"; also *Cir Sith* or *Ce Sith*)—A monstrous Black Dog of the Scottish highlands, the Cu Sith is the size of a cow and covered with dark green fur. Its paws are bigger than a human's hands, and it carries its long, braided tail coiled over its back like a saddle. The Cu Sith is as swift as the wind and hunts nocturnal wanderers on the moors, making a noise like a galloping horse and leaving huge footprints. Upon barking three times, it overtakes its prey and pulls it down. It is said to round up nursing mothers to supply fresh milk to infant fairies.

Freybug—A monstrous Black Dog that terrorized English country lanes in medieval times.

Galley-Trot (or *Gilitrutt*)—In the tradition of the Black Dogs of the British Isles, the Galley-Trot haunts the lonely roads of Dunwich and Woodbridge, and the Bathslough bog of Suffolk, harassing nocturnal travelers. This bullock-sized shaggy dog is white rather than black.

Gwyllgi (also called The Dog of Darkness and The Black Hound of Destiny)—This is an enormous Welsh version of the typical British Isles Black Dog, the Gwyllgi is a giant mastiff that likes to pad along

Fig. 3. Black Dog seen in Suffolk, 1577

beside midnight travelers. The Gwyllgi seems to enjoy terrifying people, but otherwise does not pose much of a threat.

Gytrash (also *Guytrash, Brash, Trash*)—A spectral Hellhound from the folklore of Lancashire and Yorkshire in Northern England, the Gytrash is a portent of imminent death and disaster. It is most often described as a huge Black Dog covered in thick shaggy fur, and sporting a pair of saucer-sized red eyes that glow like embers. It walks with a splashing sound ("trash") on webbed feet and terrorizes nocturnal travelers on lonely country roads. Sometimes it appears as a spectral horse or donkey.

Keelut—In Inuit folklore, a hairless version of the British Black Dog. It haunts lonely regions of polar Canada and Alaska, following and attacking nocturnal travelers.

Mauthe Dhoog (also *Mauthe Doog, Moddey Dhoo*)—A spectral Black Dog that haunted the corridors and battlements of Peel Castle on the Isle of Man in the 17th century. It was described as an enormous spaniel the size of a calf, with shaggy hair and eyes like pewter plates (see title illo). It attacked anyone who saw it, killing them outright, or driving them mad. In 1871, the remains of Simon, Bishop of Sodor and Man (died 1247) were uncovered during excavations. The bones of a large dog were found at his feet. Could this have been the original beast?

Fig. 4. Gytrash

Oschaert— A spectral Black Dog with fiery red eyes. Sometimes appearing as a giant horse, it haunted the region around Hamme, near Duendemonde, Belgium, until it was banished by a local priest for 99 years. It would leap upon the backs of unwary travelers on lonely roads, growing heavier with each step until they could no longer move.

Padfoot (or *Padfooits*)—A spectral beast with glowing red eyes that haunts the moors around Leeds, in Northern England. The Padfoot may manifest as a massive sheep, a giant white dog, or even a monstrous black donkey. Its presence is announced by soft, padding footfalls that may be accompanied by the rattle of chains or a fierce roaring as the beast draws closer to its intended victim. As with any of the other Hellhounds, the Padfoot should not be approached or touched.

Rizos—A massive Black Dog with huge claws, found in modern Greek folklore. It haunts lonely roads at night, terrifying wanderers. It may attack if it is touched, but usually it just vanishes.

Rongeur d'Os (French, "Gnawer of Bones") A gigantic Black Dog in the folklore of Normandy, in northern France. As with all of its kind, it frightens nocturnal travelers on lonely roads.

Saidthe Suaraighe ("Bitch of Evil")—A monstrous Black Dog of Irish legend, one of the pack of spectral hounds belonging to the legendary pre-Christian chieftain, Crom Dubh.

Shony—A Cornish ghost-dog whose appearance heralded a storm.

Shuck Dog (or *Shuck, Black Shuck, Old Shuck*)—A monstrous Black Dog in the folklore of East Anglia, England. Its name probably derives from the Anglo-Saxon *scucca*, meaning "demon." The Shuck Dog is roughly the size of a donkey and is covered with shaggy black hair. Shuck Dogs have fiery red eyes, but some have been reported to have only have one eye, right in the center of their head, which shoots forth greenish-blue sparks. Depending on the locale, Shuck Dogs can be evil or good. Most patrol certain areas after dark, and do not cause harm to people unless they are witless enough to challenge them.

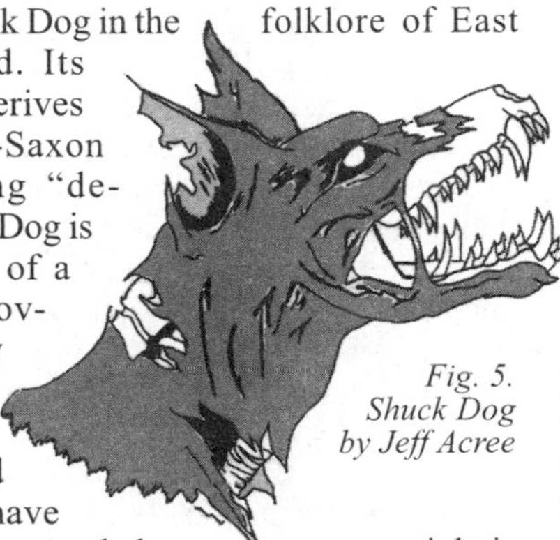

*Fig. 5.
Shuck Dog
by Jeff Acree*

Skriker (or *Shriker, Skriker*)—A gigantic Black Dog that haunts lonely back roads in Lancashire, England. With huge glowing red eyes, it may be heard shrieking in the wood or appear alongside a lone traveler at night, constantly moaning and howling.

Sus Lika—A fearsome, spectral dog in the folklore of the Taniana Indians of sub-Arctic Alaska. It haunts mountain passes, where it may be heard barking, but is never seen.

Waheela—A wolf-like creature said to inhabit Alaska and Canada's Northwest Territories. It is larger and more heavily built than ordinary wolves, with a wide head, big feet, and long, white fur. Witnesses describe it as being about 4

*Fig. 6. Waheela
(or Bear Dog)*

feet high at the shoulder. Its hind legs are shorter than its front legs, and its tracks indicate widely-spaced toes. They are solitary creatures and never seen in packs. According to native legends, the Waheela is an evil spirit, which tears the heads off its victims. Its description matches that of the Pleistocene bear dog (*Amphicyonid*), presumed extinct for 10,000 years.

Youdic Dogs—Monstrous Black Dogs in the folklore of Brittany, northwestern France. They dwell in the Youdic swamps, and, similar to all their kin, terrify lone, nocturnal travelers on desolate roads.

hounds of hell

*Black dog, Derry dog, Shuck and Cu,
Gabriel's hounds hunting after you.*

*Whist hounds, Arawn's hounds, Barghest and Grim,
See a black dog, prospects look slim.*

*Black dog, Gytrash, Padfoot, Ki Du,
Coinn Iotair chasing after you.*

*Hellhound, Mauthe Dhoog, Skirker and Grim,
See a black dog, luck turns dim.*
                —Ash "LeopardDancer" DeKirk

There are also many accounts of packs of Hellhounds on the loose. A particularly demonic aspect of the traditional British Black Dogs, they are believed to hunt and drive lost or damned souls into Hell, Annwfn, or the Underworld. Their master is the Lord of Death. These are often called "Gabriel Hounds" or the "Wild Hunt."

In Welsh folklore they are called the **Cwn Annwfn** ("Hounds of Hell"). Also known *Cwn Mama* ("Hounds of the Mothers"), *Cwn Cyrff* ("Corpse Dogs"), or *Cwn Wybr* ("Sky Dogs"), these are huge white hounds with red ears and eyes. Led by the grey huntsman, *Arawn* (or *Gwyn ap Nudd*), they drive the souls of the dead to *Annwfn,* the Underworld. The Irish equivalents are the *Coinn Iotair*.

The **Whist Hounds** (*whist*, meaning "eerie," from the Devon dialect) are a pack of huge, white

*Fig. 7.
Cwn
Annwfn*

Fig. 8.
Coinn Iotair,
Dana Keyes

hounds with flame-red eyes and ears. They can be found in the folklore of Dartmoor and Cornwall, England. They are led by Dewar the Huntsman, also called the Horned Man. When storms rage over the moors, folks say that the Wild Hunt is riding out, hungering for human blood or the souls of unbaptized babes. Anyone who catches sight of these terrible hounds will sicken and die within the year.

The **Devil's Dandy Dogs** are a pack of demonic Black Dogs of the Wild Hunt in Cornish folklore, England. They have fiery eyes and breath, and they hunt down the living as well as the damned souls of the dead. And the **Coinn Iotair** (Gaelic, "Hounds of Rage") are the pack of monstrous hunting hounds belonging to legendary Irish chieftain, Crom Dubh, the "Black Crooked One."

Fig. 8. The Devil presenting a Black Dog to a Witch

Ki Du is a Hellhound in the folklore of Brittany. It accompanies the souls of the dead on their journey to the Otherworld, where it will wait with them until they are reborn back into this one.

In Greek myth, the gates of *Erebos,* the Underworld realm of Hades, Lord of the Dead, are guarded by a monstrous three-headed dragon-tailed Black Dog named **Cerberus** (Greek, *Kerberos,* "Demon of the Pit"). He lets anyone in, but does not allow any to leave. His heads represent the past, the present, and the future, and devour all things. A child of the giant Typhon and Echidna, originally Cerberus was described as having 50 to 100 heads. As his final labor, Heracles dragged Cerberus out of Hades' realm. Wher-

ever Cerberus's saliva fell, the poisonous aconites sprouted (also called monkshood or wolf's bane). Later, the poet Orpheus charmed the beast to sleep with the music of his lyre. In Roman mythology, Aeneas and Psyche were able to pacify Cerberus with three honey cakes (one for each head!). He is featured prominently in the movie *Harry Potter and the Philosopher's Stone.*

Fig. 9.
Cerberus by
Ian Daniels

In Hindu mythology of India, **Sharama** is the mighty dog that herds the cows of Surya the sun god each morning to begin the day. Its offspring are the *Sharameyas,* two great, fearsome, four-eyed hounds that guard the entrance to the Afterworld, ruled by Yama, god of death. Their names are *Syama the Black* and *Sabala the Spotted.* Yama sends them out to find the dead and lead them to his bright kingdom. Therefore, the dead are given raw meat to pacify the hounds.

In Norse mythology, **Garm** or **Garmr** is the blood-spattered, four-eyed Hellhound that guards the gates to Niflheim—land of the dead and dread domain of the goddess Hel. From his post in the cave of Gripa, he allows no one to leave. Perhaps he was the third puppy of Sharama!

Fig. 10.
Garm

And finally, there is **Xolotl**, a huge and monstrous Underworld dog in the mythology of the Aztec Indians of Mexico, similar in many ways to the North American Coyote. His legs and feet are turned backward, and his ears point in all directions at will. Every evening, he catches the golden ball of the sun, dragging it down into the Underworld until the next morning. He was said to have created the first humans and given them fire, but he was also the cause of various disasters. Attempting to avoid death, he underwent many transformations, finally becoming the small, perpetually larval amphibian, the Axolotl (*Ambystoma mexicanum*).

history

The presence of Black Dogs in and around Anglia, England, dates back to before the time of the Vikings. One of the earliest recorded sightings appeared in a French manuscript called the *Annales Franorum Regnum* (circa 865 CE). This manuscript recounts an event in which darkness descended upon a church halfway through a service. A massive Hellhound with glowing red eyes appeared, ran about as if searching for something (or someone!), and, just as abruptly, disappeared.

A vicious, wolf-like beast ravaged the countryside of southeastern France from 1764–1767. Called the **Beast of Gévaudan**, it was said to have killed more than 100 people and many cattle, ripping out their entrails. It was described as a creature resembling a wolf, with a shaggy coat, long legs, and glaring eyes. Many believed it was a werewolf. When local hunters failed to kill it, King Louis XV sent his own soldiers, to no avail. In 1767, it was finally killed by Jean Chastel, who shot it with two silver bullets. It turned out to be a Striped Hyena (*Hyaena hyaena*) that had escaped from the private menagerie of Antoine Chastel, Jean's son.

Fig. 11. The Beast of Gévaudan

Another historical curiosity is the **Shunka Warak'in,** a great, wolf-like beast said to inhabit the great plains of North America. The name means "carries off dogs" in the language of the Ioway Indians. Some cryptozoologists speculate that the Shunka Warak'in may be a Dire Wolf (*Canis dirus*), or some other surviving Pleistocene predator. A purported specimen was shot in Montana, around the turn of the 20th century. It was mounted and displayed at a general store and museum in Henry Lake, Idaho, where the owner called it "Ringdocus." (Fig. 12) Its current location is unknown, but it certainly resembles a Brown Hyena (*Parahyaena brunnea*).

Sightings of Black Dogs continue even today, though most are not quite as frightening as their predecessors. They are also quite popular in today's media. Sir Arthur Conan Doyle's infamous *Hound of the Baskervilles* was based on the white Hellhound of

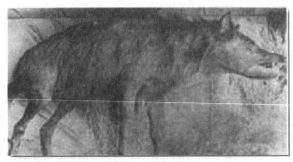

Fig. 12. "Ringdocus"

Dartmoor. Charlotte Bronte makes use of the Gytrash in her novel *Jane Eyre*. Even more recently in the literary realm, J.K. Rowling has made the Black Dog a major player in her *Harry Potter* series, in the guise of Sirius Black, an *animagus* whose animal form is a giant, shaggy-furred Black Dog. Even his name means "Black Dog." Hellhounds show up in other areas, too. They have been brought to life in movies and they are very popular RPG enemies. Cu Sith, Hellhound, and Black Dog enemies show up in such games as *Culdcept, Disgaea*, and *Disgaea 2*, all for the PS2. They also make an appearance in the popular children's anime and RPG series *Pokemon*, in the form of Houndour and Houndoom.

MONSTER MOVIES: BLACK DOGS AND HELLHOUNDS

The Omen (1976). Bad dog, bad dog! The glowing eyes of the spooky Rotweilers in this picture were a major feature of these Hounds from Hell. The villain in *The Neverending Story* (1984) is G'mork, a large, black, wolf-like creature that is capable of speech. Its mission is to track down and kill the young hero, Atreyu. In *Willow* (1988), the hideous Hellhounds of the evil Queen Bavmorda are terrifying and relentless in their pursuit of the sweet baby who is destined to become the rightful queen. The brilliant Japanese animated film *Princess Mononoke* (1997), by the legendary Hayao Miyazaki, features a pack of wolf gods and their mother, the huge wolf goddess, Moro. *Brotherhood of the Wolf* (2001) is a compelling and well-executed treatment of the historical case of the Beast of Gévaudan. *Hound of the Baskervilles* (2002) is based on the classic Sherlock Holmes story by Sir Arthur Conan Doyle. Cerberus makes an appearance in *Harry Potter and the Sorcerer's Stone* (2001), and that movie and *Harry Potter and the Prisoner of Azkaban* (2004) feature black dogs. Needless to say, the excellence of the Harry Potter films is legendary, and the appearance of Sirius Black as a shaggy Hellhound is definitely impressive! *Lady in the Water* (2006) featured a "scrunt," a terrifying, green, wolf-like creature with grassy hair that can hide on a lawn.

28. Phantom Felines

By Ash "LeopardDancer" DeKirk

In the centre of this room, lying in the middle of a golden patch of sunlight, there was stretched a huge creature, as large as a tiger, but as black and sleek as ebony. It was simply a very enormous and very well-kept black cat, and it cuddled up and basked in that yellow pool of light exactly as a cat would do. It was so graceful, so sinewy, and so gently and smoothly diabolical, that I could not take my eyes from the opening.

"Isn't he splendid" said my host, enthusiastically.

"Glorious! I never saw such a noble creature."

"Some people call it a black puma, but really it is not a puma at all. That fellow is nearly eleven feet from tail to tip. Four years ago he was a little ball of black fluff, with two yellow eyes staring out of it. He was sold me as a new-born cub up in the wild country at the head-waters of the Rio Negro. They speared his mother to death after she had killed a dozen of them."

—Sir Arthur Conan Doyle
The Brazilian Cat (1922)[1]

Ian Daniels

LSO CALLED ALIEN BIG CATS OR ABCs, these oversize felines are found in odd or unusual places. Reports of misplaced big cats are found in the Americas, Europe, Australia, and many other places. Phantom Cats can be any type of great cat, from the smaller lynx to the larger black panthers to lions. Unlike other cryptids, Phantom Cats (especially in the British Isles, Europe, and North America) are usually not unknown animals per se. Rather, these are ordinary large cats that are found in abnormal locales. Oftentimes reports of ABCs are put down as incorrect identifications, media hysteria, or fraud. Confirmed instances of Phantom Cats are often the result of zoo escapes, private collector escapes or releases, or escapees from traveling circuses.

Panthers

According to the *Physiologus*, the **Panther** (also called *Panthera*, *Pantera*, *Pantere*, *Painter*, or *Love Cervere*) is a large cat with "a truly variegated colour, and it is most beautiful and excessively kind." It was most famed for its aromatic belches (said to smell like allspice), emitted after it has slept for three days following feasting, and which attract its prey. These were bottled and sold as expensive perfumes, leading to a confusion with the musk-producing African Civet Cat (*Civettictis civetta*). The favored mount of the Greek god Dionysus, the Panther's only natural enemy is the Dragon, which is immune to its fragrant breath.

Panther is a term used not for a single species, but for any large cat—especially one in a black phase, which is called a Black Panther. These may be mountain lions, leopards, or jaguars. Thus the African lion is *Panthera leo*, and the leopard is *Panthera pardus*. The heraldic Panther is always shown "incensed," or with flames issuing from its ears and mouth. Sometimes it is depicted as an ordinary feline, but in German heraldry it has four horns, cow's ears, and a long, fiery red tongue

British Isles

Fig. 1.
Heraldic
Panther

From the 1960s until today, pumas have been reported in Surrey, England. Since the 1980s there have been reports of a panther-like creature near the village of Exmoor. Dubbed the Beast of Exmoor, it is theorized that this is a panther or possibly a large dog. Other witnesses claim it is a black leopard. Lynx have also been reported in the area.

The Beast of Bodmin was a Phantom Cat of Bodmin Moor, in Cornwall, where sightings included occasional reports of mutilated slain livestock. Henceforth, all alleged panther-like cats of the region became popularly known as the Beast of Bodmin Moor.

In 1980 there were several sightings of a puma in Cannich, Scotland. This beastie was dubbed Felicity.

In 1989 a jungle cat was struck and killed by a car in Shropshire, in 1993 a leopard was shot on the Isle of Wight, and in 2005 there were reports of a black cougar loose on a wildlife preserve. Once more, conclusive evidence remained elusive. A report in 2006, put out by the British Big Cats Society, noted that there were more than 2,000 sightings of ABCs in Britain between April 2004 and July 2005.[2]

One of the better-known legendary Phantom Cats of the Scottish Highlands is the **Cait Sith**, meaning "fairy cat." A large black cat, as big as a dog, with a white spot on its chest and sometimes a white blaze on its face, the Cait Sith was commonly thought to be a Fairy or a transformed Witch. It is often depicted with an arched back and bristled fur, and it is this image that has become familiar to us at Hallowe'en. It is now believed that the Cait Sith is actually a rare breed of cat known as the Kellas cat, a hybrid between feral domestics and Scottish wildcats. Named after the village of Kellas in Moray, Scotland, a specimen was not obtained for study until 1984, when a gamekeeper named Ronnie Douglas shot and killed one. These cats are black and roughly the size of a Labrador or golden retriever.

Fig. 2. Cait Sith

Cath Pulag was another Fairy Cat, this time hailing from Welsh and Arthurian myths. Other names include: *Chapalu*, *Cath Balug*, *Capalus*, *Cath Pulac*, and *Cath Balwg*. This spectral feline hunted both cats and people to satisfy its ravenous appetite, until it was slain by Sir Kay or King Arthur. The Cath Pulag had a spotted pelt and massive claws. It was thought to have originally been a leopard imported into Anglesey by a Welsh king.

Another ferocious big cat of the Highlands is Big Ears, King of the Cats. Big Ears is much larger and more demonic in nature than the Cait Sith. It is said that the King of Cats could be summoned by carrying out the bloodthirsty ritual of Taghairm, in which live cats were spitted and roasted alive until Big Ears appeared to grant the wishes of his summoner.

Big Ears may have been a reference to sightings of Kellas cats. However, there have also been recent reported sightings of an-

Fig. 3. Big Ears by Dana Keyes

other Scottish wildcat with larger-than-average ears. Although some of these beasties have been killed, no specimens have been kept for scientific study. One such reported is the Dufftown cat. It is thought that it might be a more primitive wildcat species. It is the same color and roughly the same size as the Kellas cat, except for the oversize ears.

Irish folklore tells of a monstrous, malevolent cat the size of an ox. Called **Írusán** ("king of the cats"). It dwelt within a great cave in the mountains of Knowth, from where, with its acute hearing, it took great offense at a poet reciting a satire on cats. It then rushed down and carried him off.

Fig. 4. Irusan

Europe

In 1982 reports of a lion at large spread like wildfire throughout Jutlan. And again, in 1992, there were reports in Denmark of a lion-like beast, dubbed the Beast of Funen. In the late 1970s and again in the early 1980s, a puma-like creature was reported in Germany. Several times since the late 1920s, leopards and pumas have been reported in the countryside in various locations around France. In 1893 a panther-like creature called the Russian Mystery Cat was said to be responsible for a series of maulings. It was reported to be about the size of a wolf, with a blunted muzzle, round ears, and a long tail.

North America

Reports of phantom cats in North America span the entire continent. American lions are said to have tufted tails and black manes. Descriptions suggest that these are African lions that have escaped or been released, though it is possible they are relict *Panthera Atrox*, a prehistoric species of lion that stalked North America during the Ice Age.

Fig. 5. Panthera Atrox by Bob Giuliani

In the late 1800s a beast called the **Santer** was reported in North Carolina. This ABC was described as striped from nose to tail and roughly the size of a shepherd dog. By 1900 reports had died off, so it is likely that the cat moved on or died. In 2004 a Mystery Cat was spotted in Georgia; it was described as a domestic cat with bobcat facial features and a long tail (although real bobcats have short, "bobbed" tails rather than long ones). The Georgia ABC has been described as roughly 2 feet tall and 4 feet long. It has been caught on video but remains unidentified.[3]

Blue lynx and blue bobcats have been reported in Alaska and other parts of North America, but these cats are color mutations of known species. There have also been reports of all-black bobcats and lynx, such as the so-called Ozark Black Howler.

Fig. 6. Lynx

Perhaps one of the most unusual places that ABCs have been reported is Hawaii. Reports of giant Mystery Cats in Hawaii have been circulating since the 1980s. The most recent sighting was in December of 2002, at which time help was sought from big cat experts William Van Pelt and Stan Cunningham. It is suspected that the cat was brought over as a pet and then either escaped or was released into the wild. The Kuna Big Cat, as it is called, eluded all efforts at capture or tracking, avoiding even the infrared cameras used to spot it. A small fur sample was obtained in 2003, but DNA analysis was inconclusive. It is assumed from descriptions that the beast is a leopard or jaguar.

The **Wampus Cat** is a legendary creature from Appalachian Mountain folklore. According to the tale, a Cherokee woman disguised herself in the skin of a mountain lion to spy on the men as they sat around the campfire and told sacred stories. When the woman was discovered, the medicine man punished her by transforming her into a half-woman, half-cat creature, which still haunts the forests of eastern Tennessee.

LATIN AMERICA

Central and South America have their fair share of Mystery Cats as well. Chief among these is the **Onza**, a gracile puma-like cat built more like a cheetah. Recent genetic analysis has revealed that the Onza is actually a mutated variation of the North American puma. Earlier reports of Onza may have been sightings of another cat known as the Jaguarundi (*Puma yaguarondi*).

Fig. 67. Onza by Craig Gosling

The Black Panther in Conan Doyle's 1922 short story, *The Brazilian Cat*, was first mentioned in 1648 by Amazon explorer Georg Marcgrave, who called it the **Jaguerete**. He described it as shiny black, variegated with even blacker spots. In Guyana, the same creature was known as *El Tigre Negri*, "the black tiger." In the 1770s, Buffon called it the *Cougar Noire* ("black cougar"). In 1775, German naturalist Johann Christian Daniel Schreber bequeathed upon it the scientific name *Felis discolor*. But as no specimen was ever obtained, it was eventually dropped from zoologists' lists. Doyle apparently got the story from Lt. Col. Percy Fawcet, who located it along the border of Brazil and Bolivia.

Fig. 8. Jaguarete by Bewick (1790)

Peru seems to have quite a few Mystery Cats. Most famous is the **Yana Puma** (Quechua for "black mountain lion"). According to native accounts collected by Dr. Peter J. Hocking, it is completely black, with large green eyes, and is twice the size of a jaguar. Said to live at high altitudes, it is a formidable nocturnal predator, slaughtering people in their sleep by chomping their heads. Perhaps this is the same animal as Doyle's Brazilian Cat.[4]

The Speckled Tiger of Peru is described as being the same size as the jaguar, but with a larger head. It is said to be ash-grey with solid black spots. The Striped Tiger of Peru fits the same description, but has whorls and stripes instead of spots. Both are likely color mutations of normal jaguars. The Jungle Lion of Peru has also been classed as a color anomaly of the normal jaguar.

The **Ccoa** is another catlike monster in the Quechua folklore of Peru. It is grey with dark horizontal stripes, and has a huge head with great fiery eyes that

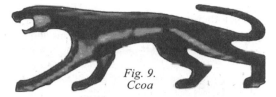

Fig. 9.
Ccoa

spit hail. It causes destructive storms and crop failure, and must be placated with offerings throughout the growing season. Its name has been adopted as an acronym for the Cougar Club of America.[5]

Seimal's Mystery Cat was a heavy-set cat, light brown, with spots and a dorsal stripe. It was believed to be a puma that retained its juvenile coloring. Another theory is that it was a puma/jaguar hybrid. Would that be called a *Juma*?

The *Shiashia-Yawa* is a white cat with black spots known to the natives of Ecuador. Another Mystery Cat, one akin to the Shiashia, is the *Pama-Yawa*, a giant grey cat known for hunting tapirs. Although the Shiashia is smaller than the average jaguar and the Pama is larger, both are thought to be natural variations of that same animal.[6]

Saber-tooths have also been reported from the mountains of Ecuador, Columbia, and Paraguay, where a mutant jaguar with 12-inch-long saber-teeth was killed in 1975. Zoologist Juan Acavar, who examined the body, believed that the animal was, in fact, a *Smilodon populator,* supposedly extinct for 10,000 years.

10. Smilodon
by Bob Giuliani

AFRICA

Africa is home to a great many Mystery Cats, many of which are hybrids. There have been numerous reports of naturally occurring leopard/lion hybrids. The *Ikimizi* of Ruwanda is grey with dark spots and a bearded chin; the *Abasambo* of Ethiopia and the *Bung Bring* of Camaroon are similar. The *Kitanga* and *Batanga* of Central Africa are leopard/lion hybrids that are reddish and spotted. The Kitanga has a full mane, and the Batanga has a slight mane or none at all.[7]

The *Marozi* (Kenyan, "spotted lion") has been reported from the montane forests of Kenya, in East Africa. First sighted by Westerners in 1903, they are darker than ordinary lions, and spotted somewhat like a leopard. In 1931, farmer Michael Trent killed two

3-yrear-old specimens, and photos of the pelts have been widely published in cryptozoological sources. Based on those photos, Bernard Heuvelmans gave the Marozi the scientific subspecies name of *Panthera leo maculatus*. To date, however, no living specimens have been captured in the wild, and most investigators believe the Marozi is a leopard/lion hybrid, such as the one in this photo.[8]

Fig. 11. "Leopon" —the real Marozi?

The *Mngwa* ("strange one"; also *Nunda*) of Tanzania has a long history, going back 1,000 years or more. It is large, roughly the size of a donkey, and has grey tabby markings. It has saber-teeth sometimes described as tusks. This big cat is unusual as it is said to be able to purr as smaller cats do. English contact with this animal began in the 1900s. Patrick Bowen, a hunter who once tracked the Mngwa, noted that the beast's prints were like those of a leopard, but much larger. It also had brindled fur quite different from a leopard's. It is believed that it may be an as-yet-undocumented African blue tiger or possibly a mutated African Golden Cat (*Profelis aurata*). From 1922 into the 1930s there were several reports of maulings and slayings attributed to the Mngwa. An expert in big cats, who was among those attacked, said that it was neither leopard nor lion.[9]

There have been several sightings over the years of cheetah/leopard hybrids— creatures with the features of cheetahs, but with giant

Fig. 12. Golden cat

stripes and whorls akin to the markings of the Clouded Leopard (*Neofelis nebulosa*). These Mystery Cats are now recognized as a natural color variation of the cheetah, and go by the name of King Cheetahs.

The *Hadjel*, *Vassoko*, and *Tigre de Montage* ("mountain tiger") are similar creatures described as having red fur, white stripes, a mane, a bobtail or no tail, long guard hairs on their feet, and saber-teeth.

Natives of Chad matched this beast to pictures of the extinct *Machairodus*, a saber-tooth of the area.[10]

Fig. 13. Machairodus by F. John, 1905

The Grahamstown Mystery Cat of Grahamstown, South Africa, rampaged through the area in the late 1880s. Two specimens were shot and killed. Examination showed a tawny cat with few rosettes, but with spots on the white underbelly and a leopard-like face. These beasts were subsequently classified as pseudomelanistic (i.e. very dark to black) leopards. There have been reports of lions, called Malagasy Lions, on Madagascar, but these are likely African lions brought over by settlers and visitors as pets that were either released or had escaped.

China and Southeast Asia

The *Hairimau Jalor* of Malaysia is a tiger described by the natives as having stripes running horizontally along its body rather than vertically. There have been reports of tigers matching the extinct Bali Tiger, leading some to believe that this tiger breed is not as extinct as it has been believed.[11]

The *Cigau* of Sumatra is a Mystery Cat that is light brown with a short tail, legs that are longer in front, and a ruff about its neck. It is smaller and stockier than the Sumatran Tiger and is noted to be a strong swimmer. This Mystery Cat is known to be highly aggressive.[12]

The Chinese wildcat known as the Mint Leaf Leopard has since been identified as the clouded leopard.[13] And Japanese legend tells of a huge and monstrous Phantom Cat that lived on the island of Oki and devoured a sacrificed maiden every year, until it

Fig. 14. Celestial tiger

was slain by a heroic Samurai knight.

The ***Celestial Tigers*** are four guardians and rulers of the cardinal quarters in Vietnam's Annamite mythology. The *Blue Tiger* rules the East, governing spring and plants. The *Red Tiger* (reported from the Sunderbans area of eastern India) rules the South, controlling summer and fire. The *White Tiger* (now commonly seen in zoos) rules the West, autumn, and metals. And the *Black Tiger* is the ruler of the North, monarch of winter and water. All except the blue one represent actual recorded color variants of the Tiger (*Panthera tigris*). But in 1910, in China's Fujian Province, American missionary Harry R. Caldwell encountered "a tiger coloured deep shades of blue and Maltese."[14]

Australia

The ***Yarri***, or Queensland Tiger, has been reported in the Queensland area since the early 1960s. This striped cat is the size of the native Dingo (*Canis lupus dingo*), but with stripes, shorter legs, and lynx-like ears. It can also climb trees. When angered it lashes its tail, just as an upset cat does. Sightings of tiger-like creatures go back to the 1700s in Australia, and actual records of such a beast, in the form of Aboriginal art, go back even further.[15] This Mystery Cat is about the size of a half-grown tiger, with a long tail and stripes along its body. It matches descriptions of the extinct *Thylacine*, but with a more feline shape to the head.

Fig. 15. Queensland Tiger by Heuvelmans

The Emmaville Panther of New South Wales is reported to be a large, black, panther-like creature. In 1966 a black panther reportedly escaped from a circus in the area.

Australia's Phantom Cats are generally attributed to World War II airmen who brought cougars and other big cats over with them and released the beasts into the wild. No absolute conclusion has been reached, but the kills made by the Australian Phantom Cats have clean punctures to the throat and the insides tidily eaten with no mess, in the same way a big cat eats. In New Zealand the Phantom Cats are often said to be black panthers, but, as with so many other cases of ABCs, there is no conclusive proof.

Hybrids

The 41 known species of felines can all be grouped into two main families, called small cats and big (or great) cats. Small cats are all less than 55 pounds in weight, and have the ability to purr like a housecat. Their young are called kittens. The eight known species of large cats (lion, tiger, leopard, snow leopard, clouded leopard, jaguar, cheetah, and cougar) are all more than 100 pounds, with adult males reaching weights of more than 270 pounds. They do not purr, but rather roar, like a lion. And their young are called "cubs."

Interbreeding is possible among most species of Small Cats, and also among most species of Great Cats. This has created some very unusual hybrids in captivity, suggesting the possibility of wild hybrids as well, which could account for some reported sightings of unusual specimens. Here are some dramatic examples:

Liger—The gigantic progeny of a female tiger and a male lion, this hybrid weighs 1,000 pounds and stands 12 feet tall, making it by far the largest cat on the planet. Its pelt is a tawny orange, and bears the stripes of its mother as well as the spots of its father. The male has a moderate leonine mane.

Tigon (or *Tion*, *Tiglon*)—An exceedingly rare hybrid of a male tiger and a lioness. As it is almost impossible to get these fierce antagonists to mate, there are only a few of these animals in existence, all owned by private collectors. Smaller than but similar in appearance to the more common Liger, the Tigon has an orange coat with alternating stripes and spots. The males has a modest mane. Its roar sounds like a synthesis of those of both parents. Like most hybrids, they have fairly short life spans.

Leopon—Hybrid progeny of a lioness and a male leopard. Bred in Japanese and Italian zoos, they have the size and strength of a lion and the climbing ability of a leopard. The males have sparse manes. Some think it is possible that such pairings in the wild could account for reports of the legendary Congolese Spotted Lion, or *Marozi*.

Jagleop (or *Jagulep*)—A hybrid of a jaguar and a leopardess, bred at a Chicago zoo in the early 1900s. Subsequently mated with a male lion, this spotted female became one of the parents of the controversial *Lijagleop*.

And here's a fascinating historical footnote:

Pard (or *Pardal*, *Pardus*, *Pantheon*)—This feline is described in the *Physiologus* as "a parti-colored species, very swift and strongly inclined to bloodshed. It leaps to the kill with a bound." It mates "adulterously" with the lion to produce the leopard. From the zoological names of the Lion *(Panthera leo)* and the Leopard *(Panthera pardus)*, it is clear that what medieval bestiaries called the Pard is known today as the leopard. The animal referred to in those bestiaries as a leopard is what we now call the Cheetah (*Acinonyx jubatis*), as the cheetah has spots like those of a leopard, and a scruffy mane like that of a lion. Also, cheetahs run in small family groups, as opposed to a pride of lions or the solitude of a leopard. Thus, this cat was thought to be a cross between *leo* (lion) and *pard* (leopard), hence *leopard*. Eventually the *pard* was dropped, the term *leopard* was adopted for the animal formerly called the Pard, and the former leopard was then renamed as the *cheetah*.[16]

Fig. 17. Pard

MONSTER MOVIES: PHANTOM FELINES
Reviewed by Seth Tyrssen

Cat People (1942) is really more of a suggestive psychological thriller, as we never quite see anyone turn into a cat; the same holds true of its sequel, *Curse of the Cat People* (1944). The general film-noire atmosphere and good writing make up for it, though. *The Cat Creature* (1973) is a film that this reviewer has not seen. For ferocious felines, you can't beat the saber-toothed tiger in *Sinbad and the Eye of the Tiger* (1977). *Quest for Fire* (1981) features very realistic prehistoric cave lions, which tree the *Homo erectus* heroes. *Cat People* (1982) is a much more thrilling version than the original: we have lovely Natassja Kinski changing into a Were-Cat, in a story that has real depth and a rather sad ending. Music by David Bowie enhances the end. *Sabretooth* (2002) is a plotless, made-for-TV film that's forgettable, except for a well-done bit of animation of the title critter. This revieewer has not seen *Attack of the Sabretooth* (2005) or *Final Fantasy—Advent's Children* (2007).

Fig. 16. Hercules the Liger

29. CURIOUS CATS

WINGED CATS AND OTHER KITTY ODDITIES

By Ash "LeopardDancer" DeKirk

This cat had growing from its back two appendages which reminded the observer irresistibly of the wings of a chicken before the adult feathers appear. These appendages were not flabby, but apparently gristly, about six or eight inches long, and placed in exactly the position assumed by the wings of a bird in the act of taking flight. They did not make their appearance until the kitten was several weeks old.

—H.C. Brooke

Matthäus Merian

HROUGHOUT HISTORY, THERE HAVE been more than 100 reported cases of Winged Cats, some very recent. There are at least 20 documented cases with physical evidence, including photos. Not only have there been reports over the centuries of Winged Cats, but also of Cabbits (part cat, part rabbit), Squirrel Cats, Kangaroo Cats, and Raccoon Cats. Oftentimes the product of an overactive imagination, and at other times the result of a simple misunderstanding of genetics, Kitty Oddities are cryptids with a real basis in fact. Quite often they can be explained by rare genetic or skin conditions rather than by unusual breeding habits.

WINGED CATS

Winged Cats are generally domesticated cats with reported wingspans of mere inches up to a few feet. Most Winged Cats are not reported to be capable of flight, though there have been at least a report or two of ones that do. One of the earliest known Winged Cats is the one described by the author Henry David Thoreau in *Walden*:

> A few years before I lived in the woods there was what was called a "winged cat" in one of the farm-houses in Lincoln nearest the pond, Mr. Gillian Baker's. When I called to see her in June, 1842, she was gone a-hunting in the woods, as was her wont…but her mistress told me that she came into the neighbourhood a little more than a year before, in April, and was finally taken into their house; that she was of a dark brownish-grey colour, with a white spot on her throat, and white feet, and had a large bushy tail like a fox; that in the winter the fur grew thick and flattened out along her sides, forming strips ten or twelve inches

> long by two and a half wide, and under her chin like a muff, the upper side loose, the under matted like felt, and in the spring these appendages dropped off. They gave me a pair of her "wings," which I keep still. There is no appearance of a membrane about them. Some thought it was part flying squirrel or some other wild animal, which is not impossible, for, according to naturalists, prolific hybrids have been produced by the union of the marten and the domestic cat. This would have been the right kind of cat for me to keep, if I had kept any; for why should not a poet's cat be winged as well as his horse?[1]

A report from India in 1868 tells of a creature the locals called a *pankha billi*, or "winged cat," that had been shot by a Mr. A. Gibson. In 1894 there came reports from England of a cat with duck-like wings, whose owner carried it from town to town to display for money. The cat apparently did not reveal its wings until after it had been roughly treated. This cat was apparently stolen soon after, though it is far more likely that it shed its wings, leaving the owner with an alto-

Fig. 1. Winged cat (Strand Magazine, 1899)

gether normal cat. A mere three years later came reports of another English Winged Kitty. It was described as a male tortoiseshell with wings like a those of pheasant bird. This cat would have been all the more extraordinary as tortoises are almost always female. In 1899 London's *Strand Magazine* featured a photo and report of a Winged Cat belonging to a lady of Wiveliscombe, Somerset, England. In the picture the cat has two fur-covered growths along its back between the fore and hind limbs. These projections flapped about when the cat ran, but didn't enable the beast to fly.[2]

In 1933 an Oxford woman spotted a Winged Cat in her stables. Startled, the cat jumped to the rafters, using its wings to aid it, according to the woman. People from the Oxford Zoo managed to catch the cat and displayed it for some time. Its wings measured roughly 6 inches in length. Three years later came a report from Scotland of a longhaired white Winged Cat with one blue eye and one red eye. Its wings were reported to be about 6 inches long, and rose when the cat ran but laid flat when it was resting. This cat apparently could not control its wings at all, though many of the previously mentioned cats could extend them just a bit.

In 1939 there came reports of a black and white tomcat in England with a wingspan of nearly 2 feet. This cat had a great deal of control over its wings and could raise them quite a bit above its body.[3]

Fig. 2. Sally, a winged cat belonging to Mrs. M. Roebuck of Attercliffe, Sheffield, England, 1939

In 1959 a Winged Cat was captured in West Virginia. This cat, a Persian, shed its "wings" a few months after capture, as they were nothing more than huge fur mats. In 1986 came yet another report of a Winged Cat from England. This cat, another longhair, shed its wings soon after, proving them to be fur mats as well. Having a lilac point Himalayan myself, I can personally attest to the fact that longhairs mat quickly, though Bakura has yet to sprout wings.

England spawned another Winged Cat in 1998, this time a black one, with wings reported to be some 8 inches long. One of the most recent reports of Winged Cats comes from Russia, but villagers, fearing it to be a messenger of the devil, unfortunately killed it in 2004. Examination of the body of the giant rufus tom did confirm the presence of wings.[4]

And as this chapter was being written, the following news item was reported from China:

Cat Grows Wings

A Chinese woman claims her cat has grown wings.

Granny Feng's tom cat has sprouted two hairy 4-in. long wings, reports the *Huashang News*. "At first, they were just two bumps, but they started to grow quickly, and after a month there were two wings," she said. Feng, of Xianyang city, Shaanxi province, says the wings, which contain bones, make her pet look like a "cat angel." Her explanation is that the cat sprouted the wings after being sexually harassed. "A month ago, many female cats in heat came to harass him, and then the wings started to grow," she said. However, experts say the phenomenon is more likely due to a gene mutation, and say it shouldn't prevent the cat living a normal life.[5]

CAUSES

There are several possible causes of wings on cats. Matted fur is one. Longhair cats mat quickly if they are not taken proper care of, although the resulting "wings" will "molt" after they loosen enough. These large mats hang by the cat's side when it is at rest, but will flare out when it runs, thus giving the appearance of wings. Matted fur is also common in hypothyroidic cats, be they long- or shorthaired.

The presence of extra limbs also accounts for some reports of Winged Cats. If the cat has vestigial appendages along its back, between the fore and hind limbs, these may resemble wings. This condition is rare, and most of these cats do not live to adulthood.

A final cause of wings is the so-called rubber skin disease, called feline cutaneous asthenia in cats (this condition also occurs among people and many other types of animals). This is a hereditary disorder that causes the skin to be extremely elastic. Loose flaps of skin will develop along the back and/or sides. These flaps, which are covered in fur, may sometimes have muscle fibers within, which allows for some degree of movement but certainly not enough to allow the cat to truly fly. At the most, these flaps mimic the fur mats and extend out when the cat runs, thus giving the appearance of wings. Cats with this disorder may also shed the flaps, as the skin is extremely fragile and prone to tearing. Tears happen often and heal quickly, leaving the cat's skin crisscrossed with a fine web of scarring.[6]

Cats with such disorders are more likely to be taken to the vet for proper treatment than to be turned into a freak-show attraction. Cats with encroaching mats of hair tend to be groomed and trimmed before things get out of hand.

Better medical care and grooming among cat owners seems to be turning the Winged Cat into a thing of the past. Cryptozoologist Dr. Karl Shuker was the first person to make a well-defined connection between the Winged Cat phenomenon and the condition of feline cutaneous asthenia.

CABBITS, KANGAROO CATS, AND SQUIRREL CATS

In 1950 there were several reports regarding a Cabbit, but these were later proven to be a hoax.[7] Older reports call such creatures *Racats*. These creatures, said to be a cross between a rabbit and a cat, had short, fluffy tails and moved with a hopping gait like that of a rabbit. Similar to the Cabbit is the Squirrel Cat, a supposed cross

Fig. 3. So-called "Cabbit"

between a squirrel and a cat. These kitty oddities have long, fluffy squirrel tails and shortened front limbs.

Similar to the above is the Kangaroo Cat, which has very short forelegs and moves with a hopping gait. The earliest reports of a Kangaroo Cat came from England in the 1930s, and again in the 1940s. In 1956 a report of a Kangaroo Cat came out of Russia. This phenomenon subsequently disappeared from Europe, only to crop up again in North America during the 1970s and 80s. By the 1990s there were reports of Kangaroo Cats in South America.

These kitty oddities supposedly come from the most unlikely of pairings. A Cabbit is said to be the result of a rabbit and a cat mating, and the Squirrel Cat speaks for itself. Both of these pairs are not likely to happen in reality, and even if they did, no viable offspring would result. Cats, rabbits, and squirrels are as genetically incompatible as a horse is with a seal. I include Kangaroo Cats here due to their link with the Squirrel Cats, but these oddities are named for their behavior, not because it was once assumed that they were actual hybrids of cats and kangaroos.[8]

CAUSES

Misunderstanding plays a large part in reports of such cats. The manx cat, a normal breed, has a stubby tail, which may lead some observers to think it has a rabbit's tail if they are unfamiliar with the breed, likewise the Squirrel Cat and longhair breeds. Many longhaired breeds have naturally fluffy, bushy tails that might be considered squirrel-like. Cats with a vestigial sixth toe on their front feet may learn to use them as primitive thumbs, thus allowing then to hold objects as a squirrel might.

In a condition called *radial hyplasia*, which is a form of polydactyly, the cat's forelimbs are shorter than normal, forcing the cat to rear back on its haunches to sit comfortably. This gives the cat a squirrel-like (or kangaroo-like, or rabbit-like, depending on your preference) appearance when sitting up, and accounts for a hopping gait when walking or running. Those with a more serious form of this condition may actually adapt by learning to hop along on just their hind legs.

Finally, these conditions may also be caused by *achondroplasia dwarfism* in cats. Here the limbs are shortened and twisted, but the body is of normal proportions. The front legs are usually affected more than the hindlegs, leading once more to the hopping gait of the cabbits.

RACCOON CATS

Of all the cat oddities, I find the Raccoon Cat to be the most amusing. This one is a case of pure misunderstanding. Maine coon cats evolved from longhair cats brought to the United States by early settlers. When these cats bred with local wildcats, which were described as grey or brownish-grey with banded tails, the result was the gorgeous cat known today as the Maine coon. The Maine coon has long, silky fur, a plumy tail, and tends to be big and stocky, often being much larger than the average domestic cat. It has a ruff of fur around its neck and chest, and its coat has two layers, an undercoat and a coat of guard hairs. Finally, the toe pads have tufts of fur around them for insulation—all in all, a perfect cold weather cat! While the Maine coon may come in many different colors, the most common pattern is that of the tabby. I have a Maine coon myself (pictured below), so I can attest to how wonderful these cats can be.

Amusingly, when the coon breed first became noticed, people thought they were the offspring of raccoons and feral domestics. The first Maine coons were likely of the grey or grey/brown variety; with this pattern, in addition to their size, they did likely resemble raccoons.

Fig. 4. RufusShinra, Maine coon

30. MYSTERY MONSTERS

By Ash "LeopardDancer" DeKirk and Oberon Zell

There are more things in Heaven and Earth, Horatio,
Than are dreamed of in your philosophies.
— Shakespeare, *Hamlet* 1:5

 ONSTERS CAN BE SORTED INTO MANY different categories. There are so-called "freaks of nature," resulting from birth defects, mutations, or other deformities and abnormalities. There are the legendary creatures of the mythic menagerie and the classic bestiaries. These are often made-up hybrids, such as the Centaur, Sphinx, or Gryphon; or, they may be exaggerated versions of little-known animals, such as the Kraken. There are the cryptids investigated by cryptozoologists—living animals reported by many and often photographed, but not yet captured and conclusively identified. Such creatures include Bigfoot, the Loch Ness Monster, the Yeti, and the Mokele-Mbembe of Africa.

And then there are those anomalies that utterly defy categorization. These are bizarre and generally unique creatures that are reported from time to time. They are usually local phenomena, witnessed late at night in strange encounters on lonely roads, and are often associated with UFO sightings. They appear and vanish mysteriously, sometimes in a flash of light. Sometimes they even appear as incomplete holographic projections. There is really no way to integrate these creatures into any coherent theory of biological evolution and natural history. They seem utterly alien from anything known to this world—or even this dimension. Perhaps they really do come from Somewhere Else. We can only call them Mystery Monsters.

Here are a few…

DEMON IN THE DARK: THE JERSEY DEVIL

By LeopardDancer

For nearly 300 years the enigmatic creature known as the Jersey Devil or the Leeds Devil has haunted the Pine Barrens of New Jersey. This cryptozoological or preternatural being has been spotted by several thousand witnesses. Indeed, the terror wrought by the Devil has caused factories and shops to close down and has driven people from the surrounding area.

So where did this mysterious being come from? There are many variations on the origins of the Jersey Devil. The most popular story is that the creature is the 13th child of a Mrs. Leeds of Estelville, New Jersey. It is said that when she found out that she was pregnant with her 13th child she declared that she

Ian Daniels

hoped the child was a devil. Her wish came true, more than she could have ever imagined. The child born to her was not human in any way: it had a horselike head, bat wings, a tail, and horns. Mrs. Leeds drove the monstrous being away and it went to dwell in the Pinelands.[1]

A somewhat different version tells of a Witch named Mother Leeds, of Burlington, New Jersey, who lay with the Devil and conceived a son who, upon his birth, resembled a normal human baby. However, shortly thereafter the baby changed form. It grew hoofed feet, a horse's head, a bat's wings, and a forked tail. These events were said to take place in the year 1735. The demonic being fled to the woodlands. Five years later, in 1740, Christian clergy performed an exorcism/banishing that was to last for more than 100 years, and the Jersey Devil was not seen again until the late 1800s.

Another story tells how a Mrs. Shrouds, of Leeds Point, New Jersey, made the wish that if she were to ever have another child it would be a devil. She got her wish: the cursed child was born misshapen. Mrs. Shrouds hid the child in the basement of the house to keep it out of view of the curious. One night, during a terrible thunderstorm, the child suddenly changed form, turning into a winged, horse-headed monstrosity that promptly escaped.[2]

Fig. 1. Birthplace of the Jersey Devil: Leeds Point, NJ

Whatever its origins, the Devil of the Pinelands has been sighted many times over the past centuries, even up until recent times. Among the earliest sightings, and perhaps one of the most unique, was that reported by Joseph Bonaparte, brother to Emperor Napoleon, in the mid-1800s while he was hunting around Bordentown, New Jersey. Between the years 1840 and 1841, a mysterious creature attacked poultry and sheep in the area, killing many. Its calling cards were odd footprints and piercing, eerie cries in the night.

For the longest time there was little-to-no activity by the Leeds Devil. Then, in January of 1909, he made a fierce comeback, terrorizing people throughout the state. On Sunday the 16th, a creature with bat wings and glowing red eyes was spotted flying down the streets of Woodbury, New Jersey. The same creature was later spotted in Bristol, Pennsylvania, where it was fired upon but not struck. Strange hoof prints were found in the snow. The next day, on January 17, 1909, those same strange hoof prints were everywhere in Burlington, and all over the cities of Columbus and Hedding, among others. Dogs were brought out to track the source of the hoof prints but they refused, going into a frenzy if people tried to force them.

In the early morning hours of January 19, Mr. and Mrs. Nelson Evans of Gloucester were awakened by strange noises outside their window. Upon peeking out, they spotted a bizarre creature standing some 3 feet tall. They described the being as having a "head like a collie dog, with the face of a horse." The creature walked, bipedal, on hoofed legs, and its arms ended in paws. The head was supported by a long neck, and bat wings sprung from its back. They watched the creature for about 10 minutes before working up the nerve to try to scare it away. The creature barked at them and flew off.[3]

Fig. 2.
Jersey Devil as described by Mr. and Mrs. Nelson Evans (Philadelphia Evening Bulletin)

On the 20th of January the Leeds Devil was seen in Pemberton, Haddonfield, Collingswood, Mooretown, and Riverside. Sightings continued into February, forcing several schools, factories, and shops to close, as people were afraid to go out even in the daylight. After February, Jersey Devil sightings became rarer and more sporadic. Had the Devil truly gone away or were people now just more cautious about revealing their sightings?

One of the next major sightings took place in 1927. A cab driver who stopped to fix a flat tire was attacked by a winged creature that landed on his car hood. Needless to say he ran, leaving the car behind. Over the next few decades the Devil's unique piercing cry would be heard in the woodlands at night. In 1961 a couple who had stopped near the Pinelands was attacked by a large flying creature. Sightings continue to the present.[4]

So what *is* the Jersey Devil? One reasonable theory is that it is a Sandhill Crane (*Grus Canadensis*), rare for those parts of the state. The sandhill crane stands about 4 feet tall and, although not naturally aggressive, *will* attack people if it feels threatened. The crane's call is a piercing,

Fig. 3. Sandhill crane (photo-Clifford Otto)

Clifford Otto / *The Record*

whooping scream. Although sightings of this elusive creature might explain some of those attributed to the Devil, they do not explain them all. What about the horns? The bat wings? The horse head and hoofed feet? What about the livestock deaths?

In 1906, Norman Jefferies, publicity manager for the Arch Street Museum in Philadelphia, read about the legendary Devil and staged an elaborate hoax, including a bogus sighting story planted in a local paper, followed by a "capture" and exhibit at the museum. Jeffries' "Devil" was actually a kangaroo painted with green stripes and affixed with bronze wings.[5]

Some other sightings were also probably hoaxes, but it has never been proven that all of the sightings of the Devil (spanning several centuries, remember) were hoaxes. Some say it is pure evil made manifest; others call it a woodland guardian of the Pine Barrens; and still others think it may be a species that we have not yet discovered. We may never know what the Devil truly is, but he will continue to be a lasting part of the national folklore of the United States.

El Chupacabra
By LeopardDancer

El Chupacabra is a Mystery Monster first reported in Puerto Rico in 1990. From there, reported sightings spread to Meso- and South America as far as Chile, and the United States as far as the Carolinas and Maine. Its Spanish name literally means "goat sucker," derived from its notorious habit of attacking and drinking the blood of goats and other livestock. A Puerto Rican comedian, Silverio Perez, is credited with coining the term.

This beastie is regarded variously as a real creature, a mythic beast, or an urban legend. Though the Chupacabra did not come to mainstream attention until about 1990, there were sighting and reports of Chupacabra-like creatures, called *cipi Chupacabra*, as early as 1987. These creatures are predated by another Chupacabra-like being, *El Vampiro de Moca*, which killed livestock and fowl near the town of Moca, Puerto Rico, in the 1970s. The slayings spread all over the island, the commonality among all being a pair of puncture marks in the victim's neck.

Itcuintlipotzotli is a bizarre Mexican creature the size of a terrier, with hairless skin, a wolfish head, no neck, a short tail, and a huge hump running the length of its back. It was illustrated in a 1780 book by a Jesuit priest, and one was reported killed in 1843 near Mexico City. Could this be the same creature as the Chupacabra?

Descriptions

There are several descriptions given of this elusive beastie. The most common Chupacabra variation is of a mostly hairless, dog-like creature that has a spiny ridge along its back, and pronounced eye sockets, fangs, and claws. This version runs along on four feet, as a dog does. In 2001, in Nicaragua, the corpse of one such Chupacabra was said to have been found. When the remains were analyzed by

Fig. 4. El Chupacabra

UNAN–Leon, the university pathologists concluded that they were of an unknown species.

Though rarer than the dog-like Chupacabra, another common variation of Chupacabra is bipedal and lizard-like, described as having leathery or scaly, green-gray skin, a doglike muzzle, glowing red eyes, and sharp quills running along its spine. Standing at roughly 3 feet in height, these Chupacabra hop as kangaroos do, rather than walk. When alarmed they will hiss and screech, releasing a sulfuric odor. Other lizard-like variations have no muzzle or only stubby muzzles.

Yet another variation of the beastie resembles a cross between the aliens known as "Greys" and a *T-Rex*-like saurian. It has the large head and huge, luminous eyes of the alien atop a saurian body, with short, stubby arms and three fingers. Its strong, muscular, reptilian legs also sport three clawed toes. Its jaw is slightly elongated, and there are only two small holes for the nostrils (again, similar to a reptile) situated above the slit of a mouth full of sharp, needle-like teeth, with fangs protruding both upward and downward. As with the other Chupa variations, it also has spines running down its back.

Fig. 5. Chupa by Ash DeKirk

It is generally agreed that all Chupacabra have glowing red eyes, spines running along their backs, a noticeable bulge in their bellies after feeding, and overly large, protruding fangs, which leave behind two puncture wounds upon their victims. In addition, it is said that they all have the power to hypnotize their prey, making it easier to feed. It seems that the Chupacabra may also be growing: The earliest reports describe creatures approximately the size of a dog, whereas more recent sightings have them at the size of a grown man, and graduated from attacking goats to attacking horses and cattle.

Sightings

Following a rash of UFO sightings in 1975, a creature began attacking livestock near the town of Moca, Puerto Rico. Originally called *El Vampiro de Moca*, this being fits the description of the ones that would be called Chupacabra later. Investigators who examined the remains of the livestock, including goats, geese, chickens, ducks and cows, found them to have been completely drained of blood. Some believed that the slayings were the work of illegally imported crocodiles.

In March of 1995, the towns of Orocovis and Morovis in Puerto Rico began experiencing similar livestock slayings. Throughout the fall of 1995, these slayings spread around the island. In the town of San German several goats were killed, and the townsfolk chased off an unusual creature attempting to kill some roosters. The town of Canovanas was an epicenter for Chupa activity, with no less than 150 livestock slayings. Several residents claimed to have seen the beastie in broad daylight. A middle-aged man, Osvaldo Rosasdo, was attacked by a Chupacabra and needed medical attention for scratches and cuts around his torso. This is one of the few known instances of a human being attacked by Chupacabra.

In 1996, Mexico had a rash of Chupacabra activity, which was followed by another rash of sightings and activity in Brazil during 1999. In the spring of 2000, residents of the town of Calamain, Chile, awoke one morning to find all of their livestock dead of puncture wounds to the neck and all the blood drained from their bodies. It was theorized that these killings may have been the work of a rogue puma, but a thorough search of the area found neither the Chupacabra nor the theorized puma.

Since its first sightings, it is estimated that Chupacabra have been responsible for more than 2,000 livestock killings in Puerto Rico alone. Chupacabra sightings have spread to mainland South and North America.[6]

Recent Sightings and Remains

July 2004—a rancher in Texas killed one of the doglike Chupacabra that had been attacking his livestock. This creature was small and hairless, with a blue-grey skin tone. Examination was unable to establish the creature's identity, although it was determined to be very malnourished. Several more creatures were spotted, and in October of 2004, another of the creatures was shot and killed. Analysis of the creatures has lead to mixed results, with some researchers saying they are unknown species of canines, and others saying they are severely deformed coyotes. This beastie also goes by the name of The Elmendorf Beast.

Summer 2004—sightings and photographs abounded of an odd creature in Mount Pleasant, in Randolph County, North Carolina. These creatures fit descriptions of the doglike Chupacabra, except for the spines. A carcass of a similar creature was found on the side of the road in Charleston, South Carolina. Analysis of it concluded that it was a fox with genetic mutations. It is commonly assumed that the North Carolina creature was a fox as well.

Fig. 6. Mount Pleasant, North Carolina Chupa (photo by "Ann")

September 2005—an alleged Chupa was shot and killed in Coleman, Texas, after killing 30–40 chickens in the neighborhood. About the size of a small terrier, it had a white, wooly coat similar to a sheep's but with a low pile. It was 28–32 inches long, and its tail was as long as its body. According to a local eyewitness, 90-year-old Reggie Lagow, "The critter was unlike any kind of animal

Fig. 7. The Coleman, Texas Chupa

in the area." Unfortunately, it was not preserved for study. "It was killed on a Tuesday and trash day took it away two days later."[7] But it was photographed, showing its kangaroo-like legs.

August 2006—a Maine woman found another possible Chupacabra dead on the side of the road. Pictures were taken of a creature, which was obviously canine but unlike any known breed of dog. Vultures had picked the carcass clean before people thought to bag it for research. For years the residents of the area had been plagued by reports of an odd creature and animal maulings.

August 2006—a fox-like creature was shot and killed near Berkshire, New York, by two teenagers, Geordie Decker and Josh Underwood. The beast was almost bald, with grayish skin and a stripe of orange fur running down its back. It had yellow eyes and hopped like a kangaroo. The bones of this possible Chupa are displayed on the Lost World Museum's Website (*www.lostworldmuseum.com*).

December 2006—a farmer in Peru saw a beast fitting the description of the Chupacabra devour a wild boar on his farm. After finishing its meal the creature fled faster than any animal the farmer knew of. This beast is also known by the name *Zahir*.

July 2007—Over four days, Phyllis Canion discovered the bodies of three hideous 40-pound animals outside her ranch in Cuero, Texas. Canion saved the head of one so she can submit it for DNA testing and then mount it

Fig. 8. Phylis Canion with the ugly head of a Cupa she found

for posterity. "It is one ugly creature," Canion said of the beast, which has big ears, large fanged teeth and grayish-blue, mostly hairless skin.[8]

Theories

There are several theories regarding the origins of the Chupacabra. One of the most prevalent is that the Chupacabra is an alien life form. Indeed, it is often described as otherworldly. There is some small resemblance between a few descriptions of the Chupacabra and those of the aliens known as Greys.

Another theory is that the Chupacabra is the result of genetic experimentation carried out by the U.S. military at a research facility located in El Yunque, a mountain in the eastern portion of Puerto Rico. Supposedly, the laboratory was damaged in a fierce storm in the 1990s, at which time the Chupacabra escaped. The U.S. military had maintained a presence on the island since the 1930s and carried out other research and development projects.

The most likely of all theories is that the creature

known as Chupacabra is an unknown creature evolved or mutated from known species, most likely native canids. Other less likely theories suggest that it may be evolved from giant vampire bats, fossils of which have been found in South America; or that it might be related to Madagascar's weird little "Aye-aye" (*Daubentonia madagascariensis*).

Fig. 9. Aye-aye

And then there are the supposed Chupacabra carcasses which may be seen in circus and carnival freak shows. The first of these Chupa gaffs, as they are called in sideshow jargon, were created by Doug Higley, a renowned genius of taxidermy art. Considering that the Chupa was first reported in Puerto Rico in 1990, we have to wonder what part these gaffs may have played in the legend:

The Chupacabra first appeared in the sideshow in the 1980's, after it had become legendary in Central and South America. The connection to the sideshow was made through the work of Doug Higley who introduced the Chupacabra exhibits into the sideshow scene. The first Chupacabra that Doug created was sold to a showman in Florida many years ago who took it to Puerto Rico.

—*Sideshow World Magazine*[9]

MOTHMAN AND OWLMAN
By Oberon Zell

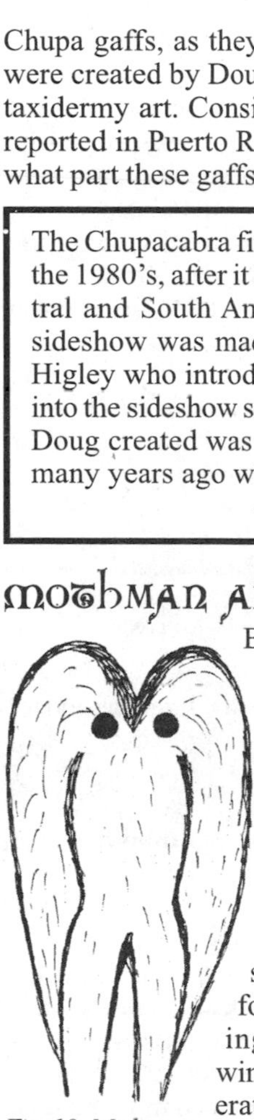

The mysterious aerial creature known as Mothman was first seen in the autumn of 1966 by two couples driving past an old generator plant in Point Pleasant, West Virginia, at 11:30 p.m. The door of the plant had been ripped from its hinges, and standing in the doorway was a 7-foot-tall monster with huge, glowing red eyes and great folded wings. As the driver hit the accelerator, the creature shot straight up into the air and began pursuing them at speeds up to 100 m.p.h. At the city limits, it veered off and disappeared.

Fig. 10. Mothman by eyewitness Roger Scarberry

Over the next few days there were a number of similar sightings and reports of a giant flying creature that attacked people, stole dogs, and mutilated animals. Its presence also seemed to interfere with radio and TV reception. On November 16, a press conference was held, during which the creature was dubbed Mothman, after the popular *Batman* TV series. Within a year of the first sighting, more than 100 reports were recorded.[10]

On October 16, 1967, the Silver Bridge over the Ohio River collapsed in rush hour traffic, dropping 46 cars into the river. It was the biggest disaster to ever hit Point Pleasant, and some people wondered if there was a connection with Mothman. Since then, there have been no further sightings, and only scattered rumors of Mothman.

However, on September 10, 1978, a terrifying, black, Mothman-like creature with huge wings blocked the entrance to a coal mine in Freiburg, Germany. As miners approached to go to work, it let out a series of unbearable piercing shrieks, driving them back. An hour later, an enormous explosion destroyed the mine. When the smoke cleared, the strange apparition was gone, having saved the lives of the men. They called it the *Freiburg Shrieker*.[11]

Fig. 11. Freiburg Shrieker, by Ian Daniels

And in the days preceding the infamous April 26, 1986 meltdown of the Chernobyl nuclear power plant in the Ukraine, employees reported seeing a large, dark, headless man with gigantic wings and fiery-red eyes. After the explosion, as Soviet helicopters circled the smoldering reactor and dropped clay, sand, lead, and extinguishing chemicals on the flames, some of the workers described a 20-foot-tall black bird gliding through the radioactive smoke.

Fig. 12. Mothman by Joe Butt

But perhaps this bird of ill omen has had even earlier appearances. In 1944, in Hollywood, Maryland, a priest saw "the outspread form of a huge man with wings, sailing down the pitch-black sky towards the church." Upon landing on the ground, it promptly vanished. The priest said it was "intensely gruesome."[12]

And at the beginning of 1926, a large, dark, manlike creature with wings was seen hovering over one of the world's largest dams, the Xiaon Te Dam in the southeastern foothills of China. On January 19, 1926, the dam collapsed, spilling more than 40 billion gallons of water onto farms and villages below and killing more than 15,000 people. Survivors came to believe that the *Man-Dragon*'s appearance had been intended as a warning.[13]

Since 1976 a giant owl-like creature has been sighted in the coastal town of Mawnan in Cornwall, England. Called Owlman, it is described as manlike with silver-grey feathered wings, pointed ears, huge glowing eyes, and a black beak. Its long bird legs terminate in large, black talons.[14]

Fig. 13. Cornish Owlman, by Sally Chapman

Similar creatures have been reported in the United States from the Alleghenies, the Ozarks, and the Pacific Northwest, by Indians and early settlers, who called them *Great Owls* or *Big-Hoot*. Mark A. Hall, in *Thunderbirds! America's Living Legends of Giant Birds* (2004), postulates that the Mothman may be such a creature.[15]

And finally, we must mention the bizarre batwinged nocturnal primate reported from the state of Washington, where it is said to dwell in the dense forests surrounding Mount St. Helens. It has purple skin, red eyes, and a simian head with bat-like features. Some cryptozoologists speculate that it may be an unknown species of giant fruit bat, but none of these are known to inhabit the Americas.

LIZARDMEN
By Oberon Zell

Fig. 14. Batsquatch by Joe Butt

Strange, hybrid, reptilian-humanoid creatures looking much like filmdom's *Creature from the Black Lagoon* have been reported from around the world. Perhaps the most famous is the *Lizard Man of Scape Ore Swamp*, near Bishopville, in Lee County, South Carolina. It was first reported on June 29, 1988, by 17-year-old Christopher Davis. He was driving home around 2:00 a.m. on a road that borders Scape Ore Swamp when he got a flat tire. While changing the tire, he heard a loud thump from across the road and saw a 7-foot-tall creature with glowing red eyes running toward him. He locked himself in the car, which the monster attacked. As Davis said later to the Associated Press, "I could see him from the neck down— the three big fingers, long black nails and green rough skin. It was strong and angry."[16] Unable to open the door, the creature jumped onto the car roof and clawed at the windshield, making large scratches as Davis drove away.

Fig. 15. Lizardman of Kentucky

A spate of similar reports began flooding in from all over Lee County, and the police had to establish a separate "Lizard Man" hotline to handle them. The creatures were even given a scientific name: *Homo subterreptus*. But by August, the sightings had tapered off, and few have occurred since.

As far back as the mid-1700s, bizarre human-reptile hybrid creatures have been reported lurking in the Florida Everglades and other large swamps in the American Southeast. Called Gatorman, they are said to be about 5 feet long, with the proportions of a child, four stubby, gator-like legs with webbed feet, and a long, muscular tail. They are covered with greenish scales, and have mouths full of razor-sharp teeth. Unfortunately, alleged photos published in tabloid papers are obviously faked *gaffs*.

In the summer of 1973, a similar gator-humanoid hybrid was sighted by numerous witnesses in New Jersey's Newton-Lafayette area. And in 1977, New York State Conservation naturalist Alfred Hulstruck reported that the state's southern region was inhabited by "a scaled, man-like creature which appears at dusk from the red, algae-ridden waters to forage among the fern and moss-covered uplands."[17]

Fig. 16. Gatorman

A carnivorous, amphibious humanoid is said to have tormented the Kwakiutl Indians of Canada's Puget Sound region for centuries. Called Pugwis, its description greatly resembles that of The Creature From the Black Lagoon.

A similar man-size, gilled, amphibious humanoid is said to inhabit Thetis Lake on Vancouver Island, British Columbia. It emerged from the lake on August 19, 1972, and attacked two boys. Nearly 5 feet tall and weighing about 120 pounds, it was covered in silver-grey scales and had webbed hands and feet with sharp protrusions, with which it slashed one of the boys. A few days later two other young men encountered the same creature, which they described as having a monstrous face with dark, bulbous eyes, a fish-like mouth, huge ears, and six sharp projections on its head connected by a thin membrane.[18]

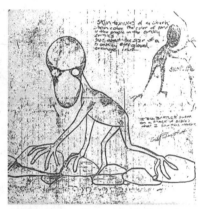

Fig. 17. The Gillman of Thetis Lake

While swimming in the Ohio River near Evansville, Indiana, on August 21, 1955, Mrs. Darwin Johnson was suddenly clutched around the knee by a large claw. Kicking free of the unseen attacker, which kept trying to drag her under, she eventually made it to shore. She was treated for multiple contusions on her leg, which bore a green, hand-shaped stain that remained for several days.[19]

In March of 1959, a strange creature was seen emerging from the Charles Mill Lake in Mansfield, Ohio. Witnesses described it as an armless humanoid, standing more than seven feet tall, with luminous green eyes. A second report came in 1963, and others have trickled in over the years. Some have even claimed to have found footprints of gigantic webbed feet on the shore.[20]

In Zulu folklore from the South African province of KwaZulu Natal, the *Intulo* is a lizard-like creature with human characteristics.

The Loveland Frogs
By Oberon Zell

The story of the Loveland Frogs began in May of 1955, when a man driving through Loveland, Ohio, at 3:30 a.m., saw three frog-like reptilian creatures standing upright by the side of the road. The man pulled over and watched

Fig. 18. One of the Loveland Frogs

them for a few minutes. One of them held up a wand with sparks shooting out of its tip.

The man reported the incident to the local police, but nothing more was seen of the creatures until March of 1972, when a Loveland policeman driving down Riverside Road at 1:00 a.m. spotted a crouching animal on the side of the road. When the headlights fell upon it, the creature rose up on its hind legs, revealing itself to be 3-4 feet tall, with a reptilian or frog-like head and leathery green skin. With a glance at the officer, it leaped over the guardrail into the Little Miami River.

Two weeks later, another police officer reported a similar incident in which one of the creatures appeared to have been injured as it limped from the road into the river. The Loveland Frogs have not been seen again, and no one knows what they really were.[21]

The Dover Demon
By Oberon Zell

The Dover Demon was first reported on April 22, 1977, in Dover, a suburb of Boston, Massachusetts. Three 17-year-old boys were driving home around 10:30 at night when the driver, Bill Bartlette,

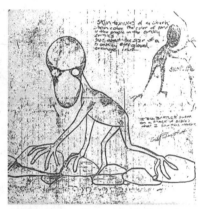

Fig. 19. Dover Demon by Bill Bartlette

tlette, saw in his headlights a bizarre creature crawling along a rock wall off the roadside. He said that it had a head like a watermelon and no features other than two large, orange eyes. Its body was thin, with long limbs and fingers that grasped the rocks. It was about 4 feet tall with peachy, smooth skin.

Bartlette's friends were talking and saw nothing. They returned to the spot, but nothing was there. Once home, Bartlette made a drawing of what he'd seen.

Two hours after that encounter, and about a mile away, 15-year-old John Baxter and his girlfriend were walking home when they saw a figure walking toward them on the road. Baxter thought it was a boy he knew so he called out his name but got no answer. The creature ran off the road and up a bank.

Following it, Baxter got a good look at the creature. He said it had a large head, thin body, and long limbs and fingers. Baxter stood and watched it for a minute before retreating in fear. He also drew pictures of it. Comparing Bartlette's and Baxter's drawings, it is obvious that they had seen the exact same creature. But what on Earth could it have been?

The day after these sightings occurred, Bartlette told his friend Will Taintor about what he had seen. That evening at midnight, Taintor was driving his girlfriend, Abby Brabham, home when Brabham saw a creature crouching on the roadside as they drove past. Even though she had not heard of the other encounters, her description matched those of the others. Taintor said he also caught a glimpse of it.

There have been no more sightings since, and the mystery of the Dover Demon remains unsolved.[22]

ᚦhe Flatwoods Monster
By LeopardDancer

In the early 1950s, amid a flurry of UFO reports, people in the tiny town of Flatwoods, West Virginia, reported seeing a reddish sphere descending slowly behind a hill. They reported seeing a luminous glow coming from the hill "as if from a landed object."[23] Three young boys went to investigate the mysterious glow and were joined by a mother, her two sons, and two more of their friends. Upon cresting

Fig. 20. Flatwoods Monster

the hill the searchers found what they called a giant ball of fire as big as a house.

Nearby, the same searchers came upon a being standing in the shadows under a tree. Some described it as having a head "shaped like an ace of spades"[24] with a pair of luminous eyes. Others reported it as having a heart-shaped face. No one saw anything that resembled arms or legs, though the creature's eyes were at a height of roughly 6 feet. It appeared to be gliding rather than walking, first moving toward the witnesses and then turning to head toward the fireball. It emitted a series of sharp hisses and a thumping noise as it sped away. They also reported smelling a sulfurous odor that was apparently emanating from the creature. The encounter lasted only seconds. When the witnesses returned the next day they found an area of flattened grass, as if a large object had rested there.

One week prior to the Flatwoods incident, a mother and daughter in Weston, about 12 miles away, had an encounter with a similar creature as they were driving home from church. The night after the Flatwoods encounter, in an area 20 miles away, a couple's car stalled mysteriously. They claimed to have been approached by a creature similar to the Flatwoods mon-

ster, also emitting the odor of sulfur. Nearly 20 years later, a Quebec woman awoke at night to find a similar creature peering into her window.

One theory asserts that the witnesses who claimed they had gotten close to the creature had, in fact, only seen a meteor—despite the fact that they had a residue covering their faces and had developed symptoms of being exposed to mustard gas. Also, when the same witnesses had gone to investigate, anxiety had turned an encounter with a barn owl into something more than what it really was. It is believed that they startled a barn owl, which then flew off. Barn owls have heart-shaped faces and make hissing noises when startled. The strange illness? Hysteria can cause similar reactions in the human body.

And finally, there is the **Enfield Horror**, a Mystery Monster spotted in Enfield, Illinois. Witnesses described it as grey, with three legs, two arms jutting out of its chest, and two pink eyes the size of flashlights. Police investigators found doglike prints with six pads. What can one say about such a sighting?

Monster Movies: Monsters of Mystery
Reviewed by Seth Tyrssen

The Creature from the Black Lagoon, (1954) *Revenge of the Creature* (1955), and *The Creature Walks Among Us* (1956) all feature one of the most memorable monsters of the low-budget era. Although there may be no actual basis for a humanoid man-fish, the costume and simple special effects were just plain great. The same cannot be said for *The Alligator People* (1959). Humans with alligator heads? Weird, but the effect was well-done for a grade-Z flick. *The Reptile* (1966) features a snake woman, and *Octoman* (1971) features an octopus-man. In *SSSSSS* (1973), the many live snakes were far and away the show stealers of this odd little film involving people being turned into snakes. There was *The Bat People* (1974)—perhaps the inspiration for the "Batboy" hoax. The low-budget but rather delightful film *Humanoids from the Deep* (1980) features a man-fish somewhat similar to the Creature from the Black Lagoon. The different look was well-done. *13th Child: Legend of the Jersey Devil* (2002) covers some of the material in this chapter. *The Mothman Prophesies* (2002) is a rather tedious film that gives us a brief look at the mysterious Mothman, said to be an actual being seen by many people. Is he an alien that got left behind, or a fiendish secret genetic experiment? We may never know. *El Chupacabra* (2003), *Chupacabra Terror* (TV-2005), and *Chupacabra AKA Mexican Werewolf* (2005) are films this reviewer has not seen. *The Snake King* (or *Snake Man)* (2005) featured more snake people.

Appendix A. Unnatural Histories - A Timeline

By Oberon Zell-Ravenheart

c 2700 BCE   *Epic of Gilgamesh*
c 800   *Odyssey* by Homer
c 700   *Theogony* by Hesiod
c 500   *Periegesis* by Hecataeus of Melitus
c 420   *Historia* by Herodotus (484–425 BCE)
c 400   *Indica* by Ctesias
333-323   Macedonian Empire of Alexander
343   *Historia Animalium* by Aristotle (384–322 BCE)
c 60   *De Rerum Natura* by Lucretius (99–55 BCE)
55 BCE-455 CE   Roman Empire
<u>51 BCE</u>   *De Bello Gallico* by Julius Caesar (100–44 BCE)
c 5 CE   *Geographia* by Strabo (63 BCE–19 CE)
c 10   *Metamorphoses* by Ovid (43 BCE–17 CE)
44   *De Chorographia* by Pomponious Mela
65   *Pharsalia* by Lucan (39–65 CE)
c 70   *Naturalis Historia* by Pliny the Elder (23–79 CE)
c 100   *The Annals* by Tacitus (55–120 CE)
c 150   *Description of Greece* by Pausanias
c 175   *A True Story* by Lucian (125–190)
2nd-5th c.   *The Greek Physiologus*
c 200   *De Natura Animalum* by Aelian (170–235)
c 200   *Collection of Remarkable Facts* by Gaius Julius Solinus
c 230   *The Life of Apollonius of Tyana* by Philostratus (170–245)
c 300   *Carmen de Ave Phoenice* by Lactantius (260–340)
2nd-10th c.   *Pseudo-Callisthenes* (attributed to Alexander the Great)
4th-11th c.   *The Latin Physiologus*
c 400   *The Phoenix* by Claudian (370–404)
455   Rome Sacked by Vandals, End of Western Empire
c 600   *Etymologies* by Isadore of Seville (560–636)
9th c.   *The Voyage of St Brendan*
9th-11th c.   *Liber Monstrorum*
ca. 1000   *The Exeter Book* (attributed to Cynewulf)
1095-1244 Crusades
11th c.   *Physiologus* by Theobaldus
11th c.   *Bodley Herbal and Bestiary*
12th c.   *The Book of Life's Merits* by Hildegard of Bingen (1098–1179)
12th c.   *A Latin Prose Bestiary*
12th-13th c.   *Letter on India to Aristotle* (attributed to Alexander the Great)
12th c.   *Itinerary* by Benjamin of Tudela (fl. 1159–1173)
12th c.   *Moralitates de Avibus*
c 1125   *Le Bestiaire* by Philip de Thaun
c 1175   *The Letter of Prester John*
c 1185   *The Worksop Bestiary*
1196-1223   *Topographia Hibernica* by Giraldus Cambrensis
c 1200   *Aberdeen Bestiary*
1200-50   *De Bestiis /Dicta Chrysostomi*

c 1230   *Rochester Bestiary*
1230-40   *Liber de Naturis Rerum*
c 1250   *Bestiaire of Guillaume le Clerc*
c 1260   *The Rutland Psalter*
1275-1300   *Westminster Bestiary*
1284   *The Alphonso Psalter*
1298   *Travels* by Marco Polo (1254–1324)
13th c.   *Middle English Bestiary*
13th c.   *De Bestiis*
13th c.   *The Journal of Friar Odoric* by Odoric of Pordenone (1286–1331)
13th c.   *The Ashmole Bestiary*
13th c.   *The Northumberland Bestiary*
13th c.   *On the Properties of Things* by Bartholomaeus Anglicus
13th c.   *The Bestiary* by Pierre de Beauvais
13th c.   *The Bestiary of Love and Response* by Richard de Fournival (1201–1260)
13th c.   *Der Naturen Bloeme*
13th c.   *De Animalibus* by Albertus Magnus (1200–1280)
c 1300   *Bestiaire*
1304-21   *The Peterborough Bestiary*
1310-20   *The Queen Mary Psalter*
1325-35   *The Lutterell Psalter*
1325-50   *Fountains Abbey Bestiary*
c 1356   *The Travels of Sir John Mandeville*
1399-1407   *The Sherborne Missal*
14th c.   *Travels* by Ibn Battuta (1304–1377)
1400-1520   The Renaissance
1420-1620   The Age of Exploration
1481   *The Mirrour of the World* by William Caxton (1422–1491)
15th c.   *Bestiarius* or *Bestiary of Ann Walsh*
15th c.   *The Noble Lyfe & Nature of Man, of Bestes, Serpentys, Fowles & Fisshes y be Moste Knowen* by Lawrens Andrewe
c 1500   *Itinerario* by Ludovicio de Varthema (fl. 1503-1508)
1532-64   *Gargantua and Pantagruel* by François Rabelais (1495-1553)
c 1534   *The Boke of Duke Huon of Burdeux* by Sir John Bourchier (1469–1533)
1551-58   *Historiae Animalium* by Conrad Gesner (1516–1565)
1578   *La Semaine ou Création du Monde* by Guillaume de Salluste du Bartas (1544–1590)
1582   *On Poysons, of Monsters and Prodigies* by Ambroise Paré (1510-1590)
1607   *The Historie of Foure-Footed Beastes* by Edward Topsell (1572–1625)
1625   *Hakluytus Postumus or Purchas His Pilgrimes* by Samuel Purchas (1577-1626)
1635   *Speculum Mundi* by John Swan
1646   *Pseudodoxia Epidemica* (or *Vulgar Errors*)

by Sir Thomas Browne (1605–1682)

1646 *Arcana Microcosmi* by Alexander Ross (1591–1654)

1661 *Six Zoological Disputations* by George Caspard Kirchmayer (1635–1700)

1718 *1300 Real and Fanciful Animals* by Matthäus Merian the Younger (1621–1687)

1730 *A Description of Three Hundred Animals* by Thomas Boreman (fl. 1736–1744)

1774 *A History of the Earth and Animated Nature* by Oliver Goldsmith (1730-1774)

1855 *The Age of Fable* by Thomas Bullfinch (1796–1867)

1861 *The Romance of Natural History* by Philip Henry Gosse (1810–1888)

1864 *Savage Africa* by W. Winwood Reade (1838-1875)

1870 *Bible Animals* by J.G. Wood (1827–1889)

1872 *Zoological Mythology* by Angelo de Gubernatis (1840–1913)

1875 *The Book of Ser Marco Polo* by Sir Henry Yule (1820–1889)

1880 *Credulities Past and Present* by William Jones

1886 *Marvelous Wonders of the Whole World* by Henry Davenport Northrop (1836–1909)

1886 *Mythical Monsters* by Charles Gould (1834–1893)

1887 *Sea and Land* by James William Buel

1886 *Un-Natural History, or Myths of Ancient Science* by Edmund Goldsmid

1890 *Curious Creatures in Zoology* by John Ashton

1892 *The Great Sea Serpent* by Antoon Cornelis Oudemans (1858-1943)

1915 *Diversions of a Naturalist* by Sir E. Ray Lankester (1847–1929)

1928 *Dragons and Dragonlore* by Ernst Ingersoll

1941 *Exotic Zoology* by Willy Ley (1906–1969)

1951 *Fabulous Beasts* by Peter Lum (Bettina Lum Crowe) (1911–)

1954 *The Book of Beasts* by T.H. White (1909–1964)

1955 *On the Track of Unknown Animals* by Bernard Heuvelmans (1916–2001)

1955 *Salamanders and Other Wonders* by Willy Ley (1906–1969)

1957 *The Book of Imaginary Beings* by Jorge Luis Borges (1899–1986)

1964 *The Land of Forgotten Beasts* by Barbara Wersba (1932–)

1967 *The Glass Harmonica: A Lexicon of the Fantastical* by Barbara Ninde Byfield

1969 *A Fantastic Bestiary* by Ernst & Johanna Lehner

1970 *The Complete Guide to Mysterious Beings* by John A. Keel (1930–)

1971 *A Dictionary of Fabulous Beasts* by Richard Barber & Anne Riches

1973 *Fabulous Beasts and Demons* by Heinz Mode

1973 *Phoenix Feathers: A Collection of Mythical*

Monsters by Barbara Silverberg

1974 *Monsters Who's Who* by Dulan Barber

1977 *Monster Manual* by Gary Gygax

1979 *The Magic Zoo: The Natural History of Fabulous Animals* by Peter Costello

1979 *Dragons* by Peter Hogarth & Val Clery

1980 *Searching for Hidden Animals* by Roy Mackal (1925–)

1981 *Alien Animals* by Janet and Colin Bord

1981 *Mythical Beasts* by Deirdre Headon

1981 *Fabulous Beasts* by Monika Beisner & Alison Lurie

1982 *Encyclopedia of Monsters* by Daniel Cohen

1982 *Dragons and Unicorns: A Natural History* by Paul and Karen Johnsgard

1983 *Dinosaurs, Spitfires and Sea Serpents* by Christopher McGowan

1984 *A Guide to the Imaginary Birds of the World* by Joseph Nigg

1987 *Mythical and Fabulous Beasts: A Source Book and Research Guide* by Malcolm South (Ed.)

1990 *Hargreaves New Illustrated Bestiary* by Joyce Hargreaves

1992 *Symbolic and Mythological Animals* by J.C. Cooper

1995 *Wonder Beasts: Tales and Lore of the Phoenix, the Griffin, the Unicorn and the Dragon* by Joseph Nigg

1995 *Monster! Monster! A Survey of the North American Monster Scene* by Betty S.Garner

1996 *The Unexplained: An Illustrated Guide to the World's Natural and Paranormal Mysteries* by Karl P.N. Shuker

1996 *Barlow's Guide to Fantasy* by W.D. Barlow

1998 *The Book of Sea Monsters* by Bob Eggleton & Nigel Suckling

1999 *The Book of Fabulous Beasts: A Treasury of Writings from Ancient Times to the Present* by Joseph Nigg

1999 *Cryptozoology A to Z* by Loren Coleman & Jerome Clark

2000 *Giants, Monsters, and Dragons* by Carol Rose

2001 *Monsters: An Investigator's Guide to Magical Beings,* by John Michael Greer

2002 *The Book of Dragons & Other Mythical Beasts* by Joseph Nigg

2003 *The Beasts That Hide from Man: Seeking the World's Last Undiscovered Animals* by Karl P.N. Shuker

2003 *Field Guide to Lake Monsters, Sea Serpents, and Other Mystery Denizens of the Deep* by Loren Coleman

2005 *Fantasy Encyclopedia* by Judy Allen

2005 *Fabulous Beasts* by Malcolm Ashman

2006 *The Field Guide to Bigfoot and Other Mystery Primates* by Loren Coleman & Patrick Huyghe

APPENDIX B. COMIC RELIEF

If Other Fabulous Creatures had a Horn Like a Unicorn - by Oberon Zell

HARPIES could carry off even more loot, since they have no hands...

DRAGONS would have lances so they could joust with mounted knights...

With a swordlike horn added to its arsenal of claws, talons, and beak, a GRYPHON would be invincible!

A nearsighted CYCLOPS would have a place to hang his monocle.

The SPHINX would have an antenna to pick up all the hottest "rock"...

SEA SERPENTS could save the whales by harpooning the whaling ships.

DRAGONS would have skewers with which to roast their own shish-kabobs and marshmallows.

MERMAIDS could have fun fencing with narwhals.

The PHOENIX could blow her own horn to announce her spectacular twice-a-millennium cremation and resurrection.

NESSIE could breathe through a snorkel horn to hide from the Loch Ness Investigation Bureau.

The KRAKEN would have a mast, and could hoist a sail to travel around the seven seas...

BIGFOOT could steal more fruit from the orchards of remote farms...

APPENDIX C. HERE BE MONSTERS

By Oberon Zell-Ravenheart

PART I. THE CLASSICAL AND MEDIEVAL WORLD

1. Atlantic Ocean
Aspidochelone
Balena
Crodh Sidhe
Echeneis
Fastitocalon
Fish Pig
Focas
Geraher
Halata
Jasconius
Merfolk
Murcat
Murena
Mustela
Physeter
Porci Marini
Rumbus
Scolopendra
Serra
Solaris
Zyphoeus

2. England
Brag
Dea
Dunnie
Liver
Grant
Oilliphéist
Questing Beast
Worm

3. Wales
Adar Llwch
    Gwin
Afanc
Carrog
Cath Pulag
Llamhigyn y
    Dwr
White Hart

4. Ireland
Aillen Trechenn
Aughisky
Bledmall
Bocanach
Brucha
Caoránach
Cornu
Dobhar-Chú
Each Tened
Easg Saint
Fachen
Kelpie
Nuckalavee
Peiste
Phooka
Merrow
Mil
Muirbech
Muirdris
Muiriasc
Muirselche
Saidthe
Suaraighe
St Attracta's
    Monster
Selchie
Sughmaire
Suileach

5. Scotland
Beithir
Boobrie
Burach Bhadi
Cait Sith
Ceasg
Corc-Chluasask
Ferla Mohr
Fuath
Gigelorum
Glas Ghaibhlann
Lavellan
Sianach
Tarbh Uisge
Urisk
Vough

6. Hebrides
Fin People
Glashtyn
Goayr Heddagh
Neugle
Roan
Sea Trow
Shoopiltey
Taroo-Ushtey
Wulver

7. North Sea
Argus Fish
Auvekoejak
Ben-Varrey &
    Dinny-Marra
Bishop Fish
Cîrein Cròin
Great Norway
    Serpent
Hakenmann
Havfine
Havfrue &
    Havmand
Havhest
Havstrambe
Kraken
Monkfish
Näcken
Neugle
Rosmarine
Sahab
Sea Hog
Sea Horse
Sea-Satyr
Skoffin
Skrimsl
Stoorworm
Swamfisk
Tursus

8. Hyborea/ Scandinavia
Audumbla
Drake
Eikthymir
Fenrir, the
    Fenris
    Wolf
Garm
Gollinkambi
Gulon
Hafgygr
Hati
Havfine
Heiddreun
Horses of the
    Sun
Hraesvelg
Jörmungandr
Lindwurm
Nidhogg
Nixie
Orm
Ratatosk
Sadhuzag
Saio-Neita
Sjøorm
Sleipnir
Svadilfari
Troll Fisk
Vuokho
Wyrm
Ythgewinnes

9. Germania
Achlis
Acipenser
Aspis
Barliate
Bialozar
Dragons
Ercinee
Fire-Drakes
Grendel
Haferbock
Hercynian Birds
Hercynian Stag
Loathly Worm
Lorelei
Salamandra
Tatzelwurm
Urus
Wudewasa

10. Gallia (France)
Arassas
Bulchin
Chichevache
Dracs
Gargouille
Gargoyle
Grylio
Guivre
La Velue
Lou Carcolh
Melusina
Muscaliet
Peluda
Tarasque
Vouivre
Yannig

11. Hispania
Aatxe
Bicha
El Cuelebre
Guita
Herren-Surge

12. Italy/ Mediterranean
Boas
Charybdis
Halcyon
Ichthyocentaur
Marine Lion
Murex
Orc
Papstesel
Peryton
Rahab
Ravenna Monster
Scylla
Sea Hare
Sirens
Tritons
Viper

13. Greco-Roman/ Aegean
Arion
Cacus
Campe
Centaur
Centauro-Triton
Cerberus
Cerynean Hind
Cetus
Echidna
Empusa
Epirotes
Fauns
Gryllus
Hippocampus
Horses of Diomedes
Horses of the Sun
Hydra
Kallicantzari
Keto
Minotaur
Nemean Lion
Orthus
Phorcids
Python

Satyrs
Sphinx
Stymphalids
Tolchines
Teumessian Vixen
Typhon

14. Illyria/ Thracia
Bitoso
Bolla
Broxa
Drekavac
Kulshedra
Laskowice
Lidérc
Lynx
Strix
Turul
Zlatorog
Zmei Gorynych

15. Asia Minor
Aries
Bonnacon
Bucentaur
Chimera
Deer-Centaur
Dog-Centaur
Dragons
Harpies
Kargas
Kerkes
Leontophontes
Onachus
Onocentaur
Stymphalids

16. Sarmacia/ Armenia
Aitvaras
Ajatar
Firebird
Gagana
Gamayun
Garafena
Gorgoniy
Pisuhand
Sarmatian Sea Snail

17. Scythia
Busse
Gryphon
Scythian Ass
Simargl

18. The Holy Land
Apocalyptic Beasts
Bar Juchne
Barometz
Behemoth
Draconcopedes
Jidra
Leviathan
Mandragora
Mermicoleon
Milcham
Nasnas
Re'em
Shamir
Ziz

19. Egypt
Akhekhu
Ammut
Apis
Axex
Babai
Benu
Buchis
Cocodryllus
Gengen Wer
Hydrus
Hypnale
Ichneumon
Ka-en-Ankh Nereru
Khepra
Maka
Mehturt
Merwer
Mimick Dog
Ouroboros
Serpopard
Sphinx
Sta
Uraeus
Ypotamis

20. Libya
Amphisbæna
Assida
Basilisk
Cerastes
Cockatrice
Cynoprosopi
Draco
Gorgon
Hyman Topodes
Karkadann
Lamia

Pegasus
Safat
Scitalis

21. Ethiopia
Cameleopard
Catoblepas
Celphies
Cynocephali
Dragons of Ethiopia
Flying Serpent of Isa
Huspalim
Karkadann
Leucrocota
Lubolf
Panther
Pard
Pa Snakes
Pegasies
Rompo
Tarandrus
Tragopan
Unicorn

22. Arabia
Abgal
Angka
Bahamut
Bahri
Boraq, Al
Caristae
Cynamolgus
Dendan
Diwe
Ghul
Jaculus
Kujata
Labuna
Murghi-l-Adami
Onyx Monoceros
Orobon
Phoenix
Simurgh
Syren
Uma Na-Iru
Winged Serpents of Arabia
Zägh

23. Mesopotamia
Anthalops
Anzu
Aptaleon
Calopus
Capricornus
Girtablili
Gugalana
Hea-Bani
Hedammu
Humbaba
Kul
Lamassu
Shedu
Sirin
Sirrush
Sta
Suhur-Mas
Tiamet
Uridimmus

24. Persia
Al
Caladrius
Chamrosh
Conopenii
Geush Urvan
Glycon
Hadhayosh
Huma
Kar-Fish
Karkadann
Khara
Koresck
Lion-Griffon
Senmurv
Shadhahvar
3-Legged Ass

25. India
Æternæ
Anguillae
Avelerion
Bull of Inde/ Cartazonus
Centycore
Crocotta
Dipsa
Dragons
Giant Ants
Karkadann
Manticora
Monoceros
Odontotyrannus
Rompo
Seps
Sevienda

Thanacth
Yale

26. Indian Ocean/ Taprobana
Farasi Bahari
Giant Ants
Mi'raj
Roc
Zaratan

27. Heraldry
Allocamelus
Alphyn
Amphisien
Apres
Ass-Bittern
Bagwyn
Boreyne
Calygreyhound
Caretyne
Cat-Fish
Cock-Fish
Dragon-Tygre
Dragon-Wolf
Enfield
Falcon-Fish
Gryphon
Guivre
Heliodromos
Hippocerf
Keythong
Lybbarde
Lympago
Lyon-Poisson
Martlet
Minocane
Morhon
Musimon
Nependis
Opincus
Pithon
Satyre Fish
Sea Dog
Sea-Dragon
Sea-Goat
Sea-Lion
Sea Stag
Sea Wolf
Snake Griffin
Stellione
Theow
Tityron
Tyger
Wyvern
Ypotryll

PART II. THE AGE OF EXPLORATION TO THE PRESENT
A MAP OF THE WESTERN HEMISPHERE CIRCA 1626

1. Oceania (Pacific)
Areop-enap
Devil Fish
Halulu
Island Beast
Many-Finned
    Sea Serpent
Moko
Mo-O
Ngani-vatu
Rainbow
    Serpent
Rigi
Tumu-Ra'i-
    Fuena
Veo

2. Canada, Alaska, Greenland
Akhlut
Amarok
A-Mi-Kuk
Angont
Ashuaps
Az-i-wû-ghûm-
    ki-mukh-'ti
Bakbakwaka-
    nooksiwae
Big Fish of
    Iliamna
Fur-Bearing
    Trout
Galokwudzuwis
Gillman of
    Thetis Lake
Halfway People
Haietlik
Hînqûmemen
Iak Im
Icegedunk
Ice Worms
Ikalu Nappa
Imap Umas-
    soursa
Keelut
Margygr
Marked
    Hominids
Michi-Pichoux
Miqqiayuuq

No-Kos-Ma
Pal-Rai-Yuk
Ponik
Pugwis
Quanekelak
Sasquatch
Sisiutl
Tirisuk
Torngarsoak
Tsemaus
Ugjuknarpak
Waheela
Wendigo

3. United States
Achiyalabopa
Ahani
Altamaha-ha
Amhuluk
Anaye
Antukai
Batsquatch
Beasts of
    Elmendorf
Big Bird
Bigfoot

Black Devil #2
Coonigator
Delgeth
Devil Monkeys
Djieien
Dover Demon
Enfield Horror
Fearsome
    Critters
Fillyloo
Flying Heads
Freshwater
    Octopus
Gaasyendietha
Ganiagwaide-
    gowa
Gatorman
Giant Sala-
    mander
Goatman
Green-Clawed
    Beast
Haakapainizi
Hakulaq
Hoop Snake

Horned
    Alligator
Horned
    Serpents
Hvcko Capko
Iya
Jackalope
Jersey Devil
Leelanau
Lenapizka
Little Manitou
Lizard Men
Loveland Frogs
Manetuwi-Rusi-
    Pissi
Mashernomak
May's Point
    Mystery
    Fish
Mill Lake
    Monster
Mi-Ni-Wa-Tu
Mishipizhiw
Misiganebic
Momo

Moogie
Mothman
Oklahoma
    Octopus
Paiyuk
Palulukon
Piasa
River Griffin
Shunka
    Warak'in
Skahnowa
Skunk Ape
Snallygaster
Stvwvnaya
Teehooltsoodi
Teelget
Thunderbirds
Thunder Horse
Tsenahale
Uktena
Underwater
    Panther
Unktehi
Wakandagi
Weewilmekq
White Panther
Wikatcha

Wishpooshi
Yenrish

4. Mexico & Central America
Ahuizhotl
Amphitere
Balam
Black Devil #1
Campacti
Chupacabra
Hoga
el Hombre Oso
Itcuintlipotzotli
Kinich Ahau
Onza
Sea Elephant
Sisemite
Sterpe
Tlatecuhtli
Wihwin
Xan
Xolotl
Ya-te-veo

5. West Indies/ Caribbean
Cigouave
Cucuio
Lusca
Racumon
Rainbow
    Serpent
Sea Gryphon

6. South America
Alicanto
Calchona
Camahueto
Camoodi
Carbuncle
Caypore
Ccoa
Chancha con
    Cadenas
Cherufe
Chonchón
Colo-Colo
El Cuero
DeLoys Ape

(map labels) NORTH AMERICA · MAR DEL NORT · THE ATLANTIC OCEAN · MAR DEL ZUR · SOUTH AMERICA · THE PACIFICKE SEA · MAGELLANICA

PART III. THE AGE OF EXPLORATION TO THE PRESENT
A MAP OF THE EASTERN HEMISPHERE CIRCA 1626

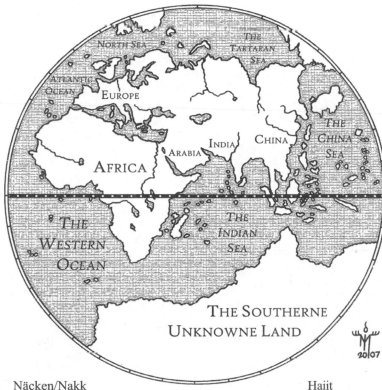

Didi
Encantado
Giant Sloth of
  Patagonia
Glyryvilu
Huallepén
Hueke Hueku
Iémisch
Igpupiara
Invunche
Iwaneï
Lampalugua
Lik
Madidi Monster
Manta
Mapinguari
Mawadi
Minhocão
Mono Grande
Monster of
  Lake Fagua
Nahuelito
Pihuechenyi
Piranu
Sabre-Tooths
Salvaje
Sa-Yin
Su
Sucuriju
  Gigante
White Chest
Xexeu

**7. Atlantic
  Ocean**
Alloés
Dragon-
  Mermaid
Flying Fish
Long-Necked
  Sea Serpent
Many-Finned
  Sea Serpent
Many-Humped
  Sea Serpent
Marine Saurian
Merhorse

**8. North Sea/
  Arctic Ocean**
Kraken
Marmaele

Näcken/Nakk
Sea Bear
Super Otter

9. British Isles
Alien Big Cats
Beast of Brass-
  knocker Hill
Black Dogs
Ferla Mohr
Hellhounds
King Otter
Loch Monsters
Owlman
Shag Foal

**10. Western
  Europe**
Beast of
  Gévaudan
Butatsch-Ah-
  Ilgs
Elbst
Freiburg
  Shrieker
Gryttie
Hippogriff

Juma
Kludde
Mjosa
Mother of the
  Fishes
Seljordsorm
Skrimsl
Storsjöodjuret
Wolpertinger

**11. Eastern
  Europe**
Barmanu
Black Bird of
  Chernobyl
Brosnie
Cows of Näkki
Dard
Frogman
Guardian of the
  Fishes
Habergeiss
Indrik the Beast
Kaptar
Kokkol

Opk•n
Ova
Phantom of the
  Lake
Rizos
Sarajevo
  Jumping
  Snake
Vodianoi

**12. Africa (sub-
  Sahara)**
Agogwe
Ambize
Badigui
Basket Monster
Booa
Coje ya Menia
Crocho
Dingonek
Dodu
Emela-Ntouka
Fating'ho
Ga-Gorib
Guiafairo

Haiit
Hai-Uri
Hirguan
Ikaki
Ilomba
Ingheena
Intulo
Jengu
Kakundakri
Karina
Kasai Rex
Kongamato
Lau
Lightning
  Monsters
Lukwata
Mahamba
Makalala
Mali
Mamba Mutu
Mamlambo
Mbielu-Mbielu-
  Mbielu
Migas
Mngwa
Mokêle-M'Bêmbe
Mourou N'gou

Muhuru
Mulilo
Nandi Bear
Ndzoodzoo
Ngoima
Ngoubou
Nguma-Monene
Nyaminyami
Nzefu-Loi
Olitiau
Pamba
Rainbow
  Serpent
Rift Valley
  Monster
Sabre-Toothed
  Cats
Sassabonsum
Sehit
Tikoloshe

13. Madagascar
Crinoida
Fandrefiala
Habéby
Mangarsahoc
Roc
Tokandia
Tompondrano
Tratratratra

**14. India
  (Hindu /
  Buddhist)**
Aja Akapad
Akupara
Ananta Sesha
Apalala
Apotharni
Asipatra
Asootee
Barmanu
Betikhân
Bhains•sura
Dadhikra
Devil Bird
Dhumarna
Gandharvas
Garuda
Hanuman
Kama-Dhenu
Kimpurushas

Kinnaras
Kirata
Kirtimukha
Kurma
Lokapala
  Elephants
Mada
Mahisha
Makara
Nagas &
  Naginis
Nee-Gued
Nyan
Samvarta
Sharama
Vritra
Yali
Yeck

15. Indian Ocean/ Ceylon
Many-Finned
  Sea Serpent
Nittaewo

16. Tibet/Nepal
Buru
Chuti
Dzu-Teh
Kere
Meh-Teh
Khyung
Serou
Tsopo
Unnati
Yeti

17. Siberia & Mongolia
Ai Tojon

Alkonost
Almas
Bergman's Bear
Chuchunaa
Kheglen
Koguhpuks
Leongalli
Mammoth
Mongolian
  Deathworm
Short-Faced
  Bear
Tien-Schu
Tuba

18. China & Korea
Bixie
Bo
Cat-Fish
Celestial Horse
Celestial Stag
Chai Tung
Chan
Chiang Liang
Chio-tuan
Ch'ou-T'i
Dragon (Lung)
Dragon Horse
Fei Lian
Fêng Huang
Fo Dogs
Gui Xian
Haetae
Hai Ho Shang
Heavenly Cock
Hsigo
Hua-Hu-Tiao
Hui
I-Mu Kuo Yan
Ink Monkey

Kanasi Lake
  Monsters
Ki-Lin
Kw'ên
Kyeryong
Lwan
Man-Dragon of
  China
P'êng
P'êng-Niao
Pi-His
Shachihoko
Shang Yung
Song-Sseu
Ssu Ling
T'ao T'ieh
Ti-Chiang
Too Jou Shen
Wuhnan Toads
Xian Yao
Y•rén
Ying-Lung
Yu Lung

19. Japan
Akuma
Amikiri
Baku
Centipede
Dragon
Hai Riyo
Hibagon
Hiyakudori
Ho-oo
Jinshin-Mushi
Jinshin-Uwo
Kamaitachi
Kami
Kappa
Kirin
Kitsune

Kudan
Kumiho
Moshiri-
  ikkwechep
Ningyo
Nue
Nure-Onna
O Goncho
Pheng
Raicho
Raiju
Samebito
Sin-You
Takujui
Tanuki
Tengu
Tsuchi-Gumo
Tsuckinoko
Uwabami
Yamamaya
Yata Garasu

20. Southeast Asia
Batutut
Celestial Tigers
Con Tram
  Nu'Ó' C
Con Rit
Elephant-Tiger
Garuda
Gergis
Jaculus
Kting Voar
Leyak
Nguoi-Rung
Orang Dalam
Seah Malang
  Poo
Stinking Ones
Sz

Vietnamese
  Night-Flyers

21. East Indies
Abaia
Adaro
Ahool
Alan
Batutut
Bird of Paradise
Boroka
Buata
Camphurcii
Cigau
Duah
Ebu Gogu
Father of Turtles
Figonas
Gainjin
Garuda
Ilkai
Kafre
Kapre
Kusa Kap
Megalania
Murray
Orang-Bati
Orang Pendek
Pinatubo
  Monsters
Pish-Meri
Rainbow
  Serpent
Ropen
Singa
Tikbalang
Upas Tree

22. Australia
Baginis
Beast of Bynoe

Bay
Bulaing
Bunyip
Cheeroonear
Eer-Moonan
Euroa Beast
Gurangatch
Jarapiri
Jongari
Kadimakara
Karora
Krantjirinja
Kunapipi
Kurrea
Lightning
  Serpents
Maldape
Megalania
Muljewang
Queensland
  Tiger
Rainbow
  Serpent
Whowhie
Yowie

23. New Zealand
Horomatangi
Hotu-Puku
Huru-Kareao
Ihu-Mataotao
Marakihan
Mastertown
  Monster
Moa
Moehau
Poua-Kai
Tanihwa
Waitoreke

PART IV. LAKE MONSTERS AROUND THE WORLD

In the hope that some reader of this book will have a digital or cell phone camera in hand when a lake monster surfaces in front of you, I thought it would be useful to provide a listing of lakes, lochs, rivers, pools, marshes, bogs, and billabongs throughout the world where such creatures have been sighted. There's probably one near you, so go check it out!

My main sources for these listings are *Alien Animals* by Janet & Colin Bord (1981), and *Monster! Monster!* By Betty Sanders Garner (1995). Another impoortant source of sightings is AmericanMonsters.com. Listings are alphabetical by countries, states/provinces, and names of lakes. Where monsters have been given colorful local names, these are in parentheses.

Africa

Cameroun: Mamfe Pool; Upper Cross River
Central African Republic: Bamingui River; Koukourou River
East Africa: Ouémé River; Lake Tanganyika; Swamps at sources of White Nile
Malawi: Lake Nyasa
South Africa: Grootvlei Reservoir; Howick Falls ("Howie"); Ingruenfisi River; Orange River; Vaaldam Reservoir
Tanzania/Uganda/Kenya: Lake Mweru; Lake Victoria
Zaïre & Zambia: Dilolo Marshes; Lake Bangwuly; Lake Kariba ("Nyaminyami"); Lake Mweru; Zambezi River

Australia

Australian Capital Territory: Molonglo River
New South Wales: Lake Bathurst; Cowal Lake; Edward River ("Tnata"); Fish River; Lake George; Hawkesbury River; Hunter River ("Yaa-Loo"); Lismore Lagoon; Midgeon Lagoon; Murray River; Murrumbidgee River; Lake Paika; Lake Tala
Northern Territory: Gudgerama Creek ("Mannie")
Queensland: Diamantina River ("Kuddimudra"); Nerang River; Tuckerbill swamp near Leeton
South Australia: Lake Alexandrina ("Moolgewanke"); Crystal Brook; Gambier Lagoon; Murray River
Tasmania: Lake Echo; Great Lake; Jordan River; Lake Tiberias
Victoria: Barwon River; Lake Burrumbert; Lake Corongamile; Eumeralla River; Eurora Reservoir; Port Fairy; Port Phillip ("Tunatpan"); Lake Werribee/ Modewarre

Canada

Alberta: Battle River; Christina Lake; Lake McGregor; Saddle Lake; Saskatchewan River
British Columbia: Boiling Lake; Cowichan Lake; Harrison Lake; Kamloops Lake; Lake Kathlyn; Kootenay Lake; Martin's Lake; Lake Okanagan ("Ogopogo"); Osoyoos Lake; Oyster River ("Klato"); Shuswap Lake ("Shuswaggi"); Skaha Lake; Somenos Lake; Lake Tagai ("Tag"); Vancouver Island ("Tsinquaw"); Williams Lake
Manitoba: Dauphin Lake; Lake Manitoba ("Manipogo"); Lake Winnipegosis; Red River
New Brunswick: Dungarvon River ("Dungarvon Whooper"); Lake Kilarney; Lake Utopia ("Old Ned")
Newfoundland: Crescent Lake ("Cressie"); Dildo Pond; Gander Lake; Grat Gull Lake; Lond Pond; Swangler's Cove ("Maggot")
Nova Scotia: Lake Ainslie; Bras d'Or Lakes
Ontario: Lake of Bays; Berens Lake; Lake Deschenes; Lake Erie; Georgian Bay; Lake Huron; Mazinaw Lake; Lake Miminiska; Muskrat Lake ("Mussie"); Nith River ("Slimy Caspar"); Lake Ontario ("Kingstie"); Ottawa River; Rideau Canal; Lake Simcoe ("Igopogo"); Lake Superior
Prince Edward Island: O'Keef's Lake
Quebec: Aylmer Lake; Black Lake; Lake Champlain ("Champ"); Lake Decaire ("Lizzie"); Lac Deschenes; Lac Memphremagog ("Memphre"); Mocking Lake; Lake Pohenegamook ("Ponik"); Lac Saint-Jean ("Ashuaps"); St Lawrence River
Saskatchewan: Cold Lake ("Kinsoo"); Rowan's Ravine; Turtle Lake
Yukon: Teslin Lake

China

Lake Chang Bai Shan Tianchi ("Heavenly Lake Monster")

Denmark

Christianshavn moat; Farrisvannet

Finland

The Lagerflot; The Thorskafjord

Ireland

Clare: Lough Graney
Cork: Lough Attariff
Donegal: Lough Keel; Lough Muck
Galway: Lough Abisdealy; Lough Auna; Ballynahinch Lake; Lough Claddaghduff; Lough Crolan; Lough Derg ("Caoránach"); Lough Derrylea; Lough Dubh; Lough Fadda; Lough Glendalough; Lough Gowlan; Lough Kylemore; Lough Mask; Lough Nahillion; Lough Nahooin; Lough Neagh; Lough Ree; Lough Shanakeever; Louch Shandangan ("Bruckee"); Lough Waskel
Kerry: Lough Brin; Lough Geal; Lough Lackagh; Lough

Looscaunagh
Mayo: Carrowmore Lake; Glendarry Lough; Achill Island; Lough Nacorra
Managhan: Lough Major
Waterford: Counfea Lough
Wicklow: Lower Lough Bray; Lough Nahanagan

Italy
Lake Maggiore

Japan
Honshu: Lake Chuzenji
Kyushu: Lake Ikeda ("Issie")

Java
Lake Patenggang

Kazakhstan
Lake Koskol ("Koskolteras Rhombopterix")

Malaya
Lake Chini

Mexico
Lake Catemaco

Norway
Berso; Jolstravatnet; Krovatnet; Krodern; Lundevatnet; Lake Mjösa ("Mjösa"); Mosvatnet; Odegardskilen; Ormsjoen; Pyvanna; Repstadvanet; Ringsjoen; Rommen; Sandnesvatnet; Seljordsvatnet ("Selma"); Skodje; Lake Snasa; Sogne; Sorsasjoen; Sor Somna; Storevatn; Lake Suldal; Tinnkejodnet; Torfinnsvatnet; Tyrifjorden

Papua New Guinea
New Britain: Lake Dakataua

Philippines
Luzon: Tikis River

Scotland
Borders: Cauldshiels Loch
Central: Loch Lomond; Loch Venachar
Highlands: Loch Alsh; Loch Arkaig; Loch Assynt; Loch na Beiste; Loch Duich; Loch Eil; Loch Hourn; Loch Linnhe; Loch Lochy ("Lizzie"); Loch Morar ("Morag"), Loch Ness ("Nessie"); Loch Oich; Loch Quoich; Loch Shiel

("Shielagh"); Loch Treig
Isle of Eriskay: Loch Duvant
Isle of Lewis: Loch Lerubost; Loch Suainaval, Loch Uraval
Isle of Skye: Loch Brittle, Loch nan Dubhrachan, Loch Scavaig
Strathclyde: Loch Awe
Tayside: Loch Rannoch; Loch Tay; River Tay

Siberia
Lake Khaiyr; Lake Labyynkyr; Lake Vorota

South America
Argentina: Esquel mountain lake; Lake Lacar; Lago Nahuel Huapi ("Nahuelito"); Santa Cruz lake; River Tamango; White Lake
Bolivia: Madidi swamps
Brazil: Amazon River
Paraguay: Paraguay River

Sweden
Lake Bullare; Lake Fegen; Lake Gryttjen ("Gryttie"); Lilla Kallsjö; Myllesjön; Stagnössjön; Lake Storsjön ("Storsie"); Lake Tingstäde

Switzerland
Selisbergsee ("Elbst")

United States of America
Alaska: Crosswind Lake; Lake Iliamna; Lake Minchumina; Nonvianuk Lake; Walker Lake
Arkansas: Lake Conway; Mud Lake; White River ("Whitey")
California: Lake Elizabeth; Lake Elsinore, Lake Folsom; Lafayette Lake; Lake Tahoe ("Tahoe Tessie")
Connecticut: Lake Pocotopang; Twin Lakes
Florida: St Johns River; St Lucie River
Idaho: Payette Lake ("Sharlie"); Lake Pendre OreilleSalmon River; Snake River
Illinois: Lake DuQuoin
Indiana: Big Chapman Lake; Lake Manitou ("Mannie"); Wabash River
Kentucky: Herrington Lake; Reynold's Lake
Maine: Sysladobosis Lake
Michigan: Lake Huron; Lake

Leelanau ("Leelanau"); Lake Michigan; Narrow Lake; Paint River
Minnesota: Big Pine Lake ("Oscar"); Great Sandy Lake; Leech Lake; Lake Minnetonka
Mississippi: Mississippi River near Natchez
Missouri: Lake of the Ozarks
Montana: Flathead Lake; Missouri River; Lake Waterton
Nebraska: Alkali Lake; Big Alkali Lake
Nevada: Pyramid Lake; Walker Lake
New Hampshire: Moore Lake
New York: Black River; Cayuga Lake ("Old Greeny"); Hudson River; Mazinaw Lake; Lake of the Woods
Oklahoma: Lake Eufaula
Oregon: Hollow Block Lake, Wallowa Lake
Pennsylvania: Lake Brompton; Wolf Pond
South Dakota: Lake Campbell
Utah: Bear Lake; Great Salt Lake; Utah Lake
Vermont: Lake Champlain ("Champ")
Washington: Lake Chelan; Crater Lake; Crescent Lake; Lake Washington
Wisconsin: Browns Lake; Delevan Lake; Devil's Lake; Elkhart Lake; Fowler Lake; Lake Geneva; Lake Kegonsa; Lake Koshkong; Lake La Belle; Madison Four Lakes; Lake Mendota ("Bozho"); Milwaukee River; Lake Monona; Lake Okauchee; Oconomowoc Lake; Lake Pewaukee; Red Cedar Lake; Lake Ripley; Rock Lake; Lake Waubesa, Lake Wingra; Lake Wobegon
Wyoming: Lake DeSmet

Wales
Dyfed: Lyn Eiddwen; Lyn Farch
Gwenedd: Lyn yr Afanc; River Conwy; Llyn Cynwch; Llyn-y-Gadair; Glaslyn Lake; Marchlyn Mawr
Powys: Llangorse Lake

APPENDIX D. MAGICKAL CORRESPONDENCES

By Ash "LeopardDancer" DeKirk

Aatxe: justice, protection against danger.

Abaia: lake conservation, water-work, storms.

Achiyalabopa: creation, life-bringing, healing.

Acipenser (sturgeon): struggles against adversity.

Adar Llwch Gwin: strength, courage, protection, and loyalty.

Aeternae: courage, strength.

Agathodemon: luck, divination, loyalty.

Ahool (also Alan): nighttime, moon, cunning.

Ai Tojon: honor, valor, sun, enlightenment.

Aja Akapad: lightning, fire, strength.

Alicanto: illumination, spiritual guidance, deception.

Alkonost: deception, forgetfulness.

Alloes: determination, focus, proper behavior.

Altamaha-ha: joy, harmony, togetherness, ability to get along with others.

Amarok (also Akhlut): cunning, ferocity, walking the planes.

Ambize (manatee): gentleness, love, peace, serenity, motherhood.

Amhuluk: transformation.

Ammut: divine retribution.

Amphisabaena: protection of pregnant women, overcoming inner conflicts, duality.

Angont: pestilence, calamity, ill fortune.

Anguilla (eel) (also Beithir): disguise, deception, strength, cunning.

Anthalops: swiftness, vigilance.

Areop-enap: cunning, fate, creativity.

Argus fish: great wisdom, psychic work, gentleness, great intelligence, patience.

Aries: aggression, passion, pioneering spirit, bravery, impulsive behavior.

Aspidochelone: nurturing, protection, patience, wisdom

Assida (ostrich): seeking the unknown, earth knowledge.

Audumbla: patience, gentleness, motherhood.

Babai: divine retribution.

Baku: dreamwork, banishing nightmares.

Balam: protection, guidance, good harvests.

Basilisk (also Cockatrice): discovering the inner self, uncovering hidden secrets, cunning, blighting.

Benu: rebirth, resurrection, divine knowledge.

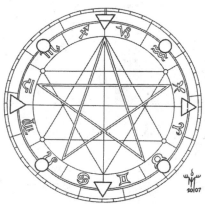

Bigfoot (also Agogwe, Almas, Barmanu, Chuchunaa, Dzu-teh, Ebu-gogu, Ferla Mohr, Hibagon, Hirguan, Ingheena, Kapre, Meh-teh, Moehau, Nee-Gued, Ngoi-Rung, Orang Pendek, Sasquatch, Sisemite, Skunk Ape, Wendigo, Yeh-teh, Yeti, Yowie): social ties, bonding, staying hidden.

Black Dogs (also Baisd Bheulach, Calchona, Keelut, Rizos, Saidthe Suaraighe): bad luck, death omen, divine justice.

Bmola: weather-work, particularly for winter weather.

Bonnacon: renewal, change, transforming personality.

Buata: determination, self-reliance.

Buchis: sun, strength, insight into past lives.

Bunyip: rain-work, learning to go with flow and make the best of all situations.

Busse (reindeer): tradition, old ways.

Cait Sith: cunning, curiosity, magick, mystery.

Caladrius: healing.

Calopus: instincts, circle of life.

Camoodi: patience, wisdom, transformation.

Carbuncle: healing, focused energy.

Centaur (also Apotharni, Bucentaur, Deer Centaur, Ghandharvas, Icthyocentaur, Onocentaur): inspiration, music, arts, healing, divination.

Chan: guarding secrets, stubbornness.

Chimera (also Bixie, Chiang Liang): ferocity, banishing negative emotions.

Chuti: instincts, communication.

Con Tram Nu'Ó'C: travel (especially long distances), abundance, link to Mother Earth.

Crodh Sidhe: curiosity, gentleness, social behavior.

Cucuio: seeing the truth in the shadows, inspiration, insight.

Didi: curiosity, imagination, learning to cope with the darker nature of personality.

Dogs of Fo: wards against evil.

Dragon, Eastern (also Dragon Kings, Lung, Ying-long): peace, prosperity, luck, wisdom, honor, royalty, rulership.

Dragon, Western (also Aspis, Bolla, Drac, Drake, Guita, Lindorm, Odontotyrannus, Orm, Scitalis, Wyvern): strength, passion.

Dragon H, Syrenorse: divine messenger, communication.

Faun (also Betikhan, Lascowic, Urisk): agriculture, fertility, music, animals, nature.

Feathered Serpent (also **Amphitere, Hai Ryo, Kinich Ahau, Kulkulkan, Palulukon, P'êng-Niao, Questalcoatl**): knowledge, wisdom, art, divination.

Gargoyle: protection of home or property, astral companionship, wards against evil.

Gryphon (also **Axex, Chamrosh, Imdugud, Kargas**): spiritual wisdom, duality, enlightenment.

Guiafairo: beginning a new life, facing one's fears.

Gulon: warns against gluttony.

Haetae: protection, royalty, time, justice.

Hippocampus (also **Afanc, Aughisky, Farasi Bahari, Glashtyn, Kelpie, Neugl Seahorse**): astral travel, meditation, assessing danger, dealing with turbulent emotions.

Hippogriff: travel between the worlds, balance.

Horned Serpents (also **Uktena**): healing.

Iak Im: power, banishing, driving away unwanted influences.

Kappa: water-working, medicine (particularly bor setting and healing).

Kitsune (also **Kumiho**): trickery, cleverness, illusion, shapeshifting.

Kraken (also **Imap Umassoursa**): hidden danger, intelligence, strength of the depths.

Mammoth: wisdom of the ages, perseverance, nobility, strength, memory.

Merfolk (also **Abgal, Adaro, Ben Varrey, Ceasg, Dinny-Marra, Fin People, Gwenhidwy, Hai Ho Shang, Havfine, Igupiara, Ikalu Nappa, Ilkai, Jengu, Kul, Lorelei, Merrow, Pish Meri, Saio-Neita, Sea Trow, Syrenka, Triton**): protection, enchantment, healing, attaining desires, magickal knowledge.

Murena: disguise, deception, strength, cunning.

Naras: poetic inspiration, astral travel, traveling to Otherworld.

No-Kos-Ma: love, caution, healing, leadership, patience.

Nue: bad luck, ill-fortune, and the banishment of both.

Ouroborus: transformation, continuity, cycle of life.

Palulukon: knowledge, wisdom, art, divination.

Pard: art of blending in, cunning, patience, intuition, grace.

Pegasus (also **Arion**): poetic inspiration, astral travel, traveling to Otherworld, speaking to the deceased.

Phoenix (also **Feng Huang, Firebird, Ho-oh, Milcham, Sevienda**): rebirth, resurrection, spiritual growth.

Quetzalcoatl: knowledge, wisdom, art, divination.

Rainbow Serpent (also **Bulaing**): rain, fertility.

Roc (also **Ababil, Angka, Bar Juchne, Crocho, Hraesvelg, Kreutzet, Ngani-vatu, Pheng, Ziz**): protection, power, strength.

Rosmarine (walrus): gregariousness, connecting with nature, socialization.

Saber-Tooth: deepest, darkest fears, primal energy.

Sadhuzag: power, stamina, taking in the "big picture."

Sassabonsum: facing one's

darkest fears, self-evaluation.

Satyr (also **Kallicantzari**): music, dancing, sexuality, lust, passion.

Sea-Bear (fur seal): creativity, imagination, learning to listen to the inner self.

Sea-Hog (manatee): gregariousness, connecting with nature, socialization.

Sea-Lion: creativity, imagination, learning to listen to the inner self.

Selkie (also **Roane**): creativity, learning to listen to the inner self, protection, enchantment, healing.

Shang Yung: weather-working, drawing rain, ending drought.

Shunka Warak'in: determination, heightening awareness, ferocity.

Skoffin: discovering the inner self, uncovering hidden secrets, cunning.

Sphinx (also **Androsphinx, Criosphinx, Gynosphinx, Heiracosphinx**): intuition, inner knowledge, guarded wisdom, knowing when to keep silent.

Stymphalian Birds (also **Asipatra**): death, disease, destruction, pestilence, rainbringing.

Tanuki: shapeshifting, prosperity, playfulness, luck.

T'ao T'ieh: ward against gluttony.

Tengu: martial arts, dancing, weapons.

Thunderbird (also **Xexeu**): storms and rains, protection, power, strength.

Turul: agility, grace, success.

Unicorn (also **Abada, Abath, Carazonus, Chai Tung, Chio-tuan, Ki'Lin, Kirin, Koresck, Sin-you, Sz**): prosperity, purity, strength of mind, developing personal power.

Winged Serpent (also **Jaculus**): knowledge, wisdom, protection.

Yata Garasu: divine messenger.

Appendix E. Monsters in Movies

For nearly a century, we've delighted in the presentation of all manner of fantastic creatures on the movie screen. What? That long? Yes, indeed. Silent film pioneers like Georges Meliere took us to the moon (*Le Voyage dans la Lune*, 1902), where his protagonists battled ant-like Selenites. The original *20,000 Leagues Under the Sea* (1916) was a silent film (and a rather dull one, but with some special effects far ahead of its time). In 1914, the first "monster-critter" ever to appear on film was a silent cartoon short, *Gertie the Dinosaur*. Abroad, in 1922, the silents *Nosferatu* and *Häxan* (also known as *Witchcraft Through the Ages*) captured the European imagination with a sinister vampire and a whole host of demonic entities, respectively. And London was probably the first city to be trampled by a dinosaur, in the classic 1925 silent *The Lost World*.

But it remained for later film-makers to re-create the monsters of traditional mythology and legend. The great pioneer of stop-motion animation, Willis O'Brien, stunned the world with *The Lost World* and *King Kong*–and it should be remembered that at one time, great apes were considered mythological! *Kong* included a number of dinosaurs and flying reptiles, all depicted with an accuracy that is surprising, considering the limited state of paleontology at the time! His techniques were carried on and perfected by his student and protégé, the legendary Ray Harryhausen, who gave us not only the sword-wielding skeletons of several *Sinbad* movies, but also the giant Cyclops, the winged Pegasus, the Ymir from Venus (who doubled as the Homunculus in a later Sinbad film), and many, many more.

There were other, lesser lights, to be sure; none achieved Harryhausen's immortality, until (perhaps!) modern-day monster-makeup and special effects creator Rick Baker came on the scene. Why do these things have such a universal fascination? Perhaps the answer lies in ancient mythology itself, the original home of all things fantastic. It is the simple realization that we may not be alone in the universe, that there are– or were–great beasties we could not always control, and those who tried, might not fare all that well. They speak to the vulnerability of humanity, and serve not only as a wonderful flight of fancy, but a reminder that we might be just a part of nature's pageant, after all.

–Seth Tyrssen
Professor of Dark Arts
Grey School of Wizardry

The escaped Brontosaurus causes havoc in the city—a plot device which would be used in innumerable later films.
The Lost World, *1925*

The Monster that Challenged the World – Giant snails **

The Giant Claw a.k.a. *Mark of the Claw* – Giant buzzard *

1958 *The 7th Voyage of Sinbad* – Roc, Cyclops, Dragon *****

1959 *Darby O'Gill and the Little People* – Phooka, spectral coach horses *****

Sleeping Beauty (animated) – Dragon ****

Journey to the Center of the Earth – Dinosaurs ****

The Giant Gila Monster – Giant lizard *

The Giant Behemoth – Godzilla-like Dinosaur *

Attack of the Giant Leeches – Giant leeches *

1960 *Dinosaurus!* – Dinosaurs ***

The Little Shop of Horrors – Predator plant **

The Lost World – Dinosaurs*

Goliath and the Dragon – Dragon **

Hercules vs The Hydra – **

1961 *Mysterious Island* – Giant crab, giant wasps, Phorusrhacos, Nautiloid ***

Alakazam the Great (anime) – The Monkey-King ***

Konga – Giant gorilla *

Gorgo – Godzilla-like monster *

1962 *The Fabulous Baron Munchausen* – Fastitocalon *****

The Magic Sword – Dragon ***

Day of the Triffids – Predator plants **

The Mermaids of Tiburon – Mermaids *

King Kong vs. Godzilla – Giant Gorilla, Godzilla*

1963 *Jason and the Argonauts* – Harpies, Hydra *****

Matango, Fungus of Terror (released in America as *Attack of the Mushroom People*) – Mushroom-people *

1964 *The 7 Faces of Dr. Lao* – Giant Serpent, Satyr, Loch Ness Monster, Yeti, Medusa *****

1965 *Beach Blanket Bingo* – Mermaid ***

1966 *One Million Years B.C.* – Dinosaurs, Pterosaurs, giant turtle ***

The Reptile – Lamia *

1967 *King Kong Escapes* – Giant Gorilla, Dinosaurs*

1968 *The Last Unicorn* (animated) – Aatxe, Unicorn, Harpy, Satyr *****

Kong Island – Giant gorilla, Dinosaurs*

Earth vs. the Spider – Giant spider *

1969 *The Valley of Gwangi* – Dinosaurs **

1970 *The Private Life of Sherlock Holmes* – Loch Ness Monster ****

When Dinosaurs Ruled the Earth – Dinosaurs, Pterosaurs ***

Space Amoeba a.k.a. *Yog, Monster From Space* – Giant cuttlefish *

1971 *Octaman* – Octopus-man *

1972 *Gargoyles* (TV) – Gargoyles ****

1973 *The Cat Creature* – Cat-monster *

SSSSSSS – Snake-people **

1974 *The Golden Voyage of Sinbad* – Centaur, Gryphon ****

The Land That Time Forgot – Dinosaurs **

The Bat People – Man-bat *

The Mutations – Plant-people *

1975 *Giant Spider Invasion* – Giant spider *

1976 *The Omen* – Black Dog ****

King Kong – Giant gorilla, giant snake ***

Food of the Gods – Giant chicken **

Queen Kong – Giant gorilla *

1977 *Sinbad and the Eye of the Tiger* – Cyclops, Sabertooth ****

The Hobbit (animated) – Dragon, giant spiders, Thunderbirds **

Pete's Dragon (animated/live) – Dragon **

Mighty Peking Man – Giant gorilla **

Tentacles – Giant octopus *

The Crater Lake Monster – Lake Monster *

Adele Hasn't Had Her Dinner Yet – Predator plant *

1978 *Lord of the Rings* (animated) – Giant octopus ***

The Water Babies (animated) – Merfolk **

1980 *Humanoids from the Deep* – Man-fish *

1981 *Dragonslayer* – Dragon *****

Time Bandits – Minotaur *****

Clash of the Titans – Pegasus, Kraken/Cetus, Hydra, Medusa ****

Quest for Fire – Homo erectus, Neanderthals, Mammoths, Sabertooths ****

Caveman – Dinosaurs, Pterosaurs ***

Loch Ness Horror – Loch Ness Monster *

1982 *Conan the Barbarian* – Giant Serpent *****

The Dark Crystal – Animate plants *****

Cat-People – Cat-people ***

Flight of Dragons (animated) – Dragons ***

The Boogens – Titanic turtles *

Q—The Winged Serpent – Amphitere *

1984 *The Neverending Story* – Eastern Dragon/Lung, Sphinx, giant turtle, Waheela *****

Splash! – Mermaid ****

1985 *Legend* – Unicorns *****

The Goonies – Giant Octopus (deleted scene on DVD) *****

Baby: Secret of the Lost Legend – Mokele M'bembe ****

The Giant Behemoth – Godzilla-like Dinosaur *

1986 *Little Shop of Horrors* – Predator plant ***

Frog Dreaming – Bunyip ***
King Kong Lives – Giant Gorilla *
1987 *Harry and the Hendersons* – Bigfoot ****
    Dot and the Smugglers (animated) – Bunyip **
1988 *Willow* – Hellhounds, Orm *****
    The Adventures of Baron Munchausen –
      Fastitocalon, Heroic Horse *****
    The Chronicles of Narnia: The Lion, the
      Witch and the Wardrobe (TV) – Faun ****
    High Spirits – Phooka ****
    Lair of the White Worm – Dragon/Orm ***
    Thunder of the Gigantic Serpent a.k.a. *Terror*
      Serpent – Giant serpent *
1989 *The Little Mermaid* (animated) – Mermaid,
      Seahorse ****
    Erik the Viking – Sea Serpent ***
    Godzilla vs Biollante – Godzilla, predator
      plant **
1990 *The Rescuers Down Under* (animated) –
      Thunderbird **
    Akira Kurosawa's Dreams (anime) – Kitsune
      ****
1991 *Hook* – Mermaids *****
    Cast a Deadly Spell (TV) – Great Cthulhu ****
    Ondine – Undine/Mermaid ***
1992 *The Lost World* – Dinosaurs ***
    Return to the Lost World Dinosaurs ***
    Pinocchio (animated) – Fastitocalon **
1993 *Jurassic Park* – Dinosaurs *****
    Carnosaur – Dinosaurs *
    Dinosaur Island – Dinosaurs *
1994 *The Secret of Roan Inish* – Roane/Selkie *****
    Jack the Giant Killer – Cyclops, Dragon **
    Dragonworld – Dragon ****
    Tall Tale – Babe the Blue Ox ****
    Hercules in the Maze of the Minotaur (TV) –
      Minotaur ***
    Hercules in the Underworld (TV) – Cerberus ***
    Pom Poko (anime) Tanuki **
1995 *Gargoyles the Movie: The Heroes Awaken*
      (animated-TV) – Gargoyles ****
    The Pagemaster (animated) – Dragon ***
    Carnosaur 2 – Dinosaurs **
1996 *Dragonheart* – Dragon *****
    Gensomaden Saiyuki (anime-1996) Kappa
      *****
    Aladdin and the King of Thieves (animated) –
      Zaratan ****
    Wyrd Sisters (animated-BBC-1996) World
      Turtle, Death's Pale Horse (Binky) ***
    The Beast (TV) – Giant Squid/Kraken ***
    The Hunchback of Notre Dame (animated) –
      Gargoyles ***
    The Adventures of Pinocchio – Fastitocalon ***
    Loch Ness – Loch Ness Monster **
    Carnosaur 3: Primal Species – Dinosaurs **
    Canhead – Golem *

1997 *Jurassic Park II: The Lost World* – Dinosaurs
    *****
    Princess Mononoke (animated) – Giant boar,
      giant wolf *****
    Soul Music (animated-BBC) – World Turtle,
      Death's Pale Horse (Binky) ****
    The Odyssey (TV) – Cyclops, Scylla, Charyb-
      dis ***
    Anaconda – Sucuriju Gigante ***
    Hercules (animated) – Centaur, Hydra,
      Pegasus, Satyr ***
    Anak ng Bulkan ("Child of the Volcano") –
      Pterosaur *
1998 *Mighty Joe Young* – Giant Gorilla *****
    Godzilla – Godzilla *****
    Mulan (animated) – Dragon *****
    Saiyuki: Reload (anime) – Kappa ****
    Saiyuki: Requiem (anime) – Kappa *****
    Quest for Camelot (animated) – Dragons,
      Gryphon**
    The Lost World – Dinosaurs *
1999 *Sleepy Hollow* – Demon Horse *****
    Journey to the Center of the Earth (TV) –
      Dinosaurs ****
    Saiyuki Reload: Gunlock (anime) – Kappa ****
    Lake Placid – Giant crocodile ***
    Dragon World II: The Legend Continues –
      Dragon **
    Beowulf – Grendel **
    Komodo (TV) – Megalania **
    Pokemon (anime) – Kitsune, Kappa, Tanuki *
2000 *Fantasia 2000* (animated) – Phoenix/Firebird
    *****
    Jason and the Argonauts (TV) – Centaur,
      Harpies, Dragon ****
    Dragonheart II: A New Beginning – Dragon ***
    Dungeons & Dragons – Dragons **
    Crocodile – Giant crocodile **
    Blood Surf a.k.a. *Krocodylus* – Giant
      crocodile *
    Python – Giant serpent **
    Spiders (2000) Giant spiders **
    Octopus – Giant octopus *
2001 *Lord of the Rings: Fellowship of the Ring* –
      Giant octopus/Kraken, Thunderbird *****
    Harry Potter & The Sorcerer's Stone –
      Cerberus, Dragon, Centaur *****
    The Lost World (BBC TV) – Dinosaurs *****
    Spirited Away (anime) – Eastern Dragon,
      Kappa *****
    Shrek (animated) – Dragon *****
    Jurassic Park III – Dinosaurs ****
    Brotherhood of the Wolf – Beast of Gévaudan
    ****
    Atlantis: The Lost Empire (animated) –
      Kraken ****
    Inuyasha (anime) – Kitsune/Tanuki ****

She Creature – Mermaid ***
The Little Unicorn – Unicorn ***
Beneath Loch Ness – Loch Ness Monster **
Raptor – Dinosaurs **
Arachnid – Giant spider *
Wendigo – Wendigo *

2002 *Lord of the Rings: The Two Towers* – Wyverns,
　　　Ents, Waheela/Warg, Heroic Horse *****
　　Harry Potter & the Chamber of Secrets –
　　　Basilisk, Phoenix, Giant spiders, Man-
　　　drakes, animate tree *****
　　Dinotopia (TV) – Dinosaurs *****
　　Reign of Fire – Dragons ****
　　Eight Legged Freaks – Giant spiders ****
　　Hound of the Baskervilles – Cu Sith/Black
　　　Dog ***
　　13ᵗʰ Child: Legend of the Jersey Devil –
　　　Jersey Devil **
　　The Mothman Prophecies – Mothman **
　　Sabertooth (TV) – Sabertooth **
　　Boa a.k.a. *New Alcatraz* – Giant serpent **
　　Octopus 2: River of Fear – Giant octopus *
　　Python II (TV) – Giant serpent *

2003 *Lord of the Rings: Return of the King* – Ents,
　　　Wyverns, Giant spider, Thunderbirds,
　　　Heroic Horse *****
　　Peter Pan – Mermaids *****
　　Aquanoids – Mermaids *
　　El Chupacabra – Chupacabra *

2004 *Harry Potter & the Prisoner of Azkaban* –
　　　Hippogriff, animate Tree, Black Dog *****
　　Shrek II (animated) – Dragon *****
　　Sky Captain and the World of Tomorrow –
　　　Phorusrhacos *****
　　Naruto (anime) – Kitsune/Tanuki ****
　　Dragon Storm (TV) – Dragons ***
　　Gargoyle: Wings of Darkness – Gargoyle ***
　　George and the Dragon (TV) – Dragon ***
　　Earthsea (TV) – Dragon ***
　　Anacondas: The Hunt for the Blood Orchid –
　　　Sucuriju Gigante **
　　Incident at Loch Ness – Loch Ness Monster **
　　Raptor Island – Dinosaurs *
　　Boa vs. Python (TV) – Giant serpents *

2005 *Chronicles of Narnia: The Lion, the Witch and
　　　the Wardrobe* – Faun, Centaur, Phoenix,
　　　Minotaur, Unicorn, Goatman... *****
　　Harry Potter & the Goblet of Fire – Dragons,
　　　Merfolk *****
　　King Kong – Giant gorilla, Dinosaurs *****
　　Dragon's World: A Fantasy Made Real (TV)
　　　– Dragons ****
　　Mirrormask – Sphinx and winged cats ****
　　Hercules (TV) – Hydra, Centaur ****
　　*Dungeons & Dragons II: Wrath of the
　　　Dragongod* – Dragons ***
　　Mee-Shee: The Water Giant – Lake Monster ***

Princess Raccoon (anime) – Tanuki ***
The Great Youkai War (anime) – Tengu ***
Attack of the Sabertooth (TV) – Sabertooth **
The Cave – Subterranean Wyverns **
Pterodactyl (TV) – Pterosaurs **
King of the Lost World – Giant Spiders, man-
　　eating vines, Dragons, giant gorilla **
Chupacabra AKA *Mexican Werewolf* –
　　Chupacabra *
Chupacabra Terror (TV) – Chupacabra **
The Snake King (or *SnakeMan*) (TV) –
　　Snake-people, Sucuriju Gigante **

2006 *Pirates of the Caribbean 2: Dead Man's
　　　Chest* – Kraken, Cthulhu *****
　　Hogfather (BBC-2006) World Turtle, Death's
　　　Pale Horse (*Binky*) *****
　　Lady in the Water – Undine/Niad (*Narf*), La
　　　Velue (*Scrunt*) ****
　　Aquamarine – Mermaid ***
　　Basilisk, the Serpent King (TV) – Basilisk ***
　　Abominable – Yeti ***
　　Tenacious D in the Pick of Destiny – Sasquatch
　　　***
　　Kraken: Tentacles of the Deep (TV) – Kraken **
　　Hellboy: Sword of Storms (anime) – Kappa,
　　　Kitsune **
　　Minotaur – Minotaur **

2007 *Eragon* – Dragon *****
　　Harry Potter & the Order of the Phoenix –
　　　Spectral horses (*Thestrals*), Centaurs *****
　　Stardust – Unicorn *****
　　Pan's Labyrinth – Faun/Satyr, Mandragore ****
　　Shrek the 3ʳᵈ (animated) – Dragon ***
　　The Water Horse: Legend of the Deep – Lake
　　　monster ****
　　Beowulf – Dragon, Grendel ****
　　Lake Placid 2 (TV) – Giant crocodile ***
　　Final Fantasy: Advent's Children – Cait Sith ***
　　Stan Lee's Harpies (TV) – Harpies ***
　　Gryphon (TV) – Gryphon **
　　Reign of the Gargoyles (TV) – Gargoyles **
　　Ice Spiders (TV) – Giant spiders **

2008 *The Spiderwick Chronicles* *****
　　Harry Potter and the Half-Blood Prince *****
　　The Power of the Dark Crystal *****
　　Jurassic Park IV – Dinosaurs ****

Monster Movies--Resources:

An excellent movie monstropedia:
　　www.monstrous.com/Joomla/
Godzilla "co-monster" cross-reference chart: www.
　　lavasurfer.com/godzilla/topher-zilla-names.html
Pictures of dozens of Japanese creatures: www.
　　giantmonstermovies.com/monster-index.html
Delahoyde, Michael, "Dinosaur Films," The Dino-
　　Source, www.wsu.edu/~delahoyd/
　　dinosource.html (2007)

Appendix F. Bibliography
Resources & References for This Book

1. Akins, William, *The Loch Ness Monster,* Signet Books, New American Library, New York, 1977
2. *All the World's Animals: Sea Mammals,* Torstar Books; New York-Toronto, 1984
3. Allen, Judy, *Fantasy Encyclopedia,* Kingfisher; Chertsey, Surrey, England, 2005
4. Allen, Judy & Griffiths, Jeanne, *Book of the Dragon,* Orbis Books; Maryknoll, NY, 1979
5. Allen, Tony & Phillips, Charles, *Land of the Dragon: Chinese Myth,* Time-Life Books, 1999
6. Alley, J. Robert, *Raincoast Sasquatch,* Hancock House; Blaine, WA, 2003
7. *American Monsters,* http://www.american monsters.com/monsters.html (2007)
8. "Ancient Bedouin Legend," www.beliefnet.com
9. Anderson, J.K., *Unicorns,* Bellerophon Books; Santa Barbara, CA, 1981
10. Ashman, Malcolm, *Fabulous Beasts,* Funimation; Fort Worth, TX, 2005
11. Ashton, John, *Curious Creatures in Zoology,* John C. Nimmo; London, 1890
12. Baldwin, Neil, *Legends of the Plumed Serpent,* Public Affairs, 1998
13. Ball, Valentine, "On the Identification of the Pygmies, the Martikhora, the Griffin, and the Dikarion of Ktesias," *The Academy* (London), vol. 23, no. 572, April 1883
14. Barber, Dulan, *Monsters Who's Who,* Crescent Books; Avenel, NJ, 1974
15. Barber, Richard, & Riches, Anne, *A Dictionary of Fabulous Beasts,* Macmillan; New York, 1971
16. Barlow, W.D., *Barlow's Guide to Fantasy,* HarperPrism; New York, 1996.
17. Bateman, Graham, proj. ed., *All the World's Animals* (series), Torstar Books, 1984
18. Bayanov, Dmitri, "Why Cryptozoology?" *Cryptozoology,* 6:1-7, 1987
19. Beisner, Monika, & Lurie, Alison, *Fabulous Beasts,* Jonathan Cape; London, 1981
20. Berridge, W.S., *Marvels of the Animal World,* Thornton Butterworth, London, 1921
21. Bille, Matthew A., *Rumors of Existence,* Hancock House; Blaine, WA, 1995
22. Boatright, Mody C., *Tall Tales from Texas Cow Camps,* The Southwest Press; Dallas, TX, 1934
23. Boese, Alex, *The Museum of Hoaxes,* Dutton, Penguin Group; New York, 2002
24. Bord, Janet & Colin, *Alien Animals,* Stackpole Books, Harrisburg, PA, 1981
25. ——, *Bigfoot Casebook,* Paul Elek, London, 1980
26. Boreman, Thomas, *A Description of Three Hundred Animals* (1786; facsimile), Johnson Reprint, 1968
27. Borges, Jorge Luis, *The Book of Imaginary Beings,* 1957; 1967 (Penguin Books, London, 1974)
28. Botkin, B.A., *A Treasury of American Folklore: Stories, Ballads, and Traditions of the People,* Crown Publishers; New York, 1944
29. Bourtsev, Igor, "A Skeleton Still Buried and a Skull Unearthed: The Story of Zana," Bayanov, Dmitri, *In the Footsteps of the Russian Snowman,* Crypto-Logos, Moscow, 1996. pp. 46-52
30. *Britannica Book of the Year,* Encyclopedia Britannica, Inc; London, 1982
31. Buel, James William, *Sea and Land,* Historical Publishing Co; St Louis, MO, 1887
32. Bulfinch, Thomas, *Bulfinch's Mythology,* Gramercy Books, 1979
33. "Bunyips," http://www.nla.gov.au/exhibitions/ bunyips/html-site/index-html.html
34. Burroughs, Edgar Rice, *Tarzan the Terrible,* A.C. McClurg; Chicago, IL, 1921
35. Burton, Maurice, *Animal Legends,* Coward-McCann; New *born,* Hutchinson; London, 1959
36. Byfield, Barbara Ninde, *The Glass Harmonica: A Lexicon of the Fantastical,* Macmillan; New York, 1967
37. Byrne, Peter, *The Search for Bigfoot: Monster, Man, or Myth?,* Acropolis Books, New York, 1975
38. "Cabbits," http://www.lairweb.org.nz/tiger/ cabbits3.html (2007)
39. "Cat Grows Wings," *Ananova,* www.ananova.com, May 25, 2007
40. "The Cattle Raid of Regamna—from the Yellow Book of Lecan," *Heroic Romances of Ireland* Vol. II, ed. trans. A.H. Leahy, London, 1906
41. Caxton, William, *Caxton's Mirrour of the World,* ed. Oliver H. Prior, Early English Text Society, Oxford, England, 1913
42. Champagne, Bruce, "A Preliminary Evaluation of a Study of the Morphology, Behavior, Autoecology, and Habitat of Large, Unidentified Marine Animals, Based on Recorded Field Observations," *Strangeark,* http://strangeark.com/crypto/ dracontology.pdf pp. 99-118 (2007)
43. Chan, Chih-Yi & Plato, *Good Luck Horse,* McGraw Hill; Columbus, OH, 1943
44. Childress, David Hatcher, "Living Pterodactyls," *World Explorer,* vol. 1, no. 4, 1994
45. Chorvinsky, Mark, "Globsters!" www.strangemag.com/globhome.html (2007)
46. Christie, Anthony, *Chinese Mythology,* Hamlyn Publishing Group Ltd.; Middlesex, England, 1968
47. Clarke, Arthur C., *The Ghost from the Grand Banks,* Victor Gollancz Ltd., London 1990
48. Clark, Leonard, *The Rivers Ran East: Travelers'*

Tales Classics, Harpercollins; New York, 1953

49. Cohen, Daniel, *A Natural History of Unnatural Things,* McCall Publishing; New York, 1971

50. ——, *Encyclopedia of Monsters,* Dodd, Mead & Co.; New York, 1982

51. Coleman, Loren, *Field Guide to Lake Monsters, Sea Serpents, and Other Mystery Denizens of the Deep,* Jeremy Tarcher; Beverly Hills, CA, 2003

52. ——, *Mothman & Other Curious Encounters,* Paraview Press, 3rd Ed. 2002

53. ——, *Mysterious America,* Paraview Press, New York, Revised Ed. 2001

54. Coleman, Loren, & Clark, Jerome, *Cryptozoology A to Z: The Encyclopedia of Loch Monsters, Sasquatch, Chupacabras, and Other Authentic Mysteries of Nature,* Fireside; New York, 1999

55. Coleman, Loren, & Huyghe, Patrick, *The Field Guide to Bigfoot and Other Mystery Primates,* Anomalist Books; San Antonio, TX, 2006

56. ——, "King Kong's playmate: Kongamato," Cryptomundo.com, http://www.cryptomundo.com (2007)

57. Comes, Natalis, *Mythologia,* Paris, 1551

58. Conway, D.J., *Magickal Mermaids and Water Creatures,* New Page Books; Franklin Lakes, NJ, 2005

59. Cooper, J.C., *Symbolic and Mythological Animals,* Aquarian Press; Kent, UK, 1992

60. Corliss, Richard, *Strange Life,* Sourcebook Project; Glen Arm, MD, 1976

61. Costello, Peter, *In Search of Lake Monsters,* Berkeley Medallion, New York, 1974

62. ——, *The Magic Zoo: The Natural History of Fabulous Animals,* St Martin's Press, London, 1979

63. Ctesias, Indica. *From Ancient India as Described by Ktesias the Knidian,* ed. J.W. McCrindle (1882; rpt., Delhi, India, Manohar Reprints, 1973).

64. Courlander, Harold, *Treasury of African Folklore,* Crown Publishing; New York, 1975

65. Cox, William T., *Fearsome Creatures of the Lumberwoods, With a Few Desert and Mountain Beasts,* Judd & Detweiler, 1910

66. Cryptozoology.com, http://www.cryptozoology.com (2007)

67. Curran, Bob, *Creatures of Celtic Myth,* Sterling Publishing Co., 2000

68. Cuvier, Georges, "Excursus IV" in Pliny: *Historia Naturae,* Paris, 1827

69. D'Amato, Peter, *The Savage Garden: Cultivating Carnivorous Plants,* Ten Speed Press; Berkeley, CA, 1998

70. Dance, Peter S., *Animal Fakes & Frauds,* Sampson Low; London, 1976

71. Davidson, Levette Jay & Forrester Blake (eds.), *Rocky Mountain Tales,* University of Oklahoma Press, 1947

72. Davis, F. Hadland, *Myths and Legends of Japan,* General Publishing Co. Ltd.; Toronto, 1992

73. De Camp, L. Sprague, *H.P Lovecraft: A Biography,* Ballantine Books; New York, 1976

74. Delahoyde, Michael, "Dinosaur Films," The Dino-Source, http://www.wsu.edu/~delahoyd/dinosource.html (2007)

75. De Gubernatis, Angelo, *Zoological Mythology or The Legends of Animals,* Vol. I, Trubner & Co., London 1872

76. DeKirk, Ash "LeopardDancer," *DragonLore—From the Archives of the Grey School of Wizardry,* New Page Books, 2006

77. Dinsdale, Tim, *The Story of the Loch Ness Monster,* Allan Wingate Ltd. & Universal-Tandem Pub. Co., Boston, 1973

78. Dove, Franklin, "Artificial Production of the Fabulous Unicorn," *Scientific Monthly,* Vol. 42, May 1936

79. Dove, Franklin, "The Physiology of Horn Growth," Journal of Experimental Zoology, Vol. 69, No. 3, 1935

80. Doyle, Sir Arthur Conan, "The Brazilian Cat," *Tales of Terror & Mystery,* 1922; Classic Literature Library, www.classic-literature.co.uk (2007)

81. ——, *The Lost World,* Hodder & Stoughton, London, 1912

82. Eaton, Matthew J., "The Bunyip: Mythical Beast, Modern-day Monster," http://www.cryptozoology.com/cryptids/bunyip.php (2007)

83. Egede, Hans, *A Description of Greenland,* London, 1745

84. Eggleton, Bob & Suckling, Nigel, *The Book of Sea Monsters,* Overlook Press; New York, 1998

85. Eggleton, Bob, *Book of the Sea-Serpent,* Overlook Press, 1998

86. Ellis, S. E., *A History of Greta,* Lowden Publishing, Kilmore, Victoria, 1972

87. Ellis, Richard, *The Search for the Giant Squid,* The Lyons Press; New York, 1998

88. ——, *Monsters of the Sea,* Knopf, New York, 1994

89. Estes, Clarissa Pinkola, "For your soul: Go out, look up, there is an ancient woman in the sky tonight" *The Moderate Voice* magazine (date not given)

90. "Fearsome Critters," Wikipedia, the free encyclopedia, http://en.wikipedia.org/wiki/Fearsome_critters (2007)

91. Firdausi, *The Shanamah,* trans. Alexander Rogers, Sang-E-Meel, 2002

92. Fleming, Carrol B. "Maidens of the Sea Can be Alluring, But Sailor, Beware," *Smithsonian,* June, 1983, 86-95

93. Franklin, Julian, *Heraldry,* A.S. Barnes & Co.; New York, 1968

94. Frey, Eberhard; Sues, Hans-Dieter; Munk, Wolfgang, "Gliding Mechanism in the Late Permian Reptile Coelurosauravus," *Science* 7,

March 1997: Vol. 275. no. 5305;. 1450-1452

95. "Gallery of Tall-Tale Creatures," The Museum of Hoaxes, www.museumofhoaxes.com/hoax/animals/P20/ (2007)

96. Garner, Betty Sanders, *Monster! Monster! A Survey of the North American Monster Scene,* Hancock House; Blaine, WA, 1995

97. Gesner, Konrad, *Gesner's Curious and Fantastic Beasts,* Dover Pictorial Archives; New York, 2004

98. Giblin, James Cross, *The Truth About Unicorns,* HarperCollins; New York, 1991

99. Giuliani, Bob, *Ready-to-Use Dinosaurs and Prehistoric Mammals Illustrations,* Dover, New York, 1995

100. Glut, Donald F., *The Dinosaur Scrapbook,* The Citadel Press; Secaucus, NJ, 1980

101. Gordon, David George, "The Search for the $50,000 Snake," Encarta, http://encarta.msn.com/encnet/features/columns/?article=sciencesnakes (2007)

102. Gosse, Philip Henry, *The Romance of Natural History,* Gould & Lincoln; Boston, 1861

103. Gould, Charles, *Mythical Monsters,* Allen & Co.,1886; Kessinger Reprints, Whitefish, MT

104. Gould, Rupert T., *The Loch Ness Monster,* Geoffrey Bles, London, 1934

105. Gould, Stephen Jay, *Wonderful Life: The Burgess Shale and the Nature of History,* W.W. Norton & Co.; New York, 1989

106. Grant, M. and J. Hazel, *Who's Who in Greek Mythology,* David McKay & Co. Inc, 1979

107. Green, Michael, *De Historia et Veritate Unicornis—On the History and Truth of the Unicorn,* Running Press; Philadelphia, 1983

108. Greer, John Michael, *Monsters: An Investigator's Guide to Magical Beings,* Llewellyn Publications; St Paul, MN, 2001

109. *The Gryphon Pages,* http://www.gryphonpages.com/index.html (2007)

110. Davis, F. Hadland, *Myths and Legends of Japan,* General Publishing Co., Ltd., 1992

111. Hall, Mark A., "The Mystery Of The Thunderbird," Fortean Times, 9/10/00, http://www.rense.com/general3/thun.htm (2007)

112. ——, Thunderbirds! America's Living Legends of Giant Birds, Paraview Press, 2004

113. Hardy, Alister, "Was Man More Aquatic in the Past?" *New Scientist,* Vol. 7, 1960, 642-5

114. Hargreaves, Joyce, *Hargreaves New Illustrated Bestiary,* Gothic Images Publications, Glastonbury, UK, 1990

115. Hartwell, Sarah, "Winged Cats—What Are They?" http://www.messybeast.com/winged-cats.htm, 2001 – 2007

116. "Has a Mythical Beast Turned Up in Texas?" Weird News, AP Cuero, TX, Sept. 1, 2007

117. Hathaway, Nancy, *The Unicorn,* Viking, 1980

118. Hausman, Gerald & Loretta, *The Mythology of Horses,* Three Rivers Press; New York, 2003

119. Hawkes, Jacquetta, & Woolley, Leonard, *Prehistory and the Beginnings of Civilization,* v. 1, Harper & Row; New York, 1963

120. Headon, Deirdre, *Mythical Beasts,* The Leprechaun Library, G.P. Putnam's Sons; New York, 1981

121. Heuvelmans, Bernard, *In the Wake of the Sea Serpents,* Hill & Wang, New York, 1968

122. ——, *On the Track of Unknown Animals,* Librairie Plon, 1955 (MIT Press, 1972)

123. Hill, Douglas, & Williams, Pat, *The Supernatural,* Pub Overstock Unlimited Inc., 1989

124. "Hippoi Athanatoi," www.theoi.com (2007)

125. Hitching, Francis, *The Mysterious World: An Atlas of the Unexplained,* Holt, Rinehart & Winston; Austin, TX, 1978

126. Hocking, Peter J., "Large Peruvian Mammals Unknown to Zoology," *Cryptozoology,* 11:38-50 (1992)

127. Hogarth, Peter, & Clery, Val, *Dragons,* The Viking Press; New York, 1979

128. Holiday, F.W., *The Dragon and the Disk,* Sidgwick & Jackson, London, 1973

129. ——, *The Goblin Universe,* Llewellyn Publications, St. Paul, MN 1986

130. ——, *The Great Orm of Loch Ness,* Faber & Faber, New York, 1968

131. Homer (Robert Fitzgerald trans.), The Odyssey, Doubleday, 1963

132. Howey, M. Oldfield, *The Horse in Magic and Myth* (orig.1923) W. Rider, London. Dover Press reprint, 2002

133. Huber, Richard, *Treasury of Fantastic & Mythological Creatures,* Dover Pictorial Archives, 1981

134. Hunt, Jonathan, *Bestiary: An Illuminated Alphabet of Medieval Beasts* (1st ed.), Simon & Schuster; New York, 1998

135. Hutchinson, H.N., *Extinct Monsters and Creatures of Other Days,* Chapman & Hall, Ltd., London, 1910

136. Huxley, Francis, *The Dragon: Nature of Spirit and Spirit of Nature,* Collier Books, MacMillan Publishing Co.; New York, 1979

137. Illinois State Geological Survey, "Illinois' State Fossil—Tullimonstrum gregarium," Geobit 5, http://www.isgs.uiuc.edu/servs/pubs/geobits-pub/geobit5/geobit5.html (2007)

138. Ingersoll, Ernst, *Dragons and Dragonlore,* Payson & Clark; New York, 1928

139. "Japanese Researchers Capture Giant Squid," *Fox News,* Dec. 22, 2006, http://www.foxnews.com/story/0,2933,238263,00.html (2007)

140. Johnsgard, Paul & Karen, *Dragons and Unicorns: A Natural History,* St. Martin's

Press; New York, 1982

141. Jones, David, *An Instinct for Dragons,* Routledge, 2002

142. Jones, Frederick Woods, *Man's Place Among the Mammals,* Edward Arnold, 1929

143. Juliano, Dave, "The Jersey Devil," *The Shadowlands,* http://theshadowlands.net/creature.htm (2006)

144. Keel, John A., *The Complete Guide to Mysterious Beings,* Doubleday; New York, 1970; 1994

145. ——, *The Mothman Prophecies,* Saturday Review Press; New York, 1975

146. ——, *Strange Creatures from Time and Space,* Fawcett; Greenwich, CT, 1970

147. Kuhn, Eskin, "Eskin Kuhn's Excellent Adventure," *About Paranormal Phenomena,* http://paranormal.about.com (2007)

148. Landsburg, Alan, *In Search Of...,* Nelson Doubleday Inc.; New York, 1978

149. Lankester, Ray, *Diversions of a Naturalist,* London, 1915

150. Leach, Maria (ed.), *Funk & Wagnall's Standard Dictionary of Folklore, Mythology and Legend,* Harper & Row, 1972

151. Le Blanc, Vincent, *Les Voyages fameux du Sieur Vincent le Blanc,* Paris, 1648

152. LeGuin, Ursula K., *Catwings,* Scholastic, 2003

153. Lehner, Ernst & Johanna, *Big Book of Dragons, Monsters, and Other Mythical Creatures,* Dover Pictorial Archives, 2004

154. ——, *A Fantastic Beastiary,* Tudor Publishing, New York, 1969

155. L'Epine, Ernest, *Croquemitaine* II. 9, trans. Thomas Hood, London, 1867

156. Leroy, P., Le Dahu, perso.orange.fr/.../pages/dahu.htm (2007)

157. LeVaillant, François, *Travels in Africa,* GG & J. Robinson, London, 1796

158. Ley, Willy, *Exotic Zoology,* Viking Press, 1941; 1959

159. ——, *Salamanders and Other Wonders.* Viking Press, 1955

160. Lilly, Ray, "New Zealand Fishermen Catch Rare Squid," *Associated Press,* 2/22/07

161. Long, Gareth, *The Encyclopedia of Monsters, Mythical Creatures and Fabulous Beasts,* http://webhome.idirect.com/~donlong/monsters/monsters.htm (2007)

162. *Lost World Museum,* http://www.lostworldmuseum.com (2007)

163. Lovecraft, Howard Phillip, *The Best of H.P. Lovecraft,* Del Rey Books; New York, 1987

164. ——, "The Call of Cthulhu," *The Dunwich Horror and Others,* Lancer Books, 1963

165. Lum, Peter, *Fabulous Beasts,* Thames & Hudson; London, 1952

166. *Lycos Excyclopedia: Oceania Index.* http://versaware.animalszone.lycos.com/continents/oceania.asp (2007)

167. MacDougall, Curtis D., *Hoaxes,* Dover Publications, Inc., 1958

168. Mackal, Roy, *A Living Dinosaur? In Search of Mokele-Mbembe,* E.J. Brill Academic Pubs.; Leiden, Netherlands, 1987

169. ——, *Searching for Hidden Animals,* Doubleday, 1980

170. ——, The *Monsters of Loch Ness,* Swallow, Chicago, 1976

171. Mackenzie, Donald, *Myths of China and Japan,* Gramercy Books; New York, 1994

172. Magnus, Olaus, *Historia de Gentibus Septentrionalibus,* Antwerp, 1555

173. Maple, Eric, "Mermaids and Mermen," *Encyclopedia of Man, Myth & Magic,* Marshall Cavendish Corp.; New York, 1970

174. Matthews, John & Caitlin, *The Element Encyclopedia of Magical Creatures,* Harper Element, Harper Collins, 2005

175. McAdams, William, "The Bird which Devours Men," *Records of Ancient Races in the Mississippi Valley,* C.R. Barnes; Cambridge, UK, 1887

176. McCormick, Cameron, "Octopus Giganteus," *Cameron's Cryptozoology Page,* http://www.geocities.com/capedrevenger/giantoctopus.html (2007)

177. ——, "The Sea Serpent Complex," Cameron's Cryptozoology Page, http://www.geocities.com/capedrevenger/seaserpentcomplex1.html (2007)

178. McCrindle, J.W. ed., *Ancient India as Described by Ktesias the Knidian* (1882 reprint), Manohar Reprints, Delhi, India 1973

179. McGowan, Christopher, *Dinosaurs, Spitfires and Sea Serpents,* Harvard University Press, 1983

180. Meehan, Aidan, *Celtic Design: The Dragon and the Griffen.* Thames and Hudson, 1995

181. *The Medieval Bestiary: Animals in the Middle Ages,* http://bestiary.ca/index.html (2007)

182. Melillo, Elizabeth, *Medieval Bestiary,* http://www.geocities.com/Paris/3963/bestiary.html (2003)

183. Mellon, Frank H., *In Witchbound Africa,* Seeley, Service & Co.; London, 1923

184. Merian, Matthäus, *1300 Real and Fanciful Animals,* ed. by Carol Belanger Grafton, Dover Pictorial Archives, 1998

185. Mitchell, John & Rickard, Robert J.M., *Living Wonders: Mysteries & Curiosities of the Animal World,* Thames & Hudson, 1982

186. Mode, Heinz, *Fabulous Beasts and Demons,* Phaidon Press; London, 1973

187. Morgan, Elaine, *The Descent of Woman,* Stein & Day Publishers; New York, 1972

188. Morgan, John, *Life and Adventures of William Buckley,* 1852

189. Morphy, Robert T., "Mermaids & Mermen," American Monsters.com (2007)

190. "Mysterious Creatures & Cryptozoology," *The Shadowlands*, http://theshadowlands.net/creature.htm (2006)

191. Nigg, Joseph, *The Book of Dragons & Other Mythical Beasts*, Barrons Educational Series; New York, 2002

192. ——, *The Book of Fabulous Beasts: A Treasury of Writings from Ancient Times to the Present*, Oxford University Press, 1999

193. ——, *Book of Gryphons*, Apple-Wood Books; Carlisle, MA, 1982

194. ——, *A Guide to the Imaginary Birds of the World*, Apple-Wood Books, 1984

195. ——, *Wonder Beasts: Tales and Lore of the Phoenix, the Griffin, the Unicorn and the Dragon*, Libraries Unlimited, 1995

196. Noble, Marty, & Gottesman, Eric, *Dragons and Wizards*, Dover Publications, 2003

197. Norman. Scott T., "Mokele-mbembe: The Living Dinosaur," 1996-2003: www.mokelembembe.com/

198. Noonuccal, Ooderoo, *Stradbroke Dreamtime*, Pymble, Angus and Robertson, Australia, 1993

199. O'Meara, John (trans.), *The Voyage of St. Brendan: Journey to the Promised Land*, Humanities Press, 1976

200. Oppian, "Cynegetica" www.theoi.com (2007)

201. O'Shea, Steve, "Giant Squid and Colossal Squid Fact Sheet," www.Tonmo.com (2007)

202. O'Shea, Steve, "Unknown Phylum," TONMO.com: The Octopus News Magazine Online, www.tonmo.com/forums/showthread.php?t=9379&highlight=unknown+phylum (2007)

203. "The Origin of the Bunyip," www.drizabone.com.au/legends/bunyip.html (2007)

204. Osborn, Chase Salmon, *Madagascar: Land of the Man-Eating Tree*, Republic Publishing Co.; Beresford SD, 1924

205. Owen, Richard, "Report on British Fossil Reptiles," *Part II. Report of the British Association for the Advancement of Science*, Plymouth, England, 1842

206. Oudemans, Antoon Cornelis, *The Great Sea Serpent*, Luzac & Co., London, 1892

207. "The Piasa Bird," *The IBEX Archive*, www.eslarp.uiuc.edu/ibex/archive/vignettes/piasa.htm (2007)

208. Paré, Ambrose, *On Monsters and Marvels*, (trans. Thomas Johnson, 1634) (Milford House, 1968)

209. Passes, David, *Dragons: Truth, Myth and Legend*, Western Publishing; Racine, WI, 1993

210. Perkins, S., "Winged Dragon," *Science News*, June 23, 2007

211. Philostratus, *The Life of Apollonius of Tyana*, trans.

F.G. Conybeare, Harvard University Press, 1960

212. Piccolo, Anthony, "Women of the Deep: A Light History of the Mermaid," *Sea History* 68, Winter 1993-4

213. Pinti, Tipi, "The Tale of the Wind Horse," *The Bishinik of the Choctaw Nation* (date not given)

214. Pliny the Elder (Caius Plinius Secundus), *Natural history*, Book 8, "Holy Cows."

215. Plutarch, Life of Pericles, vii, written 75 CE. Translated by John Dryden, *Internet Classics Archives*, http://classics.mit.edu/Plutarch/pericles.html, 2006.

216. Poignant, Roslyn, *Oceanic Mythology*, Paul Hamlyn; London, UK, 1967

217. Poltarnees, Welleran, *A Book of Unicorns*, Green Tiger Press; San Diego, CA, 1978

218. Pontopiddian, Erik, *The Natural History of Norway*. London, 1755

219. Pride, Marilyn, *Australian Dinosaurs*, Angus & Robertson; Sydney, Australia, 1988

220. Pries, Byron, Betancourt, J., & DeCandido, K., *The Ultimate Dragon*, Dell, 1995

221. Propertius, Sextus, *The Poems of Sextus Propertius*. trans. A.E. Watts, Centaur Press; Westminster, MD, 1961

222. Rabelais, François, *The Five Books of Gargantua and Pantagruel*, trans. Jacques Le Clercq, Modern Library, 1936

223. Reeves, William, ed., *Life of Saint Columba, Founder of Hy. by Adamnan, Ninth Abbot of that Monastery*, Edmonston and Douglas, Edinburgh, 1874

224. "The Riddles of Gestumblindi" from *The Saga of Hervor and King Heidrik the Wise*, trans. Peter Tunstall (2005)

225. *The Rig Vedas*, trans. R.T. Griffith, London, 1896

226. Roach, John. "Elusive African Apes: Giant Chimps or New Species?" *National Geographic News* (2003-04-14)

227. Robbins, Tom, "Superfly: The Toadstool That Conquered the Universe," *High Times*, Dec. 12, 1976

228. Rose, Carol, *Giants, Monsters, and Dragons*, W.W. Norton & Company; New York, 2000

229. Sagan, Carl, *The Dragons of Eden*, Random House, 1977

230. Sanderson, Ivan, *Abominable Snowman: Legend Come to Life*, Chilton; Philadelphia, 1961

231. ——, *Investigating the Unexplained: A Compendium of Disquieting Mysteries of the Natural World*, Prentice-Hall, 1972

232. Santillana, Giorgio De, *Hamlet's Mill*, Harvard University Press, 1969

233. *Sea Slug Forum*, http://www.seaslugforum.net/ (2007)

234. Shackley, Myra, *Still Living? Yeti, Sasquatch and the Neanderthal Enigma*, Thames & Hudson, 1983

235. *The Shadowlands,* www.theshadowlands.net/creature.htm (2007)

236. Shepard, Odell, *The Lore of the Unicorn,* 1930 (Harper Colophon edition; New York, 1970)

237. Shuker, Karl P.N., *The Beasts That Hide from Man: Seeking the World's Last Undiscovered Animals,* Paraview Press, 2003

238. ——, "Flights of Fantasy?" *All About Cats,* 4 (March-April 1997)

239. ——, *In Search of Prehistoric Survivors,* Blanford Press, London, 1994

240. ——, *Mystery Cats of the World,* Robert Hale; London, 1989

241. ——, *The Unexplained: An Illustrated Guide to the World's Natural and Paranormal Mysteries,* Carlton; London, 1996

242. Shuker, Karl P.N., "Wonderful Things are Cats with Wings," *Fate,* 49 (April 1996)

243. Silverberg, Barbara, *Phoenix Feathers: A Collection of Mythical Monsters,* E.P. Dutton & Co.; Boston, 1973

244. *Skeptic's Dictionary,* http://www.dcn.davis.ca.us/~btcarrol/skeptic/bunyips.html (2007)

245. Slessarev, Vsevolod, *Prester John: The Letter and the Legend,* University of Minnesota Press, 1959

246. Smith, Gordon, "The Case of the Reclusive Ri," *Science,* Feb. 1985

247. South, Malcolm (Ed.), *Mythical and Fabulous Beasts: A Source Book and Research Guide,* Greenwood Press; New York, 1987

248. *Story of the Trojan War: An Epitome,* Classic Writers trans. Anonymous, James Blackwood and Co.; London, 1874

249. *StrangeArk.com,* www.strangeark.com/checklist/guide.html (2007)

250. Strasenburgh, Gordon, "The Crested Australopithecus Robustus and the Patterson Film," 1979, http://www.bigfootencounters.com/biology/strasenburgh.htm (2007)

251. Strieber, Whitley, & Barry, Jonathan, *Cat Magic,* Tor Books; New York. Reprint edition, 1987

252. Sucik, Nick, "Hawaii's Giant Octopuses," www.strangeark.com/nabr/NABR.pdf (2007)

253. Suhr, Elmer G., *The Mask, the Unicorn, and the Messiah: a Study in Solar Eclipse Symbolism,* Helios Books; New York, 1970

254. Taylor, Troy, "The Legend of the Piasa Bird," 1999, *Ghosts of the Prairie: Haunted Illinois,* http://www.prairieghosts.com/piasa.html (2007)

255. Tennyson, Alfred Lord, *The Poetical Works of Alfred Tennyson,* Poet Laureate, etc. Complete in one Volume. University of Michigan Library, 2005

256. Thoreau, Henry David, *Walden,* Ticknor & Fields, Boston, 1854

257. Time-Life Books, Editors of, *Mysterious Creatures,* Time-Life Books; New York, 1988

258. "To Catch a Dragon: The Burden Expedition to remote and dangerous Komodo Island," *Virtual Exploration Society,* http://www.unmuseum.org/burden.htm (2007)

259. Topsell, Edward, *The Historie of Foure-Footed Beastes,* 1607 (Houghton Library, Harvard University)

260. Tryon, Henry Harrington, *Fearsome Critters,* Idlewild Press; Cleveland, OH, 1939

261. Unexplained Mysteries, www.Unexplained-Mysteries.com (2006)

262. *Unexplained Phenomena Calendar,* Accord Publishing, Denver, 2003

263. "Unicorns: The Complete Story of Unicorns through the Ages," http://www.unicorncollector.com/legends.htm, 2006

264. Van der Toorn, Jaap, *Jaap's Marine Mammal Pages,* http://ourworld.compuserve.com/homepages/jaap/leopseal.htm (2007)

265. Van Patter, Bruce, *Mythical American Animals,* www.brucevanpatter.com/mythanimals.html (2007)

266. Vartoman, Lewis, *The Navigations and Voyages of Lewes Vertomannus,* translated out of Latine into Englyshe by Richard Eden, London, 1576.

267. Wagner, Roy, "The Ri—Unidentified Aquatic Animals of New Ireland, Paupa New Guinea," *Cryptozoology,* International Society of Cryptozoology, 1, 1982, 33-39

268. Wagner, Roy; Greenwell, J.; Raymond, Gale; Von Nieda, Kurt, "Further Investigations into the Biological and Cultural Affinities of the Ri," *Cryptozoology,* 2, 1983, 113-125

269. Wagner, Stephen, "Did Pterosaurs Survive Extinction?" paranormal.about.com/library/weekly/aa061702b.htm (2007)

270. Waite, Arthur Edward, *The Pictorial Key to the Tarot,* University Books, Inc., 1959

271. Wamsley, Jeff & Sergent, Donnie Jr., *Mothman: The Facts Behind the Legend,* Discovery Press; Los Angeles, CA, 2001

272. Wersba, Barbara, *The Land of Forgotten Beasts,* Atheneum, Simon & Shuster; New York, 1964

273. White, T.H., *The Book of Beasts,* J.P. Putnam's Sons, 1954; Dover Publications, 1984

274. Wilford, John Noble, "Before Birds, a Weird way to Fly," *New York Times,* March 11, 1997

275. Williams, Tom, "The Hunt of the Unicorn: a Fabulous Legend Returns to Life." *Amargi,* Vol. 1, No. 3; Feb. 1, 1989 (in *Green Egg,* Vol. 21, No. 84, Feb. 1, 1989).

276. ——, "Tailing the Mermaid: A Merry Chase to the Depths of Myth," *Amargi,* May 1988, 1-4

277. Wilkins, Harold T., *Secret Cities of Old South America: Atlantis Unveiled,* Library Publishers, 1952

278. *Wiltshire White Horses,*
www.wiltshirewhitehorses.org.uk (2007)
279. "Chinese Winged Cat," Ananova,
www.ananova.com, May 25, 2007
280. Witchell, Nicholas, *The Loch Ness Story,*
Terence Dalton, London, 1974
281. Zell, Morning Glory, *The Hunting of the Ri*
(unfinished; illustrated by Oberon Zell)

BEASTLY WEBSITES

The Aberdeen Bestiary
www.abdn.ac.uk/bestiary/bestiary.hti
A complete online transcription of the most
important medieval bestiary, including full-
color reproductions of its illuminated pages.

American Monsters
www.americanmonsters.com/monsters.html
An amazing resource, with countless entries
and excellent organization. Categories are:
Formerly Extinct, Hairy Hominids, Hybrid-
Beasts, Lake Monsters, Lover's Lane, Out of
this World, Recently-Uncovered, Sea-Serpents,
Aquatic Enigmas, Avian Anomalies, Curious
carcasses, Beyond Mythology, and Unclassified.

aRiKaH.net: Liste de créatures fantastiques
www.arikah.net/encyclopedie-francaise/
Liste_de_cr%C3%A9atures_fantastiques
A good alphabetical listing of fantastic creatures
and mythological beings, with many illustrations
found nowhere else. The text is in French.

Loren Coleman, The Cryptozoologist
www.lorencoleman.com/index.html

*Clipart etc. an online service of Florida's Educa-
tional Technology Clearinghouse*
http://etc.usf.edu/clipart/index.htm

Cryptomundo.com
www.cryptomundo.com
A place to enjoy the adventures, treks, theories,
and wisdom of some of the most respected
leaders in the field of Cryptozoology.

Cryptozoology.com
www.cryptozoology.com/glossary/glossary.php
Really excellent entries on all kinds of cryptids,
plus extensive galleries of photos and art.

Dave's Mythical Creatures and Places
www.eaudrey.com/myth/alphabetical_index.htm
Excellent illustrated listings in the following
categories: Biblical Beings, Serpents &
Dragons, Part-Human Creatures, Winged
Beasts, Land Beasts, Sea Creatures, Mythical
Places, Marvels of the East, Egyptian Crea-
tures, and Japanese Mythological Symbolism.

Encyclopedia Mythica: Bestiary
www.pantheon.org/areas/bestiary/articles.html
This is a wonderful and continually-expanding
encyclopedia of mythology, folklore, legends,
and more. It contains over 6,100 gods and
goddesses, supernatural beings, and legendary
creatures and monsters from all over the world.

*Gareth Long's Encyclopedia of Monsters, Mythical
Creatures and Fabulous Beasts* (or, *the
Encyclopedia of Monsters etc.*)
http://webhome.idirect.com/~donlong/monsters
/monsters.htm
Detailed entries on just about every fabled beast
and being imaginable! With many illustrations.

Bestiary: Heraldic Monsters & Medieval Critters
www3.kumc.edu/itc/staff/rknight/monsters.htm
These are creatures referred to in various
bestiaries and/or heraldry texts.

List of Species in Folklore and Mythology (from
Wikipedia, the free encyclopedia)
http://en.wikipedia.org/wiki/
List_of_species_in_folklore_and_mythology
Contains extensive and detailed listings
arranged both alphabetically and by categories.

The Medieval Bestiary: Animals in the Middle Ages
http://bestiary.ca/index.html
This website deals with any and all aspects of
the general topic "animals in the Middle Ages,"
though there is an emphasis on the manuscript
tradition, particularly of European bestiaries.

Monstropedia
www.monstropedia.org/
Monstropedia is the ultimate online encyclopedia of monsters in myth, magick and legend.

Mostly Medieval: Beasts in Myth and Legend
www.skell.org/explore/text/beastintroT.html

Mythic Creatures: Dragons, Unicorns & Mermaids
www.amnh.org/exhibitions/mythiccreatures/
A wonderful exhibit organized by the American
Museum of Natural History, New York City,
and going on tour around the world.

Sideshow World
http://www.sideshowworld.com/
Fascinating info and interviews with amazing
people, including makers of Gaffs and this
author (OZ) regarding the Living Unicorns.

The Shadowlands
http://theshadowlands.net/creature.htm
Under "Mysterious Creatures & Cryptozoology" are excellent articles about some of the
many unknown, undiscovered, mysterious
animals that are out there.

*StrangeArk.com: BioForteana, Zoological
Oddities, Unusual Natural History*
www.strangeark.com/checklist/guide.html
Regional Checklist of Animal "Legends" of
Interest to Cryptozoology

The Strange the Wacky: Weird Wonders of Fantasy
www.harvestfields.ca/etextLinks/bzz/10.htm
Amazing collection of images, and many
excellent writeups.

APPENDIX 6. CHAPTER CITATIONS

1. The Baleful Basilisk
1. Nigg, *The Book of Dragons*
2. Wikipedia, "Basilisk"
3. Ley, *Exotic Zoology*
4. Costello, *The Magic Zoo*
5. White, *The Book of Beasts*
6. *Monstropedia,* "Salamander"
7. Shuker, *Beasts That Hide from Man*

2. Cosmic Serpents
1. Robbins, "Superfly"
2. *Wikipedia,* "Gigantophis garstini"
3. Heuvelmans, *On the Track of Unknown Animals*
4. Coleman & Clark, *Cryptozoology A to Z*
5. The Shadowlands.com
6. Gordon, "The Search for the $50,000 Snake"

3. Dragons
1. Sagan, *The Dragons of Eden*
2. Wilford, "Before Birds, a Weird Way to Fly"
3. Frey, Sues, Munk, "Gliding Mechanism in *Coelurosauravus,*"
4. Perkins, "Winged Dragon"

4. The Universal Unicorn
1. Hathaway, *The Unicorn*
2. Williams, "The Hunt of the Unicorn"
3. "Unicorns: The Complete Story…"
4. Plutarch, *Life of Pericles*
5. Ctesias, *Indica*
6. Shepard, *Lore of the Unicorn*
7. Pliny the Elder, *Natural history*
8. LeVaillant, *Travels in Africa*
9. Berridge, *Marvels of the Animal World*
10. "Unicorns" *Ibid.*
11. Le Blanc, *Les Voyages fameux du Sieur Vincent le Blanc*

12. Vartoman, *Navigations and Voyages*
13. Comes, *Mythologia*
14. Franklin, *Heraldry*
15. Cuvier, "Excursus IV"
16. Heuvelmans, *On the Track of Unknown Animals*
17. Shepard, *Ibid.*
18. Dove, "The Physiology of Horn Growth"
19. Dove, "Artificial Production of the Fabulous Unicorn"
20. *Britannica Book of the Year*
21. Green, *De Historia et Veritate Unicornis*

5. Wonder Horses
1. Propertius, *Poems of Sextus Propertius*
2. Howey, *The Horse in Magic and Myth*
3. L'Epine, *Croquemitaine*
4. Hausman, *The Mythology of Horses*
5. "The Cattle Raid of Regamna"
6. "Hippoi Athanatoi"
7. "The Riddles of Gestumblindi"
8. Hausman, *Op cit.*
9. "Ancient Bedouin Legend"
10. Pinti, " Tale of the Wind Horse"
11. Estes, "For your soul"
12. De Gubernatis, *Zoological Mythology*
13. Firdausi, *The Shanamah*
14. *Wiltshire White Horses*
15. Oppian, "Cynegetica"
16. *Story of the Trojan War*
17. Chan, *Good Luck Horse*

6. Holy Cows & Sacred Bulls
1. "Cattle," Wikipedia
2. "Bovinae," Wikipedia
3. Hawkes & Woolley, *Prehistory and Beginnings of Civilization*
4. Santillana, *Hamlet's Mill*
5. Wikipedia, "Mithraism"

7. The Piasa & the Manticore

1. McAdams, "The Bird which Devours Men"
2. "The Piasa Bird," The IBEX Archive
3. "Piasa," Wikipedia
4. "The Piasa Bird," *Op clt.*
5. McAdams, *Op cit.*
6. Taylor, Troy, "The Legend of the Piasa Bird"
7. McCrindle, *Ancient India by Ktesias the Knidian*
8. Philostratus, *The Life of Apollonius*
9. Caxton, *Mirrour of the World*
10. Rabelais, *Gargantua and Pantagruel*
11. Boreman, *Three Hundred Animals*
12. Costello, *The Magic Zoo*
13. Ball, "On the Identification of the Pygmies, the Martikhora, the Griffin, and the Dikarion of Ktesias"
14. Topsell, *Historie of Foure-Footed Beastes*
15. Costello, *Op cit.*
16. Lehner, *Big Book of Dragons*

8. The Fiery Phoenix
1. "Phoenix," Wikipedia
2. South, *Mythical and Fabulous Beasts*
3. Nigg, *The Book of Fabulous Beasts*
4. *Ibid.*
5. *Ibid.*
6. South, *Op cit.*
7. Costello, *The Magic Zoo*
8. Christie, *Chinese Mythology*
9. Rose, *Giants, Monsters, and Dragons*
10. *Ibid.*
11. *Ibid.*
12. "Phoenix," *Ibid.*
13. *Ibid.*
14. *Ibid.*
15. *Ibid.*
16. Burton, *Phoenix Reborn*
17. Shuker, *Beasts That Hide from Man*
18. *Ibid.*
19. "Phoenix," *Op cit.*

9. Gryphons & Hippogriffs
1. Nigg, *Book of Fabulous Beasts*
2. Aelian, *On Animals*
3. "Lammergeier," Wikipedia
4. Shuker, *Beasts That Hide from Man*

10. Merfolk
1. Costello, *The Magic Zoo*
2. *Ibid.*
3. Piccolo, "Women of the Deep"
4. *Ibid.*
5. Fleming, "Maidens of the sea"
6. *Ibid.*
7. *Ibid.*
8. *Ibid.*
9. Morphy, "Mermaids and Mermen"
10. Botkin, *Treasury of American Folklore*
11. *Ibid.*
12. *Ibid.*
13. Hardy, "Was Man More Aquatic in the Past?"
14. Morgan, *The Descent of Woman*
15. Smith, "The Case of the Reclusive Ri"
16. Wagner; Greenwell; Raymond; Von Nieda, "Further Investigations into the Ri"
17. Wagner, "The Ri—Unidentified Aquatic Animals of New Ireland"
18. Zell, *The Hunting of the Ri*
19. Williams, "Tailing the Mermaid"
20. Zell, *Op cit.*

11. The Kraken
1. Lilly, "New Zealand Fishermen Catch Rare Squid"
2. O'Shea, *Giant Squid Fact Sheet*
3. Lovecraft, "The Call of Cthulhu"
4. *Ibid.*
5. Ellis, *Search for the Giant Squid*
6. Gould, *Wonderful Life*

12. Hippocampus: Sea Horses & Water Horses
1. "Hippocampus," *Wikipedia*
2. *Ibid.*

13. The Enigmatic Sphinx
1. Nigg, *The Book of Fabulous Beasts*
2. Lehner, *Big Book of Dragons*
3. "Sphinx," *Monstropedia*
4. Waite, *Pictorial Key to the Tarot*
5. "Sphinx," *Monstropedia, Op cit.*
6. "Sphinx," *Wikipedia*
7. "Sphinx," *Monstropedia, Op cit.*
8. Hargreaves, *New Illustrated Bestiary*
9. "Sphinx," *Wikipedia, Op cit.*
10. Gould, *Mythical Monsters*
11. "Sphinx," *Wikipedia, Op cit.*
12. *Ibid.*

15. Plantimals
1. Buel, *Sea and Land*
2. Bayanov, "Why Cryptozoology?"
3. D'Amato, *The Savage Garden*
4. "Nepenthes," *Wikipedia*
5. Osborn, *Madagascar: Land of the Man-Eating Tree*
6. Buel, *Op cit.*
7. Ley, Salamanders and Other Wonders
8. Shuker, *Beasts That Hide from Man*
9. Buel, *Op cit.*
10. Wilkins, *Secret Cities of Old South America*
11. Shuker, *Op cit.*
12. *Ibid.*
13. *Ibid.*
14. Schwartz, *Carnivorous Plants*
15. Mackal, *Searching for Hidden Animals*
16. Wilkins, *Op cit.*
17. *Ley, Op cit.*
18. Costello, *The Magic Zoo*
19. *Ibid.*

20. *Ibid.*
21. Boese, *Museum of Hoaxes*
22. "Yggdrasil," *Wikipedia*

16. Oriental Spirit-Creatures
1. Christie, *Chinese Mythology*
2. Davis, *Myths and Legends of Japan*
3. Gould, *Mythical Monsters*
4. Mackenzie, *Myths of China and Japan*

17. Fearsome Critters
1. Van Patter, *Mythical American Animals*
2. Cox, *Fearsome Creatures of the Lumberwoods*
3. Leroy, *Le Dahu*
4. "Gallery of Tall-Tale Creatures," *Museum of Hoaxes*
5. Cox, *Op cit.*
6. Borges, *Book of Imaginary Beings*
7. *Ibid.*
8. *Ibid.*
9. Cox, *Op cit.*
10. "Fearsome Critters," *Wikipedia*
11. Cox, *Op cit.*
12. *Ibid.*
13. Borges, *Op cit.*
14. Cox, *Op cit.*
15. "Gallery of Tall-Tale Creatures" *Op cit.*
16. Van Patter, *Mythical American Animals*
17. Cox, *Op cit.*
18. *Ibid.*
19. *Ibid.*
20. *Ibid.*
21. "Fearsome Critters" *Op cit.*
22. Cox, *Op cit.*
23. *Ibid.*
24. *Ibid.*
25. *Ibid.*

18. Lake Monsters
1. Reeves, *Life of Saint Columba*
2. Witchell, *The Loch Ness Story*
3. Time-Life Books, *Mysterious Creatures*

4. Costello, *In Search of Lake Monsters*
5. "Mekong Giant Catfish," Wikipedia
6. Oudemans, *The Great Sea Serpent*
7. American Monsters
8. *Ibid.*
9. *Ibid.*
10. *Ibid.*
11. *Ibid.*
12. *Ibid.*
13. *Ibid.*
14. *Ibid.*
15. *Ibid.*
16. Boese, *Museum of Hoaxes*
17. Holiday, *The Great Orm of Loch Ness*
18. Illinois State Geological Survey, "*Tullimonstrum gregarium,*"
19. Akins, *The Loch Ness Monster*
20. Costello, *Op cit.*
21. Gould, *The Loch Ness Monster*
22. Costello, *Op cit.*
23. Dinsdale, *Story of the Loch Ness Monster*
24. Bord, *Alien Animals*
25. Dinsdale, *Op cit.*
26. *Ibid.*
27. Bord, *Op cit.*
28. Holiday, F.W., *The Dragon an the Disk,* Sidgwick & Jackson, London, 1973
29. "Sea Slugs," Wikipedia, the free encyclopedia, http://en.wikipedia.org (2007)
30. *Sea Slug Forum,* www.seaslugforum.net/ (2007)
31. *Ibid.*
32. Dinsdale, *Op cit.*
33. "Fabled Monster Caught on Video"

19. Sea Serpents
1. Champagne, "Large, Unidentified Marine Animals"
2. "Sea Serpent," *Wikipedia*
3. McCormick, "The Sea Serpent Complex"
4. Oudemans, *The Great Sea Serpent*
5. Heuvelmans, *In the*

Wake of the Sea Serpents
6. *American Monsters*
7. *Ibid.*
8. *Ibid.*
9. *Cryptozoology.com*
10. *American Monsters, Op. cit.*
11. McCormick, *Op cit.*
12. *American Monsters, Op. cit.*
13. *Ibid.*
14. *Ibid.*
15. *Ibid.*
16. Buel, *Sea and Land*
17. Egede, *A Description of Greenland*
18. "Frilled Shark," *Wikipedia*
19. Van der Toorn, *Jaap's Marine Mammal Pages*
20. Bord, *Alien Animals*
21. "Japanese Researchers Capture Giant Squid"
22. O'Shea, "Unknown Phylum"

20. Titanic Turtles & Legendary Lizards
1. O'Meara, *The Voyage of St. Brendan*
2. *Ibid.*
3. "Turtle," *Wikipedia*
4. *Ibid.*
5. "To Catch a Dragon"

21. Occult Octopuses
1. *American Monsters*
2. Clarke, *The Ghost from the Grand Banks*
3. McCormick, "Octopus Giganteus"
4. Shuker, *In Search of Prehistoric Survivors*
5. Buel, *Sea and Land*
6. Sucik, "Hawaii's Giant Octopuses"
7. Chorvinsky, "Globsters!"
8. American Monsters, *Op cit.*
9. Chorvinsky, *Op cit.*
10. *Ibid.*
11. American Monsters, *Op cit.*

22. The Bunyip of the Billabong
1. "Bunyip," Wikipedia
2. Heuvelmans, *On the*

Track of Unknown Animals

3. Gareth Long's Encyclopedia of Monsters
4. Morgan, *Life of William Buckley*
5. *Ibid.*
6. Heuvelmans, *Op cit.*
7. *Ibid.*
8. Ellis, *A History of Greta*
9. Noonuccal, *Stradbroke Dreamtime*
10. Heuvelmans, *Op cit.*
11. *Ibid.*
12. *Ibid.*
13. *All the World's Animals: Sea Mammals*
14. Ellis, *Op cit.*
15. Heuvelmans, *Op cit.*
16. Wikipedia *Op cit.*
17. Eaton, "The Bunyip: Modern-day Monster"
18. "Bunyips"
19. *Ibid.*
20. Wikipedia, *Op cit.*
21. "Origin of the Bunyip"

23. Thunderbirds
1. Jones, *An Instinct for Dragons*
2. South, *Mythical and Fabulous Beasts*
3. "Thunderbirds," Wikipedia
4. South, *Op cit.*
5. Bord, *Alien Animals*
6. *Ibid.*
7. *Ibid.*
8. Rose, *Giants, Monsters, and Dragons*
9. *Ibid.*
10. *Ibid.*
11. *Ibid.*
12. *Ibid.*
13. *Ibid.*
14. *Ibid.*
15. "Avian Anomalies," American Monsters
16. Hall, *Thunderbirds!*
17. Mitchell, *Living Wonders*
18. Nigg, *Imaginary Birds of the World*

24. Leather Wings
1. Doyle, *The Lost World*
2. Keel, *Complete Guide to Mysterious Beings*
3. Sanderson, *Investigating the Unexplained*

4. Hall, "The Mystery Of The Thunderbird"
5. *Ibid.*
6. Michell & Rickard, *Living Wonders*
7. Corliss, *Strange Life*
8. Michell & Rickard, *Op cit.* p. 50
9. Childress, "Living Pterodactyls"
10. Michell & Rickard, *Op cit.*
11. Childress, "Living Pterodactyls"
12. Kuhn, "Eskin Kuhn's Excellent Adventure"
13. Sanderson, *Op cit.*
14. *The Shadowlands*
15. Wagner, "Did Pterosaurs Survive Extinction?"
16. Childress, "Living Pterodactyls"
17. Coleman, "King Kong's playmate: Kongamato"
18. Wagner, "Did Pterosaurs Survive Extinction?"

25. Prehistoric Survivals
1. Doyle, *The Lost World*
2. Owen, "Report on British Fossil Reptiles"
3. Burroughs, *Tarzan the Terrible*
4. MacKal, *A Living Dinosaur*
5. Heuvelmans, *On the Track of Unknown Animals*
6. *American Monsters*
7. Heuvelmans, *Op cit.*
8. MacKal, *Op cit.*
9. Heuvelmans, *Op cit.*
10. Clark, *The Rivers Ran East*
11. Mitchell & Rickard, *Living Wonders,* p. 105
12. Delahoyde, "Dinosaur Films"
13. Norman, "Mokele-mbembe: the Living Dinosaur"

26. Hairy Hominids & Mystery Monkeys
1. Buel, *Sea and Land*
2. Coleman & Clark, *Cryptozoology A to Z*

3. Coleman & Huyghe, *Field Guide to Bigfoot*
4. *Paranormal About*
5. Bourtsev, "The Story of Zana"
6. Time-Life Books, *Mysterious Creatures*
7. Buel, *Op cit.*
8. "Bigfoot," *Wikipedia*
9. Roach, "Elusive African Apes"
10. "Bili Ape," *Wikipedia*
11. *American Monsters*
12. *Ibid.*
13. "Gigantopithecus," *Wikipedia*
14. Strasenburgh, "The Crested Australopithecus Robustus"
15. Coleman, & Clark, *Op cit.*
16. Heuvelmans, *On the Track of Unknown Animals*
17. Shackley, *Still Living?*
18. "Hobbits," *Wikipedia*
19. Time-Life Books, *Op cit.*
20. Byrne, *The Search for Big Foot*
21. Sanderson, *Abominable Snowman*

27. Demonic Dogs
1. Bord, *Alien Animals*
2. Keel, *Complete Guide to Mysterious Beings*
3. Keel, *Strange Creatures from Time and Space*
4. Shuker, *Beasts That Hide from Man*

28. Phantom Felines
1. Shuker, *Mystery Cats of the World*
2. *Ibid.*
3. Coleman & Clark, *Cryptozoology A to Z*
4. Hocking, "Large Peruvian Mammals Unknown to Zoology"
5. Shuker, *Op cit.*
6. *Ibid.*
7. Coleman & Clark, *Op cit.*
8. Shuker, *Op cit.*
9. *Ibid.*
10. *Ibid.*
11. *Ibid.*
12. *Ibid.*
13. Coleman & Clark, *Op*

cit.
14. Heuvelmans, *On the Track of Unknown Animals*
15. Melillo, *Medieval Bestiary*

29. Curious Cats
1. Thoreau, *Walden*
2. Shuker, "Wonderful Things are Cats with Wings"
3. Hartwell, "Winged Cats"
4. Shuker, "Flights of Fantasy?"
5. "Chinese Winged Cat," *Ananova*
6. Shuker, "Wonderful Things" *Op cit.*
7. Dance, *Animal Fakes and Frauds*
8. "Cabbits"
9. LeGuin, *Catwings*

30. Mystery Monsters
1. Juliano, "The Jersey Devil"
2. *Ibid.*
3. Bord, *Alien Animals*
4. Juliano, *Op cit.*
5. Coleman, *Mysterious America*
6. *Unexplained Mysteries*
7. Keel, *Strange Creatures from Time and Space*
8. "Has a Mythical Beast Turned Up in Texas?"
9. Coleman, *Op. cit.*
10. Bord, *Op. cit.*
11. *American Monsters*
12. Bord, *Op. cit.*
13. Coleman, *Mothman & Other Curious Encounters*
14. Bord, *Op. cit.*
15. Coleman, *Mysterious America, Op. cit.*
16. *American Monsters, Op. cit.*
17. *Ibid.*
18. *Ibid.*
19. *Ibid.*
20. *Ibid.*
21. Landsburg, *In Search Of*
22. *Unexplained Mysteries, Op. cit.*
23. Coleman, *Mothman, Op. cit.*
24. *Ibid.*

Appendix b. Art Credits

There are at least 1,500 graphics in this book, as we've tried to illustrate every creature possible! Most of these are traditional representations taken from historical sources, for which the Dover Clipart series of books have been incredibly useful. Another valuable resource for images of actual animals, extant and extinct, has been Clipart etc., an online service of Florida's Educational Technology Clearinghouse.

For many of these creatures, I was unable to find traditional or historic representations, and so we recruited a number of artist friends to draw pictures of them based upon the descriptions, utilizing their own artistic imaginations. Many of these appear throughout the Glossary, where there was unfortunately no space for credits. Foremost among these artists is the amazing Ian Daniels, who not only did the gorgeous cover art, but also about 40 of the Glossary spot illos, most of the chapter headers, and all the full-page section illos. Co-author Leopard-Dancer did 23 spot illos of critters for the Glossary, and I did about 70 graphics—including critters, maps, diagrams, and all the capital alphabet letters. Here is a list of the contributing artists other than myself, and their illustrations drawn especially for this book:

Jeff Acree:
Hellhound
Joe Butt:
Batsquatch
Cthulhu
Kelpie
Loveland Frog
Minotaur
Mothman
Nuckalavee
Ash DeKirk:
Aatxer
Adar Llwch
  Gwin
Ai Tojon
Amarok
Balam
Betikhan
Big Ears (Cat)
Bixi
Buata
Carbuncle
Chupacabra
Derketo
Dragon-wolf
Eonbarr
Estas, the Fire-
  Bringer
Feng Huang
Hippocerf
King Otter
Kitsune

Water Panther
Weewilmekq
Winged Panther
Sandy "Xander"
  Carruthers:
Ami-kuk
Biasd Bheulach
Chuchunna
Ian Daniels:
Alphyn
Arassas
Bagini
Batsquatch
Bigfoot
Buata
Centaur
Centycore
Cerberus
Cockatrice
Croc-Monster/
  Campacti
Cthulhu
Deer-Centaur
Dragon
Dragon-Mermaid
Each Tened
Ent
Faun
Fei Lian
Firebird
Freiburg
  Shrieker

Giant Bird
Girtablili
Guiafairo
Heliodromos
Hippogriff
Kelpie
Lake Monster
Lizard-Man
Mermaid
Mokele-Mbembe
Mystery Octopus
Pegasus
Peryton
Phantom Cat
Plesiosaur
Pterosaur
Sabre-Tooth
Sacred Bull
Salamander
Seahorse
Sleipnir
Sphinx
Tatzelwurm
Unicorn
Yeti
Ying Lung
Dana Keyes:
Big Ears
Bocanach
Brag
Brucha
Cabyll-Uisge

Carrog
Coinn Lotair
Cornu
Dinnymarra
Djieien
Each Tened
Fin People
Gengen Werae
Gollinkambiae
Gwenhidwyae
Muchalindaae
Natasha Kirby:
Marakihan
Safat
Meredith Lambert:
Agathodamon
Tam Songdog:
Safat
Samebito
Shojo
Silen
Snake Griffin
St Attracta's
  Monster
Song-Sseu
Surma
Tahujui
Tangie
Ti-Chiang
Unnati
Vietnamese
  Night Flyer

Tracy Swangler:
Alklha
Ass-Bittern
Audumbla
Basket Monster
Beithir
Bessie
Campacti
Concopeni
Eer-Moonan
Fachen
Fairy Dragon
Griffin-Vulture
Hippogriff
Kundav
Koschei the
  Deathless
Muscaliet
Odontotyrannus
On Niont
Opken
Ouroboros
Quanekelak
River-Griffin
Snake-Griffin
Uma Na-Iru
Yeck
Adam Swangler:
Kirata
Pi-His
Ugjuknarpak
Uridimmus

When I couldn't find traditional representations, and our commissioned artists had done all they could, I ransacked the Internet using Google Images. This valuable resource really helped fill in the blanks, but unfortunately, many of the graphics so obtained were unattributed. I apologize for the lack of attribution in such cases, and I would like to invite anyone who can provide such to please contact me so this omission may be rectified in future editions: Oberon@mcn.org.

If any of these illustrations are by living artists, I hope you are pleased by their inclusion. But if you wish to decline permission for their use, let me know and I will create replacements for them in the future.

And finally, I wish to extend appreciation to the late Bernard Heuvelmans (1916-2001), the "Father of Cryptozoology," for his encouragement of this book concept when we joined his International Society of Cryptozoology in the mid-'80s and launched the great Mermaid Expedition. I am pleased to have been able to include several of his now-classic illustrations from *On the Track of Unknown Animals* (1955) and *In the Wake of the Sea-Serpent* (1958).   --Oberon Zell

APPENDIX I. INDEX

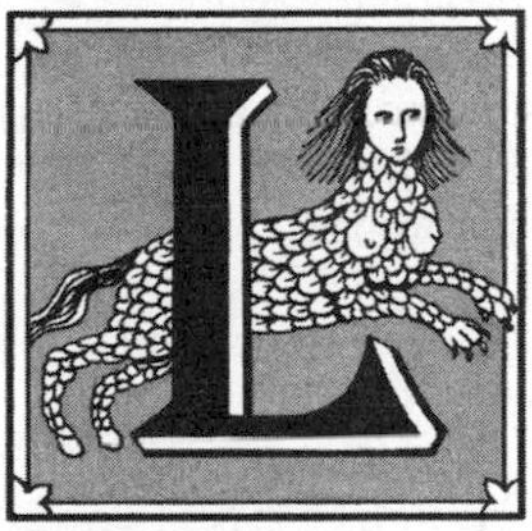

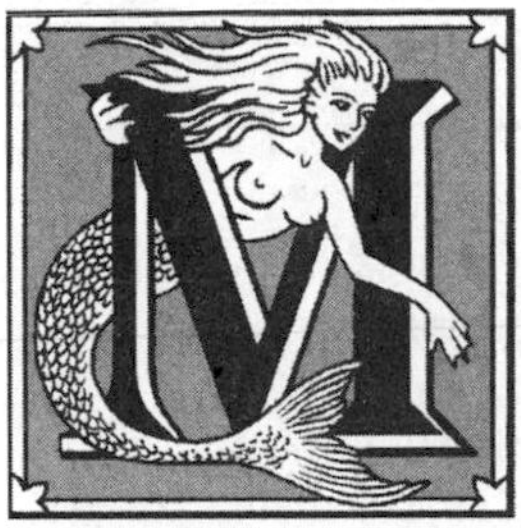

OTHER TITLES FROM NEW PAGE BOOKS

Encyclopedia of Haunted Places
Ghostly Locales From Around the World
Jeff Belanger
EAN 978-1-56414-612-0

Encyclopedia of the Undead
A Field Guide to the Creatures That
Cannont Rest in Peace
Dr. Bob Curran
EAN 978-1-56414-841-4

The Ghost Files
Paranormal Encounters, Discussion, and
Research from the Vaults of Ghostvillage.com
Jeff Belanger
EAN 978-1-56414-375-4

Lost Lands, Forgotten Realms
Sunken Continents, Vanished Cities, and
the Kingdoms That History Misplaced
Dr. Bob Curran
EAN 978-1-56414-958-9

Pet Ghosts
Animal Encounters From Beyond the
Grave
Joshua P. Warren
EAN 978-1-56414-888-9

Vampires
A Field Guide to the Creatures That Stalk
the Night
Dr. Bob Curran
EAN 978-1-56414-807-0

Walking with the Green Man
Father of the Forest, Spirit of Nature
Dr. Bob Curran
EAN 978-1-56414-931-2

The World's Most Haunted Places
From the Secret Files of Ghostvillage.com
Jeff Belanger
EAN 978-1-56414-764-6

AVAILABLE WHEREVER BOOKS ARE SOLD, OR CALL 201-848-0310

newpagebooks.com

BOOKS BY OBERON ZELL-RAVENHEART
AND THE GREY SCHOOL OF WIZARDRY

Grimoire for the Apprentice Wizard
$18.99 ❖ EAN 978-1-56414-711-0

Creating Circles & Ceremonies
$15.99 ❖ EAN 978-1-56414-864-3

Companion for the Apprentice Wizard
$18.99 ❖ EAN 978-1-56414-835-3

Dragonlore
$14.99 ❖ EAN 978-1-56414-868-1

AVAILABLE WHEREVER BOOKS ARE SOLD
OR CALL 201-848-0310

newpagebooks.com

The **Mythic Images Collection**

Oberon Zell's
Mermaid

Oberon Zell's
SeaHorse

www.MythicImages.com   1-888-Mythic-1

ABOUT THE AUTHORS

(1983)

Oberon Zell-Ravenheart (1942-)

Those who know him well consider Oberon to be a modern Renaissance man, as well as a Wizard. He holds academic degrees in sociology, anthropology, psychology, teaching, and theology. He founded a visionary church, helped to forge a worldwide religious movement, and published *Green Egg*, the award-winning legendary journal of modern Paganism. Oberon was also the first person to conceive and publish the biological and metaphysical foundations of what has become known as the "Gaea Thesis"—the unified body and emergent soul of the living Earth.

Oberon and his wife Morning Glory rediscovered the long-lost secret of the Unicorn in 1976, and in 1980 created the first of several living Unicorns. For the next four years they traveled all over North America exhibiting their authentic Medieval-style Unicorns at Renaissance Faires, before arranging a four-year exhibition contract with the Ringling Bros./Barnum & Bailey Circus.

In Feb. 1985, Oberon organized a video diving expedition to New Guinea and New Ireland which identified the species of the mysterious "Ri" and solved the ages-old mystery of the Mermaid.

Oberon's artwork has illuminated the pages of various fantasy, science-fiction, and metaphysical magazines since the late 1960's, as well as illustrating a number of books. But his favorite art project is his ongoing sculpture series of ancient Gods and Goddesses, and of mythological and legendary creatures, available as the Mythic Images Collection. He is also the founder and Headmaster of the online Grey School of Wizardry .

Living in Sonoma County, California, with Morning Glory, Oberon's previous books are:

Grimoire for the Apprentice Wizard (2004)

Companion for the Apprentice Wizard (2006)

Creating Circles & Ceremonies (with Morning Glory) (2006)

Ashley "LeopardDancer" DeKirk

LeopardDancer is a university graduate specializing in dragons and dragonlore. She holds a BA in anthropology and is hoping to go for a Masters in history or English at some point in the future.

In the Grey School of Wizardry, Prof. LeopardDancer is Dean of the Departments of Alchemy and Divination, Professor of Beast Master, and Instructor in Ceremonial Magick, Dark Arts, Lifeways, Lore, and Magickal Practice.

Her hobbies and pastimes include: reading (all the time!), writing and games of all sorts. Her first book is *Dragonlore* (New Page, 2006). She is in the process of writing a fantasy novel and a modern translation of the Chinese folk-legend "Journey to the West."

A Graelan priest of the Dun 'marra, she lives in North Carolina with two room-mates, Heather and Mike and their giant pet family: Rufus, Drizzt, Bakura, Tseng and Tia (kitties), Artemis (rat), Roy (gerbil), Cinnamon and Sirius (birds) and her own personal pet dragon—Nobunaga the python.

The Grey School of Wizardry

Do you want to study real magick and arcane lore? Enroll in the **Grey School of Wizardry** and attend our online campus! Incorporated as a non-profit educational institution with a Federal 501(c)(3) tax exemption status, the Grey School offers over 200 classes at 7 levels with readings, projects, exams, and practical exercises. Classes are developed and taught by a large and highly-qualified faculty. 16 Departments encompass *Wizardry, Nature Studies, Magickal Practice, Mind Magicks, Healing, Wortcunning, Divination, Performance, Alchemy, Lifeways, Beast Mastery, Mathemagicks, Cosmology, Ceremonial Magick, Lore,* and *Dark Arts*. Graduates are certified as "Journeyman Wizards." The Grey School is highly interactive, with Elemental Houses, Lodges, the Great Hall, clubs, and other forums in which students can communicate directly with teachers and each other. Tuition fees are modest. Full details appear on the Grey School website: **www.GreySchool.com**